D0215126

For Referenc

not to be taken

The Kurds

KURDISTAN

The Kurds

An Encyclopedia of Life, Culture, and Society

SEBASTIAN MAISEL, EDITOR

ABC-CLIO™

An Imprint of ABC-CLIO, LLC
Santa Barbara, California • Denver, Colorado

Every reasonable effort has been made to trace the owners of copyright materials in this book, but in some instances this has proven impossible. The editors and publishers will be glad to receive information leading to more complete acknowledgments in subsequent printings of the book and in the meantime extend their apologies for any omissions.

Library of Congress Cataloging-in-Publication Data
Names: Maisel, Sebastian, 1970– editor.
Title: The Kurds : an encyclopedia of life, culture, and society / Sebastian Maisel, editor.
Description: Santa Barbara, California : ABC-CLIO, an Imprint of ABC-CLIO, LLC, 2018. | Includes bibliographical references and index.
Identifiers: LCCN 2017061633 (print) | LCCN 2018016889 (ebook) |
    ISBN 9781440842573 (ebook) | ISBN 9781440842566 (hardcopy : alk. paper) |
    ISBN 9781440842573 (ebook : alk. paper)
Subjects: LCSH: Kurds—Encyclopedias.
Classification: LCC DS59.K86 (ebook) | LCC DS59.K86 K875 2018 (print) |
    DDC 909/.0491597003—dc23
LC record available at https://lccn.loc.gov/2017061633

ISBN: 978-1-4408-4256-6 (print)
      978-1-4408-4257-3 (ebook)

22 21 20 19 18   1 2 3 4 5

This book is also available as an eBook.

ABC-CLIO
An Imprint of ABC-CLIO, LLC

ABC-CLIO, LLC
130 Cremona Drive, P.O. Box 1911
Santa Barbara, California 93116-1911
www.abc-clio.com

This book is printed on acid-free paper ∞

Manufactured in the United States of America

This book is dedicated to Nadia Murad and the other Yezidi survivors of genocide. And to my Kurdish friends from all over the world who shared their stories, knowledge, anger, and friendship with me, in particular Redwan, Khalil, and Ali (Alan).

Contents

Preface

The Kurdish people are a large ethnic group that lives in mountainous regions of several countries spanning southwest Asia, from Turkey to Iran and beyond the Caucasus Mountains, making up a cross-border region known as Kurdistan. Since the creation of nation-states in the region after the collapse of the Ottoman Empire, the Kurds have faced discrimination and persecution, gave up their mostly nomadic lifestyle, and began fighting for basic human rights. All too often, the only knowledge we have of this homogenous yet diverse group is one darkened by violence and conflict, whether they are battling ISIS, fighting for control in Syria, or were gassed by Saddam Hussein. However, even today the Kurds remain hopeful to be recognized as a distinct culture living in a sovereign country. Who are the Kurds, and why have they been forced to struggle with a national identity and home for so long?

The Kurds: An Encyclopedia of Life, Culture, and Society is a timely reference to further our understanding of the Kurds and Kurdistan. It also fills a notable gap in the literature about the Middle East where multiple compilations describe the diverse people, cultures, and identity groups, such as Muslims, women, Arabs, political systems, and minorities, but few focus on the largest ethnic stateless minority, the Kurds. By examining all aspects of Kurdish life in several countries as well as in the diaspora, this encyclopedia provides reliable, up-to-date, and nonsensationalist references for the generally interested and open-minded readership. These references are compiled by a team of international scholars and researchers including many Kurds with broad experience in the topics discussed in this volume, including historians, geographers, anthropologists, political scientists, linguists, and artists.

The content of the encyclopedia includes three main parts. The first approaches Kurdish life through a number of thematic essays with emphasis on the history, geography, social organization culture, and political situation. Following these topics are country-specific entries profiling the Kurdish population in Kurdistan, the area that is split among Turkey, Iran, Iraq, Syria, and the Trans-Caucasus region, as well as in the global diaspora. Special attention is given to local contemporary issues the Kurds face in these countries. The third part surveys a diverse list of primary document excerpts where experts analyze the sources and their relevance to the Kurds throughout history and in the various areas of settlement. These documents include popular poems, works of literature, religious texts, political manifests, and speeches, as well as legislation and other laws. Sidebars, a glossary of the most common Kurdish words, and a selected bibliography will round out the text. A note on transliteration from Kurdish (and other Middle Eastern languages) and a chronology of Kurdish history are also incorporated in the book.

Introduction

The Kurds and their homeland, Kurdistan, remain a mystery for many people in the West despite their strong media presence and deep cultural ties through diaspora groups. Instead, a myriad of misconceptions, stereotypes, and ignorance dominate the common knowledge and debate about this group. Perhaps this is related to the fact that Kurdistan is part of the greater Middle East, and in these current times of conflicts, civil wars, revolutions, and terrorism, many lost track and confidence in understanding the origins of the conflict and the original stakeholders. Instead, we tend to generalize the region by describing its people as "radical Arab Muslims" who suppress their women, hate the West and the Jews, and are irrational conservative fundamentalists. These images, added with the occasional depiction of suffering refugees, prevail in our news headlines and influence the public opinion and arguably the opinion of our decision makers as well.

Kurdistan and the Kurds

The Kurds are different, however. They do not fit this blatantly scary and misleading picture. On the contrary, the contemporary Kurds in their various living areas often represent a pluralistic society that shares many values and norms with Western countries. While our focus and political alliances keeps us closer to the dominant ethnic groups and their nation-states, such as Turkey or Saudi Arabia, we overlook this potential friendly ally and partner. As a minority group, they lack a strong, unified voice and message to the rest of the world as well as a lobby group that could further strengthen their cause among the international community. The split of their living area among several nation-states remains a major obstacle in the way of developing a stronger relationship with other international actors and organizations, which in turn are also often restricted in their ability to communicate with nonstate actors.

In order to describe who the Kurds are, it is best to start explaining who they are not. Ethnically, the Kurds are not related to the Arabs or Turks, but they are indeed an Indo-European people speaking the Kurdish language, which is linguistically linked to the larger Iranian language family. Although the majority of Kurds adheres to Sunni Islam, we must recognize the religious diversity within the Kurdish lands that includes Christian and Jewish groups as well as the Yezidis, an ethnoreligious minority with pre-Islamic roots and a syncretistic belief system and other smaller religious groups like the Shabak or Kakai. Also among the Alevis, an Islamic Sufi organization, one can find many Kurds. The two Sufi brotherhoods of the Qadiriya and Naqshbandiya also remain extremely popular, and their leaders or sheikhs maintain political influence in addition to their religious significance. This kind of popular religion stands in sharp contrast to the strict, orthodox, and rudimentary interpretation of Islam as practiced by radical Islamic organizations such as The Islamic State or Ansar al-Islam. Although some Kurds joined their ranks, the majority of the Kurdish population can be regarded as less fundamental in religious affairs with a strong tendency toward secularism especially among the urbanized groups and those supporting the Kurdish Workers Party (PKK) and their affiliates.

While religion may not seem to be the major building block of Kurdish identity, at least not for the majority, the adherence to specific cultural values and customs remains an important contributor to the constant rebuilding of Kurdish identity. The social organization of the Kurds was based on tribal/kin-based affiliation, and for centuries, powerful Kurdish tribal groups controlled much of Kurdistan and beyond. Membership in a tribe was not based on religion; in fact, many heterogenic tribes included Muslim, Christian, and Yezidi clans. Instead, an imagined common language, culture, land, and ancestry was the glue that kept Kurdish society together. Tribes, clans, and families were led by dominant families called aghas, sheikhs, or mullas like the Barzanis, Barzanjis, Bedirkhan, or Shemdinan. Recently, nationalism has been added to the characteristics of Kurdish identity. This has been demonstrated by the rise of political parties and leaders who claim to represent all of Kurdistan as well as their local constituency.

The currently roughly 35 million Kurds live in a compact settlement area commonly known as Kurdistan, or Land of the Kurds, which is the size of France. It is roughly shaped by the Zagros and Taurus mountains between the upper Euphrates, Lake Van, Lake Urmiya, and the city of Kirmanshah in the east. However, this geographical description does not fit the political realities. First of all, there is no independent state called Kurdistan. Instead, the region is divided among four countries, none of which has a Kurdish majority population. The largest areas are part of Turkey, Iran, Iraq, and Syria, but with the exception of the Kurdistan Region in Iraq and the Kordestan Province in Iran, no other administrative or political unit exists. The Kurds in Syria during the ongoing civil war have created a federal de facto autonomous region in those territories with a Kurdish majority in parts of the Hassaka, Raqqa, and Aleppo governorates. Kurdish nationalists gave it the name of Rojava, the west, referring to Western Kurdistan. This matches similar attributes describing the three other Kurdish territories as Bakur (North—Turkish Kurdistan), Bashur (South—Iraqi Kurdistan), and Rojhilat (East—Iranian Kurdistan). In Turkey some 20 million Kurds are estimated, and in Iran around 10 million. Iraq has approximately 7 million and in Syria live approximately 2 million Kurds. In the three Caucasus countries of Armenia, Azerbaijan, and Georgia, we find over 220,000 Kurds. The estimates vary regarding the number of Kurds living in the diaspora ranging from 500,000 to 2 million. Comparing these numbers to an approximate total of almost 40 million people makes the Kurds one of the largest ethnic groups and the largest stateless community in the world.

A common language is another denominator that describes the Kurds. Kurdish as an Indo-European language is part of the northwestern group of the Iranian languages. Although there is no standard, unified Kurdish high language, but rather two main dialects (Kurmanji and Sorani), the Kurdish language is rich in oral traditions, such as songs, legends, and religious hymns, the most famous of which is the love epic Mem u Zin written by Ahmad Khani in 1692. This and other influential literary works are discussed in this volume. Although the two main dialects have many similarities, they are written in different alphabets based on the country of origin. Kurds in Turkey speak Kurmanji and write with Latin letters, Kurds in Iraq mostly speak Sorani and use the Arabic/Persian alphabet to write their dialect, and the Kurds in the Trans-Caucasus region mostly use the Cyrillic alphabet to write their Kurmanji vernacular. And recently, they have added an Armenian version.

The origins of the Kurds are contested, but for many they represent an indigenous group of upper Mesopotamia often described as the mountain people in the Zagros and Taurus. Certainly, a close relation with the Iranization of the region during the reign of the Medians and Scythians starting in the ninth century BCE must be noted. The name "Kurds" as a common label appeared only after the Islamic conquest of the area denoting those nomadic tribes of non-Arab or Turkish origin. The isolated mountainous character of their homeland preserved the special features of the Kurdish ethnicity with their unique language, culture, and religions. Foreign control and outside rule were enforced only in limited areas, and the Kurds lived semi-autonomously for centuries organized in tribal clans and emirates, until by the end of the 19th century a national identity across the tribes and leading families emerged in response to social transformation, Ottoman pressures and growing Western influence in the Middle East region. The revolt of Sheykh Ubeydallah in 1880 was the first to demand a free and unified Kurdistan. This was followed by a growing movement of nationalism that saw the opening of national clubs, political parties, and the publication of the first Kurdish newspaper in 1898.

World War I changed the political landscape of the Middle East significantly with the dissolving of the Ottoman Empire and the creation of nation-states. Although the Allies first assured the Kurds of their potential track towards independence in the Treaty of Sevres, three years later in the Treaty of Lausanne they divided the land among Turkey, Syria, and Iraq. In the decades to follow, Kurds in all those countries launched multiple rebellions against the central governments and for political rights, but ultimately were defeated and experienced a century of foreign rule, persecution, and discrimination. However, concurrently, they continuously pushed for cultural autonomy or political independence until the present time. During the short-lived Republic of Mahabad in present-day Iran, this dream became reality in 1946 until it was shattered after the Soviet Union withdrew its support and troops, and the Kurds had to learn again the harsh lesson of dependency on foreign support. While the Kurds seem to fall into the trap repeatedly, they also did not surrender or gave up their struggle of Kurdistan. Masud Barzani, now president of the Kurdish Autonomous Region in Iraq, was born in Mahabad and an array of political parties was founded and modeled after Mulla Mustafa Barzani's Kurdish Democratic Party (KDP). Not necessarily in agreement, and often in ideological or personal competition, these Kurdish parties, such as the Patriotic Union of Kurdistan (PUK), the Kurdish Workers Party (PKK), or the KDP's branches in other countries, used their limited means to pressure the central governments for political and cultural rights for the Kurds. The end of the First Gulf War brought the formation of the first autonomous zone for the Kurds in Iraq in 1992. For some this was a milestone, whereas others only regarded this as a stepping-stone towards further achievements.

The Kurdish identity has been suppressed in all four states in varying degrees that ranged from straightforward denial of Kurdish existence in Turkey with the subsequent prohibition of expressing anything related to the Kurds to the denigration as secondary citizens in the Syrian Arab Republic, where speaking Kurdish and engaging in political activities could easily land a person in jail. In Iran, life for the Kurds is described as "living in a giant prison," and Kurdish militias challenged the Iranian army with little success. The most brutal attacks against the Kurds were recorded in Iraq under the regime of Saddam Hussein, who stripped them of their ethnicity and citizenship, evicted them from their homes, destroyed their villages and fields, arbitrarily arrested and subsequently killed entire tribes, gassed cities, and massacred hundreds of thousands of Iraqi Kurds. However, Saddam's regime is gone, and the Kurds in Iraq were among the strongest and most capable supporters of the U.S.-led invasion in 2003. And it is here in Kurdistan-Iraq where they reached their greatest political success in the Kurdish Autonomy Zone.

As stated earlier, little is known in the West about the Kurds in general, and even less about their particulars in the four main countries and the diaspora. However, knowing their present facets and future prospects will allow us to better understand our own Western position on the rapids developments in the region. Who would have thought that the Arab Spring would give rise to Islamic extremism and that the key to defeat the militants is in the hand of long underappreciated group like the Kurds? However, as so often in the past, the key is not ready to use. It requires foreign approval, and concessions and compromises must be reached. America, Russia, Turkey, Iran, and Iraq (and yes, to a lesser extend the Syrian government) all try to build competing alliances and often successfully co-opted the Kurds into their camp and into supporting their agenda. And as long as the inner-Kurdish rivalries are bigger than the desire for a unified, safe, and prosperous country, the idea of Kurdistan remains an idea. A century of physical and cultural separation, as well as military struggle and discrimination, hardened the differences between the various groups rather than merging them into one big national movement. Although the revolutionary climate in the region favors the emergence of new forms of Kurdish nationalism, like the democratic confederalism in Syria, the four regions of Kurdistan—Bakur, Rojava, Bashur, and Rojhilat—seem more distant from each other than before.

However, at the same time they are so much closer to us in the West. And with the spread and advance of technology the events in Kurdistan no longer remain unnoticed. We can see live videos from Mount Sinjar where Yezidi Kurds die of hunger and thirst fleeing the Islamic state. We hear about anticorruption rallies in Arbil. Images of Kurdish activists executed in Iran are spread, and we were there with the young Kurdish women defending the city of Kobane. We cannot close our eyes before the images of Kurdish children drowned in the Mediterranean Sea. It is thus the humble goal of this book to provide a roadmap of understanding those images and put them in their geographic, historic, and political context.

Part I
Thematic Essays

Origins and History

Early Origins: Myths, Fables, and Theories

The origins and early development of the Middle East's Kurdish community remains a topic of considerable scholarly debate and controversy. Prior to the modern age, a variety of myths and legends pertaining to the genesis of the Kurds coexisted. Perhaps the most famous myth claimed the Kurds were the descendants of children rescued from Zahhak, the cannibalistic tyrant of Iranian folklore. Other theories can also be found in the works of medieval Islamic scholars. These included the suggestion that the Kurds possessed an Arab genealogy, being the descendants of Arab tribes that had fled Arabia in the pre-Islamic era, and a legend that the Kurds were the product of an unholy union between of King Solomon's concubines and *Jinns*, supernatural creatures of Arabian and Islamic mythology. Since the mid-19th century, a growing number of scholars in the West have put forward new theories concerning to the Kurds' origins. Such theories often seek to posit the idea that the modern Kurdish community is a continuation of one or more of the peoples inhabiting the ancient Middle East, including groups such as the Corduene of Xenophon's *Anabasis* and the Cyrtii mentioned in the works of Polybius, Livy, and Strabo. Nevertheless, perhaps the most well-known and widely accepted theory is that the modern Kurds are the direct successors to the Medes, ancient Iranic people who dominated much of the territory of modern Iran between 678 and 549 BCE. Although this theory has gained popularity amongst the Kurdish intelligentsia, it is largely speculative and has been criticized by modern scholars who suggest that the study of Kurdish community should begin with the appearance of the term "Kurd" in the historical record (Özoğlu, 2004: 25). In this regard, the earliest direct mention of the Kurds can be found in the Pahlavi language sources of Sassanid era Iran (224–651) (Asatrain, 2009: 28). However, it was only following the rise of Islam in the seventh century that the term gained wider usage.

Medieval Islamic sources often used the term Kurd in a vague manner when referring to a variety of tribal and nomadic populations inhabiting mountainous zones separating the Anatolian and Iranian plateaus. Citing the work of 10th-century scholar Hamza al-Isfahani, Russian-born orientalist Vladimir Minorsky noted that the Persians "were accustomed to call the Daylamites "Kurds of Tabaristan" as they used to call the Arabs "the Kurds of Suristan, i.e. of Iraq . . ." further observing that other Arab and Persian authors from the 10th century used the term to describe "all Iranian nomads from the Western Persia, such as the tent-dwellers of Fars" (Minorsky, 1943: 75). This has led a number of scholars to conclude that the term Kurd was originally a socioeconomic designation, being synonymous with the term "nomad," and only later came to refer to a specific ethnic community (Jwaideh, 2006: 11; Nikitin, 1956: 9). More recent scholarship has questioned these conclusions, suggesting that, while the Kurdish community was often associated with the pastoral way of life, the term Kurd was an ethnonym used to describe a specific population that inhabited a specific territory and possessed other shared attributes, including myths of common origins and linguistic specificities. Nevertheless, prior to the 12th century, it is difficult to ascertain whether any of those communities, tribes, and individuals described as being Kurds saw themselves as being part of a larger ethnic community.

Medieval Islamic World (610–1500)

According to the accounts of Muslim historians and geographers of the medieval period, Kurdish tribes dwelling in the mountains of Upper Mesopotamia and Western Iran resisted the advance of Islamic armies in the seventh century. The earliest encounters date back to the late 630s, when Arab armies advanced into regions around Mosul, defeating Kurdish tribesmen in the city's mountainous environs. Further campaigns in the early 640s, led by the Arab commander 'Utba ibn Farqad brought the regions of Shahrazur (present-day Sulaimani Governorate in Iraq) and Hulwan (present-day Kermanshah Province in Iran) under Muslim control. Prior to the Muslim conquest, the Kurdish populations seem to have possessed a variety of religious orientations, including communities of Christians, and "Fire Worshippers," possibly a reference to Zoroastrians. However, Arab subjugation set the stage from the gradual spread of Islam amongst the Kurdish tribes. The processes through which the Kurdish population was Islamized are poorly understood, although it might partly be explained by the desire of Kurdish tribal groupings to avoid liability for the *jizya*, an Islamic tax imposed on non-Muslim communities. Consequently, between the seventh and ninth centuries the vast majority of Kurds converted to Islam, and most Kurds became adherents of the Sunni branch of Islam and followers of the Shafi'ite School of Islamic jurisprudence (Poladian, 1994: 21–26).

The conversion of the Kurds *en masse* to Islam had a profound impact of the fate of the Kurds, opening the way for integration of elements within the community into the military and political elite of the Islamic World. With the decline of the Abbasid Caliphate in the ninth century, a number of Kurdish tribal leaders were able to seize effective control in their mountainous homelands and establish a series of Muslim emirates, the most significant of which were the Shaddadids (951–1174) in Azerbaijan and Armenia, the Rawwidids (955–1071) in Azerbaijan, the Marwanids (990–1096) in Diyarbakır and Lake Van, and the Hasanwayhids (959–1095) in Western Iran. This relatively brief period of Kurdish ascendancy was largely brought to an end in the 11th century by the arrival of the Selcuk Turks in Iran. The Selcuk dynasty, which established control over Iran, Iraq, and Anatolia, and Syria, as well as their subordinates such as the Zengid Atabeks of Mosul, launched numerous military campaigns against independent Kurdish leaders.

However, the relationship between the Kurds and Turks during the 11th and 12th centuries was not governed entirely by hostility. For example, a branch of the Shaddadid dynasty continued to govern the town of Ani (in present-day Armenia) as vassals of the Selcuks until the 1175. Moreover, Kurdish tribal groups were often integrated into the militaries of Turkish-dominated polities, becoming important actors in the countercrusades of the 11th and 12th centuries, which in turn provided Kurdish tribal leaders with new opportunities for advancement.

Perhaps the most successful Kurdish leader of this era was Saladin Ayyubi (1137–1193), the Muslim hero of the countercrusades. Saladin's ancestors originally served the Shaddadids rulers of Dvin (in present-day Armenia). However, following the Selcuk seizure of the town, Saladin's grandfather, Shadhi ibn Marwan, immigrated to Iraq with his two sons, Saladin's father, Najm ad-Din Ayyub (d. 1173), and his uncle, Asad ad-Din Shirkuh (d. 1169). Both men eventually entered the service of the Nur ad-Din Zengi (1118–1174), the Turkish ruler of Mosul and Syria, with both attaining high office within the Zengid polity. The former was appointed the governor of Baalbak and Damascus, while the latter served as governor of Homs and, in 1163, was selected to command a Zengid intervention forces into Fatimid

Saladin Ayyubi was a Muslim leader of Kurdish descent. This image is believed to date from around 1180. (Jupiter Images)

Egypt. Although Shirkuh was forced to withdraw from Egypt in 1164, he was appointed the head of a second Zengid expedition to Egypt in 1167. This time he remained in Egypt until his death two years later. Following Shirkuh's death, Saladin, who had accompanied his uncle on both Egyptian campaigns, was able to assume control of the Zengid forces in Egypt and, on the orders of, Nur ad-Din Zengi, overthrew the Shi'ite Fatimid dynasty and restored Sunnism to Egypt.

Saladin

The famous Muslim leader against the Crusaders, Salah al-Din al-Ayyubi or Saladin, is of Kurdish descent. His family is from a Kurdish tribe in Eastern Anatolia, and he sported many Kurdish soldiers in his army. Although he did not practice his Kurdish language, he is widely seen as a champion among Kurds who look up to his accomplishments and achievements. In fairness, Saladin is largely remembered as a unifier of Muslims and liberator of Jerusalem. But who would not like to have a successful, wise, and charismatic hero as their champion?

Despite seizing power in Egypt, Saladin initially remained loyal to Zengids. However, following the death of his overlord in 1174, Saladin established himself as an independent ruler and proclaimed himself Nur ad-Din Zengi's successor. Subsequently, Saladin was not only able bring Egypt and Zengid lands in the Levant under his control, but also establish a vast Muslim imperium, encompassing Libya, Sudan, Yemen, and the Hejaz. Today, Saladin is mostly remembered for his role in the countercrusades. In July 1187, Saladin's forces inflicted a crushing defeat on the crusaders at the Battle of Hattin. Muslim forces subsequently captured numerous crusader-held towns, including the holy city of Jerusalem, which had been in Christian hands for over 80 years. Despite these early successes, the Ayyubid dynasty was relatively short-lived. Rather than establishing a centralized imperial state, Ayyubid territories were organized into semi-independent fiefdoms governed by members of Saladin's family. This political order proved to be unstable, and following Saladin's death in 1193, the empire was shaken by internal discord as his descendants vied for supremacy. The dynasty's eventual downfall came at the hands of the Mamluks, Turkish slave-soldiers, maintained by various Ayyubid princes. In 1250, a Mamluk revolt in Cairo put an end to Ayyubid control over Egypt. Meanwhile, the Ayyubid holdings in Syria were devastated by the Mongol invasions. Subsequently, the Mamluk successfully seized control of the Levant following their victory over the Mongols at Ayn Jalut in 1260.

The fall of the Ayyubids signaled the end the supremacy of Kurdish elements in Egypt and Syria, although a cadet branch of the Ayyubids continued to govern the fortress town of Hasankeyf on the banks of the upper Tigris well into the 16th century. Nevertheless, communities of Kurds continued to exist across the Levant long after the Mamluk revolution, most notably in Damascus where the Kurdish quarter remained an important center of Kurdish language and culture well into the 20th century. Moreover, Kurdish tribal groupings and emirates remained important actors in their mountainous homelands. The political and military significance of the Kurds was further enhanced by the struggle between the Egyptian Mamluks and the Mongol Ilkhanids in Iran. Residing on the borderlands between the two empires, Kurdish tribesmen came to be seen as potential military allies. The Mamluks attempted to mobilize Kurdish support in the struggle against the Mongols through the appointment of a "Generalissimo of the Kurds" (*Muqaddam al-Akrad*), an individual responsible for uniting the Kurdish tribes. Mongol administers also reached accommodations with Kurdish tribal elites recognizing, for example, Asad al-Din Musa as the ruler of the Mazanjaniyya region near Hakkari.

In the late 14th century, the Middle East was shaken by the invasions of Timur Lang (1370–1404), who conquered a vast territory stretching from Central Asia to Anatolia. Following his death, his empire rapidly degenerated with Timurid authority over Kurdistan being replaced by that of the Turkic Karakoyunlu and Akkoyunlu tribal confederations. By 1450, the Karakoyunlu rulers, who emerged as the dominant force in Azerbaijan, extended their authority over the Kurdish emirates of Bitlis, Siirt, and Hasankeyf, while the Kurds residing in the Diyarbakir region were governed by the Akkoyunlu Turkmen. In 1460, the Akkoyunlu ruler, Uzun Hasan (1428–1478), began advancing eastwards seizing the Kurdish held towns of Hasankeyf and Siirt. In response, the Karakoyunlu ruler, Cihanşah (1397–1467), launched a counteroffensive, but was defeated and killed in 1567. Subsequently, Uzun Hasan's forces drove east into Azerbaijan and Iran, on the way seizing the Kurdish strongholds of Cizre-Bohtan, Bitlis, and Hakkari.

Early Modern Period (1500–1830)

The Akkoyunlu dominance in Iran was relatively short-lived, ultimately being defeated and overthrown by the Safavids, a Sufi religious order founded by a Kurdish mystic, Safi ad-Din Ardabili (1252–1334). Although originally a Sunni movement, by the mid-15th century the movement had come to be associated with "exaggerationist" (*ghulat*) beliefs, a radical and messianic form of Shi'ism. The Safavids attracted widespread support amongst the Turkmen tribes of Azerbaijan and Anatolia, in the process becoming an important military as well as religious power. In the late 15th century, the movement successfully ousted the Akkoyunlu dynasty and, in 1501, the order's charismatic leader, Ismail Safavi was crowned shah in the Akkoyunlu capital of Tabriz. Over the subsequent decade, Shah Ismail I (r. 1501–1526) established a vast empire stretching from Kurdistan in the west to the borders of Afghanistan in the east.

Once in power, the shah eschewed millennialism, opting instead to establish orthodox Twelver-Shi'ite Islam as Iran's official religion. This religious revolution set the stage for conflict with the predominantly Sunni Kurds who now found themselves under Safavid rule. Although some Kurdish potentates, most notable the emir of Hakkari, İzzeddin Şir, adapted to the new religious order, most were deeply distrustful of the Safavids and their religion. This tendency was aggravated by the tendency of the shah to remove Kurdish emirs from their ancestral fiefdoms, often installing his own followers, known as the "Red Hats" (*Qezelbash*), in their place. Indeed, according to one account, when a group of 16 Kurdish emirs traveled to pledge fidelity to the shah, all but two were "clamped in irons and imprisoned" (Sharaf Khan, 1860: 441). The policies adopted by Shah Ismail I towards the Kurds were in stark contrast with those adopted by the Safavid's Western neighbor, the Ottoman Empire. The rise of a powerful Shi'ite dynasty in Iran constituted a major strategic challenge for the Sunni Ottomans. This set the stage for Ottoman intervention into Kurdistan, a move that culminated in the Ottoman military, led by Sultan Selim I (r. 1512–1520), inflicting a crushing defeat on Shah Ismail's forces at Çaldıran in the summer of 1514. Unlike their rivals, the Ottomans adopted a policy of co-option towards the Kurdish emirs, with Sultan Selim I placing İdris-i Bitlisi, a former Akkoyunlu official familiar with Kurdish affairs, in charge of securing Kurdish support.

This effort proved effective, with one Ottoman chronicle noting that Bitlisi managed to win, "the hearts of twenty five of the famed Kurdish emirs and with his sweet tongue brought them to obedience and submission to the [Ottoman] sovereign" (Solakzade, 1881: 378). Bitlisi's diplomacy paid dividends on the battlefield, with Kurdish warriors playing a critical role in ejecting pro-Safavid forces from across much of Kurdistan during the first half of the 16th century. Ottoman success in securing and maintaining Kurdish support can be in large part ascribed to the administrative structures the empire established in Kurdistan. Although the territories inhabited by Kurds were organized into provinces governed by centrally appointed governors-general (*beylerbeyi*), Kurdish emirs and tribal leaders were allowed to maintain ownership of their "ancestral" lands on a hereditary basis in return for a recognition of Ottoman suzerainty. The degree of autonomy enjoyed by various elements of the Kurdish elite varied. The most prestigious Kurdish notables, the emirs who governed fortified mountain towns such as Bitlis, Cizre-Bohtan, and Hakkari, were granted tenure over their lands as dynastic hereditary fiefs (*yurtluk/ocaklık*) exempt from Ottoman taxation. Other Kurdish tribal territories were organized into "Kurdish counties" (*ekrad sancakları*) which, although subject to Ottoman taxes, were also granted to Kurdish tribal leaders as hereditary fiefs. For Ottoman officials and statesmen, the Kurds came to be seen as key allies in the defense of the empire's eastern frontiers. Reformist official Koçi Bey (d.1650) stated that the provinces of Diyarbakır and Van along with the "Kurdish enclaves dependent on them" could supply 50,000 soldiers, more than enough to combat any Iranian assault (Koçi Bey, 1939, 26). Evliya Çelebi (1611–1682), the Ottoman traveler, expressed the importance of the Kurds to Ottoman strategies in the East even more succinctly, noting that were it not for the presence of the Kurdish tribesmen, "it would be an easy matter for the Persians to invade Asia Minor" (van Bruinessen, 2000: 33).

The success of Ottoman policies in winning Kurdish military support encouraged the Safavids to soften their approach to the governance of Kurdistan. Although the Ottomans maintained control of the majority of Kurdish-inhabited lands, Kurdistan's more easterly extremities remained under Safavid rule. While some Kurdish populated districts, such as Kermanshah, were organized into imperial provinces, important Kurdish clans, such as the Ardalans of Sanandej and the Mukriyani tribal confederation in western Azerbaijan, were recognized as hereditary governors. Indeed, the Kurds' reputation as frontier warriors prompted several Safavid monarchs to transplant Kurdish-speaking tribesmen to Khorasan, establishing a network of Kurdish emirates aimed at defending Iran's northeast from Uzbek and Turkmen raids. The Safavids also attempted to win Kurdish support within the Ottoman dominated portion of Kurdistan. When the emir of Bitlis was removed from office by Sultan Süleyman the Magnificent (r. 1520–1566), he and his clansmen fled to Safavid Iran, where they were granted sanctuary and imperial favor. The emir's grandson, Sharaf Khan (1543–1603), was educated in the Safavid royal household and, later in life, was granted the title of "the high emir of the Kurds" (*amir al-omara al-akrad*) with the responsibility for representing the interests of the Kurds at the Safavid court (Sharaf Khan, 1860: 427–428). Although Sharaf Khan eventually defected to the Ottomans in return for his restoration to his ancestral seat, Iranian subversion continue to be a perennial threat to Istanbul's primary in Kurdistan. Indeed, in 1821 when the ruler of the Baban emirate, a Kurdish principality that had risen to prominence in Shahrazur district during the 18th century, defected to the side of the Iranian governor of Azerbaijan, Crown Prince Mirza Abbas (1789–1833), it sparked general war between Iran and the Ottoman Empire.

The relatively indirect forms of administration adopted by the Ottomans and Iranians in Kurdistan between the early 16th and early 19th centuries provide important context for the visible material prosperity for some important centers in the region. For example, when Evliya Çelebi visited Bitlis in the mid-16th century, he encountered a thriving town, home to numerous shops and an extensive tanning and leatherworking industry. The British traveler Claudius Rich, who visited the Baban emirate in early 19th century observed a similarly prosperous society, noting that the Baban's capital of Sulaimani was home to five covered markets, two good mosques, and "a very fine bath" (Rich 1836, 85). Kurdistan's material prosperity was mirrored by developments in the cultural sphere. Kurdish fiefs served as important centers of cultural production. Evliya Çelebi observed that the emirate of İmadiye was home to a lively literary sense, which was producing poetry in the Kirmancî dialect of Kurdish. The Ardalan emirate patronized works in the Guranî dialect, while the rise of the Soranî dialect was intimately linked with the rising fortunes of the Baban emirate in the late 18th century (Blau, 2012: 13–15). In addition to the courts of the emirs, Kurdistan's institutions of religious learning served as important centers of cultural and intellectual activity. Throughout the early modern period, Kurdistan remained a center of Shafi'i religious learning and a region in which the teaching of rational sciences, which declined in other parts of the Middle East, continued to constitute an important part of religious education (el-Rouayheb, 2008: 196–221). While much religious education was conducted in Arabic and Persian, over the course of the 17th and 18th centuries, the existence of pedagogical and religious texts in the Kirmancî dialect of Kurdish suggest that, at least in some Kurdish inhabited regions, there was a tendency towards the vernacularization of religious education (Leezenberg, 2014: 713–733). The importance of religious institutions in the development of Kurdish culture is also evident by the fact the vast majority of the Kurdish literati, most notably Sheikh Ahmed-i Khani, the author of the poetic epic *Mem u Zin*, were products of Kurdistan's network of Islamic seminaries (*madrasa*).

The Age of Reform (1830–1906)

The 19th and early 20th centuries were a time of considerable social and political change in Kurdistan. By the late 18th century, it had become apparent that the military, economic, and diplomatic balance of power increasingly favored the industrializing nation-states of Europe and North America. In response, both the Ottoman and Iranian states engaged in processes of Western-inspired reform and modernization aimed at self-strengthening in face of an ascendant West. In the Ottoman Empire, these reforms began in earnest during the reign of Sultan Mahmud II (r. 1808–1839) and gradually, but fundamentally, altered the relationship between the sultanate and the Kurds. A central theme in reform was the rationalization and centralization of provincial administration. Thus, in the 1830s, centrally appointed governors and military commanders in Kurdish-inhabited provinces launched military campaigns to remove independent Kurdish tribal leaders and emirs from their ancestral fiefdoms. This was a fundamental assault upon the unwritten constitutional arrangements, which had secured Ottoman sovereignty in Kurdistan since the early 16th century. Resistance from Kurdish notables was fierce. In 1842, Bedirhkan Bey (d. 1868), the leader of Cizre-Bohtan's traditional ruling house, revolted in response to efforts to split his "emirate" between the governors-general of Diyarbakir and Mosul. For the next four years, Ottoman government forces were tied down suppressing Bedirkhan Bey and his allies, which included other disgruntled emirs including Han Mahmud (d. 1866) of Müküs and Nurullah Bey of Hakkari. In 1846, Bedirhkan Bey was captured by government forces and sent into exile, first in Istanbul and later Crete and Damascus. Over the subsequent four years, the Ottoman government abolished the remaining semi-independent Kurdish emirates. In 1849, Nurullah Bey, who had turned against Bedirhkan Bey during the later stages of his rebellion, was dismissed from Hakkari and, in 1851, the last of the Babans were removed from Sulaimani. A similar process occurred across the border in Iran, albeit at a slower pace. Although the Kurdish emirates in Khorasan were suppressed in the first half of the 19th century, it was not until 1860s that the House of Ardalan was removed from the position of Senandej's hereditary governors-general.

While the opening decades of the nineteenth had seen an end to the autonomies enjoyed by certain powerful Kurdish noble houses, Ottoman and Iranian control over Kurdistan remained precarious. In the region's main urban centers Ottoman governors were busy establishing the institutions of a modern state—provincial councils, courts, schools, and newspapers—providing new opportunities for advancement for urban elites. However, for the majority, the tribesmen and cultivators of the countryside, modernization was a fundamentally negative experience, characterized by rising taxes and the application of conscription. Kurdish tribal unrest was further aggravated a growing fear of Christian ascendancy. Muslim social and political dominance was a central ideological pillar of the premodern Ottoman and Iranian civilizations. However, developments in the 19th century seemed to be undermining Muslim superiority. Most obviously, the European powers were encroaching on Islamic lands and exercising enormous influence over the internal affairs of the Ottoman and Iranian empires. At the same time, the Ottoman reforms of the *Tanzimat* era (1839–1876) sought to construct the basis of a civic Ottoman patriotism based on the legal equality for all imperial subjects, regardless of race or religion. This, too, was regarded by many traditionalist Kurds as a challenge to the Muslim order; a sense further agitated by the increasing assertiveness of representatives of the Armenian community.

In this atmosphere of growing sectarianism, religious leadership became increasingly important in Kurdish tribal society. Sufism, the spiritual practice of Islam, had long had a defining influence on the practice of popular religion in Kurdistan. Sufi lodges were extensive religious networks led by "sheikhs," cult leaders often regarded by their followers as possessing spiritual or mystical powers. With the removal of the emirates and the weakness of Ottoman authority, Sufi sheikhs managed to leverage their spiritual authority into political power, acting as mediators in tribal disputes. This in turn allowed them to build enormous fortunes and large tribal followings. The influence of the Sufi orders in tribal society led the Ottoman military to rely on tribal irregulars raised by the Kurdish sheikhs in the Russian-Ottoman War of 1877–1878. However, sheikhs also played an important role in organizing resistance to the government. In the aftermath of the war, Ottoman and Iranian government in Kurdistan was in disarray, many regions descended into famine conditions, and rumors spread among the Muslim community that the Ottoman government was about to acquiesce to the formation of an Armenian state in the Lake Van region. In these chaotic circumstances, Sheikh Ubeydullah (d. 1883), a veteran of the war, launched an insurrection against both the Iranian and Ottoman governments directed at creating a unified Kurdish administrative district comprising both Ottoman and Iranian Kurdistan.

The implications of the Sheikh Ubeydullah Rebellion were significant for developments in the final quarter of the 19th century. In Iran, the Shi'ite government reasserted control through a punishment campaign against the predominantly Sunni Kurds. Ottoman policy in Kurdistan also shifted. In 1876, Sultan Abdülhamid II (r. 1876–1909) had promulgated the empire's first constitution, which had opened the way for the formation of a parliamentary regime. However, the Sultan ultimately rejected constitutionalism, suppressing parliament and establishing himself as a powerful autocrat. In ideological terms, the new regime sought to re-emphasize the Islamic characteristic of the empire in an appeal to popular Muslim sentiment. However, Hamidian policies also sought to appeal to the self-interest of Muslims alienated by reform. In Kurdistan, the Sultan sought to forge strong bonds of loyalty with powerful tribal interests. Most famously, the government brought into being the *Hamidiye* Cavalry Regiments. This military formation, established in 1891 and named in honor of the sultan, was drawn from among Sunni Kurdish tribes and placed under the command of the sultan's brother-in-law, Marshal Zeki Pasha (1862–1943), the commander of the Ottoman IV Army Corps. On the surface, the *Hamidiye* scheme was designed to provide the regular military with a pool of light cavalry. However, they also served as a way to distribute patronage to important Kurdish tribes and as a counterbalance to the growing Armenian revolutionary movement. The organization gained international notoriety after its involvement in the anti-Armenian pogroms, which swept Eastern Anatolia between 1894 and 1896. Even in regions in which Kurds were not enrolled into the *Hamidiye* Calvary, the Sultan cultivated relations with important local notables, often indulging their lawlessness. For example, in the province of Mosul, the imperial palace forged strong ties with Sheikh Said Berzinci (d. 1909), who became the regime's strongman in and a detested tyrant of the region of Sulaimani.

The patronage furnished upon the Kurdish tribal leaders earned the Sultan Abdülhamid II the sobriquet "Father of the Kurds" (*Bave Kurdan*). However, Hamidian policies were far from universally popular among the Kurds. The tyranny of Kurdish notables with connections to the palace aroused opposition from many Kurds. *Hamidiye* tribesmen did not differentiate between their traditional tribal enemies and those of the state, often plundering Muslim villagers as well as Christians and other religious minorities. In Diyarbakir, urban notables such the Pirinççizades of Diyarbakir were engaged in an intense and, at times, violent competition with the *Hamidiye* commander and sultanic favorite, Milli Ibrahim Pasha (d. 1908). The Hamidian regime was also opposed by some members of the nascent Kurdish intellectual and professional classes, brought into being by the expansion of Western-style education in the Ottoman Empire. Many of this new elite came from important Kurdish notable families, including old emiral dynasties such as the Bedirhans and Babans. However, they were integrated into the new governing classes of Ottoman-Muslims who found employment within the reformed civil and military institutions of the Ottoman state. Consequently, while some educated Kurds came to oppose the Hamidian autocracy, this was expressed in participation in the constitutionalist opposition. Indeed, two Kurdish students, Abdullah Cevdet (1869–1932) and İshak Sükuti (1868–1902), played a critical role in the formation of the Committee of Union and Progress (CUP), the empire's preeminent revolutionary organization. Yet the Kurdish intellectual and professional elite's attachment to constitutionalism and the Ottoman Empire did not preclude a keen interest in the development of the Kurdish community. In 1898, Mikdad Midhat Bedirkhan and Abdurrahman Bedirkhan (1868–1936), former Ottoman officials and sons of Bedirkhan Bey, published *Kürdistan*, the first Kurdish-oriented newspaper. In political terms, it was an organ of the CUP, supported by CUP money and technical support. Hence, it maintained an editorial line critical of Hamidian policies, arguing that constitutionalism was the solution to the woes of all Ottomans, including the Kurds. However, the publication also acted as a forum for the examination of Kurdish culture, history, and politics, signifying a growing "national" revival among the nascent "Westernized" Kurdish intelligentsia.

Revolution, War, and the End of Empire (1905–1923)

Between 1905 and 1908, a wave of revolutionary fervor swept the Middle East, ushering in the advent of constitutional rule in both Iran and the Ottoman Empire. In 1905, a wave of popular protests across Iran forced Shah Mozaffar ad-Din (r. 1896–1907) into promulgating a constitution in December 1906. However, this brief experiment in constitutionalism proved disastrous. The shah died only days after granting Persia its basic law. Iran's new ruler, Shah Muhammad Ali (r. 1907–1909), moved against the new parliament and the constitutionalists and, in 1908, with British and Russian connivance, eliminated the parliament. In July 1909, constitutionalist forces re-established authority and the shah's 11-year-old son, Shah Ahmad (r. 1909–1925), was placed on the throne. However, by this time, central government authority had all but collapsed, and both Russia and British as well as the Ottoman soldiers and officials routinely violated Persian sovereignty. In Iranian Kurdistan, the feebleness of Tehran's authority meant that the region had become a refuge for Kurdish rebels and revolutionaries fleeing the more vigorous

The *Hamidiye* light cavalry troops were recruited from among Kurdish tribes to support the Ottoman army against revolts and rebellions, and to protect the borders. (Bettmann/Getty Images)

Ottoman administration. However, although the power and authority of the Ottoman government remained far superior to that of loosely administered Persia, the Ottoman Empire was not immune to revolutionary unrest. Indeed, Ottoman Kurdistan was shaken by a series of tax revolts in which some Kurdish tribesmen participated. The movement was ultimately suppressed. However, in July 1908, a military revolt in the Balkans led by young officers with connections to the CUP forced Sultan Abdülhamid II to recall parliament and allow for the establishment of a constitutionalist government.

The fall of the Hamidian autocracy was welcomed by educated Kurdish elites in the capital, many of whom were sympathetic to the CUP and the new constitutional order. In September 1908, Kurdish political leaders in the capital established a Kurdish civil society organization, the Society for Kurdish Mutual-Aid and Progress (SKMP), with the expressed aim of propagating constitution and love of the sultan-caliph among the Kurdish population. The society, which was disbanded in 1909, was only the first of a series of Kurdish organizations in the Ottoman capital, which became a hub for Kurdish activism. In 1910, a group of leading Kurdish intellectuals, notables, and parliamentary deputies established a new association, the Society for the Propagation of Kurdish Education (SPKE), dedicated to the establishment of schools for the Ottoman Kurdish population. In 1911, this organization too folded. However, a year later, Kurdish university students in the capital established the Kurdish Students' Hope Society (KSHS), a student association that remained active until the outbreak of the war in 1914. Kurdish activist circles in the Ottoman capital were, of course, far from homogenous; there were secular liberals and religious conservatives as well as pro-CUP unionists and supporters of the "liberal" opposition. However, even those who came to oppose the CUP-led government remained committed to the ideal of a unified Ottoman Empire with a constitutional government.

In contrast, the popular attitude towards constitutionalism in the Kurdistan provinces was far more ambiguous. The constitutionalist regime did, of course, have its Kurdish backers in the provinces. Urban notables took advantage of the change in regime to move against Hamidian protégés such as Milli Ibrahim Pasha in Diyarbakir and Sheikh Said Berzinci in Sulaimani, both of whom were dead within a year of the revolution. Indeed, some urban notables, such as the Pirinççizades of Diyarbakir, were able to prosper in the constitutional era by maintaining close relations with the CUP and winning election to the Ottoman parliament. However, those who had maintained close relations with the Hamidian autocracy, especially those enrolled in the *Hamidiye*, rightly feared that the CUP and the constitutional government sought to limit the privileges they had enjoy under the former regime. In the winter of 1908–1909, many disgruntled Kurdish tribal leaders established Kurdish "clubs," local committees that were formally connected to the SKMP in Istanbul. However, unlike their parent body, the provincial clubs became largely anticonstitutionalist in character and were suppressed after a brief anti-CUP insurrection led by the Bitlis club. Although the new government abandoned plans to abolish the *Hamidiye* and restore lands taken over the proceeding decades by Kurdish tribesmen to Armenian cultivators, the administration did move to rein in the tribal lawlessness and limit the privileges enjoyed *Hamidiye* tribes.

Consequently, the years leading up to the outbreak of the First World War were characterized by growing antagonism. The CUP was regarded by many Kurds as being irreligious, and there was a perception that only the Armenians had benefited from the advent of constitutionalism. Fear of Armenian dominance was further intensified by the apparent weakness of the empire. Defeats in Libya (1911–1912) and the Balkans (1912–1913) undermined the prestige of the government. However, most concerning from the Kurdish perspective was Ottoman acquiescence in February 1914 to European administration of the "Six Provinces" (*Vilayat-ı Sitte*) of Ottoman Armenia (Diyarbakir, Harput, Erzurum, Van, Bitlis, and Sivas), districts home to a considerable number of Kurds as well as Armenians. This growing atmosphere of unrest and uncertainly gave rise to an outbreak of separatist agitation. In 1911, Abdürrezzak Bedirkhan (1864–1918), an educated former Ottoman official and descendent of Bedirkhan Bey, began touring the Ottoman-Iranian frontier, building support for an anti-Ottoman rebellion. Abdürrezzak Bey's objectives were to secure an independent Kurdistan with the support and protection of Tsarist Russia. To these ends, he established a series of secret organizations, which brought together antigovernment notables, including influential tribal leaders such as Simko Şikak, Sheikh Taha of Nehri, and Sheikh Abdüsselam Barzani. Although on the eve of the First World War, Abdürrezzak Bey and his supporters had largely failed to ignite a general Kurdish uprising in Ottoman Kurdistan, they did constitute a growing challenge to Ottoman authority in the East (Reynolds, 2011: 411–450).

Ottoman entry into the First World War in October 1914 radically altered the political circumstances in both Ottoman and Iranian Kurdistan. Most immediately, the region became a battlefield as Russian and Ottoman forces clashed, ignoring Iranian sovereignty in the process. It should be noted that many individuals of Kurdish origin served in the Ottoman military across the empire. However, the Kurdish population was most significant on the Russian front. On a most basic level, many of those in the regular armies stationed in the East were conscripted from Kurdish-speaking areas. Kurdish irregulars also played an important role in the military campaign. In Iranian Kurdistan, Ottoman emissaries were successful in inciting Kurdish tribesmen to fight against the Russians, and Kurdish tribesmen played a critical role in the Battle of Dilman in April 1915, as well as in Ottoman operations in Mesopotamia. Russia, too, had Kurdish proxies. Abdürrezzak Bey received support from the tsar's military and was even appointed governor of Erzurum when the town fell to the Russians in February 1916. Elements of the Kurdish population were also caught up in one of the darker chapters of the First World War, the 1915 campaign of genocide waged by the CUP government against the Ottoman Armenian population. Across the East, many Kurds participated in the orgy of plundering, looting, and murder of Armenians orchestrated by the administration. Kurdish civilians were also subject to violence. Much was at the hands of the Russian military and Armenian partisans. However, even those who escaped the frontlines faced difficulties. In 1916, the CUP issued a directive pertaining to the treatment of Kurdish refugees, a directive that sought to break up and disperse Kurds fleeing the front across Anatolia in order to facilitate their "Turkification" (Bozkurt, 2014: 823–837).

Following the Russian victory at Sarıkamış in January 1915, Ottoman operations on the eastern front were largely defensive. However, the Russian revolutions of 1917 set the stage for a rapid reversal of fortunes. As the Russian military pulled back, Ottoman forces were able to reoccupy lost territories and managed to capture and execute Abdürrezzak Bey. Despite successes on the Russian front, British forces had successfully driven Ottoman forces from Baghdad and were advancing from the south towards Mosul and its Kurdish dependencies. In October 1918, with Ottoman troops in retreat in Iraq and Syria, Istanbul surrendered. The end of the war brought about an intense military and diplomatic struggle over the fate of Kurdistan. In Iranian Kurdistan, Abdürrezzak Bey's old ally, Simko Şikak, took control of large areas around Lake Urmia and successfully resisted Tehran's authority until 1920. Across the border, the fate of the Kurdish inhabited regions of the Ottoman Empire was also in contention. In December 1918, Kurdish elites in the Ottoman capital established the Society for the Betterment of Kurdistan (SBK). In political terms, the SBK was an organization divided between a more conservative pro-Ottoman faction led by Sheikh Ubeyduallah's son, Sheikh Abdülkadir Efendi (1851–1925), an Ottoman senator, and a more radical pro-independence faction championed by Bedirkhan Bey's son, Emin Ali Bedirkhan (1851–1926). However, despite divisions, in 1920, the organization's representative in Paris, General Mehmed Şerif Pasha (1856–1951), a former Ottoman diplomat, scored a major diplomatic victory, reaching an agreement with the Armenian delegation over the division of Ottoman lands in the East, as well as securing a pathway to Kurdish independence in the Treaty of Sèvres of August 1920.

Yet the Kurdish movement in the capital was in a precarious position. In 1920, the pro-independence faction within the SBK, led by Emin Ali Bedirkhan, established a breakaway organization, the Organization of Kurdish Society (OKS). More significantly, the Kurdish elites in the capital and in Europe were increasingly cut off from the flow of events in Kurdistan. In the Kurdish districts of Mosul, the British moved to suppress nationalist agitation in Sulaimani, led by Sheikh Said Berzinci's son, Sheikh Mahmud (1878–1956), and integrated the region into the newly formed Hashemite Kingdom of Iraq. In those Kurdish provinces farther north, which remained under Ottoman control at the end of the war, events unfolded differently. Resistance to efforts to partition the remains of the Ottoman realm was coalescing under the leadership of Mustafa Kemal Pasha (Atatürk) (1882–1939), who had arrived in Anatolia in March 1919. In the eastern provinces, the Kemalist movement was able to capitalize on fears within the Kurdish population of an Armenian takeover of the region. As one senior Kemalist general noted: "I have already immunized all the Kurds [to Kurdish nationalism] by stating that they [the Great Powers] want to make Kurdistan into Armenia . . ." (Karabekir, 1960: 113). Kurdish support proved pivotal in early military successes of the Kemalist movement in its conflict with the Armenian Republic in the autumn of 1920. Kurdish notables were also important actors in the political struggles. Kurdish tribal leaders were represented at the opposition congresses in Erzurum (August 1919) and Sivas (September 1919), which laid the foundations for a new government in Ankara. Kurdish notables also intervened in the diplomatic process, with many telegramming the peacemakers in Paris to denounce the Treaty of Treaty of Sèvres for handing over Muslim lands to the Armenians (Özoğlu, 2004: 112).

This is not to suggest that the Kemalists did not encounter opposition from among the Kurds with a serious disturbance breaking out in the Koçgiri region in 1921. However, by 1923, the position of the Kemalists was secured following their victories over Greece in western Anatolia. Upon taking control of Istanbul, following a British and French withdrawal, the new Ankara government moved to suppress the Kurdish organizations operating in the former Ottoman capital, with many former Kurdish activists being forced into exile. The Kemalists were also successfully renegotiating the terms imposed on the Ottoman government at Sèvres. The Treaty of Lausanne, signed in July 1923, made no provisions for an independent or even autonomous Kurdish homeland. Ankara's supremacy in the Kurdish-inhabited provinces of eastern Anatolia was assured. However, the Kemalists were unable to establish its claims on Mosul, along with its Kurdish-inhabited environs, and in 1926, the issue was decided by League of Nations' arbitration, with the territory being awarded to the British-controlled Kingdom of Iraq. Other southerly Kurdish districts between Gaziantep and Aleppo were attached to French Syria, with the Berlin-Baghdad railway serving as the dividing line for much of the Turco-Syrian frontier. Thus, by March 1924, when the Grand National Assembly of Turkey abolished the last vestiges of Ottoman order, the caliphate, the partition of Ottoman Kurdistan had already largely been completed.

Djene Rhys Bajalan

Further Reading

Asatrain, G. (2009). "Prolegomena to the Study of the Kurds." *Iran and the Caucasus*, no. 13, 1–58.

Ateş, S. (2015). *Ottoman-Iranian Borderlands: Making a Boundary, 1843–1914.* New York: Cambridge University Press.

Bajalan, D. R. (2016). "Princes, Pashas and Patriots: The Kurdish Intelligentsia, the Ottoman Empire and the National Question." *British Journal of Middle Eastern Studies*, vol. 43, no. 2, 140–157.

Bey, K. (1939). *Koçi Bey Risalesi: Şimdiye Elde Edilememiş Olan Tarihî Eserin Tamamı* (trans. Ali Kemalî Aksüt). Istanbul: Vakıt Kütüphanesi.

Blau, J. (2012). "La littérature kurde." *Études Kurdes,* no. 10, 5–38.

Boris, J. (2014). "Arab Ethnonyms ('Ajam, 'Arab, Badw and Turk): The Kurdish Case as a Paradigm for Thinking the Difference in the Middle Ages." *Iranian Studies*, vol. 47, no. 4, 683–712 (translation).

Bozkurt, S. (2014). "The Kurds and Settlement Policies from the Late Ottoman Empire to Early Republican Turkey: Continuities and Discontinuities (1916–1934)." *Iranian Studies*, vol. 47, no. 4, 823–837 (translation).

El-Rouayheb. (2008). "The Myth of 'The Triumph of Fanaticism' in the Seventeenth-Century Ottoman Empire." *Die Welt des Islams*, vol. 48, no. 2, 196–221.

Jwaideh, W. (2006). *The Kurdish Nationalist Movement: Its Origins and Development.* New York: Syracuse University Press.

Karabekir, K. (1960). *Istiklal Harbimiz.* Istanbul: Turkiye Basimevi.

Klein, J. (2011). *The Margins of Empire: Kurdish Militias in the Ottoman Tribal Zone*. Redwood City, CA: Stanford University Press.

Leezenberg, M. (2014). "Elî Teremaxî and the Vernacularization of Madrasa earning in Kurdistan." *Iranian Studies*, vol. 47, no. 5, 713–733.

Minorsky, V. (1943). "The Gūrān." *Bulletin of the School of Oriental and African Studies*, vol. 11, no. 1, 75–103.

Nikitin, B. (1956). *Les Kurdes, étude sociologique et historique*. Paris: Klincksieck.

Özoğlu, H. (2004). *Kurdish Notables and the Ottoman State: Evolving Identities, Competing Loyalties, and Shifting Boundaries*. Albany: State University of New York Press.

Poladian, A. (1994). "The Islamization of the Kurds (7th-10th Centuries AD)." *Acta Kurdica*, vol. 1, 21–27.

Reynolds, M. A. (2011). "Abdürrezzak Bedirhan: Ottoman Kurd and Russophile in the Twilight of Empire." *Kritika: Explorations in Russian and Eurasian History*, vol. 12, no. 2, Spring, 411–450.

Rich, C. J. (1836). *Narrative of a Residence in Koordistan, and on the site of ancient Nineveh; with journal of a voyage down the Tigris to Bagdad and an account of a visit to Shirauz and Persepolis*, vol. 1. London: James Duncan.

Sharaf Khan [Şeref Han]. (1860). *Scheref-nameh ou Histoire des Kourdes par Scheref, Prince de Bidlis*, vol. 1. St. Petersburg: Gregg International.

Solakzade, M.H. (1881). Tarihi. Istanbul: Mahmut Beg Matbaasi.

van Bruinessen, M. (1992a). *Agha, Shaikh and State: The Social and Political Structure of Kurdistan*. London: Zed.

van Bruinessen, M. (1992b). "Kurdish Society, Ethnicity, Nationalism and the Refugee Problem." In P. Kreyenbroek & Stefan Sperl (Eds.), *The Kurds: A Contemporary Overview* (pp. 26–52). London: Routledge.

van Bruinessen, M. (2000). "Kurdistan in the 16th and 17th Centuries, as Reflected in Evliya Çelebi's Seyahatname." *Journal of Kurdish Studies*, no. 3, 1–11.

Geography

The Kurds historically and politically represent one of the most significant ethnicities and count as the fourth most populous ethnicity in the Middle East with 35 to 40 million people alongside Arabs, Turks, and Persians. Despite the considerable size of the population and the historical and political significance of Kurds, literature on Kurds has not developed at the same level as the other ethnoreligious communities of the Middle East (McDowall, 2003: XI). The reason behind the undermining of Kurdish studies in the literature is the nationalist politics of the central governments and strong oral culture of Kurds. Therefore, it must be noted that even basic information about the Kurds is overlooked in the literature. This section covers the basic information on the geography of the Kurds, which illustrates the historical, social, natural, human, and political geographies.

Before moving on to the description of the historical, natural, human, and political geography of Kurds, an identification and location of the geography of Kurds are needed to illustrate. Kurdish lands are located alongside the borderland areas in the east and southeast part of Turkey, northwest of Iran, north of Iraq, and northeast of Syria heading toward Armenia and Azerbaijan. This area is historically identified as Kurdistan, which was used first across history by one of the Turkish dynasties of the Seljuk Empire in the reign of Prince Sandjar in the middle of the 12th century. Besides its historical and geographical meanings, the definition of Kurdistan has been politicized in the era of nationalism by the both central governments and Kurdish nationalist movements, especially during the last century. However, we will use the definition of Kurdistan for its historical and geographical meaning to define Kurdish-populated areas rather than its politically controversial definition.

Historical Geography

Several different ethnicities and powers have inhabited and dominated the current Kurdish-populated areas throughout history. Indeed, investigations into the origin and mass migration of Kurds to Kurdistan are discussed controversially in the literature, and there is a lack of in-depth historical studies on the Kurds (Bois, 1966: 17–18). However, the mainstream narration is that Kurds are descended from Indo-European tribes who migrated in the middle of second millennium BCE toward westward Iran (McDowall, 2003: 8).

One of the most significant developments in Kurdish history is the establishment of the Medes Empire in the ninth century BCE. Despite the critical approaches toward the link between the Kurds and the Medes in the literature (van Bruinessen, 2000: 19), Russian orientalist Minorsky (Bois, 1966: 14–18) emphasizes the connection between Kurds and the Medes Empire based on linguistic, geographic, and historical similarities.

Although the reign of the Medes Empire ended in the middle of sixth century BCE, their legacy in terms of the civilization and religion of the Middle East, specifically in Kurdistan and Iran, had been sustained until Alexander the Great conquered the area in 331 BCE. The period after the Medes Empire, from Alexander the Great to the advent of Islam, and specifically between the fifth century BCE and the sixth century CE, is identified as the time of homogenization and consolidation of Kurdish identity in Kurdistan (Izady, 2015: 109). After this period, within one century, Islam had conquered all Kurdistan, and most of the Kurds converted to Islam.

The collapse of the Sasanian Empire with the concurrent advent of Islam in the middle of seventh century led to a reassertion of the rule of Kurdistan by the Kurds under the Islamic Empire. From that period, Kurds have found a significant place in Islamic sources. Islamic sources overwhelmingly address the nomadic and seminomadic culture in the mountainous area of Kurdistan (Bicer, 2012: 52). Therefore, the Islamic period is recognized as a time of re-emergence of Kurdish political and cultural power between the 7th and 10th centuries CE (Izady, 2015: 117).

The declining power of the Abbasid Empire in the late 10th century led to a rise of power of Kurdish dynasties in the region. The most significant and famous of the Kurdish dynasties were the Buwayhids (932–1062 CE) and the Ayyubids (1171–1260). The Buwayhids succeeded the Abbasid caliphate of Baghdad as a central power in the Islamic world. Under King Pana Khusraw (Adud al-Dawlah, r. 949–983), the borders of the Buwayhid Empire expanded from Anatolia and Mesopotamia to the shores of the Indian Ocean (Izady, 2015: 122). Moreover, the Ayyubids emerged from Kurdistan and expanded its territory to Egypt, Iraq, Syria, the Holy Lands, Arabia, and Yemen. The founder of the Ayyubid Empire, Salahuddin or Saladin (1137–1193), who also recaptured Jerusalem from the Crusaders, is one of the most prominent historical figures not only in the Kurdish world but also in Islamic and world history. The military of Ayyubids was composed of Kurds, and some of the Kurds migrated under the leadership of Salahuddin to Damascus, Beirut, and Cairo. They are still living in these areas, preserving their identity.

The Mongols' invasion in the early 14th century created a realm that was chaotic and lawless and empowered the small tribal powers in Kurdistan. After the Mongols retreated, Kurdistan witnessed a power struggle between the Shi'i Qara Quyunlu (1375–1468) and the Sunni Aq Quyunlu (1378–1502), which ensued until the 15th century. This conflict was then maintained between the Sunni Ottoman Empire and Shia Safavid Empire until the 1502 Chaldiran War, which resulted in an Ottoman victory against the Safavids but separated Kurdistan between the Ottoman and Safavid empires. After that period, Kurdistan was comparatively more peaceful until the attack of the Ottomans on the Safavids in the 1630s. Although the Ottoman Empire extended its territory through Baghdad and

Basra during this war, it was not able to extend its boundaries through all of Kurdistan. At the end of this process, the Ottomans and Safavids signed the Treaty of Zuhab in 1639, which formally determined the borderland, which remained until World War I. In that period, the support of the Kurds to the Ottomans was one of the reasons behind the subsequent oppression of the Kurds by the Safavids during the 17th century. The Safavids deported several Kurdish tribes from Kurdistan to the northwestern part of the empire, to Khurosan in Iran, and some of the Kurds who were moved to Afghanistan are still living there.

The partitioning of Ottoman Kurdistan to Turkey, Iraq, and Syria as a consequence of World War I marked a watershed in the history of Kurds. During and after the war, Kurdish and non-Kurdish powers had plans to dominate and govern Kurdistan. The Sykes-Picot Agreement between British and French diplomats in 1916 determined that southern Kurdistan would exist under French control and northern Kurdistan would be under the control of the Armenian state. However, this plan was doomed to fail because of the sequence of events during the war and the outbreak of the Russian Revolution in 1917. Then, Britain planned to add southern Kurdistan (i.e., the Mosul province of the Ottoman Empire) to its colonial domains by incorporating it into the Mesopotamia/Iraq state. Therefore, one week after the Armistice of Mudros in 1918 between the Ottoman and Entente Powers, Britain invaded Mosul province and the separation of Ottoman Kurdistan became a reality.

Despite all attempts of Kurdish nationalists and some tribal leaders to establish an independent Kurdistan, the existing national, ethnic, or tribal sentiments were not enough to translate this aspiration into reality. The National Salvation Movement of Turkey under the leadership of Mustafa Kemal, founder of Turkey, gained considerable support by Kurds. This movement signed borderland agreements with France in 1921 (Ankara Agreement), and even Mosul was added by Britain to Iraq in 1918, and those changes were formalized in the 1926 Frontier Treaty by the British Mandate of Iraq and Turkish sides. Thus, the end of World War I witnessed the division of Kurds across the new nation-states of Turkey, Iraq, and Syria.

After WWI, the division of Kurdistan led to the emergence of new dynamics in Kurdistan. Kurds have resided mainly in four different countries, Turkey, Iraq, Iran, and Syria, and a smaller part of Kurdistan and Kurds have stayed in Azerbaijan, Armenia, and Russia. Moreover, the 20th century saw the political instigation of ethnic politics under the nationalist policies of states and ethnic movements. Therefore, Kurdistan has been under the violent policies of central governments and Kurdish nationalist movements, which consequentially identified Kurdistan as a zone of war. Consequently, a considerable population of Kurds internally migrated from Kurdistan to Istanbul and Ankara in Turkey, Damascus and Aleppo in Syria, Mosul and Baghdad in Iraq, and Tehran in Iran. In addition to the internal migration, many Kurds migrated to Western countries, specifically Germany, France, Netherland, Austria, Switzerland, Belgium, and Britain. In the meantime, many different ethnoreligious communities of Kurdistan such as the Assyrians, Jews, Armenians, Yezidis, Turks, and Arabs migrated to the cosmopolitan cities of Middle Eastern or Western countries.

Natural (Physical) Geography

The size of Kurdistan is estimated between 230,000 and 250,000 square miles. Kurdistan is divided as follows: 43 percent in southeastern Turkey, 31 percent in western Iran, 18 percent in northern Iraq, 6 percent in northeastern Syria, and a small portion of 2 percent in Armenia and Azerbaijan (Meho & Maglaughlin, 2001: 4). Geographically, the most prominent characteristic of Kurdistan is its elevations and altitude. The highest mountains are the Ararat (16,200 feet), Munzur (11,644), Nimrud (10,400), Sipan (11,300), and Judi (6,500) in Turkey, additionally, Mt. Alvand (11,745) in Iran, Mt. Halgurd (12,249), and Pira Magrun (9,200) in Iraq (Bois, 1966: 1; Izady, 2015: 49).

While the Middle East suffers from a lack of water sources, the mountainous feature of Kurdistan distinguishes it from the rest of the Middle East as having precious rich water sources. The Euphrates and Tigris rivers and their tributaries have been the most significant water sources in the Middle East, which derive from northern Kurdistan in Turkey. These rivers flow through Syria and Iraq and meet at the Shatt al-Arab in southern Iraq to join the Persian Gulf. The area between Euphrates and Tigris is called Mesopotamia, or the land between the two rivers, which is one of the most fertile regions and a cradle of civilization. Moreover, Kurdistan includes other rivers such as the Khabur, Murat, Greater Zab, Little Zab, Aras, Sirvan, Safid Rud, and Zarrinehrud. In addition to rivers, there are many lakes in Kurdistan—the largest of these are Lake Urmiah (5,500 square kilometers) and Lake Van (3,713 square kilometers), which are very salty.

Rugged mountains in northern Kurdistan, eastern Turkey. (Salajean/Dreamstime.com)

Aside from the mountains, rivers, and lakes, there are also very rich and fertile valleys along the Euphrates and Tigris in the plains of Urfa and Tigre and the regions of Diar and Jezireh. Moreover, the fertile valley of Mush is located at the middle course of the Murad River, and the valleys of the two Zab rivers around Arbil and Kirkuk are other fertile areas in Kurdistan (Bois, 1966: 2). Therefore, these valleys have an economic and historical significance for the region.

The climate of Kurdistan changes between extreme weather conditions from the harsh snowy winters to scorching hot and semi-humid summers. The coldest area of Kurdistan is the northern part which includes 20 percent of Kurdistan's total area; the annual average temperature there is around 5 to 10 degrees Celsius and five to six months of snow cover. Central and southern Kurdistan are warmer, with annual temperatures around 10 to 15 degrees Celsius. And for the other parts of Kurdistan in southern Turkey, all parts of Syrian Kurdistan, and half of central Kurdistan in Iraq, they are the warmest part, with annual temperatures between 15 and 20 degrees Celsius (Izady, 2015: 63–64).

Because of these geographical features and climate conditions, the mountain areas are mostly covered with forests of different sorts of trees, such as oak, chestnut, juniper, pine, cedar, and wild fruits (Izady, 2015: 72). Moreover, Kurdistan is known for its unique flowers such as tulips, hyacinths, gladioli, and daffodils, and medicinal herbs such as valerian and cowslip. The fauna of the region still has an excellent diversity of animals, with black and brown bears, wolves, hyenas, bears, foxes, beavers, jackals, cheetahs, leopards; migratory and resident birds such as eagles, bustards, larks, bluebirds, quail, and partridges; and reptiles such as turtles, lizards, and snakes (Izady, 2015: 73). Additionally, the rivers and lakes include a variety of fishes like carp, trout, and over 40 different spring and subterranean types of cave fish. It is also necessary to note that many species of plants and animals are under attack with the economic capitalization of Kurdistan and the conflict between the Kurdish nationalists and central governments.

In addition to physical features and climate conditions, there is an extraordinarily wealth of natural resources such as deposits of coal; oil reserves; a hydroelectric potential on the rivers; and sizeable minerals such as phosphates, lignite, copper, iron, and chrome. Large oil deposits are found in the Mosul, Kirkuk, Khanaqin, and Ain-Zaleh regions in Iraq; around Qasr-e Shirin in Iran; Batman in Turkey; and Rumeylan in Syria.

Social Geography

The economic activities of the Kurds have been related to the geographic features, weather conditions, and natural resources. Primarily, Kurds have had a long tradition of animal husbandry with nomadic and seminomadic lifestyles in this mountainous area. However, this has dramatically changed over the last hundred years because of the new economic opportunities and sedentary politics of the states. According to ethnographic studies of Maunsell (1901), Harris (1895), and Sykes (1908) in the late 19th and early 20th centuries, most of the Kurds were living a nomadic and seminomadic lifestyle. However, as mentioned, this has changed, and currently nomadic and seminomadic lifestyles are quite uncommon in Kurdistan.

Emphasizing the changing of the nomadic and seminomadic lifestyle in Kurdistan, currently, agriculture is one of the most significant economic activities and sources of income for the Kurds. Historically, Mesopotamia is among the first areas of agricultural development in the world, and the Kurds still depend on it. Improving the agricultural productivity in Mesopotamia, Turkey started the Southern Anatolia Project, or GAP, which is the biggest hydroelectric project in the Middle East, including mega-dams and long irrigation canals. The fertile river valleys mentioned earlier, such as the Mush Valley, are also important for agricultural production. However, the military conflict between the Kurdish movement and the central governments has had a negative impact on the productivity of agriculture as farms are destroyed and villagers are forced to leave their lands. Also, technology decreased the necessity for a huge number of people to work in agricultural industries, which has led to a significant increase in urbanization and the population of city centers as compared to the reduced population of the villages.

Besides the agricultural industry in Kurdistan, natural sources are one of the most significant economic assets for the Kurds. Primarily, rivers flowing from the very high mountains of Kurdistan have been used for hydropower generation, specifically in Turkey. Moreover, natural resources, specifically oil, play a dominant role in the Iraqi Kurdistan economy. On the other hand, oil has not been a primary economic source for the Turkish, Iranian, and Syrian Kurds. In the meantime, other natural sources are offering economic benefits such as phosphates, lignite, copper, iron, and chromes. In addition to the natural resources, Kurdistan geographically plays a major role in the transportation of oil and gas from the oil-producing countries to European countries. In addition, Kurdistan is engaged in regional trade as a borderland area to many states. Historically, Kurdistan is located on the ancient Silk Road connecting China with Europe.

Human Geography

The human geography of Kurdistan and the Kurds is remarkably diverse in terms of the various ethnoreligious communities living there. Kurdistan has always been home to non-Kurdish ethnic communities such as Turks, Arabs, Persians, Jews, Armenians, and Assyrians. Additionally, the Kurdish ethnicity consists of various types of religious, sectarian, linguistic, and lifestyle divisions.

The general perception of the demography of Kurdistan is that of a homogenous Kurdish land throughout history. However, Kurds were a relatively large majority compared to the other ethnoreligious communities before World War I. For example, Armenians were slightly less numerous than the Kurds in many parts of Kurdistan, specifically in the northern and central parts.

However, tensions between Armenians and their Muslim neighbors, the Kurds and Turks, emerged during the 19th and early 20th centuries in the Ottoman Empire. There were several reasons behind this tension. Primarily, the Ottoman Empire changed the concepts of citizenship from the *millet-i hakime* (dominant or ruling community) and *millet-i mahkume* (dominated or ruled communities)—where Muslims had status as the dominant community and non-Muslims constituted the dominated communities—to equal citizenship, which caused problematic relations between the Armenians and the Kurds (Oran, 2003: 19–20). In addition, Armenians who were educated in the missionary schools of Europeans and successful farmers, merchants, and craftsmen were more powerful socioeconomically than Kurds. Also, in the Russian-Ottoman wars, the position of the Armenians brought mistrust between the Ottoman Empire, Kurds, and Armenians. Therefore, these reasons triggered the outbreak of a violent conflict between the Armenians and Kurds.

This tension led to the killing and deportation of hundreds of thousands Armenians from Ottoman-Russian borderland areas to the Syrian provinces of the Ottoman Empire before and during World War I. The deportation of Armenians from northern and central Kurdistan was orchestrated by the central government and facilitated by the local Kurdish people. The Armenian population dramatically decreased in these areas, and most of them could not return to their homes because of political reasons. Moreover, a large number of Armenians were killed during that period, and the rest of them migrated to Armenia, Syria, Lebanon, and Western countries.

Another prominent Christian community in Kurdistan was the Assyrians. The Assyrians were mainly living in Hakkari, in the plains of Urumiya and Mosul. Tensions between Assyrians and Kurds, specifically with the Bedirkhan tribe, traced back to the early 19th century. Later, at the end of the 19th century, tensions escalated, and Russian protection of Assyrians during the Ottoman-Russian war caused more problems in the region (Aboona, 2008). Then, the after-war conditions, specifically the establishing of modern Turkey and Iraq, triggered a rebellion of Assyrians against the pressures of the state. Most of the Assyrians, who were living in Turkey's Kurdistan, moved to Iraqi Kurdistan, where they had to endure further massacres. However, today, one of the main minority groups in Iraqi Kurdistan is the Assyrians, who enjoy wide minority rights. They still have five permanent seats in the parliament. Lastly, many of the Assyrians migrated from Kurdistan to the United States, Germany, Sweden, Australia, and Jordan.

Alongside the Christians, Jewish communities existed in Kurdistan from the eighth century BCE. Jews have inhabited southern Kurdistan the mountainous area of Zagros and Taurus, northern Kurdistan in the Van and Urmia lake region, and the plains of the Tigris. Jews spoke Kurdish and were largely integrated into Kurdish society. In addition, they were mostly merchants or artisans. Although Christians have experienced an unfortunate fate in Kurdistan, Jews, on the other hand, have been living comparatively more peaceful with Kurds. Although a considerable number of Kurdish Jews moved to Israel during the 1950s, a small part of them are still residing in Iraqi Kurdistan.

In addition to the non-Kurdish and non-Muslim communities in Kurdistan such as the Armenians, Assyrians, and Jews, there are significant non-Kurdish Muslim communities such as Persians, Turks, and Arabs. Indeed, some of the Turkish and Arabic tribes assimilated into Kurdish society over the years and are speaking the

Kurdish language. In the era of nationalism, the Arab, Iranian, and Turkish states followed the nationalistic politics of settling non-Kurds (Turks, Arabs, and Persians) in the region in order to decrease the power of Kurds and limit Kurdish culture. However, this project was largely unsuccessful, and is currently revised with Kurds brought back home and Arabs relocated outside of Kurdistan.

The Kurds are also separated internally regarding religious, sectarian, linguistic, and lifestyle categories. Primarily, Kurdish Jews have been mentioned as non-Muslim Kurds, but the Yezidi Kurds are originally of Kurdish ethnicity. They speak the Kurdish language, specifically the Kurmanji dialect. They believe in the old religion of the Kurds, which is over 6,000 years old. They are mostly living in the north of Mosul and Sinjar area and the borderlands of Turkey, Iraq, and Syria. Some of the Yezidis migrated to Russia to escape Muslim persecution during the war. Also, many of them were forced to convert to Islam in the early republican period of Turkey. The distribution of the Yezidi population over the countries is as follows; 50,000 in post-Soviet countries (Russia, Armenia, Azerbaijan), 10,000 in Turkey, 5,000 in Syria, and 300,000 in Iraq. However, after the ISIS attacks in 2014 and 2015, the population of Yezidis decreased in Iraq, and many of them migrated to city centers of Iraqi Kurdistan, Turkey, and Europe.

The majority of Kurds are Muslim—around 90 percent of the entire Kurdish community—and 70 to 80 percent of them belonging to the Sunni sect of Islam. Most of the Sunni Kurds follow the Shafii school of law, and a small portion of them follow the Hanafi school of law, mostly those living around Urfa city. In addition, many of the Kurds are inspired by the Sufi teaching of Islam. Naqshbandi and Qadri *tariqas* (orders) are the most important Sufi branches among the Kurds. Also, Kurdish *madrasas* (schools) are the primary religious schools that have resisted the assertive secularism of Kemalism in Turkey. Education in these Kurdish madrasas is based on the traditional teaching and understanding of Islam.

Other prominent non-Sunni communities are the Alevis and Shias who constitute 15 percent of the total Muslim Kurds. Kurdish Alevis live in Tunceli (Dersim), Sivas, and Kahramanmaras cities in Turkey, and Shias can be seen in Kermamsah, Iran. Alevi communities in Turkey are defined as heterodox Muslim in Turkey, and their lifestyle is more secular compared to Sunni Kurds. On the contrary, Shia Kurds in Iran have been considered orthodox Muslims in the eyes of the Shia society and central government, and they have good relations with the Iranian society and state.

Linguistically, the Kurdish language comes from an Indo-European language and is very close to the Persian language. The Kurdish language is divided into two main branches: the Kurmanji group and Pahlawani group (Meho & Maglaughlin, 2001: 3). Kurmanji consists of Kurmanji and Sorani dialects, and both are the most spoken dialects among the Kurds. Most Turkish and Syrian Kurds and at least half of the Iraqi and Iranian Kurds speak the Kurmanji dialect. Sorani is quite common in Iraq, and the official language there is the Sorani dialect. In addition, the Pahlawani group is divided into Dimili and Gurani dialects. Gurani is quite common in southern and eastern Kurdistan, specifically among the Iranian Kurds. Also, speakers of Dimili, commonly known as a Zazaki in Turkey, can be seen in Turkey

(Bingol, Tunceli, and Elazig cities) and Iran. The alphabet of Kurmanji is mostly based on the Latin alphabet in Turkey; Arabic in Iraq, Syria, and Iran; and Cyrillic in post-Soviet countries.

Although Kurds have been categorized as a mountainous, nomadic, and semi-nomadic people, their urbanite lifestyle has expanded and empowered the Kurds specifically in the modernization period of the Middle East. The ethnographic research of Mark Sykes (1908) categorized Kurdish tribes by lifestyle from an insignificant sedentary population to more populated nomadic and seminomadic groups. However, currently, the period of the nomadic Kurds has almost ended; seminomadic lifestyles are still found, but are insignificant in terms of their size of the population in Kurdistan. Most of the Kurds today live in villages, cities, and towns. Specifically, after the conflict in Kurdish areas, the population of the villages has decreased. During this long urbanization and modernization period, tribal ties of Kurds have also decreased in comparison to previous periods.

Political Geography

Ibn Khaldun, the great medieval scholar, stated that "geography is a destiny" for understanding the sociopolitical and economic developments of nations. Kurdistan has always witnessed the power struggle between regional powers. Moreover, in the era of contemporary nationalism, the nationalist politics of central governments and the nationalist aspiration of Kurdish movements have been clashing in Kurdistan. At the same time, the physical nature of Kurdistan has given the Kurds a chance to retreat into the mountainous area for sanctuary during periods of conflict. The well-known Kurdish proverb summarizes the situation of Kurds with these words: "No friends but the mountains." Therefore, illustrating the political dimensions of Kurdistan interconnects directly with the geography of Kurdistan.

Historically, Kurdistan has predominantly existed as a buffer zone (O'Shea, 2004: 9) among the dominant regional powers. During the long dominance of Islam in the region, Kurdistan witnessed the power struggle between the Sunni and Shia sects of Islam. Iran has always represented a center of the Shias against the Sunni powers, which caused the conflict to materialize in Kurdistan. In addition to being a buffer zone between the Sunni and Shia sects, Kurdistan had been a periphery of central powers as illustrated by Klein (2011) in the Ottoman case. After the dissolution of the Ottoman Empire and Qajar dynasty following World War I, Kurdistan was separated between the dominating Turkish, Arabic, and Persian ethnicities as a buffer zone between the main protagonists of the Middle East in the age of nationalism. Therefore, instead of understanding a unified political meaning of Kurdistan, geopolitically Kurdistan represents a buffer zone between regional dominant supremacies.

In the nationalism era, the territory of post-Ottoman states has been defined through the ethnic-based approach of central governments. Naturally, Kurdistan has represented the biggest obstacle for Turkey, Iran, Iraq, and Syria to be ethnically unified territories. Therefore, a unified Kurdistan must be considered a controversy between these states and Kurdish nationalist movements. Before this era, using the identification of Kurdistan had no political meaning for Kurdish-populated areas. For example, the Ottoman Empire identified the Diyarbakir province, including several Kurdish cities, as Kurdistan in the period between 1847 and 1867 (Ozoglu, 2004). However, after World War I, on the one hand, newly emerged countries in the region followed the nationalist approach to define the territorially unified nation-state under the Westphalian system. On the other hand, Kurdish national movements have generated a discourse of the ethnopolitical definition of Kurdistan for the sake of a future Kurdish state with self-determination under the international legal system. Between these two approaches, Kurdistan is still a conflict zone not only in terms of definition but also understanding of regional states and Kurdish nationalist movements.

Self-determination of the Kurds has been promoted by the Kurdish nationalist movements on an international scale for the territorial autonomy or independence of "Kurdistan." Kurdish nationalist movements claim that Kurdistan has an ethnically unified territorial identity on the basis of Kurdish ethnicity. Maximizing the legitimacy of Kurdish nationalist movements in the international area against the central government, the political meaning of Kurdistan is one of the significant issues for self-determination (Kaya, 2012: 11). Also, characterizing the central governments as exclusionary to Kurdish identity is another significant discourse of the Kurdish nationalist movement to gain minority rights in each part of Kurdistan.

To the contrary of proposing the concept of self-determination by Kurdish nationalist movements, the legacy of the Westphalian system in international politics provides more legitimacy to regional states and protects their sovereignty over its territory and borderlands. Moreover, strengthening the power and control of the state over the citizens via modern tools is another significant feature of the contemporary states. Therefore, it is crucial to discuss the differentiation of political dimensions across Turkish, Iranian, Iraqi, and Syrian Kurdistan as the result of different experiences of Kurds across these countries.

Within this framework, Kurdish political movements emerged and reacted differently with regard to their political agendas, social roots, and methods of movements under the different political and institutional conditions of Turkey, Iran, Iraq, and Syria. For instance, among the items of the political agenda of Kurdish political movements is to improve the linguistic, cultural, and social rights with the high political representation or federal system across Turkey, Iran, and Syria. Nevertheless, the Iraqi Kurds had already established a federal system and, currently, independence of Iraqi Kurdistan is their most important agenda item. Although each political movement emphasizes that their agenda is limited to the country of residence, diaspora Kurds stress the independence of all Kurdistan, which is another dimension of current Kurdish politics (Kaya, 2012: 12).

The social roots of Kurdish politics vary on the basis of whether they adhere to tribal or modern bonds, depending on the political history of each country. The strength of the tribal bonds has decreased among Turkey's Kurdish political movements as a result of the strong modernist politics of Turkey. On the contrary, tribal ties are the most powerful determinant of the Iraqi Kurdish political movements because of the experience and legacy of the British mandate (1920–1932) in Iraq. Iranian and Syrian Kurdish political movements include both tribal and modern dimensions.

Applying both violent and nonviolent methods can be seen among the Kurdish movements in each part of Kurdistan. Primarily, the mountainous characteristic of Kurdistan is a great advantage for Kurdish nationalist movements to use as a military strategy against the central governments. Therefore, Aydin and Emrence (2015) identify Turkey's Kurdistan as "zones of rebellion" because of the conflict between the Turkish government and PKK (Kurdistan Workers Party). Iraqi Kurdistan has been living relatively peacefully since the U.S. intervention in Iraq in 2003, in comparison with the previous periods of terrible conflict until the emergence of ISIS. In addition, although there have been serious human rights violations against the Kurds in Iran and Syria, the level of conflict between Kurdish movements and the Iranian and Syrian states has been lower than in Turkey and Iraq.

Finally, the geography of Kurdistan is significant from a political economic perspective because of its place on the trade routes and transit areas of energy. Primarily, Kurdistan is on the route of Silk Road, an old trade route from China to Europe. Although the Silk Road lost its significance after finding new trade routes in the age of discovery and the building of the steamboat during the Industrial Revolution, China has earmarked funds for a project designed to revive the Silk Road according to announcements by President Xi Jinping on 2013. Moreover, Kurdistan is situated in the borderland area between Turkey, Azerbaijan, Iran, Iraq, and Syria as the center of trading between these countries. In addition, currently, transit routes of energy (oil and gas) are an important topic of the political debate in Middle Eastern and Western politics, which directly relates to Kurdistan. Kurdistan's is significant for transportation of Gulf energy to Europe.

Selcuk Aydin

Further Reading

Aboona, H. (2008). *Assyrians, Kurds, and Ottomans: Intercommunal Relations on the Periphery of the Ottoman Empire*. Amherst, New York: Cambria Press.

Aydin, A., & Emrence, C. (2015). *Zones of Rebellion: Kurdish Insurgents and the Turkish State*. Ithaca: Cornell University Press.

Bicer, B. (2012). "Islam Tarihi Kitaplarinda Kurtler Hakkindaki Rivayetler (7. ve 12. Yuzyil Arasi)." *International Journal of Social Science,* vol. 5, no. 6, 51–80.

Bois, T. (1966). *The Kurds* (trans. by M. W. M. Welland). Beirut: Khayats.

Harris, W. B. (1895). "A Journey in Persian Kurdistan." *The Geographical Journal,* vol. 6, no. 5, 453–457.

Izady, M. (2015). *The Kurds: A Concise History and Fact Book*. Abingdon, New York: Routledge.

Maunsell, F. R. (1901). "Central Kurdistan." *The Geographical Journal,* vol. 18, no. 2, 121–141.

McDowall, D. (2003). *Modern History of the Kurds*. London, New York; IB Tauris.

Meho, L. I., & Maglaughlin, K. L. (2001). *Kurdish Culture and Society: An Annotated Bibliography*. Westport, CT: Greenwood Publishing Group.

Minorsky, V. (1927). "Kurds." *Encyclopaedia of Islam* vol. 6, 447–464.

Kaya, Z. N. (2012). "Maps into Nations: Kurdistan, Kurdish Nationalism and International Society." PhD dissertation submitted to London School of Economics.

Klein, J. (2011). *The Margins of Empire: Kurdish Militias in the Ottoman Tribal Zone*. Redwood City, CA: Stanford University Press.

Oran, B. (2003). *Kürt Barışında Batı Cephesi: "Ben Ege'de Akilken"*. Istanbul: İletişim.

O'Shea, M. V. (2004). *Trapped between the Map and Reality: Cartography and Perceptions of Kurdistan*. New York, London: Routledge.

Ozoglu, H. (2004). *Kurdish Notables and the Ottoman State: Evolving Identities, Competing Loyalties, and Shifting Boundaries*. Albany, NY: SUNY Press.

Sykes, M. (1908). "The Kurdish Tribes of the Ottoman Empire." *The Journal of the Royal Anthropological Institute of Great Britain and Ireland*, vol. 38, 451–486.

Van Bruinessen, M. (1992). *Agha, Shaikh, and State: The Social and Political Structures of Kurdistan*. London: Zed Books.

Van Bruinessen, M. (2000). "The Ethnic Identity of the Kurds in Turkey." In M. Van Bruinessen (Ed.), *Kurdish Ethno-Nationalism Versus Nation-Building States: Collected Articles* (pp. 15–25). Istanbul: ISIS.

Yildirim, K. (2016). *Median Empire as Forefathers of the Modern Kurds*. Saarbrücken: Lambert Academic Publishing.

Political Systems and Parties

Political parties are major actors in the politics of most countries, even countries such as Iran and Syria with nondemocratic political systems. In nondemocratic political systems, political parties can play a vital function in mobilizing and voicing the grievances of the people who oppose the government. Indeed, some of the key functions of political parties include recruitment, contesting elections, and representation. According to John Aldrich, political parties are a response to "problems that current institutional arrangements do not solve and that politicians have come to believe they cannot solve" (Aldrich, 1995: 22). Kurdish political parties are not unique in this regard. They are a response to political systems that have either completely or at least significantly shut out the Kurds from participating in the political arena.

Kurds were politically active in Iran, Iraq, Syria, and Turkey in the early 20th century, but much of Kurdish political activity at this time, however, was conducted in unofficial capacities or in the form of uprisings against the central government. In the 1940s, Kurdish political parties began to emerge in Iran and Iraq. This trend reached Syria in the 1950s and, later, in Turkey in the 1970s. In all cases, Kurdish political parties have faced staunch opposition from successive central governments that did not tolerate dissent or a challenge to their power. Despite closed political systems and governmental repression, Kurdish political parties have managed to survive, mobilize support from Kurdish citizens, and openly participate in elections.

The objective of this chapter is to provide an outline of Kurdish political parties and the political systems within which they operate. Given the limited space available to the author and the large number of Kurdish political parties, the chapter will not cover all political parties. The entry will demonstrate that the repressive policies of the four governments that have Kurdish populations provided the impetus for the emergence of Kurdish political parties. In other words, Kurdish political parties have emerged and endured in closed political systems that made it difficult for groups to mobilize politically. Under open political systems (e.g., Turkey and Iraq), Kurdish political parties organize, compete in elections, and even experience success. In post-2003 Iraq, for example, Kurdish political parties regularly gain more than 60 seats in the parliament of Iraq. Recently in Turkey, the Peoples' Democratic Party (HDP) became the first Kurdish political party to meet the 10 percent threshold required for a party to enter the Turkish parliament. The HDP achieved this success in the June 2015 general election in Turkey. In Iran and Syria, on the other hand, Kurdish political parties are illegal and have no standing or representation in political institutions.

This chapter will proceed as follows. The first section will outline the political systems of Iran, Iraq, Syria, and Turkey. It will provide the background for the ways in which the political systems and landscapes shape the formation and evolution of Kurdish political parties. The second section identifies and discusses five common threads, or themes, that shed light on Kurdish political parties and the political systems of Iraq, Iran, Syria, and Turkey. The third section covers the period from 1945 to 1957 and the emergence of the Kurdistan Democratic Party in Iran, Iraq, and Syria. Next, the chapter outlines the emergence of socialist and Marxist parties from 1967 to 2004. The next section examines the emergence of modern political parties. Specifically, this section outlines the founding of Gorran in 2009 in Iraq and the Peoples' Democratic Party in 2012 in Turkey. Following that, the chapter briefly discusses Islamic political parties with a particular focus on Iraq and Turkey. It will then provide a brief overview of Yazidi political parties in Iraq. The final section will offer some brief concluding remarks about Kurdish political parties.

Political Systems of Iran, Iraq, Syria, and Turkey

Officially, the four countries with a Kurdish population are republics: Republic of Turkey, Syrian Arab Republic, Republic of Iraq, and Islamic Republic of Iran. In practice, however, Syria and Iran are far from being democratic, and Turkey's weak political institutions often raise questions about its democratic credentials. Iraq, on the other hand, has experienced a real democratic transformation since the 2005 federal election. For all its institutional weaknesses and democratic deficits, Iraq holds significant promise for establishing an open political system. Turkey's political system often demonstrates rigidities that are undemocratic (e.g., banning political parties that are deemed Islamist or pro-Kurdistan Workers' Party). Prior to the civil war, Syria's political system did not allow political parties to organize along ethnic lines, and therefore most Kurds were shut out from the political process. Iran's political system is similar in that groups cannot form political parties along ethnic or cultural lines.

In 1979, Iran's monarchic system was replaced by the current political system that functions within the principle of *velayat-e faqih* (guardianship of the jurist). This principle created two institutions that are occupied by clerics who supervise state institutions to ensure that they conform to Islamic law. The clerics supervise the directly elected president and the unicameral parliament (or Majles), which allocates seats to provinces in proportion to population size (Gasiorowski & Yom, 2011: 76). Minorities, including Christians, Jewish, and Zoroastrian, also receive representation through five reserved seats in the parliament. A supreme leader, Ali Khamenei, heads Iran and is perhaps the most powerful person in the political system. The president is elected every four years and can serve two consecutive terms. In theory, the president, who heads the executive arm of the government, occupies the second most powerful position. The president and supreme leader share responsibilities in areas such as foreign policy and defense. The speaker of the Majles is also an important post. The Majles is responsible for reviewing budgets and legislation on matters related to the executive, ratifying treaties, and evaluating the performance of the president.

The constitution permits the creation and participation of political parties in the political system, but they must adhere to the principles of the Islamic regime (Gasiorowski & Yom, 2011: 78). In 1998, the government created legislation to regulate political parties. The organization of political parties is permitted in Iran, but they are severely constrained by legal guidelines. The constitution of Iran stipulates that the formation of political parties and other organizations is permitted on the grounds that they "do not violate the principles of independence, freedom, national unity, the criteria of Islam, or the basis of the Islamic Republic. It also states that no one may be prevented from participating in the aforementioned groups, or be compelled to participate in them. In addition, political parties cannot be created on the basis of ethnicity or culture, and they cannot promote cultural or racial differences in Iran. Political parties in Iran typically adhere to a combination of Islamic values and support for the revolution. Examples of political parties in Iran include the Association of the Devotees of the Islamic Revolution (Isargaran) and National Trust. Kurdish political parties, therefore, are illegal and cannot promote the Kurdish culture or identity. Within this framework, Kurdish political parties have been forced to operate underground and often use violence against the Iranian government.

Iraq's political system underwent dramatic changes in the wake of the 2003 United States–led invasion of Iraq. The U.S. invasion toppled the dictatorial regime of Saddam Hussein and replaced the one-party political system with an open democratic system. Post-2003 Iraq is a multiparty parliamentary democracy that guarantees representation for all ethnic and religious groups in the country with a figurehead president. Kurdish political parties have been very successful in the post-2003 Iraq political system. Jalal Talabani, secretary general of the Patriotic Union of Kurdistan (PUK), was president of Iraq from 2005 to 2014. In addition, members of the Kurdistan Democratic Party (KDP) and PUK have held high-level positions in Iraq, including deputy prime minister and other ministerial positions in successive governments. In the April 2014 general election in Iraq, Kurdish political parties received more than 60 seats in Iraq's parliament. In short, Iraq's open and democratic political system provides Kurdish political parties with an arena within which they can pursue their objectives. Indeed, Kurdish political parties possess tremendous power in the politics of Iraq. Since 2005, successive governments have relied on the support of the KDP and the PUK to form a cabinet.

The Kurdistan Democratic Party (KDP)

The KDP (or sometimes referred to as PDK) is the oldest Kurdish political party. It was founded in 1946 in the Republic of Mahabad by Qazi Mohamed and Mustafa Barzani. The latter would lead the party for decades and into autonomy from the Iraqi government. Barzani's son and grandsons would continue the legacy of leadership, while in Syria and Iran branches were formed to lead the political struggle there. Today, the KDP is the most powerful political agent in northern Iraq, and is largely seen as a tribal and authoritarian party ruled by the Barzani family.

More importantly, the Kurds have institutionalized their political, economic, and cultural rights in the constitution of Iraq. This includes the creation of an autonomous region comprising four provinces: Sulaymaniyah, Duhok, Halabja, and Erbil. The Kurdish region of Iraq functions with a high degree of autonomy from the central government in Baghdad. For instance, the Kurdish region holds regular regional elections for the Kurdistan National Assembly, and the Kurdistan Regional Government legislates and administers the Kurdish region with little influence from Baghdad. The Kurdish region has an independent presidency, parliament, security forces, and diplomatic relations with other governments. Kurdish political parties in Iraq, therefore, work on two tracks. At the federal level, Kurdish political parties work with the government in Baghdad to uphold the extensive political and economic benefits the Kurds have secured in the post-2003 Iraq. At the regional level, political parties compete (and cooperate) with each other to control the institutions and resources of the Kurdish region.

The political system of the Kurdish region of Iraq is a mixed system with a president and a unicameral parliament. The president is the top executive and the most powerful individual in the political system. Masoud Barzani has been the president of the Kurdish region since 1992. His second and final term since 2005 was sched-

Masoud Barzani, president of the Iraqi Kurdistan region (2005–2017) and leader of the Kurdistan Democratic Party (KDP), at a press conference on January 5, 2008. (Sadık Güleç/Dreamstime.com)

uled to end in 2013, but was subsequently extended to August 2015. Barzani has not stepped down, and instead, the KDP is demanding that the Barzani presidency receive an additional two-year extension. As of May 2016, the issue was unresolved. The 111-seat parliament is made up members from the Kurdistan Democratic Party, Gorran, the Patriotic Union of Kurdistan, the Kurdistan Islamic Union, and the Kurdistan Islamic Group, and 11 of the seats are reserved for minorities such as the Yezidis, Turkmen, Christians, and Armenians. The parliament also reserves 30 percent of its seats for women.

Syria has been embroiled in civil war since the spring of 2011, and it is not clear how the conflict will unfold or whether it will lead to significant political changes. To date, Bashar al-Assad has offered little by way of real reform. As a result, a national front, has governed Syria since the early 1960s, and its president, Bashar al-Assad, has been in power since 2000. Since the rise of Hafiz al-Assad (1930–2000) in 1970, the Alawite minority has dominated the Syrian political system, and power has been concentrated in the hands of the Assad family. Hafiz al-Assad turned Syria into a one-party state committed to Arab nationalism under the ideology of the Baath party. The Baath party in Syria was founded in 1947 by Michel Aflaq and Salah Baitar. The party was founded on the ideology of pan-Arab nationalism and socialism and it sought to unite all Arabs. The Baath party in Iraq was founded in 1951 as an offshoot of the original party in Syria. The Baath parties in Syria and Iraq disagreed on how power ought to be exercised: whereas the Baath party in Syria established a military regime in 1966, the Baath party in Iraq attempted to establish a political party that was a regular political organization not attached to the military. Syria's one-party and closed political system constitutionally banned all political expression, including ethnicity.

There were great expectations for economic and political reform when Bashar al-Assad assumed the presidency in 2000. Instead, Bashar perpetuated the authoritarian state he inherited from his father and did little to improve the poor economy and the political repression (Lesch, 2012: 5). Hafiz al-Assad had constructed a political system (including the Ba'th party, security apparatuses, and elites) that was subservient to the president and one that would be difficult to reform (Perthes, 1995: 133). The smooth succession of Bashar to the presidency and the regime's survival are a testament to the enduring authoritarian political system set up in Syria. Syria has a president and unicameral parliament with 250 representatives elected by a popular vote for four years. The president is popularly elected to seven-year terms without term limits. The president governs without any checks on his power and possesses extensive and institutionalized powers. It is within this closed and rigid political system that Kurds have formed political parties in Syria. Political parties, for instance, are legal but cannot be founded on ethnic, religious, or tribal grounds.

For the Kurds, political activity and organization in Syria have been conducted illegally and are fraught with danger. Little changed when Bashar al-Assad assumed the presidency in 2000. Following the 2011 uprising, Assad attempted to appease the opposition with constitutional reforms that included elections to be contested by political parties. Restrictions against ethnic political parties were not removed, and as a result the reforms did little to change the Kurdish position in Syria (Allsopp, 2015: 23). In other words, Kurds and Kurdish political parties have been excluded from the political system and are still deemed illegal in Syria. It should be noted, however, that Syria's political system is closed to all non-Arabs, not only Kurds. Since the 2011 uprising in Syria, however, Kurdish political parties have openly opposed the Syrian government and have publicly declared their desire for Kurdish autonomy in a federal Syria. To this end, Kurdish political parties in Syria have established self-administration cantons in the area referred to as Rojava. These cantons are established under the principles of gender equality, democracy, and ethnic and religious equality.

Turkey is a multiparty parliamentary democracy with a ceremonial president. Henri Barkey and Omer Taspinar describe it as a "unitary republic and a parliamentary democracy" with a unicameral legislature (Barkey & Taspinar, 2011: 29). The prime minister is the head executive and leads the Council of Ministers. The Constitutional Court of Turkey is the top court in the country and possesses the prerogative to rule on the constitutionality of laws and political parties. Turkey's political system functions within the framework of the Kemalist ideology, which prioritizes secularism, nationalism, and republicanism.

Kemal Ataturk (1881–1938) established Turkey's parliamentary republic in 1923, but Turkey was effectively a one-party state (i.e., Republican People's Party) until 1945. From 1945 to the early 21st century, Turkey's political system was under the careful watch of the military. The intrusive role of the Turkish military is one of the weaknesses of Turkey's democratic political system. Indeed, the Turkish military committed three coups d'état that took place in 1960, 1971, and 1980. A second weakness is Turkey's proclivity for banning political parties that are either not secular (i.e., Islamist) or alleged to be affiliated with the Kurdistan Workers' Party (PKK). Consequently, Turkey's Constitutional Court has banned over two dozen political parties since 1961 (Sayari, 2012: 185).

In Turkey, Kurdish political parties face the constant threat of being banned by the state. Notable examples include the People's Democracy Party (HADEP) in 1997 and its predecessors Freedom and Democracy Party (OZDEP) in 1993, and Democracy Party (DEP) in 1994. Members of the DEP included prominent Kurdish politicians such as Leyla Zana and Orhan Dogan, both of whom were imprisoned for their alleged ties to the PKK. However, it is noteworthy that although Kurdish political parties are banned in Turkey, members often establish a new party based on the same principles as the previous one. And in addition, many of the same individuals join the new party.

The 1970s witnessed the emergence of a plethora of Kurdish political parties in Turkey, founded by Kurdish nationalists and former members of Turkish leftist movements. The most influential is the PKK. Founded in 1978 by Abdullah Ocalan and others, the Kurdistan Workers' Party soon turned its focus and mobilization efforts to the Kurdish region in eastern Turkey (Romano, 2006: 49). Following the 1980 military coup in Turkey, Ocalan and other high-ranking PKK officials escaped to Syria and Lebanon where they set up training camps for rank-and-file members to receive military training in guerrilla tactics. With military bases in Syria, Lebanon, and Iraq, the PKK launched its armed struggle against Turkey in 1984 with guerrilla-style attacks on Turkish governmental institutions, including military and nonmilitary personnel (Romano, 2006: 50).

Common Political Threads

Although they have emerged under different political systems and have markedly different histories and experiences vis-à-vis the central governments, Kurdish political parties have several noteworthy themes in common. This section outlines and discusses five themes that stand out when examining Kurdish political parties.

First, all Kurdish political parties are, to some degree, nationalist parties with the aim of advancing Kurdish rights. Kurdish political parties in Iran, Iraq, Syria, and Turkey have been established on the basis of Kurdish identity and to advance political, economic, and cultural interests of the Kurdish population. The clearest indication of this trend is the pervasive use of the words "Kurdish" and "Kurdistan" in the names of political parties. In addition, Kurdish political parties unequivocally emphasize Kurdish nationalism as a key principle of their political objectives. Kurdish nationalism, therefore, is important for two reasons: first, it is a source of inspiration for the emergence of Kurdish political parties and, second, it is a political objective of Kurdish political parties. Despite this common goal, Kurdish political parties often oppose each other and at times engage in armed conflict with each other.

Second, the majority of Kurdish political parties are influenced by ideas associated with Marxism/communism and socialism. Also, many Kurdish political parties are Islamic in both Iraq and Turkey. Although there are a variety of Kurdish political parties with respect to ideological foundations, most parties fall on the left side of the political spectrum. This is particularly true of the more influential political parties in the four Kurdish regions. Ideological influence ranges from parties that are staunchly Marxist (e.g., Komala in Iran) to parties that are more moderate democratic socialist (e.g., Patriotic Union of Kurdistan in Iraq).

Two factors explain this phenomenon. One, communism was very popular in Iraq, Iran, and Syria in the mid-20th century due to Soviet Union influence and activity in the region. Many Kurds were originally members and supporters of the communist movements in Iraq and Iran. For instance, in 1945, the Kurdish Communist Party (Shuresh), although short-lived, was influential in shaping the political ideology of subsequent parties (Ghareeb, 1981: 35). When the national communist parties of Iraq and Iran failed to articulate Kurdish interests, the Kurds began to organize around Kurdish nationalism. Furthermore, in the 1960s and the 1970s the revolutionary fervor of Marxism/communism was a popular ideological grounding for revolutionary movements taking hold in different parts of the world. The Kurds, like other groups, believed that Marxism's revolutionary ideas would provide the ideological legitimacy for their movements.

Third, the political systems of Iran, Iraq, Syria, and Turkey have, at one time or another, imposed restrictions or, in some cases, outlawed Kurdish political activity altogether. The exception to this rule has been Iraq since 2005 when it adopted an open and democratic political system. Kurdish political parties in Iraq, therefore, compete openly and successfully in regional and general elections. In Turkey and Iran, Kurdish political parties (and political parties in general) continue to face restrictions. In Turkey, for instance, the Democratic Society Party (DTP) was banned following allegations of connections with the Kurdistan Workers' Party (PKK). In 2008, the DTP was succeeded by the Peace and Democracy Party (BDP), which was also banned by Turkey's Constitutional Court and later became the Peoples' Democracy Party (HDP). The BDP was the eighth representation of the same Kurdish political party whose predecessors were outlawed by the Constitutional Court of Turkey for alleged connections to the PKK.

Fourth, Kurdish political parties face the difficult task of negotiating the domestic politics of the country in which they operate, and they must also navigate the challenging politics of the broader Middle East. In other words, Kurdish political parties must quickly adapt to the ever-changing political environment within the borders of Iran, Iraq, Syria, and Turkey and in the Middle East at large. For example, Kurdish political parties often function illegally (as is the case in Syria and Iran) or face institutional barriers (as in Turkey). In the broader region, Kurdish political parties must manage relations with other Kurdish political parties and neighboring states. For instance, the Kurdistan Workers' Party (PKK) and Kurdistan Democratic Party (KDP) regularly engaged in bloody clashes in the 1990s due a struggle for influence, resources, and territory. Similarly, the KDP and the Patriotic Union of Kurdistan (PUK) fought a bloody civil war from 1994 to 1998 over power and resources in the Kurdish region of Iraq.

Fifth, Kurdish political parties are often used as proxies by regional governments. That is, the governments of Iraq, Iraq (until 2003), Syria, and Turkey enlist Kurdish political parties as proxies to achieve their own political objectives. During the Iran-Iraq War, Tehran supported the PUK against Baghdad and Massoud Barzani's KDP, while Baghdad supported the KDP against Iran. Similarly, Turkey and Syria have exploited Kurdish political parties as instruments for their objectives. Turkey has a close alliance with the KDP in order to counteract the PKK. Syria, meanwhile, used the PKK as leverage against Turkey throughout the late 1980s and 1990s. Syria provided the PKK with a safe haven during its early years and throughout the 1990s when the PKK was engaged in a bloody civil war with Turkey.

The Emergence of the Kurdistan Democratic Party (1945–1957)

Kurdistan Democratic Party–Iran

The Democratic Party of Iranian Kurdistan, or the Kurdistan Democratic Party–Iran (KDPI), was founded on August 16, 1945, in Mahabad, Iran. As stated in their program, one of the central objectives of the KDPI was to establish "a modern, well-organized and popular political party with an explicit commitment to democracy, liberty, social justice and gender equality". Shortly after its founding, the KDPI declared an independent Kurdish state in Mahabad, a city in Iran with a majority Kurdish population. Kurdish nationalists of Iran captured Mahabad with support from the Soviet Union, which at the time occupied northwestern Iran. The Republic of Mahabad was short-lived, and its leader and founder of the KDPI, Qazi Mohamed (1893–1947), was arrested and hanged by Iran.

In 1956, the KDPI continued to function underground, adopted leftist ideology, and became increasingly active in the late 1950s. In the 1970s, Abdul Rahman Ghassemlou (1930–1989), a European-trained intellectual and Kurdish nationalist, led the KDPI until his assassination by the Iranian regime in 1989. As a response to the assassination of its leader, the KDPI engaged in a violent insurgency against the Iranian government. The violence of the 1990s was ended by a ceasefire between KDPI and Iran, but KDPI continued to function underground. However, the decision to sign a ceasefire and the continued repression by Tehran significantly weakened the KDPI.

The current leader of KDPI is Mustafa Hijri. Hijri has been a member of the party since 1979 and assumed the leadership position in 2006 following a decade as deputy leader from 1996 to 2006. The KDPI declares that its main objectives are "to attain Kurdish national rights within a federal and democratic Iran" (Democratic Party of Iranian Kurdistan). The party describes itself as a "democratic socialist party." KDPI continues its activities in Iran through its political and military wings. Politically, KDPI is active in recruiting members and disseminating its ideology among the Kurdish population. Militarily, KDPI peshmerga occasionally clash with Iranian security forces (Democratic Party of Iranian Kurdistan). In addition, KDPI has an international presence through its foreign relations department, which is responsible for representing the KDPI in several European countries, the United States, and Canada.

Kurdistan Democratic Party–Iraq

Created in 1946 after the collapse of the Mahabad Republic, the Kurdistan Democratic Party of Iraq (KDP—originally called the Kurdish Democratic Party) emerged as an important political entity in Iraq. Mustafa Barzani established KDP–Iraq as a response to his increasingly acrimonious relationship with Qazi Mohamed and to satisfy his desire for more influence in the Kurdish nationalist movement. Its first congress was held in Baghdad on August 16, 1946, wherein Mustafa Barzani (1903–1979) was elected as its president-in-exile. KDP–Iraq presented Iraqi Kurds with an opportunity to articulate and advance their own political and economic grievances (Ghareeb, 1981: 36). Barzani was forced into exile following a rebellion against the government of Iraq in the early 1940s and subsequently had to flee Iran following the collapse of the Republic of Mahabad.

After its founding, the KDP bolstered its ranks and adopted socialist leanings with the addition of leftist elements such as Ibrahim Ahmed. From the beginning, the KDP advocated for Kurdish nationalism within the framework of Iraqi unity and called for a democratic political system in Iraq and national unity between Kurds and Arabs (Ghareeb, 1981: 36). By the 1950s, however, the KDP shifted its program to the left and called for socialist reforms in Iraq and for Kurdish autonomy (Ghareeb, 1981: 36–37).

Mustafa Barzani's exile in the Soviet Union did little to undermine his authority as the president of the KDP. Indeed, Barzani's absence only increased his popularity and support among Iraqi Kurds. During his exile, the KDP was temporarily led by intellectuals, including Ibrahim Ahmed and Jalal Talabani, from the Sulaymaniyah region (Stansfield, 2003: 66). Despite some internal opposition from the likes of Ahmed and Talabani, Barzani's strong support within the KDP allowed him to silence all opposition to his rule. Over time, however, Barzani's iron fist created a split within the KDP between the Barzani camp and a group of intellectuals led by Ahmed and Talabani. The two groups continued to work under the KDP umbrella, largely because Barzani needed an organization to have an influence and the intellectuals needed the party to advance their political ideas and nationalist agenda. Following the Free Officers coup d'état in Iraq, Barzani returned from exile in 1958 to assume leadership over the KDP.

Following the coup d'état, the new president of Iraq, Abdul Karim Qassem, offered Barzani, the KDP, and Kurds an olive branch in an attempt to establish peace in Iraq. Following two years of cooperation and negotiations over the status of the Kurds, Barzani requested autonomy for the Kurds, which Qassem found unacceptable. As a consequence, a civil war erupted in 1961 between the Kurds and Baghdad (Ghareeb, 1981: 38). And although the Ba'ath party in Iraq overthrew Qassem, Abdul Salam Arif ultimately overthrew the Ba'ath regime and assumed power in Baghdad. Barzani unilaterally negotiated a ceasefire with Arif without consulting other KDP leaders. Ahmed and Talabani were incensed and believed that the KDP ought to function with more consensus in its decision making. When a group led by Ahmed and Talabani attempted to remove Barzani as party leader, they were expelled from the KDP (Ghareeb, 1981: 38).

The Kurdish Flag

Many Kurds support a flag in the colors of red, white, and green with a yellow sun in the middle. Red symbolizes the blood of the martyrs, white stands for peace, green represents the fertility of the Kurdish lands, and yellow is the color of the sun. The 21 sunbeams refer to the Kurdish New Year, Newroz, which is celebrated on March 21. This flag was first flown in the short-lived Ararat Republic, and today is the official flag of the Kurdish Autonomy Region (KRG) in Iraq. Many consider the flag a symbol of Kurdish statehood; however, Kurds in other regions sport their own flag, for example, the Yezidis or the PKK.

The Barzani family has effectively ruled the KDP since its creation. Following the death of Mustafa Barzani in 1979, his son Idris Barzani (1944–1987) assumed power until his death in 1987. Masoud Barzani, Mustafa's younger son, has been the leader of the KDP since 1987. The Barzanis continue to exercise significant influence within the KDP. Masoud's nephew, Nechervan Barzani, is the vice-president of the KDP, and his oldest son, Masrour, is a member of the KDP's leadership council and the head of the Kurdistan Region Security Council.

It should be noted that the KDP's *raison d'être* is Kurdish nationalism. Its most up-to-date constitution declares that it is a "patriotic and democratic party based on a fundamental commitment to human rights, individual freedom, and national rights for the Kurds and other nations as regards self-determination".

Kurdistan Democratic Party–Syria

Today, there are approximately 20 Kurdish political parties in Syria, all of which are illegal entities (Allsopp, 2015: 17). Kurdish political parties in Syria date back to 1957 with the founding of the Kurdistan Democratic Party in Syria (KDP–Syria), often described as a sister party of the KDP in Iraq. Like its counterparts in Iraq and Iran, the KDP–Syria is founded on the goals of Kurdish nationalism and, in particular, cultural and political rights.

Abdul Hakim Bashar currently leads KDP–Syria. KDP–Syria is banned due to its ethnic foundations and nationalist political objectives. As a result, the KDP–Syria has largely operated in Europe. In 2014, the Kurdistan Freedom Party (Azadi) merged with KDP–Syria. KDP–Syria is one of the primary parties fighting against Bashar al-Assad and has called for external military intervention by the international community and, at the same time, it has rejected the idea of dialogue with Assad. Domestically, its primary objectives are a democratic and secular Syria that furnishes minorities with political and cultural rights.

The Emergence of Socialist and Marxist Parties (1967–2004)

Komala (Iran)

Komala, the first Marxist Kurdish political party to endure, was established in Iran. The origins of Komala, "society" in Kurdish, can be traced back to 1967, but it did not hold its Founding Congress until 1969 in Tehran. Komala is a Marxist-Leninist political party whose founding objective was to oppose the Shah as well as the Kurdish bourgeoisie and to protect Kurdish rights. Its current leader, Abdullah Mohtadi, was one of the original founders and was elected as the party leader at its Founding Congress. Komala is also active abroad in Europe and shares its political ideas and objectives with the Kurdish diaspora through the Sweden-based satellite station, Rojhelat (Hevian, 2013: 97).

Komala became increasingly significant in the Kurdish region of Iran in the 1970s, and due to strategic imperatives, it cooperated with the KDPI following the 1979 revolution. Indeed, KDPI and Komala briefly entered into negotiations with the new government as a united front before military clashes broke out between the government and Kurdish groups (Romano, 2006: 244–245). The period of cooperation between the KDPI and Komala, however, was short-lived. Relations between Komala and KDPI were particularly poor in the 1980s as clashes led to hundreds of deaths between the two sides. Most recently, however, KDPI and Komala signed a memorandum of agreement following high-level meetings between the leaders of both parties (Hevian, 2013: 96). The agreement outlines broad cooperation as a strategic goal between the two parties.

Patriotic Union of Kurdistan (Iraq)

The Patriotic Union of Kurdistan (PUK), co-founded by Jalal Talabani, Nawshirwan Mustafa (current leader of Gorran), Fuad Masum, and others, is a prominent political party in Iraqi Kurdistan. Jalal Talabani and his supporters formally established the PUK on June 1, 1975, in Damascus, Syria. At its inception, the PUK was a coalition of different political factions, including the Marxist-Leninist Komala in Iraq, a progressive socialist wing, and the personal followers of Jalal Talabani. Ideologically, the PUK is a social-democratic party. Its support base is predominantly from the Sorani-speaking population around the Sulaymaniyah region and pockets of Erbil.

According to official party documents, the PUK was established as a response to the failed 1974 Kurdish uprising, led by Barzani's KDP, against the government in Baghdad. It is a socialist party, and its general principles are "democracy, human rights, and the right to self-determination" (Patriotic Union of Kurdistan). The official party program of the PUK indicates that self-determination for the Kurdish people is a top priority. At the same time, the PUK emphasizes the need to "maintain and promote the democratic, federal and parliamentary systems of Iraq" (Patriotic Union of Kurdistan).

The emergence of the PUK initiated a long period of competition for power in the Kurdish region between the KDP and the PUK. In 1992, the Kurdistan National Assembly was created and the Kurdistan Regional Government was formed following elections in the Kurdish region of Iraq. The KDP, PUK, the Islamic Movement of Kurdistan, and other minor political parties contested the elections, which resulted in a 50–50 power-sharing arrangement between the KDP and PUK. The arrangement collapsed in 1994 and resulted in a civil war between the KDP and PUK. The civil war was sparked by a minor dispute between the Barzanis and a tribe allied with the PUK that eventually spiraled into a full-scale civil war that killed thousands of Kurdish peshmerga from both sides (Gunter, 1999: 79). The parties signed a 1998 peace agreement mediated by Washington.

Since 2009, the PUK has fallen on hard times following the departure of the disillusioned faction led by Nawshirwan Mustafa. In addition, its leader, Jalal Talabani, fell victim to a stroke in 2012, which has debilitated his ability to lead the party. As a consequence, the PUK has faced infighting between at least two factions. Talabani's wife, Hero Ibrahim, and his son Qubad lead the first faction. Barham Salih, the former prime minister of the Kurdistan Regional Government, leads the second faction. The political infighting and weakness of the PUK were demonstrated in the 2013 Kurdish regional election where it was reduced to third-party status behind the KDP and Nawshirwan Mustafa's Gorran. The future of the PUK is unclear and will largely depend on the ability of the party to resolve its internal disputes.

The Kurdistan Workers' Party (Turkey) and Its Affiliates

The Kurdistan Workers' Party was founded in 1978 by a group of Kurdish university students led by Abdullah Ocalan. In 1984, the PKK initiated an armed struggle against Turkey, and as a consequence, Turkey, the European Union, and the United States blacklist it as a terrorist organization. Until 1999, the PKK was a Marxist-Leninist and Kurdish nationalist organization and called for the radical transformation of Kurdish society. Following the capture and imprisonment of Abdullah Ocalan in 1999, the PKK declared that its political objective would be "democratic confederalism," including political and social autonomy for the Kurds in Turkey.

Since the early 2000s, the PKK has made efforts to reform its organization in an attempt to participate in the political process and to gain international legitimacy.

In April 2002, the PKK became the Kurdistan Freedom and Democracy Congress (KADEK) and declared its intention to work through democratic institutions (Romano, 2006: 144). KADEK was dropped in November 2003 in favor of Kongra-Gel (Kurdistan People's Congress) and adopted the rhetoric of democracy, human rights, and freedom (Romano, 2006: 145). These efforts produced little change in the ways in which the PKK operated and how it was perceived in Turkey and the world. (The PKK and its affiliates remain on U.S. and EU lists of terrorist organizations.)

In 2002, the PKK committed itself to nonviolence and to achieve its political objectives peacefully through the political process. In 2012, a peace process was initiated by the Justice and Development Party (AKP). The process included meetings with the imprisoned leader of the PKK, Abdullah Ocalan, who in 2013 called on Kurds in Turkey to embrace peace and engage in the democratic process. The "Kurdish opening," as it was called, led to a ceasefire and generally improved the political and cultural conditions of Kurds in Turkey. However, the ceasefire ended abruptly in July 2015 when the PKK and Turkish forces engaged in military clashes in Turkey and northern Iraq.

Democratic Union Party (Syria)

The Democratic Union Party (PYD) has emerged as a dominant political force in the Kurdish region of Syria. It was founded in 2003 as an offshoot of the Kurdistan Workers' Party (PKK) and with much of the same goals as the PKK. The PYD has openly and vigorously called for a pluralistic and democratic society in Syria. It emphasizes the need to protect the environment and to increase the role of women in society. The PYD is also a nationalist Kurdish political party that advocates for democracy and autonomy for the Kurds in Syria. The PYD functions under a joint leadership structure with Salih Moslem and Asya Abdullah as the co-chairs. It is worth noting, however, that its members view Abdullah Ocalan as its ideological leader.

The civil war in Syria and the threat posed by the Islamic State against the Kurdish population have produced a political landscape with two camps: the PYD and their allies, and the Kurdish National Council. In 2011, Kurdish political parties formed the Kurdish National Council (KNC) in an effort to more effectively oppose the regime of Bashar al-Assad. It was formed in the capital of Iraqi Kurdistan, Erbil, under the sponsorship of Masoud Barzani. The KNC consists of 26 members, including 16 Kurdish political parties (for a list of these parties, see Allsopp, 2015: XIII).

The opposing camps represent the broader regional rivalry between the PKK and Masoud Barzani's KDP. As mentioned earlier, the PKK and KDP rivalry dates back to the early 1990s due to differences of strategy and relations with Turkey. Whereas the KDP has forged strong political and economic relations with Turkey, the PKK (occasional ceasefires notwithstanding) is at war with Ankara. And because the PKK has bases in Iraqi Kurdistan, the KDP is caught in the crossfire of the Ankara-PKK conflict. During the recent outbreak of violence in the summer of 2015 between the PKK and Turkey, the PKK attacked an oil pipeline that traverses from Iraqi Kurdistan to Turkey's Ceyhan port.

Generally, Kurdish political parties in Syria, including KDP-Syria, criticize the PYD for its ties to the PKK and alleged cooperation with the Assad regime. Indeed, there is considerable strain between the PYD and the Kurdish National Council (KNC). One of the members of the KNC, and a PUK affiliate, is called the Kurdish Democratic Progressive Party in Syria (KDPPS), led by Abdul Hamid Darwish, one of the founders of KDP–Syria. KDPPS calls for the cultural and political rights of the Kurds and political decentralization in Syria (Hevian, 2013: 5). It is noteworthy that whereas Talabani's PUK supports the PYD in Syria, its affiliate, the Kurdish Democratic Progressive Party in Syria, is a member of the KNC and therefore opposes the PYD. Another active political party in Syria is the Kurdish Yekiti Party in Syria currently led by Ibrahim Bro, who is also the current head of the KNC. Yekiti advocates for Kurdish cultural and political rights and self-determination for the Kurds in Syria.

Free Life Party of Kurdistan (Iran)

The Free Life Party of Kurdistan (PJAK) was established in 2004 under the leadership of Haji Ahmadi. PJAK is also a left-leaning party with a military wing, and it is strongly linked with the PKK. Like the PKK, PJAK is based in the Qandil Mountains of the Kurdish region of Iraq. Its members recognize imprisoned PKK leader, Abdullah Ocalan, as the supreme leader of PJAK. As a result, PJAK has adopted many of PKK's ideological and political beliefs such guerrilla-style attacks against the Iranian regime. In a 2006 piece, Seymour Hersh wrote that "Israel and the United States have also been working together in support of a Kurdish resistance group known as the Party for Free Life in Kurdistan" (Hersh, 2006). Despite this suggestion, since 2009, the United States has labeled PJAK a terrorist organization.

Modern Political Parties (2009–2012)

Jalal Talabani has controlled the PUK since its founding in 1975. Recently, however, the PUK has faced political instability and poor electoral results in regional and federal elections. The PUK has been in disarray since 2009 when an unsettled faction, led by Nawshirwan Mustafa, broke away from the PUK to form a new political party.

Gorran (Iraq)

The Change Movement (often referred to as the Gorran Movement or simply Gorran), founded by Nawshirwan Mustafa and other discontented former PUK members on April 16, 2009, is a centrist and reformist political party. Its founding members were unhappy with what they called the corrupt politics of the Kurdish region and, in particular, with the PUK's willingness to cooperate with the KDP. Gorran's main objectives are to be a viable opposition in Iraqi Kurdistan and to advocate for domestic political reforms.

These beliefs are reflected in and reinforced by Gorran's election platforms found on the party's official website. On the topic of national objectives, Gorran believes that "Protecting the national security and establishing a strong region that can withstand external threats, starts with individual freedom and is possible when an internal democratic system exists. A free nation is combined of free individuals, those who think freely and choose freely. The more people have freedom and justice in their own land, the stronger and more resistant the social structure and national forces become". Despite criticisms of the KDP and PUK, Gorran joined the two parties in the formation of the Kurdistan Regional Government following the September 2013 regional elections.

Peoples' Democratic Party (Turkey)

The successor of the BDP, Peoples' Democratic Party (HDP) is a progressive political party that emphasizes democracy, ecology, women's rights, and equality for all individuals. Although it does not have the name Kurdish or Kurdistan in its title, the HDP is a Kurdish political party that advocates for a peaceful resolution to the conflict between Turkey and its Kurdish population. It believes that peace can be achieved if minorities have the "right to education in one's native language, the right to self-govern at the local level and the constitutional recognition of equal citizenship" (Peoples' Democratic Party). HDP is co-chaired by Selahattin Demirtaş and Figen Yüksekdağ.

HDP made a significant impact on Turkish politics in the June 7, 2015, Turkish general election. It became the first pro-Kurdish political party in Turkey to pass the 10 percent threshold required for political parties to enter Turkey's parliament. HDP earned more than 13 percent of the national vote and secured 80 seats for its members of parliament. More significantly, however, HDP's support base cut across Turkey's ethnic and religious cleavages, as many ethnic Turks and liberal-democratic individuals voted for HDP (Ozcelik, 2015). However, the governing Justice and Development Party (AKP) did not win a majority of seats in the parliament and was unable to form a coalition government. As a result, snap elections were called for on November 1, 2015. The November 2015 general election produced a majority government for AKP and reduced HDP's vote to 10 percent and 59 seats. Although it is a major setback compared to the June election, HDP became the first pro-Kurdish political party to have representation in Turkey's parliament.

Religious Political Parties (1987–2012)

Although Kurdish political parties are generally secular, Islamist Kurdish political parties exist, and some have experienced success in terms of membership, support, and competing in elections. The following is a short summary of two of the more influential Islamic Kurdish political parties.

Kurdistan Islamic Union (Iraq)

The Kurdistan Islamic Union (KIU), a Muslim Brotherhood affiliate, was officially formed in 1994 but its roots can be traced back to the 1970s. Its formation coincided with the onset of the KDP-PUK civil war. The KIU condemned the KDP and

PUK for killing Kurds and Muslims and for forging expedient alliances with Baghdad, Tehran, Ankara, and the PKK. It effectively used rhetoric to garner support from a Kurdish population that was disillusioned with the civil war. Although KIU supports the Kurdish right to self-determination, its general principles emphasize the need for Islamic values and in particular the implementation of Sharia law in Iraqi Kurdistan.

In addition to KIU, two other Islamist parties have influence in Iraqi Kurdistan. The Kurdistan Islamic Movement, founded in 1987, advocates for the importance of Islamic values for Kurdish society. The Kurdistan Islamic Group, led by Mala Ali Bapir, broke away from the Kurdistan Islamic Movement in 2001. It won six seats in the 2013 Kurdish regional election and is staunchly Islamist in its objectives. Both of these political parties allegedly have ties with extremist groups in Iraqi Kurdistan and the broader Middle East region.

Huda Par (Turkey)

Between late 2012 and early 2013, Huda Par (or the Party of Allah) was founded in Turkey. Although Huda Par advocates for Kurdish rights, it is an Islamist and religious party that calls for Islamic values and the removal of restrictions on religious practices such as the headscarf. The emergence of Huda Par has increased tensions between religious organizations and the secular PKK even to the point of violent clashes (Hurtas, 2015).

Yezidi Political Parties

Following the massacre at the hands of ISIS in 2014, the Yezidis have attempted to become better politically organized in an effort to advance their interests in Iraq. One such example is the Yezidi Movement for Reform and Progress, which promotes Yezidi nationalism in Iraq and has one representative in Iraq's parliament and one representative in Nineveh province's council. In addition, influential Yezidi militia have pledged allegiance to political parties in the Kurdish region of Iraq. For example, Qasim Shesho has ties to the Kurdistan Democratic Party in Iraq; his nephew, Haydar Shesho had ties to the Patriotic Union of Kurdistan; and still other factions have pledged their allegiance to the PKK.

Conclusion

To summarize, Kurdish political parties have largely functioned under closed political systems that have not been accommodating to their social, political, and economic demands. (As mentioned earlier, post-2003 Iraq has provided the Kurds in Iraq with a political system that tolerates Kurdish political parties.) Outside of Iraq, then, Kurdish political parties exist and function under tenuous conditions. The prospects for Kurdish political parties are brightest in Iraq. They continue to gain strength, possess autonomy in the Kurdish region of Iraq, and exercise high degrees of influence on the central government in Baghdad. The position of Kurdish political parties in Turkey will continue to be uncertain given the unstable conditions of Turkey's political system. In Syria, Kurdish political parties have become influential actors in the Kurdish region of Syria. It is difficult to draw any conclusions regarding the Kurdish position in Syria, given the civil war and the uncertainties associated with Syria's future. The prospects for Kurdish political parties in Iran, meanwhile, remain bleak under the theocratic regime.

Zheger Hassan

Further Reading

Ahmed, Mohammed M. A., & Gunter, M. (Eds.). (2013). *The Kurdish Spring: Geopolitical Changes and the Kurds,* Costa Mesa, CA: Mazda Publishers.

Aldrich, J. (1995). *Why Parties? The Origin and Transformation of Party Politics in America,* Chicago: University of Chicago Press.

Allsopp, H. (2015). *The Kurds of Syria: Political Parties and Identity in the Middle East,* London: I. B. Tauris.

Barkey, H. J., & Taspinar, O. (2011). "The Republic of Turkey." In M. J. Gasiorowski & S. L. Yom (Eds.), *The Government and Politics of the Middle East and North Africa* (pp. 15–48), Boulder, CO: Westview Press.

Gasiorowski, M. J., & Yom, S. L. (Eds.). (2011). *The Government and Politics of the Middle East and North Africa,* Boulder, CO: Westview Press.

Ghareeb, E. (1981). *The Kurdish Question in Iraq.* Syracuse, NY: Syracuse University Press.

Gunter, M. (1999). *The Kurdish Predicament in Iraq: A Political Analysis.* New York: Palgrave MacMillan.

Hersh, S. (2006). "The Next Act." *The New Yorker.* November 27, 2006 Issue. https://www.newyorker.com/magazine/2006/11/27/the-next-act.

Hevian, R. (2013). "The Main Political Parties in Iran, Iraq, Syria, and Turkey: A Research Guide." *Middle East Review of International Affairs,* vol. 17, no. 2, 94–95.

Hurtas, S. (2015). "Can PKK, Turkey's Hezbollah Reconcile?" *Al-Monitor.* June 24, 2015.

Lesch, D. W. (2012). *The Fall of the House of Assad,* New Haven, CT: Yale University Press.

Ozcelik, B. (2015). "What the HDP Success Means for Turkey." *Carnegie Endowment for International Peace.* June 11, 2015, http://carnegieendowment.org/sada/?fa=60370

Perthes, V. (1995). *The Political Economy of Syria under Asad,* London: I. B. Tauris,

Romano, D. (2006). The Kurdish Nationalist Movement: Opportunity, Mobilization and Identity. Cambridge, MA: Cambridge University Press.

Sayari, S. (2012). "Political Parties." In Heper, M. and Sayari, S. (eds.). *The Routledge Handbook of Modern Turkey* (pp. 182–193), London: Routledge.

Stansfield, G. (2003). *Iraqi Kurdistan: Political Development and Emergent Democracy* London: Routledge Curzon.

Religion

Given that the lands the Kurds populate are probably the most ancient as well as rather extensive and are scattered among a couple of countries, they are among the most troublesome areas for studying religions, religious beliefs, and orders due to the variety of religions practiced in them. The majority of Kurds who are living in Iran, Turkey, Iraq, and Syria, however, follow the Shafi'i school, which is one of the four main branches of Sunni Islam. The Shafi'i school is a distinguishing feature that differentiates Kurds from their Muslim neighbors in the Middle East. Moreover, there are Kurds who are Alavis, Imamis, Shias Muslims, Zoroastrians, Christians, Assyrians, Kalimis, Yezidis, Yaresans, Nasiris, Qadiris, Naqshbandis, Khaksars, and Ne'matullahis. The diversity of religions, sects, and orders among the Kurds is to the extent that scholars call Kurdistan the "India of the Muslim world."

Introduction

Religions are fluid phenomena. Historical surveys show the metamorphosis of religions from one period to another. However, changes and reformations are not immediately observable because most people are not ready to accept any modifications in this area. Nonetheless, exposure to new lands and people through immigration as well as new social and scientific developments force people to negotiate with the existing conditions and accept gradual reforms, sometimes arising without the conscious effort of the followers of religions. Traditional rituals are an inseparable part of the history of religions, but the status and mutual borrowing between religion and tradition are still a matter of speculation. This gets even more complicated when religions are orally transmitted. Add this to the fact that when there is neither a sacred text nor valid commentary, it becomes difficult to study religion among communities whose religion is largely based on oral tradition.

The historical geography of Kurdistan is quite rich. It includes many important archaeological sites in the Middle East. Likewise, it is located within the cradle of religions and religious rituals. This area, which includes Zagros, Ararat, Mesopotamia, and Anatolia, is a region that is quite mysterious in terms of the history of religions. However, research on religions and rituals in this area is still in its infancy. Therefore, it is impossible to speak with certainty about the status of religions in this geographical area.

In the sixth and fifth centuries BC, in the western regions of Iran, the Elamites, who were the pioneers of civilization and urbanization, were still faithful to their ancient religions and, at the same time, the Urartians in the northwest were undergoing development and growth. Today, it is accepted, to a large extent, that the Achaemenids (the first and the most important empire of Iran), founded the center of their government in the western regions of Iran. It is believed that they were the followers of Zoroastrianism. Yet there are obvious differences between the texts from the Avesta (Zoroastrian holy text) and the remaining Achaemenid clay tablets and stone scriptures. These differences have convinced some scholars to argue against those researchers who believe in the Achaemenids being Zoroastrians. They believe the Achaemenids were not Zoroastrians but practiced a sort of Mazdaism. If we consider the Avesta, or those sections of the Zoroastrian scriptures entitled Avesta as our base, it should be accepted that in the west of Iran, during the Achaemenid period, Zoroastrianism was prevalent. The assumption that Zoroastrianism is a text-based religion has been accepted to some extent among scholars. This tradition reflects their relative commitment to the Indo-Iranian religions of the Medes and Persians, known as the Magi. Nor should we ignore the influence of the oral religious tradition of the Elamites over the religions emerging after them.

The presence of Ahura Mazda, or the "Great God," is probably the most important element in the formation of the official Achaemenid religion. One can claim that Mazda Ahura was picked up form Mazdaism; therefore, Mazda can be said to be an Indo-Iranian or pre-Zoroastrian god. Nonetheless, one can also claim that Ahura Mazda originally belongs to the Gathas period. Therefore, his presence in the Achaemenid inscriptions should indicate the presence and effect of Zoroastrianism in the early years of the Achaemenid period.

Today, scholars believe that the great god, Ahura Mazda, is neither an Indo-Iranian god nor a pure Iranian one, but an essential element in the worldview of the *Gathas*. The similarity between Hindu Vedas and Zoroastrianism can be a sign of the centuries-old co-existence of the Indians and the Iranians prior to the immigration date (probably from 400 BCE to 400 CE). These similarities are more closely related to the homogeneity of their worldviews and types of their gods. Once we believe that religions are prone to change, then it is not possible to determine the status of the Achaemenid religion exclusively based on Zoroastrian texts.

Mithraism

One of the most important religions in ancient India and Iran, in which the Kurds also believed, is the religion of Mehr or Mithrasm. In the early 20th century, in a region that was the ancient capital of the Hittites, clay tablets were obtained on which the name of Mithra has been seen. Experts believe that these tablets, which depict a treaty between the Hittites and their neighbors, date back to 1400 BCE. In general, it can be said that the evidence of Mithra in the East is more text based, whereas in the West it is based on archaeology and ancient monuments. Mithra can be called the goddess of light, the one who served Ahura Mazda, the greatest ancient god of Iran, fighting against darkness. There were seven other servants known as Amshaspandan also serving Ahura Mazda. Likewise, at Mithra's service, there were gods who were the mediators between Mithra and the people.

Mithraism, nevertheless, has its own religious rituals, such as sacrificing cows and lambs and the use of the intoxicating *hauma* plant. There is a great deal of evidence that their rituals were only attended by men, and they kept a masculine hierarchy in their ceremonies. Mithraism was popular among people from all walks of life, including the general public, businessmen, artists, and artisans. All of these people have been observed participating in their ritual ceremonies. Zoroaster, an Iranian prophet who appeared around 600 BCE, attacked the fundamental principles of Mithraism and inflicted a severe blow to the popularity of the religion, hence reducing the number of its followers. By forbidding sacrifices and other important parts of their religious ceremonies and preventing the use of the *hauma* drink mixed with the blood of a lamb, Zoroaster diminished the power of the religion and gained full control.

Zoroastrianism, however, failed to isolate or destroy Mithraism. The last sections of the Avesta, the Zoroastrian holy book, called "*Mehr Yasht*," describe the splendor and power of Mehr and praises it. The existence of "*Mehr Yasht*" among the sacred texts of Zoroastrianism shows the power, depth, and influence of Mithraism among the people. In many different parts of the Avesta there are other signs of Mehr and Mithraism. For instance, in the tenth *Yasht* of the Avesta, we find the following praise for Mehr: "You are supporting the people who have good will about Mehr. You fight the ones who want to harm him. Mehr is the owner of extensive lands. I wish that the triumphant Mehr, the glorious king of peoples on earth, Mehr the almighty for whom you pray, come to help all of us."

The stone inscriptions and images of Mithra are abundant in various Kurdish regions, including western Iran, the eastern and northeastern parts of Iraq, and southeastern Turkey. For example, in a stone carving in the city of Kermanshah, Mithra is seen dressed the same as Ahura Mazda standing on a lilac, her head surrounded by a halo of light, along with Ardeshir II (between 379 and 383 CE), king of the Achaemenid. In this picture, Ardeshir II receives the royal ring with his right hand from Ahura Mazda. Right before the Islamic conquest of the lands of the Kurds, the majority of them were practicing either Mithraism or Zoroastrianism. However, there were a few Kurds who were Jews, Christians, or the followers of religions and orders, which had picked up elements of the aforementioned to practice.

The Emergence of Islam in Kurdistan

Islam originated in Mecca and Medina at the start of the seventh century, and in the immediate vicinity of a century, an empire was firmly established whose borders extended from Liberia in Africa to the Sindh in the Indian subcontinent. Although the history of Islam points to the inclusion of some Kurds among the prophet's companions, the first serious encounter between the Kurds and the Muslim world was the conquest of Kurdistan during the reign of the second caliph of Islam, Omar bin al-Khattab. Shortly after the conquest of the Sassanid capital, Ctesiphon, in 636 CE, the Muslim Arabs captured the first Kurdish territories known then as Jibal, or Iraq. After the conquest of major cities of Kurdistan, such as Masibezan (near to the modern city of Ilam) and Hulwan (modern Sar-pol-i Zehab), in

Sufism is a very popular form of the Muslim religion in Kurdistan. Here, Iraqi Kurdish dervishes perform a Sufi ritual in Erbil, 2008. (AFP Photo/Safin Hamed/Getty Images)

the year 642 CE, the Arab conquerors arrived at the central and strategic city of Nihavend, where a great war broke out between the Sassanid army and the Muslim Arabs. This war is known as the "Nihavend war" in Iran and *Fatah al-Futuh* (Great Victory) in the Islamic world. The defeat of the Iranians in Nihavend was the most significant blow to the Sassanid Empire, and shortly thereafter, the Sassanid Empire was torn apart forever.

The Arab invasion of Kurdistan was so extensive that, by the end of the seventh century, most of the Kurdish regions were under the rule of Islam and the majority of the Kurds had converted to Islam. Some cities like Mawsil (modern Mosul) in the northwest of Baghdad and Urmia were conquered before other cities, and Sharezur fell into Muslim hands after a mass murder. Other cities such as Mendeli and Azerbaijan have not been conquered despite the efforts of the Arab invaders. They stopped fighting and agreed to pay ransom. The most important cities of Kurdistan, which were initially captured, quickly became centers of science and religion in the early days of Islam. These cities included Erbil, Mosul, Sharezour, Hemedan, Dinewer, Nihavend, Sirwan, Seymere, Borujird (Brudjird), and Keredj-i ebu-Dolef. Consequently, the inhabitants of the captured cities mainly converted to Islam. These new Muslim Kurds, however, were mostly Sunni Muslims.

Khorremiye and the Alevis of Zagros

Since the conquest of Iran by Muslims, there have been a lot of incidents and changes in the country, but for the sake of brevity, we only mention the highlights.

One of these major incidents is the death of the Bihzadan, son of Vendad, known as Abu-Muslim, believed to be a Kurd from Khorasan. He was credited for removing the Umayyad caliphate and replacing them with the Abbasids in Baghdad. However, Abu-Muslim, was soon ironically murdered by the Abbasid. This incident, which took place around 755 CE, triggered a series of political and religious protests and movements in Iran, especially in Kurdistan (Jibal). A group of Abu-Muslim companions who later became known as Abu-Muslimyya (the adherents of Abu-Muslim) did not believe in the death of Abu-Muslim. They believed in his eternal life and awaited his emergence as the promised savior. This, however, created the most important opposition movement against the Abbasid caliphate, lasting from 817 to 838. The movement was named *Khorremiye* or *Khorram Dinan,* those of the joyous religion. It was founded and led by Babek Khorremdin (795–838) in the mountainous regions of Kurdistan. Since then, the movement planted its seeds in the mountains of Kurdistan. The geographical vastness of the lands under the influence of *Khorremyye*, which included much of western Iran, caused a series of disagreements among the followers and gradually established the basis for the emergence of new religious beliefs.

The influential *Khorremyye* movement later materialized in two main branches: one called *Kudekyye* and the other *Kurdshahyye*. It is said that the reason for naming the first sect is that the followers were faithful to a child who was the grandson of Abu-Muslim's daughter named Muteher. The leader was known as the "knowledgeable child." It seems that the sect believed in the emergence of a savior in the shape of a "knowledgeable child." Kurdshahis, who were a smaller group, lived in the Khorremabad area and are generally known as the "*Khorremyye*." Evidence concerning the *Khorremyye* is abundant in many of the Islamic chronicles. On the basis of the Islamic texts, *Khorremyye* are the people who exaggerate the centrality of Abu-Muslim and believe in the emergence of the spirit of God in him, and they would say that Abu-Muslim is better than Gabriel, Michael, and other angels and that he is alive and they are waiting for him. They also believe that Zoroaster has sent Abu Muslim, and Zoroaster himself is alive and will not die, and will re-emerge for the restoration of his religion.

In another source (Maqdisi, 1906/1993: 575–76), it is said that the *Khorremis* are multiple sects, but all of them agree on reciprocation (reincarnation) and believe in the change of the name and conversion of the body. They believe that all the prophets have the same spirit and that the revelation is never discontinued. For them, every religious person, as long as he hopes for rewards and fears punishment, is on the right path. Some Muslim historians, nonetheless, maintain that *Khorremis* believed in the two principles of dark and light, which constitute the basis of the ancient religions of Iran, especially that of the Manicheans and the Zoroastrians (Maqdisi, 1906/1993: 575–576).

One of the most controversial issues in Islamic sources about *Khorremis* and those who later became known as "*Ghollat*" (those who exaggerate about Ali bin Abi Talib) is the question of reincarnation. As it turns out, even major scholars like Ibn Sina (980–1037) wrote works rejecting the idea of reincarnation. This shows that the idea was influential at the time. The idea of reincarnation is likely to come from the notion of the limited number of the spirits. Each earthly living being must host a spiritual guest, and each of the limited number of spirits should be present in several different bodies without dependence on any of them. Belief in reincarnation is evident not only in Kurdistan but also in many other parts of the world, but it is said that the belief in reincarnation began with the Manichaeans and was then adopted by the Mazdakis. From Mazdakis, it was transferred to Khorremyye and later from them to the Yaresans and the Alevis.

Kurdish Emirates and Islamic Caliphate

The decline of the Abbasid caliphate in the 10th century led to the emergence of the first Kurdish emirates, such as Hasanuyids in Dinewer and Merwanids in Cizire (Jazira). The occasional confrontation between the Kurds and other militants of the region, and sometimes with the central power, the Islamic caliphate in Baghdad, became an impetus for the emergence of religious changes, strife, and reinterpretations among the Kurds. Historians have argued that the emirate of Hasanuyids, from a religious point of view, was more inclined toward Imam Ali, the first imam of the Shias (Dehnawi, 2014: 105–124). The tendency toward Shia Islam is also evident in the life and works of the Erdilan emirates who ruled for centuries in Kurdistan. The most interesting point is that most of the Kurdish regions under the rule of Erdilan were Sunnis, and in recent centuries, these people have often showed interest in Sufi orders such as Naqshbandi and Qadiri (the most important Sunni traditions of Sufism). The main center of the Erdilans after the Safavids was in the city of Senendej. They kept a more liberal religious attitude. Under their rule, many Shia and Sunni mosques and centers of worship belonged to the Jews and Christians. Despite the fact that most residents were Sunni, their Erdilani rulers swore allegiance to the Shia Qajar kings from Iran and promoted their sect by building Shia mosques.

The Main Islamic Sects in Kurdistan

Kurdistan is one of the most colorful religious places in Islamic geography. This diversity and colorfulness has its roots in three different interpretations of three principles of Islam: beliefs, jurisprudence, and ethics. Different interpretations in each of these areas have led to the emergence of a number of Islamic groups. Referring to each of these three principles, there have been arguments and disputes among the Muslims. For instance, differences in beliefs led to theological arguments; differences in religions led to jurisprudential transformations; and jurisprudential issues themselves led to the creation of social and disciplinary aspects of religion. Added to all these are the Sufi brotherhoods formed by differences in the moral worldview and spiritual conduct.

Sunni

Sunnis are divided into four main schools of jurisprudence: Hanafi, Maliki, Hanbali, and Shafi'i. Sunni Kurds, with the exception of a small group of Kurds from Turkey, are usually followers of Imam Shafi'i. The Shafi'i school is attributed to

Mohammed bin Idris Shafi'i. He was born in 767 in Gaza and died in 820 in Egypt. When young, Imam Shafi'i traveled to various cities and countries, including Mecca, Baghdad, Egypt, and Yemen, observing the legal principles of various sects. By applying principles of Hanafi and Maliki, he founded a new school of thought that became known by his name. Shafi'i' relies on four criteria in practicing Sharia: the book (Holy Quran), tradition (hadith), consensus, and analogy. The Shafi'i school was spread over many parts of the Islamic lands by its disciples. Today, the religion has a great number of followers in Egypt, Iraq, Jordan, Syria, Lebanon, India, and Indonesia. The Kurds in Iran, Iraq, and Syria are mostly followers of the Shafi'i religion. In Turkey, most Kurds follow Imam Shafi'i, in contrast to Sunni Turks who prefer Hanafi.

Shias

Compared to the Sunni followers of Islam, the Shias only form a small part of the Kurdish population. The most important Shia-based sects are the Twelver Imamis, Sevener Ismailis, and Fiver Zeydis according to the number of imams they accept. The majority of Kurdish Shias follow the Jafari or Twelver orders. All these denominations, despite the obvious differences in beliefs and jurisprudence, share in the issue of the necessity of "*Imamate*," though each sect's interpretation of Imam is unique. However, Shi'ite Kurds are followers of the 12 Imams. The Kurds of Ilam, Kermanshah, and parts of the cities of Kurdistan Province, such as Bijar, Ghorveh, and Songhor in Iran; and the southern parts of Iraqi Kurdistan, such as Khaneqin, Bedre, Kut, and Wasit; and the Kurdish Feyli residents of Baghdad, are among the most important Shia towns. Unlike Sunnis, the Shias do not believe in the authenticity of the consensus and the succession of the first four caliphs. Instead, they believe that the Muhammad, Prophet of Islam and the ruler of the Islamic Empire, installed Ali ibn Abi Talib, his cousin, as his successor in an event known as the "Ghedir Khom incident." Henceforth, by highlighting the concept of *Imamat*, they believe that Imam Ali and his 11 descendants, known as the innocent imams, were the rightful governors of the Islamic empire. Therefore, they created their own theology, which has different jurisprudential and other principles from Sunni Muslims. Nonetheless, Shias follow the same principles of monotheism, prophecy, and resurrection with other Islamic sects. However, they have added the principles of justice and imamate.

The Twelver Shias are known to believe in the emergence of the promised savior, the 12th imam, by the name of Mahdi (born 869) on judgment day. Accordingly, in the system of their political thought, the theory of *Vilayet-e Feqih*, or the Guardianship of the Jurist, has been prominently raised. According to the doctrine, the twelfth imam or the promised Mahdi has had two periods of absence. The first period, called the *Soghra* (Minor) Absence, is the period when the 12th imam hid himself from the public, but he was still connected with his followers by a number of his companions. The second period, known as the *Kobra* (Major) Absence, has been around since his disappearance in 941. From now on, jurists or scholars would guard and rule the community. Belief in physical resurrection is a common point of Shia and Sunni Muslims, but the idea of the lasting savior has created many controversies among the Sunni and the Shi'a.

Sufism

The Neoplatonists and some Greek philosophers are thought to have mystical tendencies, and the fact that ascetic thoughts and tendencies can be seen in most religions of the world, Sufism must be viewed as the Islamic interpretation of this concept and tradition. Muslims understand that there are no non-Muslim Sufis. There are many definitions for Sufism. Hujwiri (990–1070), for instance, defines Sufism in his book, *Kash-al-Mahjoub*, as follows: "Sufis are a group of poor and unfortunate Zahids who have lived in the Prophet's mosque because [of not having] housing, property and a family." Sufism is in fact a method of asceticism based on rituals and conduct for the cultivation of the soul and the acquisition of truth. In other words, Sufism is a way of esoteric conduct. The origins of Sufism go back to the second and third centuries of Islam. Both the Sunni and Shia have Sufi orders, but it seems that the Sunnis have a greater tendency toward Sufism.

Sunni Sufi Schools in Kurdistan

In the Sunni-populated Kurdish regions, there are two major schools of Sufism: Qadiriya and Naqshbandiya. The Qadiriya is among the oldest schools of Sufism in Kurdistan. The central figure in the Qadiriya order is Abd al-Qadir Gilani (1077–1166) whose life is shrouded in mystery. However, it is known that he was a student at the madrasa (school) of Abu Sa'id al-Mubarek and replaced him as the leader of the circle after his master's death in 1119. Surviving the Mongolian conquest of Baghdad in 1258, the institution prospered and spread its influence on neighboring lands. This Sufi order is so widespread today that it has followers from Africa to the Indian subcontinent. There are many legends about Gilani: some people believe that he is from the north of Iran (Gilan), whereas some others believe that he was born in Baghdad. Followers call him the grand master, or the sheikh of the east. He was an outstanding preacher and scholar. Some texts are attributed to the sheikh that are mainly transcriptions of his sermons.

It is said that Qadiriya was introduced into Kurdistan by two families: Seyyid Ismail Qazanqaya (d. 1745) from the Berzinji family and Mullah Mahmoud Zengene (1723–1801) from the Talabani family. Even today, descendants from both families control the order and are dominant among the Sufi masters. The Qadiriya performs oral recitations (*majlis al-samaa*) in which they gather in their *Tekiye* (convent), form a ring, and dance with the rhythmic movements of the *Def* (drum) while singing *Dhikr* (chants or hymns). Occasionally, some of the Sufis go unconscious while they are dancing as well as doing extraordinary things like swallowing razors, stones, and glass and piercing sharp knives and daggers into their stomachs and heads, depicting their joy and selflessness.

Naqshbandi Order

Compared with Qadiriya, the Naqshbandi order is more traditional, moderate, and conservative. Following tradition and maintaining the Shari'a law and avoiding any innovation and changes in the traditional practice of Sunna are key points for them. There is no privacy in this order, no seclusion, and no singing and oral reciting. What is repeatedly emphasized in the teachings of the Naqshbandis is to adhere to the tradition of the Prophet and to preserve the Shari'a. According to the writers of this order, the teriqa (order) of Naqshbandiya is the same as that of the Prophet's closest companions, observing the principle that they will not add anything to this tradition or reduce anything from it.

Naqshbendi is attributed to Khwaje Baha al-Din Naqshband Bukharayi (1318–1389). This is one of the most important orders in the Muslim world, since it spreads from China to the Caucasus and Syria and Anatolia. The propagator of this movement is a Kurdistan, Mewlana Khalid Naqshbandi (1779–1827), who was born in Silemani and died and was buried in Damascus. After learning from his father and other scholars in the city, he moved to Senendej where he was taught by Sheikh Muhammed Qasim, head of the Ulama in Senendej. Then he returned to Silemani and began teaching there. He performed the Hajj and travelled to India. After his return, he became the khalifa for the order in Silemani.

The followers of this order preach mysticism and the acquisition of God's favor through meditation and silence, and, unlike the followers of Qadiriyah, refrain from dancing, chanting, and playing music. They form a ring round their sheikh, and while they shut their eyes, they begin to meditate to be able to connect to their sheikh directly. They build a relationship, or *rabita*. Then, the sheikh addresses the disciple, kneels before him, and gives him the necessary spiritual training while directly looking into his eyes. This step is called attention. The more affectionate the disciple is, the more important the attention he gets, sometimes to the extent that it leads to the disciple's screaming, which is called attraction. This stage is intentionally prolonged by the sheikh to the extent that the disciple of attention gets inward spiritual power by himself so that he does not need the teaching of the sheikh any longer. Due to Mewlana Khalid's efforts, the order spread rapidly among the Kurds. Many tribal leaders adopted the order, and many locals were appointed khalifas. This led Kurdistan to become one of the most important centers of the Naqshbandiya in the Islamic world in a relatively short time.

Other Kurdish Sufi Orders

One of the most important Sufi orders, which is popular among the Kurds, is the *Ni'metollahi* order. This *teriqa*, however, was founded in Iran. The order is named in honor of its 14th-century founder Shah Ni'metullah Nur ad-Din Ni'metullah Weli, who used to live in Mahan, Kerman Province, Iran, where he was buried, and his tomb is a site of pilgrimage today. Some scholars believe that Shah Ni'metullah was a disciple of the Qadiriya Sufi Abd-Allah Yefa'i, but there is no reliable text or evidence to prove this.

Nimatullahis are a Shia Sufi order that, unlike many other *teriqas*, do not believe in seclusion or *Semaa* or dancing at their gatherings, but they prefer to gather in their *Khaniqas* and pray with their masters in groups. In Iran, their most important centers are in Tehran, but they have *Khaniqas* in Kermanshah as well. There are also *Khaniqas* in Ilam and Senendej, which are not active due to political reasons.

Khaksariyya is a sect of the Shia Iranian Dervishes, which has close affinities with *Yaresanism*. The followers of the order are known for exaggerated modesty and introduce themselves as followers of Imam Ali, the modest Shia Imam, hence calling themselves Abu Turabi (someone who sits and sleeps on plain earth rather than rugs). They also relate themselves to a person called Seyyid Jelal-ud-din Heyder, and they believe that this man wrote a treatise on Khaksaryya customs and beliefs, but even the followers of the *Teriqa* themselves do not know who Seyyid Jelal-ud-din Heyderi is.

Like some Indian orders, they believe in 14 clans, and like the *Yaresans*, they believe in 40 holy men and 7 men who are holy angels. Moreover, the stages of passage of the seeker are similar to that of *Khaksaryya* and even more similar to those of the *Yaresan* (*Ahl-e-Haq*). They are obliged to take a manual in the form of a manuscript from their master and keep it with them to consult at all times. What is left of *Khaksaryya* in Iran is the remains of the teachings of the Gholam Ali Shah order and, to some extent, a smaller order called Massum Ali Shahhi. They live mostly in Tehran, Mashhad, Shiraz, and Kermanshah.

Given the variety of Sufi orders among the Sunnis as well as the Shias, there are still some other orders that cannot be categorized under these two headings, but they need to be discussed separately. Furthermore, the Yaresan and Yezidis must be explained here because of the similarities of these two religions with the Sufi traditions.

Some Social and Political Issues of the Sunnis and Shias

Both Shia and Sunni Muslims put a high emphasis on saying prayers. Shia Kurdish Muslims pray three times a day, whereas the Sunni Muslims pray five times a day. Sunni Muslims have five obligatory prayers during the day: in the morning, at noon, afternoon, the evening, and the sunset prayers as well as some noncompulsory ones. Friday prayers have become a political event, at least after the Iranian revolution. There are government-appointed Friday imams in each city who address public affairs and current issues during the sermon. Turkey's Sunni Kurds are not subject to a government ban on building their own mosques or performing their religious ceremonies and prayers due to having a lot of common points with the Turks since they are also Sunnis. However, the situation is quite different in Iran. In the capital of Iran, after nearly 40 years since the Islamic Revolution, Tehran still lacks a special mosque for Sunnis, and Sunni Kurds living in Shia cities have many problems with their religious ceremonies.

On the other hand, the issue is quite different in the Iranian part of Kurdistan. Sunni Kurds have their own mosques in their cities, and they organize their ceremonies according to Shafi'i rules. The *Adhan* (call for prayers) is calculated based on the principles of the branch of the religion as well as the geographical position of the city. Therefore, there is little difference between the Shia and Sunni *Adhan* and the time of prayer. Most of the mosques of the Sunni Kurdish cities such as Senendej, Seqiz, Mahabad, etc., are run by the Sunnis themselves, but in the state-owned places, only the Shia *Adhan* is broadcasted.

For many years, the antagonism between Shia and Sunni religious clerics has caused separation or even hatred among the Shia and Sunni Kurds. This religious hatred is often the result of the exaggeration of some radical clerics in reading the traditions and religious texts and narratives that have been transferred from government platforms and propaganda slogans to the general public.

Religious differences and similarities are important factors contributing to the relationship the Kurds have toward other Kurds in their country or their neighbors. This difference has created a lot of issues between the Kurds of Iran, on the one hand, and Kurds from neighboring countries, on the other. For example, despite the politically created border between Iran and Iraq, Sunni Kurds on both sides of the border have had more organized relationships and contacts than the Shias. The religious relationship of the Sunnis of western Iran and northeastern Iraq dates back to centuries before the Ottoman Empire. The establishment of the city of Silemani (1774) by Sulaiman Pasha Baban and the invitation of elders and religious authorities to the city, as well as the construction of mosques and numerous chambers in that city, have had significant impacts on the religious and political trends of the Sunni Kurds, especially since the emergence of Sufism. To sum up, it can be said that the most important Kurdish political trends have been influenced by Qadiriiya or Naqshbandiya in a way that the leaders of the two major political parties in the Kurdish regional government, the Democratic Kurdistan Party and the Kurdish Patriotic Union, are both dependent on the religious traditions of the Sufis.

Yaresan (Ahl-e-Haqq)

The Ahl-e Haqq, or People of the Truth, are referred to as Yaresan in Iran and Kaka'i in Iraq. Their religion is a syncretic belief system with mystical rituals. It has most of its practitioners in Iran and Iraq's Kurdistan. Scholars estimate that around 5,000,000 people follow this religion, of which around 2,000,000 live in Iran. However, there are a few non-Kurdish followers of the religion among the Persians, Azeris, or Arabs. Because they keep their religion secret due to fear of being persecuted, an exact estimation of their population is not possible. There is no solid evidence on how this religion came into existence. However, the Yaresan believe that their religion is eternal without any specific date of establishment. The religion, nonetheless, has had certain developments in its different historical periods. The oldest texts of the faith date back to 200 years after the emergence of Islam, but the origin of their places of worship (*Jamkhane*) go back to pre-Islamic times. The principles of the faith date back to the 15th century and are heavily influenced by the central figure of the faith, Sultan Sehak. He was born in Barzinja and established a community in Perdiwar near Hawraman. His followers later moved to the Guran region, which today is known as the center of the Yaresan. Hooshmandrad (2014) described the community in Guran as a distinct faith with a rich cultural heritage and formalized practice with the idea that God or the idea of the divine manifests itself in a cyclic manner.

Though the Yaresans share a certain number of common beliefs, depending on which of the 11 clans they follow, they have specific rituals, beliefs, and sets of rules that sometimes even oppose those of the others. It seems that in the beginning of the formation of the sect, the followers had a common set of beliefs and rules. As the followers of the religion emigrated to other regions and countries, differences began to emerge. The following reasons can account for these differences: oral rather than written transmission of the principles, the followers' lack of access to reliable sources, personal profits of some local leaders, followers' different languages, and the most important of all being the followers not being able to read and write.

Notably, there are branches among the Yaresan that focus on pre-Islamic traditions, whereas others focus on their proximity to Islam. Some scholars believe that the religion is derived from Shi'ism because the followers of the *Teriqa* value Ali Ibn Abi Talib, the first imam of the Shia, very highly, but at the same time, one can observe the sources of their rituals and recitations in ancient Iranian myths and religions. Some scholars believe that the order follows a mixture of the principles of Mithraism, Zoroastrianism, Manichaeism, and even Christianity. However, in Iran, the followers of the sect lead a secret religious life, because their religion is not officially accepted by the government. For instance, they cannot marry according to their own principles or inherit property as ascribed by their own rules. They cannot be employed if they openly assert that they are *Yaresans*.

The Yezidis

The Yezidis are a small ethnically Kurdish religious community scattered in several countries. Most of them are indigenous to northern Mesopotamia, and they are strictly endogamous. This means that a Yezidi who marries a non-Yezidi is automatically excluded from the community. According to Philip G. Kreyenbroek (2013) there is no precise estimation of their population. However, scholars believe that there are around 100,000 to 250,000 of them living in present-day Iraq; there are probably about 40,000 or even more living in Armenia and Georgia and about 5,000 in Syria and a few in Iran. However, for many reasons, except the community in northern Iraq, the population in other countries has been in decline since the 1990s, due to their huge emigration to Western countries especially in Europe and mainly Germany. Since they are a very small religious minority, many people around the world have never heard of them. Nonetheless, they were recently on the world news when ISIS, the radical Islamist terror group, launched attacks on

A Yezidi family baptizes an infant in the village of Lalish, Iraq, September 12, 2017. The Yezidis are an ethno-religious minority indigenous to northern Mesopotamia. (J. Carillet /iStockphoto.com)

them in northern Iraq for the purposes of genocide, claiming that they wanted to purify Iraq and its neighbors of the infidels. Moreover, around 10,000 Yezidis who once lived in Turkey migrated to Germany during the 1980s, because they could no longer live in their homeland. Despite their being a small ethnic and religious minority, the Yezidis and their faith have fascinated a considerable number of travelers and scholars since the middle of the 19th century. As a result, they have been the subject of many publications to date. Indeed, the ISIS genocide attempt has highlighted the existence of the sect for not only Westerners, but also the neighboring countries and communities in the region.

The main language of the Yezidis living in Iraq and Europe is Kurmanji Kurdish. They perform their cultural practices in Kurdish, which is also the language of the orally transmitted religious traditions they adhere to. Some Yezidis in Iraq speak Arabic as their native language though. Even though the majority of the Yezidis speak Kurdish, their exact origin is a matter of dispute and speculation among scholars. Based on the existing texts and documents, we cannot firmly maintain where the Yezidis are Kurds or a distinct ethnic group. For instance, Saddam Hussein, when in power in Iraq, launched an Arabization project for the Yezidis, which put them under high pressure. Encountering this, some Kurd leaders suggested that the Yezidis introduce themselves as Kurds, but they were not quite happy to do this.

Melek Taus

Melek Taus, or the Peacock Angel, is a superior divine figure in the Yezidi religion who is considered the chief angel and active participant in the creation of the universe. Melek Taus represents God's will on earth. On Yezidi New Year, he descends to Lalish to bless the Yezidis. They do not associate with him any representations of evil or the devil as it is often misunderstood among non-Yezidis. Melek Taus is not a fallen angel or source of evil. Yezidis revere him as the primary spiritual force that guards and protects them. Melek Taus represents Yezidi faith.

Yezidism, on a large scale, is linked to ancient Mesopotamian religions. It combines elements of ancient Iranian Mithraism with aspects of Zoroastrianism, Judaism, Christianity, and Islam. Yezidis are monotheists who believe in a single God as the creator of the world. They are in a sense similar to the 18th century European Deists. Like them, they believe that their God, as soon as creating the world, put it under the care of seven holy beings or angels, the chief of whom is Melek Taus (the Peacock Angel). This Melek Taus, they believe, is the ruler of the world and is the primary agent who causes both good and evil to befall to all individuals. The fact that he has an ambivalent character and is the source of both good and evil is close to the ancient Iranian myth of Zorvanism. The duality is inherent in the myth of the Peacock Angel himself. He is believed to have once temporarily fallen from God's favor, the consequence of which is his constant crying so that his tears flooded and extinguished the fires of hell. Finally, this remorseful act reconciled him with God. Sticking to this myth, the enemies of the Yezidis associate Melek Taus with Satan (Iblis), the evil angel who refrained from prostrating Adam despite God's absolute command to do so.

Yezidism, another opinion maintains, is a movement that follows a mystical interpretation of Islam. However, Sufism and mystical interpretations of Islam only partly account for the beliefs and ideas of the Yezidis. Traditionally, Yezidism is associated with one central figure: the Sufi Sheykh Adi bin Musafir who arrived in what is now northern Iraq, was warmly welcomed, and had a successful preaching career, earning him a considerable number of followers. Some scholars believe that he was a descendant of the Umayyad dynasty, which some Kurds used to look favorably upon. Sheikh Adi then reformed the already existing Yezidi believes and added new dogmas, rituals, and hierarchies. For many, he is considered a manifestation of Melek Taus. Today, many Kurdish organizations and leaders describe Yezidism as the original Kurdish religion.

In recent years, *Alevism* has become a distinguishing feature of identity in Turkish Kurdistan. These ritualistic and religious affiliations, even in the diaspora, have united disparate orders such as the *Alevis*, the Yezidis, and the *Yaresans* together under the ethnic and political affinity.

Alevism

Alevism is probably the most controversial religious sect discussed here. It is estimated that there are around 15 to 20 million Alevis living in present-day Turkey and Syria. Most of these people, however, speak Turkish and follow the principles of the Beqtashi order. Nonetheless, there is also a considerable number of Alevis in Turkey who are Kurds. They speak a Kurdish dialect called Zaza, which has close affinities with Persian.

Moreover, there are many Alevis who speak Arabic. These people are referred to as Alawites, and they live in western Syria and southwestern Turkey. The Alawites are from the same denomination as Bashar al-Asad, the current president of the country. If the Syrian civil war carries on with the same intensity, there is the possibility for the Alevis in Turkey to react against Turkey's policy of supporting the rebels.

The followers of Alevism believe in reincarnation—they believe that God's spirit has reemerged in the body of Ali ibn Abi Talib. This highlights the similarities between the Alevis and the Yaresans. Observing the similarity, it is possible to maintain that the Alevis and the Yaresan are among the most ancient religions of the area, their beliefs have roots in Zoroastrianism. However, because of later development after the conversion of the majority of the people to Islam, these two sects modified their principles with Islamic principles to survive.

While some scholars believe that Alevism is a branch of Shi'ism, others argue stronglythat they are not. When the Arabs invaded the people inhabiting the Zagros mountains, the Arabs were confronted by intense resistance. Though, many of the people were converted to Islam, the Alevis and the Yaresans did not follow the other people, but, instead, they made their religions more flexible and compatible to Islam, keeping most of their Zoroastrian principles. One such modification, as mentioned earlier, was promoting the role of Ali ibn Abi Talib to the same rank of the Divine.

Despite the large population of Alevis in Turkey, there is little reliable information about them due to the secrecy they keep in many aspects of their lives. However, they neither say prayers, nor fast. They gather in their centers of worship (*Jam Khane*), sing, and dance, with men and women mixed together. Due to their religious laxity and liberalism, they are popular among the seculars. Moreover, their women enjoy more freedom compared with other Islamic sects and religions. In the past, Alevis were called Kizilbash, or red heads, because of their unique headdress. Many Kurdish Alevis struggle with their double minority status and wonder where their loyalty belongs: Is it with their Turkish brothers and sisters in faith or with the Kurds with whom they share the same ethnicity?

Behrooz Chaman Ara and Vali Gholami

Further Reading

Curtis, J., & Nigel, T. (Eds.). (2005). *Forgotten Empire: The World of Ancient Persia*, Berkeley: University of California Press.

Dehnawi, N-A. (2014). "Hokumat-e Bani Hasanouyeh az Zohour ta Soghout" [The Rise and Fall of Hassanouyids]. *Journal of Historical Researches*, no. 22, 105–124.

Ghani, Q. (1999). *Tarikh-i Tasawof dar Iran [The History of Sufism in Iran]*, Tehran: Zevvar.

Gnoli, G. (2000). *Zoroaster in History*. New York: Bibliotheca Persica Press.

Hooshmandrad, P. (2014). "Life as Ritual: Devotional Practices of the Kurdish Ahl-e Haqq of Guran". In Omarkhali, Khanna. Religious Minorities in Kurdistan: Beyond the Mainstream. Wiesbaden: Harrassowitz, 47–66.

Ibn al-Nadim, Muhammad b. Abi Yaqub (1871–1872). *Kitab Al-Fihrist*, G. Flugel (Ed.) (1970)., 2 Vols. Leipzig; (Eng. Trns.) *The Fihrist of al-Nadim*. New York: Columbia University Press.

Ibn Khalikan (1948). *Wafiyat al-A'yan wa anba abna' al-zaman*, Mohammad Mohyiddin Abd al-Hamid (ed.)., Cairo: Al-Nahda al-Misriyya Publishers.

Kreyenbroek, P. G. (1995). *Yezidism: Its Background, Observances and Textual Tradition*. New York: Edwin Mellen, Lewiston.

Kreyenbroek, P. G. (2013). *Teachers and Teachings in the Good Religion: Opera Minora on Zoroastrianism*. K. Rezania (ed.) Wiesbaden: Harrassowitz Verlag.

Kreyenbroek, P. G., & Jindy Rashow, Kh. (2005). *God and Sheikh Adi Are Perfect: Sacred Poems and Religious Narratives from the Yezidi Tradition*. Wiesbaden: Harrasowitz.

Maqdisi, M.-A. (1906). *Ahsan al-Taqaasim fi Ma'rifat-ul-Aqaalim*, Michael Jan Goeje (ed.), Cairo: Dar al-Sadr; M. Sh. Kadkani (Persian Translation.) Vol. IV–VI, 1993.

Massicard, E. (2013). *The Alevis in Turkey and Europe: Identity and Managing Territorial Diversity*. London and New York: Routledge.

Shankland, D. (2003). *The Alevis in Turkey: The Emergence of a Secular Islamic Tradition*. London and New York: RoutledgeCurzun.

Soltani, M. A. (2004). *Ghiam va Nehzat-e Alavian-e Zagros* [The Rise and Movement of Zagrosian Alavids]. Tehran: Soha.

Conflicts and Issues

Kurdistan is a geocultural area of Asia and the Middle East comprising southeastern Turkey, northeastern Syria, northern Iraq, northwestern Iran, and states of the former Soviet Caucasus such as Armenia and Azerbaijan. The region covers some 74,000 square miles and is characterized by mountainous and forested terrain. For thousands of years many varied ethnic groups either have natively inhabited or have become established in Kurdistan, including the Kurds, Turks, Persians, Arabs, Armenians, Assyrians, Chechens, and Azeris. Since time immemorial, these ethnic groups have endeavored to create their own homelands. For this reason, Kurdistan has long been the location of both ethnic fighting and peaceful cohabitation.

The Kurds are an indigenous Aryan people originating from the highlands and plains of the historical region known as Mesopotamia, which was located within the modern-day countries of Iraq, Syria, Turkey, and Iran. There are thought to be between 25 and 35 million Kurds living in the area referred to as Kurdistan with many more Kurds living abroad and making up the Kurdish diaspora. Today, the Kurds form a community united through race and culture. However, the Kurds are a diverse group for they do not speak a shared standard dialect, and though the majority of Kurds are Sunni Muslims, other Kurds follow a variety of religions and creeds.

Although the Kurds are the fourth-largest ethnic group in the Middle East, they have yet to form a permanent nation-state. In recent decades, Kurds across the Middle East and Asia have increasingly influenced regional developments. Kurds have fought for autonomy in Turkey while also playing important roles in fighting against central governments in Iraq, Iran, and Syria, as well as helping to form resistance against the jihadist group sometimes referred to as Islamic State (IS, also known as ISIS or Daesh, among other names). The Kurds' higher profile in international issues comes about as the result of decades of political and military efforts by the Kurdish minorities to secure Kurdish self-rule and gain a homeland of their own. As a result of their minority status in the countries in which they live, the Kurds have experienced varying degrees of ethnic suppression while endeavoring to gain independence. Kurds have been most severely repressed by the Turks and Arabs, while the Kurdish population to enjoy the greatest degree of autonomy is, arguably, the Iraqi Kurds. Indeed Iraqi Kurdistan (formerly known as the Kurdish Autonomous Region), which was founded as a distinct entity within federal Iraq in 1970, is governed by the Kurdistan Regional Government (KRG) and has as its capital the city of Erbil. Iraqi Kurdistan is an autonomous Kurdistan region in the north of Iraq that has its own parliament consisting of 111 seats. The region's first president was Masoud Barzani, who was elected first in 2005 and then again in

2009. In 2013, Barzani's presidency was extended for another two years, though in 2015 Barzani's rule ended after the main political parties failed to agree over extending his term in office. Despite the end of his presidency, however, Barzani continues to be in control of the region. The Constitution of Iraq defines the Iraqi Kurdistan region as a federal entity of Iraq comprised of four governorates: Dohuk, Erbil, Sulaymaniyah, and Halabja. Iraqi Kurdistan encompasses about 16,100 square miles and as of 2015 is home to a population of 5.5 million people.

Iraq has suffered a great deal of political turmoil recently, something that has, to a certain extent, worked in favor of the creation of an independent Kurdistan. The turbulent state of the Iraqi nation in the wake of the 2014 northern Iraq offensive that saw Islamic State and allied factions act against Iraqi government forces means there is a greater chance of independence for Kurdistan. This is because the weakening of Iraq as a centralized state provides an opportunity for Kurdish independence that has also been boosted by a degree of cooperation from neighboring Turkey. It should be noted, however, that Turkey remains resistant toward any move that would see Kurdish autonomy in Turkey and Syria. Historically, Turkey has worried that a Kurdish state located in northern Iraq would incite and support Kurdish separatists in neighboring Turkish provinces. For this reason, Turkey has long opposed Kurdish independence in Iraq. In the wake of the political turmoil in recent Iraqi history, Turkey has worked increasingly with the Iraqi Kurds.

Historical Roots of Conflicts

The history of Kurdistan is marked by numerous invasions and occupations, as well as periods of unrest and wars, both civil and international. As a major crossroads of the Middle East, Kurdistan has long attracted occupying forces. For example, during ancient times, Persians invaded the area from the east, while Macedonian king Alexander the Great invaded from the west. During the seventh century, Muslim Arabs invaded from the south, and during the 11th century, Seljuk Turks (a Sunni Muslim dynasty) came from the east. In the 13th century, the Mongols led by Genghis Khan invaded from Central Asia, and the 16th century saw the arrival from the north of medieval Persians and the Ottoman Empire. During the 16th century, Kurdistan was also divided between the Safavid dynasty of Iran and the Ottoman Empire, for a major division of Kurdistan arose after the Battle of Chaldiran in 1514. This battle saw the Ottoman Empire trounce the Safavids, leading to a division of Kurdistan that was ratified by both the Ottomans and Safavids in the 1639 Treaty of Zuhab. From this time onwards until the aftermath of World War I, most of Kurdistan was generally under the rule of the Ottoman Empire. During World War I, the Ottoman Empire fought against the Allies of World War I (Britain, France, Russia, Italy, and the United States). In 1918, after the defeat of the Ottoman Empire, British forces came to occupy the *vilayet* (Ottoman province or administrative district) of Mosul, now a large city in northern Iraq. Thus in this way, areas of land inhabited extensively by Kurds came under British rule. Furthermore in 1919, the Mosul area was added to the new Iraqi state, which also became a British mandate.

Peshmerga

Peshmerga, or "Those who confront death," is a paramilitary organization of mostly Iraqi Kurds. During Saddam's regime, they fought as guerillas against Baghdad, but today they are recognized as an official military unit, and they joined the Iraqi Army in their fight against the Islamic State. They continue the long tradition of Kurdish warriors, although the word Peshmerga was only recently coined in the middle of the last century by Kurdish Iraqi writer and founder of the PUK, Ibrahim Ahmed.

After the Ottoman Empire's collapse, the Allies arranged to split the whole of Kurdistan under the terms of a pact known as the 1920 Treaty of Sèvres. The Treaty of Sèvres abolished the Ottoman Empire and provided for a Kurdish state, subject to the agreement of the League of Nations, with Article 64 of the treaty thereby giving Kurds living in the Mosul vilayet the choice of joining a future independent Kurdistan. All the while, the political turmoil resulting from the end of World War I and the downfall of the Ottoman Empire meant that a power vacuum was created in the areas of southeastern Anatolia and northern Iraq that the Kurds inhabited. This situation, together with the creation of the Treaty of Sèvres, seemed to present the Kurds with an opportunity to forge their own nation-state that was referred to in general as Kurdistan. It was also around this time that the Peshmerga, the military forces of the autonomous region of Iraqi Kurdistan, was formally established as the Kurdish fighting force. Over time, the Peshmerga would become a major element of Kurdish culture. This change in the perception of the Peshmerga went hand in hand with the growth of the Kurdish nationalist movement. As a result of these changes, in the collective mind-set of the Iraqi Kurds the Peshmerga developed from defenders of tribal lands to nationalist freedom fighters striving for an independent Kurdish state.

Meanwhile the Treaty of Sèvres was never ratified, and at the same time the British, who were fearful of the threat of growing Bolshevism in the wake of World War I, sought to unite territory in Iran, Turkey, and Iraq. In order to accomplish this unification of land, the British changed their tactic. The British had once encouraged Kurdish nationalism as a way to see off any threat from Turkey. For instance, the British had welcomed the intervention of ambitious Kurdish leader Sheikh Mahmud Barzanji, as they saw Barzanji as a central figure around which the Iraqi Kurds could unite, thereby bringing peace to the region. However, to the consternation of the British, Barzanji soon began to capture British soldiers and lead rebellions against the British while also declaring a Kurdish kingdom in northern Iraq. Ultimately, the British would exile Barzanji to India. Meanwhile the British view of Kurdish nationalism changed so that the British now opposed the forming of a Kurdish state, as they felt doing so would appease Kemal Atatürk, the Turkish revolutionary and founder of the Turkish nation. Thus the Allies accepted a renegotiated peace agreement known as the Treaty of Lausanne that was signed in 1923.

The Treaty of Lausanne settled officially the conflict that had existed between the Ottoman Empire and the Allied British Empire, French republic, kingdom of Italy, empire of Japan, kingdom of Greece, and the kingdom of Romania since the start of World War I. The treaty was the result of a second attempt at peace after the failed Treaty of Sèvres. Leaders of the Turkish national movement rejected the Treaty of Lausanne at a later date but, nevertheless, the Treaty of Lausanne defined the borders of modern Turkey, because according to the treaty, Turkey relinquished all claims to the remaining parts of what had been the Ottoman Empire and in return, the Allies recognized Turkish sovereignty over its land. In addition, other areas previously considered Kurdish were allocated to the new British- and French-mandated states of Iraq and Syria, as well as to Persia (later renamed Iran). Ultimately, this division of land resulted in the Kurds being left without a self-ruled region, and also meant that the Kurds retained their minority status in the countries in which they lived.

Kurds in Iraq

Over the years, Iraqi Kurds have striven to achieve self-rule. As a result of this quest for autonomy many Kurds have faced extreme oppression and endured much hardship. Despite the suffering that the Iraqi Kurds have endured, historically Iraqi Kurds have enjoyed better rights than Kurds living in other neighboring countries. Moreover, to a degree Iraqi Kurds have managed to attain their goal of establishing an autonomous state, with Kurds making up around 15 to 20 percent of Iraq's population.

The route to the establishment of Iraqi Kurdistan was lengthy, convoluted and resulted in a great many lives being lost, however. That the Kurds in general were left without their own autonomous territory after World War I led to successive waves of civil unrest in the countries inhabited by Kurdish minorities. For example, in 1932 a Kurdish rebellion formed in the Barzan region of Iraq during which Kurds protested the fact that Iraq had been permitted to join the League of Nations, while Kurdish demands for autonomy had been ignored. Some years later, in 1943, Mullah Mustafa Barzani led another Kurdish rebellion in Iraq, with rebels seizing control of the city of Erbil and the region of Badinan. In 1946, another uprising by Iraqi Kurds resulted in the British Royal Air Force (RAF) bombing the rebels over the border and into Iran. Once in Iran the Iraqi Kurds united with the Iranian Kurds headed up by Qazi Mohamed, who subsequently went on to establish a short-lived independent Kurdish state in Mahabad, Iran. That same year, Mustafa Barzani established the Kurdistan Democratic Party (KDP) with the aim of gaining Kurdish autonomy in Iraq while the party also held its inaugural congress in Mahabad. Soon after this initial congress, however, the so-called Mahabad Republic disintegrated under attack from Iranian government forces, leading Mustafa Barzani to seek refuge in the Soviet Union. While in exile in the Soviet Union, Barzani was made the nominal president of the Iraqi Kurds (in 1951), though the real power lay with Ibrahim Ahmed, who desired the forging of closer ties between the KDP and the Iraqi Communist Party. At the same time, a new wave of Iraqi Kurdish nationalism reignited interest in the KDP.

After the 1958 Iraqi coup that saw the overthrowing of the country's Hashemite monarchy, subsequent Iraqi governments vowed to give Kurds autonomy over the land they inhabited, and a new constitution recognized Kurdish rights within the structure of the Iraqi Constitution. The ousting of the Hashemite monarchy allowed Kurdish nationalists the opportunity to operate openly after many years of covert organizing, while a new Iraqi constitution recognized Kurdish national rights. In addition, Mustafa Barzani was permitted to return from exile in the Soviet Union further boosting Kurdish nationalism and potentially preparing the way for Kurdish autonomy. However, relations between the Iraqi Kurds and the Iraqi authorities became increasingly tense, leading to the KDP to complain that the Iraqi government was repressing the Kurds. In 1960, a Kurdish rebellion in northern Iraq led the Iraqi government to disband the KDP, while Barzani's plan for self-governance was vetoed by the Arab-led Iraqi government. A year later, in 1961, the KDP began an armed struggle for independence.

In March 1970, the government of Iraq prepared a peace agreement intended to end the fighting by giving the Iraqi Kurds a de facto autonomous region. This region was known as the Kurdish Autonomous Region, now referred to as Iraqi Kurdistan (or occasionally as southern Kurdistan). This autonomous Kurdish state was located in the northeast of Iraq; comprised the former Iraqi provinces of Erbil, Dohuk, Sulaymaniyah, and Halabja; and was populated by 3 million people. The peace accord asserted that the people of Iraq comprised two nationalities: Arab and Kurds, with Kurdish and Arabic being recognized as Iraq's two official languages. The region's new parliament was, however, arguably little more than another component of the Iraqi central government, for the Kurdish authority was ordained by Iraqi leaders. As such the population of the Kurdish Autonomous Region did not have any particular democratic political freedom and certainly not more than any other Iraqis. Today, elections for the Kurdistan Parliament, which was known as the Kurdistan National Assembly until 2009, take place every four years. The leading political alliance at the last elections in 2013 was the Kurdistani List that was made up of the two main political parties of the Patriotic Union of Kurdistan (PUK) and the KDP. Another, newer, competing movement, the Gorran List, won a quarter of the parliamentary seats. In the presidential election, Masoud Barzani was elected president, but in 2015, Barzani's presidency ended when the Iraqi Kurdish political parties could not agree on whether or not to extend his term in office. The issue of the presidency of Iraqi Kurdistan and the legitimate extension of a presidency beyond two terms is a contentious subject in Iraqi Kurdistan and the cause of a great deal of disquiet among Iraqi Kurds.

Just over a year after the 1970 peace agreement was enshrined, relations between the Iraqi authorities and the Kurds deteriorated to the point that Mustafa Barzani felt the need to appeal to the United States for support. Around this time, the United States made a secret pact with the Shah of Iran to secretly fund Kurdish rebellions against the Iraqi government through a partnership between the Central Intelligence Agency (CIA) and Mossad, Israel's national intelligence agency.

Eventually, the peace deal between Iraq and the Iraqi Kurds failed, and fighting began again in 1974 with Iraqi government forces launching attacks that forced the Kurds closer to the Iraqi border with Iran. Soon Iraq and Iran entered into talks to stop the Iranian backing of the Iraqi Kurds in exchange for changes to the border territory that favored Iran. These changes to the Iran-Iraq border were ratified by the 1975 Algiers Accord after which Iran cut funding to the Kurdish separatist movement in Iraq. The same year divisions within the KDP saw a splinter group, the PUK, form as a coalition of disparate political entities under the leadership of Jalal Talabani with the aim of bringing about self-determination for the Kurds. Meanwhile despite Iran's agreeing to stop supporting the Iraqi Kurds as ratified in the Algiers Accord, Barzani fled to Kurdish land in Iran along with many of his followers. As a result of the Algiers Accord, the Ba'athist Iraqi government's control over the Iraqi northern region grew. In order to cement this growth in power over the area, the Iraqi government began a program of so-called Arabization. This Arabization project saw the Iraqi government begin to resettle Arabs in areas that were mainly inhabited by Kurdish people as well as other minorities, including the Yezidis, Assyrians, Shabaks, Armenians, Turkmen, and Mandeans. This program of enforced relocation was implemented particularly around the oil-rich city of Kirkuk and resulted in the expulsion and forced relocation of the Kurds who had been living there. The oppressive measures executed by the Iraqi government against the Kurds in the wake of the Algiers Accord led to more civil unrest and, in 1977, to clashes between the Iraqi Army and Kurdish revolutionaries. In the years following these clashes, several hundred Iraqi Kurdish villages were razed to the ground while approximately 200,000 Kurds were banished to other parts of the country. The policy of forced relocation was hastened in the 1980s when the Iran-Iraq War (1980–1988) broke out.

Kurds in Iran

As the Kurds are one of Iran's largest ethnic populations, Kurdish issues have long been an important factor in the innumerable political and socioeconomic matters, both domestic and international, that have surrounded the country since it was founded as the Islamic Republic in 1979. Shortly after the onset of the Iran-Iraq War, the Iraqi government set out to court the Kurdish Democratic Party of Iran (KDPI) in the hope that the group would act as leverage in its war effort. In 1981, Saddam Hussein's Iraqi regime created its first major weapon supply route to the KDPI close to the Iranian cities of Nowdesheh and Qasr-e Shirin. Iraq did this with the aim of seizing Nowdesheh, for the city had a prime strategic location, the capturing of which would prevent Iran from using the highway that ran between the Iraqi capital city of Baghdad and the Iranian capital, Tehran. For its part, the KDPI aimed to establish so-called Kurdish liberated zones throughout Iranian Kurdistan. Over time both the KDPI and Iraq suffered losses as Iranian forces inflicted heavy numbers of casualties on Iraqi forces and managed to push the Iraqi forces back across the Iraqi border. Subsequently, Iranian forces began a series of devastating attacks on the KDPI that rendered the group a marginal military factor during the war.

By 1983, Iran had also begun to woo the Kurds in its fight against Saddam Hussein's Iraq. At the same time, the Iraqi government became concerned about possible

Kurdish attacks on a strategically important and (highly lucrative) oil pipeline that connected the oilfields of Kirkuk with the Turkish port of Iskenderun. Although Iran never acted against this pipeline, Iraq remained on high alert for a potential Kurdish attack supported by Iran on one of Iraq's most important economic assets.

In retribution for the Kurdish support of Iran during the Iran-Iraq War and to prevent further Kurdish rebellion, Saddam Hussein, leader of Iraq, began a campaign of revenge on the Kurds. The most infamous incidence of retribution came in 1988 when, with the Iran-Iraq War coming to an end, Iraqi forces launched the Anfal campaign against the Kurds. The Anfal campaign was a concerted, methodical attempt to break Kurdish resistance that took the form of a program of systematic ethnic cleansing. Indeed, the campaign has been classified as genocide by authorities in Sweden, Norway, and the United Kingdom for it resulted in tens of thousands of Kurds, both civilian and military, being killed. Hundreds of thousands more Kurds were forced into exile, often transported to dismal new settlements farther south, and forbidden, under pain of death, to return home. Many of the Kurds who were taken to these new areas starved to death within one year of their transportation or survived only through the surreptitious assistance of local inhabitants. Other noncombatant Kurds were jailed, with many dying in prison as a result of neglect. Moreover, large numbers of Kurdish men of militant age who were imprisoned by Iraqi authorities were subsequently executed and buried in mass graves.

One aspect of the Anfal campaign in particular, the deliberate targeting of civilian Kurds with chemical weapons, caused especial international condemnation. The most notorious incidence of this use of chemical weapons against the Iraqi Kurds occurred in the town of Halabja in 1988. There were several reasons why Halabja was targeted by Iraqi forces. One reason was that the town was considered a major center of Kurdish resistance in the Kurds' struggle for autonomy. Second, in the final weeks of the Iran-Iraq War, Halabja had greeted advancing Iranian troops warmly, thereby provoking the ire of Iraqi officials. The Halabja chemical attack is infamous because during the attack the Iraqi authorities killed an estimated 5,000 people, mostly women and children. The attack began when government jets first bombarded the town with conventional weapons in order to break protective windows and doors and to force townsfolk to shelter below ground, before dropping a mixture of mustard gas and the nerve agents sarin, tabun, and VX (and possibly cyanide) on the town. As the chemicals were heavier than air, being forced below ground level meant that people were even more exposed to the toxins than had they stayed above ground. As well as those townsfolk that died as an immediate effect of the attack, around 12,000 townsfolk died later from cancer and other illnesses resulting from exposure to the chemical attack. Even today, the legacy of the attack continues for the chemical contamination resulting from it is believed to have passed into the town's soil and water supply, as well as the local population's gene pool. This means that since the chemical attack an abnormally high number of local children have been born displaying genetic defects. The Halabja chemical attack scarred the collective memory of Iraqi Kurds and increased their determination to regain a degree of autonomy within a loose Iraqi federation.

Meanwhile the two men directly responsible for the attack—Saddam Hussein and Hussein's cousin Ali Hassan al-Majid (who had been nicknamed Chemical Ali on account of his ordering chemical attacks against the Kurds)—were hanged after the downfall of Hussein's regime, in 2006 and 2010, respectively.

Even though Kurdish autonomy had been granted in 1970, the Iraqi Kurdish population had yet to enjoy increased freedom from political discrimination. This situation began to change, however, in 1991 in the wake of the uprising against Saddam Hussein that occurred after the conclusion of the Gulf War. The path to this autonomy was convoluted and came at great cost to many Kurdish civilians who were either killed or uprooted during the many ensuing periods of unrest. In March 1991 following the expulsion of Iraqi troops from Kuwait, some members of the Jash (Kurdish fighters who had cooperated with the Iraqi government) defected to the side of the KDP and PUK in order to fight against Iraq. This uprising was unsuccessful however, and U.S.-led forces refused to support the rebels. As a result of the fighting some 1.5 million Kurds were forced to flee the land they inhabited, but Turkey shut its border, meaning that many hundreds of thousands of Kurds had to seek refuge in the mountains on the Iraq-Turkey border. In the meantime, Masoud Barzani (the leader of the KDP and son of Mustafa Barzani) together with Jalal Talabani began negotiating with Saddam Hussein for the creation of an autonomous Iraqi Kurdistan. That same year, after Iraq was beaten in the Gulf War, Masoud Barzani and Jalal Talabani (elected interim Iraqi president in 2005) fronted a Kurdish uprising seeking the creation of an autonomous Kurdish state.

Meanwhile Kurdish rebels managed to capture the Iraqi towns of Ranya, Sulaimaniya, and Kirkuk, but Hussein retaliated swiftly and brutally by bombarding Kirkuk, and in particular the town's hospitals, with artillery fire. Geographically, these towns were almost impossible to defend as they sat on flat terrain surrounded by mountains. Eventually the Kurdish rebels and their families were able to flee into the mountains, where they are said to have been targeted by Iraqi helicopters and doused in flour as a reminder of the powder-like chemical weapons used by the Iraqi authorities during the Anfal Campaign. The ferocity with which Iraqi authorities suppressed the Kurdish uprising was such that a great deal of international concern arose focused on the plight of the Kurdish refugees. For instance, the United Nations Security Council Resolution 688 condemned the repression of the Iraqi civilian population, most particularly in areas populated by the Kurds, while also voicing concerns that Iraqi actions could endanger international peace and security. The resolution demanded that humanitarian groups be allowed access to Kurdish refugees and ultimately led to the creation of a safe haven within Iraq. Meanwhile the international coalition of the United States and its allies, namely Britain and France, felt compelled to create a partial no-fly zone in the north of Iraq under the name of Operation Provide Comfort. This operation also included the delivery of humanitarian aid and military protection to the Kurds by a limited number of Allied ground force made up of members from the United States, Britain, France, and Turkey.

The no-fly zone was an area of Iraqi airspace in which Iraqi aircraft were forbidden to fly. The policy was enforced by United States, British, and French air patrols

Kurdish refugees in the United Nations-administered Makhmur refugee camp in Kurdistan, northern Iraq, January 26, 2007. (Sadık Güleç/Dreamstime.com)

and was established as a humanitarian effort to protect Kurds in northern Iraq and Shi'a Muslims in the south. The zone was controversial as it was not authorized by the United Nations or specifically sanctioned by a Security Council resolution. Another controversial issue surrounding the creation of the no-fly zone was that the no-fly zone did not cover Sulaymaniyah, Kirkuk, and several other areas with notable Kurdish populations. Nevertheless, the no-fly zone did manage to help and protect Kurds and other groups against the Iraqi military action that had driven large numbers of people across the borders into Turkey and Iran. The no-fly zone also allowed Kurdish leaders, together with armed Peshmerga forces, to strengthen their hold in the north of Iraq in the wake of the withdrawal of Iraqi forces. Fierce battles between Iraqi forces and Kurdish rebels continued despite the no-fly zone, however, and, after an anxious and unstable balance of power was reached, the Iraqi government withdrew its military and other personnel in full from the region in October 1991. This withdrawal allowed for the formation of Iraqi Kurdistan as an autonomous Kurdistan region that had its own flag and national anthem. The new Iraqi Kurdistan was to be ruled by the two main Kurdish parties; the Kurdish Democratic Party (KDP) and the Patriotic Union of Kurdistan (PUK). Therefore, it could be argued that in the long run the no-fly zone did ultimately allow the Iraqi Kurds to enjoy self-governance, for the KDP and PUK agreed to a power-sharing deal. Tensions between the two parties soon arose, however, leading to a four-year internal struggle beginning in 1994. The KDP and PUK would later participate with the United States and its allies in the 2003 invasion of Iraq that led to the downfall of Saddam Hussein, and both parties have subsequently taken part in all national Kurdish governments formed since this time. The two parties also formed a coalition government known as the Kurdistan Regional Government (KRG). This government was established in 2005 to govern the four Iraqi governorates of Dohuk, Erbil, Sulaymaniyah, and Halabja. In 2005, the initial session of the Kurdish parliament was held in Erbil with Barzani made president of the autonomous region. In December that year, it became known that a foreign company had started to drill for oil in the Kurdish north of Iraq, leading Iraqi leaders to fear a breakaway Kurdish state might form. Such fears were heightened when, in 2006, Barzani ordered the Iraqi national flag to be removed from public buildings and replaced with the Kurdish flag.

The granting of a degree of Kurdish autonomy within Iraq did not guarantee peace within the region, for there is a history of radical Islamic parties operating within the area. For instance, Ansar al-Islam was a mainly Kurdish militant organization based in Iraqi Kurdistan that formed in 2001 following the mergers of several Kurdish Islamist groups. From the start, Ansar al-Islam was closely linked with Osama bin Laden and Al Qaeda, something that came to international attention in 2003 when the Bush administration claimed that Ansar al-Islam was the tie between the Hussein regime and Osama bin Laden. Although it has not been established concretely, the Bush administration frequently referred to this connection as a reason for the U.S. invasion of Iraq in 2003.

Prior to 2003, Ansar al-Islam mainly targeted the PUK, which together with the KDP controlled the KRG. Ansar al-Islam originated in, and was based within, the PUK-controlled Iraqi Kurdistan and the differing philosophies of the two organizations lead to conflict in 2002. While the PUK had a strongly secularist and nationalistic ideology, Ansar al-Islam wished to create within Iraqi Kurdistan an Islamic caliphate governed by the tenets of strict Sharia law. Soon after the U.S-led invasion of Iraq in 2003, U.S. aerial bombardments combined with Peshmerga ground attacks in Iraqi Kurdistan resulted in most Ansar al-Islam members being killed or escaping to Iran from where they continued to operate.

Between 2003 and 2007, Ansar al-Islam targeted both Iraqi government troops and coalition forces. One especially infamous Ansar al-Islam attack in February 2004 saw simultaneous suicide car bomb explode at PUK offices in Erbil, killing more than 100 civilians and injuring 130 others. Then in 2007–2008, Ansar al-Islam cooperated with Al Qaeda in Iraq to attack U.S. and PUK troops. When the United States withdrew from Iraq in 2011, Ansar al-Islam stayed active and concentrated on attacking the Iraqi government and its associated security forces in and around Mosul and Kirkuk. However, after the Syrian civil war began, Ansar al-Islam began to operate in Syria too. Here Ansar al-Islam frequently fought alongside other militant groups against Syrian government forces, the YPG, and Islamic State, which had by then succeeded Al Qaeda in Iraq.

The relationship between Ansar al-Islam and Islamic State fluctuated between one of close collaboration and one of hostility. While Ansar al-Islam supported Islamic State's desire to create an Islamic caliphate in the Middle East, it disapproved of the latter's proclamation of itself as a state. Disagreements between the two groups meant that they began to fight one another in both Iraq and Syria, and at one point Ansar al-Islam declared war on Islamic State. Nonetheless, in 2014, Ansar al-Islam pledged allegiance to Islamic State and the two organizations merged.

Meanwhile in mid-2013, so-called Islamic State began to attack repeatedly three Kurdish enclaves that bordered land controlled by the group in northern Syria. In June 2014, an offensive in Iraq saw Islamic State invade the city of Mosul, defeating Iraqi army divisions and seizing arms that were later transported to Syria. Islamic State's progress in Iraq drew Iraqi Kurds into the fight against the jihadists with the government of the country's autonomous Kurdistan region sending Peshmerga forces into areas abandoned by the Iraqi army. For a while, there were only minor battles between the Peshmerga and Islamic State. Then in August 2014, Islamic State launched a shock offensive against the Kurdish forces that saw the Peshmerga withdraw in a disorderly fashion. The rushed retreat resulted in a number of towns inhabited by religious minorities falling to Islamic State, most notably Sinjar, where Islamic State fighters killed or captured thousands of members of a Kurdish religious community known as the Yezidis. Indeed, by the time the battle for Sinjar concluded some 5,000 Yazidis had been slaughtered, 300,000 Yezidis had been forced to flee, and 7,000 Yezidi girls and women had been kidnapped and taken as sex slaves by Islamic State. Worried by the advance of Islamic State and the possibility of genocide being committed against the Yezidis of Sinjar, the United States led an international coalition that both launched air strikes in northern Iraq and sent military consultants to assist the Peshmerga. The YPG, together with the Kurdistan Workers' Party (or Partiya Karkeren Kurdistane, PKK) that had been active in Turkey previously, also came to the aid of the Yezidis. Although the Peshmerga and their allies eventually stopped the advance of Islamic State into land held by Iraqi Kurds, this did not prevent Islamic State attempting to capture Kurdish areas of Syria.

Kurds in Syria

Today, Kurds make up between 7 and 10 percent of the Syrian population. Kurds have been repressed in Syria for a long time and for many years have been denied many basic rights. Moreover since the 1960s around 300,000 Syrian Kurds have been denied citizenship, and Kurdish land has been commandeered and reallocated to Arabs in an attempt to both lessen the impact of the Kurds in traditionally Kurdish regions of the country and to make these areas seem less Kurdish. Syrian authorities have also suppressed Kurdish demands for greater autonomy by preventing protests and detaining Kurdish political leaders.

Prior to the ongoing Syrian civil war and the revolution against President Bashar al-Assad that began in 2011, most Syrian Kurds lived in three unconnected areas around Kobane, the northwestern town of Efrin, and the northeastern city of Qamishli as well as the country's capital city, Damascus and the city of Aleppo. For the first two years of the conflict in Syria the Kurdish enclaves remained fairly untouched because the main Kurdish parties stayed neutral with regard to the conflict and did not speak out about the revolution publicly. In mid-2012, Syrian government forces left certain areas of Syria in order to concentrate on fighting the opposition leading to Kurdish groups taking control of the areas that the government forces had vacated. The left-wing Partiya Yekitiya Demokrat (PYD, or Democratic Union Party) soon established itself as the prevailing Kurdish force. The growing influence of the PYD and ideological proximity to the PKK strained relations between the PYD and smaller Kurdish parties that went on to form the Kurdistan

National Council (KNC). In July 2012, the two main political alliances in Rojava (the de facto autonomous region originating in and comprising the three self-governing cantons of northern Syria: Efrin Canton, Kobani Canton, and Cizire Canton that has Qamishli as its administrative center), namely the PYD and the Kurdish National Council (KNC), established the Kurdish Supreme Committee (KSC) as the supreme governing body of Rojava, and a committee was selected to write an interim constitution. The PYD together with its armed wing, the YPG, soon became the prevailing force and, in November 2013, declared a self-administration in the Kurdish region of Syria that strove to establish a political framework that included many Syrian Kurdish political parties. In January 2014, the PYD agreed to create a coalition government with the KNC, and these parties joined together to announce the formation of a Kurdish-led democratic autonomous government that had branches based in the three Kurdish enclaves of Syria. The PYD and KNC emphasized that they did not wish to win independence from Syria but rather to create a localized democratic administration within a federal structure. The co-chair of the PYD, Salih Muslim, has maintained that any political agreement intended to end the conflict in Syria will have to contain guarantees of Kurdish rights and acknowledgment of Kurdish autonomy. Furthermore, Muslim has stressed that President Assad must not stay in power during any government transition. At the same time, however, Muslim has had to deny that the PYD is associated with the Syrian government, though it is known that the YPG has attacked some rebel groups and avoided fighting with the Syrian army.

The conflict in Syria has affected the way in which Kurds have been treated in Turkey and influenced the chances for the creation of a Turkish Kurdish state. For instance in September 2014, Islamic State launched an assault on the territory around the Syrian town of Kobani, which lies just south of the Syrian-Turkish border and that had been under control of the YPG since 2012. The attack by Islamic State forced tens of thousands of Kurds to flee across the border into neighboring Turkey. Turkish authorities refused to intervene by attacking Islamic State, however, and would not permit Turkish Kurds to travel into Syrian Kurdish land to help defend the town. This refusal to help the Syrian Kurds led to protests by Turkish Kurds so eventually the Turkish government partially conceded and allowed Iraqi Peshmerga fighters to join the battle for Kobani in the wake of U.S.-led air strikes against the Islamic State advance forces. In early 2015, Kurdish forces recaptured Kobane though by this time, more than 1,600 people had died and more than 3,200 buildings had been destroyed in the town.

Since the battle for Kobani, Kurdish forces, in conjunction with U.S.-led coalition air strikes, have inflicted a number of defeats on Islamic State forces in northern Syria. Kurdish forces have gained control over a 250-mile stretch of connecting territory along the Turkish border and have advanced to within 30 miles of the Islamic State stronghold in the northern Syrian city of Raqqa. Indeed, under the name of the Syrian Democratic Forces (SDF), the YPG and their Arab partners have become a main ally of the U.S.-led coalition and are considered by the coalition to be one of the few efficient allies fighting against Islamic State on the ground in Syria.

Kurds in Turkey

In the meantime, long-term hostility still exists between the Turkish authorities and Turkish Kurds because for many decades the Turkish authorities have treated the Kurds harshly. Today, Kurdish people make up around 20% of Turkey's population as a whole. Many Kurdish people opposed the historic amalgamation into Turkey of eastern Anatolia, a region inhabited by Kurds. This incorporation of eastern Anatolia into Turkey and the ensuing ill feeling has resulted in a lengthy battle for independence that has seen many thousands of people die. The region has witnessed many large-scale Kurdish rebellions such as the Koçgiri rebellion of 1920 as well as successive waves of insurgency against the Turkish state—these rebellions include the Sheikh Said rebellion of 1924, the Republic of Ararat of 1927, and the Dersim rebellion in 1937. This last rebellion was quashed ruthlessly by the Turkish authorities at the time and resulted in the deaths and displacement of thousands of Kurds, something for which Turkish Prime Minister Recep Tayyip Erdoğan apologized in November 2011.

In response to unrest in the 1920s and 1930s, the Turkish authorities cracked down heavily on everyday Kurdish life in an apparent attempt to deny the existence of Kurds. For example, many Kurds were resettled, Kurdish names and ethnic dress were banned, and the use of the Kurdish language in public and private life was banned in 1983 meaning that people who spoke, wrote, or sang in Kurdish risked imprisonment. In 1991, meanwhile the very reality of Kurdish ethnic identity was refuted, with Kurds designated Mountain Turks by the Turkish authorities. Moreover, the Turkish authorities prohibited the use of the words "Kurds," "Kurdistan," and "Kurdish." Then through the late 1990s and early 2000s, the Turkish government banned political groups representing Kurdish interests, including the search for an independent or autonomous Kurdish state. Until 2002, it was also prohibited for broadcasts to be made in Kurdish, and it was only as recently as 2003 that Kurdish parents were allowed to give their children Kurdish names. However, these names could not include the letters W, X, or Q because whereas these letters exist in the Kurdish alphabet, they do not appear in the Turkish alphabet.

Despite the harshness with which Turkish authorities have cracked down on Kurdish insurgency, there have long been calls for an independent Kurdish state within Turkey. For instance in 1978, those seeking Kurdish self-governance and self-determination within Turkey formed the PKK militant separatist group. Six years later, the PKK started an armed insurgency with this aim in mind. Since then, many thousands of Kurds have been killed in the struggles between Turkish authorities and the PKK, with hundreds of thousands of Kurds being displaced. In 1983, Kurdish provinces within Turkey were placed under martial law. The imposition of martial rule by the Turkish government was a reaction to the activities of the PKK. Soon after, a guerrilla war began that lasted throughout the 1980s and 1990s with the PKK being led by Abdullah Öcalan, commonly referred to as Apo (meaning uncle in Kurdish), a man regarded as hero by many Kurds but as an enemy of the state by Turkish authorities. Öcalan had helped found the PKK in 1979 with

Abdullah Öcalan, one of the founders and first leader of the Kurdistan Workers' Party (PKK), in a photo from 1992. (Ramzi Haidar/AFP/Getty Images)

the aim of establishing an independent Kurdish state achieved through war against the Turkish regime. In 1979, Öcalan fled to Syria, where he remained until 1998, when the Syrian government expelled him in the face of threats from Turkey.

The Kurdish-Turkish conflict saw many Kurds evacuated from the Turkish countryside and hundreds of Kurdish-inhabited villages demolished or set on fire. Supplies of food were also restricted in areas inhabited by the Kurds. In all, in excess of 20,000 Kurds were killed in the fighting while hundreds of thousands more had to leave their homes. In the 1990s, the PKK withdrew its demands for Kurdish self-governance and instead called for greater Kurdish cultural and political independence while still continuing to fight for autonomy. In 1999, Öcalan was arrested in Kenya by agents of the Turkish National Intelligence Agency. Subsequently, Öcalan was sent back to Turkey where he was sentenced to death. This sentence led to riots and Kurdish demonstrations in Turkey and across Europe. Öcalan appealed the death sentence and announced a ceasefire that ordered all PKK forces to leave Turkey. This was followed in 2002 by the PKK's agreement to follow a peaceful political program. That same year Turkey commuted Öcalan's death sentence to life imprisonment because Turkey had abolished the death penalty in order to comply with the requirements of the European Union. In 2003, the European Court of Human Rights ruled that Öcalan's 1999 trial was unfair since his defense had been restricted inappropriately. Turkey's appeal against the ruling failed but Turkey refused to conduct the recommended retrial.

In 2004, the PKK halted its ceasefire and resumed attacks. Covert peace talks between PKK leaders and Turkish officials commenced in 2009, but these failed in 2011, and in 2012, the Turkish prime minister, Erdoğan, announced that Turkish authorities had begun negotiations with Öcalan. A year later, Öcalan called for another ceasefire, leading PKK forces to withdraw from Turkey. Despite this accord, fighting between the Turkish authorities and the PKK continued and the ceasefire collapsed again in July 2015. The end of the peace came just days after a suicide bombing occurred in the predominantly Kurdish town of Suruc, close to the Syrian border. The bombing killed 33 Kurdish activists and was blamed on Islamic State. The PKK responded to this bombing by attacking Turkish soldiers and police. This in turn led the Turkish government to lash out against both the PKK and Islamic State. Since 2015, hundreds of Kurds have been killed in clashes in southeastern Turkey and by air strikes on PKK bases in northern Iraq. In July 2015, Turkey joined the U.S.-led military alliance against Islamic State but did so only on condition that the air strikes against Islamic State be accompanied by maneuvers against Kurdish PKK militants stationed in northern Iraq. The Turkish government also began a bombing campaign against the PKK in this area of Iraq. This was the first time that Turkey had attacked the Kurds since agreeing to a ceasefire with the Kurds in 2013. In response to these attacks in August 2015, the leaders of Iraqi Kurdistan urged the Turkish authorities to exercise restraint while calling on the PKK to relocate its bases away from populated areas so that the danger to civilian areas was lessened.

The Turkish government also blamed the YPG for a suicide bombing in the Turkish capital Ankara in February 2016. The bombing resulted in the death of dozens of people, and in response, Turkish troops attacked YPG sites in northwestern Syria to prevent the YPG from seizing the town of Azaz. In the eyes of the Turkish government the YPG and the left-wing Syrian Kurdish Partiya Yekitiya Demokrat (PYD, or Democratic Union Party) are affiliated with the PKK, as the groups share the PKK's goal of gaining Kurdish independence through conflict and as a result are all regarded as terrorist organizations by the Turkish government. Nevertheless, the rise of Islamic State has changed the relationship between Turkey and Kurdistan somewhat. For instance, when Islamic State took the Iraqi city of Mosul, the Turkish authorities realized that Kurdistan presented a useful buffer between Turkey and Islamic State.

Political turmoil in the Middle East and the spread of Islamic State have led to thousands of Kurds leaving their homes in many areas of Kurdistan. The spread of Islamic State has weakened the country of Iraq, thereby presenting the Kurds with a chance to develop their independence and in turn declare an independent Kurdish state. To this end in June 2014, a spokesman for the Turkish government indicated that Turkey might be ready to accept an independent Kurdistan located in northern Iraq.

The Kurdish Future

The fighting in Syria has resulted in tens of thousands of refugees fleeing into Iraqi Kurdistan. However, in areas of northern and western Iraq that have seen Kurdish minority populations flee ahead of Islamic State, Kurds have now returned in greater numbers than lived there previously. Kurds have entered these areas and seized properties, destroyed buildings, and appropriated farmland previously owned by Iraqi Arabs. Indeed, since 2014, the Kurds have increased the size of their region in Iraq by about 40 percent by laying claim to newly vacant land that was not attributed to them previously. In this way, the Kurdish map is changing across Iraq and in Syria. Kurds argue that taking this land is merely a case of redressing past wrongs perpetrated by successive Iraqi leaders, most especially Saddam Hussein. The Kurds also see the amalgamation of their land as a vital step to gaining the independent state that they have desired ever since the demise of the Ottoman Empire. Other people, including members of the Iraqi government, argue that the Kurds are inflicting new injustices while also setting up the bases of future conflict. The increasing influence of the Iraqi Kurds is also making neighboring states nervous, as these countries fear that their own Kurdish minority populations may rise up and join the Iraqi Kurds.

The emergence of Islamic State is having a profound effect on the Kurds and their hopes of creating an independent Kurdish state in the future. While the advent of Islamic State has cleared the way for Kurds to capture land that was not previously Kurdish owned, the coming of the jihadi group has also renewed old Kurdish anxieties surrounding the loss of Kurdish territory. For instance, Masoud Barzani has said that many Iraqi Arabs are using Islamic State to reinforce their own territorial claims while also taking advantage of the rise of Islamic State to reclaim disputed areas.

In 2016, Masoud Barzani repeated the call for a Kurdish referendum. However, Barzani emphasized that the referendum would not be binding but rather would only allow Kurdish leaders to carry out the will of the people when the time and conditions were suitable. The immediate undertakings facing the Iraqi Kurdish government are great for they include reconstructing shattered infrastructure, forming a cohesive administration, and absorbing the many hundreds of thousands of displaced people and refugees that have been forced from their home after years of war. In Iraq, for the most part, Iraqi Kurdistan escaped the deprivations of the final years of Saddam Hussein's rule and the chaos that ensued after Hussein was deposed in 2003. Since Iraqi Kurdistan mostly survived intact after this period of turmoil, it has been able to build a parliamentary authority accompanied by a growing economy. Elsewhere major problems still face the Kurds, however. For example, Kurdistan is bordered by countries such as Iran and Turkey that are generally unsympathetic to Kurdish ambitions, and by other nations, particularly Syria and non-Kurdish Iraq, which are close to almost total collapse. Kurdistan is also in dispute with the Iraqi authorities over a number of territories, most notably the historic city of Kirkuk. The two sides have yet to reach an agreement over Kirkuk, but in 2014, when Kirkuk was in danger of falling to Islamic

State, Peshmerga forces anticipated Islamic State's attack by capturing Kirkuk themselves.

Anxieties in Kurdistan have been increasing recently as Iraqi forces, Kurds, and the Iranian-backed Shi'ite militia have formed an uneasy alliance with the aim of driving out Islamic State. The members of this alliance share a common enemy, but they have little else in common. For instance, there are ideological differences between the KDP and PKK for whereas the KDP is pro-capitalist, in favor of closer ties between the Kurds and the West, and aligned to Turkey, the PKK holds to a Marxist ideology and has ties to Syria's Assad regime. Furthermore, recent developments have resulted in the two Kurdish factions becoming increasingly distrustful of each other. On the one hand, the PKK fears that the KDP may help Turkey attack its strongholds in northern Iraq, while the KDP feels increasingly surrounded by PKK fighters now that the PKK has become established in Sinjar. In 2014 when the KDP lost Sinjar to Islamic State, the PKK (together with the PYD) opened a corridor enabling townsfolk to escape. Ultimately, the KDP regained Sinjar but the PKK did not vacate the town. Instead, the PKK established the Sinjar Resistance Units, a local Yazidi force. In 2015, this force registered with the Iraqi government, meaning it could receive funding from Iraqi authorities. The situation in Sinjar, together with other factors such as the influence of anti-KDP Iran in Sulaymani-yah, is complicating the KDP-PKK rivalry and the groups' mutual desire to head the broader Kurdish nationalist movement.

Observers suggest that the KRG will soon face the consequences of failing to invest in democratic institutions and for governing in a manner that is not transparent. At the same time the PKK's presence in the KRG, which seems to be endorsed by Iran, is adding to the unease in the region. Some commentators fear that Iraqi Kurds are about to lose an opportunity for greater autonomy as a result of hostile politics, failed bureaucracy, and the seemingly subversive intervention of neighboring states. With a background of such uncertainty, it seems that only time will tell as to whether peace can be achieved in the Kurdish region and whether this peace will run parallel with the establishing of an independent state of Kurdistan.

Victoria Williams

Further Reading

Aslan, S. (2014). *Nation-building in Turkey and Morocco: Governing Kurdish and Berber Dissent*. New York: Cambridge University Press.

Bartrop, P. R., & Jacobs, S. L. (Eds.) (2015). *Modern Genocide: The Definitive Resource and Document Collection*. Santa Barbara, CA: ABC-CLIO.

BBC News Service. "Who Are the Kurds?" *BBC News: World*. March 14, 2016. http://www.bbc.co.uk/news/world-middle-east-29702440.

Coles, I., & Kalin, S. (2016). "Power Struggle in Iraq: In Fight against Islamic State, Kurds Expand Their Territory." *Reuters Investigates*. October 10, 2016. http://www.reuters.com/investigates/special-report/mideast-crisis-kurds-land/

de Bretton-Gordon, H. (2016). "Remembering Halabja Chemical Attack." *AlJazeera.com*. http://www.aljazeera.com/indepth/opinion/2016/03/remembering-halabja-chemical-attack-160316061221074.html.

Ihsan, M. (2017). *Nation Building in Kurdistan: Memory, Genocide and Human Rights*. Abingdon, UK: Routledge.

Stanford University. (2010–2017). "Ansar al-Islam." *Mapping Militant Organizations*. http://web.stanford.edu/group/mappingmilitants/cgi-bin/groups/view/13.

Toumani, M. (2008). "Minority Rules." *The New York Times Magazine*. http://www.nytimes.com/2008/02/17/magazine/17turkey-t.html?ex=1361854800&en=df64cf85326e2103&ei=5124&partner=permalink&exprod=permalink.

Tripp, C. (2007). *A History of Iraq*. New Edition. Cambridge UK: Cambridge University Press.

Voller, Y. (2014). *The Kurdish Liberation Movement in Iraq: From Insurgency to Statehood*. Abingdon, UK: Routledge.

Social Organization and Family Life

For a long time the term "Kurds" has been used to describe tribespeople who spoke the Kurdish language. This tribal image indicated a society based on kinship ideology (McDowall, 1992: 13). Tribal structures have been central in the social and political organization of Kurdish society, and related to that bride price, arranged and religious marriages, and polygyny are relatively widespread. However, tribalism should not be essentialized, leaning on Orientalist, nationalist, or modernist presentations of Kurdish society. Such representations function to depict Kurds as the "Other," which has yet to be socialized, modernized, and assimilated into the modern, democratic, and developed world. A more balanced perspective is needed that pays attention both to the diversity and recent developments within Kurdish societies in which tribes often play a marginal role, as well as on the continuing influence of tribal structures in specific situations and areas, where they are perceived as one of the reasons for prevailing gender and power inequalities.

Tribes

Tribes have played, and to some extent still play, an important role in the Kurdish society (van Bruinessen, 1992; Yalçın-Heckmann, 1991). A Kurdish tribe may consist of several hundred to tens of thousands of families, subdivided into segments or clans. The subunits are (ideally) endogamous patrilineal decent groups. The social structure of the tribe was fluctuating, and the organization was based on a real or fictive idea of kinship and a common ancestor. The smaller tribes could constitute real descent groups with only a few external incorporated members. Larger tribes were hierarchically organized and emerged out of a conglomerate of a leading lineage, commoner clans, client lineages, and tributary nontribal peasantry. The shared descent of its members was assumed but has been hard to trace in reality (Yalçın-Heckmann, 1991). Tribes were socially and ideationally constructed and could grow and increase in numbers under the leadership of a strong chieftain, but also disappear and re-emerge.

Tribes

Part of the social framework in Kurdistan are tribal groups. The concept of common ancestry and supporting each other based on a construct of cohesion is common among the Kurds. In fact, throughout history, Kurdish tribal groups have been important actors. The leadership in tribes is in the hands of sheikhs, aghas, or mullahs, who inherit this position. Kurdish tribes live and work together, but they also often share the same religion. Larger confederations of tribes, however, may include branches from other religions such as Christians or Yezidis. Kurdish tribes offer a network of mutual support and protection, and they operate in a transnational context.

Tribes were also known to possess a strong sense of territorial identity (McDowall, 1992). Territories were linked to settled villages and pastures, but could expand to also include the lands of subject peasant villages and any land where tribal leaders were charged by the government to maintain order and collect taxes. The territorial aspect is also manifested in the fact that regions were named after the tribe inhabiting it (van Bruinessen, 1992). Nomadic tribes furthermore insisted on the basic right of passage for seasonal migration, something which brought tribes in frequent conflict with states, especially when tribes had to cross national borders during this passage.

Territory and the people had to be defended against both state intrusion and rival tribes. Self-defense and mutual aid within the tribal community were therefore important functions—which also competed with the influence of centralized governments. During conflicts within the tribe, especially in the cases of blood feuds, the segmentary structure became clearly visible. Closest relatives joined forces against more distant relatives, one segment fought against another segment, and so forth (van Bruinessen, 2002).

Leadership within a tribe was based on a hereditary system within the agha (also called *aghawat*) or sheikh family. Agha is the common term for a tribal leader who has been appointed from within the tribe. The ideal agha is described in van Bruinessen: "He should be a 'man' in the full meaning of the word: strong, courageous, just and generous, a good strategist and a wise judge, and nowadays it is also important that he know how to deal with 'government people'" (1992: 79). Sheikhs were religious leaders, who came as outsiders and often managed to mobilize and unite several tribes against the states. Successful sheiks, like the Barzanis or the Sayyids of Nihri, were able to mobilize several kinship groups unrelated to each other but embracing group solidarity. Although sheikhs had a religious background, members of a tribe or confederation led by the sheikh did not necessarily share the same religion or belong to the same religious sect (McDowall, 1992).

It has been argued that in addition to mediating conflicts and managing contact with the outer world, leading during conflicts and waging war actually were among the most important tasks of tribal leaders (van Bruinessen, 1992). As no clear rules exist as to who should be made leader, it was through their ability and cunningness in warfare that leaders reaffirmed their leadership, united their tribe, and enlarged the scope of both. The aghas could further consolidate their position, as state officials accepted them as negotiators and mediators between the state and the tribe (van Bruinessen, 1992; McDowall, 1992). Through their fortune and position as mediators with the state aghas could further expand their territory, increasing the number of followers and their influence. While smaller tribal units tended to be egalitarian, larger tribes showed a distinct social hierarchy, in which often several leading families competed for control over the clans that together made up a tribe.

> In this competition, which may turn quite violent, rival chieftains of a tribe commonly conclude political alliances with significant outsiders, such as neighbouring tribes or officials of one of the relevant states. An ambitious social climber wishing to establish himself as a paramount chieftain will not shy from having his armed retinue raid villages of his own tribe in order to terrorize them into obedience. It is not uncommon to find within a single tribe one chieftain who co-operates closely with the state and a rival who is a "bandit", a rebel or a collaborator with a neighbor state. (van Bruinessen, 1999)

Van Bruinessen has argued that the specific tribal formations which have existed in Kurdish society have been the products of the interaction with the different nation-states in which the Kurds are living. Furthermore, as McDowall has pointed out, the actual form of the tribal group also depended on the personality of its leaders, economic or kin relations with tribal or nontribal neighbors, and the respective nation-states within which they acted (McDowall, 1992: 13). Because of these interactions, there are major differences today in each country regarding the roles tribes play in the social and political formation of Kurdish society. Some of the tribal formations in Turkey, Iraq, and Syria will be subsequently discussed.

Tribes in Turkey

Describing the tribal structure, at least in Turkey, is no mere practice in anthropological kinship terms, but a highly political endeavor, which for the most part has been avoided by Kurdish scholars. The few anthropological publications on Kurdish tribes in Turkey have been written before or during the war between the Kurdistan Workers Party (PKK) and the Turkish state forces (Beşikçi, 1992 [1969]; van Bruinessen, 1992; Yalçın-Heckmann, 1991). Although taking into account the emergence of the village guard system, these publications have only to a very limited extent considered the political and social changes brought by the war. Furthermore, all of these studies have focused on the southern provinces, predominantly the Hakkari province, which is described as the province most dominated by tribes (van Bruinessen, 2002). Generalizing from these temporal and geographically limited studies on the entire Kurdish population is, of course, problematic.

There is no doubt that tribal organization has been important both in the social organization and in political terms throughout the centuries. However, describing today's Kurdish society as tribal or arguing for a process of retribalization through the war (van Bruinessen, 1999) is highly problematic. Although it is widely acknowledged that political parties have tried to win over tribal leaders and their followers throughout the establishment of the multiparty system in Turkey (McDowall, 1992), tribal structures have today far less influence on voting patterns. This is especially true for voting patterns among the pro-Kurdish parties. Few pro-Kurdish tribal leaders who have the economic and political resources to mobilize their fellow kinsmen have remained in the region. Furthermore, the economic incentive of voting for the pro-Kurdish party was negative—as the pro-Kurdish parties were poor and the districts where the pro-Kurdish party had won local elections could expect economic reprisals by the state. Many pro-Kurdish politicians, most notably Leyla Zana, did not come from the tribal elite. Those pro-Kurdish politicians in eastern Turkey who did have a tribal background were said to have gained political prestige and legitimacy *in spite* of this background, because of their continuous defiance of state repercussions and prosecutions. Pro-Kurdish parties were based on other than kinship loyalties. Jobs at the municipality were rather distributed among political activists and relatives of political prisoners and guerrilla fighters in need of financial support.

Tribal animosities and conflicts between families or clans soon spilled over into the conflict between the PKK and the Turkish state forces. The PKK had a strong antitribal ideology. Its first armed attacks were therefore also directed against powerful tribes in the southeast of Turkey. However, the PKK soon engaged in alliances with "patriotic" tribes, whose rivals often had little choice but to become "traitors" and collaborate with the Turkish army (van Bruinessen, 1999).

Shortly after the beginning of the armed conflict, the Turkish state exploited existing tribal animosities between the local groups in order to fight and weaken the PKK and formed a Kurdish militia, the "village guards," or *köy korucuları*. The village guards were only loosely integrated into the structure of the armed forces and commanded by their own chieftain who was given weapons and salaries for his followers. In return, the village guards were and still are expected or forced to take part in the annual "spring operations," where the mountains are searched for guerrillas. Not all village guards took up arms voluntarily. Especially in areas that were regarded as strongholds of the guerrilla and the PKK, villages could choose between becoming village guards or having their village and land destroyed.

Tribes in Iraq

Tribal organization has played and still plays a central role in the consolidation of Iraqi Kurdistan. It was through tribes, and here especially under the leadership of the Barzani tribe, that the Kurdish nationalist struggle against the Iraqi state was mobilized. Like in Turkey, the central Iraqi government tried to control the Kurdish revolt by integrating some Kurdish tribes into the army command structure as irregular cavalry regiments (*al-Fursan*). These tribes were offered arms and pay. However, "their participation in the conflict continued to depend more on the dynamics of their own relations with the Barzanis than on policy decisions by the central government" (van Bruinessen, 2002). On the other hand, it has been argued that the Barzani confederation developed according to the following principle: a weaker central government led to a strong confederation and the development of a secondary state, whereas a stronger central government weakened and diminished the confederation of states. What has become clear in the Iraqi Kurdish history was the importance of alliances, not only with other tribes, but even more so with other countries.

By the mid-1960s, Mulla Mustafa Barzani had managed to unite most tribes in northern Iraq. With the support of the Iranian government, he established a rudimentary Kurdish administration in the de facto autonomy of northern Iraq (Wimmer, 1997) which lasted until 1975. By then the Iranian government and the Iraqi government had settled their border conflict and signed the Algiers Agreement. The Iranian state withdrew its support for the Kurds, which again led to the strengthening of the Iraqi central government. During the Iran-Iraq war, Mulla Mustafa's sons Masoud and Idris managed again to unite several tribes and, again with Iranian support, to bring several border areas under their control. The government, on the other hand, incorporated a considerable part of the Kurdish population in the *Fursan* regiments, which was considered a substitute for military service. The militia commanders, the *mustashar*, received arms and pay for their men and were allowed some autonomy, not least in their (violent) interactions with rival villages or tribes. This led to the strengthening of the tribes and their leaders. With the end of the Iran-Iraq War in 1988, the Kurdish autonomous dream collapsed, and the Iraqi government started a systematic destruction of Kurdish villages and the deportation and relocation of Kurdish tribes. Tens of thousands of Kurds, especially those who were involved in the nationalist fights, fled to Iran.

This systematic repression accelerated the establishment of a common Kurdish identity, which slowly replaced tribal identities and loyalties (Wimmer, 1997). The Barzani confederation had become the face of the Kurdish nationalist struggle and merged in the early 1990s into one of the two dominating political parties, the KDP, which Barzani had co-founded in 1946. The other party was the PUK, which had been founded in 1975 by urban leftist intellectuals and also established its own Peshmerga army. According to Wimmer (1997), the Kurdish uprising of March 1991 was, however, not led by these political parties, but was dominated by the *mustashar*. McDowall (1992) does not mention the *mustashar*'s important role, but reports that the political parties had not expected the rebellion which "came from the people themselves." Only gradually could the political parties take over leadership. Be that as it may, Wimmer's description of the Kurdish political parties in the mid-1990s as tribal confederacies might perhaps have been an exaggeration; however, it showed "an appreciation of the prominent role that the large tribes have come to play in Iraqi Kurdistan" (van Bruinessen, 1992: 7).

Tribes in Syria

Within the Syrian territory, tribal relations played a much less dominating role in the Kurdish areas. In some regions, such as the Afrin Region, tribal animosities ended in 1850. The region remained relatively peaceful thereafter and was incorporated into the French mandated, territory between 1918 and 1920 without much difficulty for the French (Allsopp, 2015). In other areas, such as the Cezire region, inner-tribal conflict dominated local politics and the area came under French control only in 1930.

The French mandate had initially little impact on Kurdish social structures or on Kurdish politics. In order to secure the northern border of Syria, the French had approached the Kurdish landowners and tribal leaders about collaborating with them. Some tribes sided with the French, others aligned with the emerging Syrian nationalist movement against the French, and others again allied with Turkey, which offered arms and money in exchange for support against the French. Tribes thus apparently took advantage of inner-state conflict and allied with either Turkey or the French to advance their own position within local Kurdish politics.

According to Allsopp (2015) this did not contribute to the strengthening of the tribal system. On the contrary, she refers to the tribal system in decline due to land reforms, modernization, and economic development: in Afrin, leadership in the Kurdish society was taken over by the landowning elite, the aghas (see also Lescot, 1988 [1940]. The importance of tribal membership was increasingly replaced by attachment to land and allegiance to the landowning elite. The latter assumed social, economic, and political leadership in the Kurdish regions until land reforms ended their hold on power in the 1950s and 1960s. In Cezire, tribal relations were far stronger than in Afrin, and tribal leaders continued to hold on to military power during the mandate years. Through the acquisition of land and control over key positions in the local administration, some tribal leaders managed to consolidate their power. Land reforms and resettlement of Arabs in the Kurdish region finally put an end to the tribal leader's power. In the third Kurdish region, in Kobani, the PKK was central in weakening tribal relations.

Nontribal Kurds

It is important to note that not all Kurds had been organized tribally, and there have always existed nontribal Kurds. According to McDowall (1992) some had converted to Islam from other religions. Others had been of tribal origin, but had become sedentary and lost the value of tribal membership. Their kin-based organization does not go beyond lineages and has no political significance. This process of gradual sedentarization during the first half of the 20th century and later urbanization apparently happened both in Iran and among the Kurds in Syria. Van Bruinessen (1992) has mentioned that nontribal Kurds in some areas formed the overwhelming majority of the population. In spite of this, these Kurds were until recently subjected politically and/or economically to Kurdish tribes. They do not own land but are sharecroppers or work as landless agricultural laborers. Their relation may be described as quasi-feudal, and the situation of such dependent non-tribal Kurds has been compared with the serfs of medieval Europe (van Bruinessen, 1992). It was thus also the tribal chief's responsibility to take revenge on their behalf.

A slightly different form of nontribalism has been observed in the northeastern part of Turkish Kurdistan. There Kurds refer to their patrilineage or clan when they talk about their kinship network. They thus describe kinship relations up to approximately four generations, including consanguine and affinal kin. Tribes, understood as the politico-ideological community that shared land and resources, do not matter anymore, and the era of the aghas has vanished. This is especially the case in areas where former leading tribal families have been exiled and their bonds to their native land have weakened. In these areas, the social and political power of the remaining local tribes has also radically declined during the more than 30 years of PKK presence. Those tribal leaders who had allied with the state had left due to the PKK pressure and harassment and established a living in Europe or western Turkey. Some village guards who had gained considerable power were left in the regions, which they also used in conflicts with neighboring villagers. Unlike the village guard commanders of the southeast, who had several hundred guards under their command, the influence and authority of village guard commanders in the northeast were limited to his own village. The tribal leaders and landowners who had supported the Kurdish nationalist movement often lost all their belongings during the war. Their lands in the countryside were burned down, their pastures turned into military areas, and their belongings in town seized by the state.

Kinship

As we have seen, tribal organization has changed considerably over the last century. Although tribal leaders and the semi-feudal system they represented belonged to the past, certain values and practices traditionally linked to the tribal system still exist. The task of providing resources and mediating conflicts was an obligation aghas had toward their followers. This obligation has been taken over by pro-Kurdish politicians. In communities dominated by the current pro-Kurdish party, it is often the mayor or some other high-ranking pro-Kurdish politician who assumed the role of the mediator in family conflicts and blood feuds. The underlying rationale is that "as long as a family is split, at least one part will ally with the state." Pro-Kurdish activists therefore often accused other state officials of ignoring or even supporting blood feuds in order to secure support for the state within a predominantly Kurdish area. The party and pro-Kurdish municipalities on the other hand have been very keen in solving interfamilial conflicts. Successful mediations and the hosting of the reconciliation meal brought prestige for the mediator and thus supporters. It was thus very likely that the reconciled parties in future elections would consent to give their votes to the pro-Kurdish party. In similar ways, patron-client relations still exist. Today's patrons are either party officials or the rich businessmen mostly living in Europe. These businessmen have mainly become rich through the (illegal and legal) cross-border trade with the neighboring countries. They have become the new patrons who are asked to invest in and sponsor local projects.

Even though much of the tribal system has been replaced by political parties that are not necessarily based on kinship ties, kinship remains an important part of social life and serves as an alternative reservoir of security, mobilization, and resistance (Belge, 2011). References to one's kin group are used in order to situate oneself and others in the social landscape and to search for common relatives. It is not uncommon for two strangers after the introduction to spend the next five or ten minutes finding common ground and establishing a relation based on kinship. That relation might be a distant one—for example, through one's grandfather's brother or the exchange of brides between two lineages. But even such distant family ties create a sense of belonging and establish a closer relationship between the two.

Due to the absence of a well-functioning healthcare system, lack of social welfare, and little trust in state institutions, kinship networks are central in providing social and economic assistance in times of need. When kin groups refuse to support each other and the person in need has no other social or political networks to rely on, people end up in extremely precarious situations. Weiss described several cases of women, who, for different reasons, had been abandoned by their closest kin. They lived for years in extreme poverty. One had been homeless for more than 10 years, whereas another woman forced her daughter into marriage in order to pay off her debts with the bride price (Weiss, 2012).

As the trust in state institutions and the police had been severely shattered during the different wars that took place in the Kurdish territory, people also relied often on their kin group to solve conflicts. Having the support of a strong kin group was definitely an asset. Kinship ties may also be mobilized in relation to the conflict with the state. For example, people with informal or formal ties to state officials could draw on these relations in order to protect their relatives from state prosecution. Such practices seem to be widespread. Belge (2011) relates an example from Turkey, in which

> a former urban guerrilla member said, that when she was about to receive a heavy jail sentence for aiding the PKK, one of her nineteen siblings, who was serving in the Turkish military, saw to it that her court file disappeared. The brother in the army had been highly resentful of the nationalist activities of some of his family members and accused them of blocking his promotion in the army. He did, however, move the necessary levers when his sister was about to receive a jail sentence. (2011: 109)

Family Life

Traditionally, Kurdish family life was organized around the patrilineal family and consisted of a senior couple; their married and unmarried sons; and their unmarried, divorced, and widowed daughters. Orphans of male members of the family could also be part of the household. In general, authority and position within the family were based on gender and age. Most commonly, the male head of the

A Kurdish family enjoys a picnic in the mountains near Qaladiza, Iraqi Kurdistan, 2014. (Muhammad Khidir Wisoo/Dreamstime.com)

household had authority over all other female and male family members. He controlled the financial resources and the physical movement of the other family members. Upon the death of the senior male in the household, the role of the "patriarch" was inherited by his younger brother or eldest son. Women who had passed reproductive age and who had born sons could also gain considerable respect and authority within the household and especially its female members. Elderly women could also (indirectly) influence decisions made by the male head and, in some instances, take over their husbands' role as the head of the household . Traditionally, but also today, the elder generation, including elder brothers, enjoy great respect from the young. Younger family members often demonstrate their respect through a special greeting ritual, where the hand of the elder is kissed and put on the young person's forehead. Young people normally refrain from smoking, speaking loudly, or sitting comfortably in front of elder members of authority. They will also consult the elders in important decisions such as marriage, education, choice of job, or settlement. However, whether elders can influence or even dictate such decisions varies greatly. Children, on the other hand, are raised relatively freely when young. Responsibilities increase relative to their age, and especially girls often experience a restriction of their action space when approaching puberty.

Upon marriage, a woman left her natal home and went to live with her husband. If the man married before he has completed his military service, his wife would stay under the protection and control of her parents-in-law during his absence. The young bride was expected to be modest, obedient, and diligent and to do the heaviest household tasks. Many women regarded that time as the worst—they described this time as being strangers in a family where they had to work hard and were without the husband they had chosen (Weiss, 2012). Especially in these first years of marriage, the relationship to their mothers-in-law was often experienced as difficult and strained. Only after some years did the young couple have enough resources to establish their own household, often built as an extension of, or in close proximity to, his family's compound. Many young women therefore try to convince their husbands to move out and establish their own household as soon as possible. Many of these practices are still in place, although often in a different form after moving to a larger town or city. For example, in town it is still desirable to settle in the same neighborhood and, if possible, to have a flat in the same apartment building as the husband's parents and brothers. Geographical proximity among male kin is an ideal, but in practice, migration and urbanization processes have often spread families over several cities, and sometimes even over several countries.

Marriage is regarded as highly important and necessary for men and women to gain the status of adults and full members of society. For a woman, marriage signified the transition from being a virgin girl to an adult woman who can establish her own household and social network. It has been argued that "strong public censure awaited individuals who chose to remain single (except under certain socially regulated circumstances) or to divorce" (White, 1994: 38) and that women who are no longer children but who are not married do generally not receive the respect given to a married woman. Although marriage is considered a central rite of passage in both men's and women's lives, there are increasing cases in which men and women remain single and become respected members of society. Education, city life, employment, and political activism enable men and women to negotiate the time frame and necessity of getting married. Earning their own money and often supporting their entire family, these single men and women mostly stay with their natal family. If they are studying or working farther away, several single women often rent a flat together, while single men may live alone or in the company of other unmarried men. Single women who live on their own usually behave and dress more modestly than their married friends. In order to demonstrate their chastity and modest behavior, they do not accept male visitors and restrict their movement outside after sunset—well knowing that they are under their neighbors' surveillance. Such living arrangements are more acceptable as they are considered to be temporary. Many single men and women aim to get married at some point and establish their own household.

Honor and Sexual Modesty

The sexual modesty of women is important in Kurdish societies and traditionally linked to the concept of honor. This concept can be divided into *namus* and *sheref*, both terms used for different forms of honor. Namus cannot be increased, but can only be secured, lost, or regained. Namus is, among other things, linked to women's sexuality and the family's ability to control it. Namus is also linked to a social group's ability to control and defend their resources and to protect its members.

Within the nationalist discourse, namus is also linked to the ability of the Kurdish community to protect its boundaries.

Sheref is an aspect of honor that is graded. This means that sheref is visible in rank, respect, and prestige. It can be reduced and increased. Whereas women's sexual transgressions are mostly linked to the loss of namus, men mostly lose sheref if they are caught or suspected of having extramarital affairs.

Traditionally, namus and sheref were collective dimensions dependent on a society's norms and values. An individual's honor was of importance for the larger group—be it the extended family, the clan or tribe, or even the nation. As sexualized warfare has shown, the collective dimension may encompass entire ethnic groups and nations. It is within the so-called honor group that defines how honor is gained and lost. It is also within this group that transgressions of the honor code are sanctioned.

Whether honor is important at all or to what degree it is important to a society differs widely, as do the sanctions for trespassing honor boundaries. King (2008) described honor killings and honor suicides as typical sanctions in her ethnography of Iraqi Kurdistan. Weiss (2010), on the other hand, has not documented any honor killings during her ethnographic research in northeastern Turkey, where severe sanctions usually included the social exclusion of men and women engaged in extramarital affairs. Regardless of the consequences of transgressions, it is up to the specific honor group to decide how reputation has been gained or lost. Rumors are therefore of central importance (King, 2008). If rumors are spread about a person—for example, if a woman is accused of having extramarital sex, she and her family will lose namus and subsequently respect and status within a society. As soon as the rumors spread, it is not important whether the woman actually had an extramarital relation. It is therefore important to control the spread of rumors, mostly by controlling family members' (and here especially women's) behavior.

Control over women was mostly exerted through seclusion and veiling. Seclusion may be understood as the designation of areas of activity appropriate to men and women. Usually women in their reproductive age were most restricted, and their movement is confined within specific social boundaries (i.e., the neighborhood or village).

Within these social boundaries, women move around relatively freely. In their world, women exploit the personal freedoms in the segregated society by building their own networks within the female side. Here, they can freely express their emotions, share thoughts and events with other, and leave the house with a group of other women, but without a male guardian. Him and Hoşgör (2011: 338) describe this as the skills to cultivate their own social network, especially a nonkin network, which is more egalitarian than a kin network. This played a significant role in deciding their well-being within the patrilocal living arrangement in which they married in as the "stranger bride."

The strictness of gender segregation and hierarchical structures within the family differs from household to household. These differences not only depend on educational, class, political affiliation, or urban/rural background, though. Within one village, even one extended family, there could be big differences in how family relations unfold. There are those families who send their children to school and others who do not. In some families women participate in conversations and in entertaining male guests and strangers, whereas especially the younger women of other households are not allowed to interact with strangers and keep out of sight upon the arrival of guests. There are those couples who live a marriage marked by mutual respect and love, those whose relationship is dominated by violence and oppression, and, of course, those whose relationship can be placed along the continuum between these two examples.

The control of women's movement and behavior differs according to the importance honor plays in a social group and what the consequences for transgressing the honor codex are. King (2008) describes the omnipresent threat of honor killings in her ethnography from Iraqi Kurdistan. There, honor killings are deemed necessary to avoid irreparable harm to the reputation of the victim's and the perpetrator's lineage.

Kurdish Olympic Champions

Kurds cannot participate in international sporting events under their own flag. Instead, they represent their host country. Kianoush Rostami is an Iranian Kurd and weightlifter who won Olympic gold at the 2016 Rio de Janeiro Summer Olympics in the 85-kg category. Kovan Abdulraheem is an Iraqi Kurdish athlete who won the gold medal at the 2016 Rio de Janeiro Paralympics in Javelin. Yezidi-Kurd Misha Aloyan, from Russia, won the bronze medal at the 2012 London Olympic Games in the super light-weight category. Kurdish female athletes also participate in international competitions, among them the Iraqi Women's National Cyclists Team.

Although Kurdish nationalists take pride in the perception of the historical freedom of Kurdish women, they, too, support appropriate clothing and often veiling as important ways of ensuring a woman's modesty. Whether a woman covers her hair and how she does so depend not only on her family background, her class and social status, and the village or city she lives in, but also on the woman's own individual taste, personal belief, and values. Of course, degrees and means of covering body, hair, and face are furthermore dependent on religion.

Furthermore, it is not uncommon to see many different forms of dressing. Depending on the area one can see women dressed in tight trousers and T-shirts with short sleeves, as well as women with headscarves and overcoats in the stylish manner that has become fashionable in several Muslim countries, as well as the *carsaf*, a black cloth covering the entire body and leaving only the eyes and nose visible. In the villages the covering is mostly less heterogeneous. There, women mostly wear a t-shirt that leaves their underarms visible and a long, colorful skirt over their trousers or pajamas. A headscarf is loosely wrapped around the head, leaving the front hair and sometimes also the ponytail visible.

Although rules and customs differ, what most areas have in common is the way transgressions of decent clothing and behavior are regarded. The transgressing woman will be the object of complaint, contempt, and correction. However, her misbehavior will also reflect on her male relatives. Thus, if a woman transgresses the rules of decent behavior and clothing, her male next of kin will often be the object of critique, as he has failed in his duty to control the woman's behavior and ensure that the family honor would not be stained.

Conclusion

The Kurds have been described as a tribal and patrilineal society. As has been described in this chapter, there are great varieties in the way social organization and family life are practiced among the Kurds today. Urbanization, migration, and different political interventions have in many places reduced or abolished the importance and power of tribal structures. Also when it comes to family relations and household formations, urbanization, modernization, and migration have altered or reformed traditional patterns. Having said this, it is important to keep in mind that the Kurdish society has always been a plural society, with multiple ways of social organization and family life. Which of the traditional values are of importance today and the impact these values have on people's lives are further-more highly dependent on class, education, where the family is located, and not least, in each individual family's history.

Nerina Weiss

Further Reading

Allsopp, H. (2015). *The Kurds of Syria*. London: I. B. Tauris.

Belge, C. (2011). "State Building and the Limits of Legibility: Kinship Networks and Kurdish Resistance in Turkey." *International Journal of Middle East Studies,* vol. 43, 95–114.

Beşikçi, I. (1992 [1969]). *Doğu'da değişim ve yapısal sorunlar (göçebe Alikan aşireti)*. Ankara: Yurt Yayınları.

Bois, T. (1966). *The Kurds*. Beirut: Khayats.

Him, S. M., & Hoşgör, G. A. (2011). "Reproductive Practises: Kurdish Women Responding to Patriarchy." *Women's Studies International Forum,* vol. 34, 335–344.

Kandiyoti, D. (1988). "Bargaining with Patriarchy." *Gender and Society,* vol. 2, no. 3, 274–290.

King, D. E. (2008). "The Personal Is Patrilineal: "Namus" as Sovereignty." *Identities: Global Studies in Culture and Power,* vol. 15, no. 3, 317–342.

Lescot, R. (1988 [1940]). "Le Kurd Dagh et le movement Mouroud." *Studia Kurdica,* vol. 1–5, 101–125.

Navaro-Yashin, Y. (1992). *The Kurds: A Nation Denied*. London: Minority Rights Publications.

Van Bruinessen, M. (1992). *Agha, Shaikh and State: The Social and Political Structures of Kurdistan*. London: Zed Books.

Yalçın-Heckmann, Lale. (1991). *Tribe and Kinship among the Kurds*. Frankfurt: Germany: P. Lang.

Gender Roles

Debates on gender roles within the Kurdish community are closely related to the feminist discourse in the Middle East. For example, common concerns include the critique of patriarchal structures and the imperative of intersectionality that is important to understanding gender within a wider social and political context. Still, the Kurdish society has demonstrated some peculiarities. Especially with the intake of leftist ideologies and the armed struggle by the PKK, new gender roles have been emerging and are gaining ground. Some of these gender roles, such as the character of the political mother, have emerged from already existing socially respected positions and thus could quite easily be vested with new meanings. Other gender roles, such as the female guerrilla fighter, posed greater challenges. Kurdish history provides some examples of independent women who participated in armed conflict or acted as tribal leaders. However, all of these women had come to power through their roles as wives or daughters of powerful men. The female guerrilla fighters had become independent and powerful in their own terms, and very often, they had become so without the support and against the will of their families.

The emergence of these new gender roles has frequently been used to prove the developmental and transformative power of the Kurdish movement. The mass mobilization of women and the political participation of women in leading positions have also improved the social latitude of other women, who themselves were not politically active. Society is changing and slowly opening up for new gender roles, including those represented in the queer community.

Introduction

Gender is not a stable category, nor is it the only category of identity. Being a woman, a man, or a trans-person is closely linked to the person's social position, ethnicity, class background, education, religious practice, and last but not least to the authority's policy toward that person's group. Being a Kurd, politically active or not, thus strongly defines what it means to be a mother, an LGBT activist, or a young man. Although ethnicity and political affiliation are pivotal factors in people's identity, power relations exist and play out along *all* the different identity markers and affect status and social latitude. Thus, we have to keep these other categories in mind when exploring gender roles, their gender norms, and rules of accepted conduct within the Kurdish society.

As the Kurdish example clearly demonstrates, gender is not a stable category of identity, but is contextual and regulated by culturally defined norms. Thus, we should understand gender rather as a performance. A gender role has to be repeatedly enacted and performed in order to be valid. It is possible to perform gender roles in slightly different ways, negotiating norms, and adapting the roles to new emerging (political) contexts. Gender roles are not fixed and stable categories, but may change and transform. Gender norms are continuously given new meaning over time and in different social contexts. This will also explain how new gender positions, such as the political mother, the female guerrilla fighter, and the politically active young woman, which have been introduced and propagated by the Kurdish nationalist movement, have gradually become culturally accepted gender norms (Weiss, 2010).

Gender and Tradition

Historical travel accounts have long admired the relative freedom and social latitude of Kurdish women. Kurdish women were described as being mostly unveiled, having relative freedom of movement, and enjoying authority within the family and society as such. Love marriages existed next to arranged marriages, and women were said to have a more financially secure position than most other women did in the Middle East. The relative freedom of Kurdish women and traces of some gender equality are symbolized in the prominent roles some women have played within Kurdish politics and society. It has been relatively easy for women to succeed their deceased husbands as head of the family or lineage, even though male heirs existed. Prominent examples are that of Adela Khanum (d. 1924), also called Lady Adela, and Kara Fatma of Maraş (1888–1955). Adela Khanum has been described as a unique, powerful woman with military skills. She was the wife of Usman Pasha, leader of the powerful Jaf tribe and the Ottoman government's appointee as governor of the district of Shahrizur. During her husband's lifetime, she gradually accumulated official power. After Usman Pasha's death, she was the unchallenged tribal leader until her death in 1924. Another prominent example is that of Kara Fatma, who was leader of the Bashi-Bazouk tribe from Maraş and commanded her men in a militia group of the Turkish army.

Whereas many Western authors have been intrigued by the prominent role of these women, others have been highly skeptical of the assumption that a few women in prominent public roles were proof of the relative freedom and equality of most Kurdish women. On the contrary, feminists and Kurdish nationalists have highly criticized the Kurdish society for its patriarchal structures, which they saw as connected with the concept of honor, and in extension, to the institutionalized subordination of women (King, 2008). They demand that patriarchy and "traditional" gender roles be abolished not only within the immediate family, but even more so within the political discourse and political sphere. Women should be liberated and freed from patriarchal slavery.

In this critique, the Kurdish society has been associated with Kandiyoti's (1988) concept of classic patriarchy. This implies that

> the patrilineage totally appropriates both women's labor and progeny and renders their work and contribution to production invisible. Women's life cycle in the

patriarchally extended family is such that the deprivation and hardship she experiences as a young bride is eventually superseded by the control and authority she will have over her own subservient daughter-in-law. (Kandiyoti, 1988: 279)

According to the author, women's life cycle encourages women to reproduce their own subordination. "In classical patriarchy, subordination to men is offset by the control older women attain over younger women" (Kandiyoti, 1988: 279). The author refers to the course of a life cycle, through which men and women take on different gender roles, which are bestowed on them by different levels of respect, freedom of movement, and the ability to act within the domestic and public domain, as well as the interaction with members of the other sex. The focus of her analysis is predominantly on age and marital status as important determinates for status and freedom of movement.

These highly different descriptions of gender and social mobility among the Kurds, the focus on the historically high status of Kurdish women on the one hand and the critique of the patriarchal system with its institutionalized subordination of women on the other hand, can be described as political projects. They do not describe the reality, which is often far more complex and varied. The Kurdish society is and has been highly heterogeneous, and gender norms might not only differ according to different political ideologies, but also urban and rural settings or different classes. Gender norms may be enforced quite differently even within same village or the same family.

When it comes to the liberationist discourse, it is important to keep in mind that gender is inherently linked to power relations. There is no "liberation" when it comes to gender roles. Although gender roles range in terms of status, reputation, authority, and not least in their spaces of opportunity and movement, there always exist systems of power and control that have to be negotiated, rejected, and appropriated (Weiss, 2012). What follows is a framework to understand the multiple meanings of being a Kurdish woman, man, or trans-person.

Gender and Nation

In many nationalist discourses, the social position of women is perceived as an important benchmark for measuring the development of a nation. Within Kurdish nationalist discourse, the emancipation of Kurdish women has been regarded as a precondition for the emancipation of the Kurdish society as a whole (Aktürk, 2016). Also, Abdullah Öcalan, the leader of the PKK and ideological representative of the Kurdish nationalist struggle in Turkey, parts of Iran, and Syria, has argued that the progress of the Kurdish nation was reliant on the progress with respect to the equality of women and men. "The project of women's liberation goes far beyond the equality of the sexes, but moreover describes the essence of general democracy, of human rights, of harmony and communal equality" (Öcalan, 2010). Furthermore, current discourses on women's role in the newly established democratic autonomous regions in northern Syria and in Turkey are built around the importance of women's liberation and gender equality (Dirik et al., 2016). Not surprisingly, these new emergent gender roles, such as the politically active women, the female guerrilla fighter, or the political mother, have become symbolic characters of the Kurdish political struggle.

However, in the Kurdish movement, like in other revolutionary and nationalist movements, feminist issues have for a long time been treated secondary to the national struggle, and women's emancipation was framed within "a modernizing project dominated by men" (Aktürk, 2016). Although gender issues, and here especially women's rights, have gained more focus within Kurdish politics and nationalist discourse since the late 1990s, and women have gained a much more active place in the Kurdish nationalist struggle(s), the proclaimed aim of gender equality has yet to be reached. Furthermore, there is still a long way to go until all gender roles and identities, including those within the LGBT movement, are fully recognized and accepted in practice.

Within modern nations' and most nationalist discourses the nation has been imagined in gendered terms, often through the image of the mother, the bride, or the virgin. The nation as mother, who mediates, gives refuge, and serves, rearticulates "the notions of the children's duties to their parents into those of the duties of (male) citizens to the motherland (Najmabadi, 1997: 460). The nation, which has to be protected from foreign transgression, is also symbolized by the bride. In that sense), the homeland is imagined as the object of male desire and of the nationalist man's exclusive love (Najmabadi, 1997). This erotic love relationship is mostly unconsumed (Weiss, 2012); however, at times, fighting for Kurdistan, the bride, may be described as a wedding (Aktürk, 2016).

Whereas the nation has been imagined in feminine terms, its people were imagined as a patrilineage. A patrilineage, of course, always consists of both men and women. However, in the nationalist imaginary, the brothers and male cousins, "sons of Kurdistan" (Aktürk, 2016), were to defend their nation from exogenous threats; to sacrifice their lives for their homeland; and to defend their freedom, their honor, their homeland, and their women (King 2008). The notion of honor here closely links the protection of the homeland to the protection of its women. This is not a coincidence. The notion of honor, *namus* or *ird*, refers to the sexuality of women and a man's ability to control it, as it indicates a man's duty to protect the boundaries of the nation-state. This also refers to women as the gatekeepers of Kurdish culture and community. As mothers and wives of the patrilineage, they were to have children by the right, that is, Kurdish men. The construction of the nation and its women as bodies in need of protection and possession became painfully visible in the early years after the establishment of the Kurdish Regional Government. Kurdish women who had been suspected of having relations with men of the Iraqi regime and other outsiders "were seen as tainting the emerging Iraqi Kurdish state with wombs that were too accessible" (King, 2008: 335). These women were blacklisted and subsequently killed by the Peshmerga.

Furthermore during warfare, sexual violence, rape, and the (sexual) mutilation of corpses have been repeatedly used by the centralized governments as weapons of war, meant to symbolically humiliate men and society at large. Men are demasculinized and dishonored as they have been shown unable to protect their women. This has been happening throughout the conflict between the Kurdish Workers'

Party (PKK) and the Turkish state, when corpses of female PKK fighters have been sexually defiled and publicly displayed (Weiss, 2010). Lately, the Islamic State has abducted, enslaved, and sexually abused Yezidi women on a massive scale. The sexual violence against the Yezidi women may stand out as an exceptionally horrendous case of sexual warfare, and has been described as part of a larger genocide against the Yezidi community.

The National Family

Imagining the nation in gendered terms is nothing particularly Kurdish and can be seen in several nationalist discourses. What is interesting in the Kurdish case is how the image of this national family—the nation as the mother, the bride, and her sons and lovers that come to her protection—is expressed within Kurdish nationalist discourse today and how it has found direct expression in several of the newly emerged political gender roles.

The notion of the Kurdish national family is expressed through the political use of kinship terms. The pro-Kurdish movement is regarded as an extension of the kin group and has become the "party family" or "national family" (Çağlayan, 2007). The leaders of the movement were the heads of the family. In Iraqi Kurdistan, Mulla Mustafa Barzani (1903–1979) was considered the father, whereas his son, Masoud Barzani (1946–), is referred to as Kak (brother). Jalal Talabani (1933–), the leader of the second biggest political party in Iraqi Kurdistan and former president of Iraq, is the father's brother Mam (King, 2008: 333). Also within the PKK-dominated nationalist discourse, the affectionate title for the PKK leader Abdullah Öcalan is Apo, which, besides being the nickname for Abdullah, also means uncle in Kurdish. In addition, the claim of a political movement to represent an entire community has, for example, been visible during pro-PKK demonstrations, where slogans such as PKK halktır (The PKK are the people) have been chanted. The mothers of guerrilla fighters and political prisoners have become the mothers of the nation.

Mothers of grown-up children and elderly women traditionally enjoyed a relatively high social status. They were less restricted in moving around in the public sphere and enjoyed high respect and authority, not only with regard to family affairs, but also within the public and political sphere (Weiss, 2012). As women beyond their fertile years, elderly women were less vulnerable to be sexually violated by government authorities and security services. It was therefore "natural" that it would be the mothers (and not the wives) who would demonstrate for prisoners' rights. One of the few prominent political wives is Leyla Zana (1961–). However, she soon refused to be active only on her husband's behalf and started her independent political career. She became the first female Kurdish MP and has spent 15 years in prison for adding a few words in Kurdish after taking the parliamentarian oath in Turkish (Weiss, 2012).

The first group of political mothers was organized in Turkey after the coup d'etat of 1980. A decade later, in the 1990s, the mothers of Kurdish guerrilla fighters formed the organization Mothers of Peace. Today, there are several such organizations, not all of which have close links to the Kurdish nationalist movement.

The public presence of these mothers and their insistence in active participation in politics gave motherhood (and here especially political motherhood) new meaning. The mother was not only peaceful, gentle, and taking on the role of the mediator (Yalcin-Heckmann & Van Gelder, 2000: 90). Political mothers often present themselves as the mothers of all guerrilla fighters in the mountains during public talks as well as during interviews. They thus also present the political struggle and the Kurdish nationalist movement as rooted deeply within society. As such, it is one of the strongest symbols in the protest against injustice and war (Weiss, 2010).

Several Kurdish feminist scholars have argued that the armed struggle of the PKK and the emergent pro-Kurdish parties have been central to the political mobilization of women (Çağlayan, 2007). They "carried numerous women from behind the walls of their houses to the public sphere, to the streets. [. . .] Kurdish women, who used to stay in their houses and be fully obedient to their husbands, today stand upon their rights, struggle for their languages, cultures and identities, and all these things create an individual consciousness and an independent personality in them" (Çaha, 2011: 438). Other researchers, however, have been critical of this "liberationist" approach that links emancipation exclusively to political activism (Weiss, 2010). What is important here is the fact that mass mobilization of women led to the gradual acceptance of politically active women. Besides political mothers, the young, unmarried women became active in politics. They took advantage of the political discourse of gender equality, political emancipation of women, and the disregard of age and other forms of "traditional" markers of social status. As young women, traditionally a gender role vested with little authority and social status, these women claimed the notion of comradeship, a fundamental part of the PKK-inspired Kurdish nationalist discourse (Çağlayan, 2007). They used the term *hewal*, comrade, to address their fellow party members, thus obliterating the "traditional" hierarchy of age, rank, and gender.

The downplaying of gender differences through terminology also indicates the asexualization of its members. In fact, the PKK has long forbidden sexual relations between its members and practiced a strict moral code. Although grounded in revolutionary and leftist ideology, the standards of modesty in the party setting fitted well with local notions of morality, chastity, and honor.

Inspired by thinkers such as Che Guevara and Franz Fanon, Öcalan adopted the idea of the new man (and later new woman). The revolutionary man, the new man, should kill his patriarchal masculinity, undo himself, and remold his personality (Özcan, 2006: 137). Similarly, the new woman should put behind the backward nature of her womanhood and liberate herself. Grojean describes the new human as promoted by Öcalan as follows: "The new human does not drink, does not play and does not think of personal joys or comfort [. . .] He has internalized the philosophy and morality of the new human, the way he sits, rises, his style, ego, his attitude and his reactions. The fundament of all this is his love [. . .] to the revolution, freedom and socialism" (Grojean, 2008).

The ban on sexual relations has made it possible for young, unmarried women to be politically active, and during their activism also move far beyond their family's gaze (Weiss, 2010). Although many young women gained access to new political and social spaces, they had to manage different gender norms in order to be accepted and respected. Thus, they had to behave chastely and dutifully, as is demanded of an unmarried daughter, and at the same time demonstrate willpower and the ability to be an independent activist. Only if young girls manage to balance this thin line without breaking any rules of modest conduct may they claim the right for gender equality and emancipation (Weiss, 2010).

Hypermasculinity and Refeminization of the Nation

Young political women who enjoyed the esteem of their family and the respect of their community were often described as or compared to men. A mother would thus say to her politically active daughter: "You are a man, and I trust you" (Weiss, 2010). Hassanpour (2001) has shown that linguistically men are associated with qualities such as zeal, manliness, manhood, bravery, and fearlessness. Women, on the other hand, are associated with weakness and feebleness. Furthermore, a woman who had demonstrated bravery was framed in masculine terms: the Sorani term for "very brave and knowledgeable woman," *nêrejin*, thus literally means a "male/masculine woman."

Bravery and the use of violence were clearly linked to manhood. Vice versa, war is a masculine undertaking. Women who take up arms and fight for their nation thus trespass an important gender norm. Linguistically, such women have long been described as men-women, or women who imitate men or have a boyish

Kurdistan Workers' Party (PKK) female fighters in the Qandil Mountains of Iraqi Kurdistan. (Eddie Gerald/Alamy Stock Photo)

behavior (Hassanpour, 2001: 237). Although women have fought with the PKK since its early beginnings, and women have had their separate units from the 1990s onwards, guerrilla fighters have been until recently described in male terms (Weiss, 2010). They were defeminized (Hassanpour, 2001) and had, as the heroes of the national struggle, to live up to the hypermasculinized image of the hero. This implied also that former guerrilla women had to adhere to notions of autonomy, moral superiority, and the rejection of any vulnerability and weakness.

The re-entry of the hypermasculinized female guerrilla fighter into the civil society has therefore constituted several challenges, and female guerrilla fighters have remained anomalies in their society. Unlike the young female activist, who moved between the protected spaces of the family and the party, the female guerrilla fighter had left the community, fought in the mountains, served time in prison, and there been exposed to (often) sexual violence by state security forces. Upon their return, most guerrilla fighters still worked as cadres, and were therefore still expected to live up to the image of the asexual new human. However, male guerrilla fighters could return relatively easily to a "normal" life and marry. This step was far more difficult for women. Although female guerrilla fighters occasionally married, this step was considered a deep transgression of their gender norm and was sanctioned with social exclusion and the threat of violence (Weiss, 2010).

Regendering the Nation

Gradually, the emergence of the female guerrilla fighter has led to a change in nationalist discourse. Already in 1999 Abdullah Öcalan argued that women's active participation in the armed struggle meant "taking the most radical step to equality and freedom" (Öcalan, 1999: 176). At least in discourse, the femininity of the female guerrilla fighters was highlighted against the patriarchal oppression of their adversaries. They were not the hypermasculinized warriors, but the feminine heroes, whose feminine essence has become their main weapon. "The image of Kurdish women taking up arms against the masculine army was intolerable. [. . .] National and male chauvinism combined forces to launch a vast propaganda campaign against women guerrillas. While official nationalism labeled the men as 'terrorists', its patriarchal politics reduced the women to 'prostitutes'" (Mojab, 2001: 4–5).

Images of female guerrilla fighters soon appeared in Kurdish and Western media. More recently, one can observe the imagery of the beautiful female fighter against the backward, barbarous, and misogynous Islamic State warriors. In fact, looking at current images of fighters of the all-female Kurdish military organization YPJ, the Women's Protection Units, most of the women are smiling and appear to be in harmony with nature. The background is often impressive mountain scenery or a lush meadow. When the woman is not depicted aiming at the (invisible) enemy, she is depicted laughing, dancing, hugging, enjoying the company of their fellow warriors, or taking care of smaller animals. Their rifles, however, are always close at hand and are clearly visible in the image. The war has become female, and the formerly hypermasculinized warriors have been vested with inherent (and stereotypical) female notions. The female hero is fearless and fierce against her enemies but full of concern and care for her surroundings.

YPJ—Yekiniyen Parastina Jin or Women's Defense Forces

Many Kurdish and other women from Syria join the Women's Defense Forces, a female-only paramilitary force that participates in the Syrian Civil War and the battle against IS. They are considered an armed wing of the PYD, the largest and most powerful Kurdish party in Syria and an affiliate of the PKK. The YPJ is actively involved in the fight against IS; however, they also are trained ideologically following the ideas of women's liberation as described by the founder of the PKK, Abdullah Ocalan. As female fighters in a patriarchal society, they break with gender norms and traditions.

Kurdish activists have been very critical of the Western sensational exotification of the Kurdish female guerrilla as the "bad-ass" Amazons. They believe that the media fetishizes these female fighters without recognizing their concurrent battle against a patriarchal society. The female guerillas fight against ISIS and gender inequality.

Changes in discourse are an important step toward changes in practice. There is still a long way to go until the complementary gender images have been dissolved and gender equality and emancipation have become the norm in the Kurdish society. However, as gender roles have to be performed and continuously repeated in order to be valid, new gender roles that come closer to the ideal of equality might manifest, normalize, and gradually find social acceptance.

It has yet to be seen whether other gender roles, such as those represented in the queer community, will at some point find general acceptance. Also, here discourses have changed, and there exists a more or less open LGBT movement in all parts of Kurdistan. However, unlike female and male gender roles, which have evolved and changed gradually, queer gender identities had to carve out far more new ground. As Hassanpour has noted, human beings should be either males or females, even biologically. Terms for trans-persons are even semantically derogatory as they relate to someone "who is neither male nor female" (2001: 238). Except for the homophobic dichotomy of the active/passive part in homosexual relationships, "the Kurdish language has no word for the less homophonic English concepts of 'homosexual', 'gay' or 'lesbian'" (Hassanpour, 2001: 241). The Kurdish nationalist movements in Turkey and Syria have embraced the LGBT community, and within the pro-Kurdish party HDP, quotas have been established to facilitate their political participation. However, until now, the quota system has had little effect on the ground, mostly due to homophobia within the party ranks and the consequential difficulties for members of the LGBT community to come out publicly.

Conclusion

As this chapter has demonstrated, gender roles and gender relations have to be explored within the intersection with other important factors such as power relations, nationality, ethnicity, class, or religion. Furthermore, it is important to explore gender within a wider social and political context and against a historical background. Only then will it be possible to do justice to the heterogeneity of gender roles, gender norms, and gender relations in the Kurdish society and to grasp the enormous changes certain sectors of the Kurdish society currently undergo.

Nerina Weiss

Further Reading

Aktürk, A. S. (2016). "Female Cousins and Wounded Masculinity: Kurdish Nationalist Discourse in the Post-Ottoman Middle East." *Middle Eastern Studies,* vol. 52, no. 1, 46–59.

Çağlayan, H. (2007). *Analar, Yoldaşlar, Tanrıçalar.* Istanbul: İletişim Yayınları.

Çaha, Ö. (2011). The Kurdish women's movement: a third-wave feminism within the Turkish context. *Turkish Studies,* vol. 12, no. 3, 435–449.

Dirik, Dilar et al. (Eds.). (2016). *To Dare Imagining: Rojava Revolution.* New York: Autonomedia.

Grojean, O. (2008). "La production de l'Homme nouveau au sein du PKK." http://ejts.revues /index2753.html.

Hassanpour, A. (2001). "The (Re)production of Patriarchy in the Kurdish Language." In S. Mojab (Ed.), *Women of a Non-State Nation. The Kurds* (pp. 227–263). Costa Mesa CA: Mazda Publishers.

Kandiyoti, D. (1988). Bargaining with Patriarchy. Gender and Society, vol. 2, no. 3, 274–290.

King, D. E. (2008). "The Personal Is Patrilineal: 'Namus' as Sovereignty." *Identities. Global Studies in Culture and Power,* vol. 15. no. 3, 317–342.

Mojab, S. (2001). *Women of a Non-State Nation: The Kurds.* Costa Mesa, CA: Mazda Publishers.

Najmabadi, A. (1997). "The Erotic Vatan as Beloved and Mother: To Love, to Possess and to Protect." *Comparative Studies in Society and History,* vol. 39, no. 3, 442–467.

Savelsberg, E., Hajo, S., & Borck, C. (2000). *Kurdische Frauen und das Bild der kurdischen Frau.* Münster: LIT Verlag.

Weiss, N. (2010). "Falling from Grace: Gender Norms and Gender Strategies in Eastern Turkey." *New Perspectives on Turkey,* vol. 42, 73–94.

Housing and Settlements

As an ethno-national community, Kurds are living in an area spread into territories of five countries in the Middle East, which are Turkey (43 percent of the total area of Kurdistan), Iraq (18 percent), Iran (31 percent), Syria (6 percent), and Armenia (2 percent) (Ghassemlou et al.). Moreover, a considerable Kurdish immigrant population, estimated at about 500,000, lives in Western European countries, largely in Germany, the Netherlands, France, and Scandinavia. This aspect enables us to call them a transnational community. Kurdistan is a geocultural region in which the Kurds have historically formed a prominent majority population and Kurdish culture, language, and national identity historically have been based. Contemporary use of Kurdistan refers to parts of eastern Turkey (northern Kurdistan), northern Iraq (southern Kurdistan), northwestern Iran (eastern Kurdistan), and northern Syria (western Kurdistan) inhabited mainly by Kurds.

Historical Development of Human Settlement in Kurdistan

Although Kurdistan is a historically important region and humankind witnessed in it one of the earliest civilizations, archaeological excavation efforts in Kurdistan were limited, and many sites are still hidden. However, there were invaluable archaeological investigations in Kurdistan in the 1940s and 1950s, which have unraveled and discovered a number of mysteries not only about the antiquity of Kurdistan but also about the beginning of human civilization. The works of Professors Robert Braidwood and Linda Braidwood and their colleagues (Braidwood & Howe, 1960) hold a prominent position in this respect. They have established that Kurdistan is one of the first cradles of humankind that witnessed the beginning of the neolithic/agrarian revolution about 9,000 years ago.

The development of human settlement in the Kurdistan region has commenced in three important stages:

Cave Stage

Geological and archaeological evidence revealed that Kurdistan has been settled since the era of the Upper Paleolithic culture, which coincides with the first stage of the last glacial period in Europe. The main type of subsistence was that of hunting wild animals and gathering. The communities were formed on the basis of joint work activity and some degree of kinship (Braidwood & Howe, 1960). The natural environment in the mountainous region of Kurdistan offered appropriate circumstances to early humankind to settle in its rock shelters and caves in order to protect them first from the harsh environment and second from enemies. The Kurdistan region has numerous caves that record the early existence of humankind in it. Among them are the caves in Zirzi, Hezarmerd, Pelgawra, Barak, Hajieh, Kaiwanian, Babakhal, Spilk, and Shanidar. One of the most important caves in the region is Shanidar Cave, which is located in the valley of the Great Zab in the Bradost Mountain at an altitude of 637 meters above sea level. It was excavated from 1957–1961 by Ralph Solecki and his team from Columbia University and yielded the first adult Neanderthal skeletons in Kurdistan, dating between 60,000 and 80,000 years BCE. The excavated area produced nine Neanderthal skeletons of varying ages and states of preservation and completeness.

Commuting Stage

This stage is considered a transition period between the cave stage and building of the first permanent settlements. This period also marks a phase of human seasonal commuting between the cave in winter and the temporary structure in the moderate season. The commuting stage in Kurdistan was a time of transition from the Paleolithic or Old Stone Age cultures to the neolithic or New Stone Age during which agriculture appeared. An example of the settlement of this stage is Karim Shahir, an open site on a terrace of the Greater River Zab in Iraqi Kurdistan, which has given its name to a culture dated circa 9000 to 7000 BCE and associated with the transition from a hunting and gathering form of subsistence to one based on farming. There is little evidence for permanent structures in the Karim Shahir sites, and most of them were probably occupied seasonally by nomadic or semi-nomadic groups, who were somewhat sedentary. However, at Karim Shahir clear proof was discovered for both the knowledge of grain cultivation in the form of sickle blades and for the baking of clay in the form of lightly fired clay figurines. The economy was based on hunting with some possible evidence of herding, and the artifact evidence also suggests an increased dependence on plant resources (Braidwood & Howe, 1960).

Settlement Stage

In Kurdistan this was the first time humans began to leave their caves and instead built homes to live in. Some 3,500 years before settlement started in Europe, northern Iraq was the scene of the neolithic revolution, perhaps the most important of all times. Thus, on the foothills of Kurdistan man ceased to be a wandering hunter, depending for his living upon luck and skill, and become a farmer attached to the small piece of land from which he obtained a regular food supply. Out of clay, he built himself a house. He secured a permanent and easily available source of milk, meat, wool, and hide from the sheep and cattle he raised and herded. At the same time, his social tendencies for the care and defense of the land developed, calling for close cooperation with others. Each family probably erected their own farm, cultivated their own field, grazed their own flocks, and made their own tools, but several families were grouped together and formed a hamlet, the embryo of a social organization (Braidwood & Howe, 1960). An example of the settlement during this stage is Zawi Chami village, which is considered one of the oldest settlements in Kurdistan—and even the entire world (Rose & Solecki, 1981). Archeologists estimated that it dates back to 10,000 BCE (Saed, 1984). It is located near Shanidar cave and just 100 meters from the Great Zab River. The location of the village near the Shanidar cave can be explained by the reason that people used it for shelter during the harsh climate in winter, considering that the building material (clay) was not strong enough to provide protection from the elements. Another important early settlement in Kurdistan is Jarmo village, which is located near Chamchamal city in an intermountain area. The animal bones found in Jarmo were of fully domesticated animals—mostly goats and sheep. The culture of this period was based on productive farming, as represented by the remains of Kultepe and some other villages. The most interesting feature of this period and location was the absence of any hunting weapons. The tools were made from flint and obsidian. The plant remains belonged to fully cultivated wheat and barley, and the bones were from domesticated animals only (Braidwood & Howe, 1960). In time, rainfall increased and the area grew suitable for cultivation. As a result, the settlements gradually moved from the foothills of the mountains to the plains. Trading and bartering among different communities became more popular, especially after the inhabitants became full-time farmers and animal breeders. This provided more generous and constant sources of sustenance. The result can be seen in the rapid population increase and the continuous growth of the number of settlements (Ibid).

Settlement Characteristics in Kurdistan

Location and Spatial Relationships

From the angle of physical geography, Kurdistan is located within the mountainous transition belt of the Fertile Crescent, with the Taurus and Zagros mountains forming an arc encircling the Mesopotamian region. These mountains have been both home and safeguard of the Kurdish people.

The mountain chains of Kurdistan run in a northwest to southeastern direction along the territories of Iran, Iraq, and Turkey. These chains slope toward the south into the fertile plains of Harir, Erbil, Sharazur, and the Garmian. These plains can be described as being a piedmont zone or landform created at the foot of a mountain by debris deposited by shifting streams. The foothills of the Zagros stretch to a few kilometers outside the major urban centers of Dohuk and Erbil, with the city of Sulaymaniyah located within them. Fertile valleys lie between the mountain ridges, and this intermountain zone is heavily dissected by active drainage systems (Naqshbandi et al., 1998).

Current human settlements in Kurdistan take different forms according to their location in the mountainous region. These forms are:

- Intermountain cities: This type includes the cities that are located in the middle of mountain ranges among valleys or plains areas, for example, Duhok in Iraq, Sirnak in Turkey, and Sina (Sanandaj) in Iran.

View of Diyarbakir (Amed), one of the largest Kurdish cities in Turkey. (Fatih Polat/Dreamstime .com)

- Piedmont cities: This includes cities that have a gentle slope leading from the foot of mountains to a region of flat land. An example is Shaqlawa in Iraqi Kurdistan.
- Pre-mountain cities: This type includes the cities, which are located in the plains area before entering a mountainous region, for example, Erbil in Iraq, Diyarbakir in Turkey, and Mahabad in Iran.

Settlements in Kurdistan linked to each other and to the rest of the Kurdistan cities by roads, which include three types: national, regional, and minor. These roads in general reflect a medium-to-bad status, as most of them are lacking pavement or traffic controls, leading to irregular movement of vehicles on them. Heavy snowfall, avalanches, landslides, and floods may block these roads. Yet transportation is always a challenge in highland regions, and the societies living there may be completely isolated at times. In many mountainous areas in Kurdistan, walking and pack animals are still the main forms of transportation, making it tough to bring items into the villages and to take products to market. Roads and railways are expensive and difficult to build in steep mountain valleys. Tunnels and bridges are often necessary.

Demographic Characteristics

The population of the settlements in Kurdistan can be described by several aspects.

First, there is a high rate of urbanization. It is clear that both urban and rural residential areas underwent major changes during the second half of the last century. At the regional level, the rural population in 1965 accounted for more than 68 percent of the total population. However, this percentage decreased to no more than 49 percent in 1995. In contrast, from 1965 to 1995 the urban population in Kurdistan increased from 31.7 percent to 51 percent, indicating a high rate of migration to the cities (Ghafor, 2005: 231).

The geographical distribution of settlements in Kurdistan generally tends to be dispersed over large areas, unlike in the rest of Turkey, Iran, and Iraq, which are more linear as the settlements are along the rivers as a result of climate conditions and water resources. For instance in the arid areas of Iraq to the west and south, cities and large towns are almost invariably situated on watercourses, usually on the major rivers or their larger tributaries. Those living or cultivating on the crest of a levee have easy access to water for irrigation and household use in a dry, hot country.

There is significant variation in the total densities of the cities. The number of areas with approximately 45 persons/km^2 is smaller, whereas there is an increase in some other areas up to about 130 persons/km^2. In addition, there is considerable variation in densities of different areas within the same city, where it rises in the old areas to reach more than 350 persons/km^2 and drops in other areas on the border, with fewer than 50 persons/km^2.

The Economic Structures

In terms of its geographic and demographic characteristics and its economic development in particular, Kurdistan is being forced into major changes, most of which are considered hostile, at least in the short term (KRG, 2011). For instance, in the Kurdistan Iraqi region the activities of successive government policies and humanitarian aid inputs in the 1990s have succeeded in weakening the agricultural basis, creating a society that, in theory, has the capability and resources to be largely self-sufficient, but is dependent on external sources for all provisions, including food and everyday consumer items.

Agriculture has been the backbone of the Kurdish economy. In the past, this economy has been so strong that the region provided the markets of Mesopotamia, Syria, Turkey, the Transcaucasia, and Iran with agricultural products for centuries (Saed, 1984). The dominance of agriculture could be seen in the numbers of people working in and depending upon this sector. In 1985, more than half of the population in Kurdistan (56 percent) was dependent on agriculture, 34 percent worked in the service sector, and 11 percent in industry (Ghafor, 2005: 179).

However, this circumstance changed considerably in many parts of Kurdistan. For instance, by the end of the 1980s, only 15.8 percent of the Iraqi Kurdistan population was dependent on agriculture, whereas 77.8 percent of them were dependent on the service sector. The continued and intensified policy of systematically destroying the rural infrastructure and deporting villagers through the 1980s was the main reason for this change (Stansfield, 2003). As a result of that, the dependency on agriculture continued to decrease noticeably year after year, to reach just 8 percent in 2004.

Urban Characteristics

In all of Kurdistan, there were 386 urban settlements in 1985. Some settlements contained more than 1,000,000 inhabitants, whereas other settlements had fewer than 100 inhabitants (see Table 1). There are also differences in the area of urban blocks, ranging from 123 acres for cities such as Akra to 743 acres for a city like Zakho (the average is 348 acres). Generally, we note a high annual growth rate of urban blocks for most cities, which also indicates an increase of agricultural land erosion.

The configuration and fabric of Kurdistan settlements are mostly a reflection of natural effects and human heritage. To cope with the "contoured layout" of the land, settlements in the mountainous regions are usually arranged in a stairway form or a semicircular design. In addition to stone construction in mountainous regions, mudbrick or brick is commonly used in construction because mud is one of the cheapest building materials available.

A house using these materials is also well suited to the cool climate of mountainous areas. By placing the houses in the valleys, the damage from the wind is minimized and more sunlight falls on the houses so that people can better cope with the cool climate. Kurdistan has large number of historical sites that have witnessed human settlement and developed different types of architectural heritages. Among these are Erbil, Mashhad, Diyarbakir, and Urfa. Kurdish traditional architecture can be classified into three basic categories according to their location: towns (*shar*), villages (*gund*), and nomadic. The citadel of Erbil is a good example of this old and unique architectural heritage in Kurdistan.

Land use varies from area to area; in rural areas (countryside), common forms of land use may include foresting and farming, whereas in urban areas (towns and cities), land use could be related to housing or industry. In addition, land use in small and medium urban areas in Kurdistan varies from land use in larger cities. The most important use in small and medium cities is residential with a lower rate of uses for businesses and the service industry.

TABLE 1 Settlement Distribution by Size Category

Settlement Size	No.	Population 1000	%
More than 500	2	1225	11.5
100–500	17	2909	27.4
50–100	31	2831	26.6
30–50	29	1138	10.7
20–30	31	776	7.3
10–20	59	817	7.7
5–10	82	604	5.7
2–5	78	274	2.6
Fewer than 2	57	49	0.5
Total	386	10623	100

Source: (Ghafor, 2005: 235)

Housing Characteristics

The typical architecture in mountainous regions in Kurdistan is described by "the lack of technology, which is substituted by creativity and through trial and error in using available materials and basic building structures" (Habitat, 2001: 3). This is evident in the building materials used by people in this area, as they commonly use stone to construct their houses because that is the most readily available material.

Another feature of homes in this area is that very little mortar is used for connecting the stones used to build the walls, which provides very good thermal control. However, a negative aspect of such a stone wall is that it is easily destroyed by natural forces (Habitat, 2001: 23).

In addition to the stone construction in mountainous regions, mudbrick or brick is commonly used in construction, because, as mentioned, mud is one of the cheapest building materials available.

In the study conducted by Habitat (2001) in Iraqi Kurdistan, it was found that houses were constructed facing southward so that they would receive the maximum amount of sunlight in the winter and a minimum amount of sunlight in the summer. The contour design is also useful in preventing landslides and allowing for the drainage of excess water when it rains. This design, which is defined as "housing combination," is also desirable because such a structure is more convenient to defend against outside threats (Habitat, 2001: 10).

The Kurdistan region of northwestern Iran is another example of a mountainous dwelling place. As in the Iraqi Kurdistan region, the houses here are oriented toward the south, allowing them to receive the maximum amount of sunlight in

Traditional mudbrick housing in the mountain village of Palangan, in the Kurdistan region of Iran. (Radio Kafka/Dreamstime.com)

winter and minimum amount of sunlight in summer. In these homes, the windows are vertical for the same reason. In Kurdistan, the houses are generally designed along ground steps This interesting design factor allows a house to use the roof-tops of the house below it as its courtyard. This is also a unique aspect in the sense that a communal feature is added to the concept of a house, which is generally considered to be strictly private property. This design is called a "terrace" design, and it is preferred because in mountainous regions, where little land is available for human use, people must minimize the use of land for dwelling purposes and leave more land for productive activities. This also explains why there is usually very little space around the dwellings (Habitat, 2001:10).

In some mountainous regions of Kurdistan, concrete slabs are laid on the floor of the majority of homes, whereas in other mountainous places, mud floors are common. To prevent heat loss, windows are usually small openings, or they may even be reduced to ventilation holes. It is also common to provide cross-ventilation through vent holes. In Kurdistan, roofs are generally made of wood and mud as simple thatched roofs. Wood is a cheap available building material, and often there will be a layer of thatching in between the wooden beams and the mud coating above.

The Challenges for Kurdistan Settlements

Kurdistan settlements and cities face particular challenges in the creative planning process. From the current status of small and medium-sized cities in Kurdistan, we find that beside the urban problems, there are social and economic problems. Positive solutions to those problems cannot be achieved without understanding their core (Ismael, 2015). Migration is a significant demographic and social problem for small and medium-sized cities, as most of the population leaves for major cities, which directly influences population stabilization on the local and regional levels (Ismael & Saleem, 2015). Furthermore, inadequate regional distribution of investments and a severe lack of economic activities in small and medium-sized cities are other important economic problems that lead to a disproportion of the population in the working age.

Some of these problems include the fact that the majority of settlements are located in mountain valleys and narrow plains. This situation represents a powerful natural limitation on the cities' growth in Kurdistan.

The physical separation of most settlements in the mountainous region makes it difficult for them to connect. In addition, it is difficult to provide transportation between them. In particular, the lack of railway lines leads the cities to depend mostly on the few paved roads for regional outreach.

The cities lack unique urban functions, and buildings and public spaces are often in a decrepit, run-down state, despite the availability of basic aspects of development and the general attraction of many cities. If used properly, they would encourage construction activities and lead to economic recovery in these cities.

Small and medium-size cities in Kurdistan do not have a particular identity or characteristic because of the diverse, overlapping urban fabric. This is in reference to their physical urban environment, such as elements, materials, form, scales, density, and networks, and its psychological, socio-cultural, ecological, managerial, and economic structures.

Resource and Regional Attractiveness

Regional attractiveness refers to characteristics and resources that a region has to offer to attract corporations, residents, and tourists. Numerous settlements in Kurdistan have access to multiple resources such as human and natural resources (Ismael, 2012). These resources may be used as an economic base for urban development at local, regional, and national levels.

Human Potential

As result of most urban activities and public services being concentrated in the Kurdistan metropolis, it is clear that the unemployment rate in small and medium-sized cities is higher than the overall rate of unemployment in Kurdistan.

Natural Potential

Kurdistan is rich in a broad spectrum of natural resources, and in particular is well endowed with water and oil. The abundant rainfall that is common over the Zagros and Taurus mountains has made Kurdistan one of the few watersheds of the Middle East. The major river system includes the Tigris and Euphrates and their tributaries. Favorable geological conditions in Kurdistan connected with the abundant water runoff to form an extensive aquifer and spring system. These springs serve as the main source of artificial irrigation and domestic water for the Kurds (Naqshbandi et al., 1998). The northern regions of Iraq are also rich with other natural resources, in particular, oil. Oil is found in abundance in the rock strata of the parts of Iraqi Kurdistan. With approximately 45 billion barrels of oil, this area has among the largest oil reserves in the Middle East, and contains larger proven deposits than the United States (Mills, 2016). Other underground resources that exist in significant quantities in Kurdistan include copper, iron, zinc, and limestone, which is used to produce cement. The world's largest deposit of rock sulfur is located just southwest of Erbil. Other important underground resources include coal, gold, and marble (Ghafor, 2005).

Heskef

Heskef, or Hasankeyf, is an ancient settlement on the Tigris River in Turkey that used to house Assyrian, Armenian, and Jewish families, but today is home to a majority of the Kurdish population. The city's history goes back to Roman times, and it has many archaeological remains and ruins from Islamic history. The

---

(continued)

gigantic GAP Project (Güneydoğu Anadolu Projesi, or Southeastern Anatolia Project) saw the construction of large dams on the Tigris and Euphrates, one of which, the Ilisu Dam, eventually led to the flooding of Heskef. Over the years, the question of resettling the entire village has turned into a nationalistic battle between the Turkish authorities and the Kurdish population.

Urban Potential

There is a large, untapped urban potential even for small and medium-sized cities, which can be used to develop these cities into places that attract people rather than cause them to move away. If applied correctly, this could change the path of rural migration toward them instead of the large cities. For example, the majority of cities include empty interior pockets; these areas can be used in development projects, as can some older areas, which can be removed and redesignated to improve their positions in addressing shortcomings and deficiencies in the service and housing sector. In addition, buildings and areas with archaeological value could be used for tourism. Some areas that represent the region's urban heritage must be preserved as symbols of the distinctive urban character of the city.

The geological evolution of Kurdistan led to the emergence of a great variation in topography from one place to another, from broad plains and narrow valleys to the deep and simple slopes and sharp peaks. The mountainous nature of Kurdistan, the difference of temperatures in its various parts, and its wealth of waters make the region a destination for tourism, where many areas could be used for tourism investment projects in small and medium-sized cities.

Planning Sustainable Urban Growth in Kurdistan

Rapid urbanization, the concentration of the urban population in large cities, and the sprawl of cities into wider geographical areas are among the most significant transformations of human settlements in Kurdistan (Ismael & Saleem, 2015). Taking into account this situation, planners and administrators should consider measures to improve the livelihood of the people and to ensure the sustainable development of the region for present and future generations. This can be achieved by formulating strategic policies and implementing sustainable growth programs through an appropriate urban planning strategy.

Urban planning can be defined as the design and regulation of the uses of space that focus on the physical form, economic functions, and social impacts of the urban environment and on the location of different activities within it.

Urban planning has four primary objectives:

- Promoting efficient provision of the urban infrastructure and allocation of land use, thereby contributing to economic growth

- Managing spatial extension while minimizing infrastructure costs
- Maintaining or improving the quality of the urban environment (including the quality of the housing stock)
- Preserving the natural environment immediately outside the urban area

Urban planning essentially means generating, developing, and managing resources. The efficiency of urban settlements largely depends upon how well they were planned, how economically they were developed, and how efficiently they are managed. The proposed urban planning for small and medium-sized cities in Kurdistan aims to address the current problems by achieving the maximum utilization of resources and capabilities available in the actual development. Moreover, it also aims to improve the natural environment for those cities by raising their ability to become more suitable for human lives and even lead its functions efficiently.

Urban planning for Kurdistan's small and medium-sized cities requires that the regional planning authorities are concerned with the development of cities at the regional level and local planning authorities with the planning at the level of the cities themselves. Urban planning at the regional level includes:

- Working toward achieving a balance of distribution of urban centers
- Alleviating urban congestion and urban populations in specific places
- Encouraging trends that generate new small and medium-sized cities with reasonable spaces between them and allowing the establishment of independent economic activities
- Converting small and medium-sized cities into attractive urban centers by highlighting each city's excellence, efficiency, and performance
- Achieving coherence and unity among cities within their region by strengthening transport and communication networks among them, which is important in order to sustain regional development

Urban planning at the local level includes:

- Improving the fabric and structure of the cities by dealing with urban deprivation.
- Supporting the connection between all areas and neighborhoods in the city and protecting city's urban cohesion from splitting, divisions, and disconnect, which result from natural limitations.
- Raising the absorptive capacity of cities by increasing their ability to provide space for land use development through optimum utilization of the contour line. For example, residences may be built on the high contour slope, as these structures require less space, whereas structures for services and industrial use are built in low-sloping areas.
- Improving properties and buildings by removing and replacing those in poor condition, repairing and maintaining surrounding buildings, and continuously maintaining areas and buildings of archaeological value.
- Providing basic urban facilities and infrastructure in the cities, such as subways, footpaths, parks, gardens, playgrounds, and public amenities, including street lighting, parking lots, bus stops, and public conveyances.

Conclusion

In Kurdistan, for the first time, humans began to leave their caves and started building permanent homes to live in. Thus, long before Europe, Iraqi Kurdistan was the scene of the neolithic revolution. Many settlements and cities in Kurdistan include multiple resources with potential, such as human and natural resources, which can be used as an economic base for urban development planning at local, regional, and national levels.

However, despite this, Kurdistan settlements and cities still face particular challenges in the development of a creative planning strategy. Based on the facts related to the status of small and medium-sized cities in Kurdistan, other social and economic problems emerge that deserve to be addressed by decision makers in order to achieve positive results from the development projects of the cities. The urbanization process is irreversible in Kurdistan and therefore should be turned into opportunities for growth. By the year 2015 and beyond, more people will live in urban areas Kurdistan than in rural areas. To guarantee that the magnitude and pace of urbanization do not hinder the country's overall development, Kurdistan should continue to implement integrated sustainable development strategies in order for our cities to become generators of development, not only for themselves but also for the rural hinterlands. Future priorities should emphasize the following imperatives of sustainable development:

- Developing efficient and effective governance systems in Kurdistan cities and other settlements
- Strengthening national and local institutional capacities in the areas of sustainable urbanization
- Promoting city-to-city cooperation in order to encourage the exchange of best practices of sustainable urban development at all levels
- Mobilizing external resources and more coordinated and concerted support for sustainable development

Ayoob Ismael

Portions of this chapter are reprinted with permission from Ayoob Ismael and Dr. Ibrahim Ngah. (2011). "Understanding the Situation of Rural Settlements in the Mountainous Region." *International Journal of Rural Studies*, vol. 19 no. 2.

Further Reading

Braidwood, R. J., & Howe, B. (1960). "Prehistoric Investigations in Iraqi Kurdistan." *Studies in Ancient Oriental Civilization*, no. 31.

Ghafor, A. (2005). *Geography of Kurdistan*. Hawler: Mokryani Center, Ministry of Education Publication.

Ghassemlou, R., et al. (1980). *People without a Country—The Kurds and Kurdistan*. Edited by Chaliand Gerard and translated by Pallis Michael. London: Zed Press.

Habitat. (2001). *Learning from Tradition to Improve Housing Design, Homestead Typological Analysis Report*. Nairobi: United Nations Centre for Human Settlements.

Ismael, A. (2012). "The Importance of Promoting Entrepreneurial Activities among Rural Communities in Kurdistan Region-Iraq." *Proceedings of the Second Scientific World Kurdish Congress* (WKC2012), October 11–15, 2012, Erbil.

Ismael, A. (2015). "Planning Sustainable Urban Growth in Kurdistan." *Proceedings of the 2nd International Conference on Ecology, Environment, and Energy*, Ishek University, April, 12–13, 2015, Erbil.

Ismael, A., & Saleem, H. (2015). "Population Distribution in the Kurdistan Region, Iraq: Experiences from 1957–2009 Population Census." *Raparin Academic Journal*, vol. 2, no. 4.

KRG. (2011). *Regional Development Strategy for Kurdistan Region (2012–2016)*. Erbil: Ministry of Planning.

Mills, R. (2016). *Under the Mountains: Kurdish Oil and Regional Politics*. Oxford: Oxford Institute for Energy Studies, Oxford University.

Naqshbandi, A., et al. (1998). "Geography of Kurdistan Region—Iraq." Brayati Center Series No. 3. Hawler: Education Publication.

Saed, K. (1984). *Scenes from Mesopotamian Civilization*. Casablanca: Al-Ngah Press (in Arabic).

Solecki, R. L. (1981). *An Early Village Site at Zawi Chemi Shanidar (Bibliotheca Mesopotamica)*. Malibu, CA: Undena Publications.

Stansfield, G. R. V. (2003). *Iraqi Kurdistan Political Development and Emergent Democracy*. London: Routledge Curzon.

Life and Work

Kurdistan experienced state-initiated modernization efforts in the form of economic restructuring in the 1950s. Often compelled to abandon traditional farming villages for urban environments, Kurds tried to escape rural economic inequality. In the cities, Kurds encountered structural economic obstacles and struggled with systemic barriers as well. While Kurdish families aspired to access opportunities for their children, they frequently lived through practices of forced assimilation and myopic tendencies to denigrate Kurdish culture and traditions. Kurds faced increasingly harsh Arabization, Persianization, and Turkification policies in the region. Discrimination against Kurds in both the economic sector and in educational environments slowed their path to achieving success in urban settings throughout the 20th century.

Internal migration of Kurds from the countryside to small Kurdish towns and then to larger urban environments contributed to layers of cultural denial and political silencing. In Turkey, for example, during the late 1980s and early 1990s thousands of small Kurdish villages were violently cleared of populations by the Turkish army, which was fighting to eradicate the Kurdistan Workers Party (PKK), an ethno-nationalist Kurdish guerrilla organization. The reality of widespread violence against poor farming communities forced the expulsion and displacement of tens of thousands of Kurds from their homeland. Many Kurds moved from the southeast and east of Turkey to Western cities; others left the country to pursue labor agreements or appealed for asylum in Europe. Some Kurds departed for neighboring countries such as Iraq. Both labor migrants and internally displaced Kurds initially ended up living in marginal and impoverished neighborhoods in Istanbul, Izmir, Adana, Baghdad, and European cities.

Kurds continue to face significant patterns of discrimination today, which are linked to their sociocultural stigmatization. Human rights violations such as expulsions were rarely acknowledged in the public sphere. Instead, the experiences of Kurds tended to be euphemistically labeled as "the Kurdish issue or the Kurdish problem." As a consequence, Kurdish people were described as living in underdeveloped provinces of the country and classified as a troublesome and undesirable ethnic group (Yeğen, 1996). The Turkish state's official communications about Kurds encouraged their characterization as tribal, patriarchal, culturally reactionary, and economically backward. Made invisible in the so-called enlightened nation-state, Kurds were portrayed as embracing practices of banditry instead of industrialization and perceived as dominated by backward religious sheikhs rather than accepting modern values. Such attitudes changed little over time, as Kurds in Turkey found that peaceful activism for political and linguistic rights led to accusations of involvement in separatist activities and PKK terrorism. Practices of public denigration of the Kurdish identity have been so pervasive in Turkey that parallel worlds developed. Kurds essentially had been erased by official state-approved accounts other than in reports related to terrorism, but lived in pain, deep suffering, and humiliation for being Kurdish.

Kurds have also achieved success despite lasting patterns of discrimination and repression. Kurds work in media environments, at universities, and in healthcare and have created their own international businesses. The Kurdish diaspora, predominantly in Europe, played an important role in supporting economic and cultural opportunities in the homeland regions for decades. Despite ongoing repression in Iran and Turkey (and today to a lesser degree in Rojava, Syria, and in the Kurdistan Regional Government in Iraq), Kurds have made enormous economic strides over the past 50 years.

Kurds and Modernization

Before the outbreak of World War I, Kurdish tribal communities subsisted in the border regions between the Ottoman Empire (dissolved in 1922), Qajar Iran (deposed in 1925), and the encroaching Russian Empire (until the Russian Revolution in 1917). Powerful Kurdish tribal chiefs managed to carve out quasi-autonomous fiefdoms and often benefited from the rising tensions between the competing interests of these empires. Kurdish tribal leaders sought out alliances with empires and focused on strengthening their regional authority.

Kurdish leaders interacted regularly with emissaries of empires who enforced regional controls through various ways, including paying for the aid of Kurdish leadership. Without the collaboration and support of Kurdish tribes, it was significantly harder for Qajar Iran and the Ottomans to manage the outer margins of their territories. Traditionally, Kurds tended to rely on income that they earned through the use of mountain pastures, including their agricultural activity, and the taxes they collected from peasant populations. In addition, caravan and trade routes contributed a vital and reliable source of revenue for Kurdish chiefs. These tribal leaders certainly welcomed the rather lucrative collaboration with regional empires. (McDowall, 1997)

In some areas, Kurds earned money from acting on behalf of empires along the fringes, while other tribal leaders offered security services for traders. By serving in the military interest of empires, Kurdish leaders ensured their own economic viability and asserted the regional security of Kurds. Over time, such arrangements between empires and local power brokers incorporated tribal structures into various administrative configurations of empires. Kurdish tribal militias took on the role of what today could be considered a paramilitary or even mercenary force (Eccarius-Kelly, 2011: 79). As a result, tribal economic and political controls over geographic buffer zones increased, and Kurdish leaders asserted their growing influence through traditional patron-client relationships. In essence, a symbiotic relationship developed between regional tribal structures and powerful empires, which ended with the collapse of Ottoman rule.

When the Allied forces defeated the Ottoman Empire, British troops occupied large swaths of Mesopotamia, including the vast region from Sulamaniyah (Sulaimani or Slemani in Kurdish) all the way north to the area of Mosul. Today, Mosul is at the center of a crucial battle to dislodge the fighters of the Islamic State from the province, and Kurdish militias once again play an exceptionally important role. British forces in 1918 encountered extensive Kurdish tribal structures along with experienced Kurdish militias in this region, which today is part of the Kurdistan Regional Government in Iraq. Inclined to grant autonomy to a number of Kurdish leaders to avoid further military encounters, the Allies proposed to carve up the weak Ottoman Empire. Ottoman elites, devastated by their losses, felt that they had run out of options and signed the Treaty of Sèvres in 1920.

The European mandate system that emerged in the aftermath of the Ottoman defeat allowed Britain to control the territories of Iraq while the French took over the provinces of Syria. Ottoman Kurdish regions were simply subsumed into different political systems and became part of modern Turkey, Iraq, and Syria. Based on Woodrow Wilson's declaration of the principles of civilization, minorities such as the Kurds were granted the opportunity to claim statehood—at least in an abstract sense. In particular, Articles 62–64 of the Treaty of Sèvres defined specific geographic boundaries as territory to be controlled by Kurds and appeared to grant Kurdish society the right to establish an autonomous homeland if sufficient support was expressed. But the Treaty of Sèvres was never implemented. Instead, the Lausanne Peace Conference replaced Sèvres in 1923. Mustafa Kemal's nationalist forces successfully defeated the invading Western armies during the Turkish War of Independence (1919–1922) and rejected the prior agreement as invalid in the face of Turkey's victory. The Turkish military's triumph in combination with the Allied forces' reluctance to further engage with Mustafa Kemal's nationalist forces nullified the earlier treaty in favor of the Lausanne Conference. This outcome, of course, contributed to the formation of regional nation-states, which denied the Kurds an autonomous region (McDowall, 1997).

Ever since the implementation of the Lausanne treaty, Kurdish intellectuals and political activists have expressed varying degrees of anger, resentment, and hostility toward the Turkish state's refusal to officially recognize Kurds as a separate people. The Republic of Turkey was established in 1923, and in less than a year the use of the Kurdish language was officially forbidden—a first indicator of the forced assimilation or Turkification policies that were to come. In practical terms, the language issue created tremendous challenges for rural Kurds as only a small percentage—estimated to have been less than 5 percent at the time—spoke or understood Turkish (Eccarius-Kelly, 2011: 80). This linguistic disadvantage made communication between the central state and the peripheral Kurdish communities extremely difficult. Access to education without prior knowledge of Turkish was practically impossible, which also contributed to a growing sense of exclusion among the Kurdish populations. The relationship between the state and Kurdish groups further deteriorated as Turkish soldiers appropriated livestock from local communities without proper compensation.

Although Mustafa Kemal initially pursued a successful policy of co-optation within the Kurdish tribal areas of Turkey, any collaborative inroads between central forces and the periphery soon became impasses as a consequence of numerous regional uprisings. Immediately after 1919, the majority of Kurdish leaders supported Turkish national resistance against the invading Greeks and Armenians for several reasons. A number of Kurdish chiefs feared reprisals from Armenian nationalists because Kurdish tribes had participated in the Armenian massacres during 1894–1896 and the Armenian genocide during 1915–1918. Sunni Kurds, who made up irregular regiments known as the Hamidiye Light Cavalry Regiments (also referred to as the Tribal Regiments), had particularly targeted Christian communities. Kurdish villagers hoped to retain formerly Armenian-held lands and properties if they collaborated with Mustafa Kemal's nationalist forces, and tribal chiefs claimed that Armenian and Assyrian areas actually had been Kurdish lands all along. Finally, the majority of Kurds supported the protection of Muslim lands against an incursion of Christian forces. In exchange for their loyal service, Mustafa Kemal granted several Kurdish leaders special rights and privileges, including appointments to the Grand National Assembly. But this mutually beneficial arrangement did not last as Kurdish tribal forces encountered the tide of Turkish nationalism.

It is important to recognize that initial Kurdish support for the Turkish Republic had not been unified. Regional uprisings, including the 1925 Sheikh Said revolt, encouraged the Turkish government to emphasize state control over Kurdish areas. In essence, the new government perceived the prior modus operandi in the Kurdish regions as an unnecessary expense and ultimately antithetical to Turkey's national objectives. This shift toward a new political direction created an entirely different set of conditions on the ground. Kurdish groups who had perpetrated violence against neighboring communities a decade earlier became victims of repression themselves after the establishment of the Turkish state. Mustafa Kemal introduced draconian measures to restrict and then eliminate Kurdish regional controls entirely. To achieve its goals the Turkish state implemented the Maintenance of Order Law, which aimed to break tribal resistance to centralized modernization efforts. This martial law repressed potentially subversive activities in the Kurdish regions, ranging from unapproved gatherings to the formation of religious brotherhoods like the Naqshbandi and Qadiri Sufi orders. In addition, the publication of Kurdish literature and access to informational or political pamphlets was not permitted.

A state tribunal carried out death sentences in the aftermath of the 1925 Sheikh Said revolt, closed dervish lodges because they were considered rebellious, and signaled the emergence of a fiercely authoritarian rule by dismantling even legal opposition to state controls. Increasing numbers of Kurdish villages objected to the repressive rule that failed to provide the benefits once experienced under the patronage system. The Turkish state now demanded that Kurds pay taxes and provide young men for national conscription, but in contrast to the established tribal tradition of reciprocity, the Kurds were no longer granted any tangible advantages in exchange. Traditional Kurdish services to the state became obsolete. Turkey stopped relying on tribal military units to carry out regional raids, ended the practice of using patronage and subsidies to encourage loyalty, and closed religious schools, which subsequently deprived the religious authorities of their expected income and leverage. The Turkish government effectively disrupted, weakened, and ultimately undermined tribal culture to prevent the rise of a pan-tribal or pan-Islamic oppositional force in the Republic of Turkey.

The Kurdish regions and their populations were subsumed into the newly formed states. Along with Kurdish villagers, petroleum deposits and water resources were also carved up and integrated into the new states. This was a particularly devastating development for Kurds in the Iraqi context. The Anglo-Iraqi treaty of 1930 made no mention of a separate Kurdish identity. In fact, the modernizing Iraqi state changed its focus away from agricultural production and embraced the notion of a development model based on petroleum. Kurdish communities had to adjust to major structural changes as they lost their economic base when elites in Iraq stopped relying on Kurdish agricultural products. Instead, Iraq pursued rapid industrialization with the help of its oil resources and decided to import food (Natali, 2005: 63). Elite investments in Kurdish agricultural regions declined, and Kurds were forced to abandon their farms and had to migrate to urban environments. In large cities, Kurds joined the growing masses of uneducated seasonal and day laborers.

While Iraq initially relied on co-optation policies for Kurds, political elites shifted to repressive Arabization strategies by the 1970s and 1980s. To break the spirit of rebellious Kurdish communities, they were pushed off their traditionally held pasture and farming lands and deported in large numbers. Increasingly controlling, the state resettled Kurds in restricted areas and fully guarded collective towns. Under Saddam Hussein's leadership, an Iraqi dictator who was the country's president from 1979 until 2003, the situation grew even more desperate for Kurds. The Iraqi military pushed Kurds into uninhabitable southern desert zones; Kurds could no longer hold deeds to land; and Kurdish names of villages and towns were changed to Arab names (which were essential elements of the Arabization campaign in Iraq).

Kurds were considered a serious threat to Iraqi stability because they represented a large percentage of the national population (up to a quarter of the population). Toward the final years of the Iraq-Iran War (1980–1988), the Iraqi army focused its full and devastating attention on subduing Kurds. Under Saddam Hussein's orders, gas attacks targeted the Kurdish town of Halabja, killing at least 6,000 villagers in the surrounding areas. Weeks later, in the fall of 1988, members of the Iraqi army carried out mass deportations and razed 75 percent of all Kurdish villages (often called the infamous Anfal or Spoils of War campaigns). Today, these murderous attacks are recognized as genocide against the Kurds in Iraq.

In Syria, the Kurds made up less than 10 percent of the population, but several provinces had large Kurdish majorities such as Jazira. The region was especially fertile as barley, rice, wheat, and cotton provided opportunities for Kurdish peasants to thrive. Many Syrian Kurds in the region actually had escaped from Turkey during earlier periods of revolt in the 1920s (Vanly, 1992: 147). Other Kurdish areas in Syria, especially Afrin, were well-irrigated zones and had enormous tracts of olive groves, fruit orchards, and dairy farms. But when the Baathist regime in Syrian enforced its own version of Arabization policies on Kurds in the 1970s, land and homes were taken away from Kurdish villagers and given to Arab settlers instead. Many young Kurds began to seek jobs in major Syrian cities such as Damascus and Aleppo. Those who stayed behind relied on seasonal employment. Often they worked for Arab families and suffered through an impoverished existence without access to running water, healthcare, or basic education (Vanly, 1992: 162).

Meanwhile, Reza Shah in Iran struggled to hold the country together as both Soviet and British troops occupied Iran during World War II. Britain and Russia were determined to destabilize German-Iranian collaboration at the time. During this period of occupation, a small group of rebellious Kurds saw an opportunity to establish an independent Kurdish Republic—the Republic of Mahabad—which received Soviet protection. However, once the Soviets withdrew from Iran, the short-lived Mahabad experiment in northwestern Iran ended with Iranian troops retaking the area in 1946. Legendary Kurdish leader Mustafa Barzani (1903–1979) and his followers received safe passage into the Soviet Union, but other Kurdish leaders, including Qazi Mohamed, were publicly hung by the Shah of Iran. Kurdish printing presses and books were destroyed, and teaching in the Kurdish language was banned in Iran. After 12 years of exile, Barzani returned to northern Iraq to begin a renewed struggle for an autonomous Kurdish region. Reza Shah focused on eradicating Kurdish tribal life in Iran by undermining agricultural opportunities for Kurdish villages and communities. Non-Persian ethnic groups were culturally repressed, their lands confiscated, and their religious expressions limited in public life.

The 1970s Persianization policies focused on advancing Iranian loyalists in government and administrative positions and denied Kurds access to leadership roles (Natali, 2005: 120). In a highly controlled, militarized, and centralized Iranian state, Kurdish language instruction was not permitted. Kurds also experienced very uneven industrialization periods that were linked to the petroleum sector, but mostly remained excluded from industrial advancements and direct economic or employment benefits. The Iranian reality for Kurds worsened after the Shah was deposed in 1979 and the Islamic Republic enforced rigid Shia religious rule. The majority of Kurds in Iran are Sunni Muslims, which made them targets of the new regime. During the Iran-Iraq War with Iraqi dictator Saddam Hussein (1980–1988), Kurdish groups attempted to carve out more local control, but failed. This turned Kurds into enemies to both the Iraqi and the Iranian state. The regime in Tehran quickly focused on arresting and eliminating Kurdish leaders, both domestically and abroad. Several Kurdish opponents of the Iranian regime in exile, including in Vienna, Austria, and in Berlin, Germany, were assassinated by Iranian agents. Abdul Rahman Ghassemlou was assassinated in Vienna in 1989, and his successor, Sadegh Sharafkandi, was murdered in 1992 in Berlin.

Kurdish Economic and Migration Patterns

From the 1920s until the 1960s, the majority of Kurds lived in small, rural villages, which frequently were located in remote valleys and mountain regions. Village life tended to be organized around pastoral agricultural activities, although some Kurds continued to engage in nomadic activities such as herding goats and sheep for decades after the collapse of the Ottoman Empire (Izady, 1992: 227–229). While nomadic Kurds pursued seasonal herding to distant mountain summer pastures, settled farmers kept their herds within a day's walk to the family farms. For all Kurds involved in herding activities, the sale of lamb to regional traders was quite common; Kurds cherished the meat but also used sheep for their wool and became involved in the growing regional textile industry. Kurdish women relied on the wool to weave kilim tribal rugs, which are flat tapestry rugs rather than the high-pile carpets more commonly known from Iran. In addition, herds of sheep provided Kurdish communities with nutritious milk, and Kurdish farms were known for producing high-quality yogurt, buttermilk, and a range of tasty peasant cheeses.

While Kurds engaged in traditional herding practices along the steeper mountain slopes, they also took full advantage of fertile valleys to expand their access to arable lands. Traditionally, Kurds considered wheat and barley among their favorite crops, along with a variety of vegetables. In some areas of Kurdistan, olives and sunflowers were grown for cooking oils and to sell on the local markets. Also, fruit and nut trees played an important role in Kurdish diets because dried pears, apples, and various other fruits sustained families during the winter months. Kurds valued their many varieties of nut trees, including hazelnuts, chestnuts, almonds, walnuts, and pistachios. During the early 1980s, dried fruits and nuts emerged as one of the most marketable cash crops for Kurds in Iran (Izady, 1992: 228).

Traditional Kurdish houses tended to be made of mud bricks that had been formed by hand. These houses had sturdy wooden roofs with easy access from inside the house. During the winter months, the houses were mostly heated with wood stoves, and some families benefited from a room below the ground to escape the bitter cold temperatures. However, during the summer, family members often slept on the rooftops for access to cool wind and to escape the stuffy and hot temperatures that remained inside the house. Water was carried into the houses from village wells because indoor plumbing did not arrive in Kurdish villages until the 1970s or even later.

Kurds also became involved with a number of cash crops by focusing on products they could sell in regional markets. In particular, tobacco played a vital role since it was used for water pipes across the entire Middle East. Cotton also became a significant crop in nearly all regions of Kurdistan. Syrian Kurds produced significant amounts of cotton because of the hot and wet climate and the availability of cheap labor. Cotton tended to be picked by hand along the banks of the Euphrates River. Unfortunately, cotton also turned out to be environmentally destructive in several ways for a number of Kurdish regions. Cotton growth required that groundwater be used for regular irrigation practices, causing water shortages for farms or communities with other crops. Also, pollution concerns became an extremely difficult issue to address during consecutive cotton growth periods. The heavy reliance on pesticides for cotton production ended up polluting drinking water reservoirs, regional rivers, and lakes. Despite such environmental concerns, cotton remains an important crop for Kurdish communities even today in Rojava, Syrian Kurdistan.

Fundamental political and economic changes reshaped the entire Middle East by the 1950s. Familiar Kurdish tribal production patterns experienced setbacks as traditional patron-client relationships ended, in part because of ongoing peasant uprisings related to land reform policies that central governments violently enforced. Kurdish society changed dramatically as many Kurds migrated to urban areas once their families lost access to land and land rights. In addition, many Kurdish communities suffered through consecutive wars in the countryside, which made their physical and economic survival extremely problematic. Although Kurdish farmers had great hopes for improved lives in towns, when they first arrived in Kurdish cities, they faced immediate barriers. Kurdish towns and cities throughout Kurdistan had been neglected by central governments. Few economic opportunities existed for Kurds to join a modernizing workforce. Without the existence of industrial enterprises or governmental investment schemes related to a regional development plan, Kurdish laborers remained on the margins of society. Many lived on the streets and struggled to find employment. While some rural migrants engaged in seasonal labor or temporary construction work (often as contractual or unregistered wage labor), others became involved in street vending activities. Many families initially sent a young man to the city to earn an income, while the rest of the family stayed in the countryside to work on what remained of their farms (Grabolle-Çeliker, 2013: 12–20).

In towns and cities, Kurds started to work in a wide range of jobs and professions. They often moved from vending into shop keeping and left behind their bartering and trading activities once they found employment as construction workers. Mainly, however, Kurds were unwelcome in urban environments (Grabolle-Çeliker, 2013). As people from the countryside, they were expected to work as unskilled menial laborers in large Turkish, Iraqi, and Iranian cities. Kurdish men faced high unemployment rates, yet family members started to push many more young men to work in the cities as poverty in rural areas increased. Expected to send part of their earnings as remittances to their families, growing numbers of Kurds never experienced traditional farming but engaged in day labor activities instead to support their relatives in remote villages. The growing importance of oil fields, trucking, and pipelines in the Kurdish regions of Turkey and Iraq also attracted many Kurdish workers. Especially in the Kurdish areas of Iraq, petrochemicals represented an increasingly indispensable source of income for Kurdish communities.

The specialization in urban economies allowed a small Kurdish working class to form, which mostly emerged through opportunities related to the oil industry. But a Kurdish working class also formed because of large infrastructure projects, a boom in housing construction, and the emergence of small factories. As more migrants started to acquire mechanical and electrical skills, they were hired in various service-related sectors working as drivers within the trucking and transportation areas. When Kurdish laborers started to travel farther away from their original villages, they found economic opportunities but also filled impoverished neighborhoods in major cities such as Istanbul, Tehran, and Baghdad. And then Kurds also arrived in Europe. While Europe had already benefited from a relatively large influx of Italian, Greek, Spanish, and Portuguese workers during the 1960s, Germany struggled to fulfill its economy's extensive demand for a growing workforce. An acute labor shortage in the country persuaded German officials to launch a temporary worker arrangement with Turkey. Between 1961, the initial year of the German-Turkish worker agreement, and 1975, just a couple of years after the recruitment period ended, some 650,000 people holding Turkish citizenship (of which about a third were Kurds) settled into semi-permanent labor arrangements in Europe (Eccarius-Kelly, 2011: 4–9).

As part of the migration experience, Kurdish women in towns and cities also began to participate in a wider range of social, economic, and cultural aspects of life outside their homes. Women pursued educational opportunities and gained professional skills. In the countryside, schools had not been widely available or even accessible to Kurds. Remedial classes, if offered at all, had often been taught in Arabic in Iraq and Syria or in Turkish, but not in Kurdish. This meant that most children could not follow the materials discussed in class and received no help in the home. As a consequence, literacy rates among Kurdish families remained very low, and girls were discouraged from attending school at all. The migration process from rural areas to cities and particularly abroad provided significantly improved educational opportunities for Kurdish families and reshaped the roles of Kurdish women.

Unemployment in Kurdistan

Access to jobs and educational opportunities continued to be uneven across Kurdistan. The lack of economic opportunities for Kurds in Iran led to their increased involvement in smuggling operations, for example. Today, Kurds from Iran cross borders illegally to reach the Kurdish Regional Government (KRG) and Turkey for access to goods. Unfortunately, smuggling is also extremely dangerous, as growing numbers of so-called kolbars (Kurdish porters who carry enormous packages of goods on their backs into Iran) have been shot and killed by Iranian soldiers along the border zones. But economic desperation in Iran continues to drive Kurds to engage in such high-risk activities.

Widespread patterns of social and economic discrimination against Kurds also intensified in Turkish society following renewed high-intensity conflict between the state and the PKK in 2016. Hostilities against Kurds also deepened as a consequence of the civil war in Syria, which had provided Syrian Kurdistan (Rojava) with an opportunity to declare its regional autonomy. Turkey rejects the notion of an independent Kurdish state on its borders for fear of increased collaboration between Kurds in Syria and Turkey. A host of problems also challenge economic development plans in the KRG. Besides significant levels of corruption and a lack of transparency in its leadership, the Kurdish state has become mired in oil disputes with Baghdad leading to periods of severe economic recession. A large number of Kurdish men pursue employment options within the KRG's state bureaucracy, especially in the security sector and among the Peshmerga forces. The average salary is often less than 500,000 Iraqi dinars ($430) per month, making the pursuit of secondary means of income a necessity to sustain families. To make matters worse, Peshmerga salaries are not paid regularly by Baghdad, and the limited funds are not redistributed in a transparent manner within the KRG. As a result, many Peshmerga members have to sell goods or offer their services as drivers during their days off. This reality has negatively affected access to education for boys, as they are expected to financially support their families.

In 2016, unemployment rates reportedly hovered around 12 to 14 percent according to Ali Sindi, the KRG's minister of planning. He suggested that unemployment rates worsened once displaced Kurdish people and regional refugees entered the KRG in the aftermath of IS (Islamic State) attacks (Rudaw, 2016). An Iranian Kurdish parliamentarian suggested that unemployment rates in Kurdish-dominated western provinces of Iran had reached more than 60 percent. (Rudaw, 2017). Meanwhile, in Turkey youth unemployment was about 28 percent and even higher in Kurdish areas, where only about half of all men under 30 years of age had access to occasional service-sector jobs or lacked employment entirely in 2016 (Gurcan, 2016). While regional states have obfuscated access to Kurdish unemployment data, Kurds tend to suffer from exceptionally high unemployment rates, especially compared to other national population groups in Iran and Turkey.

Corruption is a serious challenge in the region. Elites often access and distribute funds, making impoverished Kurds dependent on rigid hierarchies reminiscent of tribal structures. Corruption tends to undermine the success of nongovernmental organizations (NGOs) and their outreach efforts. The two dominant political parties in the KRG rely on nepotism and clientelism to sustain their control in the region. NGOs have attempted to engage with Kurdish communities on the grassroots level, but often encounter obstacles or political challenges in their attempts to implement transparent policies. In the KRG, many NGOs are funded by international intergovernmental organization (IGOs) (such as the United Nations), as well as numerous international governments. To access international funds, NGOs often focus on development, education, gender equality, and capacity-building goals. In Turkey, the vast majority of NGOs focused on work with Kurdish communities have been closed down since 2016.

Despite the tremendous hardships experienced by Kurds along their migratory paths out of small villages, some Kurds have become inspirations for their brethren. Among them is Hamdi Ulukaya, the founder of Chobani, one of the world's largest yogurt companies today. Ulukaya, a Kurdish immigrant of peasant roots, arrived in upstate New York to study business. As Chobani's philanthropically oriented CEO, Ulukaya supports refugees through employment and training centers, but also continues to make large donations to many different charities. His commitment to refugees and marginalized communities is a testament to his own journey as a Kurd from Turkey who achieved enormous success abroad.

Vera Eccarius-Kelly

Further Reading

Eccarius-Kelly, V. (2011). *The Militant Kurds: A Dual Strategy for Freedom*. Santa Barbara, CA: Praeger.

Grabolle-Çeliker, A. (2013). *Kurdish Life in Contemporary Turkey*. New York: Palgrave MacMillan Press.

Gurcan, M. (2016). "Youth Unemployment Poses Latest Danger to Turkey." *Al-Monitor*. http://www.al-monitor.com/pulse/originals/2016/11/turkey-youth-unemployment -becomes-risk-factor.html.

Izady, M. R. (1992). *A Concise Handbook: The Kurds*. Washington, DC: Taylor & Francis.

McDowall, D. (1997). *A Modern History of the Kurds*. London: I. B. Tauris.

Natali, D. (2005). *The Kurds and the State*. Syracuse, NY: Syracuse University Press.

Rudaw. (2016). "Unemployment Rate in Kurdistan is 14%." http://www.rudaw.net/english /business/21092016

Rudaw. (2017). "Unemployment Rate in Iran's Kurdish Province Passed 60 Percent, Lawmaker." http://www.rudaw.net/english/middleeast/iran/11032017.

Vanly, I. C. (1992). "The Kurds in Syria and Lebanon." In P. G. Kreyenbroek & S. Sperl (Eds.), *The Kurds: A Contemporary Overview* (pp. 143–170). New York: Routledge.

Yeğen, M. (1996). "The Turkish State Discourse and the Exclusion of Kurdish Identity." In S. Kedourie (Ed.), *Turkey: Identity, Democracy, Politics* (pp. 216–229). London: Frank Cass Publishers.

Education

For Kurds, being educated is an honorable feature, which grants an important status to the literate parts of society. This can be observed in the way Kurds show respect to the *mollah*, a man of religious knowledge. Other societal leaders such as a *mir, agha*, or notables do not walk in front of a Mollah as a sign of respect for their knowledge. Similarly, if a Kurd meets a Mollah, he shows his respect by kissing their hands (Beyazidi, 2012: 160). In fact, literacy alone can be the reason for appreciation and success in Kurdish society (Dersimi, 1997: 13).

Education is a factor that provides transitivity among social classes in Kurdish society. For example, mirs have tried integrating the *mirza*, the tutors of their children, into their family by marrying them to one of their daughters. Otherwise, it is known that the upper class of Kurdish society, mirs, aghas, and *sheikhs* do not intermarry with lower-class families, but here education works as a factor in providing transitivity. In addition, families who include several generations of mollahs can earn reputation and respect like other prominent families. To distinguish themselves from the commoners, they introduce themselves with titles like *malmela* or *keyemelan*. Thus, it is obvious that education brings prestige. After the Kurdish fiefdoms broke up in the late 19th century, the local schools, or *madrasas*, were transferred to the villages, and it has been considered a source of honor for the village to host the school.

In the Kurdish language, many proverbs relate to the importance given to education in society. For example, we find in Kurmanji, *"Cerxa cihane bixwendine digere,"* or "The world's wheels turn with education" or in Zazaki, *"Ez nevana wahari herf vano,"* or "I don't speak, the owner of the letter speaks" meaning that educated people speak the truth.

Historical Background

Historically, education spread from the elites to the commoners. The situation of the Kurds attests to that. While madrasas were open to everyone, nonreligious education was given to the families of the leaders, the mir, agha, or notables, often in their private homes. The educators, who were called *Rusipi, Akilbent,* or *Mirza*, taught the children basic skills, such as reading and writing, but also consulted with the Mir in political or social issues. These teachers often did not have a regular education themselves, but they had qualities that enabled them to teach, such as wisdom or being literate.

While madrasas are often regarded as the first educational institution among the Kurds, before their time, classes were taught at mosques, inns, and khanakhs (Keles, 2015). In particular, mosques have served as an important center for education, which is why the word hucra or mosque-school is still widely used. They continued to provide classes even after the establishment of the madrasas. For example, today, Medresa Sor, located in Mahabad, still offers both functions as a mosque and a school.

Education in the Early Kurdish State

Shaddadis (951–1088)

Shaddadis was a medieval Kurdish state in the Arran and Armenia region during the 10th and 11th centuries. It ruled for nearly 200 years over the principalities of Ganja, Dvin, and Ani and their surroundings. Its rulers established zoned communities in their cities with special places for educational institutions and libraries. They, too, contributed to the Golden Age of Islam, which saw a revival of science and appreciation of knowledge during that time (Keles, 2015: 3–4).

While there is little information about the madrasah as the main educational institution in the medical Muslim world, evidence shows that they existed in the period of the Shaddadis. For example, Qadi Tahir al-Janzi, who completed his education in Ganja, the capital of Shaddadis, and Abu'l-Kasim Ali an-Nisaburi and Abu'l-Fadl Shaban al-Bardai, who lectured on Islamic sciences, revealed that there were indeed institutions like the madrasah or mosques where knowledge was transmitted. The library in Ganja was known among scholars who came here for teaching and research, enjoying the open scientific atmosphere (Keles, 2015: 3–4).

Another example is the city of Ani that was turned into a center of learning where Qadi Burhanaddin al-Anawi taught Islamic sciences, medicine, and astronomy. The well-known Ani School was established under Hovhannes Sarkavag during the rule of the Shaddadis, and it attracted many students and scholars (Keles, 2015: 4). This shows that educational institutions such as madrasahs, hangah, and hocras existed and skills were taught in many cities, among them Islamic sciences, mathematics, philosophy, music, and medicine (Keles, 2015: 18).

Marwanids (983–1085)

The Marwanids were a Kurdish dynasty ruling over a large territory in Diyabakir's Silvan Province. It is said that northern Mesopotamia reached its peak in economic and cultural affairs during the Marwanid period. The results and products of the period of enlightenment in the arts, culture, and music can be seen in the works of today's scholars and artists from Diyarbakir. The Marwanid rulers took Armenian, Assyrian, and Jewish scholars under their protection. For example, Abu Nasr Yahya bin Jarir al-Takriti was a famous Jacobite scholar of medicine, astronomy, philosophy, and theology. He later became the physician of Nasruddawla (d. 968), the second Hamdanid ruler of the Emirate of Mosul (Baluken, 2010).

Ardalan Mirs (1168–1867)

One of the Kurdish fiefdoms or emirates in Rojhelat (Iran) was Ardalan, which also was an important center for the arts, culture, and education. In the capital of Ardalan, the city of Sine, there were many madrasahs, which gave the city the capacity to accommodate many students and scholars. Kurds, Persians, Turks, and other people from different ethnic backgrounds came to Sine to study. For this reason, the city was called the House of Wisdom, *Dar al-Ilm*. Among the great scholars from Sine we find Mawlana Khalid Shahrazuri and Qadiri an Mardukhi, families who contributed to the fields of art, science, and literature (Sheerin, 2011: 241–243).

Ayyubids of Hasankeyf (1232–1524)

The Kurdish lands witnessed a golden age during the reign of the Ayyubids of Hasankeyf, especially in the fields of education, science, and art where several madrasahs were built in the city. As a result, important scholars flocked to Hasankeyf, and great works have been produced here especially in the fields of Sufism, history, medicine, and music. The famous scholar of music Muzaffar bin al-Husayn el-Haskafi wrote his masterpiece, *al-Kashshaf fi Ilm al-Aghnam* (Studies in the Sciences of Songs) about musical terms and modes. One of the Ayyubid sultans, al-Malik al-Kamil Khalil (d. 1238), wrote his own poetic collection or *diwan*. Dawud al-Aghbari wrote the books *Tawali al-Buruj* about astronomy and *Nihayat al-Idrak wa al-Aghradat* about pharmacology.

The efforts of the Ayyubids of Hasankeyf to institutionalize education should be noted. They established charitable foundations as a source of financing the madrasas and supporting the students and faculty. Several sultans also collected large libraries as a tool for education and research.

Botan

The city of Cizre has been an important center of learning under various Kurdish rulers, including the Marwanids, Ayyubids, and Botan Emirates. The name al-Jazari refers to thinkers, scholars, and scientists who originated from this city. Among them are such great names as Ibn al-Athir, Abul Khayr, and Ismail Abu'l Izz (Sengul, 2014: 61). The most well-known and influential madrasas in Cizre were Madrasa Sor and Madrasa Mir Abdal. At the court of the Mir of Botan a lively literary and cultural scene was noted. For example, Ahmed Khani's famous story, Mem u Zin, takes place in Cizre.

Suveydi/Mirdasi Emirates

This fiefdom near Diyarbakir included important urban centers like Egil, Gerger, Siverek, Palu, and Hani where a majority of Zaza-speaking Kurds lived. Again, the premier institution for learning was the madrasa, which could be found in any of those cities. Palu in particular had a large number of madrasases, which were linked to the Sufi Naqshbandi order.

Missionary or Millet Schools

British missionaries reformed the educational system in Kurdistan during the Otto-man era. Prior to this, schools were supposed to transmit religious knowledge. Only with the *tanzimat* reforms of the Ottoman Sultan did secular disciplines enter the school curriculum in the larger cities. However, this was also objected to by the religious men or *ulema*, who did promote the opening of sectarian or *millet* schools as it was permitted by the Hatt-I Humayun or sultan's decree. It stated that each recognized religious community had the right to open private schools under government control. Initially, these missionary schools were not considered a threat to the government, but rather were seen as an educational benefit free of charge. They also attracted many Kurdish families from the upper class to send their sons to those schools where they were educated as loyal citizens to the sultan. Over time, the millet schools grew and proved to be more successful than the educational measurements of the government, which were underfunded and exposed to the resistance of the ulemas. Ultimately, these schools failed, however, to build a nonconfessional citizenry.

During the last quarter of the 19th century, a number of schools and universities were opened in the Ottoman Empire, and the Kurdish graduates of those institutions formed a small class of government officials, doctors, officers, and intellectuals, who promoted the history, language, and culture of the Kurdish people. Many were further influenced by their time spent in European exile where they fled after Sultan Abd al-Hamid suspended the constitution in 1878 and reversed some of the reforms from the Tanzimat era. The Kurdish intellectuals began publishing in their own language, and in 1898, *Kurdistan*, the first Kurdish newspaper, was published. Considering the educational level of the Kurdish population, only a small fraction was actually able to read it. However, the cultural and educational awakening process spread out to the Kurdish provinces of the Ottoman Empire where many local leaders, both religious and secular, saw the benefits and necessities of opening schools for their Kurdish constituency.

Education among Kurdish Religious Groups

Religious education was among the first activities to educate society for obvious reasons of social and religious cohesion. Each religious community developed unique strategies to meet the needs of religious instruction through different methods and institutions but still according to their dogma and religious praxis. While Kurdistan is a predominantly Sunni Muslim region, many other denominations and religions exist. Earlier the historic evolution of education among Kurdish Sunnis has been described. In the following paragraphs, the education of Shias, Yezidis, and Yarasan/Kakais is discussed.

The Yarasan/Kakais are also known as *Ahl-i Haqq,* or People of the Truth, who are mostly found in the Hawraman Region. They speak Gorani, which is also the language of their sacred texts, which consists of sacred poems in the Hawrami dialect called *kelam.* The *kelam* are performed by religious clerics called *pir.* Those who wish to become a *pir* have to memorize the *kelam* and learn how to perform them with a tambour or hand drum. The ceremony of performing the *kelam* to the community is done in a *diwan,* which concurrently is the center of religious learning among the Yarsan. During the ritual, a spiritual bond between the *pir* or teacher and the audience or students is created.

Among the Kurdish Alevis, education is not institutionalized. However, in the early 20th century, they started to use madrasas as their main centers of learning and instruction. The religious leaders of the Alevis are called *pir* or *seyyid,* and they are the transmitters of Alevi beliefs. Today, Alevi society is more urbanized and subsequently more organized. In Alevi Diwans, students are taught Alevi beliefs. In the ceremonies and performances, they use the tambour to recite the sacred texts. In the larger urban areas and due to the close contacts with the Turks, Turkish language is also used in the litanies.

The Yezidis, like other syncretistic religious groups in the area, follow a socio-religious separation between the laymen and the clerics. The clerics, known as *sheikh* or *pir,* preserve the religious knowledge and pass it on to the next generation. Religious education is not institutionalized (with the exception of the *qewal*), while secular/public education created a new class of curious laymen who want to be involved in the religious education. Knowledge is preserved in oral literature, psalms, hymns, and songs mostly in the Kurmanji dialect. In 1925, Darwish Shamo, the Yezidi leader from Kurdagh in Syria, opened the first school for the Yezidi children in his hometown long before anyone else in the region.

Finally, there are Kurdish Shia groups who mainly live in present-day Iran, where they follow the official path of both religious and secular education like many other Iranian Shias do. This is conducted in Persian and not in Kurdish. Shia Kurds living in several regions in Kurdistan Iran (Rojhelat) refer to their religious authorities regarding religious education. This bond existed before the Islamic Revolution, and is now well developed into a system of madrasahs, many of which are funded and supplied by the Iranian government. Special educational programs exists that focus on Kurdish culture, history, and language, but the official language of instruction is Persian.

Kurdish Madrasahs

A common Kurdish word for education is *xwendin/wendis,* which literally means reading. This skill is arguably the most important in the madrasa, where the reading of the Quran is a main subject. Other subjects taught at the madrasa include language sciences, psychology, philosophy, and legal studies where the students learn about the main sources of Islam, Quran, Sunna, and Islamic law. The study of language includes syntax, morphology, rhyme, calligraphy, semantics, oratory, and lexicology. Colloquially, these classes at the madrasa are referred to as *diweyes ilm/duwazde ilm* (12 sciences). The madrasas provide education not only in the eastern parts of Turkey, but in other areas populated by Kurds too, in Iran, Iraq, and Syria (Cicek, 2011). Two types of madrasahs are typically found: *medrese miran* (established by Kurdish emirs) and *medrese neqshibendi* (established by Sufi orders).

Today madrasas may be found in villages under the auspices of villagers but also in cities and small towns because of the urbanization and decline in population of the villages. The curriculum in the madrasa is based on reading a certain book series in different fields. The madrasa teacher is called "*Seyda*," and he evaluates the students' performance after finishing the book series, including the syllabus. The students who pass the evaluation receive a graduation certificate and are now called molla and are authorized to work as such (Sengul, 2008).

Today, the madrasa operates under the supervision of the ministry of education. After the foundation of the Turkish Republic, the law of unifying education was passed, and its authority was passed on all religious schools. The function of the madrasa has expanded over the years, and now it includes the religious instructions and explanations and legal advice, and it became the center of the political opposition. Naturally, the government tried to diminish the influence of the madrasas by co-opting the graduates with jobs in public service. They were also officially appointed as imams, which in return required them to promote a more moderate and government-friendly perspective.

Other mollas, however, led what was known as the Civil Friday Prayer, initiated by the Peace and Democracy Party in 2011. They led prayers at public squares and not in the government mosques. This caused the government to crack down on the madrasas, and many of them were subsequently closed down. In response, the government started its own training program for imams at the Imam Hatip Schools where they tried to train a more government-friendly cohort of imams.

Modern Schools

Modern public schools were opened during the time of Iranian and Ottoman modernization and continued along during the time of the republic. Later, separate primary or elementary and high schools were opened; however, those schools were limited in number. For example, in 1900, in Dersim Hozat, a primary school with three classrooms and a junior high school with three classrooms were opened, while in Elazig, a military junior high school and a Sultani school were opened. The Kurdish population was generally very interested in enrolling their children at these schools; however, the large financial expenditures needed for studying at these schools as well as enrollment quotas had a negative impact on schooling among the Kurds (Dersimi, 1997; 17–19). Also the fact that the language of instruction was Turkish prevented Kurdish pupils from attending these government schools (Nursi, 1990).

After the second declaration of constitutionalism in the Ottoman Empire in 1908, new educational opportunities for the Kurds emerged. One of those new

A Kurdish teacher conducts class in the Syrian city of Qamishli, January 31, 2016. (Delil Souleiman/AFP/Getty Images)

initiatives was the opening of *asiret mektebi* (tribal school), and another one was the Kurdish Constitutionalism School opened by the Kurdish Education Association in Istanbul. Other Kurdish associations were founded by Kurdish intellectuals with the goal of providing literacy to the Kurdish population. Ultimately, they wanted to start schools for Kurdish language, literature, education, and publication. The first of these schools was opened in Istanbul in an area with a high concentration of Kurds. The community was excited about this opportunity, and they petitioned for the opening of similar schools in other parts of Kurdistan. With the rise of Turkish nationalism, the trend of furthering Kurdish education was reversed, and many schools were closed largely for displaying the word Kurd on their banners and signs.

In addition, another member of the association, Beduizzaman Said Nursi (1877–1960), developed a project to establish a university. After the sultan's approval, the groundbreaking ceremony for Medresetu'z-Zehra was held in Van-Edremit. However, because Nuri and many of his students joined the army at the outbreak of World War I, the project was never completed.

Education as a Means of Struggle

Kurdish demands for education are mentioned as a political problem even in the old texts. In his work, Ehmede Xani (1650–1707) indicates that the reason why the Kurds are under foreign control is their weakness in education. In the 1880s, in his letters to the Iranian and Russian ambassadors, Sheikh Ubeydullah Nahri (d. 1883) wrote about the fact that the Kurds don't have any educational organizations while at the same time mentioning their general misery and lack of honor (Celil, 2007: 43–44). Dishonor or shame is here considered equal to being uneducated. In other words, the fact that the Kurds are weak as a group is seen as the reason for their misery. During the Era of Constitutionalism, Beduizzaman Said Nursi pleaded with his compatriots "*xwendin, xwendin, xwendin*" (read, read, read) in order to eliminate the social misery of his community.

Other media mentioned education as a means to struggle for Kurdish rights. For example, in the magazine *Hawar*, published by Kurds in exile in Syria, it was emphasized that the pen as a symbol for education and information must be sharpened as an important weapon in the political struggle (Aydinkaya, 2010: 221). The elites of the Turkish republic also noted the potential of educating the masses equating the armament with knowledge symbolized by the pen to the armament with real weapons. The government's response to the implementation of basic educational structures in the Kurdish territories was that "nobody shall read or become rich." The situation worsened after the Sheikh Said rebellion. Although there was only one high school in Diyarbakir, among the students were some supporters of the rebellion. This was also quelled, and later nobody used the word Kurd in school anymore. Only people in the villages were referred to as Kurds, while the people in the cities and towns were called Turks.

Zaza (2000: 62), who went to school in Diyarbakir in 1930, described the mood in the educational sector after the Sheikh Said rebellion as "stressful," especially regarding the relations between Turkish and Kurdish students. He also exposed the other government's strategy of Turkifying the population. In his memoir, he wrote, "One day, the principal tells a third grade student who was caught speaking Kurdish that he had to speak Turkish in Turkey and that any other language was banned. The student replied that they would continue speaking in their mother tongue, after which he was expelled from school."

Over the years, the government's educational practices did not change much with regard to objectives and processes. And while they still invested in the infrastructure, it was never sufficient for the fast-growing Kurdish population. Priority was given to the Turkish sector until 1980 when private schools were allowed to operate. The Kurds, however, were never satisfied with the "equal educational rights for all citizens."

The issue of education was among the most important political demands by Kurdish activists until 1980. This was particularly true during the famous "Eastern Meetings" in the late 1960s where activists like Said Elci or Dr. Siwan accused the government of deliberately neglecting the Kurdish territories. "Schools and Roads for the West, Gendarmes and Patrols for the East" was a common slogan. Elci spoke at these meetings about the lack of educational infrastructure: "Let's look at this simple case, Siverek, which is a town of 35,000 people living in some 387 villages. There are only 39 schools in those villages! If they cannot hear us, we will tell them: We call for roads, factories, schools, and universities. We call for the means of 20th-century civilization. Not giving it to us is a crime, it is murder!" (Karadogan, 2007).

Kurdish Education in Other Countries

Northern Kurdistan

In Turkey or northern Kurdistan, primary education is compulsory for all kids and free of charge. Education is supposed to be built on the principles of contemporary science and pedagogy according to the philosophy of Ataturk with the ultimate goal of assimilating the Kurds into the Turkish state. Article 39 of the Treaty of Lausanne stipulated that all citizens were allowed to use their mother tongue in public and private, although the use of this language in schools was not directly mentioned. In Turkey, this went as far as prohibiting the instruction in and of Kurdish. The 1924 law, no. 430 *Tehvidi Tedrisat Kanunu* (Education Unification Law), prescribed the abolishment of religious schools and schools teaching in Kurdish. According to paragraph 42, Section 9 of the Turkish constitution states that no language other than Turkish shall be taught as a mother tongue to Turkish citizens at any institution of education.

In the Kurdish area in Turkey, one finds a primary school in almost every village and a secondary school in every town. Also, some vocational schools can be found in the region. The largest cities, such as Van, Elazig, Erzurum, Malatya, Diyarbakir, and Urfa, all have institutions of higher education. The educational level among the Kurds in Turkey is relatively high, but it is still lower in comparison with the country's general average.

The government "Turkish" schools remain open and work on molding the Kurds into loyal citizens of the republic. Many Kurds still believe that the public educational system aims at assimilating them into Turkish society. Only after 2002 did the government announce the official end of the assimilation policy. Then they let Kurds, like other ethnic and religious communities, protect and develop their heritage, language, and culture. Kurdish language and literature departments have been opened in some universities within this framework of recognition. In addition, in primary and secondary schools, Kurdish has been added as a second language or optional topic. And with the new regulations, ethnic groups have been permitted to provide education using their own native language in private schools. However, in 2006, three of those schools have been closed for alleged contacts with the PKK. In a newly opened college in Diyarbakir, Kurdish has been accepted as the second language of instruction. Some preschools and kindergartens started offering a Kurdish-language curriculum.

Eastern Kurdistan

As in other parts of Kurdistan in Rojhelat or eastern Kurdistan, education started in the mosque, then at the madrasah, which are present in every town. The madrasahs are still operating today, although their number is shrinking (unlike the number of students enrolled in these institutions). Public education took off in 1921 as part of the government's plan to modernize the country (Imam & Mohammadpur, 2010). Trying to use education as a tool to modernize the "backward" Kurdish areas is a strategy applied by many states in the region. The role of education here is to free the citizens from the shackles of old family, ethnic, or religious loyalties and to shape them into modern citizens. Thus, schools of all levels and ages can be found throughout Iran. In addition, there is a university or college in every larger Kurdish city. Another governmental tool of modernization is the *medreseyi ashair* (tribal school), which is common among the formerly nomadic Lur Kurds. Persian is the language of instruction, and many Kurds in Iran are eventually bilingual or trilingual (Fekuhi, 2008). Although the constitution states that education may be provided in other languages, there are not many opportunities to offer classes in and on Kurdish language. Kurdish may be taken as an elective. Sanandaj University offers undergraduate and postgraduate courses in Kurdish.

Southern Kurdistan

Bashur or southern Kurdistan is the only region where Kurds enjoy both the traditional and the modern educational infrastructure (Rauf, 2009). In Iraq after the Sheikh Mahmud Barzanji Rebellion in the 1920s, the government allowed the establishment of school teaching in Kurdish. Schools became an important factor in the negotiations between the British, the central government in Baghdad, and the Kurds fighting for autonomy. In many treaties and memorandums, they mentioned the right of the Kurds to teach their language, the need to build more schools in the Kurdish territories, the naming rights for schools, and the language of instructions to be either Kurdish or Arabic. The March Manifesto of 1970 signed by the Iraqi Kurds and the government in Baghdad explicitly grants the right of Kurdish as a second official language. Today, Kurds in Iraqi-Kurdistan have schools from all levels, from preschool to university. The government of the Kurdish Autonomy Region has appointed two ministers, one for general education (primary, secondary, vocational) and one for higher education. Ever since 1992, the educational sector is growing rapidly, and the current number of public or state universities is now 11. During the reign of Saddam Hussein, there was only one university in Erbil (Kurdistan Government, 2016). In addition to that, nine private universities have been opened in the region. Most universities offer undergraduate and graduate programs. The four largest universities are Salahadin University in Erbil (since 1968), University of Sulaymaniah (1992), the University of Dohuk (1992), and Soran University (1992). In 2000, the University of Koya and Hawler Medical University were founded. The University of Halabja, University of Raparin in Rania, University of Garmian, and University of Zakho were founded in 2011. The private universities include the American University of Iraq—Sulaymaniyah, Cihan University, Sabis University, University Dijlah College, and Nawroz University (Kurdistan Government, 2016).

Kurdish Universities

In the years following the establishment of the Kurdish Autonomy Zone in northern Iraq, many institutions of higher education were founded, among them 13 public and 12 private universities. The relative stability and large percentage of the student-aged population generated this boom. Many universities have Kurdish as the main language of instruction, while others choose an affiliation with Western universities and teach in English. In Rojava, Kurdistan Syria, the first university opened in Efrin in 2015. Plans to open a Kurdish university in Diyarbakir (Amed) are discussed as well. The University of Kurdistan (Iran) was established in 1974.

Western Kurdistan

In the Syrian Kurdish territories or Rojava, both the French mandate and the Ba'ath Party left their marks on the educational sector. Although the mandate authorities provided some limited opportunities for the Kurds, in general, most Kurds were prevented from attending school for various reasons (Hassanpour et al., 1996). Education was completely Arabized and in Arabic during the Ba'ath Party's era. It was used as a tool to brainwash and transform the Kurdish citizens. However, since there also was a lack of appreciation for Kurdish citizens, with several hundred thousand losing their citizenship, most Kurds resisted the government's assimilation policies.

Syrian Kurds had the opportunity to receive education in their mother tongue after the outbreak of the Syrian civil war and the establishment of the semi-autonomous cantons in the north of the country. Here ethnic, religious, and linguistic diversity was considered in the design of new school curricula. In addition to primary, secondary, and high schools, two universities have been opened in the region: Efrin University in the Efrin Canton and Qamishli Rojava University in the Cezire Canton. In addition, al-Furat University in Hasake remained under the control of the ministry of education, and agreements have been made to rewrite the former nationalistic, anti-Kurdish curriculum.

Nurettin Beltekin

Further Reading

Aydınkaya, F. (2010). Golgotha Tepesinden İnmenin Arifesinde Vicahiye Cevrilmis "Kurt Modernlesmesi Elestirisi." *Dipnot*, 1, 205–226.

Baluken, Y. (2010). *Mervânîler Devrinde Dinî Gruplar Arasındaki Munasebetler.* (Yayınlanmamıs Yuksel Lisans Tezi). Yuzuncu Yıl Universitesi Sosyal Bilimler Enstitusu: Van.

Beltekin, N. (2014). *Okul ve Oteki Yurttaslar: Kurt Politik Aktorlerinin Egitimsel Deneyimleri.* Istanbul: Vate Yayınları.

Beyazîdî, M. M. (2012). *Adat û Rusûmatnameê Ekradiye* (2nd ed.). Istanbul: Nûbihar.

Celîl, C. (2007). *Kurt Halk Tarihinden 13 Onemli Yaprak.* (Translated by Hasan Kaya.) Istanbul: Evrensel Basım Yayın.

Cicek, M. H. (2011). "Dogu ve Guney Dogu Medreselerine Analitik Bir Yaklasım." http://mehmethalilcicek.com/Makaleler.aspx.

Demir, B. (2010). "Devlet Destekli Kurtce Egitim: Kurd Mesrutiyet Mektebi." *Toplumsal Tarih,* 200, 72–78.

Dersimi, N. (1997). *Hatıratım.* [Turkish: My Memories], Istanbul: Doz Yayınları.

Hassanpour, A., Skutnabb-Kangas, T., & Chyet, M. (1996). "The Non-education of Kurds: A Kurdish Perspective." *International Review of Education,* Special issue, "The Education of Minorities," N. Labrie & S. Churchill (Eds.), 367–379.

Iman A., & Mohammadpur, T. (2010). "The Impact of Modern Education in the Ouramant Region of Iranian Kurdistan: A Grounded Study." *Quality & Quantity,* vol. 44, 893–904 doi: 10.1007/s11135-009-9242-y.

Karadogan, Y. (2007). 1967 "Dogu Mitingleri ve Nevzat Sagnıc." http://gelawej.net/pdf/1967_DOGU_MITINGLERI_VE_NEVZAT_SAGNIC.

Keles, N. (2015). "The Poets and Scholars that Affected the Scholarly and Cultural Life in the Reign of Shaddādids." *Journal of History School,* vol. 8, no. XXIV, 1–23. doi: http://dx.doi.org/10.14225/Joh799.

Kurdistan Government. (2016). "Ministers." http://cabinet.gov.krd/p/p.aspx?l=12&s=020000&r=308&p=218.

Nursi, S. (1990). *İctimai Receteler. 1. Baskı.* Istanbul: Tenvîr Nesrîyat.

Rauf, A. I. (2009). Merakiz Seqafiyyeh Meghuriyyeh fi Kurdistan. Erbil: Mukriyani Establishment for Research and Publication.

Sengul, S. (2008). *Bilgi, Toplum, İktidar: Osmanlı ve Cumhuriyet Modernlesmesi ile Karsılasma Surecinde Dogu Medreseleri.* Yayınlanmamıs Doktora Tezi. Ankara: Hacettepe Universitesi.

Sengul, S. (2014). "Cizre Kırmızı Medrese Baglamında Tarih Kimlik Hafıza Olusumu." *Kebikec,* 37, 57–78.

Tan, A. (2009). *Kurt Sorunu: Ya Tam Kardeslik Ya Birlikte Kolelik.* Istanbul: Timas Yayınları.

Zaza, N. (2000). *Bir Kurt Olarak Yasamım.* (Translated by A. Karacoban.) Istanbul: Peri Yayınları.

Language

Kurds call their language *Kurdî* (کوردی) in Kurdish. This chapter first provides some historical and sociocultural information about the language such as the family of languages it belongs to, its variety groups, and its current status and vitality. This will be followed by a linguistic description of Central Kurdish (Sorani, henceforth CK), for it is beyond the scope of this chapter to cover the linguistic properties of all Kurdish variety groups. We will focus on CK because it is the variety that is spoken by the vast majority of Kurds in Iraq where Kurdish has an official status. Some basic vocabulary and expressions in both Central and Northern Kurdish (Kurmanji, henceforth NK) will be presented followed by a sample text in CK. The chapter concludes with a list of books and resources on the language.

Language Family

Kurdish belongs to the western branch of Iranian languages, one of the major branches of the Indo-European language family. Although Kurdish has been influenced by majority regional languages such as Arabic and Turkish, it differs in phonology (the sound system), morphology (word formation), and syntax (word order). Arabic and Turkish do not belong to the Indo-European family of languages. Linguistically, Kurdish is closer to Persian/Farsi, Baluchi, and Pashto. It also shares some basic but ancient vocabulary with European languages: *dû* "two" in English and "deux" in French ("x" is not pronounced); *no* "nine" and "neuf" (French); *pênc* "pènte" (Greek); *pê* "pied" (French; the "d" is not pronounced); *bira* "brother"; *dan* "dent" (French; "t" is not pronounced and "e" is pronounced "a" as in "father").

Kurdish Variety Groups

Like most, if not all, languages, Kurdish is a constellation of varieties and subvarieties. Some of these varieties may not be mutually intelligible unless there has been a considerable prior communication among their speakers. This means that speakers of a certain variety may not be understood by speakers of a different variety. Sometimes the linguistic differences between varieties are so large that they are considered separate languages by some scholars. Nonetheless, the vast majority of Kurds call their speech variety *Kurdî*, the Kurdish language. From this perspective, it is more appropriate to call Kurdish a macro-language.

Based on the criterion of mutual intelligibility and also based on linguistic evidence, Kurdish varieties can be categorized into five variety groups: Northern

(Kurmanji), Central (Sorani), Southern (Kirmashani), Zazaki, and Gurani/Hawrami. Many theoretical linguists believe that the latter two groups are non-Kurdish because they are linguistically very distinct from Kurdish proper (the other three groups). However, most speakers of the Zazaki and Gurani/Hawrami groups call themselves Kurds. The latter two variety groups share a wide vocabulary in addition to some grammatical features with other Kurdish speech varieties.

The majority of Kurds identify Kurmanji as their mother or heritage tongue. These Kurds live in Turkey (approx. 10 to 15 million), Syria (approx. 2 million), Iraq (1 to 1.5 million), Iran (approx. 1 million), and Armenia and neighboring countries (approx. 500,000 to 1 million). Some of the major urban centers home to Kurmanji speakers include Diyarbakir (*Amed* in Kurdish) in Turkey, Duhok in Iraq, Al-Qamishli (*Qamishlo*) in Syria, and Urmia (*Wirmê*) in Iran. North America and Europe, particularly Germany, are also home to about 500,000 speakers of this Kurdish variety.

Kurmanji was the language of the Kurdish scribal culture at the turn of the 16th century. However, mainly because the Kurds did not have a state of their own, the variety remained spoken rather than written and standardized until the mid-20th century. For most of the 20th century, Kurmanji was banned in both Syria and Turkey. In Iran and Iraq, it was mostly used in private domains rather than in schools or government institutions. Thanks to a group of Kurdish intellectuals in exile, for example, Jeladet Ali Bedir Khan, the standardization of this Kurdish variety took serious steps in the 1940s.

In 1992, Turkey lifted its ban on Kurdish, and we started to witness an unprecedented rise in Kurdish publications in the country, Kurdish learning and teaching courses both in private and public domains, and the launching of a 24/7 government-sponsored television channel (*TRT Kurdî*), among others. However, Kurdish still does not have an official status in Turkey and is not the language of schools even in Kurdish regions of Turkey. This is also the case in Iran. In Iraq, however, since 1992 when Iraqi Kurds started to enjoy political autonomy, Badini, a subvariety of Kurmanji Kurdish, has become the de facto official language of the province of Duhok in Iraq. In addition to being the language of the local government and over a dozen newspapers and TV and radio channels, it is the language of instruction in the province's education system. Kurmanji has also become an official language in Kurdistan-Syria since 2014. The language, however, does not enjoy any positive status in Iran or Turkey. In both countries the variety is tolerated (i.e., it is not banned), but it does not enjoy any substantial state support. Although publishing in this variety is possible, and state-run media use it for broadcasting, it is not a language of the school system, the government, or private institutions.

Central (Sorani) Kurdish is arguably the second-largest Kurdish variety group, and it is only spoken in Iran (approx. 3.5 million) and Iraq (approx. 4 million). Although it began its scribal tradition about two centuries after Kurmanji, it started to enjoy its literary upper hand in the early1800s. In Iraq, since the 1930s, CK became one of the official languages of media, schools, and local governments in the provinces of Sulaimani, Hawler (Erbil), and Kirkuk where the vast majority of

Kurds in Iraq live. In 1945, when Iranian Kurds established a short-lived republic in Mahabad, Kurdish became the official language of the polity. Since then, however, the language similar to other minority languages has remained marginalized; it is neither the language of public or private institutions, nor is it the language of instruction in schools. In September 2015, the University of Kordestan (Sanandaj, Iran) started a BA program in Kurdish language and literature. One of the objectives of the program is to train Kurdish teachers so that they can help teach the language in schools once the government acknowledges such language rights. In Iraq, the situation is completely different. CK is the official and prime means of communication, schooling, and correspondence in the Kurdistan Regional Government of Iraq. The use of Arabic has been limited to mosques and some aspects of the legal and medical sectors where Kurdish does not yet have sufficient terminology in order to function effectively. Unlike 30 years ago, many children in Iraqi Kurdistan nowadays grow up and finish school without being proficient in Arabic. Instead, English is becoming more and more popular in the region. Thirty years ago, students would start taking two-hour English lessons on a weekly basis as of grade six. These days, English is introduced from grade one and in some places from kindergarten.

Similar to CK, Southern Kurdish, also called Kirmashanî, is spoken in Iran and Iraq only. Major urban centers speaking this variety group include Kirmashan/Kermanshah in Iran and Khanaqin and Baghdad in Iraq. In Iran, most of the speakers of the variety are concentrated in rural areas, while the language of many urbanized centers, such as Kirmashan, has been assimilated into Persian. For a very long time, the use of the language was relegated to the privacy of homes and other small and informal domains. In recent years, however, the population has increasingly shown more interest in this variety by publishing books, periodicals, and web pages.

Zazaki or Dimili has about 2 million speakers in Turkey. Except for a group of literary figures, most Zazaki people consider themselves ethnic Kurds. Many philologists and linguists, mostly of European origin, think that Zazaki is not a Kurdish variety but a distinct language. Diyarbakir is one of the major centers that is also home to the Zaza people in addition to Kurmanji speakers. Since the 1980s, Zazaki activists and literary figures have made efforts to standardize the variety and introduce it to domains such as the media and, to some extent, privately run language courses.

Similar to Zazaki, the Gurani/Hawrami variety group is also considered non-Kurdish by many linguists of European origin. In fact, these linguists believe that there are more similarities between these two groups than between either of them and Kurdish proper (Northern, Central, and Southern groups). However, unlike Zazaki, which is spoken in Turkey, the Gurani/Hawrami variety is spoken in Iran and Iraq. The total number of the speakers of this group is about 100,000, which is much fewer than other Kurdish variety groups. Furthermore, it is much less standardized, and except for some limited presence in media, its usage is restricted to informal settings. When children go to school, learning CK in Iraqi Kurdistan and Persian in Iran, we must consider that Gurani/Hawrami is an endangered language variety (for more details see Sheyholislami, 2015). Followers of the Kaka'i or Ahle-Haqq religion speak a variety of Gurani/Hawrami (Sheyholislami, 2015).

Linguistic Description

Standard Varieties

It is beyond the scope of this chapter to provide a linguistic description for all Kurdish variety groups. Thus, in what follows we will focus on the basic linguistic description of CK. As stated before, the reason for this choice is that CK is not only one of the official languages of Iraq, but it is the common, working, and official language in the Kurdistan Regional Government (KRG). Moreover, it is arguably the most standardized Kurdish variety. Before presenting a linguistic description of CK, however, major differences between the two standard varieties, CK and NK, will be highlighted (see Table 1).

It may suffice to say that the differences outlined in Table 1 have compelled some linguists to conclude that these two Kurdish varieties are as different as German and English and thus they should be seen as separate languages rather than

TABLE 1 Differences in the Morphosyntax of Sorani and Kurmanji (Haig & Öpengin, 2015: 5–6)

Sorani	Kurmanji
1. Presence of a definiteness suffix -aka	Absence of definiteness marker
2. Generalized plural marker -ān	Plural marking only on obliques
3. Presence of clitic pronouns	Absence of clitic pronouns
4. Loss of direct form ez of the first singular personal pronouns (all dialects); lack of distinct case forms for all other independent person pronouns (though maintained in the third person singular in some dialects, e.g., Mukri, cf. Öpengin forth c.)	Maintenance of ez / min distinction in the first person, maintenance of obl/direct case distinction on all other personal pronouns (syncretism in the second person singular in some dialects)
5. Loss of gender distinctions in most environments (maintained in certain dialects, e.g., Mukri)	Maintenance of gender distinctions
6. Presence of a morphological passive	No morphological passive, analytical passive with auxiliary hatin "come"
7. No free or demonstrative forms of the ezafe	Free or demonstrative ezafes
8. Open compound type of ezafe	Lack of open compound ezafe construction (though restricted usage in some dialects close to Sorani region, e.g., Şemzinan)
9. Loss of case marking on nouns and all personal pronouns (though marginally retained in some dialects, e.g., Mukri)	Retention of case marking on all pronouns and nouns (lost in some dialects on masculine singular nouns)

varieties of the same language (for a thorough discussion of the current debate over language and variety, especially within the context of Kurdish, see Haig & Öpengin, 2014).

Here, I will briefly expand on one item from Table 1: item 5, grammatical gender. Unlike in CK, all nouns in NK have grammatical gender; they have to be either feminine or masculine. This might be the most difficult aspect of NK to learn for adult second-language learners, including CK speakers, simply because the grammatical genders are for the most part arbitrarily assigned; there are no obvious rules to know what is feminine and what is masculine. *Pirtûk,* "book," is feminine; thus "my book" becomes *pirtûka* min; but because *hesp,* "horse," is masculine, "my horse" becomes *hespê min.* In CK, both possessive structures will be the same: *pertûkî min, hespî min* (Here î "of" attached to the end of the noun is called *îzafe,* which is explained later on) (for more on this, see Haig & Öpengin 2015).

Phonology

Vowels

The vowel system for both CK and NK consists of eight phonemes: five long vowels (a, i, e, o, u) and three short vowels (æ, ʊ, ɨ). In Table 2, Kurdish vowels are represented according to their IPA (International Phonetic Alphabet) symbols. These eight vowels are shared by CK and NK. However, in some regions, the vowel system is not as stable as one may expect. For example, the phonemes *e* as in 'red" and *o* as in "toe" might be in free variation with their long counterparts especially *i:* as in "dear" and *u* as in "tour". Whereas "red" is in Kurdish rendered as /suɾ/ in one region, it might be pronounced /soɾ/ in another (also in NK). Whereas "bring" might be said as /benæ/ in one region, it might be pronounced as /bi:næ/ in another. In the standard variety of CK, however, /suɾ/ and /benæ/ are preferred.

Consonants

Central Kurdish has 27 consonants (see Table 3). Although most of these consonant sounds are of Indo-Iranian origin, a few have originated from Arabic such as q, ς, and ħ, as in the Arabic names *Qadir, Abdullah,* and *Hamid,* respectively. Kurdish shares more or less all the other English consonants except for two sets. First, the initial sounds in the English words "that" and "think" do not exist in Kurdish. Second, the consonants ɣ as in the French word "dorier" and x as in the German word "lo**ch**" are productive phonemes in Kurdish but not in English.

TABLE 2 Kurdish Vowels Shared by Central and Northern Kurdish

	Front	Central	Back
High	i:	ɨ	u, ʊ
Mid	æ, e		o
Low	a		

TABLE 3 CK Consonants

	Biblabial	Labiodental	Dental/ alveolar	Palatoalveolar/ palatal	Velar	Uvular	Pharyngeal	Glottal
Stops and affricates	p b		t d	č j	k g	q		ʔ
Fricative		f v	s z	ʃ ž	x ɣ		ʕ, ħ	h
Nasal	m		n					
Approximants	w				y			
Flap, trill			ɾ, r					
laterals			l		ł			

Although the vowel system in both main varieties is the same, there are some notable differences when it comes to consonants in the two varieties. The consonant *v* is much more frequent in NK than CK, and at the same time, the consonant *w* is more frequent in CK. In many lexical items, *w* in CK turns into *v* in NK: *aw* (C) *av* (N) "water," *pêław* (C) *pêlav* (N) "shoe," *lêw* (C) *lêv* (N) "lip," *şew* (C) *şev* (N) "night." In CK, the alveolar flap /ɾ/ and trill /r/ are not only two different sounds but also different phonemes; they contrast on the phonemic level, as in *ker* /kæɾ / "donkey" versus *keř* /kær/ "deaf." This is also the case with the laterals /l/ and /ł/. These two similar sounds do exist in many languages but they do not contrast at the phonemic level in all languages, including English and NK. Therefore, whether you say in English /blæk/ with a light *l* or /błæk/ with a strong *ł* this will not change the meaning of the word "black." In CK, however, it does change the meaning. *kel* "hill" contrasts with *keł* "buffalo," or *guł* "flower" contrasts with *gul*, a "person suffering from leprosy."

Alphabet

Kurdish has been written in several scripts. Today, however, it is mainly written in two forms. One is based on Arabic and Persian scripts and is used in Iran and Iraq. Here we will refer to this one as Kurdo-Arabic. The other alphabet system is referred to as Kurdo-Latin and mostly used by Kurds from Armenia, where Cyrillic used to be employed, Turkey and Syria (see the following table and also the sample text at the end of this article). As might be expected, the Kurdo-Latin script resembles the Turkish alphabet. The interesting case, however, is that the Syrian Kurds write in this same alphabet, which is totally different from the alphabet of the Syria's dominant language, Arabic.

The Kurdish Alphabets

The Kurdish language lacks a unified standard form and alphabet. There are two standardized varieties: Kurmanji and Sorani. Sorani, in both Iraq and Iran, is written in Perso-Arabic *alphabet*, but in the Kurdish *script* with some variation in *orthography*. Whereas in Arabic and Persian scripts the phonemic alphabet mostly represents consonants, in Kurdish script, a modified alphabet represents the vowels as well. Standard Kurmanji is written in the Perso-Arabic alphabet in Iran, Iraq and Syria, and also in Latin-based alphabet in Turkey, Armenia and also Syria. Kurdish has multiple alphabets and scripts, because it is used in different countries with different alphabets and scripts.

In Table 4, Kurdish phonemes are represented in IPA, Kurdo-Latin, and Kurdo-Arabic alphabets along with examples from both English and Kurdish vocabularies to illustrate each sound. Note that the short vowel /ɨ/ as in the English word "sit," is only represented in the Kurdo-Latin script as *i*, for example, *min*, "I," but it has no correspondence in the Kurdo-Arabic alphabet as in من (m+n) "I." On the other hand, the glottal stop, which typically precedes vowels when in the initial position of a word, is not represented in the Kurdo-Latin alphabet. Thus, the word "yes" when rendered in Kurdish will be written as *erê* in Kurdo-Latin script, but ئەرێ (ʔ+e+r+ê) in Kurdo-Arabic script. Furthermore, although speakers of NK frequently use the sounds /ɣ/ and /ʕ/, they are not represented in the standard Kurdo-Latin alphabet, possibly following the Turkish writing system. Two other sounds and letters that are absent from the Kurdo-Latin alphabet are the alveolar trill /r/ and the velar lateral /ɫ/ (see Table 4 for examples).

TABLE 4 Kurdish Alphabet (IE: Indo-European; NK: Northern Kurdish)

IPA	Kurdo-Latin	Kurdo-Arabic	Approx. sound in Eng. words	Sound exemplified in Kurdish words
ʔ	*	ئ	The sound between the vowels in uh-oh	*azad* ئازاد "free"
a	a	ا	b**u**t, c**u**t	*ba* با "wind"
b	b	ب	**b**rother	*Bira* برا "brother"
j	c	ج	**j**am	*ciwan* جوان "young/beautiful"
č	ç	چ	**ch**urch	*çem* چەم "river"
d	d	د	**d**ad	*dû* دوو "two"
æ	e	ە / ه	h**a**d	*de* دە "ten"
e	ê	ێ	b**e**d	*sê* سێ "three"
f	f	ف	**f**ather	*fêr* فێر "learn/teach"
g	g	گ	**g**arden	*ga* گا "ox"
ɣ	x	غ	r in do**r**ier (French)	*bax* باغ "garden"
h	h	ه - هـ	**h**oney	*heval* هەڤال "friend/comrade"
ɦ	h	ح	Mu**h**ammad (not IE)	*Muhemmed* موحەممەد "Muhammad"
ʕ	ʻ	ع	**A**li (not IE)	*Elî* عەلی "Ali"
i:	î	ی	s**ee**d	*sî* سی "thirty"
ɨ	i	—	s**i**t, b**i**t	*min* من "I"
k	k	ک	**c**ake	*kêk* کێک "cake"
l	l	ل	**l**abel	*lale* لاله "tulip"
ɫ	l	ڵ	labe**l**	*baɫ* باڵ "wing"
m	m	م	**m**other	*min* من "I, me"
n	n	ن	**n**o	*na* نا "no"
o	o	ۆ	d**oo**r	*bo* بۆ "for"
p	p	پ	**p**et	*pare* پارە "money"
q	q	ق	**Q**uran (not-IE)	*Qur'an* قورئان "Quran"
ɾ	r	ر	**r**ed	*ře* ڕێ "road"
r	ř	ڕ	Trilled r	*keř* کەڕ "deaf"
s	s	س	**s**imple	*serma* سەرما "cold"
ʃ	ş	ش	**sh**ed	*şeř* شەڕ "war/fight"
ʒ	j	ژ	plea**su**re	*jîyan* ژیان "life"

(continued)

TABLE 4 Kurdish Alphabet (IE: Indo-European; NK: Northern Kurdish) (*continued*)

IPA	Kurdo-Latin	Kurdo-Arabic	Approx. sound in Eng. words	Sound exemplified in Kurdish words
t	t	ت	telephone	*telefon* تەلەفۆن "telephone"
ʊ	u	و	put	*Kurdî* کوردی "Kurdish"
u	û	وو	boot	*dûr* دوور "far"
v	v	ڤ	vowel	*govar* گۆڤار "magazine"
w	w	و	wind	wane وانه "lesson"
x	x	خ	loch	*xak* خاک "soil/dirt"
y	y	ى -ێ	yellow	*yek* یەک "one"
z	z	ز	zebra	*zengîn* زەنگین "rich"
ž	j	ژ	pleasure	*jin* ژن "woman"

TABLE 5 Personal Pronouns

Singular		Plural	
min	I/me	*ême*	We
to	you	*êwe*	you (plural)
ew	she/he/it	*ewân*	they

Morphology

Nouns

In CK, nouns have three states: absolute, indefinite, and definite. The absolute state does not require any article (e.g., a, an, the) or affix. It provides the generic aspect and lexical form of the noun (e.g., *hengwîn şîrîn e* "honey is sweet"). The indefinite state is analogous to "a" and "an" in English, and it is marked by the suffix *êk* when the noun ends in a consonant and *yek* when the noun ends in a vowel: *kuřêk* "a boy" or *kiçêk* "a girl/daughter," but *mamostayek* "a teacher." The definite state is marked by the suffix *eke* after consonants, *ke* after the vowels *e* and *a*, and *yeke* after the rest of the vowels: *piyaweke* "the man," *kureke* "the boy," *derwazeke* "the gate," *çiyake* "the mountain," *Hewlêrîyeke* "the Hewleri (person)," *rêyeke* "the road," *dêyeke* "the village," and *şûyeke* "the husband."

The plural of nouns is formed by adding—*an* to words ending with consonants and—*yan* to words ending with vowels. To make definite plural nouns, we add—*ekan* and—*yekan,* respectively. Examples include the following: *mindal* "child," *mindalan* "children"; *dê* "village," *dêyan* "villages" (also *dêhat* with *dê+at* plural ending borrowed from Arabic); *mindaleke* "the child," *mindalekan* "the children," *dêyeke* "the village," *dêyekan* "the villages."

Personal Pronouns

There are six personal pronouns as shown in Table 5.

For example, *min mamostam* "I am (a) teacher," *to qutabî(t)* "you are (a) student"; *ême Kurdîn* "we are Kurdish," *êwe Amrîkîn* "you are Americans."

TABLE 6 Possessive Pronouns

Singular		Plural	
-im	my	-man	-our
-it	your	-tan	your (plural)
-î/y	her/his/its	-yan	their

Possessive pronouns are marked by suffixes attached to the end of the noun. When added to nouns in the absolute state, they sounds they make are shown in Table 6.

For example, *kitêbim* "my book, *kitêbit* "your book," *kitêbî* "his/her book"; *kitêbman* "our book," *kitêbtan* "your book," *kitêbyan* "their book." These suffixes can be also added to nouns in the indefinite state, for example, *kitêb+êk+im* "a book of mine," and in indefinite state, *kitêb+eke+m* "the book of mine."

Demonstratives

The Kurdish demonstratives are as follows: *eme* "this," *ewe* "that," *emane* "these," and *ewane* "those." For example, *eme kitêb e* (this book is) "This is (a) book" and *ewe baş e* (that good is) "that is good." When demonstratives, however, are used as attributive adjectives and modify nouns, they envelop them, where the noun is placed between the two parts of the demonstrative: **em** *piyawe* "this man," **ew** *jine* "that woman." Also, in this structure, the plural suffix is removed from the demonstrative and is attached to the modified word: **emane** *hatin* "these came," but **em** **kesane** *hatin* "these people came."

The Îzafe Construction in the Possessive or Genitive Case

Îzafe is equivalent to "of" in English. In Kurdish, the vowel "î" connects the two parts of the genitive construction, for example, *utombêlî min* (automobile of mine/my automobile); *utombêlî to* (automobile of yours/your automobile). However, when the word ends in a the vowel î /i:/ *îzafe* becomes *yî*, for example, *şořebî-yî tenya* "the lonely weeping willow." When the word ends in other vowels, the *îzafe* becomes *y* as in *mamostay min* "my teacher," *dêy êwe* "your village," *beřey ême* "our carpet," *mûy to* "your hair."

Adjectives

The most common combination of noun and adjective is noun+î (*îzafe*)+adjective. Examples include: *kiçêkî wirya* (girl+î+smart) "a smart girl" and *filmêkî xoş* (film+î+nice) "a nice movie." Although possible, it is less common to have the opposite word order: adjective+e+noun, for example, *şořejin* (graceful+woman) "graceful woman." When it occurs, the result is written as a compound noun: *şengebêrî* (beautiful+e+milkmaid) "beautiful milkmaid" or *kerepiyaw* (donkey+e+man) "stupid man."

Comparatives and superlatives are formed by adding suffixes to the end of adjectives: *tir* for comparatives (equal to "-er" and "more" in English) and *tirîn* (comparative *tir+în*) for superlatives (equal to "-st" and "the most" in English): *xêratir* "faster," *xêratirîn* "the fastest," *cuwantir* "more beautiful," and *cuwantirîn* "the most beautiful."

Adverbs usually take a single form and may not change to other forms. However, a good number of them are formed by adding the suffix *ane* or the prefix *be* to nouns: *zîrekane* "cleverly," *saɫ**ane** "yearly/annually," *be xêrayî* "quickly."

Adpositions

Kurdish utilizes prepositions, postpositions, and circumpositions. Common prepositions include *le* "in/at," *wek* "like," *le ser* "over, on top of," *pêş* "before," and *paş* "after." A number of prepositions, however, acquire meanings because of the postpositions accompany them. For example, *le Kurdistan* means "in Kurdistan," but *le Kurdistan ewe* means "from Kurdistan." Other examples include *le ew kate da* (*le* + that + time + *da*) "at that time" but *le ew kat ewe* (*le* + that + time + *ewe*) "from that time on." Circumpositions are pairs of adpositions that occur on either side of the complement. They are uncommon in English, but frequent in Kurdish. Deleting the adposition on one side may not alter the meaning in significant ways, for example, the meanings of these phrases are almost the same: *le ew kate da* "in that time" and *ew kat* "that time." However, removing an adposition may change the meaning in significant ways, for example, the meaning of *le ew kat ewe* "since then" is very different from *ew kat* "that time" and *kat ewe* bears no meaning.

Cardinal Numbers

These are quite similar to Persian numbers. When writing in the Kurdo-Latin alphabet, as is often the case when writing Kurmanji, the numbers will be written in Arabic numbers, similar to English. However, when writing in the Kurdo-Arabic alphabet, the numbers are written as shown in Table 7.

Numbers precede words that indicate time and instance: *dû roj* "two day(s)," *sê saɫ* "three years," *no mang* "nine months," *yek saat* "one hour," *de car* "ten time(s)."

Ordinal numbers are formed from the cardinal numbers followed by the suffix–*am* when the number ends with a consonant. The suffix–*hem* is added when the number ends with a vowel, as shown in Table 8.

The days of the weeks are as follows: *Şemme* "Saturday," *Yekşemme* "Sunday," *Dûşemme* "Monday," *Sêşemme* "Tuesday," *Çarşemme* "Wednesday," *Pêncşemme* "Thursday," *Heynî/Cum'e* "Friday."

The seasons of the year are as follows: *behar* "spring," *hawîn* "summer," *payîz* "fall," *zistan* "winter." The months of the year are as follows: *xakelêwe* "March 21–April 20," *guɫan* "April 21–May 21," *cozerdan* "May 22–June 21," *pûşper̂, gelawêj, xermanan, r̂ezber, xezeɫwer, sermawez, befranbar, rêbendan, r̂eşeme*.

TABLE 7 Cardinal Numbers

English	Kurdî	کوردی	
0	sifir	سفر	٠
1	yek	یەک	١
2	dû	دوو	٢
3	sê	سێ	٣
4	çar	چار	٤
5	pênc	پێنج	٥
6	şeş	شەش	٦
7	ħewit	حەوت	٧
8	hetşt	هەشت	٨
9	no	نۆ	٩
10	de(h)	دە	١٠
11	yazde	یازدە	١١
12	diwazde	دوازدە	١٢
13	sêzde	سێزدە	١٣
14	çarde	چاردە	١٤
15	pâzda	پازدە	١٥
16	şazde	شازدە	١٦
17	ħevde	حەڤدە	١٧
18	hejde	هەژدە	١٨
19	nozde	نۆزدە	١٩
20	bîst	بیست	٢٠
21	bîs u yek	بیست و یەک	٢١
22	bîst u dû	بیست و دوو	٢٢
30	sî	سی	٣٠
31	sî u yek	سی و یەک	٣١
40	çil	چل	٤٠
50	penca	پەنجا	٥٠
60	şest	شەست	٦٠
70	ħefta	حەفتا	٧٠
80	heşta	هەشتا	٨٠
90	newed	نەوەد	٩٠
100	sed	سەد	١٠٠
101	sed u yek	سەد و یەک	١٠١
200	dûsed	دووسەد	٢٠٠
1000	hezar	هەزار	١٠٠٠
1101	hezar u sed u yek	هەزار و سەد و یەک	١١٠١

TABLE 8 Ordinal Numbers

1st	yekem	7th	ħewtem
2nd	dûhem	8th	Heştem
3rd	sêhem	9th	nohem
4th	çiwarem	10th	dehem
5th	pêncem	11th	yazdehem
6th	şeşem	12th	duwazdehem

Verb Morphology

Kurdish verbs are of three types: simple verbs (e.g., *kirdin* "to do"), constructed verbs with a pre-verb (e.g., *der kirdin* "to expel"), or complex verbs. Complex verbs are constructed with an infinitive as the second element plus either a noun or an adjective as the first element (e.g., *kar kirdin* "to work," *çak kirdin* "to make" or "to fix"). In Kurdish, verbs indicate tense, transitivity or intransitivity, voice (active or passive), mood, aspect, and number. Here we will expand on the first four.

Tense

Central Kurdish does not have a grammatical future tense (a future form of the verb), similar to English and Persian. Nor does it utilize auxiliaries, as English does—for example, with "will" and "shall," to indicate future. Instead simple present form is used in combination with a temporal adverb (e.g., *deřom* "I go" [present], but *sibeynê deřom* "I go tomorrow"). In the absence of a time indicator, such as "later," "tomorrow," or "after two hours" one could not tell whether *deřom* means "I am going" or "I will go" unless one could construe the meaning from the context. In the present tense, all verbs are conjugated similarly (i.e., *de*+stem of the verb+enclitic). A clitic is neither clearly a word nor an affix, such as *'ll* in *I'll go home*, or *'t* in *I can't do that*. Clitics that follow their base, such as *'ll*, are called enclitics. The enclitics needed to conjugate present tense in Sorani Kurdish are shown in Table 9.

Table 10 explains the conjugation of the intransitive verb *řoyiştin* "to go" in the present tense. The stem of the verb is *řo* ending in a vowel. (Note: "*o*" changes to "*w*" when proceeded by another vowel, e.g., in third person singular.)

TABLE 9 Enclitics for Conjugating Present Tense

Vowel Stems		Consonant Stems	
Sing.	Plu.	Sing.	Plu.
-m	-yn	-în	-m
-y(t)	-n	-î(t)	-in
-a(t)	-n	-ê(t)	-in

TABLE 10 Conjugation of the Verb *Royîştin* "to Go"

	Singular		Plural	
1st	*deřom*	I go	*deřoyn*	we go
2nd	*deřoy(t)*	you go	*deřon*	you go
3rd	*deřwa(t)*	she/he/it goes	*deřon*	they go

The negation of the verb is formed by replacing the modal prefix *de* with *na*: *naŕom* "I don"t go," *naŕoy(t)* "you don't go", *naŕwu(l)* "she/he/it doesn't go," *naŕoyn* "we don't go," *naŕon* "you don't go," *naŕon* "they do not go."

Table 11 presents the conjugation of the verb *bîstin* "to hear" with the stem ending in a consonant.

Negative forms of *bîstin* are similar to that of *ŕoyiştin* earlier: *nabîsm, nabîsî(t)*, etc.

Table 12 presents two more examples to illustrate the conjugation of present tense: the verb *kirdin* "to do" with the stem *ke*, and the verb *bînîn* "to see" with the stem *bîn*. Note that the former stem ends in a vowel but the latter ends in a consonant.

TABLE 11 Conjugation of the Verb *bîstin* "to Hear" with Stem Ending in a Consonant (t)

		Singular		Plural
1st	*debîsim*	I hear	*debîsîn*	we go
2nd	*debîsî(t)*	you hear	*debîsin*	you go
3rd	*debîsê(t)*	she/he/it hears	*debîsin*	they go

TABLE 12 Conjugating Verbs in Present Tense

	Singular	Plural
1st	*dekem* (I do)	*dekeyn* "we do"
2nd	*dekey(t)* "you go"	*deken* "you do"
3rd	*deka(t)* "he/she/it goes"	*deken* "they do"
1st	*debînim* "I see"	*debînîn* "we see"
2nd	*debînî(t)* "you see"	*debînin* "you see"
3rd	*debînê(t)* "he/she/it does"	*debînin* "they see"

TABLE 13 Past Tense Conjugations: Transitive Verbs

	Simple Past	Imperfect	Present Perfect	Past Perfect
1st Singular	*bîstim*	*dembîst*	*bîstûme*	*bîstibûm*
	"I heard"	"I was hearing"	"I have heard"	"I had heard"
2nd	*bîstit*	*detbîst*	*bîstûte*	*bîstibût*
3rd	*bîstî*	*deybîst*	*bîstûye*	*bîstibûy*
1st plural	*bîstiman*	*demanbîst*	*bîstûmane*	*bîstibûman*
	"we heard"	"we were hearing"	"we have heard"	"we had heard"
2nd	*bîstitan*	*detanbîst*	*bîstûtane*	*bîstbûtan*
3rd	*bîstyan*	*deyanbîst*	*bîstûyane*	*bîstbûyan*

TABLE 14 Past Tense Conjugations: Intransitive Verbs

	Simple Past	Imperfect	Present Perfect	Past Perfect
1st Singular	çûm	deçûm	çûm	çûbûm
	"I went"	"I was going"	"I have gone"	"I had gone"
2nd	çûy(t)	deçûy(t)	çûy(t)	çûbûy(t)
3rd	çû	deçû	çûwe	çûbû
1st plural	çûyn	deçûyn	çûyn	çûbûyn
	"we went"	"we were going"	"we have gone"	"we had gone"
2nd	çûn	deçûn	çûn	çûbûm
3rd	çûn	deçûn	çûn	çûbûn

Past Tenses

In Central Kurdish, there are about 10 ways to form and conjugate any verb in the past tense. Here we will only show verb conjugations for the four most common past tenses: simple past, imperfect, present perfect, and past perfect. These forms are conjugated differently depending on whether the verb is transitive or intransitive. Tables 13 and 14 show how these tenses are conjugated for the transitive verb *bîstin* "to hear" and the intransitive verb *çûn* "to go."

The Passive Voice

In most cases, the passive voice is formed by attaching suffixes -*rê* and -*ra* to the end of the present stem of the verb. The present passive voice is constructed from the modal prefix *de* + present stem of the verb + -*rê*: e.g., *dexurê* "It's (being) eaten," or **denûsrê** "It's (being) written." The past passive verb is formed by the present stem of a transitive verb + -*ra*, e.g., *xura* "It was eaten," or *nûsra* "It was written." The past passive participle is formed from the past passive stem + -*ra* + *w/we*, e.g., *xurawe* "It has been eaten," or *nusrawe* "It has been written." Finally, the past perfect passive is formed from the past passive stem + -*ra* + *bû*, e.g., *xurabû* "It had been eaten," or *nusrabû* "It had been written." In closing this segment, two additional points should be made. First, all the conjugations made in discussing the passive voice here are in the third person singular. Second, like many aspects of grammar (e.g., English irregular verbs) there are some irregularities in the way passive voice is formed in Kurdish.

The imperative mood is constructed from the prefix *bi* plus the stem of the verb. For example, from *řoyîştin* "to go," with the stem *řo,* the commad "go" becomes *biřo*. Negative imperatives are constructed from *me* plus the stem: *meřo* "don't go" or *meçû* "don't go". In complex (two-part) verbs like *kar kirdin* "to work" the imperative prefix *bi* is wrapped between the noun *kar* "work" and the stem of the infinitive (*ke*). Thus, the imperative "work" becomes *kar bike*.

Complex predicates are structured from a verb (e.g., *Xistin* "to drop/ground") plus a preverb (e.g. *da* "down") to form the verb *daxistin* "to close" as in the sentence *Dûkandareke dûkanekey daxist* "shopkeeper-the shop-the-his closed, The Shopkeeper closed his shop." Alternatively, the same verb can be combined with a preposition (e.g., *leser* "above/over" *leser kirdin* "to wear something over the head," or with an adjective (e.g., *çak* "good," *çak kirdin* "to fix, to improve"), or with a noun (e.g., *hawar* "shout," hawar *kirdin* "to shout" especially for help).

Syntax

In contrast to English word order, in which the basic clause structure is Subject-Verb-Object, in Kurdish it is Subject-Object-Verb. This is particularly true for transitive verbs, which require an object, such as "eat," "drive," and "push," as opposed to intransitive verbs like "sleep," "laugh," and "go," which do not require an object; one does not go anyone or anything but she or he just goes (e.g., *min sêwêk dexom* (I apple-one de-eat-I, I eat an apple," or, *ew dengêkî bîst* (He/She sound-one heard, He/she heard a sound"). Not always but very commonly, adverbials of time and manner precede the verb, whereas adverbials of place follow the verb: <u>emřo</u> *deçim bo bazar* "<u>today</u>, I go to the market," *Shaho <u>le nekaw</u> pêkenî* "Shaho <u>suddenly</u> laughed," *Shaho <u>be pele</u> çû bo fêrge* "Shaho <u>quickly</u> went to school." When all segments are present the most common clause structure is in this order: Time adverbial—Subject—manner adverbial—verb—place adverbial: em<u>řo, Shaho be pele</u> çû bo bazar "Today, Shaho quickly/in a hurry went to the market." In present tense, the subject marker appears on the verb: *min Shaho debînim* "I see Shaho." However, for the past tenses of transitive verbs, subject markers appear on the item in post-subject position: *pêrê, Shaho<u>m</u> dît* "two days ago, I saw Shaho." In response to the question, "When did you see him?" one could say, *pêrê<u>m</u> dît* "the-day-before I saw-him" or *pêrê dîtim* "the-day-before saw-him-I, two days ago I saw him."

Clauses in Kurdish can be in two relations: coordination or subordination. Coordination is achieved through juxtaposition and coordinating conjunctions. An example of the former would be this: *Şofîreke dabezî, silawî kird, duway çak u xoşî danîşt, daway awî kird, gutî: tînû me, gelêk* "the driver got off the car, said hello, after greetings sat down, asked for water, he said: I'm thirsty, a lot.

Coordinating Conjunctions

Although less frequent in spoken language, conjunctions are also used to coordinate independent clauses. The most common conjunction is the enclitic=*u* "and." Other conjunctions include *yan~yan* "or," *bełam* "but," *eger* or *bêtû* "if": *min çûm u danîştim* "I went and sat," *yan min deçim yan ew deçêt* "either I will go or he will go," *min çûm, bełam ew nehat* "I went, but he didn't come," *bêtû neye, minîş naçim* "If he doesn't come, I won't go either." (Note that the enclitic îş means "too, also," thus *minîş* means "me too.")

Subordinating Conjunctions

Complement, relative, and adverbial clauses are introduced using the general subordinating conjunction *ke* "that." Compound conjunctions using *ke* are also used: *her ke* "as soon as," *be mercêk ke* "on the condition that." Other subordinating conjunctions include *ta / heta* "until," *tawekû / hetawekû*"until, so that," *bêtû / eger* "if."

Vocabulary/Lexicon

Both standard varieties, CK and NK, have been enriched by drawing on the lexical repertoire of various regional varieties. Whereas spoken Kurdish still contains a great number of loan words from Arabic, Persian, and Turkish, standard Kurdish, particularly in Iraq, has been significantly and deliberately "purified" of Arabic loan words in particular. Instead of Arabic in recent years, Kurdish schoolbooks and the media have started to readily borrow and appropriate European, especially English, words. Words such as *tolerans* "tolerance," *sponser* "sponsor," *sivîl* "civil," *festîval* "festival," and *kampeyn* "campaign" are common currency. It is also common to see exact English expressions as the name of TV shows (e.g., *Top Story*; *Style*), housing complexes (e.g., *Naz City*), and so forth.

Here is a list of frequent Kurdish vocabulary and expressions in both CK and NK along with their English translation. In case of variation, differences are marked by C for Central Kurdish and N for Northern Kurdish:

erê "yes," *na* "no," *fermû* (C) / *fermo* (N) "please," *sipas* "thanks," *ser* "head," *dest* "hand," *çaw* (C) / *çav* (N) "eye," *mû* "hair," *kezî* "braid of hair," *lût/kepo* (C) / *poz* (N) "nose," *lêw* (C) / *lêv* (N) "lip," *kon* (C) / *kevn* (N) "old," *nan* "bread," *aw* (C) / *av* (N) "water," *kiç* (C) / *kiç* or *keç* (N) "girl," *kuř* (C) / *kuř* or *xort* (N) "boy," *kuř* "son," *jin* "woman," *piyaw* (C) / *mêr* (N) "man," *bira* "brother," *xuşk* (C) / *xuşk* or *xwişk* "sister," *bab/bawik* (C) / *bab* or *bav* (N) "father," *dayik* "mother," *gul* (C) / *gul* (N) "flower," *asman* (C) / *asman* (N) "sky," *herd* (C) / *erd* (N) "earth/ground," *roj* "day," *şew* (C) / *şev* (N) "night," *xanû* (C) / *xanî* (N) "house," *mał* (C) / *mal* (N) "home," *dar* "tree," *şekir* "sugar," *şirîn/şîrîn* "sweet," *birsî* (C) / *birsî* or *birçî* "hungry," *tînû* (C) / *tî* (N) "thirsty," *pîs* (C) *pîs* or *qirêjî* (N) "dirty," *pak* "clean," *xew* "sleep," *mandû* (C) / *mandî* (N) "tired," *kem* (C) / *kêm* (N) "little," *gelêk* (C) / *gelek* (N) "a lot," *xebat* "struggle," *azadî* "freedom," *siław* (C) / *silav* (N) "hello," *be xêr hatî* (C) / *bi xêr hatî* (N) "welcome (to our place/village/city," *to çonî?* (C) / *tu çawan î* or *çawa yî?* (N) "how are you?), *min baş im* (C) / *ez baş im* (N) "I'm fine," *spas* "thanks," *to çi dekey* (C) / *tu çi dikî?* (N), "what are you doing?, *maława* (C) / *malava* (N) "goodbye: may your household be prosperous," *xuwa hafîz* (C) / *bi xatirê te* or *bi xatira te* (N) "goodbye," *min Kurd im* (C) / *ez Kurd im* (N) "I'm Kurdish," *min xwêndkar im* (C) *ez xwendkar im* (N) "I'm (a) student," *min mamostam* (C) / *ez mamosta me* (N), "I am (a) teacher," *beyanît baş* (C) / *sipêde baş* (N) "good morning," *roj baş* "good day," *şew baş* (C) / *şev baş* (N), "good evening," *baş e* "Ok/it's Ok," *baş niye* (C) / *baş nîne* or *ne baş e* (N) "it's not Ok."

Sample Text

Table 15 is an excerpt from a folktale told by a Kurdish speaker from the Sulaimani region of Iraqi Kurdistan. The text is in CK, but it is here written in both Kurdo-Arabic and Kurdo-Latin scripts along with the English translation. (Adapted from Wahby & Edmonds 1966, 176–179.)

Jaffer Sheyholislami

TABLE 15 Sample Text, CK, in Two Alphabets, with English Translation

---

Bextyar u Bedbext dû bira bûn le dêyek da. بەختیار و بەدبەخت دوو برا بوون لە دێیەک دا.

Bakhtyar [Prosperous] and Badbakht [Miserable] were two brothers in one
(living in the same) village.

Rojêk biřyaryan da ke biřon bo şaran, pare ڕۆژێ لە ڕۆژان بڕیاریان دا کە بڕۆن بۆ شاران، پارە پەیدا بکەن؛

peyda biken; we her bo sibeynê serî xoyan وە هەر بۆ سبەینێی سەری خۆیان هەڵگرت و پێکەوە کەوتنە

hełgirt u pêkewe kewtne rê . . . ڕێ . . .

One day they decided to go to town to make money; And the very next morning they
left home and set out together . . .

Bo nîweřo geyishtine ser kanî u awêk. بۆ نیوەڕۆ گەیشتنە سەر کانی و ئاوێک.

By midday they reached a spring.

Wityan, "ba lêre wiçanêkî bo bideyn u nanî وتیان [/گوتیان]،" با لێرە وچانێکی بۆ بدەین و نانی

nîweřoy lê bixoyn"; we danîştin le giwêy kanîyek. نیوەڕۆی لێ بخۆین " ؛ وە دانیشتن لە گوێی کانییەک.

They said, "Let us have a halt here from our march and eat our midday meal by it"
and they sat down beside the spring.

Înca Bedbext řûy kirde Bextyar: "Bextyar, ba bo ئێنجا بەدبەخت ڕووی کردە بەختیار: "بەختیار، با بۆ نیوەڕۆ

nîweřo têşûyekey to bixoyn, têşûyekey minîş bo تێشوویەکەی تۆ بخۆین، تێشوویەکەی منیش بۆ

êwarêman . . . ئێواریمان . . .

Then Badbakht turned to Bakhtyar: "Bakhtyar, let us eat your food parcel for midday,
and (keep) my parcel for our evening meal."

Bextyar desesiřekey piştî xoy kirdewe, we le ser بەختیار دەسەسڕەکە ی پشتی خۆی کردەوە، وە لە سەر

erzekey raxist. ئەرزەکەی ڕاخست.

Bakhtyar undid the handkerchief (tied to) his waist and spread it on the ground.

Sa her çiyekî tiya bû, we hendê boy ħesanewe u سا هەرچییەکی تیا بوو خواردیان، وە هەندێ بۆی حەسانەوە و

kewtnewe řê. کەوتنەوە ڕێ.

Then they ate all of what was in it and rested for a time and (then)
resumed their journey.

Êware beser hat. ئێوارە بەسەر هات.

Evening overtook them.

Hêşta awayî dûr bû, geyîştne dûřêyanêk, kanî u هێشتا ئاوایی دوور بوو، گەیشتنە دوورڕییانێک، کانی و

awêkî lê bû. ئاوێکی لێ بوو.

The (nearest) village was still a long way off (when) they reached a fork in the road
where there was a spring.

(continued)

TABLE 15   Sample Text, CK, in Two Alphabets, with English Translation (*continued*)

Em care Bextyar r̄ûy kirde Bedbext u witî [/gutî]:   ئەم جارە بەختیار ڕووی کردە بەدبەخت و وتی [/گوتی]:
"Bedbext, min zorim birsîye; wa diyare awayîş   "بەدبەخت، من زۆرم برسییە؛ وا دیارە ئاواییش زۆر دوورە؛
zor dûre; ba lêre danîşîn, şew bikeyn, înca   با لێرە دانیشین، شەو بکەین، ئینجا ئەکەوینەوە
ekewînewe [/dekeynewe] r̄ê.   [/دەکەوینەوە] ڕێ.

This time Bakhtyar turned to Badbakht and said, "Badbakht, I am very hungry
and the village, it is clear, is a long way off too; let us sit down here,
have supper, and then resume the journey."

Bextyar witî [/gutî]: "hew, be xuwa, min le   بەختیار وتی [/گوتی]: "هەو، بە خوا، من لە
têşûwekem beşî to nadem, her beşî xom eka   تێشووەکەم بەشی تۆ نادەم، هەر بەشی خۆم ئەکا
[/deka].   [/دەکا].

Badbakht said, "O dear no; by God, I shall not give you a share from my food parcel;
it will just be enough for myself."

Bextyar, ke em napiyawîyey dî, kas bû, we her   بەختیار، کە ئەم ناپیاوییەی دی، کاس بوو، وە هەر ئەوەندەی
ewendey pê kira bit̄ê: "ke wa bû, Bedbext, îtir mn   پێ کرا بڵێ: "کە وا بوو، بەدبەخت، ئیتر من هاوڕێیی
hawr̄êy bedsiriştêkî wekû to nakem; lem dû r̄êye   بەدسرشتێکی وەکوو تۆ ناکەم؛ لەم دوو ڕێیە یەکێک
yekêk hełbijêre, miniş ewî tiryan egrim [/degrim]".   هەڵبژێرە، منیش ئەوی تریان ئەگرم [/دەگرم]".

Bakhtyar, when he saw this caddish behavior, was dumbfounded and only just
managed to say, "In that case, Badbakht, I shall not go along any more with
an ill-natured person like you. Of these two roads choose one for yourself;
you take that road and I will take the other one."

Bedbext r̄egayekyanî bo xoy hełbijard, Bextyarîş   بەدبەخت ڕێگایەکیانی بۆ خۆی هەڵبژارد، بەختیاریش ملی
milî r̄egekey tirî girt u lêk ciwê bûnewe.   ڕێگەکەی تری گرت و لێک جووێ بوونەوە.

Badbakht chose one of the roads for himself, Bakhtyar followed the other road,
and they separated from each other.

Bextyar ke tarîkî beser da hat tûşî aşekonêk   بەختیار کە تاریکی بەسەردا هات تووشی ئاشەکۆنێک
bû . . .   بوو . . .

When darkness overtook him Bakhtyar came across a deserted mill . . .

Ewendey pê neçû şêr̄ek hate jûrewe . . . lepaş ew   ئەوەندەی پی نەچوو شێرێک هاتە ژوورەوە . . . لە پاش ئەو
gurg kirdî be jûra . . . we r̄êwî geyişt.   گورگ کردی بە ژوورا . . . وە ڕێوی گەیشت.

No much time had elapsed when a lion came in . . . After him Wolf
strode in . . . and Fox arrived.

. . . Şêr r̄ûy kirde r̄êwî: ". . . demêke hiç deng u   . . .شێر ڕووی کردە ڕێوی: ". . . دەمێکە هیچ دەنگ و
basêk bo neg̃êr̄awmetewe".   باسێکت بۆ نەگێڕاومەتەوە."

. . . Lion turned to Fox: ". . . it is a long time that you have not related
any piece of gossip to me."

(continued)

TABLE 15 Sample Text, CK, in Two Alphabets, with English Translation
(*continued*)

Řewî witî [/gutî]: "qurban, . . . mişkêk heye lem   ڕێوی وتی [/گوتی]: "قوربان، . . . مشکێک هەیە لەم
aşe kone da, diwanze dînarî zêřî heye; hemû   ئاشەکۆنەدا، دوانزه دیناری زێڕی هەیە؛ هەموو سبەینێ که
sibeynê, ke xor ekewêtewe [/dekewêtewe]   خۆر ئەکەوێتەوه [/دەکەوێتەوه] ئاشەکەوه، ئەم مشکه ئەم
aşekewe, em mişke em zêřane dênête derewe, le   زێڕانە دێنێتە دەرەوه، لەبەر خۆرەکە ڕایان ئەخا [/دەخا] و
be xoreke řayan exa [/dexa] w baryan pê eka [/   یاریان پێ ئەکا [/دەکا] . . .
deka] . . .

Fox said, "Sir, . . . in this deserted mill there is a mouse who has 12 pieces of gold;
every morning when the sun shines into the mill this mouse brings out these
pieces of gold, spreads them out in the sunlight, and plays with them; . . .

Şay caneweran, ke emey bîst, spasî mam řewî   شای جانەوەران، که ئەمەی بیست، سپاسی مام ڕێوی کرد؛ وه
kird; we lepaş nexte hawpirsekêy tir encumen   لەپاش نەختێ هاوپرسەکێی تر ئەنجومەن بڵاوەیان لێ کرد.
biławeyan kird.

The king of the beasts, when he heard this, thanked Uncle Fox; and after some
further discussion they dispersed.

Bextyar, ke giwêy lem qisane bibû, îtir xew   بەختیار، که گوێی لەم قسانە ببوو، ئیتر خەو نەچووه چاوی؛
neçuwe çawî; çaweřwanî xorhełat bû . . .   چاوەڕوانی خۆرهەڵات بوو . . .

When Bakhtyar had heard this conversation he could not sleep any more [sic];
he was waiting for sunrise . . .

Le piř le kunêkewe şitêk brîskayewe. Serî   لە پڕ لە کونێکەوه شتێک بریسکایەوه. سەری مشکێک،
mişkêk, şitêkî brîskedar be demewe, le kunêkewe   شتێکی بریسکەدار به دەمەوه، لە کونێکەوه هاتە
hate derê . . .   دەرێ . . .

Suddenly from a hole something glittered. A mouse's head, with something
glittering in its mouth, came out from the hole . . .

Bextyar çû, zêřekanî ko kirdewe u xistinye   بەختیار چوو، زێڕەکانی کۆ کردەوه و خستنییە گیرفانیەوه، وه
gîrfanîyewe, we le aşeke hate derewe . . .   لە ئاشەکە هاتە دەرەوه . . .

Bakhtyar went, collected the pieces of gold, put them into his pocket, and
came out from the mill . . .

Îtir zor dewłemend bibû . . .   ئیتر زۆر دەوڵەمەند ببوو . . .

And so he had become very rich . . .

Rojêk le rojan řebiwarê hate jûrewe u piyałeyê   ڕۆژێک لە ڕۆژان ڕێبواری هاتە ژوورەوه و پیاڵەیێ ئاوی کرد به
awî kird be sera, we ke lêbuwewe henaseyêkî   سەرا، وه که لێبووەوه هەناسەیێکی هەڵکێشا.
hełkêşa.

One day a traveler came into the room and quaffed a cup of water and,
when he had finished, heaved a sigh.

Dergawan desbecê çû be layewe w pêy wit [/gut]   دەرگاوان دەسبەجێ چوو به لایەوه و پێی وت [/گوت] که
ke xawenmał tika eka [/deka] ke biçête lay.   خاوەنماڵ تکا ئەکا [/دەکا] که بچێتە لای.

The doorkeeper immediately went up to him and told him that the owner
requested that he would go to him.

(continued)

TABLE 15 Sample Text, CK, in Two Alphabets, with English Translation
(*continued*)

Řêbwaryan birde lay Bextyar.
رێبواریان برده لای بەختیار.

The traveler was taken to Bakhtyar . . .

Lepaş nextê xoşî u çonî Bextyar witî [/gutî]:
لەپاش نەختێ خۆشی و چۆنی بەختیار وتی [/گوتی]: "برا

"bira giyan, . . . ewey min heme le geł to da
گیان، . . . ئەوەی من هەمە لە گەڵ تۆدا بەشیان

beşyan ekem . . .
ئەکەم . . .

After a few inquiries Bakhtyar said, "Dear brother, . . . I will divide what
I possess with you . . .

Bedbext . . . witî [/gutî]: ebê pêm błêy, Bextyar,
بەدبەخت . . . وتی: ئەبێ پێم بڵێی، بەختیار، تۆ ئەم

to em dewłete le kiwê u çon çing kewtuwe; minîş
دەوڵەتەت لە کوێ و چۆن چنگ کەتووە؛ منیش ئەچم، وەکوو

eçim, wekû to peyday ekem.
تۆ پەیدای ئەکەم.

Badbakht . . . said, "You must tell me, Bakhtyar, where and
how you obtained this wealth."

Herçend Bextyar beserya hat . . . sûdêkî
هەرچەند بەختیار بەسەریا هات . . . سوودێکی

nebû . . . Bextyar le qisekanî bûwewe, îtir
نەبوو . . . بەختیار کە لە قسەکانی بووەوە، ئیتر بەدبەخت

Bedbext aramî negirt, derpeřye derewe berew
ئارامی نەگرت، دەرپەڕییە دەرەوە بەرەو ئاش.

aş.

However, as much as Bakhtyar sought to dissuade him . . . it was of no avail . . .
When Bakhtyar had finished speaking, Badbakht could rest no longer and
dashed out in the direction of the mill . . .

Çuwe jûrewe, we wekû Bextyar kirdbûy le pişt
چووە ژوورەوە، وە وەکوو بەختیار کردبووی لە پشت

dołyanewe xoy mat da.
دۆڵیانەکەوە خۆی مات دا.

He went inside and, just as Bakhtyar had done,
he hid behind the water-drop.

Şew tewaw tarîk bibû ke şêrêk le piřêka kirdî be
شەو تەواو تاریک ببوو کە شێرێک لە پڕێکا کردی بە ژوورا و

jûra u le nawendî aşekeda hełtûteka. Lepaş
لە ناوەندی ئاشەکەدا هەڵتووتەکا لەپاش ئەو . . .

ew . . .

The night had become quite dark when a lion suddenly strode in and
squatted in the middle of the mill. After him . . .

Înca şêr řûy kirde mam řêwî: ". . . ewe bo
ئینجا شێر رووی کردە مام رێوی: ". . . ئەوە بۆ دەمێکە

demêke deng u basêkit bo min negêřawetewe?"
دەنگ و باسێکت بۆ من نەگێڕاوەتەوە؟"

The Lion turned to Uncle Fox: ". . . why is it so long that you have
not related any gossip to me."

Řêwî witî: "qurban . . . carî pêşû katê ke lêreda
رێوی وتی: "قوربان . . . جاری پێشوو کاتێ کە لێرەدا ئەو

ew agayanem bo egêřaytewe, ademîzadê lew dîw
ئاگایانەم بۆ ئەگێڕایتەوە، ئادمیزادێ لەوودیو دۆڵیانەکەوە خۆی

dołyanekewe xoy mat dabû, giwêy le hemû
مات دابوو، گوێی لە هەمموو ببوو . . .

bibû . . .

Fox said, ". . . Last time when I was relating those pieces of information
to you here, a human had hidden himself on the other side of the water-drop
and had heard everything . . .

(*continued*)

TABLE 15 Sample Text, CK, in Two Alphabets, with English Translation
(*continued*)

Şêr, ke emey bîst, witî: "adey, namerdtan neken, aşeke bigeřên; eme xiwaye, şêwî em êwareyeman bo derçê" . . .	شێر، که ئەمەی بیست، وتی: "ئادەی، نامەردتان نەکەن، ئاشەکە بگەڕێن؛ ئەمە خوایە، شێوی ئەم ئێوارەیەمان بۆ دەرچێ" . . .

  When Lion heard this he said, "Now then, get on with it, search the mill;
  God willing this evening's supper may come out of it for us" . . .

Her ke çûne ewdîw dolyanekewe, Bedbextyan dozîyewe . . .	هەر کە چوونە ئەویو دۆڵیانەکەوە، بەدبەختیان دۆزییەوە . . .

  As soon as they went to the far side of the water-drop they found Badbakht, . . .

Minîş hatmewe u hîçîyan nedamê.	منیش هاتمەوە و هیچیان نەدامێ.

  I too have come back and they gave me nothing.

(*Note:* The last sentence is a discourse feature of storytelling marking the end of a story in Kurdish. The expression may change slightly from region to region.)

Acknowledgments

I am grateful to Erik Anonby, Michael Chyet, and Deniz Ekici for sharing their insights on an earlier draft of this paper. I'm solely responsible for its contents.

Further Reading

Chyet, M. L. (2003). *Kurdish-English Dictionary: Ferhenga kurmancî-Inglîzî*. New Haven, CT: Yale University Press.

Ekici, D. (2010). *Beginning Kurmanji Kurdish* [DVD-ROM]. Tucson: University of Arizona.

Haig, G., & Öpengin, E. (Eds.). (2014). "Introduction to Special Issue. Kurdish: A Critical Research Overview." *Kurdish Studies,* vol. 2, no. 2, 99–122.

Haig, G., & Öpengin, E. (2015). "Kurmanji Kurdish in Turkey: Structure, Varieties, and Status." https://www.academia.edu/17650650/Kurmanji_in_Turkey_structure_varieties_and_status

Hassanpour, A. (1992). *Nationalism and Language in Kurdistan, 1918–1985*. San Francisco: Mellen Research University Press.

Karadaghi, R. (2006). *The Azadi English-Kurdish [Central K] Dictionary*. Teheran: Ehsan Publishing House.

Sheyholislami, J. (2015). "Language Varieties of the Kurds." In W. Taucher, M. Vogl, & P. Webinger (Eds.), *The Kurds: History, Religion, Language, Politics* (pp. 30–51). Vienna, Austria: Austrian Federal Ministry of the Interior.

Sheyholislami, J., Hassanpour, A., & Skutnabb-Kangas, T. (Eds.). (2012). *The Kurdish Linguistic Landscape: Vitality, Linguicide and Resistance*. Special issue of *International Journal of the Sociology of Language,* vol. 2012, no. 217.

Thackston, W. M. (n.d.). *Kurmanji Kurdish—A Reference Grammar with Selected Readings*. http://www.fas.harvard.edu/~iranian/Kurmanji/kurmanji_1_grammar.pdf

Thackston, W. M. (n.d.). *Sorani Kurdish—A Reference Grammar with Selected Readings*. Accessed April 10, 2016. http://www.fas.harvard.edu/~iranian/Sorani/sorani_1_grammar.pdf

Wahby, T. & C. J. Edmonds. (1966). *A Kurdish-English Dictionary*. Oxford: Clarendon Press.

Literature

Kurdish literature developed late compared to that of other nations, has suffered from bans and obstacles, and is divided between several regions and alphabets (the Latin alphabet in Turkish Kurdistan and Syrian Kurdistan, an adapted version of the Persian-Arabic alphabet in Iraqi and Iranian Kurdistan, and the Cyrillic alphabet is also used in the former Soviet Union [FSU]). It has not developed at an even pace across the Middle East and Caucasus, and it is necessary to divide it into regions as well as periods.

The Kurdish homelands are divided between four sovereign countries, and prolonged bans and censorship in all regions have negatively influenced the development of the Kurdish language. Much later than Kurmanji, literary works in Sorani appeared in the late 18th and early 19th centuries. However, lengthy interruptions have often occurred for both main dialects. Before the 20th century, the Kurdish language was mainly a means of social communication. The dominance of the Kurdish oral tradition, the supremacy of the languages of those who ruled Kurdish areas, and the political obstacles confronting the Kurds by the late 19th/early 20th century have also affected the development of Kurdish literature.

Studies and anthologies of Kurdish literature mostly concentrate on one or two regions. This may be partly because of practical and methodological concerns, as the varying contexts and influences and the changing sociopolitical circumstances of each region have produced various branches of literature, creating additional challenges.

Sociopolitical circumstances deprived Kurds of the conditions for creating their own written literature for centuries, and knowledge of the historical development of Kurdish literature is inadequate due to lack of sources. This has led to contradictory opinions regarding the first Kurdish written text. According to MacKenzie (1959), it is a written stanza using the Armenian alphabet in the early 15th century, an idea first put forward by Georgian researcher Akaki Shanidze in 1938. Some scholars claim that the first Kurdish texts were produced before the Islamic period and that Kurdish and Median, an ancient Iranian language, are the same. This is supported by historians who consider Medes the ancestors of the Kurds because of some language similarities. There is also lack of clarity about the dates of the birth and death of Kurdish classical poets, and some of their works are untraceable.

Kurdish poets are recorded as early as the 13th century, but they wrote their works mainly on theology, astronomy, and philology in the dominant language of their rulers. For instance, Kurdish historians and biographers such as Ibn al-Athir (d. 1233) and Ibn Khallikan (d. 1282) and the geographer and historian Abu al-Fida (d. 1331) wrote in Arabic. Idris Hakim Bidlisi (d. 1520) wrote the first history of the Ottoman dynasties, *Hasht Bahasht* (The Eight Paradises), in Persian. Sharaf Khan, the ruler of Bitlis principality, wrote *Sharafname* (1596), a history of the Kurdish principalities covering five centuries, also in Persian. Even much later, works were written in other languages by Kurdish mollas (scholars educated on Islamic theology). For example, Sheikh Marifi Node Barzinji (1733–1838) is the author of 46 works in Arabic and Persian, though he also wrote one Arabic-Kurdish glossary containing only a few hundred words. Many Kurdish writers wrote in the languages of their sovereign states. Today, Kurdish writers are still sometimes obliged, or prefer, to write in the official languages of the state.

Alexander Jaba's writings in 1860, based on those of Mahmud Bazîdî, seem to provide the earliest data regarding Kurdish literary history. However, MacKenzie (1959) argued that certain information based on Bazîdî's narrations in Jaba's writings is inaccurate, and therefore it is unsafe to rely on his narrative (Kreyenbroek, 2005). Amin Faizi's (1860–1923) *Anuman-i Adiban* (The Assembly of Writers) written in 1920 in Istanbul depicts the lives of certain Kurdish poets with extracts from their poetry. Refik Hilmi's *Shi'r û Adabat-i Kurdi* (Kurdish Poetry and Literature) (vol. 1, 1941; vol. 2, 1956), a work of literary criticism, contains biographical data and depictions of different periods in Kurdish literature. Alaaddin Sajjadi's *Meezhu-y Adab-i Kurdî* (Kurdish Literary History), written in Baghdad, studies 24 poets, including writings on the Kurdish epic tradition, mythology, and journalism. Izaddin Mustafa Resul's doctoral thesis on Kurdish poetry (particularly the poetry and lives of poets such as Feqiyê Teyran, Ali Bardaşani, and Bakhtiar Zewar) from a Marxist point of view, written in Arabic, was translated in 1968 in Beirut. Sahiq Baha Ud-Din Amedi's work *Hozanvanet Kurd* (Kurdish Poets), written in Baghdad in 1980, contains biographies and poems of 19 Kurdish poets writing in Kurmanji. Qenate Kurdoev's *Tarix-a Edebiyata Kurdi* (The History of Kurdish Literature) was published in Stockholm in 1980. The novelist Mehmed Uzun's *Destpêka Edebiyata Kurdî* (An Introduction to Kurdish Literature, 1992) and *Antolojiya Edebiyata Kurdî I–II* (The Anthology of Kurdish Literature, 1995), published in Sweden, offer a restricted background to Kurdish literature, particularly contemporary work.

Oral Traditions

Many epics handed down by oral tradition over several centuries before they appeared in written form are difficult or impossible to date. They usually concentrate on love, war, and loyalty, with some of the best known being *Memê Alan* (Meme Alan), *Siyabend û Xecê* (Siyabend and Khaje), *Dimdim*, (Dimdim), *Zembîlfiroş* (The Basket-seller), and *Binevşa Narîn û Cembeliyê Hekkarê* (Binevşa Narin and Cembeli of Hakkari).

Memê Alan is often regarded as the Kurds' national epic. It is completely fictional and unrelated to history and exists in various versions. The protagonists are Mem, the son of the Kurdish Amir, and Zin, daughter of the Emir of Botan, and the story presents a panorama of Kurdish social relations, traditions, and customs. The work by Ahmad Khani (in Kurdish Ehmedê Xanî) entitled *Mem û Zîn* (Mem and Zin) tells the story of two lovers separated by factors beyond their control. Xanî bases his historical and geopolitical analysis on the narrative of the "methnewi" (a type of poem consisting of rhyming couplets) of *Memê Alan*. Considered the first written work, it reveals the sense that the Kurds were culturally distinct people.

Classical Age

For several centuries, Kurdish literature was restricted to verse. The starting date of classical Kurdish poetry differs between dialects, so one must distinguish between the Kurmanji, Sorani, and Gorani (or Hawramî) schools.

Jazira (Cizre in Turkish), the capital of Botan, had a significant role in the establishment of the Kurmanji school. Among the earliest leading poets and lyricists writing in Kurmanji are Melayê Bateyî (1414–1495), Elî Herîrî (1425–1495), Melayê Cizîrî (1566–1640), Feqiyê Teyran (1590–1660), and Ehmedê Xanî (1651–1707). Although they received their education in Arabic and Persian at "Medrese" (*madrasah*, Islamic theological school), they expressed themselves through their poetry using their mother tongue. Being also well versed in Sufism, they made great contributions toward developing Kurdish into the language of intellectuals.

Arguably, the greatest of these was Cizîrî, author of more than 2,000 verses, considered the founder of the Kurmanji school and known for his *Diwan* (collected poetry). Bateyî wrote his first work entitled *Mewlûd* (Mawlid) containing proses on the birth and life of prophet Mohammed in Kurdish. Teyran (1590–1660), a student of Cizîrî and the first Kurdish poet known to have used the Mesnevi (couplet) form in his poetry, wrote *Sêxê Senan* (The Sheikh of Senan), *Qiseya Bersiyawî* (The Story of Bersiyay), and *Qexlê Hespê Reş* (The Story of the Black Horse). He is considered to be the first to have written prose in Kurdish. According to Mehmed Uzun (2007 [1992]), Teyran developed his poetic style in accordance with Cizîrî; however, he avoided Islamic mysticism, instead using the language of the common people. Xanî is of great significance (see earlier). The methnewi, in the narrative of which Xanî puts his historical and geopolitical analysis, has been regarded as the symbol of the Kurdish language and interpreted as an expression of nationalist sentiments. He also wrote *Nûbihara Biçûkan* (The New Spring of Children), a rhymed Arabic-Kurdish word list for the use of Kurdish students, and religious works such as *Aqîdeya Îslamê* (Basics of Islam) and *Eqîdeya Îmanê* (The Path of Faith), containing 73-couplet long lyrical poetry (Shakely, 1992 [1983]).

Gorani, the dialect mainly identified with the Ahl-Haqq people (a heterodox religious group), can be classified as the folk poetry of the region influenced by Sufi literature and local poetic tradition. Under the rule of Ardalan principality (1160–1867), Sina (Senne, *Sanandaj* in Persian), now on the border of Iranian Kurdistan, became an important place for Kurdish classical poets writing in the Goran (also pronounced *Guran*) dialect, which is considered to have appeared 1,000 years ago (Minorsky, 1943: 77). Most of the poets composed their verses in Hawrami, a variant of Gorani. Yusuf Yaska (also known as Yusuf Zaka, 1636–?) is representative of the Hawrami school, writing ghazals (a lyric poem with fixed number of verses and repeated rhyme). Khana Qobadi (1700–1759), also writing in the Ardalan principality in Hawrami, wrote a Gorani version of *Khosrow and Shirin* (written by Persian poet Nizami Ganjavi). Mastura Ardalan (1805–1848, also known as Mah Sharaf Khanum Kurdistani), the wife of Khasraw Khani Ardalan, ruler of the principality, and believed to be the only woman historiographer until the end of the 19th century, was known for her Persian poems, and the fact that she also wrote in Gorani was discovered much later. One of her best-known works, a collection of poetry written in Persian and Kurdish, was *Divan-i Masturah Kurdistani*. Sheikh Ahmet Takti Marduki (1617–1692), Sheikh Mustafa Besarani (1641–1702), and Ahmet Begi Komasi (1796–1877) were among other poets mostly writing in Hawrami. Another renowned literary work was a Gorani version of *Leyla and Mecnun* by Molla Bolad Khan (1885).

Mawlawi Tawgozi (pen name *Madum*, also known as *Mewlewi Kurds*, 1806–1882), the last and most well-known member of the Gorani school, using the traditional Hija meters, particularly the 10-syllable form, gave a realistic and lively picture of the natural scenery of Kurdistan (Karim, 1985: 49). One of his most well-known works is a collection of poems written in both Sorani and Gorani. When Ardalan fell under the Qajar dynasty from 1867, literary work in Gorani ceased.

Abdulrahman Pasha (1797–1855) and the Nalî school of poetry contributed a lot to the use of Sorani as a literary language. Molla Kedri Ahmad Sawaysi Mikail (1797–1870), known as Nalî, was the founder of the Nalî school, which developed during the 19th century under the Baban emirate (1649–1850). Nalî himself was known for his lyrical poetry praising the rulers in mystical verses. His relative Abdul-Rehman Begi Saheb-Qiran, known as Salem, used the Ghazal form, Qasidas, and the Hazaj meter (a quantitative verse metric used in epic poetry) and contributed a lot to Sorani poetry. Certain epistolary poems were exchanged between Salem and Nalî that enabled readers to understand the destructive results of the occupation of Sulaymaniyah by the Ottomans. Wafayi (1836–1892), Kurdî (1812–1850), and Mahwi (1830–1909) are other renowned Sorani school poets. Sheikh Reza Talabani (1842–1910), a Qadiriya sheikh in Kirkuk from the Nalî school, lived in Istanbul for several years and introduced satire to Kurdish poetry. Nalî, Talabanî, and Salem utilized the sense of nostalgia, grief, and loss related to the Baban dynasty and glorification of the dynasty, which was defeated by the Ottomans, in their poetry.

The last Baban prince left Sulaymaniyah in 1850, so Sorani poetry left Sulaymaniyah and continued in Kirkuk and Persian Kurdistan. Hacî Qadirî Koyî (in English, Haji Qadir Koyi, 1817–1897), influenced by the poetic themes utilized by the Nalî school, is one of the well-known representatives of poets being obliged to leave their homeland. His advocacy of Kurdish language and idealization of Kurdish emirates constituted a broader nationalism than other Nalî school poets, who longed for the glory of the Baban dynasty. Koyî, who wrote in Sorani and spent his last years in Istanbul, even urged Kurds to use modern tools such as newspapers and magazines for mass communication. He became familiar with the Kurmanji language and literature and was also familiar with the nationalist struggle.

Newspapers

Kurdish literature before the 20th century was mostly poetry. During the 20th century, due to the rise of newspaper publication, the efforts of the Kurdish intelligentsia, and changing sociopolitical circumstances, Kurdish prose literature emerged in Kurmanji and Sorani. Until World War I and the partition of Ottoman Kurdistan, most national movements were led by Kurmanji speakers, and this is visible in the first Kurdish journals and periodicals, which were issued by Kurdish organizations and groups affected by emerging nationalist sentiments within other nations. They also led to the development of modern Kurdish literature. Members of the Kurdish *Rozhaki-Badirkhanid* (princely house), including Thurayya (Sureya) Bedir Khan (1883–1938), Jaladet Ali Bedir Khan (1893–1951), and Kamuran Ali Bedir Khan (1895–1978), had developed a Latin-based alphabet for Kurmanji, and the Bedir Khan brothers used this alphabet for the first time to publish the journals *Hawar* (Cry) (1932–1943) and *Ronahî* (Light) (1935), which they smuggled out of French Syria into Turkey. Cegerxwin (1903–1984), Osman Sabri (1905–1993), Qedri Can (1911–1972), and Nureddin Zaza (1919–1988) were also members of this Hawar school. Kamuran Ali Bedir Khan then published *Roja Nû* (New Day) (1943–1946), which contributed further to the development of Kurdish literature in Kurmanji dialect within Kurdish society.

Political organizations were very important in disseminating Kurdish literary works at the beginning of the 20th century. The purpose of such journals was to improve Kurdish language and literature and publish Kurdish classics, as well as to promote Kurdish history and the question of Kurdishness. Organizations included Kurdistan Azm-i Kavi Cemiyeti (Society for a Strong Kurdistan); Kürd Teavun ve Terakki Cemiyeti (Kurdish Society for Cooperation and Progress); Kürd Talebe Hêvî Cemiyeti (Kurdish Hope Student Organization); Kürd Tamim-i Maarif Cemiyeti (The Organization to Spread Kurdish Publishing and Sciences); and Kürdistan Teali Cemiyeti (Society for the Advancement of Kurdistan): they published journals and newspapers in Kurdish and Ottoman Turkish, such as *Kürdistan* (Kurdistan), *Kürt Teavün ve Terakki Gazetesi* (Kurdish Solidarity and Progress Newspaper), *Rojî Kurd* (Kurdish Day), *Hetawî Kurd* (Kurdish Sun), and *Jîn* (Life), all of which gave much space to Kurdish literature.

The first Kurdish periodical, *Kurdistan* (1898–1902), constituted a very significant attempt to develop Kurdish in written form. With its appearance, interest in prose writing increased. The first issue was published in Cairo by Miqdad Midhat Bedir Khan, whose brother Abdurrahman Bedir Khan Beg took over responsibility for it after six issues. It moved to Geneva, London, and Folkestone, appearing in both Kurdish and Turkish and focusing on cultural, literary, and political issues. The monthly *Rojî Kurd*, first published by the political group Hêvî in Istanbul in 1913 in both Turkish and Kurdish, had four issues, and contributed to the Kurdish cultural revival. Articles were mainly aimed at facilitating learning Kurdish language, history, and traditions. For instance, *Çîrok* (Story), the first Kurdish short story written by Fuadê Temo, founder of *Kürd Talebe Hêvî Cemiyeti* (Kurdish Hope Student Organization), was published in *Rojî Kurd*.

Jîn was the semi-official newspaper of the Society for the Advancement of Kurdistan (*Kürdistan Teali Cemiyeti, KTC*), regarded as the first Kurdish nationalist organization. Portraying the nationalist character of the organization, it appeared in 1918–1919 and had 25 issues. *Mem u Zin* was published by the Society for the Dissemination of Kurdish Education and Publication (*Kürd Tamim-i Maarif ve Neşriyat Cemiyeti*, KTMNC) in 1919, the agenda of which included the development of the Kurdish language and promotion of education in Kurdish. So the late 19th century and first half of the 20th gave rise to many Kurdish journal and periodical publications through the initiatives of Kurdish intelligentsia, leading to the development and publication of Kurdish prose.

Soviet Armenia

The first modern story based on *Mem û Zîn* was an 1856 rewrite by Mele Mehmûdê Bazîdî (1797–1858), a religious cleric, historian, and writer, who had a "madrasa" background, like many other Kurdish poets. The only work by Bazîdî that exists today is *Adab û Nasîna Kurdan* (Kurdish Customs and Traditions), written in Kurmanji. He also translated *Sharafname* from Persian into Kurmanji and wrote a history of the Kurds, *Kîtaba tewarîxe cedîdê Kurdistan*, the original of which is lost, but was translated into French by Alexander Jaba.

There are many reasons why the Kurdish novel emerged in the 20th century but not earlier. The sociopolitical conditions of Kurdistan, the supremacy of prose and oral traditions over prose writing in Kurdish, and the conservative nature of Kurdish society can be some of these reasons. The fragmentation of the Kurdish nation and the difficulties arising from social and political conditions meant that the various branches of Kurdish literature have developed separately from one another.

The Soviet period was crucial for the foundation of modern Kurdish literature because the Kurds of Armenia paved the way for the creation of the standardized Kurdish language and the emergence and development of Kurdish literature, in particular, novelistic discourse. Kurdish migration into the Caucasus took place mainly at the end of the 19th century and early 20th century from the Ottoman Empire into Caucasian Armenia fleeing persecution. During the 1920s, Soviet policy on minorities encouraged Kurds to play a leading role in the spread of literacy among Soviet Kurds to enhance their education and to undertake literary activities. The All-Union national minorities policy (i.e., the policy of "*korenizatsiia*" or indigenization) expanded after 1932, which had a positive effect, notably on the Kurds in Soviet Armenia. They established, for instance, the first Kurdish radio broadcast and the first Kurdish newspaper. Soviet nationality policy was part of its modernization aiming to create a literate society by turning the semi-nomadic Kurdish peasants into modern citizens. The creation of a literary language as an instrument of social progress and communist education formed part of the *korenizatsiia* policy. Literacy led to the emergence of a striking number of Kurdish writers engaged in literary and sociopolitical activities. The first schoolbooks in Kurdish were produced and first steps toward modern prose writing were taken. The first

Kurdish novel, *Şivanê Kurmanca* (The Kurdish Shepherd), was written in Kurmanji in Yerevan in 1935 by Erebê Şemo (1898–1978). Between 1937 and 1955, Stalin's policies silenced Kurdish literature, but it re-emerged during Khrushchev's de-Stalinization process.

Thus, the mid-1950s and 1960s saw significant steps toward novel writing, and Şemo was followed by other Yezidi Kurdish authors, most notably Eliyê Evdi-rehman. His *Xatê Xanîm* (Lady Xate, 1959) and *Dê* (Mother, 1965); Heciyê Cindî's *Hewarî* (Cry, 1967) and *Gundê Mêrxasa* (The Village of the Courageous, 1968); and Seîdê Îbo's *Kurdên Rêwî* (Traveler Kurds, 1981) are among early Kurdish novels published in the USSR. However, the independence of Armenia in 1991, the lack of funding for educational materials and specialists to teach Kurdish, and the impact of the war between Armenia and Azerbaijan over Nagorno-Karabakh in 1991 to 1993 led to a decline in Kurdish literary publication. Furthermore, the Armenian government has always favored the Yezidis over the Muslim Kurds.

Iraqi Kurdistan

Even Kurds in Iraqi Kurdistan, more at liberty in terms of linguistic and cultural rights compared to other Kurdish regions, suffered for decades under the Ba'th regime and were excluded from the political process.

Following the 2003 Gulf War, Kurds seized the opportunity to implement their aspirations for an autonomous state, leading to a striking increase in the development of the Kurdish language and Kurdish publications. Earlier, Iraq under the British mandate granted limited cultural and linguistic rights to the Kurds, which led to a flourishing of Kurdish literature. The first printing press in Kurdistan was set up in Sulaymaniyah in 1919 by Major Ely B. Soane (Blau, 2010), and the use of Sorani as a written language was promoted during the early British mandate. In the late 1920s, publications in Sorani Kurdish, especially translations of Western works, started to appear.

Tawfeq Mahmoud Hamza, pen name Piramerd (1867–1950), was a literary figure and journalist who contributed to the development of Sorani through initiating the Kurdish newspaper *Jiyan* and was among those who established the first private Kurdish school in Kurdistan, "Partukxane-i Zanisti" (Knowledge School). Apart from several translations from Turkish and Hawrami, he published a wide range of works, including a collection of Kurdish folklore (*Galte û Gep*, 1947) and poems and history articles such as the history of Baban principality and Jaff tribes, in the 1930s and 1940s.

Abdullah Goran (1904–1962), known as the father of modern Kurdish literature, allowed no Arabic influence in his poetry and applied Kurdish cultural themes and folkloric traditions through the use of Kurdish folksong patterns and free verse rather than Arabic meter. He is mostly known for two 1950 collections of poetry, *Firmêsk û Huner* (Tears and Art) and *Beheştî Yadigar* (Heaven and Memory). Ahmad Mukhtar Jaf (1896–1935) and Bakhtiar Zewar (1875–1948) are significant poets from the first half of the century creating their own meters and forms. Bêkas and his son Sherko Bêkas, Kamran Mokri, and Kakay Fallah are other significant poets from the post-1940s period, when free verse became very widespread in classical Sorani poetry.

The emergence of newspapers and magazines in the 1920s played a significant role in the development of Sorani prose. These included *Pêşkewtin* (Progress, 1920–1922; 118 issues), *Bangî Kurdistan* (The Call of Kurdistan, 1922; 14 issues), *Rojî Kurdistan* (The Day of Kurdistan, 1922–1923; 15 issues), *Diyarî Kurdistan* (The Gift of Kurdistan, 1925–1926; 16 issues), *Jiyanewe* (Rebirth, 1924–1926; 56 issues) *Jîyan* (Life, 1926–1938; 556 issues), *Gelawêj* (Sirius, 1939–1949), *Jîn* (Life, 1939–1963; more than 1,000 issues), and *Hîwa* (Hope, 1957–1963). They all published Sorani prose, particularly short stories, generally quite political, and critical of British colonial policy, such as "Le Xewi Me" (In Our Dream) by Ceil Saib (1887–1959), published in *Jiyanewe*.

Other significant prose works include "*Ademîzad le sayey derebegî*" (Man in Feudal Society, 1945) by Hosayn Hozni Mokriāni (1893–1947); a short story entitled "Meseley Wijdan" (A Matter of Conscience) written in 1926 but published in 1970; and Shakir Fettah (1914–1988) added a new voice with children's stories such as "Hawrêy Minal" (Children's Friends) in 1948 and "Tîshk" (Sunbeam) in 1947, and "Afretî Kurd" (Kurdish Woman), 1958, concentrating on the liberation of women. Muherrem Mihemmed Emîn (1921–1980) published "Mem Xomer" (Uncle Omar) in 1945 and "Rêgay Azadî" (Road to Freedom) in 1959. Kurdish children literature emerged almost 75 years ago, and authors such as Zevar, Bekas, Piramerd, and Goran wrote poems for children influenced by folklore for children, but their poetry, combining realistic and romantic styles, was also addressed to adult readers (Grondahl & Kadir, 2003: 13).

Subsequently, despite gas warfare, deportations, and other oppressive policies between 1958 and 1960 and between 1970 and 1974, Kurds in Iraq are linguistically and culturally in a better position than those in other regions (Skutnabb-Kangas & Sertaç, 1994: 369). Although the publication of Sorani literary works was disrupted by the new Iraqi governments between 1959 and 1961, the Kurdish language leapt forward with the demands of the Kurdish Democratic Party aiming to the use of Kurdish at school and universities, and the Directorate General of Kurdish Studies was founded as part of the Ministry of Education, a bachelor's program in Kurdish language was initiated at the University of Baghdad's Kurdish academy, and Kurdish broadcasting was introduced during the 1960s. The relationship between Kurdish groups and the Iraqi government was strained, but with the peace agreement between the Kurdish opposition and Iraqi government in 1970, Kurds were granted autonomy, with Kurdish recognized as an official language, leading to the development of literature and the standardization of Sorani. However, very soon after the signing of the Algiers Agreement in 1975, relations deteriorated again. The important literary output between the 1950s and the 1991 Gulf War included *Zari Kurmanji* (a literary and historical magazine) published by Husein Huzni and *Akhbar-a Harb*, a magazine associated with Tawfiq Wahbi (1891–1982), who served as a colonel in the Ottoman Empire and later as a member of the Iraqi army and was also a philologist working on Kurdish codification and orthography. He attempted to apply the Latin alphabet for use with Kurdish but this was not allowed by the Iraqi government for religious reasons. Ahmad Hardi (1922–2006) had a great influence on modern Kurdish poetry in the 1950s and was also a leading figure in the Kurdish liberation movement. He had to move to Iran in 1975 and then moved to the UK in 1993. Muhamad Salih Dilan (1927–1990), poet and maqam singer, wrote many of his poems in prison between 1947 and 1966. His collection "Diwanî Dilan" was published in 1987.

From the 1970s, Latif Halmet (1947–), Rafîq Sabir (1950–), and Abdulla Pashew (1946–), belonging to the post-Abdulla Goran generation of modernists, have been writing free verse and developing their literature in the context of the sociopolitical condition of Iraqi Kurdistan, which is reflected in their poetry.

Sherko Bekas (1940–2013) was the son of a pioneer of modern Kurdish poetry, Fayak Bekas. He was forced into exile between 1986 and 1992, served as a minister of information in the Kurdistan Regional Government for a year (1992–1993), and was president of Sardam publishing house. He has a distinct position in Kurdish modern poetry for breaking with the standard rhymes and introducing a freeform style called *rwanga* (vision), and he established the Rwanga school with other poets Jamal Sharbaxeri, Husein Arif, and Celal Mirza Kerim in Baghdad. This school, aiming to establish modernist poetry like Goran's school, added new dimensions with a tendency toward realism and a concern with the liberation movement (Naderi, 2011: 12). He was a patriotic and nationalist literary figure whose lyrics have become the anthem for the Patriotic Union of Kurdistan (PUK). He has published more than 30 books, and his works have been translated into many languages. Significant post-1990s literary periodicals in Iraqi Kurdistan include *Ayanda*, run by Dilshad Abdula, and *Raman*, run by Azad Abdul-Wahid.

Although even the pioneer Kurdish woman poet Mestûrey Kurdistanî (1805–1847) contributed with her literary works in the 19th century and other two Kurdish women poets, Cîhan Ara (1858–1911) and Mîhreban (1858–1905) followed, literary works of Kurdish women have been discontinuous throughout the 20th century due to the patriarchal nature of Kurdish society, bans on Kurdish language, and economic instability. The most visible and widely read Kurdish women are Pakîze Refîq Hilmî (b.1924); Xanim Resul Ehmed (b.1949), whose pen name is (Erxewan); Xurşîde Baban (b.1940); Firîşte Xan (b.1929); and Kurdistan Mukiryanî (b.1948), all of whom published their poetry in the Kurdish newspapers and magazines. Kurdish women authors and poets have become more visible since the 1990s. Najiba Ahmad (1954–), Kajal Ahmad (1967–), Mahabad Qaradagi (1966–), and many other new-generation Kurdish women authors and translators have contributed to the development of contemporary literature in Iraqi Kurdistan. Although in 1995 only 3 percent of books published were by women, there have been over 100 in the last few years (still far less than the number published by men). However, the number of publications by Kurdish women in other regions is much lower. Abdulla Pashew (1946), who is known as the founder of Resistance Literature, apart from his seven poetry collections is also known for his translations of the works of Walt Whitman and Pushkin into Kurdish.

Despite the emergence of rich Sorani prose since the 1920s, the first Sorani novel, *Janî Gel* (The Suffering of the People) was not written until 1973, by Ibrahim Ahmad, who was also founder of the Kurdish literary journal, *Gelawêj*. Bakhtiyar Ali (1960), who has lived in Germany since 1996, is another prominent and influential Sorani prose writer. Apart from his 11 magical realist novels, he has several collections of poetry. Similarly, Farhad Pirbal (1961) has been involved with literary activities as a writer, poet, and academic. Delshad Abdula and Karim Dashti (1955), like the generation of Ali and Pirbal, reflect disillusionment with the political and social atmosphere in their surrealist modern poetry. In terms of short story and novelistic discourse since the 1980s, Hisen Arif, Sherzad Hesen, Ismail Mihemed Emin, Serhed Tofiq Meruf, Hesen Caf, Abdulla Seraj, Kerim Arif, Ehmed Resul, Mihemed Mukri, Selah Jelal, and Hekim Kakeweys are the prominent Kurdish writers, all concentrating particularly on sociopolitical conditions in Kurdistan along with historical events.

After decades of political conflicts interrupting Kurdish publication, the universities of Baghdad and Sulemaniyah have Kurdish-language departments with high student enrollment. Kurdish publishing houses in Iraqi Kurdistan still face many political and, particularly economic, obstacles to their activity, some of which are related to official censorship.

Turkish Kurdistan

Prohibitions and political restrictions imposed by the Turkish Republic have hindered the presence and growth of Kurdish literature in Turkish Kurdistan (Galip, 2015: 77). Starting with the foundation of Turkish Republic in 1923, Turkish became the only language for all citizens to speak. Through severe regulations and prohibitions, Kurdish language was banned from public use, which led to bans on publications and printing in Kurdish until Turgut Özal, president of Turkey (1989–1993), lifted the ban in 1991.

The military coups of 1960, 1971, and 1980 brought stricter linguistic polices to reinforce the hegemony of the Turkish language and maintain Turkish unity, leading to discrimination against Kurdish along with other minority languages.

Due to the bans and possible prosecutions, from the beginning of 20th century until 1990s very few literary works were published, including a poetry anthology *Kimil* (Aelia, 1962) and a play entitled *Birîna Reş* (Black Wound, 1965) by Musa Anter and a short story compilation entitled *Meyro* (Meyro, 1979) by Mehmet Emin Bozarslan. According to Malmisanij (2006: 19), ". . . in the period 1923–1980 not more than 20 Kurdish books were published in Turkey." The monthly literary journal *Tîrej* (Light Beam, 1979–1980) lasted for only four issues but is significant as the first journal to be published in Turkish Kurdistan after 1923. Despite the lifting of bans on Kurdish printing and publication, the linguistic hegemony of the Turkish language was able to suppress Kurdish language until the beginning of 2000s. Only two literary works were published during 1990s. Îhsan Colemergî wrote *Cembelî Kurê Mîrê Hekarî* (Cembelî, Son of the Mir of Hakkari) in 1992 but was only able to publish it in Sweden in 1995, and Îbrahîm Seydo Aydogan's *Reş û Spî* (Black and White) was published in Istanbul by Elma in 1999.

Turkey has been forced to fulfill the Copenhagen criteria per the EU membership conditions after its official candidacy for the EU was established in 1999, which imposed a dynamic process of political reform and democratization. AKP (Adalet ve Kalkınma Partisi/Justice and Development Party), founded in 2001, a center-right with Islamic leanings, became the ruling party in the Turkish parliament in 2002 and made some language reforms along with EU membership negotiation regulations. In 2004, a regulation concerning radio and television broadcasts that contained different languages and dialects came into force regarding the Turkish national broadcasting channel (TRT: *Türkiye Radyo ve Televizyon Kurumu*).

Current Turkish language policy still places constraints on educational and linguistic rights. Nevertheless, Malmisanij's research reveals that there has been a considerable increase in Kurdish book publishing. As he notes "in 2000 more than 40 Kurdish publishing houses were established in Turkey" (2006: 26); however, nearly 50 percent of the output (305 books) came from eight publishers, with Diyarbakir and Istanbul being the main centers. The campaigns on the development of Kurdish language, opening of Kurdish language courses, and offering Kurdish at the BA and MA level in some universities (Mardin Artuklu University and Mus Alparslan University) have led to the revitalization of Kurdish in the 21st century, which have also resulted in large number of publications in the Kurdish language. Even Kurdish writers living in Europe have started to prefer their works be published in Istanbul and Diyarbakir, which can considered two central cities for Kurdish publications.

Writing fiction in Kurdish became very common among the young generation of Kurds, with people mostly involved in some sort of literary occupation; some studied literature as undergraduates, others are editors at publishing houses, making them aware of changes in the contemporary literary scene. They seek imaginative devices through which they narrate their stories, such as completely fictional settings and characters, or the use of journals and letters throughout the narration. Political conditions in Turkish Kurdistan intruding on publications in Kurdish or about Kurds also compel them to adopt indirect and symbolic styles to combat censorship.

Ince Memed

Yaser Kemal, a Turkish novelist of Kurdish descent, wrote *Ince Memed* in 1955. This is the story of a young Kurd who rebels against the feudalistic agha and becomes a hero and supporter of his people. Kemal wrote four sequels, many of which were translated in over 30 languages. The literary figure of Ince Memed became a legendary hero and symbol in the Kurdish struggle against the old Kurdish oligarchies and suppressive Turkish regime. The story was spread through public readings in coffeehouses and recounted by traveling bards. Yaser Kemal also remained immensely popular in his home country even after his death in 2015.

Berken Bereh (1954–), Arjen Arî (1956–2012), Dost Çiyayî (1972–2003), Welat Dilken, and Rênas Jiyan are significant literary figures representing contemporary Kurmanji poetry. Lokman Ayabe, Şener Özmen, Edip Polat, Yunus Eroğlu, Yaqup Tilermenî, Ronî War, Omer Dilsoz, Adil Zozani, Hesen Duseyin Deniz, and Mîran Janbar are some of the leading novelists. Roşan Lezgîn (1964) writes short stories in both Zazaki and Kurmanji dialects. Female short story writer Lorîn Doğan (b. 1975) has two books: *Kirasê Teng* (Tight Dress, 2007) and *Destên Vala* (Empty Hands, 2012); however, Gulgeş Deryaspî, with her three novels, is the only female novelist currently writing. The number of Kurdish literary critics has also increased, and Ayhan Geverî, Remezan Alan, Azad Zal, Mehmet Öncü, and Kawa Nemir have published a number of literary articles and critiques in Kurdish journals. Literary and cultural magazines and journals, including *Newepel* (New Page), *Şewçila* (Night Lamp), *Nûbihar* (New Spring), *Wejê û Rexne* (Literature and Criticism), and *Tîroj* (Gleam), have contributed to disseminating the writings of both well-known and new authors.

From the 1990s, we also see the emergence and development of Kurdish theater in Turkey with the works of the Mesopotamia Cultural Centre (Mezapotamya Kültür Merkezi, MKM), Seyr-i Mesel Theatre, Destar Theatre (2008), and Şermola Performance (2010).

The Kurdish Writers Association was established in 2004 in Diyarbakir, in Batman in 2015, and in Mardin in 2016, and the Kurdish Literature and Publishing Network (KurdîLit) was established in June 2016 with the collaboration of Lîs publishing house and Literature Across Frontiers. The annual Amed Book Fair organizes panels on literature with the support of Diyarbakir municipality and Kurdish publishing houses based in Turkey and Turkish Kurdistan.

Literary output in Zazaki is much less than that in the Gorani, Kurmanji, and Sorani dialects. Although Zazaki is the most used language in Turkey after Turkish and Kurmanji, Zazaki is categorized as an endangered dialect. Zazaki has been preserved orally for centuries, though the number of speakers has decreased and, due to the lack of legal status and education, it is also less used in social life. There are currently believed to be around 300 books in Zazaki, most of which were published in the last 30 years.

The first is the mawlid (texts on the birth and life of Prophet Mohammed) entitled "Mewludê Kirdî" (Kurdish Mawlid) by Molla Ehmedê Xasi, written in 1892 and published in 1899. The next is another mawlid called "Bîyîşê Pêxamberî" (Life of Prophet) by Siverek Mufti Osman Efendi, published in Damascus in 1933. In 1963 the journal *Roja Newe* published two articles in Zazaki.

Zazaki written text disappeared until the 1980s, when certain small pieces (poems, short stories, and folkloric texts) appeared in newspapers and journals such as *Tirêj* (1979–1981), *Riya Azadî* (1975), *Roja Welat* (1977), and *Devrimci Demokrat Genclik* (1978). It became more prevalent in the 1990s in Europe, initiated by Kurdish migrant intelligentsia through journals such as *Armanc*, *Hêvî*, *Çira*, and *Berbang*. A number of Zaza exiled speakers established the Vate Study Group in 1996 and started publishing a journal, *Vate*, in 1997 in Stockholm. In addition, Vate publishing house, established in 2003 in Istanbul, became the main publisher of Zazaki texts.

Malmîsanij and Deniz Gündüz, researchers and linguists, contributed greatly to the development of Zazaki. Murad Canşad, İhsan Espar, Munzur Çem, Roşan Lezgîn, Huseyîn Karakaş, Jêhatî Zengelan, Alî Aydin Çîçek, Bedrîye Topaç, Lorîn Demirel, Îsmet Bor, Denîz Gunduz, Burçîn Bor, Hikmet Çalagan, and Hesen Dilawer Zazaki are short story and novel writers whose works have mainly been published by Vate, Avesta, and Perî (Istanbul) and Roşna (Diyarbakir).

Zazaki was first broadcast for half an hour every week on TRT 3, one of the Turkish state channels, in 2004, and broadcasting slightly increased with the arrival of state channel TRT 6 (now TRT Kurdî) in 2009. There are now Turkish universities (Bingol and Tunceli) supporting academic work on Zazaki. But Kurdish satellite channel Stêrk TV, based in Brussels, gives little room for Zazaki.

Iranian Kurdistan

Although the Kurds in Iranian Kurdistan have had a larger degree of cultural freedom, they have been militarily suppressed, their attempts at autonomy have been crushed, and they have been deprived of participation in the political process. Although the Republic of Mahabad existed for only a very short period, it enabled the publication of various newspapers and journals. Hesen Qizilci (1914–1984), who was involved with the establishment of the republic, had to live in Iraqi Kurdistan after its collapse until 1979 and was arrested in 1984. Hejar and Hemin were two poets who contributed much in this period. Hemin Mukriyani (1921–1986) had to flee Iraq for political reasons. He went to Iran and settled in Baghdad for several years. While Mukriyani regularly contributed to various newspapers, he also established a publishing house (Salahaddin Eyyubi) in Urmia and served as an editor of the Kurdish journal Sirwe (Breeze) until he died. A collection of his articles, entitled Paşerokî Mamoste, was published in Mahabad in 1983. Hejar (1920–1991) was also involved in the Kurdish movement led by Qazi Mohamed in 1947, which resulted in years of exile in several Middle Eastern countries, before he returned to Iran in 1975. Apart from several poetry books, he has translated many works from Persian, Kurmanji, and Arabic into Kurdish. The Pahlavi dynasty (1925–1979) established by Reza Khan banned Kurdish cultural expression in order to eliminate the Kurdish ethnic identity. In the later Pahlavi period, there were some local broadcasts in Kurdish, and folkloric texts were published. After 1946, however, Kurdish cultural expression came under pressure, discouraging and disrupting Kurdish literature. The weekly Kurdistan (1959–1963, 205 issues), published in Tehran but only circulated outside Iran, had a significant role, focusing on Kurdish literary works.

The foundation of the Islamic Republic was a great attack against the Kurdish political movement, leading to the assassination of several Kurdish political figures. The teaching of Kurdish was not allowed by the mid-1980s. During the early 1980s, the publication of short stories and literary cultural magazines was permitted to some extent. Literary works appeared in Kurdish, and Kurdish publishing developed. Ahmad Qazi (1936–2015) was prominent in the formation and growth of the Kurdish press here. He published a collection of satirical short stories entitled *Baqabên* (Bond) in 1984. Ali Hasaniani, Qasim Moayedzada, and Sewara Ilkanizada established a literary movement parallel to that of Goran in Iraqi Kurdistan, applying the new syllabic rhythm (Naderi, 2011: 10, 11). Eta Nahai (b. 1960) is one of the most prominent Kurdish authors from Iranian Kurdistan. Despite his low output, his prose, particularly novels, is influential on the younger generation, while Ayaz Knonsyawashan, Nasrin Jafari, and Simin Chaichi represent a more sophisticated younger generation of Kurdish literature.

Although Kurdish can be studied at the universities and Kurdish publications are relatively tolerated, teaching the language is not permitted at elementary level, and it is not used in the administration of Iranian Kurdistan. Only a few TV and radio programs are in Kurdish. A number of Kurdish websites and political and cultural magazines have been shut down by Iranian government authorities. However, from 2015, through the efforts of Kurdish academics and activists, Kurdish language courses will now be offered in the high school curriculum in Kurdish regions of Iran. Also in 2015, the University of Sanandaj announced that a new Kurdish-language department would be admitting students in the next academic year. Such developments will open new paths for the development of Kurdish literature and increase the readership.

Syrian Kurdistan

There was short-term cultural and linguistic freedom in Syrian Kurdistan during the period between the two World Wars resulting from the support of minorities by the French mandate, leading other Kurdish intellectuals to move there. Kurdish language and literature were mainly developed thanks to Prince Celadet Bedir Khan (1893–1951), son of the last emir of Botan, who used the Latin alphabet for the first time to publish the journal *Hawar* (Cry) (1932–1943). Writers contributing to the Hawar school had to leave Syria after its independence following World War II. Between 1960 and the 2011 civil war, Kurds experienced forced Arabization and severe repression of their sociocultural and linguistic identity, with many even being denied Syrian citizenship, while the registration of children with Kurdish first names, cultural centers, bookshops, and similar activities were all prohibited. Due to the political obstacles, Syrian Kurds have mainly produced their literary works in Europe. Prominent Kurdish writers from Syrian Kurdistan moved to Europe, mainly Germany and Sweden, where they continued their literary production. They include Jan Dost (b. 1965), Hêlim Yûsiv (b. 1967), Keça Kurd (b. 1947), Cankurd (b. 1948), Zerdeşt Haco (b. 1950), Ehmed Huseynî, and Fawaz Hussain (b.1953). Syrian Kurdish authors published their works in Turkish Kurdistan due to better publishing conditions and Kurmanji as the common dialect. For example, Axîn Welat published her two poetry books at Avesta in Istanbul.

With the outbreak of civil war in 2011 and attacks by ISIS, Kurdish students have even been deprived of their formal education, which has only been in Arabic for over years. With the de facto rule of PYD (Partiya Yekîtiya Demokrat

---

Cegerxwin

Shexmus Hassan, also known by his pen name Cegerxwin, is one of the most important and popular Kurdish poets of the 20th century. Early on, he was engaged in political activities to further the Kurdish national cause in Syria, Iraq, and Lebanon. Concurrently, he wrote some of the most beautiful poetry that depicts the process of awakening among the Kurdish peasants, workers, and women, for example, *Ki me ez?* (Who am I?). After spending most of his life in exile, he was laid to rest in Qamishli. His works include eight volumes of collected poems.

(Democratic Union Party) over three Kurdish areas, Afrin (Êfrîn in Kurdish), Kobani, and Jazira (Cezire), the use of Kurdish at primary schools began with the introduction of voluntary teachers in 2014. However, the lack of well-qualified Kurdish teachers and materials decreases the effectiveness of the education, along with the fact that the ongoing civil war, threat of ISIS, and unstable governance have hindered the progress of Kurdish literature.

The Diaspora

The foundation of the Turkish Republic and the process of linguicide in Syria meant that from the 1960s the development of Kurmanji slowed and publishing in Kurmanji effectively ceased, being replaced by Sorani as the main dialect in terms of the number of publications and linguistic development. Since the 1980s, however, the lifting of embargoes in Turkey on writing and publishing in Kurdish and the contributions made by Kurdish migrants in Europe to publication and broadcasting have revived and reinforced the use and development of Kurmanji, returning it to where it was at the beginning of the 20th century. Kurmanji language and literature developed mainly outside Kurdistan, especially after the French mandates in Lebanon in 1943 and Syria in 1945. Then, after the 1980 military coup in Turkey, Sweden and Germany witnessed a striking increase in the publication of Kurmanji literature, especially among political refugees from Syrian Kurdistan (in particular after 2000).

Many writers and intellectuals from all Kurdish regions have strived to develop Kurdish literature through establishing publishing houses and journals and literary writing. Mehmed Uzun, Firat Cewerî, Mehmet Emîn Bozarslan (1934), Ferhad Shakely (b. 1951), Perwîz Cîhanî (b. 1955), Serdar Roşan (b. 1958), Xelîl Duhokî (b.1951), Têmûrê Xelîl (b. 1949), Ehmed Huseynî (b. 1955), Hesenê Metê (b. 1957), and Bavê Nazê (b. 1946) contributed to the enrichment of Kurdish, particularly Kurmanji, in its written form to reach many more speakers. The Paris Kurdish Institute, founded in 1983, supporting Kurdish intelligentsia and artistry and offering Kurdish culture and language courses, has contributed to the development of Kurdish literary production. The semi-annual journal *Hîwa-Hêvî* (Hope) was first published in 1983, and since 1987, *Kurmancî*, a semi-annual linguistic magazine,

deals with the problems of terminology and standardization of the Kurdish language. Similarly, *Nûdem* (New Era), founded by Cewerî, was published from 1992 to 2002 and played a considerable role in the development of Kurdish literature.

The Kurdish intelligentsia who fled Turkey after the 1980 military coup have especially contributed to the development of Kurdish novelistic discourse written in the Kurmanji dialect. For instance, Mehmed Uzun (1953–2006) and Mahmut Baksî (1944–2000), who were the most productive novelists, fled Turkey during the coup to avoid further prosecution and imprisonment and lived in Sweden until they passed away. Although some of them are not active right now, many Kurdish publishing houses in Europe such as Nûdem, Roja Nû, Orfeus, Apec, Helwest, Sara,

Kurdish novelist Mehmed Uzun during an interview in Istanbul, Turkey, June 28, 2005. (Cem Turkel/ AFP/Getty Images)

Welat, Pelda, Jîndan, and Newroz have been established since the beginning of 1980s.

The group of writers, particularly from Syrian Kurdistan, who migrated to Europe after 2000 includes Fawaz Hussain (b. 1953), Hêlim Yûsiv (b. 1967), and Jan Dost (b. 1965), the leading Kurdish prose writers in Europe. Hussain (Fawaz Husên), after completing his PhD in France, moved to Sweden in 1993. He is well known for his French-Kurdish translations, particularly *The Stranger* by Camus and *The Little Prince*. He wrote his first novel, *Siwarên Êşê*, in 1994, and it was published in French four years later. He also translated Uzun's *Sîya Evînê* into French. Dost has been living in Germany since 2000. Rather than his poetry, he is known best for his four Kurdish novels concentrating on sociopolitical and historical developments in Kurdistan. It can be argued that most of the novelists from the diaspora who are of the same generation (born in the 1950s and 1960s) are already politicized figures due to their background before exile.

After the autonomy of Iraqi Kurdistan in 1991, Kurdish literary circle has strikingly expanded including a number of Kurdish women writers and poets. Some, such as Necîbe Ehmed (b. 1954), managed to publish their work after autonomy who could not do so in 1980s due to political reasons. Along with those in Iraqi Kurdistan, a number of Kurdish poets emerged in other Kurdish regions as well such as Jîla Husênî (1964–1996) from Iranian Kurdistan, Fatma Savcı (b. 1974) from Turkish Kurdistan, and Dîya Ciwan (b. 1953) from Syrian Kurdistan.

A new generation of Kurdish women is living as part of the diaspora and publishing in the language of their host countries, including Nazand Begikhani (1964), Dilsoz Heme (b. 1968), Choman Hardi (b. 1974), and Nîgar Nadir (b. 1976).

Despite all the negative factors, Kurdish literature has advanced in all dialects during the past two decades. Its most significant characteristic is that the greater part of it is directly or indirectly the outgrowth of epics. There is a marked continuity in the development of fictional prose from earlier oral sources.

Özlem Belçim Galip

Further Reading

Blau, J. (1996). "Kurdish Written Literature." In P. G. Kreyenbroek & C. Allison (Eds.), *Kurdish Culture and Identity* (pp. 20–28). London: Zed Books.

Blau, J. (2010). "Written Kurdish Literature." In P. G. Kreyenbroek & U. Marzolph (Eds.), *Oral Literature of Iranian Languages* (pp. 1–32). London and New York: I. B. Tauris.

Galip, O. B. (2015). *Imagining Kurdistan: Identity, Culture and Society.* London and New York: I. B. Tauris.

Grondahl, S., & Kadir, N. (2003). "The Role of Kurdish Children's Literature for Language Maintenance." In L. Huss, A. C. Grima, & K. A. King (Eds.), *Transcending Monolingualism: Linguistic Revitalisation in Education* (pp. 129–148). New York: Routledge.

Karim, D. L. (1985). "A Comparative Study of Free Verse in Arabic and Kurdish: The Literary Careers of Al-Sayyab and Goran." Unpublished PhD thesis, University of Glasgow, Glasgow, Scotland.

Kreyenbroek, P. (2005). "Kurdish Written Literature." http://www.iranicaonline.org/articles/kurdish-written-literature.

Leezenberg, M. (2011). "Soviet Kurdology and Kurdish Orientalism." In M. Kember & S. Conerman (Eds.), *The Heritage of Soviet Oriental Studies* (pp. 86–102). Abingdon, UK: Routledge.

MacKenzie, D. N. (1959). "The Language of Medians." *Bulletin of the School of Oriental and African Studies,* vol. 22. no. 2, 354–355.

Malmisanij, M. (2006). "The Past and the Present of Book Publishing in Kurdish Language in Turkey." http://www.npage.org/IMG/pdf/Turkey.pdf.

Minorsky, V. (1943). "The Guran." *Bulletin of the School of Oriental and African Studies,* vol. 11, no. 1, 75–103.

Naderi, L. (2011). *An Anthology of Modern Kurdish Literature.* Erbil, Iraq: University of Kurdistan Publishing House.

Shakely, F. (1992 [1983]). *Kurdish Nationalism in Mem û Zin.* Brussels: Kurdish Institute.

Skutnabb-Kangas, T., & Sertaç, B. (1994). "Killing a Mother Tongue: How Kurds Are Deprived of Their Linguistic Human Rights." In T. Skutnabb-Kangas & R. Phillipson (Eds.), *Linguistic Human Rights: Overcoming Linguistic Discrimination* (pp. 347–371). Berlin: de Gruyter.

Uzun, M. (2007 [1992]). *Kürt Edebiyatına Giriş.* Istanbul: İthaki.

Vanly, I. C. (1992). "The Kurds in the Soviet Union." In P. G. Kreyenbroek & S. Sperl (Eds.), *The Kurds: A Contemporary Overview* (pp. 193–218). London: Routledge.

Media

The Kurds, one of the world's largest ethnic groups without their own country, have long endured the consequences of systematic sociopolitical and cultural repression. Consecutive governments in Iraq, Iran, Syria, and Turkey have relied on both military and political mechanisms of subjugation to quell Kurdish nationalist aspirations. At various times throughout the 20th and 21st centuries Kurdish groups rebelled against centralized state structures. In recent decades, Kurds have relied on unauthorized media outlets such as satellite TV and radio stations to advance their goals. In particular, transnational and European-based Kurdish media efforts have succeeded in shaping a Kurdish consciousness to a limited degree. New Kurdish media opportunities also emerged in both the Kurdistan Regional Government in Iraqi Kurdistan and in the autonomous Syrian Kurdish region known as Rojava. But consumers of Kurdish media have mostly experienced a decline in the quality and a reduction in the accessibility to free media throughout the region. Turkey manifests the most troubling trend in that decline today, as even limited access to Kurdish media has been terminated. Since the failed coup d'état in 2016, Turkey has become an increasingly dangerous place for independent journalists and private users of social media to produce and consume Kurdish-language media (unless it is the state-approved version). Indeed the future for free and independent Kurdish media in Turkey looks extremely bleak. Iran has never granted free media rights to its Kurdish communities, and changes should not be expected any time soon despite the re-election of professed moderate President Hassan Rouhani in 2017.

The rise of Kurdish media over the past several decades highlights an increasingly complex relationship between the central authorities in Iraq, Iran, Syria, and Turkey and ethnic Kurdish communities in the four nation-states. Ethnic media outlets often focus on producing divergent information and cultural meaning, which questions the dominant state's narratives and historical claims. Since the governments of nation-states endorse, privilege, and legitimize a specific cultural group (such as Turks in Turkey), they simultaneously disadvantage other groups such as the Kurds. This is specifically the case when an ethnic group refuses to be assimilated or resists sociocultural subjugation. Regional nation-states have systematically disadvantaged Kurds, weakened their economic opportunities, and curtailed their sociocultural and political influence in all four countries. In such environments, independent and free Kurdish media outlets rarely receive permission to operate. Instead, they frequently function illegally and on the margins of society, struggling against patterns of discrimination. Nation-states frequently classify Kurdish media as hostile and dangerous entities and accuse them of spreading subversive propaganda.

Over a period of many decades, regional states in the Middle East have applied a variety of ruthless strategies to silence Kurdish nationalists in the hope of defeating popular support for an independent Kurdish state. The vast majority of Kurdish communities in the Middle East share similarly devastating experiences with Arab, Persian, and Turkish authorities as their distinct claim to a Kurdish identity raised questions about the legitimacy of the national borders of Iran, Iraq, Turkey, and Syria. Until today—while an exception can be made for Kurds living in the semi-autonomous Kurdistan Regional Government (KRG) in Iraq—all Kurdish regions

1. Tend to be economically marginalized in comparison with other regions, which has resulted in the deep impoverishment of Kurdish populations
2. All Kurdish regions have been exposed to a highly threatening security apparatus, which aims to eradicate expressions of a separate ethnic identity
3. All Kurdish regions experienced strategic patterns of repression at various times, inspiring regional uprisings and long-term insurgencies against central authorities
4. All Kurdish regions continue to be vulnerable to meddling and strategic manipulation by neighboring states, and their militia forces have been used as proxy forces in the interest of both regional and global powers

Despite devastating patterns of repression in their homeland regions, Kurds have succeeded in significantly advancing their claims to a separate ethnic identity. Over the past several decades, ethnic Kurdish media rose to prominence by playing a particularly noteworthy role in disseminating nationalist ideology and strengthening public support for ethnic Kurdish recognition. In particular, the increasing availability of communication technologies and the pattern of transnational migration created new opportunities for Kurds interested in disseminating nationalist ideas more widely. Instead of solely aiming to advance Kurdish identity claims within their homeland regions, exiled Kurds pursued their nationalist aspirations from an extraterritorial space in the diaspora. The rise of ethnic Kurdish media beyond the Kurdish homeland can be directly traced to the dispersion of media technologies by Kurds in Europe.

Kurdistan

The first Kurdish newspaper, *Kurdistan*, was published on April 22, 1898, first in Istanbul and later in Cairo by Mikdad Bedirkhan. He used the Ottoman Turkish alphabet to publish the articles in Northern Kurdish or Botani. A total of 31 issues appeared irregularly with some 2,000 copies. Early on, the main objective of *Kurdistan* was to educate the readership about culture and literature. The newspaper was the first to publish the Kurdish national epos "Mem u Zin" by Ahmed Khani. Political articles described the early national struggle of the Kurds against the Ottoman Sultan Abdulhamid II.

Transnationalism

Over the past three decades, Kurds in European exile pursued ethnic media tools to disseminate nationalist content in various Kurdish languages (Kurmanji, Sorani, and Zaza) to populations in the Kurdish homeland regions. Ethnic media programs are frequently embraced by marginalized linguistic, racial, and ethnic minority communities such as the Kurds (Matsaganis et al., 2011: 5–10). Their own publications and broadcasting programs often focus on creating content that is otherwise curtailed or entirely repressed in nation-states. The target audience for ethnic media tends to be a particular community that faces widespread political and linguistic obstacles to accessing positively framed or unbiased information about itself. Kurdish media organizations have directly challenged the validity of anti-Kurdish bias, which is advanced by authoritarian and state-controlled media outlets. In addition, Kurdish media have defied and circumvented rules that have been established to control minorities in countries with sizable Kurdish populations (such as Iraq, Iran, Syria, and Turkey).

Over 50 years ago, Kurdish laborers left impoverished towns in Turkey's southeastern provinces to pursue temporary jobs in Europe. Public attitudes in Europe toward Kurds were characterized by a general sense of disinterest in domestic Turkish politics. The subjugation of Kurds through a Turkification-focused assimilation policy was not considered relevant for labor migrants in Europe. Few public officials understood that Kurdish-language prohibitions existed in Turkey, that Kurdish children had been forced to attend regional boarding schools to civilize them (i.e., to make them into Turks), that names of Kurdish villages and cities had been Turkified, and that a homogenization process was underway in Turkey (Zeydanlioğlu, 2012).

Turkey's military coup in 1980 initiated another wave of migration to Europe. This time tens of thousands of Turkish citizens, many of them ethnically Kurdish, entered Austria, Belgium, Germany, and the Netherlands as asylum applicants to escape persecution in Turkey. Access to human rights–based asylum protections facilitated the creation of clandestine political networks by ethnonational Kurds abroad. The makeup and structures of Kurdish groups in Europe shifted from predominantly apolitical migrant clubs to hierarchical and homeland-oriented challenger organizations. Migration experts suggested that one-quarter to one-third of all asylum seekers from Turkey were ethnically Kurdish and that many of them sympathized with the ethno-nationalist ideals pursued by the Kurdistan Workers Party (PKK), a feared guerrilla organization in Turkey (Castles & Miller, 1993: 276–277).

Kurds who had been granted asylum reached out to Kurdish laborers to establish broader political networks in Europe. With the expertise typical of trained PKK cadres, nationalist Kurds in Europe disseminated detailed information about the mistreatment of their brethren in homeland regions. Pro-PKK publications such as *Azadi* and *Kurdistan Rundbrief* regularly suggested that it was necessary to confront Turkey's discriminatory and repressive policies toward Kurds. Kurdish ethnonationalist newspapers and journals such as *Serxwebun*, *Özgür Politika* (later renamed *Yeni Özgür Politika*), and *Rohani* printed long lists of fallen Kurdish guerrilla fighters (called martyrs) in the war against the Turkish state. Kurdish publications articulated many grievances but emphasized culturally based demands such as the right to study and speak Kurdish, for families to select Kurdish-language names for their children, and the need for independent Kurdish radio and TV programs.

During the 1990s, Kurdish media succeeded for the first time in articulating claims for self-determination on an international level. Sustained campaigns of political activism among Kurds allowed media outlets to thrive by flouting authoritarian controls in the homeland regions. Kurds in Europe staffed and financially supported newspapers, radio broadcasts, and satellite TV stations with the intent of strengthening a sense of Kurdish ethnic and political consciousness. Kurdish media professionals in the European diaspora succeeded in scaling up their messaging because of remarkable improvements in media technologies. Their reliance on increasingly widely available satellite technology and the integration of social media tools advanced Kurdish identity claims over time. A gradually more aware and mobilized Kurdish diaspora reached out to Kurdish audiences now larger than ever before. It also allowed for highly targeted ethnonationalist, secular, and Marxist notions to flourish alongside more traditional religious and cultural Kurdish programming.

The most obvious area of contention related to Kurdish satellite media broadcasts from Europe into the Middle East. As a transnational community, diaspora Kurds shifted from relying on newspapers and journals to fully embrace satellite TV stations and social media tools. At the same time, Kurdish media also began to more accurately reflect the linguistic diversity among regional populations and successfully ended the silencing of Kurdish representations.

While tolerated in European countries, Kurdish media outlets were also considered suspicious. Many European governments expressed grave concerns that the mounting consumption of ethnic media sources could undermine the desired progress toward immigrant integration in Europe. Disagreements also emerged repeatedly over official Turkish demands for Kurdish radio and TV stations to be shut down across Europe. Turkey insisted that the PKK directly financed and controlled numerous media outlets with the intention of spreading anti-Turkish propaganda and terrorist ideology. Ankara successfully forced the closure of Med-TV in the UK in 1999 and managed to convince the French government to withdraw its broadcasting permits from Medya-TV in 2004. But Turkey failed to push Danish authorities to shut down Roj-TV despite vigorously arguing that the station presented a direct terrorist threat to Turkey.

Among the most controversial Kurdish media outlets according to the Turkish government were Firat News Agency in the Netherlands, Roj-Group and Denge Mezopotamya radio in Belgium, Roj-TV and MMC-TV in Denmark, Newroz-TV in Norway, and the *Yeni Özgür Politika* newspaper in Germany. Extensive diplomatic efforts by the Turkish government to have Kurdish-language media closed down contributed to disputes between Ankara and European national governments. As hostile relations over access to free speech and media rights increased, Turkey's application for full European Union (EU) membership stalled in 2005. But at the same time Kurdish media also faced growing bureaucratic obstacles in Europe.

In anticipation of further licensing challenges including lawsuits, police raids, and mounting fines in Denmark, Roj-TV's Kurdish team decided to shut down its operations. However, within weeks of Roj-TV's closure the same group of producers launched two new Kurdish stations operating today as Sterk-TV and Med-Nucu TV. Their range of programming is quite similar to Roj-TV and is mainly transmitted through Eurobird satellite to the Middle East. Both stations also continue to be widely available to viewers across Europe as well. Many Kurdish diaspora viewers access Sterk and Nuce through streaming technology instead of relying on satellite technologies. This is the case because streaming is significantly less costly than accessing satellites and also because it can be quite dangerous in Kurdish regions to display satellite dishes when security personnel suppress dissident channels.

Kurdish Satellite TV Inside Turkey

Kurdish media that aim to operate inside Turkey have been consistently prohibited and currently face a renewed and particularly ferocious pattern of state repression. Gün-TV experimented very carefully with Kurmanji-language broadcasting starting in 2006. The station was operated in Diyarbakir, one of the major Kurdish cities in the southeastern provinces of Turkey. Initially, the station faced severe restrictions in terms of its hourly operations, but then received permission to broadcast more frequently in the Kurdish language (Smets, 2016: 743). It gained the right to access satellite technologies and to disseminate its culturally oriented programs. For years its content continued to be monitored and severely censored, but Gün-TV programs eventually managed to receive a pass from the Radio and Television Supreme Council (RTÜRK).

Gün-TV represented a first attempt to create an ethnic Kurdish station within Turkey, but when the relationship between the AKP government and various parties in the Kurdish dominated regions deteriorated dramatically in 2015, Kurdish media also faced mounting constraints. In August 2016, shortly after the failed coup d'état against the Turkish government, Gün-TV's access to satellite capabilities was cut off and security forces began to dismantle the station (Cupolo, 2016). The Turkish government justified the closure of Gün-TV by calling it a mouthpiece of Fetullah Gülen, the Erdoğan government's Islamic challenger, who has been accused of masterminding the coup against the Turkish government in 2016. Gülen lives in Pennsylvania today and has become a U.S. citizen. So far, U.S. courts have rejected the evidentiary documentation submitted by the Turkish government and called it insufficient to extradite the religious leader (who is ethnically Turkish and not Kurdish) to Turkey.

In a report issued in 2016, Freedom House warned that Turkish media in general have been curtailed at an alarming rate. Most opposition newspapers and media outlets were either banned or closed down after the July 2016 coup attempt. Many well-known and respected journalists, writers, and bloggers have left the country to seek asylum abroad, while others languish in prison cells without legal representation or information about their cases. The vast majority of journalists, it appears, face accusations of having supported separatist or terrorist activities. Over the past year, at least 45,000 people have been detained in Turkey, and 130,000 employees have been dismissed from government payrolls for allegedly supporting the coup and engaging in anti-Turkish activities. In addition, dismissed former journalists, writers, and government employees have been blacklisted and their family members ostracized, which in essence means that they cannot find employment in the country under the current climate of fear.

Among the most widely recognized Kurdish media outlets the Turkish governments closed down are the Kurdish daily Azadiya Welat, the news agency Dicle (DIHA), and the multilingual, all-women news agency JINHA. In addition, Ankara routinely blocks Twitter and a range of social media sites, and most recently banned access to Wikipedia so that citizens cannot gain information about leaked information. The government has been accused of involvement in various corruption schemes and may even have played a role in the coup (documents posted to Wikileaks appear to suggest that the coup was orchestrated by the current government).

For nearly a decade, Turkey also experimented with ethnic co-optation strategies and tried to reach out to particular Kurdish population groups through state-managed Kurdish-language media. Turkey established a state-funded Kurdish-language TV station, TRT6, in 2009. The aim of the Turkish Radio and Television

Opening ceremony of the Kurdish-language, state-run television channel TRT 6 or TRT Kurdi, on January 1, 2009. (Adem Altana/AFP/Getty Images)

Corporation (TRT) was to compete with European-based, transnational Kurdish media, which had focused predominantly on secular and Marxist interpretations of Kurdish life. Initially known as TRT6 this state-sponsored station was renamed TRT Kurdi in 2015 (Smets, 2016: 743–744). The government planned to demonstrate a deeper commitment to Kurdish-language broadcasting, yet simultaneously managed its content to complement national Turkish narratives. Predictably, nationalist Kurds questioned the intentions and sincerity of TRT 6/TRT Kurdi. Many Kurds reject TRT Kurdi as a tool that is employed by state authorities to culturally and ideologically manipulate a marginalized Kurdish population. While a large number of socially conservative Kurds in Turkey tend to watch TRT Kurdi, Kurdish critics of the AKP government perceive the channel as advancing an inauthentic and repressive attitude toward Kurdish identity.

Kurdish Media in the KRG and in Rojava

The rise of the semi-autonomous Kurdistan Regional Government (KRG) in Iraq created additional opportunities for Kurdish media to emerge and thrive. Instead of predominantly relying on programming produced by Kurds in Europe, the KRG experienced an increasingly diverse and independent media environment. Kurds in the KRG created their own content and programming, which included newspapers, web-based media sites, radio, and TV. For the first few years after the fall of Saddam Hussein's regime, Kurds in the KRG experienced a comparatively open media environment and took full advantage of new communications opportunities. Recently, however, the KRG has undergone a pronounced decline in terms of its population's access to independent and free media.

Kurdish media in the KRG fully emerged in the early 2000s. The Kurdistan Syndicate of Journalists suggested that some 800 media outlets initially operated in the Kurdistan region (at least 600 print media such as newspapers and magazine and 150 satellite TV and radio stations) (KurdJS.com, n.d.). But the two dominant Kurdish political parties, the Kurdistan Democratic Party (KDP) and the Patriotic Union of Kurdistan (PUK), were alarmed by their inability to manage the flow of information in the region. Both parties began to sponsor various media outlets with the intent to undermine independent and local media. Party-affiliated media operations, often described today as "shadow media groups," have risen to prominence. They closely follow particularistic political agendas that are advanced by powerful Kurdish elites and politicians (Chomani, 2014).

With the rise of the "shadow media," independent journalists faced growing personal threats and also frequently engaged in self-censorship because of widespread intimidation strategies. Several high-profile journalists became targets of brutal beatings and assassinations after they reported on government corruption schemes. In 2011, the free satellite TV station NRT was set on fire just three days after it was officially launched. Another strategy that has been used by political parties to reduce the influence of independent media is to outspend them and thereby eliminate competition from independent sources in the media market.

Political parties in the KRG have relied on satellite TV and digital media teams to create appealing and flashy news that successfully pushed newspapers and journals out of the market. Powerful individuals have established entire media empires, which advance agendas that are preferred by particular subgroups, elites, or allied blocs within the KRG. According to a 2015 Gallup poll about media usage in Iraq and Iraqi Kurdistan, Kurds most frequently receive their news and general information from satellite TV stations (BBG Gallup, 2015: 1–2). Younger, better educated, and urban Kurds also access and rely on the Internet very frequently. It is obvious that controlling media messages has become essential to maintaining a position of political power and influence in the KRG. While Gallup observed that an extreme media plurality exists in the region, it also cautioned that the Kurdish population lacked access to trustworthy, objective, and reliable news sources (BBG Gallup, 2015: 1–2).

Despite a region-wide financial crisis related to disputes with Baghdad over the distribution of oil revenues, two KDP competitors from within the powerful Barzani family run two separate satellite stations called Rudaw and Kurdistan 24. The Rudaw media network is directly funded by Nechirvan Barzani, the long-standing prime minister of the KRG. Rudaw competes with Kurdistan 24, which is sponsored by Masrour Barzani, who serves as the chancellor of the Kurdistan Regional Security Council. In addition, the second-largest Kurdish party, PUK, also operates its own satellite TV station, which is called Kurdsat News. Facing too much media competition (and lacking the same access to funds), a smaller splinter party, Gorran, appears to be reducing its staff at Kurdish News Network (KNN), which is its very own satellite station. Similarly, Payam TV, an Islamic TV station, is also no longer able to compete with the Barzanis. It appears that the media empires of the KDP and, to a lesser degree, of the PUK will control the entire satellite market in the KRG in the near future.

Supporters of independent and free Kurdish media in the KRG are beginning to discuss the importance of a regulatory body that would introduce a sense of professionalism and fairness into the broader media market (Chomani, 2014). However, few Kurds in the KRG believe that the Barzanis are willing to give up their media control that has allowed them to effectively shape public opinion among vast segments of the population.

Just across the border in Syrian Kurdish areas, access to free media is a very new reality for Kurdish communities. The Bashar al-Assad government relied on the so-called National Media Council to ensure that all media was fully controlled and operated by the central authorities. The council issued press passes and licenses and determined which foreign journalists were permitted to enter the country. When the civil war began in 2011, Syria became one of the world's most dangerous places for media professionals as well as citizen journalists. Numerous journalists, writers, and private bloggers were imprisoned, kidnapped for ransom, and brutally executed by the Bashar al-Assad regime, Syrian opposition groups, or adherents of IS (Islamic State). When the Assad regime lost control over several regions of the country, including the Kurdish-dominated provinces, Rojava (Western Kurdistan) declared its autonomy from Damascus. This led to the rise of independent yet privately funded Kurdish media in a part of the former Syrian state.

The de facto establishment of a self-governing area in Rojava, the Kurdish-controlled cantons of northern Syria known as Efrin (in the West), and Cizire and Kobani (in the East) provided opportunities for Syrian Kurds to access and produce web-based social media sites. As the war in Syria intensified, Syrian Kurds pursued broader nationalist notions by defying the Assad regime but also by challenging Turkish territorial interests. Rojava predominantly relies on European, U.S., and Canadian transnational media connections to reach an international audience, but also actively uses websites and social media tools inside the self-governing areas to advance its Kurdish nationalist agenda.

Rojava established its own constitution in 2014, which also included basic protections for independent and free media. Some restrictions have always applied to media in Rojava, especially when security reasons are raised to curtail the flow of information. All media outlets tend to be carefully managed by the Democratic Union Party (PYD), which is the dominant Kurdish political party in Rojava. A PYD media agency provides permits for all outlets and manages which organizations are permitted to function. Despite such restrictions, a variety of print and broadcast outlets operate without significant government interference today. The PYD media agency also provides training for journalists and collaborates with international groups such as the North American Rojava Alliance, which has a significant social media presence, and disseminates videos, documentaries, and other information about the ongoing revolution in Rojava.

Status Quo in Iran

While Kurds in Syria have managed to assert significant media freedoms in their de facto autonomous regions, the media landscape in Iran is tightly controlled by the theocratic regime in Tehran. Journalists and web activists are frequently questioned and detained in the country. The Islamic Republic supervises all programming content, and government officials carefully vet operations managers. Kurdish media, just like all other independent media outlets, are not permitted to operate without special government approval. Several Iranian Kurdish diaspora groups founded satellite TV stations in Europe in the early 2000s, including Komala TV, Rojhelat TV, and Tishk TV (Sheyholislami, 2011: 87). Kurds in Iran also have attempted to publish articles in clandestine cultural journals related to Kurdish life, but most issues are quickly confiscated. Both consumers and writers of such articles and journals can face detention and arrest. Kurdish journalists, bloggers, and activists are frequently tortured in Iranian prisons, and executions of political prisoners are common.

The Shia Ministry of Culture and Islamic Guidance closely watches the mostly Sunni Kurdish population and frequently relies on security forces to subdue any unauthorized activities in Kurdish provinces (including Kermanshah, Hamadan, and parts of Ilam, West Azerbaijan, and North Khorasan). Visitors to Internet cafes, for example, have to show their national ID numbers and sign logs to access a computer. Iranian security rules also require that owners of Internet cafes install CCTV cameras so that government officials can supervise all activities and identify consumers who dare to examine unauthorized websites.

In addition, it is challenging for Iranian Kurds to receive transnational satellite TV stations since satellite dishes tend to be forcibly removed from houses throughout the Kurdish provinces (and periodically throughout the entire country). Despite attempts to camouflage satellite dishes, security forces sometimes enter homes to check for unapproved technology. Kurdish houses with so-called resisters are sometimes raided, occupants can be beaten, and the heads of households face detention by security personnel in Iran. However, satellite dishes tend to be illegally trucked into Iran with the assistance of border smugglers who make a living by selling banned goods. Most of the illegal items that enter Iran are trucked across the border from either the predominantly Kurdish areas of Turkey or come from the KRG (Hawramy, 2013).

Despite the recent landslide re-election of President Hassan Rouhani, the reformist candidate, Kurds in Iran expect few sociopolitical changes to take place in the future. Accessing unauthorized and independent Kurdish media outlets remains a highly risky business for Kurdish communities living in the Islamic Republic.

Vera Eccarius-Kelly

Further Reading

Castles, S. & M. J. Miller. (1993). *The Age of Migration: International Population Movements in the Modern World.* New York: Palgrave Macmillan Press.

Chomani, K. (2014). "Independent Media Fades in Iraqi Kurdistan." *Al-Monitor.* http://www.al-monitor.com/pulse/originals/2014/07/iraq-kurdistan-free-independent-media-krg-rudaw.html.

Cupolo, D. (2016). "Silencing Kurdish Voices." *Jacobin.* https://www.jacobinmag.com/2016/09/turkey-erdogan-coup-kurdish-press-ozgur-gun/.

Freedom House. (2016). "Turkey: Freedom of the Press 2016." https://freedomhouse.org/report/freedom-press/2016/turkey.

Gallup. (2015). "Media Use in Iraq and Iraqi Kurdistan." *Broadcasting Board of Governors (BBG).* https://www.bbg.gov/wp-content/media/2015/03/Iraq-brief-FINAL.pdf.

Hassanpour, A. (2003). "Diaspora, Homeland, and Communications Technologies." in K. H. Karim (Ed.), *The Media of Diaspora* (pp. 76–78). London: Routledge.

Hawramy, F. (2013). "Border Smuggling Rises in Iranian Kurdistan." *Al-Monitor.* http://www.al-monitor.com/pulse/tr/originals/2013/10/iran-kurdistand-smuggling-rises.html.

Kurdistan Journalists Syndicate. (n.d.). http://kurdjs.com/index.php/en/who-we-are.html.

Matsaganis, M. D., Ball-Rokeach, S., & Katz, V. S. (2011). *Understanding Ethnic Media: Producers, Consumers, and Societies.* Thousand Oaks, CA: Sage.

Sheyholislami, J. (2011). *Kurdish Identity, Discourse, and New Media.* New York: Palgrave Macmillan Press.

Smets, K. (2016). "Ethnic Media, Conflict, and the Nation-State: Kurdish Broadcasting in Turkey and Europe and Mediated Nationhood." *Media, Culture & Society,* vol. 38, no. 5, 738–754.

Zeydanlıoğlu, W. (2012). "Turkey's Kurdish Language Policy." *International Journal of the Sociology of Language,* vol. 217, 99–125.

Food and Dress

Food and Drink

Kurdish food and cuisine are closely linked to the group's culture and identity, as mentioned in the famous universal saying "you are what you eat." However, it is difficult to classify Kurdish food as a specific ethnic food because of the similarities with other, neighboring cuisines, especially those food items from the eastern Mediterranean and the Iranian regions. And while some describe Kurdish food as a blend of Turkish, Arab, and Persian cuisines, others highlight its unique features and ingredients.

The geography of Kurdistan, with its elevated mountains, high plateaus and pastures, relative abundance of precipitation, and other water sources like rivers and lakes, contributes to the distinct diet of many of its inhabitants. Climate and ecologic conditions also dictate what grows where and where animals can graze. The formerly many nomadic groups among the Kurds who grazed their flocks on summer and winter pastures ensured a constant supply of meats, especially sheep and lamb. Dairy products and chicken are also staples in the Kurdish diet. The area has fertile soil and significant amounts of rainfall that allow for growing many different vegetables and fruits. Many fresh and dried vegetables, fruits, and herbs are used for daily cooking, such as okra, aborigines, mint, and turnips. Truffles (*chema*), considered a delicacy in many cultures, grow locally and are often collected by poor people.

Traditionally, different cereals and vegetables have been grown, with wheat, barley, and watermelons being the most popular. However recently, rice, both homegrown and imported, has replaced those as the most common staple—at least for those who can afford it. In the villages and refugee camps, wheat flour to bake bread is still the most popular food staple. Other cash crops include tobacco, cotton, and olives. In the fertile river valleys, a variety of fruit and nut trees are raised such as mulberries, walnuts, pistachios, and grapes.

Being part of the cradle of civilization, food production in Kurdistan goes back to the beginning of time where evidence of some of the oldest varieties of wheat, barley, lentils, and grapes were found in archeological sites. There was also evidence of early domestication of sheep, goats, cattle, and pigs as early as 7000 BCE. Nomads and farmers in Kurdistan contributed much to this process. And today, agriculture with large animals, farms, gardens, and irrigated fields are an obvious sign of the long experience in this sector.

The ability to produce most of its food locally plus the relative peaceful and stable situation allowed for the development of a food industry that offers employment opportunities and helps preserve the traditional character of the Kurdish diet. Local animal and vegetable markets provide most of the daily food; however, processed goods gain more importance as well as fast-food restaurants.

When asking Kurds about the best food, they most likely will reply, "my mother's food." And within the large Kurdish families, cooking is done as a communal chore where female relatives and neighbors often join in the preparation of the food.

Most Kurds are Muslims and thus follow the Islamic dietary restrictions. They include the prohibition of pork, the meat of dead animals, and that of animals not slaughtered properly. Yezidis have their own dietary restrictions when they refrain from eating lettuce or prepare special meals on religious holidays.

Meal times are considered important moments of gatherings for family members, neighbors, and friends. The shared social experience adds to the cohesion of the community. They might share meals at home, at family outings, and on ceremonial occasions. Drinking tea or coffee together is a ritual of almost every formal and informal meeting. It allows for the host and the guests to engage in a special relationship, and Kurdish hospitality is well known for this. While Kurds all over the world welcome visitors to share meals and drinks, their personal daily rhythm or eating habits might be different from place to place.

A typical Kurdish breakfast starts at home in the morning with fresh bread (*naan*), yogurt, eggs, cheese, and black sweet tea. Fresh flatbread (also known as *dorik* or *lavash*) is available almost everywhere at local bakeries. Lunch is usually

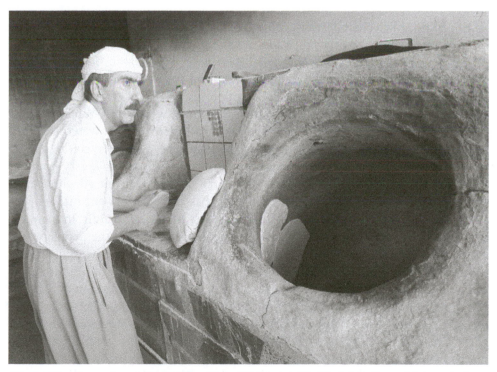

All over Kurdistan there are small traditional bakeries. The fresh bread is sold directly from the bakery window. (Rastislav Kolesar/Alamy Stock Photo)

the most important and largest meal of the day, whereas dinner tends to be a lighter meal at the end of the day. However, changing living and working patterns led to many Kurds having their main meal at the end of the working day. A common lunch or dinner meal may consist of rice (*pilaw*), beans, lentils, cabbage or other vegetables, and perhaps some meat, usually chicken or lamb. Vegetables, such as zucchinis, onions, tomatoes, peppers, eggplants, and others, are stuffed with rice, crack wheat, and occasionally meat. They are called *dolma* and can be found all over Kurdistan. Some call dolma the "national" food of Kurdistan.

Dolma

On Friday, the holiday of the week, Kurdish women gather to prepare dolma, or stuffed vegetables. In this communal effort, the vegetables are prepared first by carving the eggplants, zucchinis, peppers, onions, cabbage, and tomatoes. Then, the filling of rice, chopped onions, herbs, cubes of meats, tomato paste, and oil are mixed together. Next, all the vegetables are stuffed with the filling and placed in a large pot. They are covered with grape leaves and salt, after which hot water is added. It should be cooked for a while until it can be served on a large platter. Dolma is considered the "national Kurdish dish."

Lamb and chicken are the most common meats followed by beef and some other birds, such as goose or turkey or the local variety kaw, and to a lesser degree fish. The meat is usually grilled over charcoal. Vegetables are grilled too, but also cooked, pickled, stuffed, or eaten fresh in salads. Herbs and spices include salt, black pepper, curry, and the sweet pomegranate syrup.

The most common beverages are water, of course, with Kani Water the most popular brand, and *doogh* (or *ayran*), a mixed drink with yogurt, water, and salt. In the Sorani-speaking area, this drink is known as *mastaw*. When coffee and tea were introduced during the Ottoman period, they quickly became very popular, and today the sweet black tea can be considered a "national" drink. Alcoholic beverages such as wine and *araq,* distilled from grapes and spiced with anis, are produced locally by non-Muslim communities like Christians and Yezidis. In the wave of the Kurdish society's growing Islamization, these shops and the people working there have been targeted by fundamental, militant Muslims, who vigorously object to the consumption of alcohol. Several attacks and killings at restaurants or shops selling alcohol have been reported. The ongoing Westernization of Kurdish eating and drinking culture with its introduction of sodas and other soft drinks brought changes to the drinking habits as did the opening of Western-style coffee shops. In the past, teahouses (*chaykhana*) used to be the most popular gathering place for men where they sip on sweet black tea; play *shesh besh*, backgammon, or card games; and smoke cigarettes or water pipes. These places are still common;

however, Western-style coffee shops have emerged at the urban centers and are frequented by the better-of middle class and elite.

Food preparation was traditionally a women's chore; however, chefs and cooks at public restaurants and eateries are almost always men. In addition, the location and design of kitchens have changed over time, which influences how, where, and by whom the food is prepared. However, it remains a domain for the women of the family except for the preparation and grilling of the meat during the holidays, ceremonies, and picnics, which is usually done by men. Kurdish men can also be seen doing the food shopping at local markets and large shopping malls.

Describing the perfect natural conditions for agriculture in Kurdistan leads us to assume that the region is self-sufficient in the supply of fruits and vegetables. To the contrary, however, the Kurdish region at large experienced rapid social transformation due to conflicts, migration, and more generally urbanization. Diyarbakir (Amed) has multiplied in terms of population since 1984 when Kurdish villagers were forced to relocate to the city. Erbil (Hewler) as the capital of the Kurdish Autonomy Region has attracted thousands of new residents, migrants, and refugees and now has almost 2 million inhabitants. The new demographic and political conditions led to a decrease of arable farmland, and this, of course, brought along changes in lifestyles, occupations, and standards of living as well as a transformation of food consumption and food selection. And thus it comes as no surprise that the Kurdish territories alone had to import produce to the tune of 10 billion dollars over the past decade since local farmers were only able to supply 20 percent of fruits and 50 percent of the region's demand for vegetables.

Traditional Foods

Each area has preserved unique traditional recipes. For example Amed's most popular dish, *meftune*, consists of lamb with rice and vegetables spiced with garlic and sumac. During Newroz, Kurds in Iraq gather to share communal meals where *yaprakh* (or dolma) is served. Kurds in Syria and Israel swear on *shamburak*, dough pockets filled with spiced ground beef. Yezidis in the Tur Abdin and Sinjar (Shingal) region prepare a special type of bread for the religious holiday of Batizmi called *sewik*, which is made from sourdough, yeast, and fat.

Dress

Language, rituals, food, games, and religious festivals are common cultural representations for the various identity groups among the Kurds. Another identity marker for different genders, generations, tribes, sects, and political affiliation is dress. In the past, it was possible to retain a lot of information about a person by looking at his or her outfit. And recognizing the status of the person allows for proper communication and interaction. As Kurdish people, like societies around the world, are usually placed in a social hierarchy, looking at the clothing of a person enabled the other to identify this position.

The Kurds in all traditional settlement areas wear unique clothing in order to identify and distinguish themselves from the majority population of their host countries (i.e., the Turks, Arabs, and Persians). They also want to reflect their tribal, regional, and religious identity. Because of this desire, the traditional Kurdish dress for both men and women is still widely popular and easily recognizable in the cities and villages of Kurdistan and beyond. Especially older people like to wear these outfits, but the younger generation too has adapted some of the older, traditional styles for their ceremonial and professional clothing.

In contrast to the dress of neighboring Arab communities, Kurds prefer bright colors. Western travelers of the past centuries described the colorful dresses in red, green, yellow, and white among Kurdish women in the cities, villages, and the nomadic groups. They also noted the large turbans as a typical Kurdish man's headgear.

The climate of the Kurdish territories also influences the dress code. With its cold winters and often hot summers, the Kurds adapted to the special weather conditions by wearing appropriate outfits. Some areas see heavy rain and snowfall, whereas others experience long droughts and heat waves. Heavier materials such as wool and cotton are chosen in the colder seasons, whereas lighter, long-sleeved, and loose-fitting garments that allow for air circulation are preferred during the hotter days.

Covering the body is also a cultural obligation for all communities in Kurdistan who adhere to specific religious morals and values. All major religions in the area—Muslims, Christians, and Yezidis—require their followers to appear modest in public, which is demonstrated by covering most body parts. In the traditional Kurdish society, which is built on the concepts of honor and shame, women's dress is a particularly sensitive issue. The family reputation depends on the proper behavior of its female members, and appropriate, modest dress is another marker of cultural conservatism. Especially Muslim women make great efforts to hide everything except their hands, feet, and face. Another aspect of women's dress was the idea that contemporary Kurdish women appear to be more free and equal to their male counterparts and often did not cover their body in a way conservative Arab women would dress with additional coats and head and sometimes face covers. This image was also promoted by Kurdish women fighting in the guerilla movements and militias wearing khakis and headscarves similar to their male comrades. Iranian and Iraqi Kurds wear clothes that are designed according to the dress code of the Peshmerga. It consists of three main parts, jacket (*kava*), wide pants (*shalvar* or *pantool*), and the large waistband or *shaal*.

Wearing traditional Kurdish dress was prohibited in Turkey and Iran during the reign of the countries' modernizing rulers, Kemal Ataturk and Shah Reza Pahlevi. Both issued decrees to restrict the Kurdish population from wearing traditional clothing and to enforce a unified, Westernized dress code. Wearing the traditional Kurdish dresses was considered an offense against the country's modernization and progress. However, many Kurds defied these orders and continued wearing their traditional clothing as a sign of political and cultural opposition to the governments.

Women's Clothing

The dress of Kurdish women, especially in rural areas, is to be modest and not reveal any skin or body parts. Ultimately, even hands and feet could be covered to demonstrate modesty in public. Showing skin is considered shameful and will most likely in result in disapproval or other repercussions. This conservative, theoretical statement does, however, not reflect reality. Protecting the honor of the family can also be done by wearing other appropriate and modest attire. Generally, a local society determines the rules of proper dress and behavior. And increasingly, many Kurdish younger women, and more so in the cities, choose not wear headscarves as a sign of their religiosity or modesty.

Traditionally, Kurdish women wear colorful cotton dresses often embroidered and decorated with little coin, beads, or amulets. The design of these dresses and the applied embroidery varied from one area to the other, and in the past, people were able to recognize from looking at the decorative patterns that this woman was from Urmiya and another was from Mahabad, for example. Mass migration, conflict, and changing living conditions have forced the emergence of a more homogenic style of dresses.

Women also wear baggy trousers underneath and often a cloak on top of the dress covering much of their bodies. 19th-century Western travelers to the region reported that Kurdish women were more relaxed with their head and face covering than their Arab Muslim neighbors. However, especially on religious or cultural holidays and festive occasions, Kurdish women were decorative scarfs and turbans, which also are embellished with various small coins, beads, and other items. The dresses worn on those special days are also very bright, colorful, and immensely decorated with bead, metal threads, and epaulettes. Kurdish women wear simple sandals or slippers made from leather or plastic, often all year long.

Traditionally, the outfit reflected to the public the personal status of the wearer, her age group, and class distinction. Upper-class women from the local elite wore more expensive and elaborate dresses, whereas ordinary women usually preferred cotton. Younger women choose brighter colors, but the older generation leans toward darker tones. The headgear was also an indicator for the woman's religious affiliation, her geographical origin, and her marital status.

The women's dress in Iraqi Kurdistan consisted of several layers: trousers, knee-length shirt, overshirt with long, open sleeves, vest, jacket, and overcoat. Extra layers included a scarf around the shoulders and another one wrapped around the hips. In the past, the headdress was made of a skullcap, a turban, and a veil; however, today, most Kurdish women, if they are not religious-conservative, do not cover their hair except on special occasions.

Men's Clothing

The traditional standard or universal outfit for Kurdish men included an open-chest jacket, wide pants, a sash around the waist, and a checkered scarf worn as a turban. They are famous for their large, baggy trousers with tight ankles and matching

Iraqi Kurdish men, wearing traditional baggy trousers, headscarves, and prayer chains, sit outside a tea house in the bazaar of Dohuk, Iraqi Kurdistan. (Tekstbureau De Eindredactie/Moment Editorial/Getty Images)

open-collar jackets made from the same material and design. This loose outfit is held in place by a shawl or belt up to 30 feet long made of printed silk or synthetic material wrapped around the waist. This sash could also hold smaller accessories like tobacco, knifes, money, and cell phones. Underneath the outfit, Kurdish men wear cotton undershirts and pants. On their feet, they used to wear heavy cloth shoes, *kalash*, that were hammered together and had protective leather stripes at the edges. In the summer time plastic (formerly leather) sandals are the preferred footwear, whereas in the colder winter days and especially in the mountains, leather boots are more common. As common in Muslim societies, men cover their heads too. A skullcap and a colorful scarf wrapped around it is the most popular form. Often the black and white checkered *kuffiye* is worn around the head, but usually tied firmly and not loosely worn like the Arabs or Bedouin. Also, the Kurdish *kuffiye* has long tassels. The black-and-white *kuffiye* is more popular in the north, whereas the red-and-white version can be found in the south and among the Yezidis. Other hats and caps are made from felt and can be found among rural groups more exposed to harsh weather conditions.

New Trends in Kurdish Dress

Generally, Kurdish dress in the main regions has been exposed to modernization and Westernization, which came with a concurrent abandoning of traditional outfits. Political instability and living in a constant state of war and migration have also contributed to the adaptation of simpler and more functional clothing, leaving the traditional outfits for special occasions or distinct expressions of Kurdish nationalism.

Other observations on changing dress styles include a trend in women's dresses to become slim rather than wide. Fabrics are no longer produced here but are imported, and dresses are no longer tailored locally with the exception of decorating and embellishing them. Materials and ready-made garments are imported from Asian markets. But to say that traditional clothes are only worn by the older generation is not correct. It is still very popular among the young generation to participate in dance and folklore troupes who proudly wear the traditional Kurdish outfits of their region as part of their efforts to reclaim their heritage. Furthermore, young Kurdish fashion designers started to incorporate traditional elements of Kurdish dress in their collections.

Sebastian Maisel

Further Reading

Barzinji, A. (2015). *Traditional Kurdish Food: An Insight into Kurdish Culinary Heritage.* www .kurdishfood.co.uk: Ala Barzinji Publisher.

O'Shea, M. T. (1996). "Kurdish Costume: Regional Diversity and Divergence." In P. G. Kreyenbroek & C. Allison (Eds.), *Kurdish Culture and Identity* (pp. 135–155). Atlantic Highlands, NJ: Zed Books.

Vogelsand-Eastwood, G. (Ed.). (2000). *The Encyclopedia of World Dress and Fashion: Volume 5: Central and Southwest Asia.* Oxford, UK: Oxford University Press.

Music

Many types of performance of sound and word in the distinct cultural area of Kurdistan may be considered to coincide with the Western concept of music. These performances entail vocal and/or instrumental performances, which unequivocally correspond to what the concept of music entails (e.g., dance songs) and other speech genres such as "melodized speech" used in expressing sentiment relating to death, exile, heroism, etc. The general lines by which such performances are conceptualized and embedded with meaning show some degree of similarity across the entire Kurdistan area despite significant variation in terminology and local classificatory practices. There are also genres and styles of performance that are unique to certain linguistic/cultural areas (e.g., Serhed, Botan, Hekarî, etc.) and specific Kurdish-speaking groups (Yezidis, Alevis, etc.) in Kurdistan. The Kurdish terms quoted in this text are all in the Kurmanji dialect of Kurdish; however, other terms are used in dialects such as Sorani and Zazaki.

Genres of Melodized Sound and Word Performance

The genres of melodized sound and word available in Kurdistan are seldom purely instrumental. Therefore, in the scholarly literature, these genres are very often conceptualized either as music or oral literature. In accordance with the subject matter of this chapter, however, the present discussion of vocal performances will be limited to those that in terms of their mode of performance are usually described in Kurdish as *bi stranî* (in the manner of song/singing), as opposed to *bi çîrokî* (in the manner of story or tale), which refers to the nonmelodized (unsung) mode of delivery.

In the following sections, various genres of melodized sound and word performance in Kurdistan will be described in a concise fashion in terms of their formal and musical features, performers, and performance contexts.

Sung Narratives and Poetry of Battles, Heroism, and Tragic Love

Sung performances of texts concerning battles, heroism, tragic love, and death are quite common across the entire Kurdistan area. Although subject matters may vary, they resort to similar literary and emotive tools and they share common characteristics of musical performance.

The prime occasions for the performance of these genres in the past were evening gatherings in villages. These gatherings were held in a designated room in the house of ideally the most prominent person/family in a village, and they were the main occasions, where men of the village would socialize with each other and guests from outside the village were hosted. These social occasions and the places where they used to be held are quite uniform across Kurdistan. In the urban society of today, these genres have largely lost their significance.

Sung narrations of heroic battles between tribes or between a tribe and another nontribal power, such as a nation-state, are often held by Kurds to be the most prestigious of these performance genres. Their subject matter is more often than not locally based, and their protagonists are often locally known or are considered to be historical personalities. Although these performance genres may be referred to generically as *stran* or *kilam* in certain areas, they may also have specific names given to them in other areas, such as *şer* (in Mêrdîn [Mardin], Hekarî [Hakkâri], Botan, and parts of Iraqi Kurdistan), *kilam* (often in the Serhed area and among the Yezidis in Armenia), *kilamê mêrxasiyê, kilamê şer, lawje şerê, xoşmêr, mêrxoş, mêrkanjî,* and *beyt.*

There are also oral traditions, which entertain much wider popularity across Kurdistan than those described earlier. Kurdish native oral traditions such as Memê Alan, Kerr û Kulik, Cembelî, Derwêşê Evdî, etc., and Iranophone oral traditions such as Koroghlu, and Yusuf and Zulaikha, among others are examples (Allison, 2001: 13). These oral traditions may be distinguished from the ones described previously by their subject matter involving more supernatural elements. These genres are linguistically distinguished from others in some areas, such as among the Yezidis in Iraq where they are known as *beyts* or *destans*, and in the Serhed area (eastern Turkey), where they are referred to as *destans*.

The theme of love is commonly found in the second category of these performance genres. However, there are also other sung narrations whose subject matters specifically concern a tragic love relationship. In some areas, these sung narrations are distinguished from those about heroism and battles and are given specific categorical names. Some love-themed performance genres are considered inappropriate to be sung among men in evening gatherings in certain areas. The same distinction used to be made by some performers, who found the performance of love songs to be beneath them.

Some performances of these genres may last as long as a few hours. These performances are often comprehensive and, depending on the area and the particular oral tradition performed, may incorporate different modes of performance (or even other smaller musical genres) within them. For instance, Turgut (2002: 27) mentions how the performance of a particular piece in the lower Mardin area features sung and unsung narration as well as rhythmically delivered rhyming poetry within the same performance.

In terms of musical form, these performance genres are often conceived in strophes and display stichic (strophic) melodies, that is, melodies that are repeated more or less exactly the same for each line of text. While quick recitative style singing often constitutes the musical substance of each line of text, each strophe usually begins and ends on extended melismas (moving between several pitches on a single syllable) sung on emotive vocables.

Performers of these genres are mostly professionals, but semi-professional performers may also be commonly found. The names given to these professional performers vary between different areas and include, among others, *dengbêj*, *şa'îr*, *lawikbêj*, *destanbêj*, and *stranbêj*. Their social status also changes drastically according to the area in question. Professional performers from peripatetic groups (groups that are spatially mobile for subsistence purposes; e.g. the Dom) are also often expert performers of these genres, and they may even monopolize their performance in certain areas, such as in the case of performers known as *mitirb*s in the lower Mardin area. Professional performers, regardless of whether they are members of peripatetic communities or not, were predominantly mobile in the past. By the virtue of their mobility and their performance skills, professional performers performed certain prestige- and information-related functions for traditional leaders (e.g., *axa*s and *beg*s) in the old society and hence could get into a patron-client relationship with these powerful classes.

Although most Kurds today believe that these genres are conventionally performed without instrumental accompaniment, this was not the case in most areas in Kurdistan in the past. Among the Yezidis in Armenia and in some parts of the Serhed area, the double-reed woodwind *duduk* or *bilûr* (a woodwind instrument traditionally associated with shepherds) and in the lower Mardin area the three-stringed bowed instrument *kemaçe* (alternatively *ribab*) ordinarily accompany performances of these genres.

In addition to the love-themed performance genres mentioned in the beginning, there are other kinds of love-themed genres, such as *payîzok*s and *heyranok*s. *Payîzok*s are strophic, highly melodic songs, which are unique to the Botan and Hekarî regions (Turgut, 2010: 120–125). *Heyranok*s are found in Bitlis, Van, Hekarî, Botan, and the Behdinan regions. Their textual form is dialogic, where each strophe is sung successively from the mouth of a young woman and a man, and their texts often have erotic elements in them (Turgut, 2010: 126–130).

Laments

Kurds frequently distinguish laments as a specific performance form. Despite their unique performance occasions and hence the distinct social conventions pertaining to them, laments share common ground with other speech genres, such as moments in daily conversation when tragic memories are recalled or the main genres discussed in a later section (Amy de la Bretèque, 2012: 143). Laments are given different names in different areas such as *şîn*, *dîrok*, or *dîlok* among the Yezidis in northern Iraq (Allison, 2001: 75) and *şînî* in the Botan and Hekarî regions (Turgut, 2010: 135).

Laments for the dead are exclusively performed by women. The performer may be a relative of the deceased, or alternatively a well-known lamenter may be invited by the grieving family to perform the lamentation. Laments are performed strictly during times of mourning, and there may be taboos concerning performing laments out of context. Performances of laments conventionally create strong emotional responses in the participants, regardless of whether they participate in the performance of the lament in any way (Allison, 2001: 76–77).

The women's lament may be performed alongside an instrument, as in the case of the double-reed woodwind instrument *duduk* among the Yezidis in Armenia (Amy de la Bretèque, 2012: 132) or by voice only, which is the convention among the Yezidis in northern Iraq. In terms of the melodic and formal properties of laments in the case of the Yezidis in northern Iraq, Allison (2001: 77) gives the following description:

> Sense-units or 'lines' may be of variable length, with a fall in pitch on the final syllable; several of these may be grouped together with two or three falls in pitch on the final syllables of the 'stanza'. Between stanzas the performer or others present may sob or beat their breasts rhythmically.

Lullabies

In accordance with their universal context and reason for performance, Kurdish women sing lullabies to their children to put them to sleep. The names given to lullabies change from area to area and include, among others, *lorî*, *lorîk*, *narînik*, and *hayîn*. While the subject matters of lullabies may involve beauty or love and contain wishes for the child to have a prosperous future, they also often speak of loss (e.g., the loss of someone close) or war (Bilal & Amy de la Bretèque, 2006: 132). Lullabies constitute "a unique chance for individual expression, in which women speak of their sorrows, their problems, their feeling of nostalgia [and] . . . [f]or these reasons, lullabies share many characteristics with laments" (Ibid.). Today, for instance, lullabies with subject matters concerning the war between the PKK (the Kurdish Workers Party) and the Turkish army in Kurdistan and forced displacement are commonly found.

Dance Songs

Songs that people ordinarily dance to constitute a distinct category of musical performance in Kurdistan. In contrast to the genres described in the first three sections, dance songs embody a mood of joy and celebration. Therefore, the prime occasion for the performance of these songs is festivities, among which wedding celebrations (*dawet* or *dîlan*) are perhaps the most important. Today national celebrations such as Newroz (the Kurdish new year), political protests, and TV shows with music often feature dancing and hence performances of these songs.

Dance songs are predominantly in strophic form and have regular metered melodies. Although they often feature melodies unique to them, it is not uncommon that songs with different words sometimes share the same melody. The musical aspects of these songs, such as tempo, meter, etc., depend on the particular dances they accompany. Although many dances enjoy widespread popularity, there are also many regional and local forms and styles.

Dance songs are usually love themed and contain elements of eroticism and, as Allison puts it, many are "about pretty girls" (2010: 42). However, historically or heroically themed dance songs are also found in some areas. In addition, at the present time dance songs with a political subject matter are commonly performed in weddings and on other occasions.

Dance songs are also linguistically conceptualized as a self-contained category in certain areas (e.g., as *peste* or *beste* among the Yezidis in northern Iraq) (Allison, 2001: 65) or are generically referred to by reference to dancing or weddings as in *lawkê govendê* (Blum et al., n.d.) or *stranên dawetê* in Hekarî (BGST, 2004: 28–29). However, they may have specific names or may be referred to after the particular kind of dance that they are associated with. For instance, the songs that accompany the dance *ya mila* (lit. that of the shoulder; alternatively *cî de*) in the lower Mardin area are referred to as *ya raqsê* (that of dancing), whereas the songs which accompany the dance *delîlo* are referred to as *delîlo* after the name of the dance.

Dance songs are very often performed with instrumental accompaniment, although antiphonal (two groups of singers singing alternating musical phrases) or responsorial (call and response) performances used to be common in some areas in the past. The instruments used depend on the area. However, until recently the *dehol* (double-headed drum) and *zirne* (a type of shawm) pair constituted the most

Men play traditional Kurdish music in the Kurdistan region of Iraq, 2016. (Dreamstime Agency/ Dreamstime.com)

popular instrumental accompaniment to dance music. In the lower part of the Mardin area *kemaçe* is the primary wedding instrument, whereas somewhat to the west of the area around the town of Kızıltepe and in the adjoining areas in Syria (today popularly known as Rojava), the amplified long-necked lute *bizk* is a popular wedding music instrument. Today digital keyboards are an integral part of wedding musicianship in the entire Kurdistan area and are used both as a melodic instrument and to provide rhythm.

At the present time, most performers of dance songs are professional wedding musicians. In the past, however, nonprofessionals (lay people) also used to perform at weddings. In any case, the professional performers of these genres often considered dance songs (or love-themed songs in general) to be beneath them. In many areas, peripatetic musicians have been the primary providers of dance music at weddings and other festivities. Nevertheless, today wedding musicianship has become a relatively more socially acceptable line of work among the Kurds themselves, and therefore there are many wedding music bands in Kurdistan in general.

Bridal Songs

In addition to the songs that are conventionally played at weddings and are associated with dancing, there are bridal songs performed at specific moments during a wedding. The musical features of these songs and the names given to them may vary between areas. The following is Christensen's description of the musical features of bridal songs in a specific tribe (Blum et al., n.d.):

> Weddings among the Ertoşi of western Hakkâri require that men and women sing at certain moments of the ritual. Women of the bride's family sing *narînik* before the departure of the procession that will take the bride to her husband. *Serke zava* ('over the groom') is a genre sung upon her arrival at the groom's house, when the couple first sits together. Thereafter *şeşbendî* are performed by men or women, or by two men and two women from the groom's family, in alternation. In all these cases, the singers stand still or sit, the performance is antiphonal and the traditional texts are sung syllabically on loosely metred [sic.] melodies.

Today, some bridal songs such as those that accompany the specific wedding ritual, where henna is applied to the hands of the bride and the groom as married and unmarried women circle around them with candles in their hands, may also be performed by the professional wedding musicians themselves.

Singing that Accompanies Work

In the village society in the past, singing accompanied certain kinds of work, such as milking animals, churning butter, crushing wheat, sickle harvesting, etc. Although as expected the main function of work songs is to facilitate labor (e.g., by synchronizing labor), Christensen also mentions that some of these songs were believed to have apotropaic (preventing bad luck and evil) qualities and performed for that reason (Christensen, 1967: 118). With large-scale urbanization in the second half of the 20th century, these songs started becoming forgotten as the activities that they accompanied became largely irrelevant to urban populations. Therefore, today only some rhythmic songs performed during harvesting crops and milling grains are still remembered (Allison, 2001: 44).

Ritual and Religious Performances

For faith groups in Kurdistan, such as the Yezidis, Yaresan (Ahl-e Haqq), and the Alevis, musical performances constitute a very important part of ritual performance and each has its own ritual performance genres, which depend on the faith group and the area in question.

For the Yezidis, musical performances consist of the sung performances of long sacred poems known as *qewls* and *beyts* and musical rituals performed within the context of religious celebrations. *Qewls* have the highest status in Yezidi textual tradition and are ordinarily memorized, transmitted, and performed by specialists named *qewwals* (Kreyenbroek, 2010: 84). Each *qewl* originally had its unique melody (Kreyenbroek, 2010: 83). Although, strictly speaking, *beyts* do not have religious themes, they contain references to the Yezidi faith (Gökçen, 2009: 140). Musical performances also take place among the Yezidis on two main occasions: the New Year and the yearly pilgrimage to the tomb of Sheikh Adi, the founder figure and saint of Yezidi faith. These performances feature woodwind instruments such as the *ney* and the *şebbabe* and rhythmic accompaniment provided by the framedrum *def* (Blum et al., n.d.). The Yezidi consider these instruments to be sacred.

Likewise, among the Yarsan, musical performances play a very important role in ritual contexts: they are an integral part of the religious assemblies known as *cem*, which consist of performances of short parts from sacred poems that are known as *kalams* by professional, specialized *kalamxwans* (Kreyenbroek, 2010: 84; 2015: 503). These performers not only sing these *kalams* but also accompany themselves on the long necked-lute *tembûr*, which is considered sacred. Previously only members of the Ahl-e Haqq were allowed to hear these performances. However, starting with the famous *tembûr* player Ali Akbar Moradi, recordings of these performances now can be found on some international labels.

Among the Kurdish or Turkish-speaking Alevis, musical performances are common during the main rituals of Alevi religious life and are referred as *cem* or *ayn-i cem* and feature dancing known in Kurdish as *semê* (or *semah* in Turkish). The longnecked lute *bağlama* is the only permissible instrument in ritual contexts and is played either by the religious leader *dede* or by another performer known as the *zakir*. Those present in the *cem* ritual may sometimes dance the *semê* or join in the musical performance by uttering vocables with religious significance (Aksoy, 2014: 124–126).

Among Muslims, musical performances in ritual contexts and songs with religious themes or ritual significance are also found. Perhaps the most common musical performance in the context of Islam is the *adhan* (call to prayer), which is recited five times a day by an *imam* from the top of a minaret. In addition to that, the recitation of the Qur'an by religious specialists also often involves melodization of the texts concerned.

Religious songs such as those referred to as *qesîde, lawje, beyt,* or *qazel* in different areas are performed among Muslim Kurds. However, because of lack of research into these genres, regional differences in the performance of these songs are still unknown to nonlocals. In the past, these genres were often performed by dervishes (members of Sufi *tariqas*) to the accompaniment of the frame-drum widely known as *erbane, def,* or *defe.* Today, only a small number of people are still alive who perform within that particular style. In terms of the performance practice of dervishes Al-Salihi (1989, 88) offers the following information:

> These songs almost exclusively consist of three parts. The first and the third parts are performed in metric free recitative. The middle part is fixed and strongly rhythmic. In the recitative part, the dervish holds his *def* vertically in front of him and uses it as a resonator and a percussion instrument. In the rhythmic part or the interludes, he holds his daff obliquely with some distance from his body. The daff is held with both thumbs and played with the fingers of both hands.

Recent Developments in Kurdish Musical Practices

Kurdistan has been politically divided between four different nation-states since the beginning of the 20th century. Some of these nation-states pursued a very oppressive policy toward their Kurdish citizens. The prime example of this is Turkey, which banned the use of Kurdish in public for many years following the state's foundation in 1923. The ban on publishing in Kurdish was officially lifted in 1991; however, unlawful and illegal restrictions and political pressure have continued since then.

Tanbur

The tanbur is a Kurdish string instrument that is played by many at home, at weddings, and at other festivities and some religious occasions. The instrument is shaped like a teardrop with a long neck and has 13 frets and three strings, two for the melody and one for the base line. It is plucked or strummed. For the Ahle-Haqq or Yaresan, the tanbur is a sacred instrument played in their religious performances and chants. Other famous Kurdish singers like Shivan Perwer play the tanbur with their songs. Ali Akbar Moradi from Iran is one of the most accomplished tanbur players.

In such an atmosphere of political oppression, two radio stations came to hold vital importance for Kurds: Radio Baghdad in Iraq and Radio Yerevan in the Armenian Soviet Socialist Republic. The broadcasting of performances of sung narratives and poetry, dance songs, and other genres of melodized sound and word on these radio stations had a lasting effect on the musical life of the Kurds, and the particular genres and styles that were broadcast attained widespread popularity in large areas.

As mentioned previously, a good degree of variety already existed in many aspects (e g , instrumentation, style, terminology, etc) of melodized sound and word performance between different areas in Kurdistan. Nevertheless, as a result of living in four different nation-states for almost a century and interacting with the national cultural forms in these nation-states, other kinds of differentiation and diversification also emerged in Kurdish musical practices.

Perhaps one of the most important developments in the 20th century has been that some of the most vital genres of sung performance lost their popularity. First, with technological advancements such as the increased accessibility of radio and television in the 1970s and subsequently with rapid—and sometimes forced—urbanization, sung narratives and poetry lost their significance. Although since the mid-1990s these genres and their performers have been revitalized as the prime element of Kurdish national culture, the social circumstances surrounding their performance and listening practices have changed drastically. Moreover, almost no new compositions in traditional genres are being made and today only old sung narrations and oral traditions are being rehashed and performed. Nonetheless, dance songs seem to have maintained their popularity during this period of change.

Another important change has been that professional musicianship, especially wedding musicianship, used to be largely considered a lowly occupation and severely inappropriate for the majority of the Kurdistan society to participate in. Moreover, in the past, among certain pious sections of the society music and musicianship (especially playing an instrument) were considered to be sinful. Today, however, musicianship has become more acceptable in the society of Kurdistan as a profession. Nevertheless, most Kurdish families would still prefer their children not become professional musicians. Certain other taboos concerning musicianship still hold for Kurds, such as playing the *kemaçe* in the lower Mardin area, as the instrument is associated with performers from peripatetic communities and Kurds consider it shameful to play the instrument.

Today, Kurds both inside and outside Kurdistan pursue a diverse range of modern forms of popular music. There is a significant trend among new-generation musicians to incorporate traditional singing techniques or references to traditional performance styles into their performances and compositions.

Argun Çakır

Further Reading

Al-Salihi, N. (1989). *Die Musik in Kurdistan*. Frankfurt: Peter Lang Verlag.

Aksoy, O. (2014). "The Music and Multiple Identities of Kurdish Alevis from Turkey in Germany." Unpublished PhD dissertation, Graduate Faculty in Music, City University of New York. http://academicworks.cuny.edu/gc_etds/5.

Allison, C. (1996). "Old and New Traditions in Badinan." In P. Kreyenbroek & C. Allison (Eds.), *Kurdish Culture and Identity* (pp. 29–47). London: Zed Books.

Allison, C. (2001). *The Yezidi Oral Tradition in Iraqi Kurdistan*. Richmond, Surrey, UK: Curzon Press.

Allison, C. (2010). "Kurdish Oral Literature." In P. G. Kreyenbroek & U. Marzolph (Eds.), *Oral Literature of Iranian Languages: Kurdish, Pashto, Balochi, Ossetic, Persian and Tajik* (pp. 33–69). London: I. B. Tauris.

Amy de La Bretèque, E. (2012). "Voices of Sorrow: Melodized Speech, Laments, and Heroic Narratives among the Yezidis of Armenia." *Yearbook for Traditional Music*, vol. 44, 129–148.

Amy de La Bretèque, E. (2013). *Paroles Mélodisées: Récits Épiques et Lamentations Chez les Yézidis d'Arménie*. Paris: Classiques Garnier.

Bilal, M., & Amy de la Bretèque, E. (2006). "The Oror and the Lorî—Armenian and Kurdish Lullabies in Present-Day Istanbul." In P. Kreyenbroek & C. Allison (Eds.), *Remembering the Past in Iranian Societies* (pp. 125–140). Wiesbaden: Harrassowitz Verlag.

Blum, S., Christensen, D., & Shiloah, A. (n.d.). "Kurdish Music." *Grove Music Online. Oxford Music Online*. http://www.oxfordmusiconline.com.

Christensen, D. (1961). "Brautlieder aus dem Vilayet Hakkâri, Südost-Türkei." *Journal of the International Folk Music Council*, vol. 13, 70–72.

Christensen, D. (1963). "Tanzlieder der Hakkâri-Kurden." *Jahrbuch für musikalische Volks- und Völkerkunde*, vol. 1, 11–47.

Christensen, D. (1967). "Die Musik der Kurden." *Mitteilungen der Berliner Gesellschaft für Anthropologie, Ethnologie, und Urgeschichte*, vol. 1, 113–119.

Gökçen, A. (2009). [Liner notes]. In *Yezidiler: Êzîdî: dini müzik, halk müziği; religious music, folk music; muzîka dînî, muzîka cimeâte* [CD]. Istanbul: Kalan.

Kanakis, I. (2005). "Chanter la Nation: La Parole Chantée dans le Nationalisme Kurde." *Outre-Terre*, vol. 1, no. 10, 361–373.

Kreyenbroek, P. (2010). "Orality and Religion in Kurdistan: The Yezidi and Ahl-e Haqq Traditions." In P. G. Kreyenbroek & U. Marzolph (Eds.), *Oral Literature of Iranian Languages: Kurdish, Pashto, Balochi, Ossetic, Persian and Tajik* (pp. 70–88). London: I. B. Tauris.

Kreyenbroek, P. (2015). "The Yezidi and Yarsan Traditions." In Stausberg, M. (Ed.), *The Wiley Blackwell Companion to Zoroastrianism* (pp. 499–504). Hoboken, NJ: John Wiley & Sons.

Scalbert-Yücel, C. (2009). "The Invention of a Tradition: Diyarbakır's Dengbêj Project." *European Journal of Turkish Studies*, no. 10, http://ejts.revues.org/pdf/4055.

Turgut, L. (2002). "Cembelî fils du prince de Hekkarî." Unpublished MA thesis, Institut National des Langues et Civilisations Orientales, Paris. In *Georg- August-Universität Göttingen*, http://www.uni-goettingen.de/de/138346.html.

Turgut, L. (2010). *Mündliche Literatur der Kurden in den Regionen Botan und Hekarî*. Berlin: Logos Verlag.

RECORDINGS

Aslan, B. (recordist). (2008). *Pirler divanı: Sinemilli pirlerinden deyişler; Dîwana pîran* [Paraliturgical tunes by Sinemilli Pirs: The Gathering of the Pirs]. [CD]. Istanbul: Kom Müzik.

Boğaziçi Gösteri Sanatları Topluluğu (BGST) (producer). (2004). *Eyhok: Traditional Music from Hakkari*. [2 CDs]. Istanbul: Kalan.

Christensen, D. (recordist). (2004 [1966]). *Kurdish Folk Music from Western Iran*. [CD]. Washington, DC: Smithsonian Folkways Recordings, FW04103.

Gökçen, A. (recordist). (2009). *Yezidiler: Êzîdî: Dini Müzik, Halk Müziği; Religious Music, Folk Music; Muzîka Dînî, Muzîka Cimeâte*. [2 CDs]. Istanbul: Kalan.

Moradi, A. A. (performer). (2002). *Les 72 maqam rituels des Yarsan*. [4 CDs]. Paris: INEDIT, Maison des cultures du monde.

Solecki, R. P. (recordist). (2004 [1955]). *Kurdish Folk Songs and Dances*. [CD]. Washington, DC: Smithsonian Folkways Recordings, FW04469.

Cinema

Within the last decade one of the most significant and effective ways of representing Kurdish identity and its social, cultural, and political resistance has been taking place through Kurdish cinema. By means of the rising visibility of Kurdish films that travel the world in international film festivals, the Kurdish people's past and present moments of resistance are revealed and circulated.

Kurdish cinema is categorized as such since the 2000s, and it is an international cinema that emerges from multiple geographic spaces, concentrated in countries with Kurdish populations, such as Turkey, Iran, Iraq, Syria, Armenia, Australia, and European countries like England, Germany, Austria, France, Sweden, and Norway. A number of historical, political, and cultural circumstances have led to the emergence of Kurdish cinema. These include the visibility of Kurdish directors like Bahman Ghobadi and Hineer Salem at international film festivals; the increase in the number of Kurdish people receiving film education; and the new digital technologies that bypass or limit the influence of censorship by state apparatuses.

A Short History of the Formation of Kurdish Cinema

The international success of the Iranian Kurdish director Bahman Ghobadi's films *Zamani Barayé Masti Asbha* (*The Time of The Drunken Horses*, 2000), *Gomgashtei Der Aragh* (*Marooned in Iraq*, 2002), and *Lakposhtha Parvaz Mikonand* (*Turtles Can Fly*, 2004) and Iraqi Kurdish director Hiner Saleem's *Vodka Lemon* (2003) and *Kilometre Zero* (2005) ignited the first spark of "Kurdish cinema." Ghobadi's and Saleem's representation of the lives of Kurdish people combined with the awards these films received at international film festivals generated recognition of Kurdish identity in the international film arena. These successful attempts created a significant motivation for Kurdish people, disseminated throughout various countries, to be assembled under the rubric of Kurdish cinema. Thus, Ghobadi's and Saleem's success is one of the most significant factors behind the international recognition of Kurdish cinema (Cicek, 2009: 3).

A Time for Drunken Horses

Kurdish-Iranian director Bahman Ghobadi released the film *A Time for Drunken Horses, Zamani Baraye Masiye Asbha*, in 2000, which became internationally acclaimed by winning the Golden Camera at the Cannes Film Festival. The film is set in the Iranian-Iraqi Kurdistan border area describing the life of some orphans where a young boy and his sister try to raise money for their youngest brother's surgery. The young boy goes with smugglers across the mountains where the mules are given alcohol to survive, and his sister is getting married, hoping to use the dowry money for the treatment.

The first significant resource that was published on Kurdish cinema was compiled and edited by Mizgin Mujde Arslan in 2009, published in the Turkish language, and it is titled *Kürt Sineması: Yurtsuzluk, Sınır ve Ölüm / Kurdish Cinema: Homelessness, Borders and Death*. Arslan is a Kurdish director and film critic from Turkey, and in her foreword, she states that the success of Kurdish directors like Bahman Ghobadi and Hiner Saleem motivated young Kurdish people of different social classes from all over the world to engage in filmmaking. In the 2000s, Kurdish films were accepted at international film festivals like Cannes and Berlin. As a result, cinema workshops were held in various newly emerging Kurdish art and cultural centers mainly established in towns with a predominantly Kurdish population in Turkey. These workshops organized by Kurdish directors provided an education in the technical aspects of filmmaking for both Kurdish and Turkish people who were interested. Apart from receiving a filmmaking education in these centers, Kurdish students also began to obtain degrees in film studies. Hence, Arslan concludes that for Kurdish people cinema became a method of self-definition and liberation (Arslan, 2008: xi). Furthermore, Hamid Dabaşi states that Kurdish cinema creates a visual topography, and in this way, it animates the reality of Kurdish people (Dabaşi, 2009: x). Based on this background, it can be argued that Kurdish cinema creates a platform to share Kurdish reality with both Kurdish and non-Kurdish audiences. It also motivates the formation of a Kurdish audience, which represents the disseminated Kurdish nation, embodying different aspects of Kurdish identity, including the different accents and dialects, local culture, traditions, and lifestyles that merge with each other through Kurdish films (Cicek, 2009: 3).

Devrim Kılıç asserts "As cinema narrates emotions, ideas, history, in short life itself with image and sound, it is a highly significant tool for Kurdish people who are in a state of liberation" (Kılıç, 2009: 3). He argues that there is a strong relationship between the emancipation attempts of Kurdish people and developments in Kurdish cinema. The rising number of Kurdish-themed films after the 1990s is a reflection of the continuous changes in the status of Kurdish people's lives. The emergence of Kurdish cinema is directly linked with the rise of the Kurdish question in international politics. The Kurdish community attracted international

Scene still from the film *Marooned in Iraq* (2002), directed by Bahman Ghobadi. (Photofest)

attention in terms of its political and cultural status especially after the first Gulf War in 1991. Due to the interventionist politics of the United States in countries like Iraq, Iran, and Syria, the cause of Kurdish people has become more of an issue in international arenas. Starting from the Gulf War to the current turmoil in Syria, the position of the Kurdish people and their resistance has always been at the core of the geopolitical conflicts. As a result of these changes in political circumstances, the Kurdish people have found the opportunity to reflect their lack of social status through cinema (Cicek, 2009: 3).

In this realm, the first Kurdish film ever made is known to be *Zare* (1926) directed by the Armenian director Hamo Bek-Nazaryan (1892–1965) as it reflects the story of the Kurdish people living in a Yezidi village. Nazaryan is known to be the pioneer and founder of Armenian cinema, and *Zare* is about the love story of Saydo and Zare and their struggle for a relationship in a Yezidi Kurdish village at the time of the Russian Revolution. The first screening of *Zare* as a part of a Kurdish cinema event took place in 2006 during the fourth London Kurdish Film Festival, thanks to the efforts of Mustafa Gündoğdu, who is the founder and the director of this festival.

Another prominent Kurdish filmmaker who inspired many Kurdish directors is Yılmaz Güney (1937–1984). His film *Yol/The Way* (1982) got the Palme d'Or at Cannes Film Festival in 1982, during which Güney was expelled from Turkish citizenship. As an actor, script writer, and director from Turkey, his cinema is embraced by both the Kurdish and Turkish cinema contexts. Mizgin Mujde Arslan would include Guney's late films *Umut/Hope* 1970, *Sürü/The Herd* (1979), *Yol*, and *Duvar/The Wall* (1983) in the realm of Kurdish cinema, because in those films the social, cultural, and political aspects of the Kurdish context is represented and problematized.

Güney's cinema occupies a highly significant space in Kurdish cinema, not only for representing and problematizing the Kurdish context in Turkey, but also for the stylistic and aesthetic level of filmmaking his films have reached. *Yol* is the story of five male prisoners who are on leave for a week during the 1980s coup d'état. Yet, in the history of cinema *Yol* is the first film that has characters through whom Güney represents the extremely problematic military regime, as well as the patriarchal context of the eastern and Kurdish geography of Turkey.

Another significant aspect of Güney's cinema is that as a communist figure he spent more than 10 years in prison, mostly in the wards for political prisoners. During this time he devoted much of his time to reading and writing, and he wrote the scripts of *Sürü* and *Yol* in prison. Especially during the script writing process of *Yol* he was inspired by fellow prisoners he stayed with. Thus, he used the prison space like a laboratory of various compelling characters and cases, which he later represents in his films. Being a prisoner never stopped him from producing—on the contrary, the scripts he wrote in prison became much longer and more elaborate in order to reflect on every detail he had in mind as he couldn't be present at the actual film shooting. In 1981 he fled from Turkey when he was on leave from prison, and he escaped to Paris where he spent the rest of his life until 1984.

Although Güney's cinematic works were internationally very well received, due to his prison time and his peculiar representation of the working-class people in his films, his works were deliberately excluded from "national cinema" debates that questioned the boundaries of "Turkish national cinema." His exclusion from Turkish national cinema prompted various questions, including: How could Güney's cinema be situated in Turkey? If it's excluded from Turkish national cinema debates in his time, where does it stand in Turkey? Is there a Kurdish national cinema?

Positioning Kurdish Cinema as a "National Cinema"

In the realm of Kurdish cinema studies, a significant debate revolves around the question of how Kurdish cinema can be situated in the "national cinema" framework. National cinema is a concept that emerged mainly in Europe, but especially in England during the 1970s, and the motivation behind its emergence was to indicate the tension between the popular and wide distribution channels of Hollywood films vs. the in-house productions of various European cinemas, including British, French, or German. In order the resist the hegemony of the Hollywood phenomena in the European film market, the concept of national cinema aimed to indicate the interaction between nation, state, and cinema that could resist the American films and its extremely wide distribution channels. Yet the national cinema framework (maybe unconsciously) has always regarded its theoretical formulation to be stemming from a recognized state. Until the 2000s, the existence of nonstate filmmaking was not taken into account in the realm of national cinema studies. With the emergence of Kurdish cinema, Basque cinema, or Quebec cinema, "the possibility of a national cinema without a state" has become an issue of dissent for national cinema frameworks, and several different film theorists have supported concepts like transnational cinema, subnational cinema, or supranational cinema. In this framework, many theorists have already positioned Kurdish cinema as a national cinema. For instance Mehmet Aktaş explains that while world cinema was celebrating its 100th anniversary, Kurdish cinema was just emerging in the early 2000s (Aktaş, 2008: 28). For Kurdish people, the 20th century was a difficult time, filled with resistance, prohibition, defeat, and sorrow. States like Turkey, Iran, Iraq, and Syria tried hard to eradicate the Kurdish language and identity through assimilation politics. Aktaş comments "that is why the late coming of a national cinema, which is more complex and which has different needs than other modern art forms, should be tolerated" (Aktaş, 2008: 56). Furthermore, Suncem Koçer would also define Kurdish cinema as a national cinema, and she would argue, "Kurdish cinema has emerged as a national cinema in transnational space" (Koçer, 2014: 474). Thus, both of these approaches for defining Kurdish cinema indicate that Kurdish cinema does not necessarily take the state formation as a condition for defining its cinematic entity as a national cinema. From Koçer's point of view, Kurdish cinema formation situates itself as a national cinema under which the transnational cinematic works can be united. Because as Koçer elaborates, "Kurdish cultural production in European Diaspora exemplifies transnational imaginations informed by the existing discourse of the nation" (Koçer, 2014: 475). Ayça Çiftçi would also state, "Kurdish cinema can be considered as a cinema that reflects and reproduces a national consciousness in a transnational space" (Çiftçi, 2015: 116). Thus, Çiftçi would also indicate the relational aspect of the transnational nature and the national discourse of Kurdish cinema, and she would further state, "It would be theoretically justifiable to regard Kurdish cinema as a sub-national cinema, national cinema, or a transnational cinema. However, rather than pressing it in one of these categories, we can see Kurdish cinema as an example that demonstrates the importance of understanding the relationships between the national, sub-national, and transnational from a relational perspective" (Ibid).

These approaches to Kurdish cinema reveal that on one side its nonstate and transnational entity challenges the existing framework of the interaction between cinema and nation and marks Kurdish cinema as an "irregularity." On the other side, as Koçer would indicate, Kurdish cinema production reveals a transnational nature through its multistate contexts of production and distribution. At this point significant follow-up questions would be: How do Kurdish films meet with their audience? How are they distributed? How are they received? How are they funded?

The Distribution of Kurdish Cinema

It is significant to note that film festivals are extremely important venues for Kurdish films to meet their audience, for Kurdish filmmakers to pitch their new projects and apply for funding, and for Kurdish cinema to arouse international recognition and appeal. From this perspective since the 2000s, Kurdish films have been screened at leading international film festivals, including Cannes Film Festival, Berlin International Film Festival, Cinéma du Réel, San Sebastián International Film Festival, Nuremberg Film Festival, and Istanbul Film Festival.

Yet especially in Turkey, the screenings of some Kurdish films are still prevented through censorship politics. For instance in 2015, the screening of *Bakur/North/Kuzey* (2015) directed by Çayan Demirel and Ertuğrul Mavioğlu, which is a documentary set in the camps of Kurdish Workers Party (PKK), was censored hours before its premier at the Istanbul Film Festival. This last-minute censorship that prevented the premier screening aroused quite a controversy, and dozens of directors from Turkey withdrew from the national competition to protest this censorship. Thus, on one side, film festivals function as venues where Kurdish fiction and documentaries meet with their audience, but on the other side, for contexts like Turkey, the policies of oppressive state apparatuses toward Kurdish cinematic representations are revealed during these festival venues.

Besides the appearance of Kurdish films at the earlier mentioned international film festivals, since the 2000s many international "Kurdish Film Festivals" are being organized by Kurdish art and culture centers in various cities, including New York, Montreal, Melbourne, London, Manchester, Paris, Vienna, Berlin, Frankfurt, Cologne, and Stockholm. Among these film festivals, the first Kurdish Film Festival was organized in London in 2001 by Mustafa Gündoğdu, right after Bahman Ghobadi's success at the Cannes Film Festival in 2000. In Turkey, there are also Kurdish film festivals like the Amed Documentary Film Festival and the Yılmaz Güney Short Film Festival organized in Batman. Apart from these, the first International Kurdish Film Conference took place in Diyarbakir in 2009, and it was organized by the Diyarbakir Metropolitan Municipality (Koçer, 2014: 482).

In addition to these Kurdish cinema events, various Kurdish culture and art centers in Turkey provide cinema workshops, including at the Mesopotamia Culture Center in Istanbul, the Aram Tigran City Conservatory, and the Cegerxwin Culture Center in Diyarbakir. At these cinema workshops especially young people who are interested in filmmaking can receive education that includes courses on directing, script writing, editing, or theoretical classes on film history and film analysis.

Kurdish Cinema Today

Along with the rising number of Kurdish art and culture centers that provide cinema education for potential young Kurdish filmmakers, the number of short Kurdish films, feature films, and documentary films is increasing. With this increase in the number of films and filmmakers, certain diverse visual/vocal and aesthetic aspects shape the distinctive framework for Kurdish cinema. In this respect, Mizgin Mujde Arslan describes various stylistic characteristics of Kurdish cinema. She states that one of the most important aspects of Kurdish cinema is that its language is Kurdish. For Arslan the use of Kurdish language would mark "Kurdish cinema"; otherwise, for instance, films made by Kurdish directors but shot in any other language would be indicative of the assimilation of the Kurdish context (Arslan,

2014). Furthermore, Arslan notes various other patterns for Kurdish cinema, including the representation of the borders, mountains, villages, and rural life, which have been common in Kurdish films. The themes of fatherlessness, statelessness, mourning a loss, the dependence on oral culture, storytelling, and the *Deng Bej* tradition would be other common aspects of Kurdish cinema. It is also important to note that many Kurdish filmmakers as well as Kurdish art and culture centers are still dealing with censorship practices, as well as the harsh circumstances of the "emergency state" in Turkey.

Other prominent Kurdish filmmakers who were not mentioned before would include Hisham Zaman, Shahram Alidi, Kazım Öz, Hüseyin Karabey, Zeynel Doğan, Ahu Öztürk, Ali Kemal Çınarö, and many other young and inspirational filmmakers who keep on producing films in spite of many obstacles and censorship practices.

Özgür Çiçek

Further Reading

Portions of this chapter were originally printed in Özgür Çiçek. (2011). "The Fictive Archive: Kurdish Filmmaking in Turkey." In *Alphaville: Journal of Film and Screen Media*, vol. 1 (pp. 1–18).

Aktaş, M. (2009). "Kürt Sineması: Artık Bir Gerçek [Kurdish Cinema: A Reality From Now On]" *Kürt Sineması: Yurtsuzluk, Ölüm ve Sınır*. Istanbul: Agora Kitaplığı.

Arslan, M. (2009). *Kürt Sineması: Yurtsuzluk, Ölüm ve Sınır*. Istanbul: Agora Kitaplığı.

Çiçek, O. (2011). "The Fictive Archive: Kurdish Filmmaking in Turkey." In *Alphaville: Journal of Film and Screen Media*, vol. 1 (pp. 1–18).

Çiçek, O. (2014). "The Old and New Ways of Kurdish Filmmaking in Turkey: Potentials and Risks." In Akser, M. and Bayrakdar, D. (eds.) *New Cinema, New Media: Reinventing Turkish Cinema* (pp. 126–138). Newcastle, UK: Cambridge Scholars Publishing.

Çiftçi, A. (2015). *The Politics of Text and Context: Kurdish Films in Turkey in a Period of Political Transformation*. Dissertation submitted to Royal Halloway, University of London.

Dabaşi, H. (2009). "Önsöz [Foreword]". In M. J. Arsaln (Ed.), *Kürt Sineması: Yurtsuzluk, Ölüm ve Sınır*. Istanbul; Agora Kitaplığı.

Kılıç, D. (2009). "Kürt Sinemasının Yükselişi." In M. J. Arsaln (Ed.), *Kürt Sineması: Yurtsuzluk, Ölüm ve Sınır*. Istanbul: Agora Kitaplığı.

Koçer, S. (2014). "Kurdish Cinema as a Transnational Discourse Genre: Cinematic Visibility, Cultural Resilience, and Political Agency." *International Journal of Middle East Studies* vol. 46, no. 3, 473–488.

Koçer, S. (2015). "I Flew You Stayed as an Example of Domestic Ethnography." *Moment Journal*, vol. 2, no. 1, 338–346.

Filmography

5 Nolu Cezaevi / Prison Number 5. Dir. Çayan Demirel. 2009.

Dengê Bavê Min / Voice of My Father. Zeynel Doğan and Orhan Eskiköy. 2014.

Bahoz / The Storm. Dir. Kazım Öz. 2008.

Bakur / The North. Dir. Çayan Demirel—Ertuğrul Mavioğlu. 2015.

Be Deng / Silent., Dir. Rezzan Yeşilbaş. 2012.

Dersim 38. Dir. Çayan Demirel. 2006.

Diyar. Dir. Devrim Akkaya. 2014.

Ez firiyam tu ma li cih / I Flew You Stayed. Dir. Mizgin Müjde Arslan. 2012.

F Tipi Film / F Type Film. Dir. Hüseyin Karabey. 2012.

Fasle Kargadan / Rhino's Season. Dir. Bahman Ghobadi. 2012.

Gitmek / My Marlon and Brando. Dir. Hüseyin Karabey. 2008.

Gönderen İlhan Sami Çomak / Sender: İlhan Sami Çomak. Dir. Çiğdem Mazlum and Sertaç Yıldız. 2016.

Güneşe Yolculuk / Journey to the Sun. Dir. Yesim Ustaoğlu. 1999.

He bu Tune Bu / Once Upon a Time. Dir. Kazım Öz. 2014.

Iki Dil Bir Bavul / On the Way to School. Dir. Özgür Doğan and Orhan Eskiköy. 2009.

Kilometre Zero. Dir. Hiner Saleem. 2005.

Kirasê mirinê: Hewîtî / A Fatal Dress: Polygamy. Dir. Mizgin Müjde Arslan. 2009.

My Sweet Pepperland. Dir. Hiner Saleem. 2013.

Sessiz Ölüm / Sessiz Ölüm. Dir. Hüseyin Karabey. 2001.

Sürü / The Herd. Dir. Yılmaz Güney. 1979.

Toz Bezi / Dust Cloth. Dir. Ahu Öztürk. 2015.

Umut / The Hope Dir. Yılmaz Güney. 1968.

Were Denge Min / Come to My Voice. Dir. Hüseyin Karabey. 2014.

Yol / The Road. Dir. Yılmaz Güney. 1982.

Zamani barayé masti asbha / A Time for Drunken Horses. Dir. Bahman Ghobadi. 2000.

Zare. Dir. Hamo Bek-Nazaryan. 1925.

Zonê ma koti yo / Where Is My Mother Tongue?. Dir. Veli Kahraman. 2012.

Part II
Country Profiles

FRANCE

History and Demographics

The Kurdish community in France is believed to be the second most numerous in Europe, after the Kurds in Germany. However, due to the prohibition of ethnic censuses, the exact number is difficult to ascertain. Furthermore, Kurdish migrants are often categorized according to their Turkish, Iraqi, Iranian, or Syrian citizenship, which makes it even more difficult to present a definite number. According to the Kurdish Institute of Paris, between 230,000 and 250,000 Kurds lived in France as of May 2016, the great majority of which are from northern Kurdistan (Turkey) (IKP, 2016; see also Karim, 2016: 39–40; Khayati, 2008: 142). A majority of Kurds live in the suburbs of the larger French cities, especially Paris (for example, in the towns of Villiers-le-Bel, La Courneuve, Aulnay-sous-Bois, Sevran, Mantes-la-Jolie, etc.) and Marseille, as well as sizable communities in cities like Creil, Lyon, Montpellier, Nantes, Rennes, Rouen, and Strasbourg.

Except for a brief visit by Ehmed Paşa of the Baban, who spent some time in France in 1853–54 (see Chodźko, 1857), the first prominent Kurdish figure to take up residence in France was Kurd Şerif Paşa (1865–1951), another Baban prince, who spent 40 years of his life in exile, mainly in Paris and in Monte Carlo (principality of Monaco). He actively campaigned for Kurdish national rights, and in 1919, he headed the Kurdish delegation at the Paris Peace Conference. This is the context in which he published his work entitled "Memorandum on the Kurdish people's demands" (*Mémorandum sur les revendications du peuple kurde*). Şerif Paşa was instrumental in securing the Kurdish position in the Treaty of Sèvres (1920); however, these efforts ultimately proved unsuccessful, as it was replaced by the Treaty of Lausanne in 1923 (see Alakom, 1998).

The Kurdish-French relationship continued in the Levant, most importantly in mandate Syria, where important diplomatic and military figures, such as Pierre Rondot (1904–2000) and Roger Lescot (1914–1975), maintained friendly relations with the Bedirxan brothers, Celadet (1893–1951) and Kamuran (1895–1978), as well as other members of the Kurdish nationalist league Xoybûn ("Independence"). This collaboration was beneficial to both parties, yielding important productions in the domain of Kurdish studies, such as the *Kurdish Grammar* (*Grammaire kurde*) prepared by C. A. Bedirxan and R. Lescot and published in 1970 in Paris (Tejel Gorgas, 2006).

In 1930, the eldest of the Bedirxan brothers, Sureyya Bedirxan (1883–1938), migrated to Paris, where he acted as a representative for Xoybûn. That same year, he also published a book called *The Kurdish Question. Its Origins and Motives* (*La Question kurde. Ses origines et ses causes*). After the end of the French Mandate on Syria, in 1946, his brother Kamuran followed in his footsteps, and in 1947, Kamuran Bedirxan replaced Roger Lescot as chair of Kurdish Studies in the Langues'O, or School of Oriental Languages, in Paris. That chair had been created in 1945, marking the first time Kurdish was taught as an academic subject in Western Europe. Kamuran Bedirxan wrote several books, including a French manual of the Kurdish language (*Le Kurde sans peine*, 1990) and an unpublished Kurdish-French dictionary (with Roger Lescot). Among his students was Joyce Blau, who later took up his professorship at the university.

Kurd Şerif Paşa, Sureyya Bedirxan, and Kamuran Bedirxan were all prominent members of the Kurdish intelligentsia in exile, and they came to France on an individual basis, benefiting from their cordial relations with French officials. As for the first wave of permanent and relatively large Kurdish migration, it can be traced back to the 1960s, when around 15,000 Kurdish migrant workers arrived in France as part of the 30,000 workers' contingent who settled there following an economic agreement between France and Turkey. These workers mostly took up residence in the Alsace-Lorraine region (Khayati, 2008: 142). The adoption in 1976 of the law of family reunification allowed them to be joined by their families under certain conditions.

Later waves of Kurdish migration closely mirrored the political developments in Kurdistan and the occupying states. The end of the 1970s and beginning of the 1980s saw a surge in the influx of Kurdish asylum seekers as a consequence of the genocidal policies of the newly established Islamic Republic of Iran (1979) and of the Turkish military regime led by Kenan Evren (who came to power with a military coup on September 12, 1980). Another contributing factor was the election in 1981 of the socialist president François Mitterrand, whose government embraced a more welcoming policy toward migrants.

The number of Kurdish political refugees in France remained high for much of the 1980s and 1990s, as the repressive policies of the Turkish state, in response to the guerrilla war launched by the PKK in 1984, led to the displacement of around 3 million Kurds and deprived millions more of the right to live and perpetuate their culture on their ancestral lands. Meanwhile, between 1986 and 1989, Saddam Hussein led a genocidal campaign against the Kurds in South Kurdistan (Iraq), causing more than 150,000 victims. François Mitterrand's wife and founder of the association France Libertés (1986), Danièle Mitterrand (1924–2011), was particularly active in her support for the Kurds during this period.

It is estimated that approximately 50,000 Kurds arrived in France between 1990 and 2002, the year in which the Party of Justice and Progress (AKP) of Recep Tayyip Erdoğan came to power in Turkey (Khayati, 2008: 144). After a continued increase between 2002 and 2005, the number of asylum seekers has been on a constant decline, from 5,356 in 2005 to 1,195 in 2015 (about 90 percent of these applications come from Kurds; see the annuals reports by the French Office for the

Protection of Refugees and Stateless Persons [OFPRA], 2001–2015). However, given the renewed and brutal oppression faced by the Kurds after the peace talks with the PKK were abruptly ended by the Turkish authorities in June 2015, a return to higher numbers of asylum seekers is likely. Furthermore, in recent years, there has also been an increase of Kurdish refugees from Rojava (Western/Syrian Kurdistan) and Bashur (Southern/Iraqi Kurdistan).

Kurdish Associations

As a result of the specific circumstances of Kurdish migration, the Kurdish community in France has always included a comparatively high number of politically conscious and active people. This explains why the Kurds in France quickly felt the need to organize themselves into associations, with the objective of defending their rights and drawing attention to the Kurdish question and to the struggle for Kurdish rights. The oldest of these associations is the Kurdish Cultural Center (KCC), located in the predominantly Kurdish neighborhood of Strasbourg Saint-Denis in Paris. In 2001, the Kurdish Cultural Center became the Ahmet Kaya Kurdish Cultural Center in honor of the popular Kurdish singer Ahmet Kaya (1957–2000), who passed away in Paris after being forced into exile because of his political positions.

Still located in its historical building, the center now is known as the Academy of Arts and Cultures of Kurdistan. It offers Kurdish and French classes, folklore lessons, sports activities, and provides a broader community atmosphere. It serves as the focal point in the grassroots political mobilization of the Kurdish community in Paris and its surroundings, as is the case for other Kurdish associations throughout France and Europe. Demonstrations frequently start at the center and take place in nearby Place de la République or Gare de l'Est.

Located in the same area is the other major Kurdish-French institution, the Kurdish Institute of Paris (KIP). The KIP was established in 1983, and among its founding members are many Kurdish artists and intellectuals, such as Yılmaz Güney, Cigerxwîn, Hejar, Tawfiq Wahby, Qanatê Kurdo, Nureddîn Zaza, etc. The institute is presided over by Kendal Nezan. Since 1993, it has been recognized for its public utility, a specific legal status by which the French Council of State commends the positive social impact of an association or foundation, and between 2008 and 2013, it received financial support from the Kurdistan Regional Government (KRG). The institute focuses mostly on cultural and scholarly activities, with various periodical publications (*Kurmancî*, *Studia Kurdica*, *Études kurdes*), exhibits, conferences, Kurdish classes, and a short-lived TV station (*Kurd Yek*). It also possesses an impressive Kurdish library, which has been digitized as the Bibliothèque numérique kurde, with many books freely available for download on its website.

While the Kurdish Cultural Center and the Kurdish Institute of Paris are the two oldest Kurdish associations in France, the increasing diversification in the territorial distribution of the community has in the last several years led to the creation of many new associations in different cities, serving as community hubs for cultural activities, socialization, and political mobilization. One should mention the Maison culturelle kurde du Val d'Oise in Villiers-le-Bel, the association Amara—Maison du peuple kurde in Rennes, the Centre culturel de Mésopotamie in Marseille, the Centre culturel kurde Engin Sincer in Nantes, and many more. All these associations are members of the Federation of Kurdish Associations in France (Fédération des associations kurdes de France, FEYKA), whose main offices are located inside the Kurdish Cultural Center of Paris.

Finally, worthy of mention is the presence in several universities of the French branch of the Kurdistan Students' Union (Yekîtiya Xwendevanên Kurdistan, YXK), an association founded in Germany in 1991 and active in various European countries, which started working in France from 2011. One should also mention the Kurdish Information Center (Centre d'Information du Kurdistan, CIK), a diplomatic office also located in Paris, near the Gare du Nord, which was the site of the assassination on January 9, 2013, of three Kurdish women activists, Sakine Cansız (founding member of the PKK), Fidan Doğan (Paris representative of the KNK), and Leyla Şaylemez.

Political and Community Life

The Kurdish cultural centers in various cities organize most of the community, cultural, and political activities. The French Kurds frequently organize demonstrations in connection with current events in Kurdistan, as well as take part in French demonstrations, such as the annual First of May marches, the 2016 protests against the reform of labor law, etc. FEYKA also participates at the Fête de l'Humanité (named after *L'Humanité*, the daily of the French Communist Party), which draws around a million people in mid-September every year. There is also an annual march and meeting in the European capital of Strasbourg on the weekend of February 15 to protest the arrest of Abdullah Öcalan in 1999.

Newroz

The Kurdish New Year, Newroz, is celebrated on March 21. It coincides with the Northward Equinox and marks the beginning of spring. It is believed to be a pre-Islamic, Zoroastrian custom that uses fire to symbolize purification and renewal. This occasion is an important element of Kurdish identity, when Kurds in all home countries and in the diaspora get together to celebrated their culture through music, dances, special food, colorful costumes, games, and gatherings. Often celebrated outside, huge bonfires are lit, and the young people jump across the fire. Newroz also has political aspects as a mass gathering of Kurds to reassert their identity and demonstrate for cultural and political rights in confrontation with the various governments.

Since 2007, the Engin Sincer Kurdish Youth Festival has been taking place in June in different French cities. It is named after the famous Kurdish politician and guerrilla commander Engin Sincer (1969–2003). The festival draws Kurds from all over Europe; likewise, Kurds from France also take part in the major Kurdish festivals and demonstrations in other European countries. Other annual manifestations include the International Working Women's Day (March 8), the celebration of Newroz, the Kurdish New Year (March 21), the birthday of Abdullah Öcalan (April 4), the start of the Kurdish armed struggle (August 15), and the foundation of the PKK (November 27).

France holds a special place among the Kurdish diaspora for its famous émigrés. Yılmaz Güney and Ahmet Kaya, who are both buried in the Père Lachaise cemetery in Paris, have already been mentioned. The cemetery is also the resting place of Abdurrahman Qasimlo, leader of the Kurdistan Democratic Party of Iran (KDP-I), assassinated in Vienna in 1989 and of his successor Sadiq Sharafkandi, assassinated in Berlin in 1991. This serves as a strong reminder of the impact of violence and conflict on the history of the Kurds, including in the diaspora.

This is especially true in Paris, where the history of political violence against Kurds goes back to the days of Kurd Şerif Paşa, who was the target of an assassination attempt organized by the Committee of Union and Progress leadership in January 1914. On December 23, 1985, Mustafa Aktaş, a member of the Army of Liberation of the People of Kurdistan (ARGK), was assassinated by killers linked to the Turkish military junta. He is also buried in the Père Lachaise. The crime perpetrated against Sakine Cansız, Fidan Doğan, and Leyla Şaylemez is the latest of these political assassinations. Its culprit, Ömer Güney, died in prison on December 17, 2016, a month before the scheduled beginning of his trial. It is suspected that he worked for the Turkish intelligence services, and every Wednesday, a demonstration is held in Paris asking for the instigators of the crime to be brought to justice.

French Attitudes Toward the Kurds

The French people are generally sympathetic toward the Kurdish community, although the extent of the support for the Kurdish cause is debated along partisan lines, with the left and far-left sections of the political class usually being the more supportive. The inclusion of the PKK on the list of terrorist organizations of the European Union in 2002 has, however, occasionally led to arrests and trials of Kurdish politicians and militants. During the Syrian crisis, France has offered limited support for the Rojava project. Nasrin Abdalla, YPJ commander, and Asiya Abdellah, co-president of the PYD, were received by President François Hollande at the Palais de l'Élysée in 2015. In May 2016, a representative office of the Rojava administration was opened in Paris near the city hall; however, it has not been officially recognized by the French government. There has been a representative of the KRG in Paris since 2001 and a French consulate in Hewler (Erbil) since 2007, as well as a section of the Institut Français du Proche-Orient (IFPO) since 2011. The Kurdish community in France maintains friendly relations with the Armenian and Assyro-Chaldean communities of the country, notably in Sarcelles where the latter is mainly present.

Culture, Sports, and Education

In terms of education, the Institut National des Langues et Civilisations Orientales (INALCO, formerly Langues'O) has a Kurdish department offering BA, MA, and PhD programs. Both Kurmanji and Sorani are taught along with classes on the history, geography, and civilization of Kurdistan. The department is headed by Professor Halkawt Hakem, and the chair for Kurmanji is held by Professor Ibrahim Seydo Aydoğan. In the past, Langues'O/INALCO has been home to scholars and educators such as Roger Lescot, Kamuran Bedirxan, Joyce Blau, Michael Chyet, and Christine Allison. At the University of Rouen, Professor Salih Akin gives Kurdish classes as part of the diploma of French teaching as a foreign language (FLE). Kurdish classes are also offered at the Kurdish Cultural Center and the Kurdish Institute of Paris. In the social sciences, Professor Hamit Bozarslan of the School for Advanced Studies in Social Sciences (École des hautes études en sciences sociales, EHESS) has written extensively on the Kurds and the broader Middle East; he also supervises a great number of Kurdish-French PhD students.

There is, as of yet, not much Kurdish literature translated into French. We can mention Ehmede Xani's *Mem û Zîn* (*Mem et Zin*, L'Harmattan, 2001), translated by Sandrine Alexie and Akif Hasan, and Mehmed Uzun's *Siya evînê* (*La poursuite de l'ombre*, Phébus, 1999), translated by Fawaz Husen. Likewise, French literature has rarely been translated into Kurdish. There is a very good dictionary of Sorani Kurdish, made by Halkawt Hakem (*Dictionnaire kurde-français*, L'Asiathèque, 2012); the only dictionary of Kurmanji Kurdish is the thorough but dated work of Auguste Jaba and Mela Mehmude Bayezidi, edited by Ferdinand Justi (St. Petersburg, 1879). A number of academic and journalistic works on contemporary Kurdish issues have been written, and recently, the Rojava revolution has attracted renewed attention from writers, with several books and documentaries produced on the subject. Abdullah Öcalan's *The Road Map to Negotiations* has been translated into French (*La feuille de route vers les négociations*, 2013), and the translations of his series of Defenses to the European Court of Human Rights are in preparation.

Several Kurdish artists are living in France and working in French, Kurdish, or both, such as writer Fawaz Husen, director Hiner Saleem, comedian and director Ahmet Zirek, poet Şeyhmus Dağtekin, singer Nuarin, and rapper Zimanbaz. The actress Amira Casar is part Kurdish, as was the late choreographer Maurice Béjart (1927–2007). Some festivals of Kurdish cinema have been organized, and projections of Kurdish films or films on the Kurds are frequent. The Kurdish Institute of Paris organizes a "Month of the Kurdish book" every year in January and February. There are several Kurdish restaurants in Paris, such as *Dilan*, *Zagros*, etc. In terms of sports, the Kurdish Cultural Center organizes a football tournament every year in May in La Courneuve, and the Engin Sincer festival also includes sports activities.

Sacha Alsancakli

Further Reading

Alakom, R. (1998). *Şerif Paşa. Bir Kürt diplomatının fırtınalı yılları*. Istanbul: Avesta.

Chodźko, A. (1857). "Études philologiques sur la langue kurde (dialecte de Soléimanié)." *Journal asiatique*, série 5, tome 9, 297–356.

Institut Kurde de Paris (IKP). (2016). "Diaspora Kurde." http://www.institutkurde.org /kurdorama.

Karim, J. S. (2016). *Qui suis-je, kurde ou français(e) ? Étude sur les identités personnelles chez les jeunes Kurdes en France (1989–2003)*. MA dissertation, University of Oslo.

Khayati, Kh. (2008). *From Victim Diaspora to Transborder Citizenship? Diaspora Formation and Transnational Relations among Kurds in France and Sweden*. PhD dissertation submitted to Linköping University.

Office Français de Protection des Réfugiés et Apatrides (OFPRA). "Rapports d'activité 2001–2015." https://ofpra.gouv.fr/fr/l-ofpra/nos-publications/rapports-d-activite (20/1/2017).

Tejel G., J. (2006). "Les constructions de l'identité kurde sous l'influence de la 'connexion kurdo-française' au Levant (1930–1946)." *European Journal of Turkish Studies,* vol. 5, https://ejts.revues.org/751.

GERMANY

If the diaspora is the fifth part of Kurdistan as Martin van Bruinessen (2015: 126) suggested, then Germany certainly covers a major part of it. It is the country with the largest Kurdish population outside of Kurdistan. What makes this especially interesting is the enormous demographic diversity including people of all ages and classes, all social subgroups, and speakers of all languages and dialects that are found in the four parts of Kurdistan. Each relevant state and region, including old and new diasporic communities, each town and more or less each village are represented. There are people of all social classes and of all educational levels, young Germans with a Kurdish background, newcomers, political activists, nationalists, atheists, secular believers, and religious fanatics. All of these groups are socially or politically organized in one way or another. Regardless of how many different points and frames of reference, they are in an ongoing dialogue with each other and with others, and they are constantly and powerfully reaffirming aspects of Kurdish identity. Transgenerational and transnational transmission of this intra- and inter-ethnical identity discourse is giving distinction to important aspects of their lives.

As is the nature of ethnicity and the context of migration, Kurdish identity with its cultural and ethnic heritage must be perceived as particularly amorphous: identifying oneself as Kurdish means different things to different people, and still there is a strong feeling of togetherness. Kurmanji becoming the *lingua franca* further strengthened this notion through active language planning on an academic level.

Second- and third-generation immigrants born and raised in Germany often acquire their Kurdistan view from an outward position, and it becomes more significant for an imagined homogenous landscape, a longing for peace and freedom, omnipresent contact with kin, and neighborly ties, as well as a general sense of belonging somewhere (Ammann, 2004: 1018). They are confronted with identity questions different from those faced by older generations and first-generation immigrants, and some certainly turn away from what is commonly considered Kurdish (Bengio & Maddy-Weitzman, 2013: 83). Those in Germany who feel mostly Kurdish relate to common frames of reference in their thinking and feeling. These are language idioms, territories of origins and destinations, transnational histories, material culture sometimes with folkloristic elements, common future perspectives and hopes, collective memories of persecution, and flight and displacement.

Specific data on the number of Kurds in Germany are limited for a number of reasons: no nation-state backing, the massive historical ethnic suppression in their homelands, and the general circumstances of all migration processes. Even though there should be no need to prove large numbers in order to justify collective demands for recognition and social justice, there is an obvious and comprehensible general desire to document and emphasize quantity.

Considering the large numbers of transnational, transethnic, and in general hybrid identities in individuals as well as collectives, especially in second and third generations of migrants, it is impossible to produce exact numbers. While some organizations consider 1 million people in Germany to be Kurds (Baser, 2013: 5), politicians and scholars treat these numbers with reservations. In 2000, an estimation came up with an overwhelming 85 percent of the German Kurds with roots in Turkey, about 60,000 to 70,000 from Iraq and a few thousand from each Iran and Syria (Ammann, 2001: 138). In the meantime, the growing numbers of refugees suggests that the diaspora community keeps growing. Within the last 10 years, more than 56,000 Kurds from Syria and about the same number of Kurds from Iraq immigrated to Germany according to the German Ministry for Migration and Refugees. According to official German statistics, there are about 140,000 Iraqis—originally registered as refugees—living in Germany. Considering estimates that 70 percent of those are Kurds, the result would be around 100,000 Iraqi Kurds. Family reunifications and transnational marriages are not included in these considerations. Neither is the growing number of returning migrants.

Another interesting fact is that among all 1.1 million adult refugees who entered Germany in 2015 a little over 3 percent—that makes 31,000 immigrants—named Kurmanji as their first language.

In 2015, about half of the 30,000 refugees from Iraq were Yezidis according to official German statistics. Due to the recurring persecution of Yezidis and Alevis in their home regions, both groups are clearly overrepresented among the Kurdish diaspora compared to their homelands. At the same time, especially Alevi and Kurdish identities sometimes mingle because these people suffer from double discrimination (Ammann, 2004: 1015). The wider public is unaware of the fact that Kurds have grown into one of the largest group of refugees and immigrants in Germany (Ammann, 2004: 1012). The only way to derive an accurate numbering of the Kurds would be a census collecting numerically representative data that are based on self-identification and giving people the option to report more than one ethnic or religious affiliation. The outcome might provide surprising results.

The Kurdish presence in Germany started with a handful of privileged academics from different Kurdish regions living in Europe before the 1950s: diplomats, lobbyists for Kurdish nationalist aspirations, scholars, and university students. However, today's diaspora primarily stems from Germany's active labor recruitment with its peak in the 1970s. Kurdish migration at that time had not been overt; only years later did it become clear that at least 20 percent of the migrant labor workers—the so-called guest workers from Turkey—were of Kurdish origin.

Because of Turkey's restrictive politics regarding its ethnic minorities and a rigid Turkish-nationalistic education system, no comprehensive, ethnic self-confidence developed. The expression of Kurdishness had been almost entirely wiped out or was fear driven. In Østergaard-Nielsen's words (2006: 4) the guest workers have only discovered or started emphasizing their Kurdishness in the diaspora. When the recruiting activities were halted in 1973, migration continued through family reunification and later the search for political asylum. Many of the Kurdish migrants had already moved to western parts of Turkey and into the big cities for economic reasons. Now, Kurdish refugees began setting off directly from rural areas in the far east of the Turkish Republic right into Germany during the 1990s. A simultaneous influx of Kurdish refugees happened from Iraq.

During the historical phase of labor recruitment, additional political and ecological push factors promoted Kurdish emigration movements. These included two military coups, severe earthquakes, and pogroms against the Kurdish Alevis. Around 30,000 Kurds fled to Germany as a result of the military coup in 1980 alone. At the same time, the first Gulf War and the new fundamentalist regime in Iran forced Kurdish refugees from Iraq and smaller numbers from Iran to flee. Two additional waves of Kurdish migration set off in Turkey and Iraq. In 1984, the PKK launched their armed struggle against the Turkish military forces. This has to be seen as a reaction to the sufferings of the Kurdish population after long years under martial law. After thousands of their villages had been forcibly depopulated by the Turkish regime, millions of Kurds turned to the metropoles of Turkey, where a whole generation became uprooted and ended up as society's precariat. Hundreds of thousands of them turned to Germany and other Western countries as asylum seekers. The second wave occurred in northern Iraq in 1991 just after the Second Gulf War. The regime then still under Iraqi President Saddam Hussein brought down a Kurdish uprising that had been encouraged by the Gulf War Allies. Recalling chemical agents used against them after the First Gulf War and a number of other atrocities, again hundreds of thousands of Kurds set off from the region as soon as borders opened for the first time (Ammann, 2004: 1012).

It is now widely agreed that Germany has witnessed the strongest activities of the Kurdish movement in Europe, or in other words "the Kurdish diaspora is one of the most visible and active Diasporas in Europe" (Baser, 2015a: 113). Bengio and Maddy-Weitzman (2013: 69) describe the European Kurdish diaspora as "the most politically vocal group of all non-native European communities." Considering the German segment of the Kurdish diaspora as being the largest by far, its role cannot be emphasized enough.

There is a fine line between community activism and political engagement among the diaspora. In Germany, there are hundreds of community organizations, social and cultural programs, and clubs run by and focusing on Kurds. There is also a large number of regular publications such as newspapers, magazines, newsletters, and websites dealing with all kinds of Kurdish issues. Most of the community organizers have transnational connections relating to other European segments of the

Kurdish women participate in German language classes in Berlin, Germany, June 1, 2004. (Brigitte Hiss/ullstein bild via Getty Images)

diaspora and to the homeland. A small professional elite group of artists, writers, and musicians forged corresponding networks (Ammann, 2004: 1013f).

For the majority of the diaspora population politics became an issue and the reason for their own or their families' often forced migration. Political persecution, expulsion, and other acts of massive violence play an important role and are a constant element in the diaspora's collective memory. Refugees have always played a catalytic role in the process of affirming identity and they continue to do so (Ammann, 2001: 136).

The first influential Kurdish political organization in Europe—founded in Germany in the second half of the 1970s—was *Komkar*, the Union of Workers' Associations from Kurdistan, which supported the left-wing movement in Turkey. As opposed to PKK—then called *Kongra Gel*—Komkar's political strategies were more or less exclusively aimed at the country of destination and not the homeland, whereas PKK in Germany acted and still acts deterritorialized and does not focus on immigrant needs. The same can be said about the Kurdish political parties in Iraq, the KDP (Kurdistan Democratic Party) and PUK (Patriotic Union of Kurdistan), as well as the recently established left-wing *Gorran*, Movement for Change (Ammann 2004: 1014; Baser 2015a; Østergaard-Nielsen, 2006: 4).

The violent activities of PKK during the 1990s did not appeal to the German public and government, which outlawed the organization in 1993 (Bengio & Maddy-Weitzman, 2013: 80). Reasons for the rise of PKK and their eminent success among the larger part of the Kurdish population in Germany can be traced back to the negative perception as migrants in Germany in addition to the historic and ongoing violent treatment of the Kurds in Turkey (Ammann, 2004: 1014, 1017). Even though the PKK is illegal in Germany, but not in Austria, similar policies can be observed. Pro-Kurdish—including pro-PKK—activities are neither officially supported nor prohibited but rather tolerated and observed. The democratic nature of the German political system and state institutions allowed for applying transnational politics, and activists keep good relations with high-ranking politicians, whereas at the same time they are under surveillance by the domestic intelligence service. Supported by a number of respectable media, serious attempts to lift the ban on the PKK can be noted. However, due to the latest violent clashes in Turkey, these campaigns probably will slow down for some years.

Kurds from Turkey and among them PKK and its numerous subgroups and organizations dominate the public perception of Kurds in Germany, which makes their image instable. Even though the drama of the Anfal and chemical attacks on Halabja, the arrest of Öcalan, the fate of the Yezidis of Sinjar/Shingal in Iraq, and the battle for the city of Kobane in Kurdish-controlled Rojava in Syria (Baser, 2015b) have raised public awareness and sympathy for the Kurdish cause, the Kurds in general are looked at with ambivalence (Ammann 2004: 1017; Bengio & Maddy-Weitzman, 2013: 21).

Transnational relations on all levels between the diaspora and the homeland are of immense importance and have been widely acknowledged especially regarding Turkey. Other studies about the relations with the Kurdish Region in Iraq further document this in detail. Candan (2013: 65) has shown that the Kurdish regional government has been actively encouraging the diaspora community to get involved in the reconstruction process to improve the living conditions in the former homeland. The remittances result in the transfer of knowledge and sociopolitical, cultural, and entrepreneurship back to the country of origin. A recent study on remigration shows that the larger part of the returnees re-immigrate on a voluntary basis, which indicates that more long-distance commuting on a regular basis is to be expected. People head back for family reasons, marriage, inheritances, patriotic reasons, and because their social capital and status is higher in their country of origin than in Germany. Permanent or semi-permanent remigration often takes place after having acquired German citizenship. In addition, they consider the fact that despite relative safety in the Kurdistan region, the frontline with the so-called Islamic State is only 50 km away, violent warlike clashes in the Kurdish parts of Turkey are ongoing, and the Syrian border is within sight. Apart from all the transnational activities that have been described by many, Kurds from both Turkey and Iraq actively take part in politics by voting in their countries of origin—a fact that should be subject for further research.

The Kurdish presence in Germany has come a long way: First being unrecognized and unorganized until they have been defined as a diaspora group with ambivalent attitudes: victims and perpetrators; or in the words of Østergaard-Nielsen as both peace wreckers and peacemakers (2006: 4). Due to Germany's close political relations to the Kurdish Regional Government in Iraq (to whom it has been providing arms and where it is running a consulate) and the growing public sympathy for the Kurdish suffering under Erdoğan's regime in Turkey, it appears that the German public opinion seems to be shifting toward a greater acceptance and support of the Kurds rather than skepticism and fear.

As Martin van Bruinessen (2015: 126) puts it, the diaspora is a "space of social and political mobilization . . . the interface of exchanges between the different parts of Kurdistan."

Backed by the democratic institutions in Germany where the Kurds are getting together in large numbers for the first time, intra-ethnic solidarity and exchange among the Kurds has grown and at the same time left a remarkable imprint on the divided homeland. Information on activities in the fields of politics, arts, and culture, as well as academic research, is circulating in different parts of the homeland as well as in the different segments of the diaspora. The diaspora is contributing to medical, humanitarian, social, academic, and political undertakings in different parts of the homeland. Kurds from the diaspora serve as interpreters and cultural mediators in international development missions and business affairs. Kurdish politicians, administrative, academic, and medical staff from the diaspora are actively and permanently engaged in the autonomous region of Northern Iraq and other Kurdish regions. The German armed forces are occasionally recruiting diaspora Kurds for missions in the relevant areas (Ammann, 2004: 1017).

Germany's Kurdish diaspora in its dimension and unique composition has composed its own narrative of Kurdishness, which faces the dilemma of resting between two poles. On the one hand, it raises claims of cultural relativism defined by opposing colonialist and imperialist forces, and on the other hand, it relies on cultural universalistic concepts, which envision the overcoming of national or ethnic peculiarities on the way to a cosmopolitan world society.

Due to a constant and growing stream of migrants and refugees coming to Germany, the diaspora group has to adjust and transform. Young first-generation Germans take in unaccompanied parachute kids, who were sent ahead by their families hoping to reunify in the diaspora later. Couples of different national backgrounds are starting Kurdish families. Other refugees with unrealistic hopes return in disappointment, while highly skilled long-time residents happily return at retirement age. Various first-language idioms exist, religious diversity is debated in transforming contexts, and the never-ending inner Kurdish political friction is getting new fuel, while additional foment is continuously created.

Birgit Ammann

Further Reading

Ammann, B. (2001). *Kurden in Europa. Ethnizität und Diaspora*. Münster: LIT.

Ammann, B. (2004). "Kurds in Germany." In M. Ember, C. R. Ember, & I. Skoggard Eds.), *Encyclopedia of Diasporas. Immigrant and Refugee Cultures around the World, Volume 2* (pp. 1011–1019). New York: Kluwer Academic/Plenum Publishers.

Atilgan, C. (2002). *Die türkische Diaspora in Deutschland*. Hamburg: Deutsches Orient Institut.

Baser, B. (2013). "Diaspora Politics and Germany's Kurdish Question. Presented at the "Diasporas and Security" workshop at the University of Kent, https://www.kent.ac.uk/politics/carc/diasporas-and-securitisation/documents/diaspora-politics-and-germanys-kurdish-question.pdf.

Baser, B. (2015a). "Komkar: The Unheard Voice in the Kurdish Diaspora." In A. Christou & E. Mavroudi (Eds.), *Dismantling Diasporas: Rethinking the Geographies of Diasporic Identity, Connection and Development* (pp. 113–125). Farnham: Ashgate.

Baser, B. (2015b). "The Kurdish Diaspora Response to Kobane: Uniting Kurds under One Roof?" Presented at the University of Oxford, Oxford Diasporas Programme, Exploring Migrants Networks and Experience, http://www.migration.ox.ac.uk/odp/kurdish-diaspora-article.shtml.

Bengio, O., & Maddy-Weitzman, B. (2013). "Mobilised Diasporas: Kurdish and Berber Movements in Comparative Perspective." *Kurdish Studies,* vol. 1, no. 1, 65–90, http://dayan.org/file/16304/download?token=1kn9HpjJ.

Bruinessen van, M. (1998). "Shifting National and Ethnic Identities. The Kurds in Turkey and the European Diaspora." *Journal of Muslim Minority Affairs*, vol. 18, no. 1, 39–52.

Bruinessen van, M. (1999). "The Kurds in Movement: Migrations, Mobilisations, Communications and the Globalisation of the Kurdish Question." Working Paper no. 14, Islamic Area Studies Project, Tokyo, Japan, 1999.

Bruinessen, van Martin. (2015). "Editorial. Kurdish Studies." *Special Issue: Kurdish Diaspora,* vol. 3, no. 2, 125–127, http://www.tplondon.com/journal/index.php/ks/article/viewFile/593/429.

Candan, M. (2013). "Die irakische Diaspora in Deutschland und ihr Beitrag im Wiederaufbauprozess im Irak nach 2003." In *Wiso Diskurs, Expertisen und Dokumentationen zur Wirtschafts-und Sozialpolitik*, 65–75, http://library.fes.de/pdf-files/wiso/10092.pdf

Østergaard-Nielsen, E. (2006). "Diasporas and Conflict Resolution. Part of the Problem or Part of the Solution?" Danish Institute for International Studies, DIIS Brief, https://www.ciaonet.org/attachments/6628/uploads.

IRAN

After Turkey, Iran has the largest Kurdish population among the Kurds' countries of origin. The population of Iranian Kurds is estimated at between 8 and 10 million, counting up to 11 percent to 15 percent of Iran's overall population. As Iran's largest ethnic group after Persians and Azerbaijanis, Iranian Kurds play a large role in Iran's national life. Most Iranian Kurds live in their historical home in mainland Kurdistan in west and northwestern Iran, but a large number lives in Khorasan, far away in the northeast.

In its broad sense in the Iranian context, "Kurdistan" refers to the western and northwestern regions of the country, which have historically been home to Kurdish tribes. Also known as Eastern Kurdistan and Rojhelat (Kurdish: the east), Iranian Kurdistan extends from Iran's northwestern borders to the slopes of central Zagros in the west, neighboring Armenia, Turkey, and Iraq. It is an area of over 112,000 square kilometers, including the provinces of West Azerbaijan, Kurdistan, Kermanshah, and Ilam. To this is added the total area of Kurdish-speaking regions of Hamedan Province.

Kurdistan's life-giving rivers, thick woodlands, and strategically important mountains, as well as easy access to vast plains on both the east and the west of

Zagros have appealed to men of power in different ages. The ruins of numerous ancient temples, bridges, houses, castles, and walled cities all speak of thriving economies and powerful governments in Kurdistan's distant past. Located at the heart of central Zagros in Kermanshah is the Behistun Inscription, one of the main relics of Persian civilization, which narrates Darius the Great's exploits (522 BC) in three languages: ancient Elamite, Akkadian, and Achaemenid cuneiform. Bahram Chobin's Valley in Ilam is a lasting record of the final days of the Sassanid Empire—of the power struggles and ruinous warfare among the descendants of Persian royal houses, which led to the intervention of Roman troops. Iran's single main Mithraic temple and the best preserved four-pillared fire temple are both located in Kurdistan—the first in Kangavar, Kermanshah, and the second in Darreh Shahr, Ilam.

Located near ancient Persian and medieval Caliphate capitals (including the Sassanid capital of Ctesiphon and the Abbasid capital of Baghdad), the Kurdish cities of central Zagros have always played a major role in the social life of the region. North and central Zagros included two main branches of the Silk Road, serving as the main communications highways of the ancient world. The cities of Hamedan, Nahavand, Kangavar, Kermanshah, Dinawar, Sirvan, Masbazan, and Shahrizour in the southwest and the cities of Mahabad, Saqez, and Urmia in the northwest have played significant roles in the economic life on the two sides of Zagros.

Khorasani Kurds, who live in Iran's northeastern provinces, including Khorasan Province, are descendants of Kurdish tribes that had been displaced from their homes in western Iran at different historical moments from the early days of Islam to the Safavid Era. In the 16th century, for instance, the Safavid government enforced large-scale displacements of the Kurds from northwest to northeast Iran to fight the Uzbek invaders. Between 1598 and 1610, the government of Shah Abbas displaced tens of thousands of the Kurds in western Iran, relocating them to areas on Iran's borders with Afghanistan and present-day Turkmenistan. Unofficial sources estimate the population of Khorarasi Kurds at around 2 million, most of them Shia Muslims who speak Kurmanji as their mother tongue.

Scattered over a vast area of 80,000 square kilometers, Kurdish towns and settlements of Khorasan are among the least developed parts of the country. While the majority of Khorasani Kurds live in villages, significant numbers of them have settled in the cities of Nishapur, Mashhad, Sabzevar, Quchan, Bojnoord, and Esfarayen. Nomadic tribes form a very small portion of the populace. The tribal family system is still well in place in the villages so that most individuals identify themselves as members of a tribe—with a surname (which in most cases ends with the suffix *loo*) betokening their descent.

Political History

With the advent of Islam in the Arabian Peninsula and the subsequent Muslim conquest of Persia, Kurdistan was among the first areas to be attacked by Muslim warriors. The Muslims' victory over the Sassanid army in Nahavand (642 CE) was a giant step forward in their historical conquest of Persia. Kurdistan's history from that day to the early days of the 10th century, usually referred to as Persia's dark ages, is vague and couched in mystery.

In the early 10th century, the first local governments were formed on the basis of tribal allegiances in southern parts of Kurdistan. The Hassanuyid dynasty (959–1015), ruling over the cities of Kermanshah, Hamedan, Dinawar, and Shahrizour, is probably the first regional Kurdish government. There were other local governors who ruled on behalf of the caliph in Kurdish-inhabited areas. Bani Anaz (991–1017) was an example of such local administrations.

With the rise of the Seljuqs in eastern Iran in 1037 and their subsequent movement toward the west, Kurdish cities fell, one after the other, between 1076 and 1079, making way for the Seljuqs' retaking of the Abbasid capital of Baghdad from the Buyid dynasty in 1055. The Seljuqs ruled over Kurdistan and Iraq from 1117 to 1194 when they were driven out by the Khwarezmids. It was during the reign of Mahmud I of Great Seljuq that the word "Kurdistan" was first used for an area in present-day Iran. Formerly known as "Iraq," this area included central and western Iranian cities of Kermanshah, Hamedan, Isfahan, Rey, Qazvin, Kashan, and Qom. "Kurdistan" thus included a vast area from Hamedan to Shahrizour, with Kermanshah as its seat. As a divide between central Persia and the Arabs, Kurdistan played a significant role in the Middle Ages.

The Khwarezmids' one-and-a-half century rule over Kurdistan and Iraq came to a close with the Mongol invasion, inaugurating the Ilkhanid era in Iran. After gathering all forces of the Far East, the Mongols swept through east and central Iran, arriving in Kurdistan—then ruled by Soleiman Shah Ivayi from his capital of Bahar—burning city after city on their way to Baghdad and far beyond to the west. Nothing could stop the Mongols, not even Caliph al-Musta'sim's troops, which he had sent to defend Kurdistan alongside Soleiman Shah's soldiers. Very soon, Hulagu Khan destroyed Bahar and subdued all of Kurdistan. In 1259, the Mongols moved toward other Kurdish regions occupying the cities of Van, Meyafarikin, Diyarbakir, and Erbil. The Ilkhanid's rule over Kurdistan and the rest of Iran was not easy. Only later, when Öljaitü the eighth Ilkhanid ruler converted to Islam, changing his name to Muhammad Khodabandeh, the people of Kurdistan began to embrace the Ilkhanids' rule.

After the Ilkhanids, between 1378 and 1501 came the Ak Koyunlu, who were soon driven out by the Kara Koyunlu; then came Tamerlane. The most significant event, however, was the rise of the Safavids. On their way to Azerbaijan, before seizing power in Tabriz, the Safavid family was warmly received in Kurdistan. After establishing themselves in Azerbaijan, they focused on Kurdistan—then ruled by the Kurdish houses of Mokri, Ardalani, and Shekak. The Safavids occupied Kurdistan following tough and bloody wars with local administrations that enjoyed the support of Kurdish tribes. Always seeing the Kurds as a potential threat, the Safavid king Tahmasp I ordered large-scale displacement of powerful Kurdish tribes from their historical home in Kurdistan to other parts of Iran. Iranian history is marked by frequent cases of such displacements as a way of dealing with rebellious local tribes.

Following the Safavids' defeat by the Ottomans in the Battle of Chaldiran, a large part of Kurdish-inhabited lands, including the important cites of Diyarbakir and Van, was separated from Iran and became part of the Ottoman Empire. Soon after, Tahmasp I of Iran embarked upon his violent demographic intervention, ruining Kurdish cities, destroying Kurdish cultural heritages, and displacing Kurdish tribes to mountainous areas in Alborz, northern Iran, and Khorasan. The homes and the lands of removed Kurdish tribes were then given to the Afshars, a number of Oghuz Turkic tribes who were likewise relocated by the Safavids. In the early 18th century, while the Safavid armed forces were busy fighting Nader Shah in the East, the Ardalans found the moment opportune to restore their power. They took Hamedan and, following Nader Sha's death in 1747, expanded their territory to Fars Province. Ardalan administration restored peace and prosperity to Kurdish settlements.

The Ardalans' rebellion against the Safavids in the final years of the Safavid era became a model for a few other Kurdish rulers during the Qajar and the Pahlavi dynasties. The year 1879 saw the first modern national movement in Kurdistan. In this year, Sheikh Ubeydullah Nehri declared his nationalist project, demanding recognition from both the Ottoman Empire and the Qajar dynasty of Iran. He brought the lands between Urmia Lake and Lake Van under control and chose Oshnavieh as his capital. Sheikh Ubeydullah's short reign came to a close when he was defeated by the Ottomans in December 1880.

The example of Sheikh Ubeydullah Nehri's movement was followed by some other Kurdish leaders in the following decades. Between 1918 and 1922, Simko Shikak, the leader of the Shikak tribe in the west of Urmia Lake, and Ja'far Sultan, the ruler of Hawraman, led powerful rebellions. Ja'far Sultan's rule in Hawraman came to an end in 1925 when his rebellion was quelled by the armed forces of the central government. Seated in Sanandaj, Ardalan governors were generally on good terms with the Qajars' central government in Tehran, but the situation could sometimes get uneasy over both personal and public issues.

Reza Shah's coming to power in 1925 was a turning point in Kurdistan's social structure. In line with his policy of assimilation and modernization, Reza Shah took strict measures against Kurdish tribes, relocating rebellious houses and imprisoning powerful leaders. Life in Kurdistan under Reza Shah (1925–1941) was one of unrest and insecurity. The situation worsened during World War II when Iran was invaded by Soviet, British, and other Commonwealth armed forces in 1941.

Iran's neutral stance during this time of invasion by the Allies wore out the national army, providing opportunity for Kurdish leaders to take up arms against the central government. Mohammad Rashid of Baneh took Baneh, Sardasht, and Marivan before he was defeated by the Shah's army in 1944. Two years later, the Society for the Revival of the Kurds (Komeley Jiyanewey Kurd or KJK) with the support of the Soviets founded the Kurdish Republic of Mahabad with Qazi Mohammed as the president. The Republic of Mahabad could not expand beyond a small area in northern Kurdistan, and within a year, it was overturned by the Shah who ordered the execution of Qazi and other leaders of the Kurdish Democratic Party of Iran.

The Republic of Mahabad

During World War II, Iran's northern part was invaded by the Soviet who encouraged the Kurds to form their autonomous government. Under the leadership of Qazi Mohamed, and with military support of Mulla Mustafa Barzani's tribal fighters, the Republic of Mahabad declared its independence on January 22, 1946. It called for a Kurdish national movement, support of the farmers, equality of its citizens, and the use of Kurdish as the official language. The Kurdish Democratic Party of Iran was the leading political organization, which later branched off into neighboring countries. The republic was short-lived. After the Soviet withdrawal, the Iranian army took over Mahabad on December 15, 1946, and shortly after Qazi Mohamed and other leaders were executed.

The 1970s are marked by many contradictions in the Shah's relations with the Kurds. Prior to the Algiers Agreement—which brought the Iran-Iraq territorial disputes to a peaceful resolution in 1975—Iran waged a proxy war against Iraq through financial and military support of the Barzanis who led a Kurdish rebellion against Saddam's Baath regime. For most Kurds, the Algiers Agreement revealed the Shah's true feelings toward the Kurds. Following the two countries' agreement to a contract of good neighborliness, Iran closed his border crossing on Iraqi Kurds and withdrew its military supports. Following this fatal blow, many Barzani leaders and Peshmergas were forced to move to Iran, an event that gave a new impetus to political activism in Iranian Kurdistan.

In response to the Pahlavis' hostile measures, Iranian Kurds played a major role in the 1979 revolution. Transition from Pahlavi regime to a democratic government that would grant the rights of ethnic and religious minorities was the project followed by the Kurds during the Revolution. After the revolution, the Iran–Iraq War (1980–1988) brought death and destruction to the lives of many Kurdish civilians in cities close to the Iran-Iraq border. Many cities were reduced to dust from frequent bombardments by Iraqi air force. Saddam occupied a few cities and threw chemical bombs on those he could not take.

Following the war, the reconstruction project in damaged cities has been slow. The government's troubled relations with a number of exiled Kurdish parties and the historical distrust toward public investment projects in border areas have been an obstacle on the path to development and economic growth. Today, many Iranian Kurds are active members of official political parties and paly active roles in the political life of the country. Although the degree of tolerance toward Kurds among Iranian statesmen is higher than is seen among neighboring nations (such as Turkey and Syria), many people question the government's restrictions on Sunni Muslims who aspire to run for high administrative positions.

Language

Iranian Kurdistan displays an astonishingly high degree of linguistic variety. Different dialects of Kurdish are spoken by different communities of Iranian Kurds in the west, northwest, and northeast of the country. Researches on Kurdish language have focused on the western parts of the country where the main dialects of Kurdish are spoken. Among the main dialects of Kurdish is Sorani which covers a cultural territory extending from Urmia and Mahabad in the north to Divandareh in the south. Further to the north, close to the Iran-Turkey border, are different Kurmanji (or Shikak) dialects. The majority of Kurmanji speakers are found in northeastern parts of Iran, in the cities of Bojnord, Quchan, and Mashhad.

Farther into the south are Ardalani speakers who live in a linguistic territory, with Sanandaj at the center, which separates northern dialects from the southern ones. Sanandaj, the center of Kurdistan Province, had been the capital of Ardalan administration during the Qajar dynasty. Ardalani is highly affected by Hawrami and Kalhori.

To the south of Sanandaj is Kermanshah, a metropolis city around which are centered the linguistic territories of Kalhori, Hawrami, and Laki. To the west of the land between Sanadaj and Kermanshah are Jaff and Hawrami speakers. The largest concentration of Hawrami speakers is in Paveh, a small town with a population of 25,000. Laki-speaking tribes mostly live in eastern and southeastern parts of Kermanshah, adjoining Khorramabad, the center of Lorestan Province.

On a slanted direction from Kermanshah to the southeast are the cities of Eslamabad-e Gharb and Eyvan, which are home to a variety of Kalhori speakers. The name Kalhor signifies both a number of very closely related dialects and a number of allied tribes. Thus, when referring to certain groups of people in Hamedan, Ilam, and Kermanshah, it does not necessarily mean tribal descent.

In Ilam, the dominant language is Kurdish, with Arabic and Lori as minor languages spoken in the provincial area—the first in the south, to the vicinities of Khuzestan Province, and the second in the southeast, to the borders of Lorestan Province.

Literature and Arts

Iranian Kurdistan has given birth to famous poets. In the Middle Ages, most Kurdish men of letters composed their works in Arabic, Farsi, or Gorani, a Kurdish dialect with exclusively literary use. Unlike their fellow compatriots in eastern and central parts of Persia, Kurdish poets were not highly influenced by Arabic literary tradition in the centuries following the Arab conquest of Persia. While throughout the 13th and 14th centuries, powerful local governments in Khwarezm and Khorasan promoted aesthetic values issued by the Islamic Caliphate in Baghdad, poets in the more provincial west, including Kurdistan, continued local literary traditions of pre-Islamic Persia. Composition of Awraman songs and Pahlawi quatrains (the *pahlawiyat*) by Iranian poets in Jibal and Iraq in the 12th and 13th centuries is an indication of the persistence of pre-Islamic literary traditions in western parts of the country.

Pahlawi quatrains were written in a developed form of Pahlawi, the official and literary language of the Sassanid Empire. Orally composed Awraman songs were most probably lyrical quatrains in Gorani, a specialized form of literary language used by bards in Hawraman, a mountainous area in Kurdistan. Gorani incorporated elements from a number of Zagros dialects, including Hawrami, Laki, Kalhori, and Lori, and it was understood by most speakers of these dialects until the mid-20th century.

Contrary to mainstream Persian prosody, in Gorani poetry the meter is syllabic, which indicates its adherence to pre-Islamic poetic rules. Like many dominantly oral languages, Gorani has no prose literature. In Kurdistan, as in most oral communities, poetry has played a significant role in maintaining and transferring cultural data, from literature to history and from philosophy to mythology. The fact that there is no prose literature in Gorani has another explanation: it reflects an old Zoroastrian belief according to which Ahura Mazda, the supreme god, orders Zarathustra not to record his teachings and to carry them in his heart instead. This belief lived well into the Islamic tradition, embodied in the Islamic practice of *hadith*, through which disciples and close relatives of the Prophet Mohammad and the imams conveyed their teachings to the wider public through oral accounts.

The works of Gorani poets were in vogue in all Kurdish lands, except for the Kurmanji territory, until the mid-20th century. A vast majority of the illiterate could recite hundreds, sometimes even thousands, of lines of lyric, epic, or religious poetry, from the *Kurdish Shanama*, to the romance of *Leyli and Majnoun*, and from the romantic epic of *Shirin and Farhad* to the Yarsan *kalam* (sacred hymns). The poems of Mala Pareshan of Dinawar, famous 16th-century poet and mystic, are the oldest extant examples of Gorani poetry. The last, and perhaps the most significant, Gorani poet is Mawlawi Tawagozi (1806–1882), known as the Kurdish Mawlawi. Available in multiple versions, Mawlawi's poems are well known all over Kurdistan.

Many of the orally composed Gorani poems are available to modern readers and scholars thanks to Kurdish governors and men of power in the past. Many Kurdish magistrates of the old times appointed copyists to transcribe for them well-known poems recited by the bards. Available under different titles, such as *razm-nama* (war account), *kashkoul* (anthology), *ketab* (script) or *daftar* (notebook), hundreds of these booklets are kept in numerous national archives as well as in people's homes.

In the last few decades, Iran's national literacy movement has tended to supplant local literary languages with Farsi, to the effect that a smaller number of people understand Gorani today. With the decline of Gorani language in mid-20th century, Kurdish poets began to try their hands at poetic and prose compositions in the relatively new literary languages of Hawrami, Laki, and Kalhori, painting the colorful landscape of contemporary Kurdish literature. Due to the strong influence of the Sorani tradition in Sulaymaniyah (in Iraqi Kurdistan), the Sorani dialect has become the dominant literary language in Iranian Kurdistan too. Many contemporary writers in Iranian Kurdistan have followed the examples of Iraqi Kurdish poets and have established themselves as key figures in this dominantly Iraqi tradition. Among Iranian Kurdish poets of the Sorani tradition are Wafayi, Qani, Hemin Mukriyani, Hajar, and Swara Ilkhanizada.

Kurdish men of letters have played significant roles in Persian literature too. Ali Mohammad Afghani's masterpiece *Shohar-e Ahoo Khanom* is among the first and most important Farsi novels, and Abulqasim Lahouti's poems are the earliest examples of free verse in Farsi. Kurdish men of letters, Mohammad Ghazi and Ebrahim Younesi, have made many world masterpieces available to Farsi speakers with their skillful translation.

Kurdistan is known as the cradle of music. Kurdish musicians, who are among the best-known Iranian artists, have dominated the nation's contemporary music. Keyhan Kalhor, Shahram Nazeri, and the Kamkars (a group of seven brothers and a sister accompanied by their children) are among many Kurdish artists whose works have reached audiences around the globe. Despite its resemblances to various musical traditions of its neighbors, Kurdish music has its own unique elements terms of in melody and rhythm and the kind of instruments used.

Religion

About 66 percent of Iranian Kurds are Sunni Muslims of the Shafi'i and Hanafi schools of Islamic law. Twelver Shias comprise about 27 percent of the population and the remaining 6 percent is formed by the Yarsans, Christians, and Jews.

Due to their strategic locations, the mountainous areas of Iranian Kurdistan have always been havens to nonconforming religious sects—including different Sufi orders—as well as political dissenters. Following the suppression of Abu Muslim Khorasani's rebellion by the Abbasid Caliph in the eighth century, his followers took refuge in Kurdistan where they pursued their activities with freedom.

Kurds in Iran celebrate the festival of Pir Shaliyar in the village of Uraman Takht. (Rahman Hassani/SOPA Images/LightRocket via Getty Images)

Reorganized into various new orders, such as the Khurramites, they had a significant imprint on Sufism in Kurdistan. Nourbakhshiyya, Suhrawardiyya, Khaksrai, Ne'matollahi, Naqshbani, and Qadiriyya are among many Sufi orders that have prevailed in Kurdistan in different ages.

Among the most mysterious religions in Kurdistan is the Yarsan. Also known as Ahl-e Haqq, Ali-Allahi, and Kaka'i, it is an esoteric religion with many traces of pre-Islamic beliefs. Despite outside pressure and inquisition by Islamic centers, the Yaresans have maintained their ancient beliefs and practices, among them reincarnation and a radically different system of good and evil. Interestingly enough, they do not believe in the world to come. Unlike the apocalyptic religions, the Yaresan seems to locate the hereafter on earth, and life after death is conceived of as a long chain of reincarnations. Thus, the Yaresan shares common elements with various other local religions and Sufi orders. The Khaksari, for instance, has close structural ties with the Yarsan so that many Khaksar Pirs (Murshids, religious chiefs) identify themselves as old Murids (disciples) of Yaresan Pirs.

The most popular Sufi orders in Kurdistan are the Naqshbandi and Qadiriyya. As one of the oldest Sufi dynasties, the Qadiris identify themselves as the descendants of Abd al-Qadir Gilani, a famous 12th-century Persian Sufi. The Qadiriyyah was founded by Baba Rassoul Barzanji in Shahrizour. Barzanji was a Murshid of an older Tariqa (order) called "Noorbakhshiyya" into which he incorporated elements from the Alaviyya, a branch of the Khalvatiyya.

A major branch of the Qadiriyya is the Kasnazani (meaning "the unknown") who relate their dynasty, through the Shah of Kasnazan, to the Prophet Mohammad. Regarded as a means of direct contact with truth, music and *sama* (a holy Sufi dance) dominate the rituals in the Kasnazani *tariqa*. Their rituals are accompanied by the performance of *karamat* (supernatural wonders) such as self-wounding, devouring rocks or blades, and self-electrocution. Most adherents of the Kasnazani live in the province of Kurdistan.

The adherents of the Naqshbandi are found over a vast area, including the Middle East and the Indian peninsula. In Iran, the order was founded in Shahrizour by Mevlana Khalid-I Baghdadi (1779–1827), who is considered as the best-known and most influential figure in the history of the tariqa from its early days in the 14th century to the present. A lifelong traveler, Mevlana Khalid was known and revered over a vast territory from Sulaymaniyah in present-day Iraq to Khorasan and India. Baghdadi spent parts of his life in different cities of Kurdistan, including Sanandaj, before settling in Sulaymaniyah where he died of the plague in 1827. There are many Naqshbandi *khanqahs* (shrines) in Sanandaj, Saqez, Baneh, Marivan, and other cities and villages in the province of Kurdistan. Unlike the adherents of the Qadiriyaa, Naqshbandis are moderate in their beliefs and practices. They observe Sunni Sharia and have no use for music and *sama* in their rituals.

Mythological Beliefs

Some mythological beliefs have been popular in Kurdistan. Until recently, people took great pleasure in the heroic tales of the *Kurdish Shanama*, which the bards recited in public places. The existence of numerous ancient architectural sites in Kurdistan has been influential in fostering mythological beliefs. One favorite local belief has it that the people of Kermanshah are the descendants of Farhad, the legendary sculptor and stonemason, and his beloved Shirin, whose heroic love story is among the most popular Iranian narratives. Many people in Sanandaj consider themselves as the descendants of Tous, son of Nowzar, the mythological Iranian prince and hero from the Pishdadian dynasty. Along with the official Persian calendar, there is an agricultural calendar, which has been in use for many ages until recent past. Even today, each of the rituals of Nowruz and Chaharshanbe-Suri is held on two different dates as a result of the difference between the modern and the ancient calendars. This discrepancy is explained by the climatic differences between the mountainous areas of Kurdistan and the desert plains of central Iran. Thus, some Iranian rituals, such as the Yarsan ritual of *Khavankar* (possibly a Mithraic festivity), are exclusive to Kurdish communities.

Literacy

As in most border provinces, literacy in Kurdistan is below the average rate of the country. Before Iran's national literacy movement (Nehzat-e Savad Amoozi), traditional *maktabs* and *madrasas* were responsible for public education in Kurdish societies. Funded by the mosques and programmed for training public and religious figures, these traditional institutions focused on religion and literature, disregarding sciences and technical knowledge.

In Iran's national literacy movement, literacy is defined as the ability to read and write in Farsi, the official language of the country and the only language of education. As a result, Iranian Kurds have had no easy access to their own literary tradition, and most of them have been unable to read and write Kurdish. Many Kurdish university graduates, including high-profile intellectuals, have little knowledge of Kurdish writing and Kurdish literature. As a result of the ban on local languages in schools, young children have ceased to speak Kurdish in many families, especially in big cities. In the absence of educational courses on Kurdish in public schools, private schools and tutors have played a major role in the education of Kurdish language and literature.

Only very recently has the Iranian Ministry of Education approved a course on Kurdish language in middle schools; and it was not until 2015 that the Ministry of Science, Research and Technology finally granted the permit for establishing the BA program in Kurdish Language and Literature at University of Kurdistan in Sanandaj. It was a belated enforcement of a disregarded, and somewhat vague, principle in Iran's Constitution (Principle No. 15) which identifies Farsi as the official language but grants the right to education and publication in local languages. Kurdish magazines and newspapers are published in Kurdish cities, and local TV and radio channels have programs in a few Kurdish dialects.

Behrooz Chaman Ara and Cyrus Amiri

Further Reading

Gresh, G. F. (2009). "Iranian Kurds in an Age of Globalisation." *Iran and the Caucasus*, vol. 13, no. 1, 187–196.

Koohi-Kamali, F. (2003). *The Political Development of the Kurds in Iran: Pastoral Nationalism.* New York: Palgrave MacMillan.

Natali, D. (2005). *The Kurds and the State: Evolving National Identity in Iraq, Turkey, and Iran.* Syracuse, NY: Syracuse University Press.

Stansfield, G. (2014). "Conflict, Democratization, and the Kurds in the Middle East." In Romano, D. and Gurses, M. (Eds.), *Kurds, Persian Nationalism, and Shi'i Rule: Surviving Dominant Nationhood in Iran* (pp. 59–84). New York: Palgrave MacMillan.

Vali, A. (2014). *Kurds and the State in Iran: The Making of Kurdish Identity.* London: I. B. Tauris.

Yildiz, K., & Taysi, T. B. (2007). *The Kurds in Iran: The Past, Present and Future.* London: Pluto Press.

IRAQ

The Republic of Iraq is home to the third largest Kurdish population in the Middle East, after Turkey and Iran. Although the precise number of Iraqi citizens that identify as being of Kurdish origins is difficult to ascertain, there are most likely between 6 and 8 million Kurds constituting approximately between 15 percent and 20 percent of the Iraqi population. Although Kurdish communities can be found in most of Iraqi's provinces and cities, the highest concentration are located in the "Kurdistan" region, located in the country's northeast.

In the Iraqi context, the precise boundaries of the Kurdistan region, also known as *Başûrê Kurdistanê* (Kurdish: Southern Kurdistan), are hotly contested. The March Accords of 1970, signed between the Iraqi central government and representatives of the Kurdish movement, laid the foundations for an autonomous Kurdish region, governed from the capital city of Erbil. However, the geographical extent of Kurdish autonomy zone continues to remain a topic of disagreement between the two sides. Currently, the regions that are officially recognized as part of the Kurdistan Regional Government (KRG) include the governorates of Erbil, Sulaymaniyah, and Dohuk. However, Kurdish political leaders continue to claim the governorate of Kirkuk as well as the districts of Aqra, Al-Sheykhan, Sinjar, Al-Hamdaniya, Tel Kayf in the Nineveh governorate, Tooz in the Salahaddin governorate, and Khanaqin, Kifri, and Baladrooz in the Diyala governorate, as well as Badra in the Wasit governorate. Following the U.S.-led invasion of 2003 and the toppling of the Ba'athist regime, the issue of the final status of these "disputed territories" was referred to Article 140 of the 2005 Iraqi Constitution. This article committed the Iraqi government to holding a referendum in November 2007 on the future status of the "disputed territories." Although no referendum was ever held, Kurdish forces occupied most "disputed territories" following the Islamic State of Iraqi and the Levant's (ISIL) occupation of Mosul in 2014.

Much of Iraqi Kurdistan is mountainous, with its eastern extremities dominated by the western partition of Zagros mountain chain. However, some of the southwestern districts of the KRG, most notably in southwestern Erbil as well as the disputed territories in Kirkuk, Nineveh, Saladdin, and Diyala governorates, are home to low rolling hills and steppe land. The region is also home to major tributary rivers to the Tigris, including the Khabur and Greater Zab, which enter Iraqi Kurdistan from Turkey, as well as the Lesser Zab and the Diyala, which enter from Iran.

The majority of Iraqi Kurdistan's population are Sunni Kurds. There are, however, minorities of Shia Kurds, as well as those who follow more heterodox religious traditions, most notably the Yezidis and the Ahl-e al-Haqq. There are also a number of non-Kurdish ethnic and religious minorities, including Arabs and Turkmen (both Sunni and Shia) as well as populations of Christians, including members of the Assyrian and Chaldean community. Since 2003, Iraqi Kurdistan has also seen increasing immigration from outside of Iraq. These include Kurds from across the Middle East, including large numbers of Syrian Kurdish refugees as well as growing numbers immigrant workers from North America, Europe, South East Asia, and China. The most widely spoken language in the region is the Sorani dialect of Kurdish, which is spoken the governorates of Erbil, Kirkuk, and Sulaymaniyah and written in the modified Arabic script. However, in the Dohuk and Nineveh governorates, a variant of the Kurmanji variety of Kurdish spoken in Turkey and Syria, known in Iraq Bahdini, is spoken. In addition to Sorani and Bahdini, there are other variants of Kurdish spoken in Iraq, including Hawrani, Bajalani, Gurani, and Luri. Arab, Turkish, Aramaic, Persian, and English are also spoken in the region in addition to Kurdish.

From Antiquity to the Ottoman Conquest, 7000 BCE to 1514 CE

Archeological evidence from sites such Jarmo and Tel Hassuna, which date from between 7000 BCE and 6000 BCE, demonstrate that the territory of modern-day Iraqi Kurdistan was home to some of the world's first agricultural communities. By the third millennium BCE, the region was known for its thriving Bronze Age culture, which was ultimately integrated in the Akkadian Empire (2334–2154 BCE), although conflict between the Akkadians and the nomadic Guti people ultimately led to the collapse of the empire. The region was later conquered by a variety of peoples, including the Assyrians (2025–609 BCE), the Neo-Babylonians (626–539 BCE), and ultimately, the Persian Achaemenids (520–331 BCE). In 331 BCE, the forces of Alexander the Great (r. 336–323 BCE) broke the power of the Achaemenids, following their victory of over Darius III (r. 536–331 BCE) at the Battle of Gaugamela, which took place northwest of the city of Arbela (modern-day Erbil). The region subsequently formed part of the Seleucid Empire (312–63 BCE), the Hellenic successor state established in Iran following Alexander's death. However, Seleucid authority in the east was broken by the rise of a new Persian dynasty, the Parthians (247 BCE-224 CE), in the mid-second century BCE. With the eastward expansion of the Roman Empire, modern-day Iraqi Kurdistan came to constitute a frontier region separating Persia from the Roman Near East. However, with the expectation of a brief Roman interlude in the second century CE, the region remained under Parthian rule until the dynasties collapse. Subsequently, the Parthians successors, the Sassanid dynasty (224–651), absorbed modern-day Iraqi Kurdistan into their vast imperium, ruled from the city of Ctesiphon located 20 miles south of the modern city of Baghdad.

Sassanid rule ultimately ended following the rise of Islam in the seventh century. The Muslim accounts of the Muslim conquest of Sassanid Iran contain some of the earliest direct mentions of the Kurdish community in the historical record. Muslims scholars mentioned the presents of tribes of Kurdish Christians and "fire worshipers" inhabiting the mountainous distinct to the northeast of Mosul and their resistance to Arab rule. Over the subsequent centuries, the majority of the Kurdish population adopted the faith of their Arab conquerors. Kurds initially played a marginal role in the broader affairs of the Islamic world. However, in the 10th century, a number of Kurdish tribal groups were able to establish independent emirates in their mountainous homelands. This included the Hasanuyids (959–1015) and the Annazids (990–1117), both of whom sought to dominate the central Zagros region, including districts such as Shahrazur and Daquq, which roughly correspond to the present-day Iraqi Kurdish governorates of Sulaimani and Kirkuk. This period of Kurdish preeminence was brought to a conclusion by the invasions of the Ghuzz (Oğuz) Turks and the formation of the Seljuq (Selçuk) empire in Iran in the 11th century. By the 12th century, with much of the territory that comprises modern-day Iraqi Kurdistan falling under the control the Seljuqs subordinate, Imad ad-Din Zengi (r. 1127–1146), became the Atabeg (governor) of Mosul. Mosul's Atabegs launched numerous campaigns against the Kurdish tribesmen residing within Mosul's environs bringing large numbers of them into submission. However, Imad ad-Din Zengi as well as his successor Nur ad-Din (r. 1146–1174) also made extensive use of Kurdish tribal units within their military structures as well as integrating important Kurdish notables into the state's governing elite. Indeed, Salah ad-Din al-Ayyubi (r. 1174–1193), who, in addition to capturing the holy city of Jerusalem from the Crusaders, established a vast Muslim imperium, stretching from North Africa to the borders of Iran in the late 11th century, began his career in service to the Zengids.

In the 13th century, the Kurdish highlands were again shaken by an invasion, this time from the Mongols, who like the Turks before them, entered the Middle East from Central Asia. The Mongol invasion proved to be extremely disruptive. Kurdish relations with the Mongols was often fraught. In 1245, for instance, Mongol forces plundered Shahrizur, depopulating the region. A decade later, during Mongol paramount Hülegü Khan's campaign to take Baghdad (1258), Mongol troops were dispatch to secure the city of Erbil, where the local Kurdish garrison unsuccessfully attempted to resist. Nevertheless, some Kurdish notables were able to reach political accommodations with their Mongol overlords, and conversion to Islam of Iran's Mongolian Ilkhanid dynasty in 1295 served to improve relations. Following the degeneration of the Ilkhanids state in the late 14th century, a succession of Turkic dynasties were able to lay claim to Kurdistan, including the Timurids, the Qaraqoyunlu (Karakoyunlu), the Aqqoyunlu (Akkoyunlu), and in the early 16th century, the Safavids. Unlike early Turkic dynasties, who were, like the Kurds, predominately Sunni Muslims, the Safavids were Shias, a fact that lay at the root of growing of religious tension between many Kurdish elites and their new overlords. This religious tension played into the hands of the Sunni Ottomans, who sought to limit the threat posed to their control of Anatolia by the rise of a vigorous Shia empire to its east. Thus, when Ottoman Sultan Selim I (r. 1512–1520) attacked the Safavid dynasty's founder, Shah Ismail I (r. 1501–1526), he was able to call upon Kurdish nobles and tribesmen for support. This supported, rallied by a former Aqqoyunlu administrator and Sufi scholar, İdris-i Bitlisi (1452–1520), proved pivotal in the Ottomans' ability to conciliate their hold over much of western Kurdistan following their victory over the Safavids at Çaldıran in the summer of 1514.

The Ottoman Period, 1514 to 1918

Despite their victory at Çaldıran, Ottoman control over Kurdistan was never absolute. The Safavids maintained control of the region's more easterly extremities. Moreover, many of the Kurdish-inhabited districts that lie within Iraq's present boundaries were only secured during the reign of Süleyman I (r. 1520–1566). Following their conquest by Ottoman forces, Istanbul organized these territories into provinces, Mosul, established in 1535, and Şehrizor (Shahrazur), established in 1554. As in other parts of Ottoman Kurdistan, the imperial authorities granted local Kurdish nobles and tribesmen a significant degree of autonomy over their ancestral lands. During the 16th and 17th centuries, the most powerful of these Kurdish nobles were the rulers of Badinan emirate, centered upon the town of Amadiya (present-day Dohuk governorate), and those of the Soran emirate, ruled from fortress of Rawandiz (present-day Erbil governorate). Although these emirates continued to exist well into the 19th century, in the late 17th, their reputations as the dominate forces in southern Kurdistan eclipsed by the rise of the Baban emirate. In 1694, the Baban chieftain, Suleiman Bey, defeated pro-Iranian Ardalan Kurds, successfully curtailing their influence in Shahrazur. As a result, the Ottoman authorities recognized him as the district's overlord and, over the course of the 18th century, the Babans were able to extend the influence over much of southern Kurdistan, including the districts of Kirkuk, Koya, Qasr-e Shirin, and Zehaw. However, perhaps one of the most significant legacies of the Babans was the founding of the city of Sulaymaniyah. The town, constructed in the late 18th century to serve as the Baban capital, soon emerged as one of the preeminent centers of Kurdish language and culture, a reputation it still enjoys to this day.

Relations between the Ottoman officials and their Kurdish vassals were, however, not always cordial. For instance, in 1805, the Baban emir, Abdurraham Pasha (r. 1789–1813), was forced to briefly seek sanctuary in Iran following Ottoman efforts to impose one of his relatives, Khalid Pasha, in charge of the emirate. The operation ultimately failed, and Abdurrahman Pasha returned to Sulaymaniyah a year later with the support of the Shah of Iran, Fath-Ali Shah Qajar (r. 1797–1834). Thus, while the Babans generally pledged fidelity to the Ottomans, they often sought to balance Ottoman influence through appeals to their Iranian rivals. Indeed, competition between the Ottoman and Iranians helped precipitate the Ottoman-Qajar war of 1821 to 1823, a conflict triggered by the defection the Baban emir, Mahmud Pasha (r. 1813–1834), to the Iranians. The Babans were not the only Kurdish dynasty to challenge for Ottoman authorities in early 19th century. The weakening of the Babans in the 1820s, opened the way for a revival of the Soran emirate, under the leadership of Kor (Blind) Mir Mohammad, who emerged as the dominate figure in southern Kurdistan in the early 1830s. However, his ascendance was relative brief. In 1836, Ottoman military successes forced his surrender. Over the subsequent decade and a half, the Ottoman authorities sought to put an end to the independence of the Kurds, seeking to replace the feudalistic system, which had defined relationships Istanbul and its Kurdish vassals for centuries, with a European-style system of centralized provincial administration. This drive, which accelerated following the promulgation of the *Tanzimat* Reform edict in late 1839, prompted significant resistance from Kurdish potentates across Kurdistan. In the early 1840s, Ahmad Pasha (r. 1838–1846) made efforts to revive the power and influence of the Baban emirate. However, he was ultimately defeated by the forces of Necip Pasha, the Ottoman governor of Bagdad in 1846. The Ottoman subsequently installed Abdallah Pasha, a more compliant member of the Baban clan, as governor of Sulaimani. However, the Ottoman central government gradually eroded his autonomy and in 1851, Baban rule in Sulaymaniyah was terminated.

The fall of the Babans marked more than three centuries in which Ottoman officials had shared the task of governing Kurdistan with local princelings. However, it proved difficult for the Ottoman authorities to provide a stable alternative administration, in particular with regard to territories that would become Iraqi Kurdistan. Between 1850 and 1878, Istanbul placed the region under the authority of the governor of Baghdad and, when compared to other Kurdish-inhabited districts farther north, reforms in provincial administration were relatively slow. It was only after 1878, when the province of Mosul, which included the formally Kurdish-held districts located to the city's northeast, was re-established, that the region was brought more firmly under central government control.

However, as in other parts of Kurdistan, the fall of the emirates and the relative weakness of the Ottoman central government laid the foundation for the rise to political prominence of the sheikhs, the leaders of the Sufi brotherhoods, religious orders that defined the spiritual life across much of the Kurdish highlands. As Muslim spiritual guides, Sufi sheikhs have along since played an important role in Kurdish society. However, will the fall of the emirates and the growth of European influence over the Ottoman Empire, the Kurdistan's Sufi sheikhs were able to both take up the role as intermediaries in tribal disputes and present themselves the defenders of traditional Muslim sociopolitical supremacy in the face what they perceived as an ascendant "Christendom." The most well-known Kurdish Sufi leader of this period was Sheikh Ubeydullah of Nehri (d. 1883), a leader in the Naqshbandi-Khalidi Sufi order, which had risen to prominence in Kurdistan in the early 19th century. His rebellion against both Ottoman and Iranian authorities in the early 1880s drew on the support of numerous Kurdish tribes, including in the distinct surrounding Mosul. Following his defeat and exile in Hejaz, resistance to the Ottoman authorities continued under the leadership of Sheikh Ubeydullah's deputies (*khalifa*), the sheikhs of Barzan, a dynasty that would come to play a critical role in Iraqi Kurdish politics. Other significant Kurdish dynasties that rose to prominence in Iraqi Kurdistan included the Talabani sheikhs, who dominated the districts surrounding Kirkuk. However, perhaps the most powerful Kurdish sheikhs in southern Kurdistan were the Talabani's rivals, the Berzinji sheikhs of Sulaimani.

The rise of the Berzinjis of Sulaymaniyah was facilitated by the shrewd alliances cultivated by the dynasty's leaders. Not only did they forge ties with powerful tribal groupings residing in the districts surrounding Sulaimani, most notable the warlike Hamawand tribe, they also formed close bonds with Sultan Abdulhamid II (r. 1876–1909). Indeed, in 1901 the Ottoman sultan hosted the family's patriarch, Sheikh Said (d. 1909) in Istanbul and giving a special code through which he could contact the palace directly, circumnavigating the regular channels Ottoman bureaucracy. This meant that Ottoman officials, who often complained about the Berzinjis lawlessness, were unable to take action against the family. As a result, Sheikh Said Berzinji was to emerge as the unofficial master of Sulaymaniyah, dominating its local government and expropriating land from local cultivators. The power of the Berzinjis was temporary checked following the 1908 "Young Turk" Revolution, which put an end to the personal rule of Sultan Abdulhamid II. As a close associate of the sultan, the new Ottoman government removed Sheikh Said from Sulaymaniyah to Mosul, where he was killed during the course of a riot in early 1909. Nevertheless, the power of the Berzinjis was not broken and Sheikh Said's son, Sheikh Mahmud (1878–1856), remained at large. Nevertheless, with the Ottoman entry into the First World War in October 1914, Sheikh Mahmud made peace with the Ottoman government, supplying irregular cavalry to fight the British invasion of Mesopotamia. After 1908, the Ottoman authorities also faced renewed resistance from the Barzanis, led by Sheikh Abdusselam Barzani (1882–1914). Significantly, faced with the hostility of the Ottoman administration, Sheikh Abdusselam Barzani sought allies, including Abdurrezzak Bedirkhan, a Kurdish aristocrat who sought to spark a general Kurdish revolt with the support for Russia. However, Ottoman forces put an end to Abdusselam's resistance, capturing and executing him in 1914. However, unlike the Berzinjis, Sheikh Abdusselam's successor, Sheikh Ahmed (1889–1969) did not make peace with Istanbul following the outbreak of the war, instead seeking sanctuary in Russia for the duration of the hostilities.

The Hashemite Monarchy, 1918 to 1958

Although at the end of the First World War most of Ottoman Kurdistan remained in Turkish hands, the British, who had been advancing northwards from lower Iraq, occupied some of the more southerly Kurdish-inhabited districts. In May 1918, British forces entered the oil-rich city of Kirkuk. This was followed by occupation of Mosul, in violation of the Mudros Armistice signed in October 30, 1918, in early November. With the fall of Mosul, Turkish authority across much of southern Kurdistan came to an end. Initially, British plans for the region were to include it within an Arab state, albeit with a certain degree of Kurdish political and cultural autonomy. Indeed, in 1919, the British recognized Sheikh Mahmud Berzinji, who had been appointed by the retreating Turks the governor of Sulaimani, as the local ruler. However, Sheikh Mahmud's efforts to expand his authority and establish an independent Kurdish kingdom soon earned him the hostility of not only the British authorities but also neighboring tribesmen who resented his authority. This resulted in his removal from office in 1919 and his subsequent exile to India. However, following Turkish efforts to re-establish control over southern Kurdistan in 1921 and 1922, the British returned Sheikh Mahmud to Sulaymaniyah in order to counteract Turkey's influence. However, Sheikh Mahmud's renewed efforts to establish an independent kingdom again led him into conflict with the British. By 1924, British forces had forced Sheikh Mahmud to quit Sulaymaniyah and take refuge in the mountains surrounding the city.

Although Sheikh Mahmud continued to agitate for Kurdish independence, only making peace with the Iraqi government in 1932, his withdrawal from Sulaimani marked the end of serious military Kurdish resistance to British attempts to integrate the Kurdish-inhabited districts of Mosul into newly formed Hashemite Kingdom of Iraq. In 1926, Turkey's claims to the region were also resolved, with League of Nations' mediators ultimately finding in favor of the Iraqi government. However, despite commitments from the Iraqi government to implement recommendations from the League of Nations that the Kurds be granted a limited degree of cultural and administrative autonomy, relations between Iraqi authorities and the Kurds remained problematic. The Iraqi government did little to realize these pledges and, in the 1930, the Anglo-Iraqi Treaty, which laid the basis for Iraqi's formal independence from Great Britain in 1932, made no mention of Kurdish cultural and political rights. Despite this, many Kurds made came to accept Iraqi rule, with some rising to prominent positions in the Hashemite administration. These included Mohammad Emin Zeki Bey (1880–1848), a prominent historian of the Kurds from Sulaymaniyah, who held a number of ministerial positions in the 1920s and 1930s, and General Bakir Sadqi Askari (1890–1937), the architect of Iraq's first military coup d'état in 1936. It also included Ahmad Muktar Baban (1900–1976), who served as prime minister between May and July 1958 and enjoyed the dubious distinction of being the last prime minister of Iraq's Hashemite era.

However, while some Kurds made peace with the monarchy, there was also a continuation of tensions. For instance, in 1931 government efforts to imposed taxation and police on the district of Barzan coupled with a program to settle Assyrian refugees from Hakkari on lands adjacent to the village resulted in conflict with the village's sheikhs. Under the leadership of Sheikh Ahmed and his younger brother, Molla Mustafa (1903–1979), the Barzanis revolted, resisting the forces of the central government for over a year, before withdrawing over the border and seeking asylum in Turkey in the summer of 1932. A year later, the Turks handed the Barzanis back to Iraqi authorities, after which they were exiled from their homes, living in various towns and cities across Iraq. In 1943, Molla Mustafa escaped the Iraqi authorities and returned Barzan, where upon hostilities resumed. However, as in the early 1930s, Iraqi military superiority gradually pushed the Barzanis back and, in 1945, he and his followers fled across the border into Iran. In Iran, he became involved in the Soviet-backed Mahabad Republic, led by Qazi Mohammad. There he served as the autonomous republic's minister of defence until its collapse in early 1947. However, unlike Qazi Mohammad, whom Iranian authorities captured and executed, Molla Mustafa engaged in a fighting retreat, evading the Iranian army and eventually crossing the Aras River into the Soviet Union. He would remain there in exile until the Iraqi Revolution of 1958.

The Barzani revolt, which helped raise the prestige of the Barzani clan, occurred at a time of growing political mobilization amongst the Iraqi Kurds, especially the growing urban intelligentsia. The rise of Arab nationalism in Iraq alienated many educated Kurds. Some were attracted to socialist ideas, and the Iraqi Communist Party (ICP), founded in 1934, won many Kurdish adherents through its calls for Kurdish national self-determination. Although the ICP later reversed this policy, it continued to maintain a Kurdish section, *Azadi* (Freedom). The 1930s also witnessed the formation of a number of Kurdish clubs and political association, including the *Komala-ye Lawan* (The Young Men's Association), a Baghdad-based youth club; the clandestine, albeit aristocratic, *Komala-ye Briyeti* (The Brotherhood Association), founded by one of Sheikh Mahmud's sons; and *Darkar* (the Woodcutters), a more radical group of nationalists with ties to the ICP. In 1938, another significant group was the *Hiwa* (Hope), led by a veteran of the Sheikh Mahmud Revolt, Rafiq Hilmi (1898–1960). *Hiwa* brought together separate Kurdish groups in Erbil, Kirkuk, Kifri, Kalar, Khanaqin, and Baghdad and served to spread nationalist ideas among educated Kurds, including those serving in the civil service and military. *Hiwa* was also supportive the Barzani revolt, seeking to transform a tribal revolt into a nationalist *cause célèbre* and worked to build relations with Kurdish activists in Iran. However, tensions between pro-British liberals such Hilmi and pro-Soviet leftists within *Hiwa* resulted in splits and the formation of a new political party in 1945, *Rizgari Kurd* (Kurdish Liberation). *Rizgari Kurd* was short-lived, although did manage to make an appeal for national self-determination to the newly formed United Nations. It was superseded by the formation of the Kurdistan Democratic Party of Iraq (KDP) in 1946.

The KDP was originally a sister organization to the party of the same name established by Kurdish revolutionaries across the border in the Iranian Kurdish town of Mahabad. Its first congress, held in Baghdad during the summer of 1946, resulted in the election of Molla Mustafa Barzani, who at the time was in Iran, as the organization's president-in-exile. However, despite this conservative leadership, the KDP soon attracted the support of many left-wing Kurdish nationalists, who coalesced under the leadership of Ibrahim Ahmed (1914–2000), a Baghdad-educated lawyer from Sulaymaniyah. In 1951, Ahmed became the party's general-secretary, also becoming the organization's de facto leader. The political program of the KDP initially called for Kurdish self-rule, but avoided calls for social and economic reforms that might alienate some of Kurdistan's more conservative tribal and landowning elites. However, under the influence of leftist intellectuals such as Ahmed, the KDP increasingly moved to the political left, even forging an electoral alliance with the ICP. By the mid-1950s, the KDP program called for the nationalization of the burgeoning Iraqi oil industry, the abolition of the monarchy, and closer diplomatic ties with the Soviet Bloc.

Republican Iraq, 1958 to 1991

In July 1958, a military coup d'état carried out by Brigadier-General Abdul Karim Qasim (1914–1963) toppled the Iraqi monarchy. Many educated Kurds welcomed the fall of the Hashemite dynasty, hoping that it might open the way for the resolution of the Kurdish question. Molla Mustafa's return from the Soviet Union after 12 years in exile further served to raise Kurdish expectations. Once back in Iraq, Molla Mustafa moved quickly to secure control of the KDP and worked closely with the new republican regime. However, despite symbolic gestures such as including a Kurd on Iraqi's new sovereignty council, creating a new national flag, which included Kurdish symbols, and the insertion of a clause in the new Iraqi Constitution, which described Arabs and Kurds as "partners" within the nation, relations between Molla Mustafa and Qasim soon deteriorated. Once back in Kurdistan, Molla Mustafa moved against tribes that had supported the Hashemite against earlier Barzani rebellions such as the Zibaris Baradost, Herki, and Surchi. In response, the Iraqi government began arming anti-Barzani tribal elements, and by 1961, Molla Mustafa and his supporters were in open revolt against the central government. Molla Mustafa was able to draw on the support of conservative landowning elements in Kurdistan enraged by Qasim's efforts to implement land reform. In contrast, the more urban and left-wing political leadership of the KDP, most notably Ibrahim Ahmed and his protégée Jalal Talabani (1933–), was more circumspect about the rebellion and suspicious of the growing power and prestige of Molla Mustafa. Nevertheless, Qasim's hostility toward the KDP and his failure to make progress on Kurdish autonomy helped push them into open revolt. Between 1961 and 1963, Kurdistan descended into political chaos, with government forces losing control over many of the more mountainous districts. The war in Kurdistan was not the major issue facing Qasim's regime. Pan-Arabists, Nasserites, and Ba'athists in Baghdad were also increasingly hostile to the government, and Qasim found himself increasingly politically isolated. Qasim's downfall came in February 1963, following a successful CIA-backed Ba'athist *coup d'état.*

Mulla Mustafa Barzani

One of the most popular and successful leaders of the Kurds was Mulla Mustafa Barzani. As a member of a traditional sheikh family, he combined his charismatic leadership skills with the work in the Kurdistan Democratic Party (Iraq), whose president he was since 1946. Until 1975, he fought several wars with the Iraqi government and neighboring countries in order to secure cultural and political autonomy for his people. After the Algiers Accord, he withdrew from politics but not until his sons took over the leadership of the KDP. He died from cancer in 1979 and was buried in his home village, Barzan.

Molla Mustafa and the KDP welcomed to removal of Qasim, and moves to put an end to the violence were set in motion. However, mutual mistrust remained. Many Ba'athists regarded Iraqi Kurdistan as Arab land and the Kurdish movement as a tool of Western imperialism. Negotiations stalled, and in June 1963, Baghdad renewed its assault on Kurdistan. The Iraqi army, however, again failed decisively to defeat the insurgents, and the offensive ended in November 1963, following President Abdul Salem Arif's removal of the Ba'athists from government. Molla Mustafa had been generally supportive of the Arif *coup d'état*, signing a peace agreement with Iraqi government in February 1964. This move was, however, heavily criticized by the Ahmed-Talabani wing of the KDP, who were incensed by the fact that Molla Mustafa had signed the agreement in his personal capacity rather than as leader of the KDP and that the agreement he had put his name on made no mention of Kurdish self-rule. This division ultimately resulted in conflict. At the sixth KDP Congress, held at Qala Diza in June 1964, Molla Mustafa ordered the arrest of supporters of Ahmed-Talabani faction. A few days later, he dispatched his son, Idris, to attack Ahmed, Talabani, and 4,000 of their supporters, driving them across the border into Iran. With his power within the Kurdish movement secured, Molla Mustafa demanded that the government include Kirkuk and Khanaqin into an autonomous Kurdish region. This demand proved to be unacceptable to Baghdad.

With discussions between the Kurdish rebels and the central government stalled, the conflict resumed. For much of the mid-1960s the violence was intermittent. Neither the Iraqi government nor the Kurdish movement could obtain a decisive military victory. Following Arif's death in April 1966, an offensive against Molla Mustafa by the Iraqi Army, supported by Ahmed and Talabani, collapsed. This opened the way for the new Iraqi prime minister, Abd al-Rahman al-Bazzaz (1913–1973), to open up a new round of talks, which culminated in the Bazzaz Declaration in June. The Bazzaz Declaration was an expansive 12-point program that recognized the binational character of Iraq and promised

Molla Mustafa Barzani, leader of the Kurdistan Democratic Party (KDP), 1970. (Keystone-France/Gamma-Keystone via Getty Images)

Kurds cultural and linguistic rights as well as self-government. Molla Mustafa and the KDP accepted the proposal. Nevertheless, pressure from hard-line members of the military pressured Iraqi's new president, Abd al-Rahman Arif (Abdul Salem's brother), to dismiss al-Bazzaz, a civilian known for his hostility to military power. The new administration broke off talks with Molla Mustafa and the KDP and armed tensions continued.

In July 1968, the Ba'ath Party regained power in Iraq. Although the party was mistrustful of Molla Mustafa and the KDP, it included in its program a commitment to resolving the Kurdish question peacefully. Already the conflict had resulted in the destruction of 700 villages, the displacement of 300,000 people, and as many as 60,000 dead and wounded. Hence, the Ba'athists, eager to consolidate power, and the Kurdish movement, weary of war, entered into a new round of talks in 1969. This culminated in the announcement of the peace accords of March 11, 1970. This agreement promised extensive political autonomy and cultural rights for the Kurdish population. However, while Baghdad moved quickly to implement some parts of the agreement, tensions soon began to resurface. The Ba'ath party continued to be suspicious of Kurds, who were receiving military aid from Iran, Israel, and the United States, while Molla Mustafa and his supporters questioned the sincerity of the Ba'athists' commitment to the March Accords. Disputes also arose regarding boundaries of Kurdish autonomy and, in particular, the future status of the oil-rich city of Kirkuk. In March 1974, with relations between the two sides deteriorating rapidly, the Ba'athist government unilaterally promulgated an Autonomy Law, albeit a watered-down version of what had been agreed to four years earlier. This resulted in a renewal of the armed struggle. Initially, the Iraqi army enjoyed considerable success, despite that fact that Molla Mustafa now had almost approximately 100,000 men under his command. Iraqi success, however, prompted the Iranians, who had been quietly backing the Kurdish since the mid-1960s, to step up military support to the Kurds. With Iranian support, Kurdish *peshmergas* (militiamen/ lit: those who face death) were able to reverse some of the Iraqi gains. It soon became apparent that Iranian support was critical to Kurdish success, prompting the Iraqi government to dispatch then Vice-President Saddam Hussein (1937–2006) to Algiers to meet with the Shah Mohammad Reza (r. 1941–1979). This meeting resulted in an agreement between the two countries, signed on March 15, 1975. In return for Iraq ceding claims to the entirety of the Shatt al-Arab waterway, Iran agreed to halt its support to Kurdish rebels. A few days later, the KDP agreed to end the armed struggle, following a meeting between the Shah and Molla Mustafa. Barzani subsequently retired to Iran and then the United States, where he died in 1979.

Molla Mustafa's death marked the end of an era for Iraqi Kurdish politics, leaving a political vacuum that his son and successor as KDP leader, Masoud Barzani, was unable to fill. Even before his death, Molla Mustafa's decision not to fight in March 1975 resulted in political splits. For example, former KDP loyalist Sami Abdul Rahman established the Kurdistan Popular Democratic Party (KPDP), angered by the continued dominance of the Barzani clan over KDP internal affairs. However, without a doubt the most significant group to emerge from the KDP in the 1970s was the Patriotic Union of Kurdistan (PUK), founded in June 1975. The origins of the PUK can be traced back to the Ahmed-Talabani faction of the KDP. Ahmed and Talabani evidentially reconciled with the KDP, but tensions remained, resurfacing after Molla Mustafa's defeat in 1975. Although Ahmed withdraw from frontline politics, immigrating to Great Britain, Talabani, who had been representing the KDP in Syria, split from the party, bringing together a number of leftist Kurdish groups under the PUK's umbrella. By the late 1970s, the PUK had *Peshmerga* fighters in the field and were waging a low-level guerrilla war against both the Iraqi army, but also elements of the KDP. Still, the overall position of the Kurdish insurgency was at its most unfavorable since it had begun in 1961. As many as 250,000 Kurds had fled to Iran, while some 60,000 were internally displaced. Moreover, the Iraqi government undertook anti-Kurdish policies, including the establishment of a 20-km-deep *cordon sanitaire* along the border, the settlement of Arabs in Kurdish districts, and deportation of between 40,000 and 300,000 Kurds to the south of Iraq (although the Iraqi government eventually allowed most to return).

Any major renewal of the armed struggle in Iraqi Kurdistan was difficult so long as the Iran remained committed to the Algiers Agreement and kept the border closed. However, the Iranian Revolution of 1979, which was welcomed by both the KDP and PUK, and the outbreak of the Iran-Iraqi War in 1980 opened the way for a renewal of Iranian military support. For example, with Iranian support the KDP was able to capture the border town of Hajj Umran and expand its influence in the Bahdinan region, while the PUK consolidated its position in districts further to the south. For the first two years of the war, Kurdish forces, backed up by the Iranians, enjoyed a number of successes against government forces. By early 1983, the Iraqi government's hold on Kurdistan was looking extremely tenuous, with the outbreak of anti-government demonstration and questions regarding the loyalty of pro-government tribal militias in doubt. In response, Iraqi president Saddam Hussein, who had seized power in 1979, sought to restart negotiation with the Kurdish groups. While he was rebuffed by the KDP, his overtures to the PUK proved more successful and in December 1983, the two sides agreed to a ceasefire. However, negotiations collapsed in October 1984, amidst continued Iraqi repression of Kurdish activism. Indeed, the intransigence of the Iraqi government helped solidify Kurdish opposition to the regime and a gradual improvement in relations between the KDP and PUK. This culminated with the formation of the Iraqi Kurdistan Front in July 1987.

Faced with an insurrection in the north, which was tying up valuable resources, the Ba'athist regime increasingly resorted to violence against civilians in order to intimidate the Kurdish population into submission. As early as 1983, Saddam Hussein had ordered the murder of 6,000 men and boys from the Barzani clan, including those who had supported the Ba'athists. The level of violence only increased as the war continued. In March 1987, Saddam Hussein appointed his cousin, Ali Hasan al-Majid as Kurdistan's ruler. Once in the north al-Majid began destroying Kurdish villages and towns, importing Arab settlers into strategic districts around Kirkuk, and using chemical weapons against the *peshmerga*. This violence only increased in the spring of 1988. Perhaps the most well-known incident to occur that year was the poison-gas attack on the border town of Halabja, in which between 3,200 and 5,000 civilians of all ages were killed. Nevertheless, the Halabja massacre must be understood within the broader context of the *Anfal* campaigns, military operations conducted against the Kurdistan's civilian population and realized in eight phases between February and September 1988. During the course of the campaign between 50,000 and 182,000 Kurdish civilians were killed and over 4,000 villages destroyed. Even after the end of the Iran-Iraq War, in August 1988, the violence and deportations continued with the Iraqi government forcibly resettling as many as 1.5 million Kurds. With Iranian military support withdrawn there was little the KDP, PUK, or other smaller parties could do halt these campaigns.

The Kurdistan Regional Government, 1991 to present

In August 1990, Saddam Hussein ordered his troops into Kuwait, a move condemned by the international community. The United Nations subsequently passed a resolution demanding the Iraqis to withdraw. Saddam refused, and ultimately a military coalition, led by the United States, attacked Iraqi forces in early 1991. By the end of February, the Iraqi army had been defeated and a ceasefire implemented. A few days later, in early March, a mass uprising broke out in both the predominately Shia south of the country as well as in Iraqi Kurdistan. The Kurdish uprising began on March 4 in the small town of Ranya and soon spread across the region, with the towns of Sulaymaniyah, Erbil, Duhok, and Kirkuk falling to KDP and PUK Kurdish fighters, who were aided by the defection of upwards of 60,000 former pro-government tribal militias to the rebels side. Nevertheless, after crushing the rebellion in the south, Saddam refocused his attention on Kurdistan. By early April, Iraqi forces had reoccupied most of Iraqi Kurdistan, prompting approximately 2 million Kurds to flee to Turkey, Syria, and Iran. This looming humanitarian disaster forced international action in the formation of "Operation Provide Comfort" and the formation of a Kurdish "safe haven," protected by a no-fly zone, above the 36th parallel. In response, the Iraqi government withdrew government officials from Kurdistan and placed the region under a blockade. Saddam evidently hoped to starve the Kurds into submission. However, the Kurdish political parties moved into fill the power vacuum, and in May 1992, the first democratic election for the Kurdistan regional parliament was held. Although eight political parties participated, the KDP obtained 50.22 percent of the vote and the PUK 49.78 percent. Given the closeness of the election, the major parties agreed to divide the seats in the 105-seat Kurdistan National Assembly (KNA) equally, each receiving 50 seats with the remaining 5 seats being assigned to representatives of the Christian minority.

The new Kurdish government, which functioned under the dual leadership of Masoud Barzani and Jalal Talabani, moved quickly to reform government, open schools, and organize the budget. In October 1992, the KNA also issued a declaration redefining the goals of the Kurdish movement from "autonomy" to "federalism." Nevertheless, the Kurdish administration was still extremely vulnerable and faced the hostility of not only Baghdad, but also that of the governments of Turkey, Iran, and Syria who feared a successful Iraqi Kurdish movement might embolden their own Kurdish populations. There were also serious internal divisions within Iraqi Kurdistan, with both the KDP and PUK establishing extensive networks of political patronage to the detriment of democracy. At the same time, the Kurdistan Workers Party (PKK), which had been waging a war against the government of Turkey since 1984, was also trying to expand its influence into Iraqi Kurdistan, which resulted in a rapid breakdown of relations with the Iraqi Kurds, in particular the KDP. At the same time as the KDP was facing off with the PKK, the PUK had its own problem, engaging in a struggle for power with Islamic Movement of Kurdistan (IMK), a Jihadist organization, which had emerged in the late 1980s. By 1994, even the power-sharing arrangements between the KDP and PUK had collapsed, making the beginning of the *Brakuji* (civil war). In August 1996, the situation deteriorated even further following KDP leader Masoud Barzani's request that the Iraqi army support him against Jalal Talabani's PUK, which was receiving support from Iran. The KDP, alongside Iraqi military units, drove the PUK out of Erbil and, for a brief time, its stronghold of Sulaymaniyah. The intervention of the United States in the fall of 1996 compelled the Iraqis to withdraw their forces from Kurdistan, and Iraqi Kurdistan was in effect partitioned between a KDP zone (Dohuk and Erbil) and a PUK zone (Sulaymaniyah). The American-brokered Washington Agreement of September 1998 in effect formalized this partition.

Between the end of the civil war period in 1998 and the U.S.-led invasion of Iraq in March 2003, witnessed a period of political reconciliation between the KDP and PUK. The two parties also cooperated in the struggle against radical Islamic groups, most notably *Ansar al-Islam*, a Kurdish Salafi group established in 2001, which had taken control a number of villages along Iranian border. In 2003, the KDP and PUK supported the U.S.-led invasion and, aided by the 101st Airborne Division, ejected Iraqi troops from Kirkuk and Mosul. In addition, PUK fighters, supported by U.S. Special Forces, also forced *Ansar al-Islam* from their stronghold on the Iranian border. Following the fall of Saddam, Iraqi Kurdish leaders emerged as important actors in Baghdad and successfully lobbied to have the principle federalism included in the new Iraqi constitution, which came into effect in 2005. This in effected legalized Iraqi Kurdistan's autonomous government, the Kurdistan Regional Government. They also secured the inclusion of an article on the future status of disputed territories (Article 140), which was to be decided by a plebiscite that was scheduled (although never held) for 2007. Kurdish politicians from both the KDP and PUK secured high-profile positions in the Iraqi central government. The former KDP spokesperson, Hoshyar Zebari, served as foreign minister between 2003 and 2014 and finance minister between 2014 and 2016. PUK leader Jalal Talabani became Iraqi president, serving between 2005 and 2014. He was succeeded by former communist and veteran PUK politician, Fuad Masum.

The post-invasion period also witnessed a certain degree of reunification of KDP and PUK zones of control, although both parties continued to maintain separate militias. In 2005, the KRG held regional elections with the KDP and PUK running a joint list (Kurdistan Alliance), along with several smaller parties, winning

90 percent of the votes. Subsequently, a coalition government was formed with ministerial portfolios shared among the members of the Kurdistan Alliance. The KDP and PUK also reached a power-sharing agreement over the position of KRG prime minister, with the KDP's Nechirvan Barzani (Masoud Barzani's nephew) serving between 2006 and 2009 and then again after 2012, while veteran PUK politician Bahram Salih held the post between 2009 and 2012.

Nevertheless, despite cooperation, Iraqi Kurdistan's political leadership has faced numerous internal challenges. The KRG government has periodically faced public protests. For instance, in 2006, crowds in the town of Halabja attacked and destroyed the Anfal memorial in the town, complaining that the KRG had neglected the town. In 2011, a more serious wave of anti-government protests broke out in Sulaimani, although the security forces eventually quelled the unrest. The KDP-PUK government was also challenged by the formation of the *Gorran* (Change) Party, which emerged after the PUK's number two, Nishirwan Mustafa, quit the party over the issue of corruption. The party, founded in 2009, first ran in regional parliament elections the same year, coming third behind the KDP and PUK, which had ended their electoral alliance. In the 2013 elections, they overtook the PUK, coming in second to the KDP. *Gorran* has since emerged as the main opposition to the KDP, which since 2013 has emerged as Iraqi Kurdistan's dominant party. In 2015, they were the main opposition to a two-year extension beyond the constitutional limit to Masoud Barzani's term in office, a constitutional crisis that resulted in the closure of parliament.

In addition to internal divisions, tensions between the KRG and Baghdad intensified. The referendum on the status of Kirkuk and other disputed territories, which was scheduled for 2007, was never held. Following the U.S. withdrawal from Iraq in 2010, relations between Baghdad and Erbil went into decline. In 2012, tensions in the disputed town of Tooz resulted in clashes between Kurdish forces and those of the Iraqi Army. Although a full-scale military clash was avoided, disagreement over not only the borders of the Iraqi Kurdistan region, but also the future of oil exploration and revenues continued to undermine relations between the two sides. In early 2014, this resulted in the central government cutting the KRG's allocation from the national budget. However, the crisis with the Baghdad government was soon eclipsed by the rise of ISIL. In June 2014, ISIL, a radical jihadist group, seized control of the city of Mosul, leading to the collapse of the Iraqi army in the north of the country. In response, the KRG advanced into the disputed territories to stop them from falling into the hands of ISIS fighters. At the same time, the KRG announced its intentions to hold a referendum on Kurdish independence. Initially ISIL focused its energies on attacking regions held by the Iraqi government. However, in August 2014 it widened its objectives, launching an offensive directed against the KRG. This included a thrust directed against the capital of Erbil as well as an assault on the Yezidi community of Sinjar. A U.S.-led military intervention helped halt ISIL's advance on the Kurdish capital, but the attack on Sinjar was more successful. Subsequently, ISIL massacred some 5,000 Yezidis with a 200,000 being forced to flee their homes. By autumn 2014, the frontline had stabilized, and Kurdish forces, in conjunction with those of the Iraqi central government and the United States, began a counteroffensive. In April 2017, as Kurdish forces were participating in a joint operation to retake Mosul, the KRG announced that it would hold a referendum on independence in September.

Djene Rhys Bajalan

Further Reading

Aziz, M. (2011). *The Kurds of Iraq: Nationalism and Identity in Iraqi Kurdistan.* London: I. B. Tauris.

Barzani, M. (2003). *Mustafa Barzani and the Kurdish Liberation Movement.* New York: Palgrave-Macmillan.

Bengio, O. (2012). *The Iraqi Kurds: Building a State within a State.* London: Lynne Rienner.

Edmonds, C. J. (1959). "The Kurds and the Revolution in Iraq." *Middle East Journal,* vol. 13, no. 1, 1–10.

Hardi, C. (2012). *Gendered Experiences of Genocide: Anfal Survivors in Kurdistan-Iraq.* Farnham, UK: Ashgate Publishing.

Jwaideh, W. (2006). *The Kurdish Nationalist Movement: Its Origin and Development.* Syracuse, NY: University of Syracuse Press.

McDowall, D. (1998). *A Modern History of the Kurds.* London: I. B. Taurus.

Natali, D. (2010). *The Kurdish Quasi-State: Development and Dependency in Post-Gulf War Iraq.* Syracuse, NY: Syracuse University Press.

Romano, D. (2006). *The Kurdish Nationalist Movement: Opportunity, Mobilization and Identity.* Cambridge, MA: Cambridge University Press.

Soane, E. B. (2007). *To Mesopotamia and Kurdistan in Disguise.* New York: Cosimo Classics.

ISRAEL

The Kurdish Jewish community has been shaped by its distinctive experience with persecution, dispossession, and expulsion from Iraq in 1950–1951. Growing hostilities toward Jews in all of Iraq followed the establishment of the state of Israel in 1948 and forced nearly the entire Kurdish Jewish (and the much larger Iraqi Jewish) community to depart for Israel. Kurdish Jews initially faced significant bias in Israel because of their lack of formal education, but should be considered a well-integrated community today. Descendants of expelled Kurdish Jews are also successfully engaged in a range of cultural and business activities that re-established relationships with Muslim communities in the Kurdistan region of Iraq. Many nationalist Kurds in Iraq increasingly appreciate Israel's public support for the creation of an independent Kurdish state. However, others fear that closer relations between Kurdistan and Israel could provoke hostile responses from neighboring Arab countries and from Iran. In essence, Iraqi Kurdish leadership quietly hopes to be able to emulate Israel's success in terms of establishing an independent Kurdish state, yet aims to avoid becoming involved in Israel's ongoing conflict with Palestinian communities (Bengio, 2014).

Traditionally, Kurdish Jews belonged to culturally isolated communities and numbered a mere 25,000 people in Iraq. Mostly poor and reliant on long-established animal husbandry and subsistence farming practices, they spoke Aramaic (an ancient Semitic language) and Kurmanji (northern Kurdish) at home (Zaken, 2007: 8–9).

Dispersed among about 200 remote villages in Kurdistan, Kurdish Jews depended on Muslim Kurdish tribal protections to eke out an existence for themselves. Kurdish Jews also lived in the Jewish quarters of the town of Zakho, near the Turkish border today, where they engaged in basic commerce and trade (Gavish, 2010: 32–43).

From a historical perspective, Kurdish Jews experienced relatively high levels of tolerance and were able to carry out their farming and trade activities as well as religious practices without significant interference by powerful Kurdish *aghas* (overlords). Prior to the 1930s, when Nazi-inspired ideological notions began to shape perceptions about Jewish communities, Jewish-Muslim relations in Kurdistan had been fairly harmonious. Yet by 1941, Kurdish Jews began to face periods of hostility and harassment, persecution and even a pogrom (organized massacres targeting a specific ethnic/religious group) as a direct result of the rise of a pro-Nazi German government in Baghdad (Zaken, 2007: 9–17).

By the 1920s, a few Kurdish Jewish families became involved in the Zionist movement. Zionism represented an ideology advanced by Jewish nationalists in support of creating a homeland in the historic areas of Israel. Jewish migration from Iraq, including Kurdish Jewish migration, increased with the establishment of the British Mandate for Palestine (1922–1947), which meant that the League of Nations had granted Britain full control over former Ottoman territories. The disregard of Palestinian interests unsettled Arab communities throughout the region and caused conflict over several decades.

Among the best-known Zionist Kurdish Jews was a young Moshe Barazani (also Barzani) (1926–1947). Barazani was born in Baghdad to a family that originated from Kurdistan and then moved to mandate Palestine. As a teenager, he engaged in anti-British acts of sabotage and terrorism. He joined Lehi (Freedom Fighters of Israel), an organization the British called the Stern Gang. Members of the group focused on expelling British forces from the region and participated in increasingly dangerous and violent acts. Lehi/Stern Gang members embraced violence as a legitimate tool to pursue the establishment of the state of Israel and enforce a path of unlimited immigration of Jews to the region. In 1947, Barazani was arrested by the British just moments before carrying out an assassination against a British military officer. Barazani was condemned as a terrorist and scheduled to be executed when someone managed to smuggle a hand grenade into his prison cell. Barazani committed suicide along with another convicted terrorist.

Levels of violence between Arab, Palestinian, and Jewish communities dramatically increased throughout the Palestinian Mandate territories in the 1940s. As the numbers of Palestinian refugees seeking shelter and aid in Iraq and Kurdistan swelled, Jews faced growing intolerance and hostility in Iraq. In 1941, after the pro-German coup in Baghdad, open hostilities shaped interactions between Muslins and Jews throughout Iraq. Iraqi political officers encouraged the so-called Farhud pogroms (campaigns of violent dispossessions) in Baghdad, but they also spread to Kurdistan where Muslim Kurdish tribes took advantage of the changing political climate. About 130 Jews were murdered in Baghdad, several others killed in the countryside, and some 2,500 Jews were injured (Yehuda & Moreh, 2008: 6–7).

Iraqi Muslims suspected that Jews and Kurdish Jews supported Zionism and with it the establishment of the state of Israel. Kurdish Jews, just like all Jews in Iraq at that time, faced accusations of being traitors and favoring the expulsion of Palestinians. Jews began to leave Iraq in growing numbers by entering Syria, then Lebanon, before reaching Palestine. Others left for Iran. Many received support from Zionists who were ideologically committed to assist as many Jews from Iraq as possible in their journeys to Israel.

Once the state of Israel declared its independence on May 14, 1948, war broke out between Arab communities and Israel. Several allied Arab states led by Egypt, Jordan, and Syria, and supported by expeditionary forces from Iraq, entered the former Palestinian Mandate territory with the aim to destroy the newly established state of Israel. In the three years following this war an estimated 700,000 Jews were expelled from countries throughout the Middle East and began a mass migration to Israel. This process is called *aliyah* in Israel and describes the mass migration of Jews from the diaspora to the homeland.

Before the mass exodus from Iraq, Iraqi Jews (including Kurdish Jews) numbered around 120,000, and nearly everyone left the country for Israel because of campaigns of economic dispossession, threats, and expulsions (Zaken, 2007: 343). Between 1950 and 1951, the Jews of historic Kurdistan were airlifted to Israel as an expansion of an earlier campaign known by its code name "Operation Magic Carpet." Magic Carpet had focused on bringing Yemeni, Djiboutian, and Ethiopian Jews to Israel starting in June 1949. In 1950, all Iraqi and Kurdish Jews received permission to leave Iraq within one year on the condition that they renounced their citizenship. In 1951, the Iraqi government froze Jewish property, requisitioned belongings, and placed further economic restrictions on community members. Israel then negotiated airlifts to bring Iraqi and Kurdish Jews to Israel in "Operation Ali Baba," also more formally known as Operation Ezra and Nehemia (in reference to the return of Jewish people from Babylonian exile in the fifth century, BCE) (Pasachoff & Littman, 2005: 301). Most Iraqi and Kurdish Jews arrived in Israel without resources, and Kurdish Jews in particular experienced high levels of destitution. Many Kurdish Jews lived in former military barracks and refugee tent encampments in Israel before being permanently resettled within the country.

The integration of Kurdish Jews into Israel proved to be a painful experience as the community faced social intolerance and patterns of discrimination. Considered uneducated country bumpkins, Kurdish Jews encountered a low public image in Israel and became the brunt of cruel jokes about their supposed lack of intelligence and knowledge about the modern world. Kurdish Jews settled throughout many small towns and villages to continue to engage in traditional agricultural and business practices for their first decades in Israel. Few arrived with modern skills, but they embraced educational opportunities for their children. The largest number of Kurdish immigrants settled in the surrounding area of Jerusalem. Kurds established themselves in the city's undesirable Katamonim neighborhood, known for concrete, Soviet-style apartment buildings. In the 1950s and 1960s, Israel relied on the construction of low-cost, prefabricated apartment block buildings to ameliorate the extreme housing shortages that followed the wave of immigration to the newly established state. Nearly 200,000 Kurdish Jews live in Israel today, and half of them can still be found in the vicinity of Jerusalem, although many also reside in various neighborhoods of Tel Aviv.

Hadassa Yeshurun

Kurds who immigrated to Israel contributed much to the country's cultural and political development. Among the most popular artists of Kurdish descent in Israel is singer Hadassa Yeshurun who performs in Kurdish although she does not speak the language. Her parents moved to Israel from Kurdistan Iraq, and through her songs, she preserves the heritage of her ancestors. Recently, she released a cover of the famous song "Peshmergayna" that was originally sung by Tahseen Taha. In this song, Yeshurun praises the bravery of the Peshmerga who protect the Kurdish homeland.

The majority of young Kurdish Jews live a secular life today and tend to intermarry with members of other Jewish community members. Israeli born Jews of Kurdish descent tend to be well integrated into Israeli society, and speak Hebrew and English as their main languages (JCJCR, 2016). In contrast, the lives of community elders are often still shaped by deeply religious practices; some speak Aramaic and/or Kurdish at home. Among the best-known Israelis of Kurdish descent is former military general, Knesset (parliament) member, and minister of defense Yitzhak Mordechai (born in 1944). He resigned from his government position once he faced accusations of sexual assault and was later convicted. Another well-known Kurdish Jew is the linguist and scholar Yona Sabar (born in 1938 in Kurdistan), whose son Ariel Sabar wrote a family memoir under the title *My Father's Paradise*, expressing the longing that exists within the Kurdish Jewish community to better understand their cultural heritage (Sabar, 2008).

Jews of Kurdish descent play a crucial role in maintaining the community's cultural traditions in Israel. Some have renewed and strengthened links between modern Israel and the Kurdish region of Iraq. While official governmental relations between Israel and the Kurdistan Regional Government (KRG) of Iraq have fluctuated over time, private and unofficial cultural contacts and business relations between Israelis of Kurdish descent and Kurds in Kurdistan are positive. Today, many Kurdish communities in Iraq welcome visits from members of long-departed Kurdish Jews. In Zakho, located in the KRG and bordering on Turkey, Muslim Kurds still describe part of the city as the Jewish neighborhood of Zakho, even though Kurdish Jews have not lived in Zakho for over 65 years.

Sherzad Omar Mamsani, a Jewish Kurd and a former Peshmerga (Kurdish militia) fighter involved in the struggle against Saddam Hussein's Baathist regime, serves today as the director of Jewish affairs in the KRG's ministry of endowment and religious affairs (Robinson, 2016). In 2015, he initiated the first official commemoration of the Farhud pogroms in Erbil, Kurdistan (Sokol, 2015). Some 400 or more Jewish Kurdish families live in the KRG, although such estimates are notoriously difficult to confirm as many families continue to officially register as Muslims, especially in light of the regional threat of ISIS (The Islamic State in Iraq and Syria) which continues to attack religious and ethnic minorities.

A major Kurdish Jewish holiday, Seharane (also Saharana) festival, is celebrated on September 29 and exclusively recognized in Israel today. The festival takes place over multiple days and encourages Kurdish communities to gather, share traditional Kurdish meals, and sing and dance together. Many Kurds from various parts of the world travel to Israel to experience this unusual holiday. Everywhere else, Kurds celebrate Newroz (New Year) on March 21. But, when Kurdish Jewish immigrants arrived in Israel in the 1950s, the Mimouna holiday fell on the same day as the Kurdish New Year. Mimouna was celebrated by a more populous and centuries-old North African Jewish community. To avoid cultural oblivion in Israel, Kurdish Jews agreed to shift the date for their own holiday celebrations to September.

Vera Kelly-Eccarius

Further Reading

Bengio, O. (2014). "Surprising Ties between the Kurds and Israel." *The Middle East Quarterly,* vol. 21, no. 3, 1–12. http://www.meforum.org/3838/israel-kurds.

Gavish, H. (2010). *Unwitting Zionists: The Jewish Community of Zakho in Iraqi Kurdistan.* Detroit, MI: Wayne State University Press.

Jerusalem Center for Jewish-Christian Relations (JCJCR). (2016). "Kurdish-Jewish Community." http://www.jcjcr.org.

Morad, T., Shasha, D., & Shasha, R. (2008). *Iraq's Last Jews.* New York: Palgrave Macmillan.

Pasachoff, N. E., & Littman, R. J. (2005). *A Concise History of the Jewish People.* Lanham, MD: Rowman & Littlefield.

Robinson, R. (2016). "Sherzad the Kurdish Jew." http://www.aish.com/jw/s/Sherzad-The-Kurdish-Jew.html.

Sabar, A. (2008). *My Father's Paradise: A Son's Search for His Family's Past.* New York: Algonquin Books of Chapel Hill.

Sokol, S. (2015). "Jew Appointed to Official Position in Iraqi Kurdistan." *Jerusalem Post.* http://www.jpost.com/Diaspora/Jew-appointed-to-official-position-in-Iraqi-Kurdistan-426320.

Yehuda, Z., & Moreh, S. (2008). *Al-Farhud: the 1941 Pogrom in Iraq.* Jerusalem: Magnes Press of Hebrew University.

Zaken, M. (2007). *Jewish Subjects and Their Tribal Chieftains in Kurdistan: A Study in Survival.* Leiden, the Netherlands: Brill.

LEBANON

Kurds have a long history of settlement in Lebanon. In the 16th century, they were reportedly described as a community of four tribes (*eshiret*), including the Banu Sayfa clan north of Tripoli; the Ras Nahash, who settled near Tripoli; the Amadi coming from the Amadiya region in Iraqi Kurdistan in the 17th century; and the

Can Polad who came from the Hakkari region. The latter are believed to be descendants of Saladin and considered ancestors of the Junblat family. A second group of Kurds immigrated to Lebanon in more recent times. After the breakdown of the Sheikh Said revolt in 1925, many Kurds fled from Turkey to Lebanon and established a new, thriving community. The nationalist organization Khoybun was founded in Beirut.

Although historically, various Kurdish settlements were found in Lebanon, the Kurdish population there should be studied in connection with those Kurds in Syria because most of them came from the neighboring country or travelled to Lebanon from southeastern Turkey via Syria. The latter lived in the Tur Abdin area near the city of Mardin and migrated to Syria after a series of failed revolts against the Turkish authorities in the 1920s and 1930s. They also crossed into Syria during the 1950s in search of work and better living conditions. Word-of-mouth propaganda proved to be a successful tool to recruit more Kurdish migrants from Turkey and Syria to come to Lebanon. This group of recent immigrants today dominates the Kurdish Lebanese community.

Other Kurds in Lebanon were part of the group of Syrian Kurds that were stripped of their Syrian citizenship after the 1962 population census. Many were forced to leave the country, and due to its proximity and open market, they decided to move to Lebanon. The Kurds in Lebanon mostly worked as day laborers and dominated the service sector.

Demographically, the Kurdish community is divided into a Kurdish-speaking group, the Kurmanj, and a group that speaks a mixed form of Arabic and Kurdish called the Mhallami or Mardalli. It is contested whether the latter's ethnicity is indeed Kurdish or Arabic. Little has been done to strengthen the Kurdish identity in Lebanon. For example, no language courses in Kurdish language are offered in the Lebanese school system or elsewhere, and thus the ability to communicate in their own language is quickly disappearing. Instead, Kurds in Lebanon speak a vernacular, colloquial type of Arabic. They often do not possess strong writing or reading skills in Arabic either and generally lack education.

The last population census in Lebanon was held in 1932, and it revealed a six-to-five majority of Christians over Muslims. The Lebanese political system is built upon this sensitive sectarian balance, and every attempt to change the status quo is fiercely attacked. It is estimated that during the middle of the Lebanese civil war around the year 1985 between 60,000 and 90,000 Kurds, almost all of the Sunni Muslims, lived in Lebanon with two-thirds of them in the greater Beirut area. However, the realities and demographics have changed significantly. Today the religious balance is estimated at 65 to 35 in favor of the Muslim sector; however, the internal divide between Sunni and Shia Muslims has become more important, and since almost all Kurds are Sunni Muslims, they are at least nominally a key political interest group.

Politicians generally avoid discussing the status quo, especially when it comes to the issue of citizenship. Lebanon is home to hundreds of thousands of refugees and migrants; however, the window of opportunity to claim citizenship is closed for almost all of them. Most Kurds in Lebanon are still noncitizens. During the

1940s when the status of citizenship for most Lebanese was determined, they did not apply for it because they mostly did not know about it or did not understand the benefits. The lack of education and the illiteracy were other reasons. Other Kurds did not apply because they considered their residence in Lebanon only temporary and hoped to go back to Syria or Turkey sooner rather than later. And others were afraid of a possible conscription into the army. However, already during World War II, it became apparent that not being a citizen had severe consequences. For example, food rations were only given to ID card holders. Later, access to public education, healthcare, and services was often limited to citizens.

Local Kurdish organizations lobbied for their naturalization; however, Lebanese decision makers were too worried about changing the demographic balance. And granting citizenship to several thousand Sunni Kurds would be problematic for the Christian and the Shia sectors.

It took the Kurds years to have sympathetic Sunni prime ministers issue them temporary or "under study" ID cards, which allowed them to enroll their children in school and earn some social benefits. However, these documents were not sufficient to let them work in the public sector. In 1994, Prime Minister Rafik Hariri issued a naturalization decree, and many Kurds, between 10,000 and 18,000, were able to acquire citizenship.

As farmers or laborers and because of their low level of education, most Kurds worked in the service sector. They also did not possess technical skills, and thus worked as day laborers, porters, construction workers, or servants. Being part of the lower class also dictated where they could live, in the low-income areas of the larger towns. From here, it was almost impossible to break the circle of poverty, illiteracy, and low status. Even the Kurdish women had to seek work as cleaners and servants in order to earn a living. And not having citizenship denied them the rights to healthcare benefits, insurances, and better education.

Low status in Lebanese society was a stigma, and those lower-class members of society were frequently discriminated against and deprived. As ethnic Kurds, they were even more disadvantaged than Arabs from the same social class. It is estimated that 85 percent of the Lebanese Kurds lived below the poverty line and 60 percent were illiterate. Because of their insecure status and low number, the Kurds experienced a precarious situation, which led to a mass immigration to Europe. Not having Lebanese citizenship was the biggest obstacle for their integration into Lebanese society and labor market. Estimates speak of less than 50 percent of Lebanese Kurds having a Lebanese passport. Authorities were reluctant to issue them the document because of the complicated and fragile ethnoreligious system of proportional representation on which Lebanese civil and political society is built.

The growing awareness of their dire situation led to the formation of political and social organizations to improve their socioeconomic conditions. However, this process did not start until the early 1960s when other mostly educated Kurds from Syria came to Lebanon to flee the ongoing persecution in Syria and the United Arab Republic. These Kurds were politically active and acutely aware of the Kurdish lot in other Middle Eastern countries. Mulla Mustafa Barzani's war with the Iraqi Kurds against the Iraqi central government was another factor that helped politicize the Kurds in Lebanon. The liberal city of Beirut was a great forum to promote Kurdish nationalism, and this boosted the group's self-awareness significantly. In 1970, Jamil Miho's Kurdish Democratic Party–Lebanon (KDL–L; el-Parti) was officially licensed after working for almost a decade in support of Barzani's KDP. Among their main goals were the facilitation of better communication, improvement of economic conditions and education level, the naturalization, and the publication of works on the Kurdish national movement. However, since no unity among the Kurdish groups existed, the party soon disagreed over many issues. Jamil Miho sided with the Iraqi government; his son Riyad took over the leadership of the KDP–L, and another son, Muhammad, founded a new political movement. By the early 1990s all Kurdish political parties either dissolved or were disbanded.

However, the Lebanese political and socioeconomic system is dominated by strong patron-clientele relations. The patron, za'im in Arabic, often belongs to an influential family and a particular religion. Each patron controlled a village, region, or part of town. The Kurds always looked toward Sunni za'ims in the greater Beirut region for leadership and protection. In the 1940s and 1950s this leadership was provided by the al-Sulh family, and in the 1960s and 1970s Saeb Salam, also the prime minister, was the Kurdish champion. During the civil war, some Kurds joined the Druze bloc and their Progressive Socialist Party under the leadership of Kamal Djunblat and his son Walid. Kamal Jumblat was at certain times in his political career labeled a Kurd and supporter of Mulla Mustafa Barzani. Although he knew Barzani personally, he never intended to join forces with his movement. Instead, the Kurdish label caused him some domestic problems. Kurds, on the other hand, with their perception of Jumblat being a Kurd, always respected him. It was Jumblat, then minister of interior, who issued the "under-study" ID cards.

During the civil war, the Kurds sided mainly with the Sunni bloc and fought alongside the al-Murabitun movement and several Palestinian groups against the Christian Phalange militia, hoping that their contribution would lead to improvements after the war. However, due to their alliance with the Palestinians, they later were dragged into clashes with the Shia Amal movement. The Syrians arrested Jamil Miho, and after the completion of the Syrian occupation, other members and supporters were targeted too. This led to another wave of emigration to Europe and the end of the political activism of the KDP–L.

After the war, then Prime Minister Rafik al-Hariri became the new za'im of the Lebanese Kurds. He managed to pass the naturalization law, which was seen as a major accomplishment. However, since class structure still is very static and deeply engraved into the Lebanese mind, daily life has not changed much for most of the Kurds. Although they now have an ID card, they are still denied many services and benefits. Hariri was also instrumental in attempting to unify the fractured Kurdish community, although the resistance from within the community was too strong and a unified Kurdish movement in Lebanon did not materialize.

Since the mid-1980s, the Kurdish Workers Party (PKK) from Turkey gained influence and support, mostly because they offered a practical and ideological solution to unify all Kurds. However, after the party's chairman Abdullah Ocalan was arrested in 1999, the support for the party vanished and instead, Masoud Barzani, the president of the Kurdish Autonomy Region in Iraq became the new political champion. The Lebanese Kurdish organizations appealed to him for political and economic support, to which he did not respond. Comparing the living conditions in Lebanon, it was found that the situation was better than in neighboring Syria and Iraq and that they did not need Barzani's help immediately. Here in Lebanon, the Kurds had citizenship and were able and allowed to speak their own language and practice their faith and culture. Furthermore, they had the chance to participate in the public life with political parties and other social and cultural organizations, all of which were officially recognized by the Lebanese government. Among the current active organizations are the Rawdah Delegation, The Rezgari Party, the Lebanese Kurdish Philanthropic Association (LKPA), and The Future Generation. They all stated as their main goal the improvement of the general living conditions for the Kurds in Lebanon; however, most of them operate without an agenda, with little resources and no cooperation with other similar groups. There are also plagued by the segmented nature of the organization, each representing a particular interest group. For example, Rezgari and Future Movement are dominated by the Mardallis and the LKPA by the Kurmanj.

Today's Kurds in Lebanon are losing their identity, language, and social cohesion. Although their status is more secure than in the past and obviously better than for the Kurds in neighboring countries, the general conditions and future prospects are weak. Without a unified voice or movement, their marginalization will continue, and immigration will become the only solution. In times of increased migration due to the civil war in Syria, the Kurds of Lebanon will be pushed further to the sidelines of society where they might cave in traditional societal fractions.

Sebastian Maisel

Further Reading

Hourani, G. G. (2011). "The Kurds of Lebanon: Socioeconomic Mobility and Participation via Naturalization." *LERC Research Paper Series 1/2011*, The Lebanese Emigration Research Center, December 2011.

Meho, L. I., & Kawtharani, F. W. (2005). "The Kurdish Community in Lebanon." *International Journal of Kurdish Studies*, vol. 19, no. 1/2, 137–171.

Vanly, I. C. (1998). *Kurdistan und die Kurden, Band 3: Syrien, Emigration, UdSSR, US-Botschaftspapiere* (in German). Gesellschaft für bedrohte Völker, Pogrom. Göttingen, Germany: Verlag.

RUSSIA AND TRANSCAUCASIA

Transcaucasia (also known as Southern Caucasia) is a region south of the Caucasus Mountains that presently includes the three independent political states of Georgia in the northwest, Azerbaijan in the east, and Armenia, situated largely on a high mountainous plateau south of Georgia and west of Azerbaijan. This region of about 72,000 square miles is south of Russia, west of the Caspian Sea, north of Iran and Turkey, and east of the Black Sea.

Up until the 19th century, Russia occupied most of Caucasia, except the western portion of Armenia, which was governed by Turkey. When the Russian Empire collapsed in 1917, the Transcaucasian Commissariat was formed as the first government of the territory of Armenia, Azerbaijan, and Georgia. It was short-lived, and in 1918, the Transcaucasian Democratic Federative Republic was declared; it dissolved after a matter of months and independent states emerged in Armenia, Azerbaijan, and Georgia. From 1922–1936, these nations consolidated to become the Transcaucasian Soviet Federated Socialist Republic (TSFSR) under the Soviet Union. With the fall of the Soviet Union, Armenia, Azerbaijan, and Georgia achieved full independence in 1991.

The peoples of the region have historically exhibited a vast amount of ethnic and cultural diversity due to successive waves of people migrating across Eurasia. This diversity was preserved by the geographic isolation of the many small ethnic groups that settled in the mountainous areas of the region. Although an accurate count of Kurdish populations has been difficult to get, as of the 1990s, around 500,000 Kurds lived in former Soviet republics, with 200,000 (2.8 percent) living in Azerbaijan, 75,000 (1.8 percent) living in Armenia (with a large Yezidi population), and 40,000 (0.9 percent) living in Georgia (McDowell, 2004: 490). However, according to the Azerbaijani Census, Kurds currently account for around 0.2 percent of the population of the Azerbaijani Republic at 13,100 people (Minority Rights Group International, n.d.). There has been speculation that up to 1 million Kurds may have integrated into various societies as far away as Central Asia.

Although Kurds identify with a common nationality, historically they have been divided along tribal and religious lines. Globally, Kurds are predominantly Sunni Muslims; however, the Kurds of the Soviet Union are primarily Shiite Muslims. Sunni Kurds have sided with non-Kurdish Sunnis over relationships with other Kurdish groups, such as the Yezidis and over other religious groups that live in Kurdistan. Often there was intertribal warfare even among Muslim Kurds. For instance, in the 19th-century Ottoman Empire, Muslim Azeri Kurds raided Christian Armenian and Assyrian villages, which were often under the protection of certain Kurdish tribal leaders. This conflict would force the tribes to defend themselves.

Many Kurds came as refugees to Britain, Sweden, Germany, and France in the 1980s–1990s as a result of genocide during the Iraq-Iran War. There they were able to begin teaching about Kurdish culture and publishing content in Kurdish. In recent years, terrorism has been associated with Kurdish political organizations, bringing the Kurdish question into the public eye.

Armenia

The Republic of Armenia is located in the Caucasus Mountains south of Georgia, bordering Turkey, Iran, and Azerbaijan. Ethnic Armenians account for 93 percent of a population of about 3 million inhabitants. The official language is Armenian. The majority religion is Christianity, the largest denomination of which is the Roman Apostolic Church (Armenian Orthodox). The capital of Armenia is Yerevan.

In Armenia, the majority of Kurds are Yezidi; they are also the largest religious and ethnic minority in Armenia. According to the 2011 Armenian census, there are 35,272 Yezidis, who are a distinct group from Muslim Kurds. In Armenia, Yezidis enjoy freedom in their religious and cultural traditions.

Armenians were persecuted by the Ottoman Empire in the late 19th century as a cultural suppression tactic. In 1894 to 1896, Turkish troops and Kurdish groups massacred Armenians, resulted in the killing of around 58,000 people, or between 2 and 12 percent of the Armenian population of the Ottoman Empire.

More systematic killings of Armenians occurred as some of their group joined the Russians to fight the Turks during World War I. During 1915–1923, various populations of the former Ottoman Empire, including Turks, Muslim groups, and Kurds, killed some 1.5 million Armenians; this has come to be known as the Armenian genocide.

Some Kurds participated in the killings in exchange for freedom from Turkish prisons, while others opposed the events, even hiding and protecting Armenians from the massacre. Yezidis were killed alongside Armenians. Many political and academic Kurdish groups recognize the act of Kurds attacking and killing Armenians as genocide and have submitted statements of acknowledgement or apology. Yezidis have mostly dissociated themselves from Muslim Kurdish groups in Armenia and are listed as a separate ethnicity. Some theories include that Yezidis see themselves as aligned with Armenians because of past violent acts they both experienced at the hands of the Kurds, but there is also speculation that this is to avoid discrimination or any negative associations with Muslim Kurds.

The 1990 Nagorno Karabakh War between Armenia and Azerbaijan resulted in the creation of another ethnically de facto Armenian state, Nagorno Karabakh (also known as Artsakh). During this conflict, 18,000 Kurds fled Armenia and Nakhichevan as Armenia occupied Azeri land. Many Yezidis fought on the Armenian side of the war against Muslim Azeris and Kurds.

Azerbaijan

The Azerbaijani Republic (also known as Azerbaijan) is located south of Russia, east of Armenia, southeast of Georgia, and north of Iran, and it is bordered on the eastern side by the Caspian Sea and includes the autonomous region of Nakhichevan. The capital of Azerbaijan is Baku, which is an important harbor town on the Caspian Sea. Ethnic Azeris make up about 90 percent of the country's population of approximately 8.5 million people; however, this population shifted beginning in 1988 during the ethnic conflict leading up to the Nagorno-Karabakh War as many Armenians were pushed out. Azeri citizens are predominantly Muslim, and the remaining population is Russian or Armenian Orthodox. The official spoken language of Azerbaijan is Azeri, and Arabic, Cyrillic, and Roman alphabets have been used in the written form of Azeri.

Almost all Kurds in Azerbaijan are Sunni Muslim and are very integrated into Azeri society; whether this is by choice due to being of the same religion or due to forced integration is a speculation. By 1926, only 17 percent of the Kurdish population identified the Kurdish language as their mother tongue. The term "Kurd" currently mostly refers to a geopolitical distinction, as those people who were formerly of the Red Kurdistan.

From 1919 to 1920, a minority Armenian population of part of Azerbaijan was driven out by Azeri and Kurds, and in 1923, this region became "Red Kurdistan," or the Kurdish Autonomous Province under the Soviet Union. Kurdish education and culture was encouraged, with classes taught in Kurdish, a Kurdish-language broadcasting service, and Kurdish-language newspaper. However, this autonomous region only lasted until 1929 before it was absorbed back into Azerbaijan due to suspicions on the part of Joseph Stalin that Kurds would ally themselves with other nations. Beginning in 1992, Kurdish populations lobbied to restore the Kurdish autonomous area. During the Nagorno-Karabakh War, many Kurds in the Kelbajar region were forced to flee during conflicts with the Karabakh Armenians.

Georgia

Georgia is located south of Russia, north of Turkey and Armenia, and northwest of Azerbaijan. Georgia also contains two autonomous entities, Abkhazia and Ajaria, as well as the region of South Ossetia, which remains unrecognized politically by Georgia. These regions tend to differ from Georgians in ethnicity, language, and/or religion, which have led to conflict and violence. Approximately 5 million people live in Georgia, most of whom are ethnically Georgian. Armenians, Azeris, and Russians are the largest minorities. Georgian is the official language, and most of the population belongs to the Christian Georgian Orthodox Church.

The Kurdish population of Georgia primarily consists of a Yezidi subgroup, with Muslim Kurds being a minority within the overall population. The Yezidis make up less than 2.3 percent of ethnic groups in Georgia and 1.5 percent of religious groups, out of a population of 4,928,052 (est. 2016). Around 80 percent of the Georgian Kurdish population lives in the Georgian capital of Tbilisi (Immigration and Refugee Board of Canada, 1998).

The Yezidis (also sometimes known as Yezidi-Kurds) are a specific religious group within the larger Kurdish ethnic group. Unlike Armenian Yezidis, in Georgia there does not appear to be as great of a distinction drawn by Yezidis between themselves and Muslim Kurds. The Yezidi observe an insular religion that honors both Christian and Islamic teachings and practices oral traditions. Their supreme creator god is called Yazdan, who is worshipped most often through seven great spirits who emanate from him. This worship includes praying five times a day to the main spirit, Tausi Melek, the Peacock Angel, and offering animal sacrifices. One must be born into the Yezidi religion and marry other Yezidis.

The Yezidis began immigrating into Georgia beginning in the late 1800s and continued as the Russian Empire absorbed lands traditionally belonging to them. Yezidi groups in the Ottoman Empire fell under religious persecution at a similar time to Armenians and so immigrated to Georgia in the early 20th century. As residents of the Soviet Union, Yezidis occupied areas at the bottom of the social ladder, living in poverty and engaging in occupations such as street cleaning. The Soviet authorities tried to improve their standing through education and government housing.

Muslim Kurds were largely forced out of Georgia during the time of the Soviet Union due to perceived ties to Turkey, in which Sunni Islam is also the majority religion. Sunni Muslim Kurds may marry other Muslims, regardless if they are Kurds, and so at times had closer ties to other surrounding Muslim groups. While Yezidis are Kurds, they belong to a religion from Muslim Kurds, who have discriminated against them for religious and cultural reasons.

After the fall of the Soviet Union, a capitalistic Georgian state became less inclined to support cultural and religious diversity and economic opportunities declined, so around one-third of the Yezidi population emigrated to Russia, Western Europe, and North America (Szakonyi, 2007). The 1989 Soviet census counted the Yezidi-Kurds population at 33,331; 13 years later in 2002, the Georgian census counted 18,329 persons self-identifying as Yezidis and 2,514 persons self-identifying as Kurds, a decline of 37 percent (Szakonyi, 2007). Within Georgia, Yezidis are still discriminated against or stereotyped as poor, uneducated, or lower class, limiting social and economic opportunity.

Several factors, such as emigration out of Georgia and religious discrimination by the government of Georgia, have weakened Yezidi cultural cohesiveness. As an endogamous religion (people must marry within the community), this emigration allowed for less choice when it came time for marriage. Yezidi culture is a caste system, and the people who could afford to emigrate were largely the wealthier priest castes, thus providing a further separation of the people of the Yezidi masses from the leaders of their religion.

Russia

The Russian Federation is the world's largest country—it covers all of northern Asia and most of Eastern Europe and borders 12 other countries. Russia is a democratic federation of republics, formed in the wake of the collapse of the Soviet Union in 1991. Russia is bordered on the north by the Arctic Ocean and by the Pacific Ocean on the east. Georgia and Azerbaijan lay directly south of Russia. Russia is a multiethnic country, with a population of around 142.5 million people; around 80 percent of the populace is ethnic Russians. Tatars, Ukrainians, Bashkirs, Chuvash, and Chechens make up the largest minority populations; however, Russia has over 200 ethnic minority groups. Russia's official language is Russian and its primary religion is Russian Orthodox Christianity.

According to the 2010 Russian Census, there are almost 64,000 ethnic Kurds in Russia. Historically, Kurds were welcomed to the Russian Empire during conflicts between the Ottoman and Persian Empires. Yezidis began moving to Russia to escape the pan-Islamic religious violence at the end of the 19th century. When the Russian Empire fell and the Soviet Union was formed, many Kurds became part of the region of Transcaucasia, known as the Transcaucasian Democratic Federative Republic.

By the late 1890s, Russia began to show interest in Iranian Kurdistan and sent its Russian Orthodox missionaries to the region of Azerbaijan. Due to the Anglo-Russian Agreement of 1907, Turkey and Russia divided Iran and Kurdistan fell to Russia. By 1913, Russia had allied itself with Britain to take Azerbaijan from Turkey and ran it as a protectorate. Although Russia maintained 10,000 troops in the region, it also co-opted Kurdish tribes to enforce order. In October 1914, World War I spread to the region, putting disputes over ownership of Iranian Kurdistan on hold.

Although some Kurds defected to the Russian forces during World War I, most tribes fought with Turkey. Russia encouraged local dissidence within the Ottoman Empire, but wouldn't directly support Kurdish or Armenian independence, as it had designs on East Anatolia—the renamed region of eastern Turkey that occupied the Armenian Highlands after the Armenian genocide of 1915 to 1923. It is ironic that during their involvement that the Kurds did not yet know the plan of the new Turkish government under The Young Turks' Committee of Union and Progress Party. After the war was concluded, they planned to relocated Kurdish groups to West Anatolia after World War I and forcibly assimilate them into the Turkish population, isolating their tribal leaders in cities and ensuring that ethnic Kurds wouldn't exceed 5 percent of the population.

During World War I, Turkey pitted predominantly Muslim Kurds against Russian Armenian Christian troops, resulting in ethnic cleansing in Azerbaijan. Ostensibly to prepare the Ottoman Empire for an anticipated onslaught by Russian forces, on May 27, 1915, the Council of Ministers in Istanbul approved the "deportation of populations 'suspected of being guilty of treason or espionage'" (McDowell, 1994: 103). The Turkish government used this argument to compel Kurdish tribes to fight the Russians through relocating and killing Christian groups such as the Armenians. With the Armenians gone, Kurdish groups occupied their former dwellings. Failure to participate in the *jihad* was tantamount to disobeying the Shah.

Some Christians were spared because they were neighbors or had been under the protection of Kurdish tribes; however, the Kurds were threatened with punishment if they comply with the government's orders. Additionally, it is speculated that it was in the interest of the Kurds to remove populations who had alliances with hostile powers (such as Russia). The ethnic cleansing of Armenians occurred more intensely in the eastern parts of the Ottoman Empire, nearest to the Russian forces. When the Russians withdrew in July 1915 from Anatolia 200,000 Christians went with them to avoid more religious persecution.

In February 1917, Russia made inroads west and the Turkish government initiated a "scorched earth" policy, which meant destroying or removing all available resources such as food, buildings, and people. The military forcibly relocated residents, with many dying along the way. Some 700,000 civilians were removed from the provinces of Van, Bitlis, and Ezerum.

Meanwhile, Russia was undergoing its own political unrest, leading to the beginnings of political instability of Russia and making its involvement in the war tenuous. This unrest culminated in two revolutions that led to the formation of the

Union of Soviet Socialist Republics in 1922. In March 1917, Tsar Nicholas II abdicated, leaving the country in possession of the newly formed Russian Provisional Government, which was led by members of the Imperial parliament. Due to setbacks during the war, much of the military was mutinous and the common people wanted to pull out of the war. When the Provisional Government chose to continue, the Bolsheviks revolted in October 1917. The revolution weakened Russian forces and the Armenians could not hold the front. Turkish army recaptured Erzinjan in February 1918.

Russia's involvement in World War I ended with the signing of the Treaty of Brest-Litovsky on March 3, 1918. After the end of the war on November 11, 1918, Turkish and Russian forces pulled out of Kurdistan, razing and scavenging crops, food stores, and houses. Many Kurds died of exposure, disease, and starvation.

In 1942, Kurds were told by the Soviet Union self-determination for minority groups was supported. As World War II began to end in 1944, the Soviet Union encouraged Azerbaijan and northern Kurdistan to demand formal separation from Iran. The Soviet Union planned to incorporate them and implied that it would help Kurdistan achieve sovereignty. However, this was also a ploy to influence Iran to provide oil to the Soviet Union. The Soviet Union planned to leave Iran after the end of WWII in 1946, but only did once there was an agreement with Iran to form a joint company: the Iran-Soviet Oil Company.

The Soviet Union also encouraged the formation of a short-lived Kurdish state in northwestern Iran called the Republic of Mahabad in 1946, led by Qazi Mohammad. The government of Azerbaijan reverted to Iran in 1946 and the Iranian government executed Mohammad. The Soviet Union provided asylum to military and Kurdish Democratic Party leader, Mustafa Barzani during 1947–1957, although for a period of time he was separated from his followers, and they were forced to do hard labor. He lobbied the Communist Party for better treatment of the Kurds after Joseph Stalin's death in 1953.

Although the Soviet Union has allied with Kurds at times, it has generally favored the regional governments and used offers of Kurdish nationalism to control Kurds and use them as bargaining chips. The Kurdish experience in the Soviet Union under Joseph Stalin (1878–1953) was a difficult one. Kurds in Soviet Union were cut off from the rest of Kurdistan. Nomadism was extinguished and the border was sealed. During the 1930s–1940s, thousands of Kurds were forcibly removed from Armenia and Azerbaijan to Kazakhstan, Central Asian republics, and Siberia. Along with many other ethnic groups within the Soviet Union, Kurds were forced into labor camps, almost half of them dying from disease and malnutrition.

Since the collapse of the Soviet Union in 1991, various Kurdish groups have been given a certain amount of sanctuary in Russia. The Kurdistan Parliament in Exile was allowed to meet in 1995. Abdullah Öcalan, the fugitive leader of the Kurdistan Workers Party unsuccessfully sought refuge there in 1998. In the 1990s, Russia opposed UN sanctions against the regime of Saddam Hussein in Iraq for economic reasons, although his regime was responsible for genocide among the Kurds.

Erin Whitney

Further Reading

Gunter, Michael M. 2011. *Historical Dictionary of the Kurds*. Lanham: Scarecrow Press.

Immigration and Refugee Board of Canada. (1998). "Georgia: Treatment of the Kurds, in Particular of Yezidi Kurds." http://www.refworld.org/docid/3ae6aae694.html.

McDowall, D. (2004). *A Modern History of the Kurds*. London: I. B. Tauris.

Minority Rights Group International. (n.d.). "Azerbaijan—Kurds." *World Directory of Minorities and Indigenous Peoples.* http://minorityrights.org/minorities/kurds/.

Szakonyi, D. (2007). "Ethnic Mobilization in Post-Soviet Georgia: The Case of the Yezidi-Kurds." *Jemie*, vol. 6, no. 2, http://www.ecmi.de/fileadmin/downloads/publications/JEMIE/2007/2-2007-Szakonyi.pdf

Unver, H. A. (2016). "Schrödinger's Kurds: Transnational Kurdish Geopolitics in the Age of Shifting Borders," *Journal of International Affairs,* vol. 69, no. 2, https://jia.sipa.columbia.edu/schrodingers-kurds-transnational-kurdish-geopolitics-age-shifting-borders.

SWEDEN

Kurds are considered the biggest stateless diaspora in the world, and they are one of the most prominent diasporas in terms of political dynamism and visibility. Due to the oppression targeting their identity and culture and political turmoil in their homelands, they are scattered around the world, mostly in Europe and the United States. Sweden is one of the European countries that hosts a visible and active Kurdish diaspora. Some authors estimate that there are around 40,000 Kurds who currently reside in Sweden (Emanuelsson, 2005), while others suggest that it is closer to 55,000 (Khayati, 2008). Other studies also talk about higher numbers from 60,000 to 100,000 (Pelling, 2013). It is very hard to come up with an exact figure for Kurds who reside in this country for a variety of reasons: First, these estimates cannot be verified, as Sweden does not register immigrants or asylum seekers according to their ethnicity but rather according to their nationality. As such, Kurds are registered as Iraqi, Turkish, Iranian, or Syrian in the statistical records. There could be other methods, such as statistics on the mother tongue language. However, such figures will leave out assimilated Kurds who do not speak Kurdish but consider themselves Kurds, or the second generation who might consider Swedish their mother tongue.

The Kurdish community in Sweden is heterogeneous and consists of Kurds from different parts of the Middle East, including Iran, Iraq, Turkey, Lebanon, and Syria, who came to Sweden for a variety of reasons. It is said that some Kurds migrated from Kurdistan for education purposes during the 1950s. Another wave of Kurds came to Sweden as labor migrants with the first wave of migration from Turkey. The reason behind this influx was mostly economic. At that time, the favorable destination was Germany; however, through personal links and other friendship networks, a significant number of Kurds, especially from Central Anatolia, chose Sweden as their host country. These migrations were followed by family reunification, which increased the Kurdish population in Sweden. After the 1971 and then the 1980 military coups in Turkey, the number of Kurdish immigrants from Turkey rose significantly, as there has been a significant increase in asylum applications. Kurds from Iran migrated to Sweden after the Iranian Revolution of 1979.

Moreover, at the end of the 1980s, many Iraqi Kurds also fled the brutal Saddam regime and migrated to Sweden as asylum seekers. They were fleeing from the genocidal campaign called Al-Anfal, which included a chemical gas attack on Halabja. As the statistics show, especially during the beginning of the 1990s, Sweden has granted asylum to many Iraqi Kurds (Pelling, 2013: 27). It is said that currently the number of Kurds from Turkey exceeds the number of Kurds from other parts of the Middle East but for the reasons explained earlier, it is hard to obtain exact figures.

Similar to many other stateless diaspora groups such as Tamils or Palestinians, Kurds were highly dynamic in terms of mobilizing in the interest of their homeland. Especially with the arrival of the asylum seekers who involuntarily left their homeland due to oppression and genocidal attacks, Kurdish diaspora activities in Sweden gained an immediate political tone. As a conflict-generated diaspora, the Kurdish community maintained their ties with their homeland and established transnational networks that kept their identity alive. This retention of ethnic identity does not appear to have caused a barrier toward integration into their host societies. Swedish integration policies and the immigrant incorporation framework have also been very supportive in terms of the cultivation of Kurdish identity, supporting civil society organizations and migrant associations in particular. This multicultural attitude, which has existed in Sweden since the early 1970s, celebrates migrants' identities. Sweden has never forced assimilation on foreign communities. The Kurdish community could mobilize and even receive support from the Swedish authorities. In the early 1980s, an umbrella organization for all Kurdish organizations was formed and officially recognized by the Swedish government. Furthermore, Sweden's citizenship policies, which were relatively more liberal compared to other European countries, gave the Kurdish community the opportunity to naturalize as Swedish citizens in a short period without taking language or citizenship tests. This positive attitude also determined Kurdish perceptions toward Sweden and paved the way for further integration without feeling threatened or risking their ethnic identity. In this environment, gradually, one of Sweden's most political diaspora groups was born.

Regarding the transnational activities of the Kurdish diaspora, Sweden is a remarkable host country. The majority of Kurds who reside there differ from those in other European countries, which received predominantly labor migrants. Sweden tends to host a comparatively highly educated Kurdish intelligentsia consisting of journalists, authors, academics, artists, and directors, which is why the first generation of Kurds here are considered a political generation (Baser, 2015). For instance, Sweden hosted a very famous Kurdish author called Mehmet Uzun who is a prominent figure in the Kurdish nationalist movement. He has written numerous books in Swedish, Kurdish, and Turkish, and each of his books touches upon important topics related to the situation of Kurds in Turkey. Sweden also became a stimulating environment for many other Kurds who, like Uzun, were free from oppression in their homeland. Sweden granted them the opportunity to cultivate their culture through the preservation of their traditions and the survival of their mother tongue (van Bruinessen, 1999: 10). Given that the use of the Kurdish language was forbidden in Turkey until the 1990s, this has been a great opportunity for the Kurdish community to achieve what they could never do where they came from. The Swedish government also enabled opening a Kurdish library in Sweden, which still exists today (http://kurdlib.org). It also provided financial support for the publication of books in Kurdish, which in the end resulted in production of thousands of books or other literary material in Kurdish, which was not possible otherwise in the Middle East. When the number of Kurds became significant, the Swedish system provided mother tongue language courses at schools for children. This policy did not exist in any countries in Europe where Kurds resided and thus was an important contribution to the preservation, but also to the revival of the Kurdish culture and language.

Although living in this positive environment, Kurdish migrants in Sweden also experienced challenges. First of all, many of these Kurds had had traumatic experiences, and these traumas merged with the exile experience in Sweden (Alinia, 2004: 320). In addition, some experienced discrimination and xenophobia in Sweden. The rise of anti-immigrant political movements in the 1990s, and the rise of Islamophobia after 9/11 affected the Kurdish community and other communities from the Middle East and Africa in a negative way. Due to structural and popular discrimination in Sweden, they experienced stigmatization in the labor market, media, and housing and education opportunities. On top of that, some developments seriously damaged the image of the Kurds in Sweden. During the 1980s, a few politically motivated murders were allegedly committed by the members of the PKK (Kurdistan Workers Party), and they occupied the newspapers for a while. Furthermore, the assassination of Prime Minister Olof Palme, a very popular political figure in Sweden, in 1986 was associated with the PKK as well, despite the fact that this was never proven. Discussions on the Kurdish question gained a negative tone for a short period. In addition, a number of honor killings were attributed to the Kurdish communities in Sweden, such as the case of Fadime Sahindal (http://memini.co/memini/fadime-sahindal), which ultimately tarnished the positive reputation of the group. Currently, clashes between local Turkish and Kurdish groups are also making the news in Sweden. These clashes never received popular support from the Turkish or Kurdish community, and interethnic violence remained marginal in Sweden compared to other European countries such as Germany and Belgium. All in all, Kurds have carved a positive environment in Sweden where they can be politically and socially active and productive while successfully balancing their Kurdish and Swedish identity.

The first generation of Kurds was politically vocal, and they established organizations in order to contribute to both homeland and hostland affairs. Kurdiska Riksförbundet (the National Kurdish Federation, KRF) and Kurdiska Rådet (Kurdish Council) are among the most popular organizations that are visible in public sphere. The second generation is also highly political. Apart from Kurdiska Student och Akademiker Förbundet (the Kurdish Students and Academics Association, KSAF), an umbrella organization for students with Kurdish origin, there are other Kurdish youth organizations with different affiliations and aims operating in different parts of Sweden. They organize meetings, seminars, folk dance courses, concerts, and demonstrations, and in that way, they render the Kurdish community and their issues visible in Sweden.

Swedish Kurds also lobby political parties and other relevant organizations for the Kurdish cause. The heterogeneity of the Kurdish population brings different colors to those activities and diversifies their targets and repertoires of actions. Besides the works by famous and authoritative authors and intellectuals, the Kurdish community also contributed to Sweden with its comedians such as Ozz Nujen or Nisti Sterk; singers such as Sidar Yigit; politicians such as Nalin Pekgul, Amina Kakabaveh, Jabbar Amin, and Gulan Avci; and journalists such as Sakine Madon. Kurdish politicians play a vital role in terms of pushing forward the Kurdish demands and putting the Kurdish question on the agenda of many political parties. There are prominent figures of Kurdish origin in a variety of different political parties from right to left of the political spectrum, which increases their leverage in political matters. One of the important successes of the Kurdish diaspora was to lobby the Swedish Parliament to recognize Saddam Regime's Al-Anfal Campaign as genocide in 2012. It happened as a result of rigorous efforts by politicians of Kurdish origin as well as civil society organizations such as the Kurdocide Watch Organization (CHAK) which is led by Ali Mahmoud, an Iraqi Kurdish activist. Sweden became the first country that recognized Al-Anfal as genocide. It was later followed by Norway and the United Kingdom.

Diaspora Kurds in Sweden also celebrated the rise of the Kurdish Autonomous Region in Iraq, which is currently discussing a potential separation from Iraq. For the stateless Kurds who suffered under various countries due to the lack of a state of their own, the foundation of this autonomous region came as a positive development. The Kurdistan Regional Government (KRG) has opened representations all around Europe and in the United States, which act as de facto embassies. There is also KRG representation in Sweden, and an official body representing the Kurds in Sweden has encouraged their self-confidence and leverage in Swedish politics.

Bahar Baser

Further Reading

Alinia, M. (2004). "Spaces of Diasporas: Kurdish Identities, Experiences of Otherness and Politics of Belonging." *Studies in Sociology* 22, Department of Sociology, Göteborg University.

Baser, B. (2015). *Diasporas and Homeland Conflicts: A Comparative Perspective.* Surrey, UK: Ashgate Publishers.

Emanuelsson, A.-C. (2005). *Diaspora Global Politics: Kurdish Transnational Networks and Accommodation of Nationalism.* Göteborg: Department of Peace and Development Research, Göteborg University.

Khayati, Kh. (2008). *From victim diaspora to transborder citizenship? Diaspora formation and transnational relations among Kurds in France and Sweden.* PhD dissertation, Linköping University.

Pelling, L. (2013). *Post-Remittances? On Transnational Ties and Migration Between the Kurdistan Region in Iraq and Sweden.* PhD thesis submitted to University of Vienna.

Van Bruinessen, M. (1999). "The Kurds in Movement: Migrations, Mobilisations, Commu- nications and the Globalisation of the Kurdish Question." Working Paper no. 14, Islamic Area Studies Project, Tokyo, Japan.

SYRIA

Over the last five years, with the political shifts in the region, the escalation of war in Syria, and the significant role assumed by Kurdish political actors in these pro- cesses, the country's Kurdish population has become the object of considerable interest to researchers, policy makers, and political activists alike. This largely politically motivated interest has already been foreshadowed since the mid-2000s, in particular following the Kurdish uprising in Syria in spring 2004. This recent increase in interest contrasts with previous decades of scholarly negligence regard- ing Syria's Kurdish communities and their areas of residence, especially with regard to more distant historical periods. Even with the incipient development of Kurdish Studies in the 1980s and 1990s, hardly any research has been conducted on this part of Kurdistan, and despite the recently growing scholarly attention to this part of Syrian society and territory, many aspects of the history, sociology, and anthropology of Syria's Kurdish population remain under- (or un-)researched until today. Throughout the 20th century, many scholars of post-independence Syria assumed that Kurdish speakers residing within the national borders would, over time, assimilate into the Arab majority. For some, this assumption was reinforced with the rise of Arab nationalism as the dominant ideology in Syrian politics since the 1950s and the introduction of political measures aiming at the accelerated Ara- bization of the Kurdish populated regions. When Syria's Kurds recently became of political interest to observers in the West, it may thus have appeared as if they came "out of nowhere" (Gunter, 2014), even though Kurdish communities look back on centuries of historical presence in today's Syria.

Geography and Society

Claims about the numbers and the territories historically inhabited by Syria's Kurds are highly politicized, and any figure can only be based on estimates. In the pre- 2011 era, no reliable numbers on politically highly sensitive issues such as the demography and geography were published by the Syrian government (no census since the mandate period has provided any data on ethnic identity). After 2012, the dynamics of Syria's unfolding (civil) war have—despite the emergence of Kurdish-dominated administrative structures—not exactly been conducive to any systematic and critical research into the issue. Moreover, during the fighting, pop- ulation shifts have affected all parts of Syria, including the Kurdish areas, and (forced) migration movements into and out of these areas continue until today.

In 2011, Syria had a population of about 22 million. The percentage of people who speak Kurmanji as their native tongue and/or identify as Kurds range from an estimated 8 percent to 10 percent (McDowall, 2004: 466) or 8.5 percent (HRW, 1996) to 12 to 15 percent (Allsopp, 2014: 18) of the Syrian population. Today, three main areas in northern Syria are settled by compact Kurdish populations, namely

Shepherd from Efrin, Syria, where many of the country's Kurds live in a traditional, rural environment. (Michael Major/Dreamstime.com)

the region of Efrin/Çiyayê Kurmênc/Kurd Dagh northwest of Aleppo, the region of Kobanê/Ayn al-Arab farther east, and part of the Jazira (spelled Cizîrê in Kurmancî) around the city of Qamishlo/Qamishlī in Syria's northeastern corner bordering Turkey and Iraq. Apart from these, there are a number of smaller Kurdish or Kurdish-origin communities interspersed in otherwise predominantly Arab-populated parts of Syria. Vice versa, Arab, Assyrian, Turkmen, and other communities can be found in predominantly Kurdish areas. As a result of the manifold and diverse history of Kurdish communities in Syrian territories, settlement patterns and degrees of identification with a Kurdish ethnic background today are heterogeneous. Communities in a number of Kurdish-populated villages in the Homs area and in that mountainous region of today's Lattakia province known as Jabal al-Akrad (the Mountain of the Kurds), for instance, assimilated into Arabic culture quickly and lost their Kurdish language while retaining a memory of distant Kurdish origins. The case is somewhat different for the historical Kurdish quarter of Damascus, where residents were integrated into the Damascene social and political fabric over centuries and often adopted Arabic as their lingua franca, but where a continuous influx of migrants from rural areas nevertheless led to a constant refreshing of Kurdish language and (self-)identification. In the 1920s, and especially following the defeat of the Sheikh Said rebellion in 1925, Kurdish tribal communities escaped Turkish army pressure by settling in the Syrian Jazira along with other—notably Christian—communities crossing into Syria from Turkey, while Kurdish nationalist intellectuals sought refuge in Beirut and Damascus.

The majority Kurdish-populated quarters of Aleppo, namely (Western) Sheikh Maqsud and Ashrafiyya, were established considerably later than the Kurdish quarter of Damascus. However, over the course of the 20th century, they developed dynamically as urban Kurdish communities in northern Syria, maintaining close ties to the majority Kurdish hinterlands in Efrin and Kobani. Until the early 20th century, the Jazira was largely populated seasonally by nomadic communities (among them Kurmanji as well as Arabic speakers), while today's urban centers Qamishli/Qamishlo and Hasake were only (re)established under the French mandate. During the 1920s, the area saw a considerable influx of populations fleeing from Turkish army persecution across the border into Syria, among them a large number of Kurdish but also Christian communities.

Political History

Although the nation-state of Syria is rather young, the region looks back to millennia of human history. There is no room to discuss in greater detail developments prior to 1918, but a brief overview is necessary in order to better situate and understand the position of Kurds as a distinct ethnic group within the Syrian nation-state. As summarized by Winter (2010), smaller, Kurdish-speaking, tribally structured groups had been moving into the territory of today's Syria since antiquity, while classical Arabic historical texts documented the immigration of Kurdish-speaking semi-nomads from the Taurus mountains (today's Turkey) during the medieval period. In the 11th and 12th centuries, a number of military dynasties or "warlords" of Kurdish background settled in the *Bilad al-Sham* (roughly: the Syrian lands) through a land distribution system, which allocated strategically important lands to feudal military leaders. The medieval stronghold Crac des Chevaliers near Homs, known since the 11th century as Husn al-Akrad (The fortress of the Kurds), attests to this. The best-known military leader of the 12th century, the famous Salah ad-Din al-Ayyubi or Saladin (d. 1193) who unified Muslims in Syria (and beyond) in the fight against Crusaders from Europe, was of Kurdish origin. During Ottoman rule (1516–1918), a number of local military leaders, religious figures, and administrators of Kurdish background held significant positions in *Bilad al-Sham*. Not least, the historical "Kurdish quarter" of Damascus bears witness to the lasting establishment of Kurds who have come to this area since the Middle Ages. Until today, the Damascene quarters of Rukn al-Din, Zorava, and Salihiya are wholly or partly identified as "Kurdish neighborhoods."

As one of the successor states of the Ottoman Empire, Syria's borders were effectively established by the victorious European powers, namely Britain and France, following the Ottomans' defeat in World War I (1914–1918). The political history of the Kurds is deeply marked by these larger political developments in the region. The often reluctant subjection and integration of Kurdish communities into different nation states of the modern Middle East—besides Syria, Turkey, Iraq, and Iran—have resulted in significantly different historical experiences and deepened linguistic division. Thus, like most Middle Eastern nation-states, the state of Syria has existed for less than a century, but it has exerted considerable power over the years by imposing legal constraints and measures on its citizens—as well as those residing within its borders who were not recognized as Syrian citizens, as will be explained later.

Following the First World War, the future Syria was shaped from the remnants of a number of Ottoman administrative units, such as the Ottoman province (*vilayet*) of Greater Syria (Sham) in the south and parts of the province of Aleppo (Halab) in the north. This entity was ruled by an Arab administration under British protection, headed by Faysal, one of the sons of Sherif Husain of Mecca, who was proclaimed king of Syria in 1920. However, in the same year, Syria was formally declared a League of Nations mandate under French administration; French troops occupied the country and ousted Faysal, who subsequently became king of Iraq under British protection. Syria, now administratively separated from what was to become Lebanon and Jordan, remained under French mandate administration—de facto until the last French troops left Syria in April 1946, although legally Syria had become an independent state in October 1945 when it joined the United Nations as a founding member.

The earlier mentioned relative "invisibility" of Syria's Kurdish population to scholars to some extent corresponded with a view informed by international political rationales following World War I. According to these, Kurdish nationalist aspirations were initially considered, but eventually not included, in the emergent political landscape of the post-war order. A considerable number of people along Syria's northern border with the newly emergent Republic of Turkey were Kurmanji speakers, while others spoke Arabic, Turkish, Armenian, or Assyrian. Many locals were fluent in more than one of these languages. The new border, established "from above," separated communities on the ground that had previously been linked by ties of kinship, economic exchange, and shared language and religion. Formerly all Ottoman subjects, members of these communities now found themselves to be citizens of different nation-states, separated from their relatives and former neighbors by a demarcation line that largely followed the tracks of the Baghdad railway: those who lived south of the tracks (*bin xatê*, "below the line") were now citizens of Syria, while those "above the line" (*ser xatê*) had become citizens of Turkey; to the east, the Syrian-Iraq international border now separated the Jazira, the Mesopotamian "island" enclosed by Euphrates and Tigris. The emergence of Syria as a nation-state and the establishment of national borders separating Syria's Kurds from their relatives in neighboring Iraq and Turkey led to the definition of Syria's Kurdish population as a "minority" in a larger, predominantly Arab whole.

Ottoman Syria

As van Bruinessen (1994) suggests, there is evidence that some kind of shared (self)consciousness of Kurdish distinctiveness vis-à-vis neighboring ethnic groups existed for several centuries before the end of the Ottoman Empire. Although Kurds in the territories of the Ottoman Empire and Iran were not a homogenous group, but differed from each other in terms of religion, dialect, and social organization. As in other settings, in Ottoman and post-Ottoman Syria, too, derivation from a Kurdish background or Kurdish family connections did not necessarily imply identification with Kurdish ethnicity as a primary characterizing feature or political motivation. Gunter (2004: 10) cites the examples of well-known historian Muhammad Kurd Ali (1876–1953) and Khalid Bakdash (1912–1995), leader of the Syrian Communist party in the 1930s as examples; both of them conducted their public and intellectual pursuits in Arabic and did not emphasize their Kurdish ethnic ties. Moreover, as urban intellectuals they had little in common with rural inhabitants of Syria's Kurdish regions. The case has been, and is, different for other notable figures of the Syrian Kurdish community, as will be explained later.

In the Ottoman period, economic, social, and political structures in the rural areas (not only in Syria) had been strongly shaped by nomadic or semi-nomadic tribes or tribal confederations, as well as religious identities and loyalties. In Syria, particular social identities, based on tribal belonging, religious, and class affiliations, persisted throughout the era of the French mandate (1920–1946) and have—albeit unevenly and partly—continued to do so until the present. In the areas today covered by Syria, a number of Kurdish tribes have been influential. Among the best known are the Milli, the Heverkan, the Berazi, and the Rashwan, to name just a few. Generally speaking, the influence of tribal loyalties is unevenly distributed between Syria's three main areas settled by compact Kurdish populations: while it is virtually nonexistent in the region of Efrin, it is still felt in the other two areas, namely Kobani and the Cizire around Qamishlo. The supposed influence of tribal loyalties on political behavior is, of course, ambivalent; but until the recent past, the ability to quickly muster large numbers of followers or supporters on the basis of tribal ties has been an undeniable asset in Syria's volatile and violent political environment. In the colonial and especially postcolonial era, however, political ideologies and party affiliations have provided a growing influence on structuring political and partly even social loyalties and subjectivities, as will be explained later.

Another distinguishing identity marker since at least Ottoman times has been religion. As in other communities and regions, this characteristic denotes social identity as much as (or sometimes more than) it describes personal beliefs and spirituality. The majority of Kurmanji speakers in Syria are Sunni Muslims; but there has also long been a sizeable Yezidi community as well as a smaller number of Alevites and individual converts to Christianity. In addition those who privately might not consider religious belief part of their identity (or who would even describe themselves as atheists) should be mentioned, but who under Syrian personal status law are until today considered to be members of their fathers' religious communities. As in other parts of Kurdistan, the influence of persons regarded as spiritual authorities, and the popular followings they were able to mobilize, has been an important aspect in the field of spirituality and religiosity. Although these movements are overtly situated in the field of religion, in the context of Syrian history they have always also had political implications. Syria's Sunni Kurds have been strongly influenced by the Naqshbandi Sufi tradition. Syria's Kurds have been, engaged to a surprising degree in "official" Sunni Islam in post-independence Syria. One reason is that many of them, due to their Sufi imprint, did not share the strict refusal of Wahhabi and Salafi Sunni Syrian circles to cooperate with the Ba'thist regime. The most prominent example is Sheikh Ahmad Kaftaru (1921–2004), a Naqshbandi Sufi sheikh who had taken over the leadership of the *Kaftariyya* tariqa (Sufi order) in the Kurdish quarter of Damascus from his father. Kaftaru was named Mufti of the Republic in 1964, an office that he held until his death in 2004. By virtue of this office, Kaftaru was co-opted as a figurehead by the Ba'thist regime under Syrian president Hafiz al-Asad. Another prominent religious scholar of Kurdish origin, who stood for a more Salafi-oriented religiosity, is Sheikh Muhammad Said Ramadan al-Buti (1929–2013). In contrast to Kaftaru, al-Buti never held any public office of similar prominence, although he was made preacher of Damascus's famous Umayyad Mosque in 2008. However, through his prominent presence in Syria's state-controlled TV, as well as his reported closeness to both presidents Hafiz and Bashar al-Asad, al-Buti, too, was visibly close to the regime. Another notable figure was Sheikh Muhammad Ma'shuq al-Khaznawi (1957–2005), a prominent representative of the Khaznawiyya *tariqa* based in the Syrian Jazira. He stood for a relatively liberal, modernist interpretation of Islamic teachings, was popular with Kurdish as well as Arab Sunnis in Syria, and gained a growing number of followers in other countries. Initially tolerated by the Syrian regime, in the 2000s he more and more vocally called for Kurdish rights within Syria and became increasingly popular among Kurds internationally. Described as "a non-conformist who was critical not only of the authoritarian Sufi model promoted by his ancestors, but also of the Ba'thist dictatorship" (Pierret, 2013b: 133), this made him appear more and more dangerous to the Syrian authorities. In 2005, when traveling in Europe, he gave an extremely critical interview to *The Canadian Globe* about the Syrian regime, which, he said, would have to "change or be terminated." He also met with Kurdish politicians as well as the exiled head of Syria's Muslim Brotherhood, Ali Sadr al-Din al-Bayanouni, in Brussels. In 2005, a few months after his return to Syria, Sheikh Khaznawi was murdered. Family members as well as outside observers have attributed the murder to the Syrian security services, although the Syrian authorities denied involvement His death triggered large-scale protests, mostly by Kurds.

The Mandate Period (1920–1946)

During the French mandate, the states of the Levant served as an important organizational base for Kurdish nationalist activities. The French administration supported such activities to a certain extent, particularly in the realm of culture. In the 1920s, a number of Kurdish activists and intellectuals crossed the newly established Syrian-Turkish border to escape Kemalist persecution. Arguably, the most notable figures among them were the Bedirxan brothers Jaladet (1893–1951) and Kamuran (1895–1978), grandsons of the last Emir of Botan, Bedirxan Beg (ca 1800–1868), and brothers of Sureyye Bedirxan (1883–1938), who had published the Ottoman Kurdish journal *Kurdistan* following the Young Turk revolution in 1908. Tolerated by France, the Bedirxan brothers and other Kurdish intellectuals founded the committee *Xoybun* ('to be oneself') near Beirut in 1927. With French support, Jaladet and Kamuran Bedirxan were also able to publish two other journals—*Hawar* ("The Calling," 1932–1940) and *Roja Nû* ("New Day," 1943–1946)—from Damascus and broadcast Kurdish radio emissions through

Radio Levant (Beirut) from 1941 on (Tejel, 2009: 21–23). These projects aimed—among other things—at the promotion of Kurdish language and culture through the publication and dissemination of Kurdish classical as well as contemporary literary production. Although they reached only a limited readership, these journals had an important role in propagating a Kurdish alphabet written in Latin letters in the Syrian contexts and, Gunter (2014: 12) argues, for contributing "to a sense of Kurdish identity" in Syria. Until today, Syrian Kurdish (Kurmanji) alphabetization and publications use Latin letters like the Kurds of Turkey, while Kurds in the Iranian and Iraqi contexts use Arabic script. French political support did not, however, extend to establishing Kurmanji as a language of teaching or as a subject in Syrian curricula or to supporting anything resembling the establishment of an autonomous Kurdish state.

It has been remarked that Kurdish nationalist activities during the mandate, such as the Xoybun organization (1927–1944) as well as its successor, the Kurdish League (1945–1946), did not aim specifically at changing the situation of the Kurdish community in Syria, but focused instead on the struggle against Kemalist Turkey. On the other hand, Syrian Kurdish-based movements challenging the central state and its political order were strongly conditioned by local struggles. Two examples illustrate this claim: between 1932 and 1939, a Kurdish-Christian movement led by Kurdish tribal leaders, notably Hajo Agha of the Heverkan, and local Christian notables called for autonomous status of the Jazira. Among the movement's demands were the "advancement of Kurdish in school and the appointment of Kurdish officials" in the Jazira; its leading figure, Hajo Agha, raised a Kurdish flag in front of his home in the Jazira. The movement thus had regionalist as well as Kurdish nationalist aspects. Another example is the so-called *murud* movement in Kurd Dagh (Efrin). Between 1933 and 1940, it mobilized mostly lower-class adepts (*muridin*) of one Sheikh Ibram (Ibrahim) Khalil who had come to Syria from neighboring Turkey. Sheikh Ibram preached not only religious austerity, but promoted a political agenda which was inimical to the powerful landowning elite (*aghas*) and opposed French rule in Syria, but did not articulate Kurdish nationalist demands. The uprising was finally suppressed through French military intervention, aided by the local elite and its followers.

From Independence to the Qamishli Uprising (1946–2004)

After independence, the country was ruled by a succession of quickly changing governments—a number of them coming into power through military coups. Two of the presidents of independent Syria, Husni Za'im (1949) and Adib al-Shishakli (1949–1954), had a Kurdish background, but this did not automatically translate into pro-Kurdish policies. On the contrary, during Shishakli's rule, Kurdish language use, Kurdish music and other expressions of Kurdish culture and identity were restricted through a number of legal provisions in order to forge a more homogenous and unified Syria under Sunni Arab auspices. Arab nationalism and enmity with Israel were increasingly used as legitimizing factors for authoritarian policies. The state security apparatus was built up and diversified; political dissent was severely suppressed, and torture of prisoners was routinely used as a means of intimidation and terror. These measures targeted any opposition against the regime, regardless of ethnic identity. Additionally, however, Syrian Kurds were marginal ized in specific ways. In 1973, a constitution was adopted (which remained valid until 2012) that defined Syria and its people as Arab, a claim that was echoed in any interaction between citizens and the state, including identity documents which explicitly identified subjects of Kurdish origin as "Syrian Arabs." Thus, the legitimate existence of Syrian Kurds was implicitly denied; a policy that translated into an increasing number of policy and legal measures. Many Kurdish place names were Arabized; parents who wanted to register newborn children with Kurdish names were unable to do so or faced considerable difficulties. In September 1992, the government prohibited the registration of children with Kurdish first names; the case was similar for business owners and shopkeepers who gave Kurdish names to their businesses; teaching and publishing in Kurdish were also prohibited.

The most momentous measure, however, was the Census of 1962, carried out in the province of Hasake in the Jazira in just one day. The way in which it was conducted on October 5, 1962, resulted in about 20 percent of Syrian Kurds being stripped of their Syrian nationality, leaving them stateless. "The government claimed that a large number of Kurds had entered Syria illegally and obtained Syrian identity documents. They hoped to identify these illegal immigrants by demanding that all inhabitants of the region provide proof of residency prior to 1945. On the day of the census, many could not provide the required proof; many were away from home and others chose not to participate, hoping to avoid military conscription and government taxes" (Allsopp, 2014: 24; cf. also HRW, 1996). As a result, those who were not able to produce the necessary documents were registered as "foreigners" (*ajanib*), amounting to about 120,000 people. Another group was classified as "unregistered" (*maktumin*), probably those who had not taken part in the census at all. Yet despite the claim that these people had recently moved into Syria from neighboring Turkey or Iraq, no effort was made to "repatriate" them; instead, they and their offspring remained in Syria, facing disadvantages and discrimination at all levels of daily life. With slight differences in status (*maktumin* being even more disadvantaged than *ajanib*) they were not allowed to participate in elections, either actively or passively; to be employed in the public sector; or to own or rent a property, including a business; registration of marriages and childbirth were rife with difficulties. And while both *maktumin* and *ajanib* were allowed to attend school until 12th grade, *maktumin* did not receive a school leaving certificate, nor were they entitled to attend university; while *ajanib* could attend university, they were not permitted to practice all professions. *Ajanib* and *maktumin* status are inherited at birth by children born to *ajanib* or *maktumin* parents. Taken together, both groups were estimated to amount to more than 300,000 stateless Kurds in 2008. In April 2011, a presidential decree granted *ajanib* (but not *maktumin*) Kurds the right to apply for Syrian citizenship in an apparent effort to placate Syria's Kurds in the face of the rapidly spreading protest movement against Bashar al-Asad (Allsopp, 2014: 148); it is unclear at present how many Syrian Kurds registered as *ajanib* subsequently actually did become citizens.

The Jazira was also the arena for another, large-scale Arabization process. Between 1973 and 1976, several tens of thousands of Arabs from the Euphrates Valley, most of whom had been forcibly displaced by the construction of the Euphrates Dam at the city of Tabqa and the subsequent flooding of Syria's largest reservoir, Lake Asad, were resettled in a string of newly constructed villages in the Jazira on land previously used by Kurds, a scheme commonly referred to as the "Arab Belt." The establishment of such a scheme had already been suggested in 1963 in a report written by the then head of security in Hasaka Province, Muhammad Talab Hilal. Hilal had proposed 12 points for the Arabization of the Jazira, among them the expulsion of Kurds and settlement of Arabs. Although the report was never officially adopted government policy, many of its suggestions were at least partially implemented in subsequent years.

In March 2004, Syria's Kurdish areas saw a wave of unprecedented mass demonstrations and protests against the regime, triggered by clashes between Arab and Kurdish soccer fans at a match in Qamishli. After violent reactions by the security forces, protests soon escalated into attacks against public buildings throughout the Jazira. Images and statues of former president, Hafiz al-Asad, were toppled by the protestors. In the following days, protests spread to Kobani, Efrin, and Damascus, partly fueled by Kurdish TV station Roj TV (associated with the PKK). Syrian security forces reacted violently, using live ammunition against protesters, until finally the Syrian Kurdish parties as well as civil society organizations called for an end to the violence and the protests died down. A year later, large-scale protests erupted once more following the murder of Sheikh Khaznawi (see earlier). The 2004 protests showed that especially younger Kurds were discontent with the role of Syria's Kurdish political parties and took to the streets to express their protest against ongoing marginalization and disenfranchisement through other means than party politics.

Development of Kurdish Political Parties in Syria

In the post-independence period, dissatisfaction with the rule of the old elite—wealthy merchants, landowners, and notables—which had persisted in the first decades of independence grew throughout Syria among rural and urban lower (middle) classes; communist and Arab nationalist ideologies attracted more and more followers. On the international stage, too, pan-Arab nationalism came to the fore. In 1958, Syria joined Egypt to form the United Arab Republic (UAR) under President Gamal Abd al-Nasser, a union that was ended by a Syrian coup in 1961. In 1963, the Syrian Ba'th party seized power. With a platform of socialist and Arab nationalist strands, the Ba'th party, founded in 1947, managed to mobilize a following from the peasantry, the urban lower middle class, and the officers' corps, many of them from rural and minority backgrounds. After six years of internal power struggles within the Ba'th, defense minister Hafiz al-Asad finally seized power in another internal coup (the so-called Corrective Movement) in 1970. He remained Syria's president until his death in 2000, after which power was transferred to his son, Bashar. Under Hafiz al-Asad, who enjoyed considerable popularity in the early years of his rule, Syria was transformed into a de facto (though not de jure) one-party state where a number of other parties beside the Ba'th—some of them represented in the Syrian parliament—acted to shore up support for Ba'thist rule as members of the "progressive front" under leadership of the Ba'th. Parties who did not acknowledge this arrangement, such as the Communist Labor Party, or the increasing number of Kurdish Syrian parties, had to operate illegally.

After Syrian independence, the significance of Kurdish ethnonationalist sentiments as a mobilizing factor in local politics increased. To some extent, this echoed the increasing significance of Arab nationalism as a dominant political force in Syria, as well as political developments in Turkey and Iraq, during the 1950s. In 1957, the Kurdish Democratic Party in Syria KDPS (*Partiya Demokrat a Kurd li Suriye*) was founded by a group of Kurdish nationalist activists and men who had previously been affiliated with the Communist Party. It has been suggested that the issues debated by the KDPS since its inception are still relevant today: Should the party advocate for Kurdish cultural and political rights within the Syrian nation-state, or should it aim at joining Kurdish movements in other nation-states of the Middle East? Overall, the decision has been for the former: "None of the parties demand an independent Syrian-Kurdish state or the inclusion of the Syrian-Kurdish regions in a united Kurdistan. None of the parties—and here the Kurdish movement in Syria differs from the Kurdish parties in Iraq and Turkey—wants to claim the rights of the Kurdish population by force of arms nor have they ever propagated this" (KurdWatch, n.d.: 15). Over this issue, the KDPS split into a right and a left wing in 1965, a split that persisted despite a brief attempt at reunion in 1970—an attempt that led essentially to the establishment of a third branch of the KDPS. In subsequent years, further offshoots were established—in fact, the majority of Kurdish Syrian parties today (which in total numbered 15 in 2014) are offshoots of the KDPS. They resemble each other with regard to programmatic aims as well as to their names, but differ in political nuances as well as personal loyalties to particular leading figures. Reasons for the extreme differentiation of Kurdish political parties in Syria are manifold. Until 2011, there has never been an armed mobilization within Syria that could have served as a unifying factor; the Syrian state and its intelligence agencies have actively intervened to keep Syrian Kurdish parties small; and the influence of external Kurdish parties (KDP and PUK in Iraqi Kurdistan, as well as the Turkish-Kurdish PKK) is a factor. Last but not least, the illegality in which Kurdish Syrian parties have been forced to operate have not only influenced cautious programmatic, but also led to decentral and cell-like structures which have been conducive to further splitting processes.

Another important political party is the Kurdish Future Movement (Şepela Pesheroje ya Kurdi li Suriye), founded by charismatic politician, Mish'al Temo in 2005. Temo advocated cooperation with Arab opposition against the Asad regime, and the Future Movement decisively supported the Syrian uprising in 2011. In October 2011, however, Temo was assassinated in Qamishli. His murder silenced not only an outspoken voice for Kurdish-Arabic cooperation and against the regime, but turned out to weaken the Future Movement considerably, which consequently has lost much of its mobilizing power. At the time of writing, the Future Movement is not officially represented within Syria, but is still active in Kurdish Syrian politics abroad.

The third, even more significant, strand in the development of Kurdish political parties is the role of the Kurdistan Workers Party (Partiya Karkeren Kurdistane, PKK), which was long tolerated and even supported by the Syrian regime on the condition that its activities not target Syria. In 1978, Abdullah Öcalan had fled to Syria from Turkey; from 1980 on, the PKK was coordinated from Damascus, and military training for PKK recruits was organized in the Beqaa Valley. Many young Syrian Kurds joined the PKK to fight for Kurdish rights in neighboring Turkey. PKK recruitment in Syria was at once expressive of, and conducive to, a wider mobilization for Kurdish nationalist politics, although the PKK advocated the view that there might be Kurds living in Syria but that they did not form part of larger Kurdistan. The close relations between the PKK and the Syrian regime ended in 1998, when Turkish pressure against Syria mounted, leading to the expulsion of Öcalan from Syria, his arrest by Turkish agents in Kenya, and his subsequent trial and imprisonment in Turkey. In 2003, a new Syrian Kurdish party—the Democratic Union Party (Partiya Yekitiya Demokrat, PYD)—was founded in close ideological, organizational, and personal proximity to the PKK. Now engaging explicitly in the Syrian political scene, it has played a dominant role in Syrian Kurdish politics since 2012.

The Uprising against Asad and the Syrian War (2011–present)

Following the Syrian uprising against the Asad regime in spring 2011, the regime's violent reaction against it and the subsequent spiral of (civil as well as proxy) war in Syria since 2012, the situation in Syria's predominantly Kurdish areas has evolved dynamically. Contrary to occasional later claims, the Kurdish street in towns of the Jazira such as Amude and Qamishli turned out early on in large numbers in support of the protests against the Asad regime, and the Future Movement led by Mish'al Temo joined the Syrian opposition as member of the Syrian National Council (SNC) in July 2011. However, the trajectory of the other Kurdish parties was different. Sixteen of them, notably those who had been derived from the KDPS, joined to form the Kurdish National Council (KNC) under the protection of Iraqi Kurdish leader, Masoud Barzani, in October 2011. The Future Movement joined the KNC in 2015. The PYD did not join the KNC, but joined the National Coordination Committee for the Forces of Democratic Change (NCC) which promoted nonviolent change in cooperation with the Syrian regime and which has been denounced as a pseudo-oppositional front for the regime by members of the Syrian opposition. Simultaneously, the PYD and its armed wing, the People's Protection Units (Yekineyen Parastina Gel, YPG), have taken the leading role in building up administrative structures and effectively controlling the regions of Afrin, Kobani, and the Kurdish areas of the Jazira around Qamishli/Qamishlo, as well as Aleppo's predominantly Kurdish quarters, Ashrafiyye and Sheikh Meqsud. In December 2011, the PYD announced the establishment of the "Popular Council of West Kurdistan" (Meclisa Gel a Rojavaye Kurdistan) which served as a de facto umbrella organization for groups close to the PYD. In July 2012, the Syrian regime ceded control over most parts of Syrian Kurdistan (Efrin, Kobani, and the Kurdish quarters Sheikh Meqsud and Ashrafiyya in Aleppo, as well as the Kurdish areas in the Jazira with the exception of some strategic points in Qamishli) to the PYD without a struggle. For the regime, this freed up military resources to counter opposition in other parts of the country; for the PYD, it opened the way to establishing administrative structures in close military, ideological, and personal cooperation with the PKK. For the critics of the PYD—both Kurds and non-Kurds—this transition underlined the collaboration of the PYD with the Syrian regime. In January 2014, the previously mentioned three regions were declared to be three separate "cantons" making up Syrian Kurdistan, which has been popularly referred to by the PYD and its sympathizers in Syria as well as outside of it as "Rojava"—Western (Kurdistan). This name was hardly used as a self-reference by Syrian Kurds before 2011 and was dropped again as official self-designation in favor of "Democratic Federal System of Northern Syria" in December 2016. The successive name changes did not indicate significant changes at the administrative level, however.

Kobani

The city of Kobani is a Kurdish city in Syria that gained international attention during a six-month-long siege imposed by the Islamic State in 2014. The surrounding area was completely captured by IS, and only the city center was under the control of YPG-led fighters. In a courageous battle, they were able to push back IS militants and step by step liberated the outskirts of the city, its suburbs, and surrounding villages. This victory symbolized the heroic resistance of the Kurdish fighters to protect their homeland. Today, reconstruction has started, and the citizens return. Kobani is part of the self-administered cantons in Rojava.

In the politically highly charged atmosphere of the Syrian war, evaluations and even descriptions of these developments are often colored by sympathy for the leftist agenda and the feats of the Kurdish administration in Syria. Among these, the realization of women's rights and political representation of women and the introduction of a "council democratic" structure, as well as the inclusion of non-Kurdish demographic groups (Arabs and Assyrian Christians) have been applauded in the administration of Syria's three Kurdish "cantons." Often added to this is admiration for the military discipline and prowess displayed by the Kurdish-led units of the YPG and YPJ in the fight against the so-called Islamic State, an admiration that sometimes appears to be mixed with a (somewhat Orientalist) fascination for the female fighters of the YPJ in particular. On the flip side, human rights violations—including the often-violent silencing of voices critical to the PYD and Öcalan; application of administrative policies such as obligatory military service; and cases of underage recruitment, harsh taxation, the explicit ideological, organizational, and military closeness to the PKK; and not least the tactical alliances with the Asad regime (which, proponents of the PYD say, have spared the Kurdish areas the devastation caused by Asad's bombs in oppositional parts of Syria)—are among the issues which motivate criticism of the PYD and its rule. Local critical voices have even denounced PYD administrative practices as resembling Ba'thism, with Asad being exchanged for Öcalan in the public iconography. Seen in a regional or even global perspective, the ongoing war has provided Syria's Kurds with potential new international allies, but it has also deepened and made more visible inner Kurdish divisions and is, at the time of writing, pitting them into an ever harsher confrontation with Turkey.

Katharina Lange

Further Reading

Ali Abdo, M. (n. y. [2003]): *Jabal al-Kurd. Dirasa tarikhiyya ijtima'iyya tawthiqiyya* [The Kurdish Mountain. A documentary social-historical study]. Afrin, Syria: private publisher.

Allsopp, H. (2014). *The Kurds of Syria: Political Parties and Identity in the Middle East.* London: Tauris.

Altug, S. (2011). *Sectarianism in the Syrian Jazira: Community, Land and Violence in the Memories of World War I and the French Mandate (1915–1939)* Unpublished dissertation, Faculty of History and Culture, Utrecht University, The Netherlands.

Crisis Group Reports. (n.d.). 151/2014, 49/2016, 176/2017, www.crisisgroup.org.

Gunter, M. (2014). *Out of Nowhere: The Kurds of Syria in Peace and War.* London: Hurst.

Human Rights Watch (HRW). (1996). "Syria: The Silenced Kurds." *Human Rights Watch Reports,* vol. 8, no. 4, 1–57.

KurdWatch Reports. (n.d.). 1/2009, 5/2010, 7/2010, 8/2011, 10/2015, www.kurdwatch.org.

Lange, K. (2010). "Peripheral Experiences: Everyday Life in Kurd Dagh (Northern Syria) during the Allied Occupation in the Second World War." In H. Liebau, Katrin Bromber, Katharina Lange, Dyala Hamzah, and Ravi Ahuja (Eds.), *The World in World Wars. Perspectives, Experiences and Perceptions from Asia and Africa* (pp. 401–428). Leiden: Brill.

Lescot, R. (1938). *Enquête sur les Yézidis de Syrie et du Djebel Sindjār.* (Mémoires de l'Institut Français de Damas; 5). Beirut: Imprimerie Catholique.

Maisel, S. (2014). "One Community, Two Identities. Syria's Yezidis and the Struggle of a Minority Group to Fit In." In K. Omarkhali (Ed.), *Religious Minorities in Kurdistan: Beyond the Mainstream* (pp. 79–96). Wiesbaden: Harrassowitz.

McDowall, D. (2004 [1996]). *A Modern History of the Kurds.* Third revised and updated edition. London/New York: I. B. Tauris.

Montgomery, H. (2005). *The Kurds of Syria. An Existence Denied.* Berlin: Europäisches Zentrum für Kurdische Studien.

Pierret, T. (2013). *Religion and State in Syria. The Sunni Ulama from Coup to Revolution.* Cambridge, UK: Cambridge University Press.

Pinto, P. (2011). "Sufism among the Kurds in Syria." *Syrian Studies Association Bulletin,* vol. 16, no. 1, https://ojcs.siue.edu/ojs/index.php/ssa/article/view/1468/492.

Savelsberg, E. (2016). "The PKK as the Lesser of Two Evils? Kurds, Islamists and the Battle for Kobanî." In M. Gunter (Ed.), *Kurdish Issues. Essays in Honour of Robert Olson* (pp. 221–234). Costa Mesa, CA: Mazda Publishers.

Schmidinger, T. (2014). *Krieg und Revolution in Syrisch-Kurdistan. Analysen und Stimmen aus Rojava.* Wien: Mandelbaum.

Selcuk, M. (2015). "Die Hegemonie der PYD unter den Kurden Syriens und ihr Verhältnis zur PKK und zu Damaskus." In G. Seufert (Ed.), *Der Aufschwung kurdischer Politik: Zur Lage der Kurden in Irak, Syrien und der Türkei* (pp. 37–46), http://nbn-resolving.de/urn:nbn:de:0168-ssoar-435313.

Tejel, J. (2009). *Syria's Kurds. History, Politics and Society*. London: Routledge.

Van Bruinessen, M. (1994). *Agha, Shaikh and State. The Social and Political Structures of Kurdistan*. London, New Jersey: Zed Books.

Vanly, I. C. (1980). "The Kurds in Syria" (published under the pseudonym Mustafa Nazdar). In G. Chaliand (Ed.), *People without a Country: The Kurds and Kurdistan* (pp. 194–201). London: Interlink.

Vanly, I. C. (1992). "The Kurds in Syria and Lebanon." In P. Kreyenbroek & S. Sperl (Eds.), *The Kurds. A Contemporary Overview* (pp. 112–134). London: Routledge.

Winter, S. (2006). The Other Nahdah: The Bedirxans, the Millîs, and the Tribal Roots of Kurdish Nationalism in Syria. *Oriente Moderno* 86: 461–474.

Winter, S. (2010). "Die Kurden Syriens im Spiegel osmanischer Archivquellen (18. Jh.)." *Archivum Ottomanicum*, vol. 27, 211–239.

Yildiz, K. (2005). *The Kurds in Syria: The Forgotten People*. London: Pluto Press.

TURKEY

The advances of the jihadist terrorist group Islamic State of Iraq and Syria (ISIS) in Iraq and the civil war in Syria have significantly increased the role of Kurds as a pro-Western and secular regional actor and as a stabilizing factor. In spite of the increased strategic importance of the Kurds in the regional and international politics, the historical conflict on their political future and autonomy aspirations has not been peacefully regulated yet.

In addition, the conflict in Turkey over the Kurdish question has not been resolved through peaceful means yet. Although the Kurdish question is not a taboo subject anymore and Kurds enjoy more freedoms than before, the war that has been continuing since 1984 between the Turkish army and the militant Kurdistan Workers Party (Kurdish: Partiya Karkeren Kurdistan; PKK) has left its marks: around 40,000 deaths, 3,500 destroyed villages, and over 2.5 million displaced people (forced migration and flight). The conflict has intensified the ethnic polarization and nationalism on both sides. The peace talks that had continued since autumn 2012 between the ruling Justice and Development Party (Turkish: Adalet ve Kalkinma Partisi; AKP) and PKK have been abandoned. Since July 2015, the violence has been dominating the Kurdish question in Turkey again.

Population

There are no certain figures or exact numbers of Kurds living in Turkey. During the 1965 census, people were asked what their native language was. However, this question was later erased and never asked again. According to the latest report of the Turkish Statistical Institute, Turkey's total population has risen to 78.7 million, of which the proportion of the Kurds is estimated to be between 15 and 25 percent, or 11 and 20 million. According to the CIA's World Factbook, based on 2008 estimates, the Kurds constitute 18 percent of Turkey's total population (The World Factbook, 2016). In 1996, David McDowall estimated the proportion of Kurds in Turkey as 23 percent, emphasizing the higher reproductive rate of the Kurdish people (McDowall, 1996: 3). According to a survey by KONDA, a Turkish research and consultancy company, in 2011 Kurds made up 18.3 percent of Turkey's total population (KONDA, 2011).

There are a few reasons for the ambiguity of the numbers. First and most importantly, the Turkish state and its institutions do not recognize the Kurdish identity. So when conducting a census, the Kurds are not listed as a separate ethnic group. According to the 1923 Treaty of Lausanne, Turkey recognizes only the Armenians, Greeks, and Jews as minorities. Second, many Kurdish people are still afraid to articulate their Kurdish identity as a result of the ongoing oppression and discrimination. Third, the total number of Kurds residing in Western Turkey is not easily to obtain. There is a considerable number of Kurds living in large cities such as Istanbul, Ankara, Izmir, Mersin, and Adana. According to some sources, Kurds make up 15 percent of the total population in Istanbul, a city that is home to 14 to 15 million people (KONDA, 2011: 16). There have been also some Kurdish communities particularly in and around Konya and Ankara for almost a century. These consist of Kurdish families that were forcefully displaced by the Turkish state following the consecutive Kurdish rebellions in 1920s and 1930s.

The number of Kurds living outside the Kurdish provinces has risen continuously particularly since 1980s due to several factors, including economic hardships, outbreak of the war between PKK and the Turkish state, consequent forced displacement of local people by the Turkish state, and the destruction of Kurdish villages by the Turkish military. Statistical data on Kurdish migration demonstrate that 41 percent of Kurdish migrants moved to Istanbul, 18 percent to Ankara, 15 percent to Adana, and 4 percent to Izmir (McDowall, 1996: 401). According to the latest KONDA report, 34.1 percent of the total Kurdish population lives outside the Kurdish provinces. Half of these, 17.5 percent of the total Kurdish population, lives in Istanbul (KONDA, 2011: 15). Moreover, a considerable number of ethnic Kurds define themselves as Turks as a result of assimilation and/or in order to avoid any oppression or discrimination.

Language

The Kurdish language is a branch of the Indo-European language family and it contains three important dialects called Kurmanji (Northern Kurdish), Sorani (Central Kurdish), and Pehlewani (Southern Kurdish). Kurmanji is the most widespread dialect that is spoken by Kurds in Bakur (Turkish Kurdistan or Northern Kurdistan). Kurmanji is furthermore spoken in Rojhilat (Iranian Kurdistan or Eastern Kurdistan), in the northern part of Bashur (Iraqi Kurdistan or Southern Kurdistan), and in Rojava (Syrian Kurdistan or Western Kurdistan). Since 1930s, Kurmanji has been written with the use of Latin alphabet in Turkey.

There are also Zazaki-speaking Kurds (Zaza-Kurds) in Turkey, mainly living in the provinces of Tunceli (also known as Dersim), Bingöl, Mus, Elazig, and Diyarbakir. It is, however, important to note that some linguists classify Zazaki as a distinct language rather than being merely a dialect of the Kurdish language.

While Kurdish is a member of the Indo-European language family, the Turkish language belongs to the Ural-Altaic languages. For decades following the founding of the Republic of Turkey (1923), however, the Turkish state insisted that the Kurdish language was only a dialect of Turkish, which was in accordance with the policy of denial Turkey had adopted in order to assimilate the Kurdish population. In the years that followed, Turkey forbade publishing in Kurdish and changed Kurdish village and province names into Turkish. The military government that composed Turkey's current constitution in 1982 prohibited even the verbal use of the Kurdish language. This restriction was abolished in 1991 by the government under Turgut Özal. Only in the early 2000s, Turkey introduced some reforms and minor improvements that relaxed the restrictions on Kurdish, including in the education and media sectors. On January 1, 2009, for instance, the state-run TRT introduced TRT-6, a channel that is broadcasting in Kurdish 24 hours a day. Three years later, in 2012, Kurdish became an elective subject in public schools. In addition, some universities launched new departments and programs dedicated to studying Kurdology.

Despite the relaxation of its use, there are still vast restrictions on the practice of the Kurdish language in Turkey. An example is the situation at courts. If Kurdish is spoken by one of the attendants at Turkish courts, it is usually noted as "X" or "an unknown language" in court records. Another example is the restriction imposed upon the Kurdish prisoners. Prison officers often reject Kurdish letters because they were written in a different language than Turkish. Furthermore, the Kurds' demand for Kurdish to become the language of instruction in schools in the Kurdish inhabited provinces remains unrealized.

Religion

One of the common bonds Turks and Kurds share is the religion. This is also one of the more conspicuous characteristics that kept Turks and Kurds together during the Ottoman Empire and during the subsequent Independence War of Turkey. Most of the Kurds are Sunni Muslims, approximately 75 percent, just like the Turkish population (McDowall, 1996: 10). Yet most Kurds follow the Shafi'i school of Sunni denomination in contrary to Turks, who are followers of the Hanafi school (Strohmeier & Yalcin-Heckmann, 2003: 43). It is, however, necessary to stress that these schools differ from each other only slightly in their religious practices and rules. For example, Shafi'i followers have to make their *niyat* (intention) before fasting in Ramadan by the morning prayer, whereas Hanafi followers can make their niyat at midday.

Kurds are, nevertheless, not exclusively Sunni Muslims, and there is also a considerable number of Kurds that follow a different sect of Islam or a different religion, the most significant group of whom is the Alevi Kurds. Whether or not Aleviness is a part of Islam is, however, a very controversial issue even among the Alevis. Some consider Aleviness a branch of Islam, whereas some others deny this relationship. Due to the great importance of the Prophet Ali and the Twelve Imams in Aleviness, some consider it a divergent school of Shi'a Islam (Massicard, 2013: 60).

There are no precise numbers regarding the Alevi population in Turkey. They compose approximately 15 percent to 25 percent of the Kurdish population in

Turkey and at least 15 percent of Turkey's total population, including the Turkish Alevis. According to the report of the European Commission of October 2004, Massicard (2013: 2) specified the number of Alevis in Turkey between 12 and 20 million.

Alevi Kurds are concentrated mainly in Tunceli (the largest Alevi city in Turkey), Mus, Bingol, Sivas, Malatya, Kahramanmaras, and Elazig. There are both Zazaki- and Kurmanji-speaking Alevi Kurds. It is pertinent now to specify that Alevi Kurds have been discriminated and persecuted in Turkey due to both their Kurdish and Alevi identities, where they constitute a minority both in ethnic and religious aspects.

Yezidism is a non-Islamic, ancient Mesopotamian religion that used to have significant followers in Turkey. Yezidis or Yazidis believe in God as the creator of the world, which makes the Yezidi religion a monotheistic one. Yezidis in Turkey are exclusively Kurmanji speakers. There is, however, almost no more Yezidis left in the Kurdish provinces of Turkey. Most of them migrated to Germany in the 1980s and 1990s. They used to live in Tur Abdin and its environs. The most prominent residential area of Yezidis is Sinjar (Kurdish: Shingal), a town in the Nineveh region of Iraq. Today they number about 750,000 worldwide.

Some Kurdish provinces of Turkey (mainly Tur Abdin and its environs) were also home to Assyrians, who are Christians and ethnically non-Kurds but mostly also speak Kurdish. Nevertheless, today only a small number of Assyrians live in the region. Most of them migrated, like Yezidi Kurds, to Europe, mainly Sweden and Germany.

Geography and Economy

Northern Kurdistan (or Turkish Kurdistan) is one of the four parts of Greater Kurdistan, and it comprises the southeastern and eastern provinces of Turkey. It is a mountainous region, with the Eastern Taurus Mountains covering the southeastern provinces. Sirnak and Hakkari provinces are renowned for their high mountains that reach over 3,500 to 4,000 meters. The highest mountain, however, is located in the eastern province of Agri, known as Mount Ararat (Kurdish: Ciyaye Agiri; Turkish: Agri Dagi) with an elevation of 5,137 meters, which makes it the highest mountain in Turkey.

Although the Kurdish region in Turkey does not have any coastline, it is actually a very water-rich region. In addition to numerous rivers and lakes, the Kurdish region contains the Euphrates, Tigris, and Great Zab rivers. Moreover, it possesses the largest lake in Turkey, Lake Van, located between Bitlis and Van, whose surface accounts for 3,755 km².

Unlike Southern Kurdistan (or Iraqi Kurdistan), Northern Kurdistan does not possess significant oil reserves. A minor oil refinery was set up in Batman in 1955. However, other natural resources are abundant in Kurdistan such as chrome, copper, iron, coal, and lignite (van Bruinessen, 1992: 14).

The Kurdish area in Turkey used to be covered with forests. The cutting of trees for construction and heating purposes and the damage caused by animals,

Landscape with the old Kurdish town of Hasankeyf, in southeastern Turkey. (Radio Kafka/ Dreamstime.com)

particularly by goats, led to considerable deforesting of the wooded areas (Stroh-meier & Yalcin-Heckmann, 2003: 23). The outbreak of the war between the PKK and Turkish state has worsened the deforestation further in the region. Beside the harmful effects of war itself, the Turkish military has burnt down some forested areas in order to deny PKK fighters a hideout and shelter.

A continental climate dominates in the Kurdish provinces. As a result, significant temperature differences can be felt between summer and winter. While it is very cold and snowy in the winter in the eastern provinces, temperatures reach up to 25 degrees Celsius in the summer. In the southeastern provinces, however, it is less cold in the winter, whereas very hot temperatures prevail in the summer, reaching over 35 degrees Celsius.

The economy in the Kurdish provinces is characterized by livestock breeding and agriculture. Some scholars define the Kurdish region as excellent for livestock breeding while at the same time stress the detrimental impacts of the war on agricultural production and livestock breeding in the region (Strohmeier & Yalcin-Heckmann, 2003: 23–24). Also the smuggling of goods across the borders has been a source of income for Kurdish families living near the boundaries. These include mostly sugar, tea, and diesel oil. Indeed, the so-called smuggling takes place within the Kurdish-inhabited areas that were carved up among Iran, Iraq, Syria, and Turkey in the years following the First World War.

According to the Turkish Statistical Institute, 17.95 percent of the total agricultural production in Turkey take place in the eastern and southeastern Anatolia regions, two of Turkey's seven geographical regions, which are predominantly Kurdish. On the other hand, the proportion of industry and service sectors in these regions within Turkey's economy is only 8.05 percent and 8.89 percent, respectively. According to a study conducted by KONDA, 23 percent of the Kurds in Turkey live below the starvation line and 53 percent of them live below the poverty line.

Political Parties

The Kurdish national struggle in Turkey remained dormant from the end of 1930s until the 1960s when it started to reorganize within Turkish leftist organizations, of which the Workers Party of Turkey (Turkish: Türkiye Isci Partisi; TIP) was the most important. The reason for this inactivity was mainly due to the draconian suppression of consecutive Kurdish rebellions and the general suppression of political activities by the Turkish state throughout the years 1921 and 1938. The suppression was fortified with the 1934 Resettlement Law that aimed at relocating non-Turkish minorities in order to *Turkify* them. Then Interior Minister Sukru Kaya revealed the aim of the Resettlement Law with the following statement:

> This law will create a country speaking with one language, thinking in the same way, and sharing the same sentiment. (Ülker, 2008: § 8)

Another member of parliament at the time, Sadri Maksudi, expressed his support for the Resettlement Law with the following words:

> Turkification of the language is among the greatest devices for assuring the future of the Turkish race and the living of Turk as Turk. This is our aim. (Ülker, 2008: § 6).

In the 1965 general elections, TIP succeeded in winning 14 seats (out of 450), obtaining 3 percent of the total vote, but it was subsequently shut down following the March 12, 1971, military coup. Kurdish activism within the party was one of the reasons for its prohibition (Strohmeier & Yalcin-Heckmann, 2003: 106). As the Kurdish awareness commenced to revive, the number of political organizations established and dedicated to the Kurdish cause also rose. Kurdistan Democratic Party–Turkey (Kurdish: Partiya Demokrata Kurdistane–Tirkiye; KDP-T), founded in 1965, can be seen as the first Kurdish party that resembled the Kurdistan Democratic Party (Kurdish: Partiya Demokrata Kurdistane; KDP) founded by Mustafa Barzani in 1946. KDP-T was, however, an illegal underground organization that failed to become a popular movement.

In 1969, another Kurdish movement named Revolutionary Eastern Cultural Hearths (Turkish: Devrimci Dogu Kültür Ocaklari; DDKO) was established. DDKO was in close connection with TIP and also dissolved in 1971 by the military junta. This marked the beginning of successive party prohibitions that were to continue in the following decades. The oppression did not only take place within the sphere of political activism. The Kurdish identity and language were also subject to strict discrimination.

The 1970s saw a great escalation of the violence between Turks and Kurds, Sunnis and Alevis, rightists and leftists, with the former being tolerated and even supported by the state. In order to combat "terrorism," Ankara took measures in the Kurdish cities, which paved the way for arbitrary arrests, torture, and general humiliation of the Kurdish people. Due to the strong attack on political activism, the number of people who believed in the necessity of an armed struggle increased continuously. It was this kind of political and social atmosphere that was prevailing in Turkey when the PKK was established in 1978.

The events culminated in another military coup in 1980, which subsequently introduced strict measures to limit political freedom and shaped the reputation for arbitrary torture, murders in custody, and repressive political practices. For example, the electoral threshold of 10 percent, which is the highest in Europe, was introduced by the junta of 1980 with the aim of keeping the dissident political parties outside the Grand National Assembly of Turkey. Another example of the strict measures is a 1983 law requiring all political parties to use the Turkish language alone during party congresses, meetings, or campaigns.

The 1980s passed by in the shadow of the military government that ruled the country from 1980 until 1983. Yet Turkey entered a new era in 1984 when PKK launched a simultaneous attack on military posts in Eruh and Semdinli in southeastern Turkey. This incident marked the beginning of the PKK insurgency that continues until today.

The 1990s witnessed the banning of four pro-Kurdish political parties by the Constitutional Court on charges of separatism, promoting the Kurdish language, and threatening Turkey's territorial integrity. These parties included:

- People's Labor Party (Turkish: Halkin Emek Partisi; HEP) founded in 1990 and banned in 1993
- Freedom and Democracy Party (Turkish: Özgürlük ve Demokrasi Partisi; ÖZDEP) founded in 1992 and banned in 1993
- Democracy Party (Turkish: Demokrasi Partisi; DEP) founded in 1993 and banned in 1994
- Democratic Mass Party (Turkish: Demokratik Kitle Partisi; DKP) founded in 1997 and banned in 1999

Predictably, the banning was not merely limited to political parties, but individuals too. In 1979, Serafettin Elci, an influential Kurdish politician who served as minister of public works between 1978 and 1979, declared publicly that "there are Kurds in Turkey. I too am a Kurd" (McDowall, 2004: 415). Subsequently, he was sentenced by the military junta of 1980 for these words and spent 30 months in prison. In 1994, several Kurdish deputies were sentenced to 15 years for separatism, including prominent politicians such as Leyla Zana, Selim Sadak, Hatip Dicle, and Orhan Dogan, after the Grand National Assembly of Turkey revoked their parliamentary immunity. The fact that Leyla Zana finished her parliamentary oath with a Kurdish sentence, "I am taking this Constitutional oath for the brotherhood of the Turkish and Kurdish peoples", caused serious protests from the parliamentary ranks.

The closure of one Kurdish political party has always led to the establishment of another one, albeit under a different name. As a successor of DEP, People's Democracy Party (Turkish: Halkin Demokrasi Partisi; HADEP) was founded in 1994 and became the first Kurdish party to participate in the general elections of 1995, receiving 4.2 percent of the total vote (Strohmeier & Yalcin-Heckmann, 2003: 112). As the party did not reach the 10 percent threshold, it did not win any seats in the parliament. Subsequently, HADEP was also banned on the charges of separatism by the Constitutional Court in 2003.

HADEP was then succeeded by the founding of Democratic People's Party (Turkish: Demokratik Halk Partisi; DEHAP) in 1997. DEHAP took part in the general elections of 2002 and received almost 2 million votes that accounted for more than 6 percent of the total vote. Yet this was not enough for DEHAP to be represented in the parliament because of the 10 percent electoral threshold. Later, DEHAP dissolved itself in order to avoid a prohibition in 2005.

Following the dissolution of DEHAP, the Democratic Society Party (Turkish: Demokratik Toplum Partisi; DTP) was established in 2005. In order to overcome the 10 percent electoral threshold, DTP adopted a different strategy. Instead of participating in the elections as a party, DTP members ran as independent candidates. This strategy actually worked out, and 21 DTP candidates made it to the parliament after the 2007 elections. A political party needs at least 20 deputies in order to build a parliamentary faction, which was enough for the DTP to form a parliamentary faction in the Grand National Assembly of Turkey that has 550 seats in total. Nevertheless, DTP had to share the same destiny as its predecessors when the Constitutional Court decided unanimously to ban it from the political arena in 2009, again on separatism charges.

The closure of DTP gave birth to Peace and Democracy Party (Turkish: Baris ve Demokrasi Partisi; BDP) in 2008. BDP did not change its election strategy and participated in the 2011 elections with independent candidates. This time, BDP increased its electoral success and gained 36 seats in the parliament.

In 2012, the Peoples' Democratic Party (Turkish: Halklarin Demokratik Partisi; HDP) was formed with the aim of bringing dissident social and political groups together and thereby becoming an umbrella organization. Although it is still predominantly a Kurdish party, HDP has managed to become a party for those who have felt discriminated and marginalized by the political system in Turkey, including leftists, workers, students, and so forth. There had already been a tradition of joint efforts between Kurds and leftists since the 1960s. In addition, HDP has included a wide variety of groups ranging from Muslims to Armenians, Assyrians, and LGBT members. As part of this strategy, BDP changed its name to Democratic Regions Party (Turkish: Demokratik Bölgeler Partisi; DBP) in 2014. From that moment on, the movement has been represented in the Kurdish provinces as DBP and as HDP in the rest of Turkey, which organizationally resembles a case in Germany where the Christian Social Union (CSU) is represented in the state of Bavaria and the Christian Democratic Union (CDU) in the rest of Germany.

In the light of these developments, HDP modified its election strategy and decided to take part in the general elections of 2015 (June 7) as a party and not as individuals. HDP achieved a great electoral success by receiving 13.1 percent of the total vote, earning 80 seats out of 550 in the parliament. Because a coalition could not be built, however, the elections were repeated in November of the same year. It is important to note that during the attempts to build a coalition, the HDP was excluded from the coalition talks by the AKP (Justice and Development Party) that has perpetually ruled the country since 2002. The AKP (Turkish: Adalet ve Kalkinma Partisi) is a right-wing conservative political party built on the principle of moderate Islam, which was founded in 2001. Since then, the AKP has won the majority in the Turkish parliament in the general elections of 2002, 2007, and 2011. The AKP has lost its majority in the June 2015 elections but regained it in the snap elections of November 2015.

HDP and the Turkish General Elections in 2015

The Turkish general or parliamentarian election took place on June 7, 2005. President Erdoğan's ruling AKP won only 40.9 percent, while the main opposition parties CHP gained 25 percent and the MHP 16.4 percent. The surprise outcome of the election was the success of the People's Democratic Party (HDP), a left-wing, pro-Kurdish minority party, that won 13.1 percent of the votes or 80 seats disallowing the AKP a single-party rule. HDP was backed by many Kurdish voters as it represented the PKK in the peace negotiations with the Turkish government. In the following snap election, HDP managed to get 10.76 percent of the votes or 59 seats.

In the snap elections of November, the HDP under the leadership of Selahattin Demirtas and Figen Yüksekdag again overcame the 10 percent threshold by obtaining 10.8 percent of the total vote, earning this time 59 seats. This electoral success constituted a milestone in the political history of the Kurds in Turkey as it was for the first time that a pro-Kurdish party passed the electoral threshold.

Women constitute 38.9 percent of HDP's members of parliament (23 out of 59 HDP seats), having the highest ratio among the political parties represented in the Grand National Assembly. In addition, HDP has the system of co-chairmanship, with Demirtas and Yüksekdag being the co-chairs of the party. This system is applied to local administrations as well, making it compulsory to have one female and one male chairperson for each district municipality.

As mentioned earlier, the persecution against Kurdish politicians has not merely been confined to political parties. Over the decades, thousands of Kurdish politicians, activists, and journalists have been sued, jailed, tortured, banned, or murdered. Pro-Kurdish party buildings outside the Kurdish provinces have been subject to racist attacks, arson, and armed assaults. Since November 2016, HDP's 11 members of parliament, including co-chairpersons Demirtas and Yüksekdag, have been taken into custody on terror charges following the approval of the proposal of the ruling AKP to revoke the legal immunity of 148 parliamentarians, a situation similar to that of 1994 (see earlier). In May 2016, the Turkish parliament stripped 148 parliamentarians (29 AKP, 55 CHP, 53 HDP, 10 MHP, and 1 independent) of their legal immunity on the grounds of provoking people to be rancorous and hostile, inciting terror, praising an offence, and libel charges (according to Turkish laws). Yet only HDP parliamentarians have been arrested so far. Apart from jailed HDP parliamentarians and its numerous party members, also almost all elected HDP and DBP mayors have been arrested and replaced by government-appointed trustees in recent months on terror charges.

There are also smaller Kurdish parties in Turkey, such as the Rights and Freedoms Party (Turkish: Hak ve Özgürlükler Partisi; HAK-PAR) founded in 2002, which stands for Kurdish autonomy within Turkey, or the Free Cause Party (Turkish: Hür Dava Partisi; HÜDA-PAR) founded in 2012, which is an Islamist political party but also stands for the constitutional recognition of the Kurds and the Kurdish language. The former has lacked any popular support or electoral success, whereas the latter could reach a minor electoral success in the local elections of 2014 only in a few Kurdish cities. HÜDA-PAR obtained 7.8 percent of the total vote in Batman, 3 percent in Bingöl, 4.3 percent in Diyarbakir, and 5 percent in Bitlis, which, however, was not enough to win over any municipality.

Party Name	Establishment	Prohibition
KDP-T	1965 (founded illegally)	-
DDKO	1969	1971
HEP	1990	1993
ÖZDEP	1992	1993
DEP	1993	1994
HADEP	1994	2003
DKP	1997	1999
DEHAP	1997	2005 (dissolved itself to avoid a ban)
HAK-PAR	2002	-
DTP	2005	2009
BDP (DBP)	2008 (2014)	-
HÜDA-PAR	2012	-
HDP	2012	-

Genesis, Development, and Current State of the Kurdish Conflict in Turkey
Foundations of the State Ideology, Politics of Forced Assimilation, and the Ethnopolitical Mobilization of Kurds

The founding of the Turkish nation-state in 1923 meant an important caesura for the Kurds of Turkey. In the new centralized unitary state, not only the tradition of autonomous self-administration of the Kurdish principalities during the Ottoman Empire was abolished. The Kurds were declared nonexistent. Their forced assimilation was cemented through new qualitative and systematic policies, which were implemented alongside a socioeconomic negligence of the Kurdish inhabited southeast of Turkey. The result was a series of local Kurdish revolts in the 1920s and 1930s. According to the Turkish General Staff, as many as 30 Kurdish rebellions took place within 1924–1938. During that time, the entire Kurdish region was under emergency rule, which was abolished only in the beginning of 2000s.

The state policy of forced assimilation and use of violence was justified by the new Kemalist state ideology named after the founder of the Republic of Turkey, Mustafa Kemal Atatürk. The fundamentals included a rigid nation and state concept, an unalterable constitutional principle of the indivisible unity of territory and people, and a restrictive approach toward the minorities. The legitimacy of the centralistic nation-state and its unitary ideology was and is still based on the unalterable constitutional principle of the indivisible unity of territory and people. Particularly this constitutional clause, which is applied in numerous provisions (e.g., in penal code, antiterror law, and law on political parties) on the legislative level has extensive impacts. Its scope of application is not clearly defined so that fundamental rights can be easily restricted, such as freedom of press and speech. For instance, the constitutional principle can be applied when ethnic minorities demand cultural autonomy or self-administration rights. Especially in the context of the Kurdish question, this constitutional principle is applied frequently and helps to restrict freedom of press and speech. The minority clauses of Lausanne Treaty of 1923 are concerned with and related to non-Muslim minorities (Greeks, Armenians, and Jews). Despite their considerable number, the Kurds in Turkey are not considered.

The repressive denial and assimilation policy, which is justified by the state ideology, triggered the ethnopolitical mobilization of the Kurds, and is one of the main causes of the emergence of the conflict. In addition, the establishment of the militant PKK should be viewed in this context.

The end of the Cold War and the Gulf War of 1991 introduced a tendency toward political change in the era of Turgut Özal, who was prime minister and president between 1983 and 1993. While retaining the military repression, Özal aimed at liberalization in the cultural realm and followed the goal to incorporate the PKK politically. However, no government after Özal followed this ambitious liberalization policy, which eventually remained stagnant.

Objectives and Contents of the Kurdish Policy of the AKP Government (2002–2016)

The AKP administration took up Özal's Kurdish policy under far more advantageous conditions, triggered by the capture of PKK-Leader Abdullah Öcalan in February 1999 and the acceptance of Turkey as a European Union (EU) candidate country in December 1999. Nevertheless, AKP's Kurdish policy remained embedded within the ideological framework of the Turkish state and constitutional order, which are defined by the primacy of Turkish nationalism. In addition to a rigid nationalism, Islam and neo-Ottomanism form two other ideological driving factors of AKP's Kurdish policy. Both elements comprise a recollection of the Ottoman past and an emphasis on the common religious affiliation. They stress national unity, but at the same time negate the political national dimension of the Kurdish question. On the one hand, a "religious brotherhood" and "national unity" should be formed by stressing the common religion, Islam. On the other hand, the recollection of the Ottoman past implies an "Ottoman solution" of the Kurdish question. This would internally allow a limited liberalization in the realm of cultural rights and expand the range of influence explicitly as "patron saint and hegemon" in the Kurdish question. Even though AKP differs from Kemalists with regard to the elements as "Islam" and "neo-Ottomanism," it agrees with respect to the primacy of the Turkish nation and the exertion of influence on the Kurdish question beyond the national boundaries. This is because AKP is a Turkish nationalist party with an Islamic-conservative character while it does not possess Kemalist attributes. The protection and preservation of Turkish nationalism and the Turkish nation is the common ideological denominator of both AKP and Kemalist powers. This common denominator is defined by a negative perception of the Kurdish question, the denial of the political-national dimension of the issue, and the preference of a military-security policy approach that rests on the use of violence and repression. Hence, the AKP government, just as all the previous governments, views the Kurdish question and PKK as a threat to national unity and territorial integrity. Furthermore, the AKP strictly differentiates the PKK from the Kurdish question, and it considers the former a terrorism problem and the latter a socioeconomic issue. Thereby it negates the relationship between the unsolved conflict and the emergence of the PKK and the historically deep-rooted political-national dimension of the conflict. This can be viewed as the troubled legacy of the peace settlements in the aftermath of the First World War and the collapse of the Ottoman Empire, which denied the Kurds self-determination right and the establishment of a Kurdish nation-state.

Despite certain changes in AKP's Kurdish policy strategy, its main understanding of the Kurdish question and its objectives are continuously based on a national consensus and not affected by the limited liberalization policies. These objectives include:

- Preventing of the emergence of a Kurdish state
- Exerting of influence on the developments related to the Kurdish question
- Weakening and controlling of the Kurdish national movements
- Combatting politically and military against the PKK

The Kurdish policy of the AKP administration is determined by a double strategy based on a policy mix of political and military measures, as well as rhetoric actionism. The cornerstones are (1) to allow a limited liberalization policy in the realm of cultural individual rights while preserving the foundations of the state ideology; (2) to contain and control the legal political sphere of Kurds by marginalizing the legal Kurdish party HDP and all the Kurdish political activities in civil society; and (3) to combat the PKK politically and militarily in order to defeat it. For this purpose, the AKP initiated talks with the PKK and its jailed leader Abdullah Öcalan for the first time in the history of the modern republic, which later, however, were terminated.

The AKP government's liberalization policies regarding the Kurds include four components:

1. Political reforms in the years 2002–2005, which were adopted as part of Turkey's EU accession process and led to an amelioration of individual freedoms. These reforms include, among others, some amendments of the 1982 constitution, the abolishment of the state security courts, the allowance of broadcasting in languages other than Turkish, the revision of the penal code on torture, the abolishment of the capital punishment, the revision of antiterror laws, and the prioritization of supranational treaties over domestic laws.
2. An initiative announced in summer 2009 promising the expansion of the use of the Kurdish language.
3. The democratization package of September 2013, which included measures that were relevant to Kurdish policy, for example, lifting the prohibition on the letters x, q, and w (used in the Kurdish alphabet); reintroducing formerly banned Kurdish place names; and expanding the use of the Kurdish language.
4. The peace talks with Öcalan and the PKK between November 2012 and July 2015 in order to achieve the disarmament of the PKK.

Taken as a whole, the adopted reforms and measures had a positive impact on the situation of the Kurdish population. In addition to Kurdish broadcasting, Kurdish-language courses, giving children Kurdish names, the reintroduction of Kurdish place names, the introduction of Kurdish as an elective subject at schools, the opening of Kurdology departments at universities, and the use of the Kurdish language during election campaigns or in prisons was permitted. Furthermore, emergency rules were lifted, and Abdullah Öcalan's capital punishment was converted into life imprisonment as part of Turkey's accession process to the EU.

Thus, the framework for a political solution of the Kurdish question from the AKP's position was set through a process of reforms. However, the expansion of individual cultural rights and freedoms occurred while maintaining the ideological fundaments of the state. These rights were never meant to recognize the Kurds as a distinct ethnocultural group. This had the effect that the reforms were not implemented systematically and were still managed restrictively. Further political demands for a federation or autonomy were rejected as separatist aspirations and a threat to the national unity and territorial integrity. This represents the national consensus of Turkey's Kurdish policy.

The Consensus on Demands of the Kurds

The adopted reforms, however, represented the demands of the Kurds only very narrowly. The Kurdish demands are built upon a consensus between the Kurdish political spectrum that includes the HDP and PKK and the Kurdish civil society. The consensus represents the following demands:

- Granting the right for Kurdish education in the public education system
- Enlarging the competences of the local administrations

- Decreasing the 10 percent electoral threshold
- Recognizing the Kurdish nation in the constitution
- Dissolving the village guards who are deployed in the fight against the PKK and receive salaries in return
- Ending political and military operations
- Releasing all political prisoners, including Abdullah Öcalan

The ultimate demand, however, is the granting of collective sovereignty rights in the context of autonomy or a federal state structure, whose final form is negotiable. The consensus furthermore includes the request to consider the PKK as part of the Kurdish question and that any political conflict resolution must include the PKK and Abdullah Öcalan. Nonetheless, particularly the issue of preferred autonomy in a federal state structure received a strong backlash from the AKP government and the two opposition parties, the Republican People's Party (Turkish: Cumhuriyet Halk Partisi; CHP) and the Nationalist Movement Party (Turkish: Milliyetci Hareket Partisi; MHP). They view autonomy as a threat to Turkey's national unity and territorial integrity, and thus reject it.

The Rise of the Kurdish Politics

Currently, the HDP is the strongest political party of the Kurds. In eastern and southeastern Turkey, the HDP has consistently managed to obtain the majority of electoral votes of the Kurdish population in general and local elections. Despite a smear campaign by the AKP, the HDP succeeded in overcoming the 10 percent electoral threshold in the last general elections of June 2015 and the subsequent snap elections of November 2015 and managed to enter the parliament for the first time. Considering the number of seats, HDP became the third largest party represented in the Turkish parliament. The number of seats in the Turkish Parliament is divided as follows: AKP 317 seats; CHP 133 seats; HDP 59 seats; MHP 40 seats; independent MPs 1 seat (550 seats in total).

All predecessors of the HDP have been banned consecutively since the beginning of 1990s on charges of close relations to and support for the PKK. The HDP, too, is labeled as a continuation of PKK and pressured to distance itself from the PKK and to condemn them as a terrorist organization. On the whole, the legal Kurdish political arena has become more resilient over the years in spite of many prohibitions and systematic marginalization attempts. They have gained more political experience since the 1990s. Both the parliamentarian and political work on the local level (through numerous city halls in the region) have reinforced the ability to organize Kurdish politics in limited areas between survival and prohibition and to solidify influence in the east and southeast. In particular, city halls have constituted the successful nucleus of the HDP. Thus, the HDP has become a vital integral component of the local political landscape. Similar to its predecessors, the HDP concentrates on the recognition of the Kurdish identity and the inclusion of Öcalan and the PKK for a conflict resolution. On the one hand, the HDP strives to serve its grassroots base. On the other hand, it works to bring the resolution of the Kurdish question onto the national political agenda, and thereby exerts pressure on the Turkish politics.

The HDP sees the resolution of the conflict in the transformation of the political administrative state structure through decentralization and democratic autonomy. The latter refers to the autonomy on the basis of self-administration with regional and local parliaments. Regarding the decentralization in Turkey, the HDP suggests 20 to 25 regions with their own regional parliament and government, which are legitimized via elections. The local administration should be strengthened by given the right to electing the governor directly. The central government should only be responsible for foreign affairs, finances, and defense. Furthermore, a new constitution is proposed with a new definition of the concept of the nation ("Nation of Turkey" instead of "Turkish Nation"), guarantees for the protection and development of identities and cultures, and the use of Kurdish in public.

The HDP's increasing success has sharpened the political rivalry between the AKP and HDP over the Kurdish voter support. AKP's reaction to this political rivalry has been very confrontational and included the following goals: (1) to curb HDP's political influence, (2) to delegitimize HDP's numerous city halls, (3) to narrow down the legal political sphere of Kurds, and (4) to preserve the political control over the Kurdish politics and the Kurdish people.

A Stronger PKK and the Fight for Democratic Autonomy

The PKK came into existence under the influence of the radicalizing political climate in the 1970s, which was furthermore exacerbated by the military coups of 1971 and 1980. With the aim of establishing an independent Kurdish state, the PKK (founded as a Marxist-Leninist organization) launched its guerrilla warfare against the Turkish state in August 1984. The PKK departed from this ultimate demand in the early 1990s. Although they were not endorsed by all Kurdish political forces due to the violent means deployed, the PKK received support from the general populace, to which the Turkish government contributed significantly with its oppressive Kurdish policy. The PKK modified its demands in 1993 and has since been pursuing a solution within the borders of the Turkish state. Since the first ceasefire declaration in March 1993, the PKK has announced, without abandoning its strategy of violence, eight unilateral ceasefires, which have, however, come to nothing. Shortly after the arrest of Öcalan in February 1999, they even withdrew its fighters from Turkey and ceased the armed struggle for several years.

But even after the capture of Abdullah Öcalan, the government's desired military solution to the PKK question has not succeeded. This is related to facts such as the regional character of the unsolved Kurdish conflict, the growing politicization of the Kurdish people, and the PKK itself. In the meantime, the PKK has become a political force, which is not only present in the "mountains," but also in the cities that possesses a societal basis that cannot be underestimated. Its regional significance and power have also been rising. In addition, regional developments like the Gulf War in 1991, the Second Gulf War in 2003, the prominence of the federal region Kurdistan-Iraq, the Arab Spring, the Syrian Civil War, and the fight against ISIS boosted the politicization of the Kurdish population and Kurdish nationalism in all parts of the country and challenged the governance.

Recently, the PKK has gained importance through their participation in the civil war in Syria and the war against ISIS. The PKK became a strategic factor combating ISIS in Iraq and Syria, which extended regional maneuverability. This can be observed by looking at the accomplishments of the PKK's offshoot, the Democratic Union Party (Kurdish: Partiya Yekitiya Demokrat; PYD) in Syria. Since summer 2012, the PYD with its military wing the YPG has been controlling and governing the Kurdish region in northern Syria called Rojava in Kurdish that consists of three autonomous cantons in Efrin, Kobane, and Cizire. The aim of the PYD and the PKK is not the formation of a separate Kurdish state in Syria, but rather autonomy for the cantons as constituents of a new democratic Syria. In Rojava, the PYD and the PKK attempt to implement their political model that is based on the core elements of gender justice, ecology, and grassroots democracy. However, this has encountered strong resistance from the AKP government who considers Rojava and the strengthening of the PKK/PYD a threat. The success of the PKK and the PYD in Rojava could inspire the Kurdish population in Turkey for autonomy endeavors and solidify the PKK's position.

The Regionalization of the Internal Conflict, a Fragile Peace Process, and the Return of Violence

The commencement of the peace talks with the PKK and Öcalan in November 2012 did not only have domestic political motives. More importantly, the talks served to curb the Kurdish threat in Northern Syria and potential strengthening of the PKK. During the peace talks, the HDP played a mediating role between the PKK leadership in the Qandil Mountains in neighboring Iraqi Kurdistan and Öcalan. During the Newroz celebrations on March 21, 2013, Öcalan, from the Imrali Prison, invited the PKK leadership to end the armed struggle. They followed this call by proclaiming a unilateral ceasefire and beginning a partial withdrawal of approximately 2,000 fighters from Turkey into the camps in Iraqi Kurdistan. The government, on the other hand, abandoned its basic principle of not speaking with "terrorists," which had been a political principle until then, and thereby recognized Öcalan as an interlocutor and representative of the Kurdish national movement and the HDP as the political voice of the PKK. Indeed, both sides adhered to the agreed ceasefire to a great extent. Nevertheless, the talks stagnated and came to a standstill prior to the general elections of June 2015. On the one hand, the peace process was influenced by the developments in Syria and Rojava. On the other hand, it was fragile from the outset because of diametrically opposed interests. While the government strictly rejects federal or autonomous forms of self-administration and the right to education in Kurdish in the context of a new constitution, these demands are central to all of the Kurdish parties and organizations—the PKK, the HDP, and Kurdish civil society establishments. The government utilized the peace process in order to reinforce its capacity to act in the Kurdish southeast of Turkey. The state built new technological well-equipped military bases and dams in the southeast that were designed for security purposes. The PKK, on the other hand, expanded its urban structures and proclaimed autonomy in some of their strongholds.

The show of force between the government and PKK intensified with the political achievements of the PYD and PKK in Syria and Northern Iraq. The electoral success of the HDP in the general elections of June 2015 was another negative development from the government's viewpoint. This was a shock for President Recep Tayyip Erdoğan and his AKP for several reasons: First, the AKP missed the absolute majority in the parliament, and the distant goal of establishing a presidential system was jeopardized. The election results meant a setback for Erdoğan's Kurdish policy. The hope to neutralize the Kurdish endeavors through the politics of involvement and negotiation did not succeed. Instead, the Kurdish question experienced an unexpected renaissance in Turkey in the wake of the bold and successful battles of the PYD in Syria. President Erdoğan and his AKP reacted by adopting the so-called "fight against terrorism" strategy: On the one hand, the PKK as a terrorist organization should be fought through military means, and on the other hand, the HDP should be discredited as alleged political extension of the PKK. Since late July 2015, the Turkish army has been bombing PKK positions in northern Iraq. They have also attacked Kurdish towns and provinces in the east and southeast of Turkey with considerable support for the PKK and HDP with special forces, commando units, snipers, and heavy weapons. The PKK applied a new strategy of carrying the war into the cities for the first time through its youth structures. Thereby, the PKK tries to stimulate a popular revolt in order to exert pressure on the government to accept the proclaimed autonomy in some places. This plan has not worked out, and the anticipated support of the people has been absent, as the population has become the target of the escalation of violence. The HDP has repeatedly asked both the Turkish state and the PKK to end the violence. Moreover, many Kurds and Kurdish civil society organizations have criticized the PKK's new strategy and demanded an immediate ceasefire. At the same time, many Kurds are deeply disappointed by Turkish state's actions and the lack of solidarity in the western part of the country. In February 2016, the government declared an action plan against terrorism with focus on security policies but without any advanced political arrangements. The government promises therein the reconstruction of the destroyed cities in combination with new security measures. Moreover, it announced not to negotiate with the PKK or HDP, but with other Kurdish actors. The end of violence is not in sight yet.

The AKP succeeded in regaining the absolute majority in the parliament following the snap elections of November 1, 2015. Despite losing some votes, the HDP managed again to enter the parliament and thus became the third largest party. Yet the internal tensions have not disappeared. On the contrary, human rights organizations such as Human Rights Watch and Amnesty International draw a dramatic picture of the situation in their 2015 Turkey reports: the criminalization of the opposition, the repression of the press and the freedom of expression, and the violation of Kurdish people's right to life.

The HDP and the city halls it controls were also profoundly affected by the confrontational policies the government has adopted. Prior to the general elections of

June 2015, the HDP was already subject to defamations by President Erdoğan, the government, and the pro-government media. The main goal of the defamations was to keep the HDP under the 10 percent electoral threshold so that the AKP could gain the majority in the parliament. The HDP and its infrastructure became the target of numerous attacks across the country, including a bomb assault on a rally in Diyarbakir in June 2015. This left the party largely marginalized. Furthermore, after the legal immunity of 53 HDP parliamentarians was revoked in May 2016, the state launched an investigation process against them. More than 10 HDP parliamentarians, including co-chairs Demirtas and Yüksekdag, have been arrested on terror charges since November 2016.

In addition, many mayors of HDP and DBP who have been elected for years in their regions by the overwhelming majority of the Kurdish population, have been arrested. Since the declaration of emergency rule following the failed coup attempt on June 15, 2016, the measures taken against Kurdish politicians have increased sharply. In the meantime, the government has replaced those democratically elected mayors with trustees in more than 70 eastern and southeastern cities, towns, and districts on the grounds of terrorism and threats to national security. The Turkish government accuses them of using the budget to support terrorism. The PKK, on the other hand, has declared to target these government-appointed trustees and AKP representatives in the region. Also on terror charges, many Kurdish media outlets (including not only pro-PKK but also many critical of the government) have been shut down, and 14,000 Kurdish teachers have been dismissed. The government's main aim is not only to deal the HDP a final blow. It is also about destroying the democratic achievements and the local governance that the Kurdish politics has achieved in the last two decades.

In addition to the domestic containment policy against the Kurds, the AKP government has expanded its military strategy beyond the Turkish borders. On August 24, 2016, the Turkish army launched a campaign, the so-called Euphrates Shield, into Syria with some factions of the Free Syrian Army (FSA) and captured the city of Jarablus in Northern Syria without considerable ISIS resistance. Meanwhile, the Turkish army and its FSA allies have captured also the strategic town of al-Bab (35 kilometers northeast of Aleppo) after fierce clashes with ISIS. With this proactive foreign policy strategy, Turkey aims at preventing the YPG and Syrian Democratic Forces (SDF) from linking up the Kurdish cantons in northern Syria. Founded in October 2015, the SDF is a multiethnic and multireligious alliance of Kurdish, Arab, Assyrian, Turkmen, and Armenian militia groups. The Kurdish YPG is the largest group within the alliance. The Turkish government's main goal has been the creation of a de facto buffer and no-fly zone in the area that divides the westernmost canton, Efrin, from the other cantons. However, this idea has lacked international support. With the creation of such a zone, Turkey ostensibly aims to establish a violence-free area for Syrian refugees. Yet the Turkish state views the YPG and SDF as terrorist organizations and also wants to obstruct a Kurdish zone along its southern borders. Thus, the Turkish government has repeatedly announced the advance of the YPG forces west of the Euphrates River as its red line. Although the YPG and SDF captured the city of Manbij, west of the Euphrates River, with the help of U.S. air support in August 2016, Turkey has seemingly achieved its goal of thwarting the Kurdish territorial unity in northern Syria with its intervention in the Syrian War. Furthermore, Turkey sporadically shells YPG-held places and threatens to advance toward Manbij.

Recognition of the Kurdish Autonomy Endeavors

The Kurdish question has been occupying the political agenda in Turkey since its establishment in 1923. The new Turkish nation-state denied the Kurdish population any cultural or political autonomy. Instead, the Turkish state denied even the existence of the Kurds and aimed at the forced assimilation of its large Kurdish population. As a result, a series of Kurdish rebellions took place in the 1920s and 1930s, which were brutally suppressed in order to consolidate the newly established unitary state system. Moreover, Kurdish place names were changed into Turkish as part of the assimilation policies.

Because of the brutal suppression, the Kurdish struggle remained dormant in the 1940s and 1950s but it started to politically reorganize in the 1960s. Yet any cultural or political Kurdish activity was suppressed. Even publishing or obtaining an elementary Kurdish book was a reason for imprisonment on separatism charges. The 1970s experienced a great escalation of the political violence and the Turkish state systematically squashed both the leftist and Kurdish activities. The 1980 coup left no space for political activism and the scope of the oppression reached a new level. In addition to numerous atrocities, arbitrary arrests, and murders, the military government banned the use of Kurdish even in private conversations. In this political context, the PKK launched its armed struggle in 1984, which continues until today.

The density of the conflict between the Turkish state and PKK increased in the 1990s. In addition to the fierce clashes, human rights abuses, and forced displacement in the Kurdish inhabited eastern and southeastern regions, the Turkish state banned several pro-Kurdish political parties and arrested some prominent Kurdish parliamentarians, including Leyla Zana, Orhan Dogan, Ahmet Türk, and Hatip Dicle. Furthermore, the entire Kurdish region was under martial law.

Following the EU compliance reforms by the new AKP government and the abolishment of the martial law in the Kurdish towns, the tensions eased in the beginning of 2000s. In the meantime, the pro-Kurdish political parties have steadily increased their electoral success and managed to create a parliamentary faction in the Turkish parliament in three consecutive general elections: 2007, 2011, and 2015.

The conflict in Turkey came to a halt in November 2012, when the Turkish state recognized PKK's ceasefire for the first time. In addition to the ceasefire, the two parties had a series of negotiations for a political reconciliation of the violent conflict. Yet the peace talks failed in July 2015. With the eruption of fierce clashes between the PKK and Turkish state, several Kurdish provinces and districts have been put under martial law again. Furthermore, the scope of the political repression expanded and many democratically elected HDP parliamentarians and mayors have been recently arrested. The Turkish government has repeatedly reiterated that it would no longer negotiate with the PKK or HDP.

However, it is difficult to reach peace without the PKK and HDP, the legitimate third largest party in the Turkish parliament. On the one hand, the regionalization of the intra-Turkish conflict has already proceeded extensively. On the other hand, the conflict over the future of the Kurds in Turkey and other three parts is essentially a troubled legacy of the peace settlements following the First World War and the collapse of the Ottoman Empire. The autonomy endeavors of the Kurds are firmly entrenched in this historical context and therefore cannot be ignored or overlooked. Any peaceful and durable conflict resolution requires the recognition of the historically deep-rooted autonomy endeavors of the Kurds and necessitates the inclusion of the PKK. Last but not least, a renewed peace process needs an external influential mediator in order to actively lead both parties, the PKK and the government, on the way to a peace settlement and to prevent an escalation of violence.

Gülistan Gürbey and Vedat Dayan

Further Reading

Eccarius-Kelly, V. (2011). *The Militant Kurds: A Dual Strategy for Freedom.* Santa Barbara, CA: Praeger.

Gürbey, G. (2012). *Die türkische Kurdenpolitik unter der AKP-Regierung: alter Wein in neuen Schläuchen?* GIGA Focus Nahost, Hamburg, Nr.11, German Institute of Global and Area Studies, https://www.giga-hamburg.de/de/system/files/publications/gf_nahost_1211 .pdf.

Gürbey, G., & I. Ferhad (Eds.). (2000). *The Kurdish Conflict in Turkey. Obstacles and Chances for Peace and Democracy.* New York/ Münster, Germany: LIT.

International Crisis Group. (2012), *Turkey: The PKK and the Kurdish Settlement,* Europe Report, 219, https://www.crisisgroup.org/europe-central-asia/western-europemediter ranean/turkey/turkey-pkk-and-kurdish-settlement.

KONDA. (2011). *Biz Kimiz'2010; Kürt Meselesi'nde Algi ve Beklentiler Arastirmasi, Bulgular Raporu—Mayis 2011* (Who Are We 2010; Research of Perception and Expectations on the Kurdish Question, Report of Findings—May 2011). KONDA Arastirma ve Danismanlik, http://akgul.bilkent.edu.tr/Konda/2011_06_KONDA_Kurt_Meselesinde_Algi _ve_Beklentiler.pdf.

Massicard, E. (2013). *The Alevis in Turkey and Europe; Identity and Managing Territorial Diversity.* London, New York: Routledge, Exeter Studies in Ethno Politics.

McDowall, D. (1996). *A Modern History of the Kurds.* London, New York: I. B. Tauris.

Strohmeier, M. & Yalcin-Heckmann, L. (2003). *Die Kurden; Geschichte, Politik, Kultur.* München: Beck.

Ülker, E. (2008). "Assimilation, Security and Geographical Nationalization in Interwar Turkey; The Settlement Law of 1934." *European Journal of Turkish Studies,* vol. 7, http://ejts .revues.org/2123.

Van Bruinessen, M. (1992). *Agha, Shaikh and State: The Social and Political Structures of Kurdistan.* London, New Jersey: Zed Books.

UNITED STATES

Kurdish-Americans and Kurdish immigrants represent a socioculturally and religiously diverse community today, and estimates suggest that around 25,000 Kurds live in United States. A steady stream of Kurdish refugees and political exiles has arrived in the United States since the 1970s, particularly following dramatic regime changes and ethnonational wars throughout the main Kurdish regions of the Middle East, including in Iran, Iraq, Syria, and Turkey. Kurds settled predominately in urban areas of southern California such as Los Angeles and San Diego, and in the upper Midwest, including in Nebraska, Minnesota, and North Dakota. The most sizable Kurdish community in the United States lives in Nashville, Tennessee, but many intellectual Kurds also decided to live in New York and in Washington, DC. Kurds have been successful in their integration efforts in the United States while also managing to protect their cultural and linguistic heritage over time.

Nashville, Tennessee

Due to a large concentration of Kurdish immigrants, the city of Nashville, Tennessee, is considered the Kurdish capital of the United States and is often called "Little Kurdistan." Most Kurds are from Iraq, and they started moving into the city in the 1970s. Other waves of Kurdish mass migration followed, and today, some 13,000 Kurds live in the greater Nashville area. They have established cultural centers, mosques, and shops to cater to the Kurdish community's needs.

A wave of Kurds from Iran settled in the United States in 1979 following the Iranian Revolution. Secular and leftist Kurds feared repression under the theocratic regime and quickly qualified for asylum abroad. Many Kurdish refugees also arrived in the United States from Iraqi Kurdish areas following the outbreak of the Iran-Iraq War from 1980 to 1988. The former dictator of Iraq, Saddam Hussein (1937–2006), aimed to crush ethnic resistance and attacked Kurdish communities in the infamous *al-Anfal* (Spoils of War) campaigns, which culminated in the horrific poison gas attacks in the area of Halabja (also Halepce) in 1988. About 5,000 civilians died in nerve gas attacks on the city of Halabja after the Iraqi air force dropped colorless and odorless Sarin gas on unsuspecting Kurdish communities (Hilterman, 2007). Throughout the entire war period, the Iraqi regime destroyed some 4,500 villages to undermine agricultural activities and viciously murdered between 100,000 and 180,000 Kurds (estimates range widely), including vast numbers of women and children (Black, 1993). By April 1991, and in the aftermath of the Gulf War (August 1990–February 1991), the United States initiated Operation Provide Comfort to deliver desperately needed humanitarian aid to Kurds fleeing their homes. However, the humanitarian intervention on behalf of the Kurds was considered inadequate by experts (Frelick, 1992: 25). Thousands of Kurdish refugees from Iraq arrived in the United States between 1991 and 1992, following the Kurdish genocide and the Gulf War.

Another major migration of Kurds to the United States took place between 1996 and 1997, after an internecine war broke out pitting the two major Iraqi Kurdish political parties against each other. The Kurdistan Democratic Party (KDP) and the Patriotic Party of Kurdistan (PUK) struggled to gain control over the region and internationalized the conflict by looking for allies. The PUK established an alliance with Iran and the KDP collaborated with Saddam Hussein, which resulted in 30,000 Iraqi troops entering the northern Kurdish city of Erbil. Kurdish refugees escaped from the region and crossed the border into Turkey. President Clinton ordered a military intervention to prevent the Iraqi regime from re-establishing a power base in Kurdistan and instituted the northern no-fly zone. A significant number of Kurdish refugees from this particular conflict were resettled in Nashville, Tennessee, which, as mentioned, claims the largest concentration of Kurdish immigrants in the United States (Campbell, 2014). The Tennessee Kurdish Community Council (TKCC) asserts that its community makes up nearly 15,000 people today.

Following the U.S. intervention in Iraq in 2003 and the capture of Saddam Hussein, many Kurds considered returning to areas of Kurdistan. Kurds expressed optimism because a federal constitutional framework for the new Iraq allowed the region to reconstitute itself as the Kurdistan Regional Government (KRG). Yet ongoing regional instability, disputes over land and oil resources, and the threat of the Islamic State in Iraq and Syria (ISIS) slowed and then reversed this trend of return migration. Finally, during the past decade, many Kurdish immigrants arrived in the United States who had previously worked with members of the U.S. military, had been employed by international humanitarian organizations, or served as translators or local mediators for other nonprofit organizations in Kurdistan and Iraq.

In comparison to Kurds in European countries, the North American Kurdish community represents a more divided and less politically active community. However, several influential Kurdish organizations have been engaged in public relations and lobbying activities in the United States since the 1990s. Among the best known Kurdish political groups in the United States are AKIN (American Kurdish Information Network), KNCNA (Kurdish National Congress of North America), the offices of the Kurdistan Regional Government of Iraq (KRG), and the HDP (Peoples' Democratic Party). Most recently, a solidarity group for Syrian-Kurdistan was formed in New York, and Washington, DC, gained a Kurdish policy think tank.

AKIN is headed by Kani Xulam, a Kurdish activist who originated from Diyarbakir, Turkish-Kurdistan. During both Clinton administrations (1993–2001), AKIN established enduring relationships with members of Congress, human rights organizations, and scholarly communities. The KNCNA was formed shortly after Saddam Hussein's regime carried out the Halabja massacres against the Kurdish minority. The KNCNA aimed to represent Kurdish interests in the United States by advancing efforts to remove the Iraqi dictator.

The KRG established offices in Washington, DC, more recently to represent the official government of northern Iraq's Kurdistan region. Since 2003, the KRG has obtained certified assistance from the United States' government to encourage the Iraqi Kurdish leadership to maintain the federal arrangement within post-Saddam Hussein Iraq. The KRG lobbies actively on behalf of Kurdish economic interests and also pursues broader security-related causes. In 2013, the KRG's high profile spokesperson, Qubad Talabani (born in 1977 in Damascus, Syria), left the United States for the KRG to become more involved in domestic Kurdish politics in Iraq. Iraqi Kurdish lobby groups are often constrained because of the very complex relationship between competing Kurdish groups within the Kurdistan region and the KRG's interactions with the central government in Baghdad. Currently, the KRG's interests are represented by Bayan Abdul Rahman in the United States. She left a career as an accomplished journalist and experienced high representative in Britain to advance Kurdish interests in the United States. Hailing from a politically active Kurdish family, both her father and her brother tragically died in a terror attack in Erbil, Kurdistan, in 2004. Nearly 100 people were killed in the attack, and Rahman decided to pursue a political career after the tragedy.

With the emergence of ISIS as a major threat to Kurdish communities in 2014, Kurdish groups in the United States intensified their efforts to influence international perceptions related to Kurdish demands for self-determination. The dramatic siege of Shingal (Sinjar), a mountain top to which thousands of Yezidi Kurds fled after ISIS attacked them, and the ferocious battles for the town of Kobani in Syrian-Kurdistan created opportunities for Kurdish activists in the United States. American Kurds of various ideological convictions demanded military assistance from the United States to be able to equip Kurdish militias to fight more effectively against ISIS. While Kurdish lobbying efforts became increasingly visible in the United States, it was not necessarily discernible that these Kurdish activities resulted in shaping American foreign policy choices.

A new arrival in Washington, DC, was the representative of the Kurdish Peoples' Democratic Party (HDP), Mehmet Yüksel. As a highly trained and skilled spokesperson for Kurdish political interests in Turkey, he added even more diversity to the varying Kurdish lobbying efforts. While the HDP spokesperson emphasized shared values of democratization and overlapping security interests, the party's entire leadership was removed from public office and then imprisoned following the failed military coup in Turkey in July 2016. Turkish President Erdoğan (born in 1954) established emergency rule in Turkey after the coup attempt. Since then, he has pursued a strategy that focuses on removing his critics from positions of influence. A wave of arrests and detentions has silenced journalists, removed Kurdish politicians from their elected positions, and fired vast numbers of people affiliated with a competing Islamist group, the Gülen movement, which has been accused of orchestrated the coup. Mehmet Yüksel and other Kurdish (and leftist) representatives of the HDP are remaining in the United States for fear of arrest and mistreatment in Turkey.

The newest organization that aims to educate the public and advance Kurdish research agendas is the Kurdish Policy Research Center (KPRC), a think tank in Washington, DC. Established in 2016, the KPRC regularly brings together groups of scholars who focus on identifying and analyzing global issues concerning

U.S.-Kurdish relations. In addition, it is important to note that various groups have formed in the United States with the intent to support Rojava's (Syrian-Kurdistan) struggle for autonomy. Rojava Solidarity, located in New York City, is among the most active groups in the United States.

Several highly successful Kurdish immigrants to the United States have shaped public perceptions about the community. Dr. Najmaldin Karim, (born in 1949) and originally from Kirkuk, Iraq, arrived in the United States in 1976 and became a practicing neurosurgeon. He co-founded the Kurdish National Congress of North America (KNCNA), and testified before the U.S. Senate Foreign Relations Committee in June 1990 on Saddam Hussein's atrocities in Kurdistan, including the Anfal Campaign, the Kurdish genocide and the use of chemical weapons by the Iraqi dictator. In 2009, he returned to Kirkuk, and in 2011, Dr. Karim was elected governor of Kirkuk Province. Perhaps the best known Kurd in the United States today is Hamdi Ulukaya, the founder and CEO of Chobani Yogurt (born in 1972). He arrived in the United States in 1994 to study English in Albany, New York. In 2005, he initiated the production of Greek-style yogurt in upstate New York and received notable recognition for his support of refugees. In 2014, he aided Kurdish communities who were displaced by the war against ISIS, and in 2015 Ulukaya pledged $700 million to provide assistance to Kurdish refugees (The Kurdish Project, 2015). Influenced by Warren Buffet and Bill and Melinda Gates, Ulukaya became the first Kurdish immigrant to the United States to sign on to the philanthropic movement.

Hamid Ulukaya at Chobani

Hamid Ulukaya is a Kurd from Turkey and founder and CEO of Chobani, a popular yogurt brand in the United States. Based on his personal experiences, he started his business employing refugees and supporting resettlement programs. For this, he and his company were targeted by hate crimes; however, Mr. Ulukaya increased his efforts to help refugees from Iraq, Syria, and other countries by signing the Giving Pledge, essentially promising to donate most of his wealth to charities working with refugees.

The main challenge that continues to face politically engaged American Kurds is the complexity of the political situation in the Kurdish regions in Iran, Iraq, Syria, and Turkey. Often Kurds are simplistically portrayed in the media as ferocious Peshmerga in Iraqi Kurdistan, willing to die in the fight against ISIS. In Syrian-Kurdistan, Kurds are sometimes identified as trustworthy regional allies, but only as long as they pursue an agenda that is approved by the Pentagon. If Kurds push for national independence, they become labeled as petulant trouble makers or even as terrorists (McKiernan 2006). In recent years, Kurds in the United States have begun to control more of the narratives about Kurdish experiences in their homeland. The growing number of Kurdish-Americans with university degrees is likely to further improve on this trend.

Vera Eccarius-Kelly

Further Reading

Black, G. (1993). *Genocide in Iraq: The Anfal Campaign against the Kurds.* New York: Human Rights Watch.

Campbell, M. (2014). "Touring a Kurdish Capital in the US." http://www.bbc.com/news/magazine-28891241.

Cook, S. A. (2016). "Who Exactly Are 'the Kurds'? *The Atlantic.* http://www.theatlantic.com/international/archive/2016/02/kurds-turkey-pkk-ypg/470991.

De Rouen, A. (2016). "Leaving the Homeland: Kurdish Diasporic Experience in Binghamton." *Anthropology of the Middle East,* vol. 11, 119–126.

Frelick, B. (1992). "The False Promise of Operation Provide Comfort: Protecting Refugees or Protecting State Power?" *Middle East Report,* vol. 176, 22–27.

Garmiany, P. (2016). "Kurdish Billionaire Gives Millions to Employees." http://rudaw.net/english/business/28042016.

Hilterman, J. (2007). *A Poisonous Affair: America, Iraq, and the Gassing of Halabja.* Cambridge, UK: Cambridge University Press.

The Kurdish Project. (2015). "Chobani's Founder Donates 700 Million to Kurdish Refugees." http://thekurdishproject.org/latest-news/us-kurdish-relations/chobanis-founder-donates-700-million-to-kurdish-refugees.

McKiernan, K. (2006). *The Kurds: A People in Search of their Homeland.* New York: St. Martin's Press.

Pipher, M. B. (2002). *The Middle of Everywhere: The World's Refugees Come to Our Town.* Orlando, FL: First Harvest and Harcourt Press.

Part III
Documents

Sharafnama

A Persian-language historical work on Kurdish dynasties, composed between 1596 and 1599 by Sharaf Khan Bidlisi (1543–ca. 1600), prince of Bidlis in northern Kurdistan (southeast Turkey).

Author. The author was a scion of the line of Diyadinid/Rojikid princes of Bidlis on his father's side and related to the Turkman Mawsillu clan on his mother's. Born in Karahrud, near Qom, Sharaf al-Din was educated in the royal palace alongside Shah Tahmasb's sons. He rose to prominence in the Safavid state, before losing royal favor during the reign of Ismail II (r. 1576–1577). The Ottoman sultan Murad III (r. 1574–1595) reinstated him as ruler of the principality of Bidlis in 1578. Sharaf Khan was removed from this position in May 1596, shortly after the accession of Mehmed III (r. 1595–1603). This is about the same time he started working on the *Sharafnama*, of which at least five different manuscripts were composed in the years 1596 to 1599. Sharaf Khan then revolted against the Ottomans; he was killed by the troops of Ahmed Khan, Ottoman governor of Van, toward the end of the year 1600 (Dehqan & Genç, 2015a, 2015b).

Contents, style and sources. The book consists of a preface, an introduction on the Kurds (*muqaddima*), four books (*sahifa*) devoted to various Kurdish dynasties, and a work of Ottoman annals as a conclusion (*khatima*). The *Sharafnama*'s style is in line with the prevalent trends in Safavid historiography at the time, adopting the simpler expression and structure of the works of the "school of Qazvin" (Quinn, 2000: 23–24), although the beginnings of chapters are written in a more elaborate prose, reminiscent of the books by Mirkhwand and his grandson Khwandamir. The author's narrative is also interspersed with lively anecdotes relating to the character of the various Kurdish clans and lightly illustrated with verses of poetry and Quranic citations.

Thematics. The *Sharafnama* touches on the three main subgenres of Islamic historical writing: dynastic history, annalistic history, and local history (Meisami, 1999). It has received a lot of attention for its early description of Kurdish identity, which most prominently appears in the introduction, a sort of ethnographic essay. Sharaf Khan is also the first to offer a precise description of the geographical boundaries of Kurdistan, later taken up by Ottoman writers such as Katip Çelebi. In the bulk of the work, Sharaf Khan is mostly concerned with the princely families and tribal clans of Kurdistan. These dynasties evolved in a world of politics, war, and violence in a land on the frontlines of two belligerent empires. Such is the world depicted in the *Sharafnama*: a "treacherous world that lures us with honey, and then feeds us poison" (Véliaminof-Zernof, 1860–1862: I, 187).

Sacha Alsancaklı

Excerpts from Sharafnama

On Sharaf Khan's education in Shah Tahmasp's palace. "It was, indeed, the habit of the late padishah to admit the children of his princes and nobles into his private quarters, caring for them as for the princes of the blood and ranking them among the most dignified lords, ensuring that they would always be properly instructed and taught respect. He encouraged them to learn the Qur'an and to read legal decisions, stimulating their piety and purity and motivating them to favor the company of religious people and those entrusted with virtues. Always diverting them from the discord brought about by the crooked, the seditious, the wicked, the wrecked and the sinners, he enjoined them to serve scholars and men of learning. As soon as they reached the frontier of reason and discernment, he taught them the arts of war, such as the practice of archery, polo and horsemanship, as well as the rules of fencing and the guidelines of civilized and courteous conduct. He told them to also commit from time to time to the art of painting, which develops good taste" (Véliaminof-Zernof, 1860–1862: I, 449–450).

On Sharaf Khan's project and his use of sources. "Since the waiting maids of the bride of discourse and the parrots of the sugar plantations of chronicles new and old had not, at any time or epoch, narrated the story of the rulers of Kurdistan, nor the events that had happened to them, and because they had not written a manuscript compilation to this effect, it came to the feeble mind of this worthless particle, devoid of credit, to take up his pen and write a book narrating, to the best of his capacities, their story and events. He used what he saw in Persian histories and what he heard from trustworthy old men, as well as what he had himself witnessed, in order to commit the information thus produced to pen and ink, in a book called the *Sharafnama* [The book of Sharaf/The book of honor], so that the history of the great dynasties of Kurdistan would not remain hidden under the veil of concealment" (Véliaminof-Zernof, 1860–1862: I, 7–8).

On the Kurds. "The Kurdish people (*ta'ifa*) is made up of four branches (*qism*), whose tongues and manners differ from one another. These are first the Kurmanj, second the Lur, third the Kalhur, and fourth the Guran. (. . .) The majority of this community [the Kurds] is intrepid, bold, liberal and conceited, and the extent of their audacity and bravery, as well as their strong sense of honor and manliness, has led them to bestow upon themselves the names of thieves and roadcutters, courageously risking their lives in such undertakings rather than to extend the hand of mendicity to base and contemptible men for a piece of bread" (Véliaminof-Zernof, 1860–1862: I, 13–14).

On the borders of Kurdistan. "The country (*vilayat*) of Kurdistan starts in Hormuz, on the coast of the Indian Ocean, and from there it follows a straight line to the provinces of Malatya and Mar'ash, where it ends. To the north of this line are the provinces of Fars and Persian Iraq and Azerbaijan and Armenia; to the south, there is Diyarbakir, Mosul and Arabian Iraq. However, Kurdish groups (*shu'bat*) have also reached the farthest extremities of Orient (*vilayat-i mashriq*) and the outer limits of Occident (*diyar-i maghrib*)" (Ibid.).

Source: Véliaminof-Zernof, V. (1860–1862). *Scherefnameh ou Histoire des Kourdes, par Scheref, prince de Bidlis.* St. Petersburg: Imperial Academy of Sciences. Translated by the author.

Further Reading

Alsancaklı, S. (Upcoming). *Le Šarafnāma de Šaraf Xān Bidlīsī. Composition, transmission et réception d'une chronique des dynasties kurdes entre Ottomans et Safavides.* PhD dissertation submitted to Sorbonne nouvelle—Paris 3.

Dehqan, M., & Genç, V. (2015a). "Reflections on Sharaf Khān's Autobiography." *Manuscripta Orientalia*, vol. 21, no. 1, 46–61.

Dehqan, M., & Genç, V. (2015b). "Why Was Sharaf Khān Killed?" *Manuscripta Orientalia*, vol. 21, no. 2, 13–19.

Meisami, J. S. (1999). *Persian Historiography to the End of the Twelfth Century.* Edinburgh, UK: Edinburgh University Press.

Quinn, Sh. A. (2000). *Historical Writing during the Reign of Shah 'Abbas: Ideology, Imitation and Legitimacy in Safavid Chronicles.* Salt Lake City: University of Utah Press.

The Kurdish Shānāma

The *Kurdish Shānāma* (The Book of Kings) [in Kurdish: Şaname, شانامه] also known as *Razm-Name or Jang-Nama* (The Book of Battles), refers to a group of poetic opuses that mainly tell the mythical history of Iran or, in a larger sense, the world from the first king [Kayumart] until the end of the reign of Bahman—the last legendary Kayanid King. According to the legendries, King Bahman was the son of the greatest Zoroastrian hero, Isfandyar, who fought for the spread of Zoroastrianism and was killed by Rustam, the legendary superhero of Iran.

The *Kurdish Shānāma* particularly focuses on the tales of Rustam, the unique superhero and patron of Iran. He belongs to a heroic dynasty, and his father, Zal, was rejected by his father (Sām) while still an infant because of his abnormal skin color. He was then raised and cultivated by the Simorgh, a huge supernatural legendry bird. The *Kurdish Shanama* narratives not only describe the most important events during the Iranian kings' dynasties in their struggles against their enemies, but also depict the heroic battles of Iranian superheroes who endure hardships and fight against Tūrānians (the major Iranian enemies), demons, and strange creatures to defend their homeland, Iran.

The narratives of the *Kurdish Shānāma* seem to rely on an old oral tradition, which includes parts of the old epic and romantic narratives of eastern Iran, known as the Sistani cycle of epics.

Scholars believe that the Kurdish epic narratives significantly differ from the *Sistani Cycle of Epics* and Ferdowsi's *Shāhnāma* in form, language, and narrative structure of the stories. Thus, they should be regarded independently from other orally transmitted Iranian epics. These narratives were probably written down in the 16th century CE for the first time.

The Iranian epic narratives have often been individually produced and transformed, each with its own specific booklet (e.g. *Barzū-nāma*, *Faramrz-nāma*, *Rostam and Sohrāb*, *Rostam and Isfandiyār*). Each of these books talks about the adventure of its own hero, and although the fictional space and bilateral system of the battle between Iran and Tūrān, or "good and evil," is similar in all, there is no continuous storyline to link those books together.

The first poet or poets of the *Kurdish Shānāma* are unknown. Locals believe that *Shānāme* comes from a tradition called *rāz* (secret). Due to this secret tradition, the early poet or poets of the narratives remained anonymous to the public.

In recent decades, however, diverse versions of the booklets of *Shānāma*, containing more than 50 titles and more than 60,000 verses have been discovered. All narratives are serious poetic compositions. Some stories, such as *Haft-Lashkar* (the Severn Armies) and *Razm-i Iran-u Tûran* (the Battle of Iran and Tūrān), are longer than others, with more than 5,000 verses.

The language of the stories and the booklets of the *Kurdish Shānāma* is Gurānī, which is said to have been a Kurdish literary language. The poetic form of *Shānāma* typically consists of rhyming distiches, following the rhyme scheme a, bb, cc, etc. Unlike Arabic and Persian poetry, which follow the quantitative metrical system, Gurānī normally has a syllabic meter containing 5 + 5 syllables per hemistich.

The *Kurdish Shānāma* narratives exhibit a unique West Iranian characteristic of myths and legends; therefore, it must be considered independent from other Iranian epics. These narratives have been transmitted orally from generation to generation for centuries in the Zagros area.

Behrooz Chaman Ara

Two sample texts of the *Kurdish Shahnama* from the *Book of Shaghad and Rustam*:

1)
bišnaw ja dawrān, čarx-i čapī-gard
ža baxt-i řustam, či nardê āward

Listen to the adverse turning of the heavens
what chances Rostam had in this
backgammon

zamāna-ŷ zabūn-i makr-i hīlagar
zīnat-i majłis-i šāhān batał-kar

the dreadful and deceitful sphere
that ruins the stately court of the kings

nijūm-i afsūn-i řamął-i axtar
nayāmad ža baxt-i zął-i zař āward

portentous stars and fateful planets
bestowed bad luck and evil fortune on Rostam

2)
zął wāt aŷ farzand, tū čêš mazānī
Pūsa ba taqdīr-i amr-i sobḥānī

Zal said, oh son! you know nothing
About the Will of Almighty God?

hakākān-i dawr, mardān-i 'āqił
kas kār-i taqdīr, nakardan bātił

Whether ancient storytellers or wise men
nobody can override the will of destiny

Source: Chaman Ara, B. (2016). *The Kurdish Shanama and Its Literary and Religious Implications*. Charleston, SC: CreateSpace, pp. 66–67. Reprinted with permission of the author.

Further Reading

Chaman Ara, B. (2016). *The Kurdish Shahnama and Its Literary and Religious Implications*. Charleston, SC: CreateSpace.

Ferdowsi, A. (2016). *Shahnameh: The Persian Book of Kings*. New York: Penguin.

Mem and Zin

The story of Mem and Zin, a Romeo and Juliet–like adaptation, is considered the Kurdish national epos. Written in 1692 by Ehmed Khani (1651–1707), the story is based on the ancient oral tradition of Meme Alan, which can be traced back to pre-Christian times in Iran. Khani adapted the folklore text in line with the Islamic tradition and Persian love epics. The book is written in classical Kurdish with many Persian and Arabic inclusions and references. He wanted to prove that the Kurds were not uncivilized, bloodthirsty tribes, but also have a literary tradition that produces high-standard works:

"So that people will not say that the Kurds
have no knowledge and have no history;
that all sorts of peoples have their books
and only the Kurds are negligible."

It was first published in the first Kurdish newspaper Kurdistan (issue no. 2, 1919 and following issues). Today it is regarded as one of the most important works of classical Kurdish literature. The work is composed of a 5,400-line narrative rendered in couplets.

The plot follows a tragic love story between Mem and Zin in the tradition of other oral masterpieces such as Kalila wa Dimna by Ibn al-Muqaffa or Yusuf and Zulaykha by Nizami. The Kurdish Bey of Botan, Zeynidin, had two beautiful sisters, Siti and Zin. A young Kurdish man, Mem, from a different tribe, fell in love with Zin during the festivities of Newroz, the Kurdish New Year. Bekir (also Beko) from the house of Botan tried to stop this love affair and eventually kills Mem. Upon hearing of Mem's death, Zin dies from grief. They were buried next to each other, with Bekir buried at their feet after he was killed in revenge by Mem's friend Tajdin.

In his work, Khani furthermore transmitted allegorical aspects of his mystic beliefs as a Sufi. It also contains a strong message about the Kurdish identity and a potential Kurdish state. In the preface, he laments the Kurdish suppression by their neighbors and lack of unity among them, which contributes to the absence of a Kurdish state.

> If only there were unity among us,
> and we would obey one another,
> then all of the Ottomans and Arabs and Iranians would become our servants,
> we would reach perfection in religion and politics,
>   and we would become productive in knowledge and wisdom.

Kurdish nationalists have declared Khani their champion in order to demonstrate a 300-year-long history of Kurdish national struggles. For them, Mem represents the Kurdish people, while Zin symbolizes the Kurdish land. Only when the two overcome the separation will Kurdistan be united.

Ehmed Khani's version is arguably the most popular, although the French orientalist Roger Lescot published a longer version in 1942 under the title *Meme Alan* that is based on oral traditions recited by Kurdish bards, *dengbej*, from Syria. Today, the city of Cizre, where the plot originally took place, opened a Mem and Zin mausoleum that became a major tourist attraction.

In 1992, the story was adapted for a film by director Umit Elci. Because of the prohibition on the use of Kurdish, it was first recorded in Turkish and later dubbed into Kurdish.

Sebastian Maisel

Excerpts from Ehmed Khani's text:

Mem's Ode to the Tigris River (from Mirawdeli)

O river so spontaneous as my tears
Restless and anxious the lover's way.
Are you impatient, agitated, never having a break
Or are you crazy just like me?
Why are you so restless?
It seems that there is a lover inside your heart.
What thoughts and fancies to you have every minute?
You are so astray in the valleys of Jezire.
If this city is your lover
Then your heart's wish has come true.
Your lover is inside your heart.
Right and left, you have put her in your arms.
But still you do not consider God's generosity towards you.
You do not pray thousand times a day thanking Him.
Tell me, why do you moan and groan so much?
What more do you wish to achieve?
Why do you cry aimlessly?
You migrate toward the exile in Baghdad . . .
. . . I am a dervish who lost his angel.
I am a Tigris abandoned by my boat.

Zin's Funeral (from Spotteswoode)

. . . At the funeral, at which not only the Mir and his sister, but all the principle people and all the population of Jezira were present, Zin told her brother that she should not survive the death of her lover.

"And now," she added, "that I am at the brink of the grave, I bear witness that our love was pure and blameless: You have done Mem a great wrong. But grant me, as my last request, three things. First, institute a festival on the day of my death, as you have done on the day of my sister's marriage, and let all the people take part in it. Secondly, that all the people of our city follow my funeral. Thirdly, that my body may be laid near to Mem's; and, at the moment when I am let down, say these words aloud: 'With full consent I give Zin to Mem'." The next day Zin died, and the testimony for which she asked was granted . . .

Sources: Mirawdeli, K. (2012). *Love and Existence: Analytical Study of Ahmadi Khani's Tragedy of Mem u Zin*. Bloomington, IN: Author House.

Spotteswoode, W. (1863). "Sketch of the Tribes of Northern Kurdistan." *Transactions of the Ethnological Society of London*, pp. 244–248. Translated by the author.

Further Reading

Chyet, M. (1991). *And a Thronbush Sprang Up Between Them—Studies on Mem u Zin, a Kurdish Romance*. PhD thesis submitted to University of California, Berkeley.
Van Bruinessen, M. (2003). "Ehmedî Xanî's Mem û Zîn and Its Role in the Emergence of Kurdish Nationalism." In A. Vali (Ed.), *Essays on the Origins of Kurdish Nationalism* (pp. 40–57). Costa Mesa, CA: Mazda Publishers.

Report by the British Consul on the Sheikh Ubeydullah Revolt in 1880–1881

In the month of October in 1880, Sheikh Ubeydullah, a Naqshibandi sufi sheikh from the Nehri region of the Hakkari province in the Ottoman Kurdistan region, gathered tens of thousands of armed men from among the Ottoman and Iranian Kurds and seized several cities in the northwest of Iran. The Iranian army marched on the occupied regions after a short while and silenced the rebellion. Iran's response involved great violence against the Kurdish tribes and villages. As a consequence, thousands of families were displaced.

Historians attribute several reasons for the rebellion by the Kurds: a Pan-Islamic agenda of the empire, growing dissention between the Shi'a and the Sunni population, the rise of nationalism among the non-Muslim minorities, and the activities of Christian missionaries in the region. Historians disagree over whether Sheikh Ubeydullah revolted due to nationalist sentiments or sectarian motives. Whether there was a sense of a common identity among the Kurds or not, most scholars consider the uprising the beginning of Kurdish nationalism. Official correspondence of various states and memoirs of missionaries in the region indicate that Sheikh Ubeydullah had projected a form of self-governance and autonomy under the banner of caliphate. Thus, his conversation with the British consul in Tabriz, William Abbot, in the aftermath of the revolt gives clues about the sheikh and his motives.

Metin Atmaca

Report from William Abbot

Tabreez, 1 October, 1881
I mentioned in my Dispatch No.27 of last year, which I had the honor to address to your Lordship that on quitting Oroomiah [Urmiya] I had an interview with the Sheikh Obeidullah [Ubeydullah]. Considerable interest appears to attach to that Kurdish chief who is now at Constantinople. I have therefore thought that a brief account of the conversation I had with him as well as a description of his person and character may prove interesting to her Majesty's government . . . He speaks Turkish and Persian fluently but with a Kurdish accent, and has a considerable knowledge of Arabic . . .

I had heard so much about him, but never anticipated that it would fall to my lot to be in personal relations with him. I appreciated the kindness and courtesy he had shown me and thanked him for the readiness with which he had listened to my representation on behalf of Christian and Mussulman non-combatants as well as for restoring property, which his troops plundered from Nestorian villages. I then asked the Sheikh what his programme was. He replied that he wished to reorganize Kurdistan. I enquired how he intended doing this, adding that he was neither justified in making war upon Persia nor raising a rebellion in Turkey, to attain his object. He then observed that he had been badly treated by both these powers. The Porte not has given him credit for good intentions. Kurdistan required to be ruled with an iron hand. No one understands its requirements better than he did. There remarked the Sheikh that he was treading on delicate ground. Did he imply that his object was to form Kurdistan into a separate Principality, independent of the Porte or merely to weld together its rude component elements, reduce order out of chaos and became the responsible head of Kurdish nation answerable to the Sultan for their good conduct as well as for the collection of the taxes? To this the Sheikh replied that nobody ever doubted his loyalty to the Sultan, but that he had a very poor opinion of the Pashas. He felt that the moment had arrived when something ought to be done for Kurdistan. He loved his countrymen. They were sorely in need of reforms. It was true that they were uneducated, undisciplined, addicted to brigandage and altogether in a most barbarous condition. He was anxious to remedy these evils and place his people in the position to which human beings they were entitled. The Kurds in Persia had been shamefully treated. Exaction, oppression, cruelty, violence, lust, every species of wrong, these had been the prevailing characteristics of Persian rule in Kurdistan. Persia had done nothing to conciliate her tribal subjects. She had irrevocably alienated them . . .

Knowing the deep interest which HM's government take in the welfare of the Armenians and that it would be of small importance if a better understanding could be brought about between them and the Kurds in whose midst they live, -it appeared an opportune moment to report to your Lordship the statements made to me by the Sheikh. I cannot say how far his professions may be sincere or otherwise. Opportunities occur whilst he is at Constantinople, of testing his sincerity and above all his loyalty to the Sultan. Even if there were doubts on this latter point, it must be remembered that his religious and political influence throughout Kurdistan are very great. His majesty would probably exercise a sounder discretion by watching his movements and ascertaining his future plans than by treating him with harshness. He has been removed from frontier of Persia and it would be desirable to prevent his exercising in future any influence calculated to disrupt the peace of the Shah's dominions. But the Porte might have restrained him at the outset of his career if they had chosen to do so, and it would be difficult to understand upon what principles of justice or fair dealing he could now be visited with punishment . . .

William Abbot

Source: The British National Archives, Foreign Office (FO) 60/441.

Further Reading

Ateş, S. (2014). "In the Name of the Caliph and the Nation: The Sheikh Ubeidullah Rebellion of 1880–81." *Iranian Studies,* vol. 47, no. 5, 735–798.

McDowall, D. (2004). *A Modern History of the Kurds* (pp. 53–59). London: I. B. Tauris.

Olson, R. (2013). *The Emergence of Kurdish Nationalism and the Sheikh Said Rebellion, 1880–1925* Austin: University of Texas Press.

Soleimani, K. (2016). "Islamic Revivalism and Kurdish Nationalism in Sheikh Ubeydullah's Poetic Oeuvre." *Kurdish Studies,* vol. 4, no. 1, 5–24.

Sureya, Jaladet, and Kamuran Bedirkhan

Grandsons of Bedir Khan (1806–1869), the last emir of the Bohtan Principality in Ottoman Kurdistan. Their father, Amin Âli (1851–1926), was an Ottoman bureaucrat and a prominent figure of late-Ottoman-era Kurdish activism. Ahmed Sureya (1883–1938) and his half-brothers, Jaladet Âli (1893–1951) and Kamuran Âli (1895–1978), were born and raised in the Ottoman imperial capital, Istanbul. They studied in the European-style *Mekteb-i Sultânî* (Galatasaray High School) in Istanbul. Later, Sureya studied agricultural economics at Istanbul University. He was employed as an Ottoman subdistrict officer. Jaladet attended the Ottoman military academy and studied law at Istanbul University. Kamuran, too, studied law at the same university. In 1906, they had to leave Istanbul when the Ottoman Sultan Abdulhamid II exiled the whole family after two prominent Bedirkhanis were involved in the assassination of Ridvan Pasha, prefect of Istanbul. They were able to return to Istanbul after the 1908 Young Turk Revolution. Sureya resumed the publication of the Ottoman-Kurdish newspaper, *Kürdistan*, in Istanbul (1908–1909). His involvement in the opposition party, Entente Liberale, however, forced him to leave Istanbul again. Sureya published *Kürdistan* in Cairo (1917–1918). Jaladet and Kamuran fought in the Balkan Wars (1912–1913) as Ottoman officers. Jaladet served in the Ottoman army in the Caucasian front during World War I (1914–1918). However, the Ottoman Empire's defeat by the Allied powers and the prospect of Kurds' self-determination turned the Bedirkhan brothers into advocates of Kurdish independence. After the armistice, Sureya established the Committee of Kurdish Independence in Cairo. In 1919, he sent a petition to the British prime minister to reclaim his grandfather's territories in Kurdistan, which had been confiscated by the Ottoman government in 1847. Jaladet and Kamuran accompanied the British Major Noel during his Kurdistan mission in 1919. The rise of the Kemalist movement in Anatolia, the War of Independence, and, eventually, the foundation of the Turkish Republic in 1923 caused the failure of the Bedirkhan brothers' activities. Jaladet and Kamuran moved to Germany where they stayed between 1922 and 1925 and pursued their graduate degrees in law. They were among the Kurdish leaders gathered in Syria and Lebanon under the French Mandate after the failure of the 1925 Sheikh Said Rebellion in Turkey. Jaladet became the first president of the Kurdish National League Khoybun, which was founded in Beirut in 1927, and spearheaded the Ararat Rebellion against Turkey (1928–1930). Sureya traveled to the United States in 1928 to represent the Kurdish movement. He died in Paris in 1938. After the failure of the Ararat Rebellion, Jaladet in Damascus and Kamuran in Beirut dedicated themselves to a cultural renaissance movement for Kurds in Syria and Turkey. They published periodicals in Kurmanji Kurdish and French until the end of the French Mandate in 1946. Jaladet died in 1951 near Damascus. Kamuran also undertook Radio du Levant's Kurdish-language broadcasting in Beirut. In 1947, Kamuran moved to Paris to teach Kurdish at the Institute of the Oriental Languages. In Paris, he also established *Centre d'Etudes Kurdes* and relentlessly worked as a self-appointed ambassador for the Kurdish cause. He assumed the role of representing the famous Iraqi Kurdish leader Mullah Mustafa Barzani in the 1960s and 1970s. Kamuran died in Paris in 1978.

After the consolidation of the Kemalist Republic in Turkey, one of the main tasks of the Bedirkhan brothers was to confront the new Turkish states' denial of Kurdish identity and policy of assimilating Kurds into Turkishness. Following is an excerpt from Jaladet Bedirkhan's 1933 open letter to the president of Turkey, Mustafa Kemal (later Atatürk). In the short selection, Jaladet informs Mustafa Kemal about the ancient history of Kurds and Kurdistan in a partly sarcastic tone.

Ahmet S. Aktürk

Excerpt from Jaladet Bedirkhan's Letter to Mustafa Kemal

[. . .] *Your Excellency* [Mustafa Kemal] *Pasha, I do not know why up to now you couldn't explicitly confess the existence of a Kurdistan question in Turkey despite your well-known courage and bravery* [. . . .] *I said "explicitly" because you always confess the existence of such a question without referring to it, and you give it an important place in your internal and external policies.* [. . .]

Yet, I, too, should confess that Kurdistan is a very old historical concept and [thus] *the question of Kurdistan started neither during the time of your rule nor that of the Committee of Union and Progress* [1908–1918] *whose policies you have inherited.*

Reminding of Poland's old situation, my homeland Kurdistan, divided among several states today, [and] *my nation, Kurds, have an old history, known territory, and social organization.*

There is no need to go back to the origins of the Medes [whom Kurdish nationalists claim to be the ancestors of the Kurds]. *It would be sufficient to start with Xenophon's Cyropaedia. However, I do not think it is necessary to explain this point. Your recent preoccupation with history, especially your close interest in the issue of Aryan* [race], *and for some reason your efforts to detach Turks from their well-known Mongolic origins and to affiliate them with Aryan race should have made your Highness completely knowledgeable about Kurds and Kurdistan.*

Thus, the question of Kurdistan started neither during the time of your rule nor that of your predecessors [the Committee of Union and Progress]. *The question of Kurdistan in Turkey existed since the Kurdish emirs pledged allegiance to a Sunni Sultan, Selim I* [in the early 16th century], *through the agency of Idris Bidlisi* [. . .]

Source: Âli Bedirkhan, J. (1933). *Mektub: Türkiye Reisi Cumhuru Gazi Mustafa Kemal Paşa Hazretlerine* (pp. 39–40). Damascus: Hawar Press.

Further Reading

Blau, J. (2000). "Mémoires de l'émir Kamuran Bedir-Khan." *Etudes Kurdes*, vol. 1, 73–90.

Bozarslan, H. (2003). "Some Remarks on the Kurdish Historiographical Discourse in Turkey (1919–1980)." In A. Vali (Ed.), *Essays on the Origins of Kurdish Nationalism* (pp. 14–39). Costa Mesa, CA: Mazda Publishers.

Civil Commissioner's Office. (1919). *Personalities in Kurdistan*. Baghdad: The Government Press.

Jwaideh, W. (2006). *The Kurdish National Movement: Its Origins and Development*. Syracuse, NY: Syracuse University Press.

Malmîsanij. (2000). *Cizira Botanlı Bedirhaniler ve Bedirhani Ailesi Derneği'nin Tutanaklari*. Istanbul: Avesta.

McDowall, D. (2004). *A Modern History of the Kurds*. London: I. B. Tauris.

Nikitine, B. (1979). "Badrkhani Thurayya (1883–1938) and Djaladet (1893–1951)." In *Encyclopedia of Islam*. New Edition. Volume I, 871. Leiden: E. J. Brill.

Noel, E. W. C. (1920). *Diary of Major Noel on Special Duty in Kurdistan*. Baghdad: Government Press.

Özoğlu, H. (2004). *Kurdish Notables and the Ottoman State: Evolving Identities, Competing Loyalties, and Shifting Boundaries*. Albany: State University of New York Press.

Reş, K. (1997). *Celadet Bedirxan, Jiyan û Ramanên Wî*. Stockholm: Jîna Nû Press.

Strohmeier, M. (2003). *Crucial Images in the Presentation of a Kurdish National Identity: Heroes and Patriots, Traitors and Foes*. Leiden: Brill.

Van Bruinessen, M. (1978). *Agha, Shaikh and State: On the Social and Political Organization of Kurdistan*. Utrecht: Rijksuniversiteit.

Treaty of Sèvres, August 10, 1920

After World War I ended in 1918, a peace conference was held in Paris, and afterwards a series of treaties were signed between the defeating main Allied Powers (British Empire, France, Italy, and Japan) and defeated Central Powers (Germany, Austria-Hungary, Kingdom of Bulgaria, and Turkey). The Treaty of Sèvres was signed between the Allied Powers and Turkey on August 10, 1920, in an exhibition room of a porcelain factory, which serves today as the National Museum of Ceramic in Sèvres near Paris.

The treaty meant the partition of the Ottoman Empire among several successive states created and mandated by the Allied Powers, such as the British Mandate of Palestine and Iraq and the French Mandate of Syria and Lebanon. Besides these states, independent Armenian and Kurdish states were envisaged. Because of disagreement among the powers, the negotiations took more than 15 months. Since the terms of Sèvres were severe and caused Turkey to lose most of its territories, it had created a strong backlash among the Turkish national movement, which was secretly organized under the leadership of Mustafa Kemal Pasha in Anatolia and eventually paved the way for the War of Independence. After the Kemalists succeeded in gaining back most of the lands in Anatolia, they disbanded the government in Istanbul, considered the Treaty of Sèvres obsolete, and finally signed the follow-up treaty of Lausanne in 1923, which disregarded all rights claimed by the Armenians and the Kurds.

During the long period of the Paris Peace Conference, the Kurdish delegate, which was led by Sherif Pasha, split into several fractions, and it was finally dissolved before the treaty was signed. Some disputed the legitimacy of the delegate's leadership, while some other delegates found the borders of future Kurdistan unrealistic and claimed more territories. In the end, the Allied Powers recognized the rights of the Kurds and specified this in Articles 62, 63, and 64 of the treaty.

Metin Atmaca

Section III of the Treaty of Sèvres
Kurdistan
Article 62

A Commission sitting at Constantinople and composed of three members appointed by the British, French and Italian Governments respectively shall draft within six months from the coming into force of the present Treaty a scheme of local autonomy for the predominantly Kurdish areas lying east of the Euphrates, south of the southern boundary of Armenia as it may be hereafter determined, and north of the frontier of Turkey with Syria and Mesopotamia, as defined in Article 27, II (2) and (3). If unanimity cannot be secured on any question, it will be referred by the members of the Commission to their respective Governments. The scheme shall contain full safeguards for the protection of the Assyro-Chaldeans and other racial or religious minorities within these areas, and with this object a Commission composed of British, French, Italian, Persian and Kurdish representatives shall visit the spot to examine and decide what rectifications, if any, should be made in the Turkish frontier where, under the provisions of the present Treaty, that frontier coincides with that of Persia.

Article 63

The Turkish Government hereby agrees to accept and execute the decisions of both the Commissions mentioned in Article 62 within three months from their communication to the said Government.

Article 64

If within one year from the coming into force of the present Treaty the Kurdish peoples within the areas defined in Article 62 shall address themselves to the Council of the League of Nations in such a manner as to show that a majority of the population of these areas desires independence from Turkey, and if the Council then considers that these peoples are capable of such independence and recommends that it should be granted to them, Turkey hereby agrees to execute such a recommendation, and to renounce all rights and title over these areas.

The detailed provisions for such renunciation will form the subject of a separate agreement between the Principal Allied Powers and Turkey. If and when such renunciation takes place, no objection will be raised by the Principal Allied Powers to the voluntary adhesion to such an independent Kurdish State of the Kurds inhabiting that part of Kurdistan which has hitherto been included in the Mosul vilayet.

Source: Martin, L. (Ed.). (1924). *The Treaties of Peace, 1919–1923, Volume II* (pp. 807–808). New York: Carnegie Endowment for International Peace, 1924.

Further Reading

Ahmad, K. M. (1994). *Kurdistan during the First World War* (pp. 198–205). London: Saqi Books.

Jwaideh, W. (2006). *The Kurdish National Movement: Its Origins and Development* (pp. 131–132, 186–188). Syracuse, NY: Syracuse University Press.

McDowall, D. (2004). *A Modern History of the Kurds* (pp. 131–137). London: I. B. Tauris.

Nikitin, B. (1975). *Les Kurdes: Étude sociologique et historique.* Paris: Éditions d'Aujourd 'hui.

Safrasian, A. (1948). *Kurds and Kurdistan* (pp. 77–78). London: Harvill Press.

Sherif Pasha's "Memorandum on the Claims of the Kurd People" to the Conference of Peace in Paris on February 6, 1919

Sherif Pasha (Şerif Paşa), who was born in Istanbul in 1865 to a noble Kurdish family, went through a French-style education, first in the prestigious Galatasaray Mekteb-i Sultani in Istanbul, Turkey, and later at Saint-Cyr Military School in Paris, France. Since his father, Said Pasha, served as the minister of foreign affairs during Sultan Abdulhamid II (1876–1909), Sherif Pasha also chose to work in the bureaucracy, respectively, as an aide-de-camp in the palace, military attaché in Paris, and finally as the Ottoman ambassador to Stockholm. He secretly supported the Committee of Progress and Union (CUP), which deposed Abdulhamid II in 1909. A few months after the change of regime, Sherif decided not to participate in the CUP government because of the dominancy of a certain group with authoritarian and Turkish nationalist leanings in the CUP and finally departed for Paris, which was going to be the permanent place for his exile. He established the Ottoman Liberal Party and financed the oppositional groups in Europe. As part of this opposition, he established a monthly journal named *Mècheroutiette* (*The Constitutional*) and had several political dissents write articles for it in French and Turkish. Once the Ottomans were defeated as part of the Central Powers in World War I, the Allied Powers organized a Peace Conference in Paris in 1919 in order to decide the fate of the post-Ottoman nations, such as Turks, Armenians, Kurds, and Arabs. Besides the representation of them by the European powers, several ethnic groups decided to have a delegate represent them. Led by Sayyid Abdulkadir of Nehri, the Kürdistan Teali Cemiyeti (The Society for the Advancement of Kurdistan) chose Sherif Pasha as the head of their delegation. On August 10, 1920, the Treaty of Sèvres was signed, and Turkey agreed to give independence to several minorities, including the Kurds.

Following is an extract of a letter written by Sherif Pasha to the Allied Powers, especially to the United Kingdom, and the conference committee. The letter was later elaborated with more supporting arguments and published with the title of *Memorandum on the Claims of the Kurd People*. The letter, which Sherif Pasha wrote in French and English, argues that a state for the Kurds will stabilize the region, secure the rights of the Kurds, and create a buffer zone against the threat of Bolshevik Russia. He suggests that the Kurds have the will and the majority in the region proposed in order to form a separate state.

Metin Atmaca

Excerpt from Letter Written by Sherif Pasha to the Allied Powers

Seeing that the Armenian affairs are shortly to be discussed before the Peace Conference; and that the Kurdish interests have no other qualified defender at Paris than myself . . . I think it (is) my duty to bring forward before the High Interallied Assembly the national claims of my race. This race forms not only the greatest majority in the regions inhabited by the Armenians, but the homogeneity of which still more gives it the right of asking for a most minute examination with respect to it . . .

If in the course of the Peace Conference a political independence were accorded, the Armenians and Arabs of Turkey, it would be natural and just for the Allies to take into serious consideration the homogenous agglomeration constituting the principle of nationalities that is invoked in a feeling of justice, and which is incontestable the principle of nationalities that is invoked in a feeling of justice, and which proves a long foreseeing policy of President Wilson, gives the Kurds the hope of their national interest being safeguarded in the name of this same principle of that justice and peace which is to come. There can, therefore, be no doubt of there being question, during the Peace Conference, of political autonomy for Kurdistan any more at least than those for Armenia and Arabia.

If it be desired to be able to apply the principle of nationalities useful to bring out in relief the vital conditions which require the setting up of a Kurdish State which will be found to be a natural neighbor. A "luminaire" (preliminary) observation is necessary . . .

Were the Kurdish people deprived of its sources of wealth, it would, by fate, be forced to seek compensation in the border countries, giving itself up to "razzias" (raids) to the greatest detriment of the neighboring states.

Of all the peoples of Asia, the Kurds are the one that might form a buffer state of the first water to bar the path of the bolshevist current, for it should be noted that the Armenians are seriously contaminated by these dangerous ideas and that by reason of antagonism between their political parties and the rivalries among their revolutionary committees they will never be in a state to offer the same safeguards and guarantees to their neighbors . . .

So that a Kurdistan may be viable and consecrate itself to its economic development, adopt modern civilization and abandon nomadic life it should be formed out of the vilayets (provinces) of Darbékirè, Kharpout, Bitlis, Mossul, and of Sanjak of Ourfa.

Is there a frontier so natural as river or even a water course and mountains? It would be necessary, if the worst come to accord to Kurdistan a very definite frontier line, comprising all the mountains where the Kurds have their summer pasturages, and a borderline extending over a score of kilometers from Kochlikan, Kalé-Korant, on the river Zey, Back-Kalé, Vostan, Kindrants, Akhlad, rejoining the Murad Sou at Cop, and thence, following the Eastern Euphrates, the Mourad Tchai and the real Euphrates, taking in into Kurdistan the left bank of these rivers as far as Hana, and reaching in a straight line Tekrit where Saladin the glory of Turkistan was born, and the South of the Persian by following Djebahamerin and Adalia between Kifrim and Kanikin . . .

In the valleys where they are grouped in compact tribes, notably in the basin of the great Zab, then the Kurds constitute a nationality powerful enough to have the ambition in the face of Turks and Persians of forming a distinct state . . .

Moreover, an international commission should be charged with the work of tracing out the demarcation of its frontier according to the principle of nationalities so as to include in Kurdistan all the lands where Kurds are in the majority.

To this end, one might proceed by means of a popular vote under control of this commission, which we are certain, would end up in the same conclusion as the French Minister for Foreign Affairs, who at the "Chambre des Députés", Nov. 3rd 1895 said "in the Turkish Provinces that alone, are under discussion at the present time, according to the statistics we have in hands the Armenian population represent certainly but a proportion of more than 13% of the inhabitants. In the vilayet of Asia, their distribution is besides very unevenly carried out, sometimes denser, sometimes more scattered. In a word, we do not discern in these provinces a point where this unhappy population is really in a majority and where it might form a center knot around which the constitution of a certain autonomy might be carried out."

The official testimony as well as the principle of nationalities hold out to us the hope of the legitimate claims the Kurdish race being thoroughly and impartially examined and fair solution being arrived at with regard to them.

Paris, February 6, 1919
General Cherif Pacha

Source: The British National Archives, Foreign Office (FO) 608/95. Reprinted in Destani, B. (2006). *Minorities in the Middle East 4 Volume Set: Kurdish Communities 1918–1974, Vol. 1* (pp. 34–38). Cambridge, UK: Cambridge Archive Editions Limited.

Further Reading

Alakom, R. (1998). *Şerif Paşa: Bir Kürt Diplomatının Fırtınalı Yılları*. İstanbul: Avesta Publishers.

Eppel, M. (2016). *A People without a State: The Kurds from the Rise of Islam to the Dawn of Nationalism* (pp. 115–130). Austin: University of Texas Press.

Göldaş, I. (1991). *Kürdistan Teâli Cemiyeti* (pp. 257–262, 268). İstanbul: Doz Yayınları.

Özoğlu, H. (2012). *Kurdish Notables and the Ottoman State: Evolving Identities, Competing Loyalties, and Shifting Boundaries* (pp. 110–113). Albany: SUNY Press.

Yıldız, H. (1992). *Fransız Belgeleriyle Sevr-Lozan-Musul Üçgeninde Kürdistan* (pp. 197–204). Istanbul: Koral Publishers.

Khoybun (also known as Hoybun and Hoyboon)

A Kurdish nationalist organization founded in Bihamdun, Lebanon in 1927. Khoybun ("Be Oneself") was an heir to the previous associations aiming at Kurdish independence following the defeat of the Ottoman Empire in World War I and its eventual demise. After the failure of the 1925 Sheikh Said Rebellion against the new Turkish Republic, Syria and Lebanon under the French Mandate became centers of Kurdish exiles from Turkey. Khoybun brought together Kurdish gentlemen from various social, economic, and ideological backgrounds, including former Ottoman officers, members of the Kurdish princely families, urban notables, tribal chiefs, and religious leaders. The primary objective of Khoybun was to liberate Kurdish territories from Kemalist Turkey. Khoybun took steps to collaborate with other opponents of the Kemalist regime, most notably with the Armenian Dashnak Party. Khoybun had branches in Syria, Lebanon, Turkey, Iraq, France, the United States, and England. The Turkish Republic closely followed Khoybun members' activities along the Turkish-Syrian border and informed the French mandate authorities. To expose Kemalist Turkey's ill treatment of its Kurdish citizens and to garner support from the international community, Khoybun published anti-Kemalist propaganda pamphlets in English, French, and Turkish. Khoybun organized the Ararat Rebellion (1928–1930) under the leadership of former Ottoman officer Ihsan Nuri Pasha. The rebels created an "independent government" with its flag on the Ararat Mountain. Taking place along the Turkish-Iranian border, the Turkish forces were able to contain the rebellion only with the cooperation of the Iranian authorities. The suppression of the Ararat rebellion and tensions among some leading members of Khoybun, particularly the Bedirkhan and Jamilpashazade families, weakened the organization. Khoybun, however, continued to exist until the end of World War II. Western powers took Khoybun into consideration vis-à-vis their regional policies. To repair its image damaged by internal divisions, Khoybun was renamed in 1945. Khoybun's leadership paid a visit to the short-lived Kurdish Mahabad Republic in northwestern Iran in 1946. Khoybun was dissolved after the end of the French mandate. However, Kurdish activism in Syria persisted partly under the influence of Mullah Mustafa Barzani's Kurdistan Democrat Party in Iraq.

Following is an excerpt from *The Case of Kurdistan Against Turkey* prepared by Sureya Bedirkhan, who traveled to the United States to represent Khoybun. It was published "by authority of Hoyboon, Supreme Council of the Kurdish Government" in Philadelphia, Pennsylvania, in 1928 when the Ararat Rebellion was in full swing in Turkey.

Ahmet S. Aktürk

Excerpt from The Case of Kurdistan Against Turkey

Kurds Demand an International Inquiry

In the name of the Kurdish People, and of civilization, The Hoyboon, the Government of Kurdistan, invites the Governments of the United States, Great Britain, France, Italy, indeed, all the civilized governments, to take the initiative to create an International Commission, which shall investigate the campaign of atrocities, which Kemalist Turkey has been perpetrating in Kurdistan since 1925. The findings of the Commission could well determine the merits of the Kurdish case. As those of the professions and pretensions of the so-called Kemalist republic.

Kurdistan Proclaims Her Independence

In October 1927, Kurdish leaders of diverse political faiths and affiliations, met in Convention, without Kurdistan, to elaborate a National Pact, and to take necessary steps to realize their national aims. This convention unanimously (a) created The Hoyboon, the supreme national organ, or the Kurdish government, and, (b) clothed that Government with full and exclusive national and international powers.

The Hoyboon, thereupon, proclaimed, on October 28, 1927, the independence of Kurdistan, as laid down in the Sèvres Treaty; designated Kurd Ava [a village near the Mount Ararat], at Egri Dagh, as the provincial capital of Kurdistan, and, by resolution, expressed the friendly sentiments of the Kurdish people for Persia, Armenia, Iraq, and Syria, and their determination to wage relentless war against the Turks-until they had abandoned, in perpetuity, the Kurdish soil, now under their grip.

The war between Turk and Kurd is going on- and will go on-until the objective of the Kurds has been attained.

Kurdish-Armenian Relations

The first task of the Hoyboon, following its creation, was an effort toward a final reconciliation, and, if possible, cooperation, with the Armenians.

I write upon Kurdish-Armenian relations with a mingled feeling of regret-and of gratitude. That, through the sinister influence of the Turk and the ignorance of the Kurd, the Armenian, in certain localities and at certain periods, has suffered, is a cause of deep regret. That we have already buried the past is cause for congratulation and gratitude.

Source: Khan, S. B. (1928). *The Case of Kurdistan Against Turkey* (pp. 53–55). Philadelphia: Authority of Hoyboon, Supreme Council of the Kurdish Government.

Further Reading

Alakom, R. (2011). *Hoybun Örgütü ve Ağrı Ayaklanması*. Istanbul: Avesta.

Fuccaro, N. (2003). "Kurds and Kurdish Nationalism in Mandatory Syria: Politics, Culture and Identity." In A. Vali (Ed.), *Essays on the Origins of Kurdish Nationalism* (pp. 191–217). Costa Mesa, CA: Mazda Publishers.

Jamilpasha, A. (1992). *Muhtasar Hayatım: Kemalizme Karşı Kürt Aydınının Mücadelesinden Bir Yaprak*. Ankara: Beybun.

Jegerkhwin. (2003). *Hayat Hikayem*. Translated by Gazi Fincan. Istanbul: Evrensel.

Jwaideh, W. (2006). *The Kurdish National Movement: Its Origins and Development.* Syracuse, NY: Syracuse University Press.

McDowall, D. (2004). *A Modern History of the Kurds.* London: I. B. Tauris.

Silopi, Z. (Qadri Jamilpasha). (1969). *Doza Kürdüstan: Kürt Milletinin 60 Seneden Beri Esaretten Kurtulus Savasi Hatirati.* Beirut: Stewr.

Tejel, J. (Ed.) (2007). *La Ligue Nationale Kurde Khoyboun Mythes et Réalités de la Première Organisation Nationaliste Kurde.* Paris: Fondation-Institut Kurde de France.

Tejel, J. (2007). *Le Mouvement Kurde de Turquie en Exil: Continuités et Discontinuités du Nationalisme Kurde sous le Mandat Français en Syrie et au Liban (1925–1946).* Berne: P. Lang.

Tejel, J. (2009). *Syria's Kurds History, Politics and Society.* London: Routledge.

The Legacy of Qazi Mohamed

At the eve of World War II with Soviet Russia and Great Britain fighting over influence in Iran, the national ethnic minorities of the Azeris and Kurds were able to carve out some territories to establish short-lived independent republics. Kurdish leaders declared the Republic of Mahabad or Republic of Kurdistan in northwestern Iran on the western shore of Lake Urmiya on January 22, 1946. Its capital was the city of Mahabad, and its first president became Qazi Mohamed (1900–1947). After unsuccessful attempts by Kurdish nationalist movements to shake off the colonial rule of the British in Iraq or the Turkish occupation, here for the first time, a Kurdish state became reality. Soviet troops and Kurdish tribal fighters under Mulla Mustafa Barzani supported and protected the new nation-state. The Kurdish Democratic Party in Iran (also Democratic Party of Iranian Kurdistan) was the main political group that formed the government of the republic. Kurdish language and culture were promoted and an educational sector established. Even today, the republic is viewed by many Kurds as a symbol of Kurdish nationalism and the ideal scenario for a future Kurdish state. After the Soviet withdrawal, the republic collapsed under the military pressure of the Shah's army. It was officially dissolved on December 16, 1946, and on March 30, 1947, the president Qazi Mohamed and two other ministers were publicly executed and hanged in Mahabad. However, before his death Qazi Mohamed wrote his political will addressing his family and the Kurdish people. In it, he defends the rights of the Kurds to their own country and calls for his people to get educated in order to know and claim their rights in the future. He also reminds them not to trust other ethnicities, and speaking to all Kurds, to remain united.

Sebastian Maisel

Excerpts from Qazi Mohamed's Last Letter

My dears,

These are the last hours of my life and I ask this of you. For the love of God, come, and stop being each other's enemies. Be as one and have each other's back in face of an unfair and ruthless enemy. Don't sell yourself cheap to the enemy. Our enemies only want you as long as it benefits their own purposes. The enemy will never feel compassion for you. The enemies of Kurds are many; they are tyrannical, ruthless and without any conscience. The success for any people is oneness, unity and support of their whole nation. Any nation that does not have oneness and unity will forever be under his enemies' rule. You as Kurds are no less than any other free nations; on the contrary, you are in many ways more ready than other nations that freed themselves from oppression. But those who freed themselves had unity among them. For you to be free, you have to stop fighting amongst yourselves, stop being jealous of each other, stop selling yourself to the enemy . . .

1. Believe in God and all the things that came from him; his protection and the prophet (pbuh). Be strong in carrying out your religious duties.

2. Defend the unity and respect among each other; don't treat each other badly; don't be greedy but responsible and helpful.

3. Increase your knowledge and become knowledgeable so that the enemy can no longer cheat you.

4. Do not trust your enemies. Even the most reasonable enemy remains your enemy, the enemy of your people, your homeland and religion. History has shown that they always tried to betray the Kurds. Even with the smallest incident, they murdered the Kurds and did not stop attacking them.

5. Do not sell your religion to your enemies for a few cheap days. The enemy remains the suppressor, and there is no place for any trust.

6. Do not betray each other, not in politics, in life or society nor in your honor. The traitor is guilty before God and the people; and the traitor will fall to treason.

7. If there is one among you who does his work without treason, help those, and do not turn against them because of greed or envy or consider them foreign spy, May God forbid!

8. Be hopeful that in those places that I dedicate in my will one day a mosque, a hospital or a school will stand.

9. Do not get tired of making efforts of resistance, so you can be equal to all other people in escaping from your enemies. Material goods have no value, because if you have your homeland and your freedom, you have all you need, be it a house, wealth, country, honor or a nation.

10. I doubt that any claims against me are justified, except for God's claims. But, if I am indebted to anyone, small or large, then he shall claim it from my house.

If you do not support each other, you will not succeed. Do not be cruel to each other, because Allah will get rid of the cruel. Oppression will disappear because this is God's law. God will punish the cruel.

The servant of the people and his nation

Qazi Mohamed

Source: Xemxwar. *Das Vermächtnis des kurdischen Märtyrers Qazi Mohammed* [in German]. The Legacy of the Kurdish Martyr Qazi Mohammed. http://www .kurdmania.org/News-Das-Vermaechtnis-des-kurdischen-Maertyrers-Qazi -Mohammed-item-944-full-432.html#c432. Translated by the author.

Further Reading

Burhaneddin, Y. A. (1995). *Vision or Reality: The Kurds in the Policy of the Great Powers, 1941–1947*. Lund, Sweden: Lund University Press.

Eagleton, W. (1963). *The Kurdish Republic of 1946*. Oxford, UK: Oxford University Press.

Roosevelt, A., Jr. (1947). "The Kurdish Republic of Mahabad." *Middle East Journal*, vol. 1, 247–269.

The Manifesto of March 11, 1970

After the Ba'th party took over the central government in Baghdad in 1968, various political reforms were initiated, among them plans to improve the foreign relations as well as the domestic Arab-Kurd relations. The Kurds under Mulla Mustafa Barzani and the KDP were fighting for autonomy, and the Ba'th party leadership under Hassan al-Bakr and Saddam Hussein, needing to consolidate their position, was willing to negotiate with the KDP, the leading Kurdish party in Iraq. Several proposals were exchanged, and on March 11, 1970, a manifesto or ceasefire agreement was signed by both sides as a precursor for a future, more comprehensive autonomy law. The manifesto included 15 paragraphs and six secret additional clauses. The Kurdish language and culture were recognized as well as a separate Kurdish region that was composed of the three administrative provinces of Dohuk, Erbil, and Sulaymania. This autonomous Kurdish region would have its own local government, administration, and capital in Erbil. Furthermore, legislative rights and posts in the central government were granted to the Kurds—for example, one of Iraq's vice-presidents would be a Kurd. The status of the Peshmerga, the Kurdish militia, was upgraded, and provisions to their families would be paid from Baghdad.

In general, after signing the manifesto, the situation for the Kurds in Iraq largely improved, to the extent that Sami Abdul Rahman, senior leader of the KDP, called the following years the "golden era." However, disagreements over territories, especially around the oil-rich Kirkuk region, which was to be included into the Kurdish autonomous region, as well as nationalistic rhetoric on both sides led to the deterioration of the relationship. The government unilaterally issued an autonomy law in 1974 and without consultation gave the Kurds only two weeks to accept it. When Barzani refused to ratify the law, a new round of violent clashes broke out. The Kurds, having secured military assistance from Iran and the United States, fought against the Iraqi army until the Shah of Iran settled his own scores with the Iraqis by signing the Algiers Accord in 1975. This brought an end to the crucial Iranian military support and subsequently sealed the defeat of the Kurdish insurgency. It also ended the short-lived Kurdish autonomy, and with it, the March Manifesto became obsolete. However, for years to come, it remained the most comprehensive and beneficial autonomy plan for the Iraqi Kurds and the basis for current negotiations between the Kurdish Autonomy Region and the Iraqi central government.

Sebastian Maisel

The March Manifesto or Iraqi-Kurdish Autonomy Agreement of 1970

1. Kurds will be appointed to senior positions in the government and military.

2. Participation of the Kurds in all government agencies including the ministries, the military leadership and other senior appointments according to the percentage of the Kurdish population and the qualification.

3. Addressing the deficits in the educational sector of the Kurdish nation in the past, a plan is developed to overcome these deficits.

   A. The general directorate for Kurdish culture and information will oversee the Kurdish radio and television programs.

   B. Expelled students will be re-admitted.

   C. More schools will be built in the Kurdish sector. Kurdish students will receive scholarships and stipends.

4. Civil servants in the Kurdish region should be Kurds or at least speak Kurdish.

5. The Kurdish people has the right to form unions and organizations for students, youth, women, workers and teachers.

6. Kurdish workers and officials who have been expelled can return to their job.

7. Payment of reparations to those who suffered in the Kurdish territories. A special pension for families of the victims and the disabled are considered as well as housing and working projects for the unemployed.

8. Repatriation of Kurdish and Arabic villagers.

9. Land and tax reforms in the Kurdish territories with the abolishment of feudalism and distribution of land among the peasants.

10. Changing the provisional constitution: The Iraqi people consists of two main nationalities, Arabic and Kurdish. The constitution guarantees the rights of the Kurdish people and all minorities. Kurdish will be the official language in the Kurdish territories alongside Arabic.

11. The broadcasting station and heavy weaponry will be returned to the government.

12. One of the republic's vice presidents will be a Kurd.

13. The Law of the Provinces will be amended.

14. The Kurdish provinces and administrative regions will be merged after completing an official census in order for the Kurds to practice autonomous rule. However, natural resources will be extracted by the central government.

15. The Kurdish people will participate in the Legislature according to their percentage of the population.

In addition, six secret clauses were included in the manifesto:

A. The Kurdish Region is an autonomous region.

B. The Region includes those territories with a Kurdish population majority.

C. The region is an independent administrative, legal and autonomous unit within the Iraqi republic.

D. The region is integrated part of the Iraqi territory and population.

E. Arbil is the administrative center of the autonomous region.

F. The institutions of the autonomous government are part of the institutions of the Iraqi republic.

History will bear witness that you [Kurds] did not have and never will have a sincere brother and dependable [an] ally as the Arab people.

Source: Asadi, A. (2007). *Der Kurdistan-Irak-Konflikt: der Weg zur Autonomie seit dem Ersten Weltkrieg* (pp. 293–294). Berlin: Verlag Hans Schiler. Translated by the author.

Further Reading
Farouk-Sluglett, M., & Sluglett, P. (2001). *Iraq since 1958: From Revolution to Dictatorship.* London: I. B. Tauris.
Gunter, M. (2008). *The Kurds Ascending: The Evolving Solution to the Kurdish Problem in Iraq and Turkey.* New York: Palgrave Macmillan.
McDowall, D. (2004). *A Modern History of the Kurds.* New York: I. B. Tauris.

The 1975 Algiers Agreement

On July 17, 1968, the Ba'th Party took control of Iraq, overthrowing the previous government. In the wake of the coup, the Ba'th Party demanded sovereignty over the entire Shatt al-Arab River, which is the disputed border with Iran. On April 1969, the Shah of Iran, who was a big military power in the Middle East and strategic ally of the United States, abolished the Iran and Iraq Border Treaty, fearing Saddam's leftist political tendencies. This treaty was signed in 1937 in order to solve the Shatt al-Arab River dispute, giving absolute sovereignty over the river to Iraq. Iran sent warships to the region, and a low-intensity war broke out between the two countries; diplomatic relations were cut off until 1973. In 1970, the two states started to provoke their ethnic minorities against each other. In 1972, the Treaty of Friendship and Cooperation was signed between Iraq and the USSR, which gave Baghdad access to heavy-duty Soviet weapons. President Nixon, as part of his "twin pillar policy," signed a secret agreement with Iran helping the Shah break Saddam's regional power with the help of the Kurds in the Gulf region and larger Middle East region. During this time, the United States, Iran, and several Gulf states supported Mustafa Barzani and his Kurdish movement with arms to revolt against the Baghdad government.

The Kurds in northern Iraq started an uprising or civil war against Saddam's regime until March 6, 1975, when the Algiers Agreement was signed at a meeting of the Organization of Petroleum Exporting Countries (OPEC) in Algiers. With the agreement, both countries gained much political advantage; however, the Kurds were on the losing side of the table because Iran cut its military assistance to them. Iran and Iraq agreed to put an end to supporting all proxy groups and re-establish traditional ties of good neighborly relations and friendship. The agreement was an appropriate way to solve political bilateral disputes within the system of balance of power. Not only did Iraq stop the Kurdish threat, but Iran also prevented the penetration of Soviet influence in the Gulf and Middle East regions. Both countries also used the agreement to improve their relations with the other states in the region (Ari, 2004:160).

However, the Algiers Agreement had severe implications for the Kurds. Iran shut off its military assistance and announced that the border between Iran and Iraq would be sealed after the signing of the agreement throughout the Kurdish region in order to stop the flow of Kurdish refugees. That meant there was no secure way for the Kurds to flee from Saddam's deadly attacks. During the decade-long conflict with Saddam, the Iraqi Kurds under the leadership of Molla Mustafa Barzani suffered much from the military campaigns and offensives by Iraqi military operations, and more than 180,000 people were killed (Mardini, 2012:2). Iran's ending of military assistance for the Iraqi Kurds and subsequent defeat of the Kurds by Iraqi forces also damaged the reputation of the leader of the Kurdistan Democratic Party (KDP), and he went to Iran as a political refugee in June 1975. A political rival party, the Patriotic Union of Kurdistan Parti (PUK), was founded in Damascus under the leadership of Jalal Talabani. The establishment of the PUK divided Kurdish political and military power in Iraq and created many internal problems among the Kurds.

Engin Koç

The Algiers Accord

March 6, 1975

During the convocation of the OPEC Summit Conference in the Algerian capital and upon the initiative of President Houari Boumedienne, the Shah of Iran and

Saddam Hussein (Vice-Chairman of the Revolution Command Council) met twice and conducted lengthy talks on the relations between Iraq and Iran. These talks, attended by President Houari Boumedienne, were characterized by complete frankness and a sincere will from both parties to reach a final and permanent solution of all problems existing between the two countries in accordance with the principles of territorial integrity, border inviolability, and noninterference in internal affairs.

The two High Contracting Parties have decided to:

First: Carry out a final delineation of their land boundaries in accordance with the Constantinople Protocol of 1913 and the Proceedings of the Border Delimitation Commission of 1914.

Second: Demarcate their river boundaries according to the thalweg line.

Third: Accordingly, the two parties shall restore security and mutual confidence along their joint borders. They shall also commit themselves to carry out a strict and effective observation of their joint borders so as to put an end to all infiltrations of a subversive nature wherever they may come from.

Fourth: The two parties have also agreed to consider the aforesaid arrangements as inseparable elements of a comprehensive solution. Consequently, any infringement of one of its components shall naturally contradict the spirit of the Algiers Accord. The two parties shall remain in constant contact with President Houari Boumedienne who shall provide, when necessary, Algeria's brotherly assistance whenever needed in order to apply these resolutions.

The two parties have decided to restore the traditional ties of good neighbourliness and friendship, in particular by eliminating all negative factors in their relations and through constant exchange of views on issues of mutual interest and promotion of mutual co-operation.

The two parties officially declare that the region ought to be secure from any foreign interference.

The Foreign Ministers of Iraq and Iran shall meet in the presence of Algeria's Foreign Minister on 15 March 1975 in Tehran in order to make working arrangements for the Iraqi-Iranian joint commission which was set up to apply the resolutions taken by mutual agreement as specified above. And in accordance with the desire of the two parties, Algeria shall be invited to the meetings of the Iraqi-Iranian joint commission. The commission shall determine its agenda and working procedures and hold meetings if necessary. The meetings shall be alternately held in Baghdad and Tehran.

His Majesty the Shah accepted with pleasure the invitation extended to him by His Excellency President Ahmad Hasan al-Bakr to pay a state visit to Iraq. The date of the visit shall be fixed by mutual agreement.

On the other hand, Saddam Hussein agreed to visit Iran officially at a date to be fixed by the two parties.

HM the Shah of Iran and Saddam Hussein expressed their deep gratitude to President Houari Boumedienne, who, motivated by brotherly sentiments and a spirit of disinterestedness, worked for the establishment of a direct contact between the leaders of the two countries and consequently contributed to reviving a new era in the Iraqi-Iranian relations with a view to achieving the higher interests of the future of the region in question.

Sources: United Nations Treaty Series. (1986). Treaties and International Agreements Registered or Filed and Recorded with the Secretariat of the United Nations, Vol. 1017, No: 14903, New York: United Nations.

Mideast Web. (2017). "The Algiers Accord." http://www.mideastweb.org/algiersaccord .htm.

Further Reading

Arı, T. (2004). *Irak, İran ve ABD* [in Turkish: Iraq, Iran and the USA], Bursa: Alfa Kitabevi.
Charountaki, M. (2010). *The Kurds and US Foreign Policy: International Relations in the Middle East since 1945*. London, New York: Routledge.
Mardini, R. (2012). *Relations with Iraq's Kurds: Toward a Working Partnership, Backgrounder*. Washington, DC: Institute of the Study of War.

Hawar

A Kurdish literary and cultural magazine published in Damascus, Syria, by Jaladet Bedirkhan. During the French mandate (1923–1946), Syria and Lebanon hosted Kurdish exiles from Turkey who established Khoybun, a nationalist organization, and organized the Ararat Rebellion (1928–1930) against Kemalist Turkey. After the failure of the rebellion, Jaladet and his brother, Kamuran, from the princely Bedirkhan family initiated a Kurdish cultural renaissance movement under the auspicious of the French authorities. The Bedirkhan brothers published periodicals in Damascus and Beirut. The first one was Jaladet's *Hawar* ("Cry for Help") which appeared in 57 issues with intervals (1932–1935 and 1941–1943). *Hawar* relied financially on readers' support and donations as well as subsidies granted by the French and the British. In addition to Syria and Lebanon, the majority of *Hawar*'s subscribers were from Iraq and Iran. The magazine was smuggled to Turkey, where its distribution was officially banned. By means of *Hawar*, the exiled Kurdish nationalists from Turkey crafted a new Kurdish national identity in the post-Ottoman era that mirrored its rival Kemalist Turkish nationalism. One of the major tasks of *Hawar* was the dissemination of a Latinized Kurdish alphabet for Kurmanji Kurdish designed by Jaladet Bedirkhan in addition to putting together a grammar and a dictionary for Kurdish. Thus, the first 23 issues of the magazine had two sections, one in the old Arabo-Persian alphabet and the other in the new Latin alphabet. Unlike the late-Ottoman-era Kurdish periodicals that had used both Kurdish and Turkish languages, *Hawar* appeared as a Kurdish-French bilingual magazine. *Hawar* featured several articles in Sorani dialect of Kurdish to reach out to Sorani-speaking Kurds of Iraq with the aim of creating a unified dialect for all Kurds. *Hawar* mobilized its readers to pen Kurdish folk literature and contribute to the magazine with articles on Kurdish tribes, geography, social customs, dialects, and subdialects. Moreover, *Hawar* published anthology articles on Kurdish classical literature. There were also many articles on ancient and modern Kurdish history. All these turned *Hawar* into a reference work used to this day and led many to call it "the little encyclopedia of the Kurds." *Hawar* became a school for promising Kurdish authors such as Nuraddin Zaza, Osman Sabri, and Cegerxwin who published poems and short stories in the magazine. *Hawar* also served as a platform for discussions on social issues among readers from various socioeconomic backgrounds. French Kurdologists in Syria and Lebanon also contributed to the magazine. During the Second World War, *Hawar* informed readers about world events and eventually had an illustrated supplement, *Ronahî* ("Enlightenment") (1942–1945) which, besides war news, included many invaluable pieces on Kurdish history, literature, and language. Since the 1970s, *Hawar* has been rediscovered as a major source on Kurdish language, literature, history, and folklore and republished in Europe, Iraqi Kurdistan, and more recently, in Turkey.

The following excerpts are two editorials from *Hawar*. In the first one, Jaladet Bedirkhan introduces the magazine. The second one was on the occasion of the first anniversary of *Hawar*. In both pieces, Jaladet stresses the significance of language for Kurdish national life.

Ahmet S. Aktürk

"The Goal, and the Style of the Work and Writing of *Hawar*" (Issue 1, May 15, 1932)

Hawar is the voice of knowledge. Knowledge is knowing oneself. For us knowing ourselves opens path to salvation and goodness.

Anyone who knows themselves can make themselves known.

Our Hawar before everything will make known the existence of our language. This is because language is the first condition of existence.

From now on Hawar will be occupied with everything that is tied to Kurdishness and Kurdism. Only politics is far from it; it does not put itself into politics.

Hawar has left politics to the associations of the country. Let them be preocuppied with the politics. As for us, we will work in the fields of knowledge, arts, and crafts.

"A One Year Old Existence" (Issue 20, May 8, 1933)

[. . .]*With this issue our Hawar* ["Cry for Help"] *reached its first year.* [. . .]*Yes, in the life our nation Hawar is such one year old child that laid the foundations of our language.*

Our language now is not only a spoken language but also has become a written language. Moreover, that child [Hawar] brought us those [Latin] letters with which writing our language has become easier and each vowel of our language, one by one, is fixed on paper.

Wasn't our language never written before Hawar? Yes, it was written in the very old days. A few centuries ago some gentlemen penned great books in our language. However, those works did not build up a [national] language for us. Those books [. . .], which had only a few Kurmanji [Kurdish] words, was full of foreign vocabulary, far from colloquial language or the pure language. Even so, all literate and considerate Kurds must keep those authors' names in their hearts and appreciate them. Especially Ahmed Khani. If Hawar laid the foundations of our language, Khani had created its spirit. This is why conscious Kurdishness started with Khani.

Source: *Hawar.* (1932–1943). Reprint Edition by Firat Cewerî, vol. 1 (pp. 23–24 and 403–405), Stockholm: Nudem Press, 1998. Translated by the author.

Further Reading

Bois, T. (1946). "L' âme des Kurdes à la lumière de leur folklore." Beirut: Les Cahiers de l'Est.

Hassanpour, A. (1992). *Nationalism and Language in Kurdistan, 1918–1985*. San Francisco: Mellen Research University Press.

Hawar. (1932–1943/1998). 2 Volumes, Reprint Edition by Firat Cewerî, Stockholm: Nudem Press.

Hebeş, H. (1996). *Raperîna Çanda Kurdî di Kov[a]ra Hawarê de*. Bonn: Belavgeha Hogir.

Lescot, R. (1943). "La Presse Kurde." *Le Jour Nouveau*, vol. 1, no. 1, 4.

Ronahî. (1942–1945), Reprint Edition, Uppsala: Jîna Nû Press, 1985.

Tejel, J. (2007). *Le Mouvement Kurde de Turquie en Exil: Continuités et Discontinuités du Nationalisme Kurde sous le Mandat Français en Syrie et au Liban (1925–1946)*. Berne: P. Lang.

Tejel, J. (2009). *Syria's Kurds: History, Politics and Society*. London: Routledge.

Zengi, D. (2009). "Wasaiq Min Arsheev Majallat Hawar." In *Atyaf al-Madi* (pp. 183–209). Beirut: Ameral Press.

Muhammad Talab Hilal's 12-Point Memorandum and the Syrian Population Census of 1962

Muhammad Talab Hilal was a Syrian army officer and Ba'th party official who published a treatise, *A Study about the National, Social, and Political Aspects of Al-Jazeera Province*, about the Syrian government's position toward the Kurdish population in the eastern part of the country. This document and the earlier population census in 1962 led to the stripping or denying the citizenship of 120,000 Syrian Kurds as well as subsequent harsher living conditions and discrimination for future generations of Kurds in Syria. At the time of writing, Hilal was the head of the security police in the Hasake Province with the highest amount of Kurds in the population, and he expressed a growing concern over the ethnic majority/minority situation in the area. For him, the Arabs were the masters of the land, and the Kurds only represented immigrants with strong tendencies toward secession and uproar. The original treatise is 120 pages long and makes a number of controversial statements about the Kurds. It later became a key document and part of the official anti-Kurdish state propaganda and stereotypes. Most notable is a 12-point plan with guidelines how to deal with the perceived threat of the Kurdish population.

The politics of anti-Kurdish discrimination in Syria started in September 1961 as a reaction to the rebellion in Iraqi Kurdistan led by Mulla Mustafa Barzani. Based on government decree 93, a population census in the Hasaka Province was launched, and some 120,000 Kurds who were unable to provide the necessary status documentation had their citizenship revoked and lost other privileges. They became foreigners in their own country or unregistered citizens. In this time of ethnic tension, the Hilal memorandum intensified the nationalist Arabic and anti-Kurdish propaganda and ultimately shaped the perception of state officials toward the Kurdish minority.

In his study, Hilal claims that the Kurds were threatening the Arabic character of the region, stressing the impossibility of a unified, integrated population. "People such as the Kurds—who have no history, civilization, language or ethnic origin—are prone to committing violence and destruction as are all mountain people" (pp. 4–5). He also accused them of favoring Kurdish nationalism over the Arab nation, comparing the Kurds to a "tumor on the side of the Arab nation that must be removed" (p. 6). Those traitors were supported by foreign interest groups, such as Israel and other imperialists (p. 14). He also stated that "Kurds became like rabid dogs, and it's time to put an end to their annoying barking."

The Syrian Ba'th party started gradually with the implementation of the plan by building an Arab belt in the northern territory, where Kurdish farmers were evicted from their homes and farms and replaced with Arab farmers, who came mostly from Raqqa and Aleppo provinces. The school curriculum was strongly Arabized and nationalized, while the use of Kurdish language was discouraged and at times prohibited. Kurdish names of people and places were changed to Arabic names. In addition, those who lost their citizenship and became stateless, as did their descendants, who had to endure multiple restrictions and hardships.

In the course of the current civil war where the Syrian government tried to appease potential opposition groups, they granted citizenship to several thousand Syrian Kurds. However, by then, the Kurds had already established an autonomous region of self-governance in the northern parts of Syria.

Sebastian Maisel

Study of the al-Jezira Province from its Political, National and Social Perspectives

Chapter 8

Suggestions regarding the Kurdish Problem

Regarding all the things we have mentioned in the midst of the events we must approach things with a cold mind and strong faith. . . . So we don't fall into the trap or the agenda of the other.

First we need to avoid the slippery citizen in order to throw the foundations of planning on the comprehensive understanding and studying during this historic period which we are going through. The situation is obviously known to us, and certainly we are fighting an armed and religious battle in the northern part of our Arabic, Iraqi homeland. We must immediately begin to harmonize in the planning with the operations in Northern Iraq. In this very era, it is of interest to complete there and remain here on the level of meanings or similar to meanings in the name of citizenship. And now when everything has appeared and all the papers here and there were revealed in Turkey and Iran with regards to the Kurds.

Thus, we propose a comprehensive and radical plan for the Jezira for the problem not to reappear after a while. As we know the entire area in Turkey, Iraq, Syria and even Iran is connected with each other along the border. We must take advantage of the Turkish position now because it might change in the future according to the colonial politics where they send every dangerous element into the interior of the country.

Thus we propose:

1. The deliberate dispersion or relocation of the Kurds to the interior according to a risk factor. There is nothing wrong with the plan taking two or three years when starting with the more dangerous elements and finishing with the less dangerous one.

2. The stultification of the community by not building schools or scientific institutes in their sector because this has proved to be opposite of what is desired.

3. The vast majority of Kurds residing in the Jezira enjoy Turkish citizenship. Thus, the civil registries must be changed. This is now being done, and we are demanding to evacuate anyone who cannot prove his citizenship and to extradite him to the country of his [original] citizenship. In addition to that it should be studied how this citizenship was proved and how it was received, because citizenship can only be obtained by presidential decree. Every citizenship not obtained by decree must be reviewed. Keep those of less danger and sent the other to their home country.

4. Stop the employment: We also have to contribute to the plan of stopping the employing of Kurds by putting them in a precarious situation ready to move away at any point. This should first include the reform of the agricultural sector in the Jezira as far as the Kurds and the Arab elements cannot lease or own a lot or sufficient, praise to God.

5. Launching a large anti-Kurdish campaign among the Arabs on someone's account in order to worsen the situation of the Kurds, secondly in order to make their life more unstable.

6. Eliminate the Kurdish religious leadership and deliberately replacing them with pure Arabs; or sending them to the interior instead because their assemblies are not religious assemblies but literally Kurdish assemblies. They have not send cables against al-Barzani instead; they have sent cables against the shedding of Muslim blood.

7. To incite the Kurds against each other. This may be very affordable by fomenting the claim that the dangerous elements among them are of Arab descent. This may also reveal documents, which claim that they were Arabs.

8. Settling Arab nationalist groups in the Kurdish region on the border. They are the fortress of the future and guardians against the Kurds during their deportation. We suggest that these elements come from the Shammar Bedouins because they were among the poorest tribes in the area, but they are very patriotic.

9. Making the northern region a military zone that supports the settlement of Arabs and the expulsion of Kurds according the government's plan.

10. Building of collective farms for the Arabs that the state settles in the northern region. These farms should be trained and armed exactly like the Jewish settlements on the border.

11. Not allowing Arabic speakers to vote or to run for election in those Kurdish territories.

12. Never granting citizenship to those who want to live in this region regardless of their former citizenship (except for Arabs).

Source: Hilal, M. T. (2013). *Study of the al-Jezira Province from its Political, National and Social Perspectives.* Markaz Amuda lil-thaqafa al-kurdiya [in Arabic]. Amuda Center for Kurdish Culture, no. 31, http://www.amude.net/erebi/mihemed-taleb -hilal-lekolin.pdf. Translated by the author.

Further Reading

Bengio, O. (2014). *Kurdish Awakening: Nation Building in a Fragmented Homeland.* Austin: University of Texas Press.

Kurdistan Commentary. (2011). "Death of Arabisation Mastermind, Mohammed Talib Hilal." https://kurdistancommentary.wordpress.com/2011/02/13/death-of-arabisation -mastermind-mohammed-talib-hilal

Kurdwatch. (2009). "The Kurdish Policy of the Syrian Government and the Development of the Kurdish Movement since 1920." *Kurdwatch Report*, no. 1, http://www.kurdwatch .org/pdf/kurdwatch_einfuehrung_en.pdf

Tejel, J. (2008). *Syria's Kurds: History, Politics, and Society.* London, New York: Routledge.

Democratic Confederalism

Abdullah Öcalan is one of the founders and first known leader of the political organization known as the Kurdistan Workers Party (PKK or Partiya Karkerên Kurdistanê). The PKK was founded in 1978 and is known for its armed struggle against the Turkish state for equal rights and self-determination of Kurds in Turkey. Abdullah Öcalan was arrested in Nairobi, Kenya, by the National Intelligence Organization (Millî İstihbarat Teşkilatı [MİT]) and has been imprisoned at İmralı island since 1999. His initial punishment for leading the PKK was the death penalty, but this was then transformed into a life sentence after the death penalty was abolished in August 2002. Throughout his captivity, Öcalan has developed several writings pertaining to the Kurdish question and his political thought.

Öcalan outlines *Democratic Confederalism* by providing definitions of the nation-state. In his definition, Öcalan ties in the current capitalist global economic system as a cause of the corruption of nation-states. After discussing the nation-state, the text is divided in seven parts. Following the text of *Democratic Confederalism*, Öcalan then describes the benefits that ethnic groups in the Middle East would gain by adapting some form of democratic confederalism.

Democratic Confederalism is a continuation of Öcalan's writings pertaining to political thought and the Kurdish question. He describes democratic confederalism as the idea of Kurdish democratic projects fighting against the notion of a separate nation-state and advancing the democratization of the Middle East through the success of Kurdish democratic projects across the countries in which they are located. The principles of democratic confederalism are also laid out.

Kyle Meppelink

Democratic Confederalism

1. The right of self-determination of the peoples includes the right to a state of their own. However, the foundation of a state does not increase the freedom of a people. The system of the United Nations that is based on nation-states has remained inefficient. Meanwhile, nation-states have become serious obstacles for any social development. Democratic confederalism is the contrasting paradigm of the oppressed people.

2. Democratic confederalism is a non-state social paradigm. It is not controlled by a state. At the same time, democratic confederalism is the cultural organizational blueprint of a democratic nation.

3. Democratic confederalism is based on grass-roots participation. Its decision-making processes lie with the communities. Higher levels only serve the coordination and implementation of the will of the communities that send their delegates to the general assemblies. For limited space of time, they are both mouthpiece and executive institutions. However, the basic power of decision rests with the local grass-roots institutions.

4. In the Middle East, democracy cannot be imposed by the capitalist system and its imperial powers, which only damage democracy. The propagation of grass-roots democracy is elementary. It is the only approach that can deal with diverse ethnical groups, religions, and class differences. It also goes together well with the traditional confederate structure of the society.

5. Democratic confederalism in Kurdistan is an anti-nationalist movement as well. It aims at realizing the right of self-defense of the peoples by the advancement of democracy in all parts of Kurdistan without questioning the existing political borders. Its goal is not the foundation of a Kurdish nation-state. The movement intends to establish federal structures in Iran, Turkey, Syria, and Iraq that are open for all Kurds and at the same time form an umbrella confederation for all four parts of Kurdistan. (pp. 33–34)

Democratic confederalism does not aim for an independent Kurdish state; its purpose is to unite the Kurdish people across state borders in a society based on a form of self-governance. But what sets democratic confederalism apart from an established state? Democratic confederalism is a form of governance by a consensus of the people rather than by an established centralized government. Öcalan explains the state in the Hobbesian tradition as existing to exploit the people; whereas Hobbes views the state as a necessary evil, Öcalan asserts it as an unnecessary evil. Political affiliations are not cast aside, nor are the traditions that may come into being with a republican or democratic form of government, for democratic confederalism is a syncretic system that would be able to cooperate with any other political institution. This political syncretism challenges the idea that state borders should be drawn in terms of nation-states; in fact, Öcalan states:

> [that] since the nation-state transcends its material basis, the citizens, it assumes an existence beyond its political institutions. It needs additional institutions of its own to protect its ideological basis as well as legal, economic and religious structures. The resulting ever-expanding civil and military bureaucracy is expensive and serves on the preservation of the transcendent state itself, which in turn elevates the bureaucracy above the people. . . . Bureaucracy and nation-state cannot exist without each other. If the nation-state is the backbone of capitalist modernity, it certainly is the cage of the natural society. Its bureaucracy secures the smooth functioning of the system, secures the basis of the production of goods, and secures the profits for the relevant economic actors in both the real-socialist and business-friendly nation-state. The nation-state domesticates the society in the name of capitalism and alienates the community from its natural foundations. Any analysis meant to localize and solve social problems needs to take a close look at these links. (p. 12)

Öcalan recognizes that politics are necessary in order to address issues that arise within the state, yet the way that politics are viewed and nomenclated needs to be changed. An understanding of democratic confederalism means an alteration to the definition of democracy and confederalism.

In contrast to a centralist and bureaucratic understanding of administration and exercise of power, confederalism poses a type of political self-administration where all groups of the society and all cultural identities can express themselves in local meetings, general conventions, and councils. This understanding of democracy opens the political space to all strata of society and allows for the formation of different and diverse political groups. In this way it also advances the political integration of society as a whole. Politics becomes a part of everyday life. Without politics, the crisis of the state cannot be solved since the crisis is fueled by a lack of representation of the political society. Terms like federalism or self-administration as they are found in liberal democracies need to be conceived anew. Essentially, they should not be conceived as hierarchical levels of the administration of the nation-state but rather as central tools of social expression and participation. This, in turn, will advance the politicization of the society (p. 26).

The Middle East becomes a phenomenal experiment for democratic confederalism. Öcalan sees the inefficiencies in the Middle East founded on the principles of nation-states and capitalism and how the nation replaced the religious community. But in order to remedy these inefficiencies:

> . . . the method in handling the issue should not be ideological, but scientific and not nationalistic but based on the concept of democratic nation and democratic communalism. The concepts of such an approach are the fundamental elements of democratic modernity. Over the past two centuries nationalism and tendency for nation-states has been fueled in the societies in the Middle East. The national issues have not been solved but rather have been aggravated in all areas of the society. Instead of cultivating productive competition, the capital enforces internal and external wars in the name of the nation-state. The theory of communalism would be an alternative to capitalism. In the framework of democratic nations, which do not strive for power monopolies it may lead to peace in a region, which has only been the field of gory wars and genocide. In this context we can speak of four majority nations: Arabs, Persians, Turks, and Kurds. (p. 35)
>
> These four nations are not the only ethnic groups Öcalan describes, yet includes the Arameans, Armenians, Jews, Turkmens, Bedouins, Caucasian peoples, and Hellenic peoples in order to show how each group would benefit by adapting democratic confederalism. *Democratic Confederalism* was not written by Öcalan to create an independent Kurdistan, but to lay the foundation for a syncretic form of government that would correct the problems existing in the Middle East. "The future is democratic confederalism." (p. 44)

Source: Öcalan, A. (2012). *Demokratischer Konföderalismus*. Porsgrunn, Norway: New Compass Press. Translated by the author.

Further Reading

Öcalan, A. (2012). *Prison Writings III: The Roadmap to Negotiations*. Cologne: Transmedia Publishing Ltd.

Öcalan, A. (2012). *War and Peace in Kurdistan*. Cologne: Transmedia Publishing Ltd.

Öcalan, A. (2013). *Liberating Life: Woman's Revolution*. Cologne: Transmedia Publishing Ltd.

Krive

Yezidis have their sons circumcised sitting on the lap of a godfather or patron—Krive in Kurdish. The song "Krive" is an old Kurdish tune that was performed by many great Kurdish musicians, including Mihemed Arife Ciziri, Hesene Ciziri, Ayse Shan, and Shivan Perver. Shivan Perver is arguably one of the most famous and popular Kurdish musicians. He achieved his legendary status over the course of a long career that started in the 1970s. But when he started singing Krive, many Yezidis felt uncomfortable or even offended. The text describes the love story between a Muslim man and a Yezidi, woman similar to the plot of Romeo and Juliet by Shakespeare, where two lovers from opposing groups endured hardship and discrimination over their romance due to the intolerance of the society they live in.

The Yezidis transmit their own version of the song where the protagonists come from two Yezidi families in the Sinjar/Shingal region. Here, the man belonged to the group of the *mirid* or laymen, while the woman was a member of the Sheikh group. And since the man was circumcised with the help of a godfather from that same Sheikh family, they were not allowed to marry. Yezidi custom prohibits marital relations between members of different groups. Since the song describes a controversial topic, it was rarely performed by Yezidis singers. Among the last ones were two bards, or *dengbej*, from Sinjar: Pir Guro, who died in the 1970s, and Khidir Feqir, who died in 2009.

According to Yezidi tradition, the storyline was later modified so that a Muslim man fell in love with the daughter of his Yezidi godfather. Equally, marital relations are not permitted between Muslims and Yezidis. In another version, it was a Yezidi man who fell in love with a Muslim woman, which caused an outcry among the Muslim community, as it is not allowed for Muslim women to marry non-Muslims.

Shivan Perver, however, liked the melody (and new lyrics) of the song and started to perform it frequently. After Yezidis intervened and explained the circumstances and negative repercussions for their community, he acknowledged their concerns and stopped singing the song.

Sebastian Maisel

Krive (Yezidi girl)
Oh, come, young man, come, come
Say, Oh Krive, my darling,
This morning I went to Mount Shingal and gazed across at Lake Smokya
Where the landscape rose and fell in never-ending crests and vales.
And my attention was caught by the daughter of Smokya village
Approaching as the dawn began to break, from the opposite direction,
The daughter of the Yezidis, my beloved Krive,
Wearing beautiful red garments

The lovely head-dress of the Kurdish maidens
And flowing kaftan with wonderful embroidery.
And she took herself to the edge of Lake Smokya flying like a green pigeon
Swimming sleek beneath the waters of the Khabur River like a duck.
Krive, do you know, what is this sin of yours and mine
That the road and its gate are shut upon us?
Our one sin is that I am a Muslim man and you are a Yezidi girl.
Oh my Krive!
Krive, at first light, hasten, wait for me at the foot of Mount Shingal.
For the people would betray us just as the moorhen betrays its kind
With its cry: kekeba, kekeba!
You are of the sheikhs, so let it be by the memory of Sheikh Tawsi Melek,
That you vouch me a kiss—come, despite care and sorrow—
You are my fate, my body and my soul, Krivo.
Let my spirit be at rest, oh Krivo.
Krivo, if you can't do this, then for your mother's and your father's sake let it be,
If this too is a sin, then upon your poverty,
Vouch this to me, Krivo
Young man, I am a woman, I can do nothing!
But I am yours alone.
Have no fear—this I swear by Sheikh Tawsi Melek,
If I die, I will marry the cold earth,
If I live, body, spirit and soul are yours,
My forbidden love, my Krivo.
In the blue hour of the dawn
As the call of the muezzin sounds
Before the day is born
For our Yezidi girl's kisses I was created,
Do you not know this, o Krivo?
I am like the gazelle, smooth and soft of breast,
Sensual and graceful,
I have never been touched,
I am a teal-green pigeon,
A sleek duck swimming
Beneath the waters of the stream,
My Krivo,
My hands are swift,
My fingers lithe as a magician's
As I set forth the cups for coffee,
My mouth, my lips, are sweet as Diyarbakir sugar
First unwrapped from soft paper brought from the mountain pass.
O Krivo.

Source: Lazier, S. (1991). *Into Kurdistan: Frontiers under Fire.* London, New Jersey: Zed Books. Translated by the author.

Further Reading

Allison, C. (2001). *The Yezidi Oral Tradition in Iraqi Kurdistan*. Richmond, Surrey, UK: Curzon Press.

Issa, C. (2007). *Das Yezidentum—Religion und Leben*, Oldenburg: Denge Ezidiya.

Article 140 of the New Iraqi Constitution from 2005

Article 140 of Iraq's new permanent constitution, approved in 2005, remains a controversial clause that vaguely describes the territorial and demographic conflict of disputed areas in Iraq after the liberation from Saddam Hussein's Ba'th party regime. The country since has declared a federal system that granted autonomy to some territories with a Kurdish majority. During Saddam's regime, families, tribes, and entire villages were displaced in order to Arabize the Kurdish region. A separate referendum for the status of Kirkuk required the reversal of Saddam's displacement policies. However, while thousands of displaced Kurds have returned home, the referendum has not taken place. However, claims for these territories to be included into the Kurdish Autonomy Region have not ceded.

Article 140 refers to an earlier legal document, Article 58 of the Transitional Administrative Law, which stipulated the return of and compensation for displaced people and called for the resolution of territorial disputes through arbitration.

However, the date for the referendum has been expired, and no further legal action has been taken. The ongoing territorial dispute among the various ethnic and religious groups has been stalled by referring the issue of territorial control to a future referendum. In the wake of the military conquest and subsequent push-back of the Islamic State, Kurdish authority has been imposed in several of the disputed territories, among them Kirkuk and Sinjar. After the final defeat of the Islamic State, the issue of allocating territories to particular provinces will be renegotiated according to the new demographic realities on the ground.

Sebastian Maisel

Permanent Constitution of Iraq from 2005

Article 140:

First: The executive authority shall undertake the necessary steps to complete the implementation of the requirements of all subparagraphs of Article 58 of the Transitional Administrative Law.

Second: The responsibility placed upon the executive branch of the Iraqi Transitional Government stipulated in Article 58 of the Transitional Administrative Law shall extend and continue to the executive authority elected in accordance with this Constitution, provided that it accomplishes completely (normalization and census and concludes with a referendum in Kirkuk and other disputed territories to determine the will of their citizens), by a date not to exceed the 31st of December 2007.

Article 58 of the Transitional Administrative Law from 2003

A. The Iraqi Transitional Government, and especially the Iraqi Property Claims Commission and other relevant bodies, shall act expeditiously to take measures to remedy the injustice caused by the previous regime's practices in altering the demographic character of certain regions, including Kirkuk, by deporting and expelling individuals from their places of residence, forcing migration in and out of the region, settling individuals alien to the region, depriving the inhabitants of work, and correcting nationality. To remedy this injustice, the Iraqi Transitional Government shall take the following steps:

1. With regard to residents who were deported, expelled, or who emigrated; it shall, in accordance with the statute of the Iraqi Property Claims Commission and other measures within the law, within a reasonable period of time, restore the residents to their homes and property, or, where this is unfeasible, shall provide just compensation.

2. With regard to the individuals newly introduced to specific regions and territories, it shall act in accordance with Article 10 of the Iraqi Property Claims Commission statute to ensure that such individuals may be resettled, may receive compensation from the state, may receive new land from the state near their residence in the governorate from which they came, or may receive compensation for the cost of moving to such areas.

3. With regard to persons deprived of employment or other means of support in order to force migration out of their regions and territories, it shall promote new employment opportunities in the regions and territories.

4. With regard to nationality correction, it shall repeal all relevant decrees and shall permit affected persons the right to determine their own national identity and ethnic affiliation free from coercion and duress.

B. The previous regime also manipulated and changed administrative boundaries for political ends. The Presidency Council of the Iraqi Transitional Government shall make recommendations to the National Assembly on remedying these unjust changes in the permanent constitution. In the event the Presidency Council is unable to agree unanimously on a set of recommendations, it shall unanimously appoint a neutral arbitrator to examine the issue and make recommendations. In the event the Presidency Council is unable to agree on an arbitrator, it shall request the Secretary General of the United Nations to appoint a distinguished international person to be the arbitrator.

C. The permanent resolution of disputed territories, including Kirkuk, shall be deferred until after these measures are completed, a fair and transparent census has been conducted and the permanent constitution has been ratified. This resolution shall be consistent with the principle of justice, taking into account the will of the people of those territories.

Sources: "The Constitution of Iraq." http://www.iraqinationality.gov.iq/attach /constitution_ar.pdf. Translated by the author.

"Transitional Administrative Law." http://www.aljazeera.net/specialfiles/pages /651be42e-de88-495c-85ba-54e6aad12888. Translated by the author.

Further Reading

Hamoudi, H. A. (2013). *Negotiating in Civil Conflict: Constitutional Construction and Imperfect Bargaining in Iraq.* Chicago: University of Chicago Press.
Jawad, S. (2013). "The Iraqi Constitution: Structural Flaws and Political Implications." *LSE Middle East Centre Paper Series*, 01. http://eprints.lse.ac.uk/54927/1/SaadJawad _Iraqi_Constitution_LSE_Middle_East_Centre_WP01_Nov2013.pdf

The Social Charta of West Kurdistan (Rojava)

As a result of the ongoing civil war, those areas in the northern part of Syria that are inhabited mostly by Kurds unilaterally declared autonomy from the central government in Damascus. On January 29, 2014, the local provisional government adopted the Declaration of the Social Charta of West Kurdistan (Rojava) as the region's constitution covering the currently four cantons or administrative centers: Cizire (Qamishli), Kobane, Shahba (Minbaj), and Efrin. The political system of Rojava is based on the idea of democratic confederalism, a political theory crafted by Abdullah Ocalan, the founder and spiritual leader of the PKK. The constitution of Rojava is the first attempt to institutionalize the concept of democratic confederalism, and it was strongly supported by the region's main political party, the PYD, the Syrian branch of the PKK.

Rojava is home to diverse ethnic and religious groups, such as the Kurds, Arabs, Assyrians, Armenian, Turkmen, Chechens, and Yezidis, and each of these groups is recognized as an integral part of Rojava's society. Based on this ethnic plurality, the constitution recognizes three official languages: Kurdish, Arabic, and Syriac. Although a decentralized, federal system is promoted, the integrity of the Syrian national borders is not contested. The constitution is based on secularism, democracy, and the separation of powers. Although committed to peaceful conflict resolution, the constitution stipulates ways for exercising defensive military action through the People's Protection Units (YPG) and the police force (Asayish). The

Universal Declaration of Human Rights is another pillar of the constitution where it stresses its support for the protection of the environment, women's rights, and religious freedom. The system of governance in Rojava with its local councils, committees, legislative assembly, executive council, and canton administration is explained in more detail next, and it notes a 40% women quota. The independence of the region's judiciary is confirmed in Article 63.

Sebastian Maisel

The Social Charta of West-Kurdistan

Article 3

A. Syria is a free, sovereign and democratic state, governed by a parliamentary system based on principles of decentralization and pluralism.
B. The cantons of the Autonomous Regions (Efrin, Cizire and Kobane) are geographically part of Syria, and the city of Qamishli is the center of the Autonomous Region in the Cizire Canton.
C. The Canton of Cizire is a canton joined ethnically by Kurds, Arabs, Chechens, Armenian and Assyrians; and religious diverse with its Muslim, Christian and Yazidi communities peacefully co-existing in brotherhood. The elected Legislative Assembly represents all three Cantons of the Autonomous Regions.

Article 9

The official languages of the Canton of Cizire are Kurdish, Arabic and Syriac with guarantees for all communities to teach in their native language.

Article 12

The Autonomous Regions form an integral part of Syria. It is a model for a future decentralized system of federal governance in Syria.

Article 15

The People's Protection Units (YPG) is the sole military force of the three Cantons, with the mandate to protect and defend the security of the Autonomous Regions and its peoples, against both internal and external threats. The Asayish forces are charged with civil policing functions in the Autonomous Regions.

Article 23

A. Everyone has the right to express their ethnic, cultural, linguistic and gender rights
B. Everyone has the right to live in a healthy environment, based on natural balance.

Article 28

Women have the right to organize their affairs free from all forms of gender discrimination.

Article 31

Everyone has the right to security and stability.
Education is free and obligatory for the elementary school.
The right for work, housing, and health and social insurance.
Mothers and children are protected.
Health and social insurance for the elderly and disabled.

Article 32

C. The Yezidi religion is a recognized religion and its followers' rights to organize their social religious affairs as well as a special personal status law.

Article 49

All governing bodies, institutions and committees shall be made up of at least forty percent (40%) of either sex.

Article 63

The independence of the Judiciary is founding principle of the rule of law, which ensures a just and effective disposition of cases by the competent and impartial courts.

Article 94

A. The Charter enshrines the principle of separation of religion and State.
B. Freedom of religion shall be protected. All religions and faiths in the Autonomous Regions shall be respected.

Source: https://peaceinkurdistancampaign.com/charter-of-the-social-contract/ Translated by the author.

Further Reading

Abdullah O. (2011). *Democratic Confederalism*. London, Cologne: Transmedia Publishing.
Knapp, M., Flach, A., & Ayboga, E. (2016). *Revolution in Rojava: Democratic Autonomy and Women's Liberation in Syrian Kurdistan*. London: Pluto Press.
Phillips, D. L. (2017). *The Kurdish Spring: A New Map of the Middle East*. London, New York: Routledge.

Yezidi Sacred Hymns

The Yezidis are an ethnoreligious minority group that is mostly associated with the Kurds. Some claim that the Yezidis were the original Kurds and that their religion was the religion of all Kurds prior to Islamization. Yezidism is a religion based on pre-Islamic Kurdish traditions that have been influenced by the mystic Adi bin Musafir (died in 1162) and that have absorbed practices from other religions. It is an endogamic religion, which does not allow conversion and requires marriage within the community. Because of its oral character and transmission of religious knowledge, and due to the spread of the Yezidi communities stretching from Syria to Iraq and Armenia, the dogma is largely unknown to the masses. The believers focus instead on religious practices and rituals, which also differ from one area to the other. However, they all accept basic tenets like the Peacock Angel, Tausi Melek; the reformer Sheikh Adi; the caste system; and the sacred hymns called qewl in Kurdish. In the past, these hymns were transmitted orally by trained clerics, the qewal, who traveled to the distant Yezidi communities and instructed them in the profane and sacred aspects of Yezidi religion.

The qewals are members of a group of clerics who memorize, preserve, and recite the religious hymns, the qewls. Considering the importance of oral narration, the qewals have arguably the most important task in protecting and preserving the religious texts and identity. Qewals are not members of the castes of sheikh or pir; in fact, they are mirids or laymen from two particular villages, Bashiqa and Bahzani, in Iraq. They should, however, be dedicated, pious Yezidi men with an interest in preserving the tradition and possibly some talent for reciting the qewls and playing instruments. This significantly limits the number of possible candidates for the job, and it comes as no surprise that the number of qewals is dropping. It is predicted that their profession may be extinct in a couple of years. The current trend to write down religious texts and no longer rely exclusively on oral recitation contributes to the dilemma.

The excerpt from the first qewl transmits the Yezidi creation story, which includes references to God, the original shape of the pearl, and the beginning of humanity and the Yezidis.

Sebastian Maisel

Qewle Zebuni Meksur

1 Oh we of broken hearts,
When the call from our dear Melek Fekhredin is heard
We should praise the deep oceans of hidden knowledge.

2 Oh we of little endurance
When the permission from our dear Melek Fekhredin comes
We should describe the deep oceans of hidden knowledge.

3 Reputable people gathered around me.
We should tell them about these oceans of knowledge
That have pearls and jewels in it.

4 Reputable people gathered around me.
We should give them a full account of the great oceans
That have the Mir (prince) in it.

5 Praise the all-knowing.
The Mir has come to the throne.
He is all-knowing and all-seeing.

6 My king came from the pearl.
Other good things came out of it.
The tree of love came from it.

7 The tree of love was in it.
On Sultan Ezid's head is the crown of sovereignty.
In his hand is the scepter of power.
Praise to God that we remained faithful to tradition.

8 The lovers saw the Mir and got to know him
Love and cup were shared.
And the foundation was laid.

9 He built the foundation and the pillars.
The pearl burst open in awe.
And it was unable to contain itself.

10 It did not have the strength to remain patient.
The pearl was adorned with colors,
Red and white and yellow.

11 Now the pearl was shining in all colors.
Before that there was no earth, sky or throne.
Who did my king adore?

12 My king speaks all languages.
Love and cup were put together.
And then my king issues the laws.

The second text is called the **Yezidi Declaration of Faith**.

1 I confess that Khodeh is God.
Melek Sheikhisn is the truth and a friend of God.
Praise to Meqlub and Mirgeh.

2 We bow before the saints towards Lalish and Meqlub.
We face the two domes.

The Yezidis refer to Sheikh Adi to honor him.

3 Sultan Sheikh Adi is my King.
Sheikhobakr is my Master.
Sultan Ezid is my Lord.

4 He is my Pir.
He is my teacher.
Tawsi Melek is my faith and belief.

5 The White Spring is the place of baptism.
The caves and the Zemzem well are the destination of my pilgrimage.
The dome is the direction of my prayers.

6 Melek Sheikhisn is my ancestor.
He is my Sheikh.
Sheshims is my religion, the light of my eyes.

7 Praise to God for the House of Adi.
We were separated from the infidels.
We were led on the straight path.

8 We thank the saints
for separating us from the infidels.
Sheikh and Pir led us on the straight path.

9 We are thankful and obedient.
We stay away from the infidels and the Sharia.
The sheikhs of tradition let us on the straight path.

10 God willing, we are Yezidis.
Followers of the name of Sultan Ezid.
Praise to God, we are content with our religion and path.

Sources and Further Reading

Issa, C. (2007). *Das Yezidentum—Religion und Leben*. Denge Ezidiyan: Oldenburg. Translated by the author.
Kreyenbroek, P., & Jindi, K. (2005). *God and Sheikh Adi Are Perfect: Sacred Poems and Religious Narratives from the Yezidi Tradition*. Harrasowitz: Wiesbaden.

Glossary

Agha	Feudal landlord among the Kurds
Ajnabi (A)	Foreigner; legal category for Kurds in Syria after the 1962 census
Amed	Kurdish name for the city of Diyarbakir
Anfal (A)	The genocidal campaign by the Iraqi government under Saddam Hussein against the Kurds in Iraq
Azad	Freedom
Bakur	Northern Kurdistan, Kurdish territories in Turkey
Bashur	Southern Kurdistan, Kurdish territories in Iraq
Chaykhana	Tea house
Chem	Alevi music
Chema	Truffles
Dengbej	Musical storyteller or bard
Dolma	Stuffed vegetables
Eshire	Tribal group
Ghulat	Extremists, label to describe radical Muslim minority groups
Gund	Traditional village
Gurani	Kurdish language variety (dialect) spoken by the Ahl-e Haqq (Yaresan) in Iraq and Iran
Hamidiye	Kurdish tribal levies in the service of the Ottoman Sultan
Hewal	Comrade
Hewler	Kurdish name for the city of Erbil
Hucra	School associated with mosque
Jash	Kurdish fighters cooperating with Saddam Hussein's military
Kelam	Sacred poems of Ahl-e Haqq
Kizilbash	Members of a militant Shia group in medieval Iran
Komala	Political association
Köy korucuları	Village guards employed by the Turkish military to combat the PKK
Kurmanji	Kurdish language variety (dialect) mostly spoken in western and northern Kurdistan
Madrasa, medrese	Religious school
Maktum (A)	Unregistered; legal category for Kurds in Syria after the 1962 census
Mastaw	Mixed drink of water, yogurt, and salt
Millet	Autonomous ethnic or religious minority group in the Ottoman Empire

Mir	Community or tribal leader
Molla	Title for religious teachers
Namus	Honor related to women and sexuality that cannot be increased, only lost
Newroz	Kurdish New Year on March 21
Peshmerga	Those who seek to die (in defense of the Kurdish homeland)
Pir	Title for religious men
Qewal	Yezidis religious men who perform rituals through music and songs
Qewl	Religious hymns among the Yezidis
Rojava	Western Kurdistan, Kurdish territories in Syria
Rojhilat	Eastern Kurdistan, Kurdish territories in Iran
Sema	Alevi dance
Sheikh	Respectful title for learned men or community leaders
Sheref	Honor related to reputation that can be increased
Shesh besh	Backgammon
Shingal	Kurdish name for Sinjar
Sorani	Kurdish language variety (dialect) mostly spoken in Southern and Eastern Kurdistan
Stran	Folklore song
Tanzimat	A set of reforms issued by the Ottoman sultans that granted more rights to minority groups
Tariqa	Sufi brotherhood or order
Ulema	Learned religious men or scholars
Vilayet	Ottoman governorate
Yekiti	Political union
Zazaki (Dimili)	Kurdish language variety (dialect) spoken in Turkey

Selected Bibliography

Aboona, H. (2008). *Assyrians, Kurds, and Ottomans: Intercommunal relations on the periphery of the Ottoman Empire.* Amherst, NY: Cambria Press.

Ahmad, K. M. (1994). *Kurdistan during the First World War.* London: Saqi Books.

Allison, C. (2001). *The Yezidi Oral Tradition in Iraqi Kurdistan.* Richmond, Surrey, UK: Curzon Press.

Allsopp, H. (2015). *The Kurds of Syria.* London: I. B. Tauris.

Ammann, B. (2001). *Kurden in Europa. Ethnizität und Diaspora.* Münster: LIT Verlag.

Aslan, S. (2014). *Nation-building in Turkey and Morocco: Governing Kurdish and Berber Dissent.* New York: Cambridge University Press.

Ateş, S. (2014). "In the Name of the Caliph and the Nation: The Sheikh Ubeidullah Rebellion of 1880–81." *Iranian Studies,* vol. 47, no. 5, 735–798.

Aydin, A., & Cem, E. (2015). *Zones of Rebellion: Kurdish Insurgents and the Turkish State.* Ithaca, NY: Cornell University Press.

Barzinji, A. (2015). *Traditional Kurdish Food: An Insight into Kurdish Culinary Heritage.* www.kurdishfood.co.uk: Ala Barzinji Publisher.

Baser, B. (2016). *Diasporas and Homeland Conflicts: A Comparative Perspective.* London, New York: Routledge.

BBC News Service. (2016, March 14). "Who Are the Kurds?" *BBC News: World.* http://www.bbc.co.uk/news/world-middle-east-29702440.

Belge, C. (2011). "State Building and the Limits of Legibility: Kinship Networks and Kurdish Resistance in Turkey." *International Journal of Middle East Studies,* vol. 43, 95–114.

Black, G. (1993). *Genocide in Iraq: The Anfal Campaign against the Kurds.* New York: Human Rights Watch.

Bois, T. (1966). *The Kurds.* Beirut: Khayats.

Braidwood, R., & Howe, B. (1960). *Prehistoric Investigations in Iraqi Kurdistan.* Chicago: University of Chicago Press, Studies in Ancient Oriental Civilization, No. 31.

Candan, C. (2016). *Kurdish Documentary Cinema in Turkey: The Politics and Aesthetics of Identity and Resistance.* Newcastle, UK: Cambridge Scholars Publishing.

Christensen, D. (1963). "Tanzlieder der Hakkâri-Kurden." *Jahrbuch für musikalische Volks- und Völkerkunde,* vol. 1, 11–47.

Cicek, C. (2016). *The Kurds of Turkey: National, Religious, and Economic Identities.* London: I. B. Tauris.

Eccarius-Kelly, V. (2011). *The Militant Kurds: A Dual Strategy for Freedom.* Santa Barbara, CA: Praeger.

Eppel, M. (2016). *A People without a State: The Kurds from the Rise of Islam to the Dawn of Nationalism.* Austin: University of Texas Press.

Galib, O. (2015). *Imagining Kurdistan: Identity, Culture, Society.* London: I. B. Tauris.

Gavish, H. (2010). *Unwitting Zionists: The Jewish Community of Zakho in Iraqi Kurdistan.* Detroit, MI: Wayne State University Press.

Ghassemlou, R., Kendal, N., Roosevelt, A., & Vanly, I. (1980). *People Without a Country—The Kurds and Kurdistan*. Edited by Chaliand Gerard and translated by Pallis Michael. London, Zed Press.

Gürbey, G., & Ibrahim, F. (Eds.). (2000). *The Kurdish Conflict in Turkey. Obstacles and Chances for Peace and Democracy*. New York, Münster: LIT Verlag.

Hilterman, J. (2007). *A Poisonous Affair: America, Iraq, and the Gassing of Halabja*. Cambridge, UK: Cambridge University Press.

Ihsan, M. (2017). *Nation Building in Kurdistan: Memory, Genocide and Human Rights*. Abingdon, UK: Routledge.

Issa, C. (2007). *Das Yezidentum—Religion und Leben*. Oldenburg: Denge Ezidiyan.

Izady, M. (2015). *The Kurds: A Concise History and Fact Book*. Abingdon, NY: Taylor & Francis.

Jwaideh, W. (2006). *The Kurdish National Movement: Its Origins and Development*. Syracuse, NY: Syracuse University Press.

King, D. (2008). "The Personal Is Patrilineal: Namus as Sovereignty." *Identities. Global Studies in Culture and Power*, vol. 15, no. 3, 317–342.

King, D. (2014). *Kurdistan on the Global Stage: Kinship, Land, and Community in Iraq*. New Brunswick, NJ: Rutgers University Press.

Klein, J. (2011). *The Margins of Empire: Kurdish Militias in the Ottoman Tribal Zone*. Redwood City, CA: Stanford University Press.

Kreyenbroek, P., & Jindi, K. (2005). *God and Sheikh Adi Are Perfect: Sacred Poems and Religious Narratives from the Yezidi Tradition*. Wiesbaden: Harrassowitz.

Lokman, I. M., & Kawtharani, F. W. (2005). "The Kurdish Community in Lebanon." *International Journal of Kurdish Studies*, vol. 19, no. 1–2, 137–171.

Massicard, E. (2013). *The Alevis in Turkey and Europe; Identity and Managing Territorial Diversity*. London, New York: Routledge, Exeter Studies in Ethno Politics.

McDowall, D. (1996). *A Modern History of the Kurds*. London, New York: I. B. Tauris.

McKiernan, K. (2006). *The Kurds: A People in Search of their Homeland*. New York: St. Martin's Press.

Minorsky, V. (1927). "Kurds." *Encyclopaedia of Islam* vol. 6, 447–464.

Mojab, S. (2001). *Women of a Non-State Nation: the Kurds*. Costa Mesa, CA: Mazda Publishers.

Nikitin, B. (1975). *Les Kurdes: Étude sociologique et historique*. Paris: Éditions d'Aujourd 'hui.

Ocalan, A. (2011). *Democratic Confederalism*. London, Cologne: Transmedia Publishing.

Olson, R. (2013). *The Emergence of Kurdish Nationalism and the Sheikh Said Rebellion, 1880–1925*. Austin: University of Texas Press.

Omarkhali, K. (2014). *Religious Minorities in Kurdistan: Beyond the Mainstream*. Wiesbaden: Harrassowitz.

Ozoglu, H. (2004). *Kurdish Notables and the Ottoman State: Evolving Identities, Competing Loyalties, and Shifting Boundaries*. New York: SUNY Press.

Savelsberg, E., Hajo, S., & Borck, C. (2000). *Kurdische Frauen und das Bild der kurdischen Frau*. Münster: LIT Verlag.

Sharaf Khan [Şeref Han]. (1860). *Scheref-nameh ou Histoire des Kourdes par Scheref, Prince de Bidlis*, vol. 1. St. Petersburg: Gregg International.

Stansfield, G. (2003). *Iraqi Kurdistan: Political Development and Emerging Democracy*. London: Routledge.

Sykes, M. (1908). "The Kurdish Tribes of the Ottoman Empire." *The Journal of the Royal Anthropological Institute of Great Britain and Ireland*, vol. 38, 451–486.

Tejel, J. (2008). *Syria's Kurds: History, Politics, and Society.* London: Routledge.

Vali, A. (2014). *Kurds and the State in Iran: The Making of Kurdish Identity.* London: I. B. Tauris.

Van Bruinessen, M. (1992). *Agha, Shaikh and State: The Social and Political Structures of Kurdistan.* London, New York: Zed Books.

Van Bruinessen, M. (1998). "Shifting National and Ethnic Identities. The Kurds in Turkey and the European Diaspora." *Journal of Muslim Minority Affairs,* vol. 18, no. 1, 39–52.

Vanly, I. C. (1998). *Kurdistan und die Kurden, Band 3: Syrien, Emigration, UdSSR, US-Botschaftspapiere.* Gesellschaft für bedrohte Völker, Göttingen: Pogrom Verlag.

Voller, Y. (2014). *The Kurdish Liberation Movement in Iraq: From Insurgency to Statehood.* Abingdon, UK: Routledge.

About the Editor and Contributors

Editor

Sebastian Maisel is Associate Professor for Arabic and Middle East Studies at Grand Valley State University. He received his PhD in Arabic and Islamic Studies and Anthropology from Leipzig University, Germany. As an area specialist of the Middle East, he teaches courses on the diverse cultures and religions of the region as well as Arabic language. His research focus is on social and linguistic transformation among rural communities and minority groups, for which he conducted fieldwork among the Bedouin tribes in Saudi Arabia and the Yezidis in Syria and Iraq, as well as Dinka slave soldiers from Sudan. Currently, he helps build a museum for women in Saudi Arabia. His publications include *The Customary Law of the Bedouins in Northern Arabia* (2006), *Yezidism—Religion and Society,* with C. Issa and T. Tolan (2007), *An Encyclopedia of Life in Saudi Arabia and the Arab Gulf States,* with J. Shoup (Greenwood Press, 2009), *The Kingdom of Saudi Arabia,* with D. Long (2010), *Yezidis in Syria—Identity Building among a Double Minority* (2017), and *The Inspiring Thread—Embroidery and Embellishment in Saudi Arabia* (forthcoming).

Contributors

Ahmet S. Aktürk is Assistant Professor of History at Georgia Southern University in Statesboro, Georgia.

Sacha Alsancakli is a PhD Candidate in Modern History/Iranian Studies at the university of La Sorbonne Nouvelle—Paris 3, France.

Birgit Ammann is Professor for Political Science in Social Studies at the Fachhochschule Potsdam, Germany.

Metin Atmaca is Assistant Professor of History at Ankara Sosyal Bilimler Üniversitesi in Ankara, Turkey.

Selcuk Aydin is a research student and PhD candidate at King's College in London. His research focuses on post-Ottoman states and Kurdish movements.

Djene Rhys Bajalan is Assistant Professor at the Department of History at Missouri State University.

Bahar Baser is Research Fellow at the Centre for Trust, Peace and Social Relations at Coventry University and Swedish Institute Postdoctoral Research Fellow at the Stockholm University Institute for Turkish Studies (SUITS), Sweden.

Nurettin Beltekin is Assistant Professor for Educational Sciences at Mardin Artuklu University in Mardin, Turkey.

Argun Çakır has a background in ethnomusicology and anthropology and conducted research in vocal and instrumental performance of oral literature traditions, music, and peripatetic groups in Kurdistan. He is Research Associate at the School of Arts at Bristol University.

Behrooz Chaman Ara is Assistant Professor at the Department of Kurdish Language and Literature at the University of Kurdistan-Iran. His area of expertise is Kurdish language and literature. His research focuses on classic Kurdish and Persian poetry and prosody, epics, and comparative literature.

Özgür Çiçek is a PhD Candidate in Philosophy at the Interpretation and Culture PhD Program at Binghamton University in New York.

Vedat Dayan is a PhD Candidate in Political Science at the Freie Universität Berlin, Germany.

Vera Eccarius-Kelly is Professor of Comparative Politics at Siena College in Albany, New York. Her research interests focus on Kurdish political activism in the diaspora, social movements, and Muslim minority refugee communities.

Özlem Belçim Galip is the Calouste Gulbenkian Postdoctoral Fellow in Armenian Studies at the Faculty of Oriental Studies at the University of Oxford.

Vali Gholami is Assistant Professor of English at the University of Kurdistan-Iran in Sanandaj, Iran.

Gülistan Gürbey is Professor of Political Science at the Otto-Suhr-Institut für Politikwissenschaft at Freie Universität Berlin, Germany.

Zheger Hassan is Professor for Political Science at King's University College at the University of Western Ontario in London, Ontario, Canada.

Ayoob Ismael is Assistant Professor for Geography at Salahaddin University in Erbil, Iraq.

Engin Koç is a Research Assistant at the Department of International Relations at Dicle University and PhD candidate at the Department of International Relations at Uludag University, Turkey.

Katharina Lange is a Cultural Anthropologist and Research Fellow at the Zentrum Moderner Orient in Berlin, Germany.

Kyle Meppelink is a graduate from Grand Valley State University in Allendale, Michigan, where he received a BA in International Relations with a focus on Middle East Studies. He has done research on Kurdish-Turkish relations, the Circassian Diaspora, and the effects of language on nationalism.

Jaffer Sheyholislami is Associate Professor for Applied Linguistics and Discourse Studies at Carleton University in Ottawa, Canada.

Nerina Weiss is a social anthropologist and researcher at the FAFO Research Foundation in Oslo, Norway.

Erin Whitney is an independent scholar who writes about world culture. She currently lives in Los Angeles.

Victoria Williams, PhD, is an independent writer living in London. She is author of ABC-CLIO's *Weird Sports and Wacky Games around the World: From Buzkashi to Zorbing* and *Celebrating Life Customs around the World: From Baby Showers to Funerals*.

Index